THE SOCIAL DEVELOPMENT
OF CANADA

AMS PRESS
NEW YORK

THE SOCIAL DEVELOPMENT
OF CANADA

An Introductory Study with Select Documents

By

S. D. CLARK

Lecturer in Sociology
University of Toronto

THE UNIVERSITY OF TORONTO PRESS
TORONTO   **CANADA**
1942

Library of Congress Cataloging in Publication Data

Clark, Samuel Delbert, 1910-
   The social development of Canada.

   Reprint of the 1942 ed. published by the University
of Toronto Press, Toronto.
   Includes bibliographical references and index.
   1. Canada—Social conditions. 2. Canada—Social
life and customs. I. Title.
HN103.C55   1976   309.1'71   75-41060
ISBN 0-404-14655-4

Reprinted from an original copy in the collections
of the Ohio State University Libraries

From the edition of 1942, Toronto
First AMS edition published in 1976
Manufactured in the United States of America

AMS PRESS INC.
NEW YORK, N. Y.

To

ARTHUR S. MORTON

Professor Emeritus in History
The University of Saskatchewan

PREFACE

THE undertaking represented by this volume grew out of the conviction that in the social development of Canada there are a number of fruitful problems for sociological investigation. The purpose of the volume is to stake out the field, and suggest lines of approach. Though the arrangement of the documents within the various parts was dictated largely by convenience, a general theory of interpretation runs throughout. From a great mass of data, that was selected which seemed the most relevant to distinctively sociological problems. At the same time, an effort was made to use as many different kinds of evidence as possible in order that the documents may serve as a guide in more detailed investigations by indicating what kind of sources are likely to yield greatest returns. No attempt was made to exhaust any of the sources nor to deal conclusively with any particular problem.

I am deeply indebted to Professor H. A. Innis for encouragement, counsel, and criticism. It was upon his advice that I first undertook to do something in the general field of the social development of Canada and he has given much time to reading and criticizing manuscripts in various stages of preparation which I have submitted to him; all of the final draft has gone through his hands. Professors A. Brady, G. P. deT. Glazebrook, and C. W. M. Hart examined the manuscript with considerable care and offered much useful criticism. Professor R. M. Saunders read and criticized the section on New France. My wife was throughout helpful and supplied invaluable aid in the translation of the French documents. The staffs of the Public Archives of Canada, the Parliamentary Library, and the University of Toronto Library cordially made available the facilities at their disposal. Finally, I am grateful to Mrs. A. W. B. Hewitt and her staff in the Editorial Office of the University of Toronto Press for seeing the volume through the press.

S. D. CLARK

Toronto, January, 1942.

CONTENTS

INTRODUCTION

THIS volume is intended to serve as an introduction to further study of the social development of Canada. For this reason, an effort has been made to present the evidence in as wide a frame of reference as possible. The chief focus is upon the very general problem of social development. To have pushed the analysis much further than this would have considerably restricted the type of evidence introduced and made the study less useful as a spring-board for further research. Yet to have failed to introduce a more limited principle of selection would have resulted in the accumulation of a mass of facts hopelessly unrelated and lacking in meaning. An emphasis, therefore, has been placed upon the particular problem of the relationship of frontier economic expansion in Canada, or more strictly the opening up of new areas or fields of economic exploitation, to the development of social organization.[1] This thesis serves to tie together much of the evidence presented in the volume without diverting attention from a number of other problems which suggest themselves.

[1]It should perhaps be emphasized that considerable liberty has been taken with respect to the term "frontier." Because of the variety of meanings which have been attached to it, its use would have been avoided if a more convenient term had suggested itself. Instead of being employed in the Turner sense to designate the furthest extended line of settlement, it is taken here to refer to the development of new forms of economic enterprise. Thus "frontier economic expansion" means simply the expansion of new forms of economic enterprise and the "frontier" the area in which such expansion is taking place. The emphasis is not upon the period of early settlement—what might be called the pioneer stage of development—but rather upon that period when new techniques were being fully employed in economic exploitation—what is here called the frontier stage. Cf. S. D. Clark, "Economic Expansion and the Moral Order," *Essays in Sociology*, ed. C. W. M. Hart (Toronto, 1940). For studies of the frontier see F. J. Turner, *The Frontier in American History* (New York, 1920); W. P. Webb, *The Great Plains* (Boston, 1931); James G. Leyburn, *Frontier Folkways* (New Haven, 1935); H. E. Bolton, *Wider Horizons of American History* (New York, 1939); John Lobb, "Frontier Adjustment in South Africa," *Studies in the Science of Society*, ed. G. P. Murdoch (New Haven, 1937); T. C. Weiler, "The Fur Trade Frontier of Siberia," *ibid.*; A. S. Aiton, "Latin-American Frontiers," *Report of the Canadian Historical Association*, 1940; A. L. Burt, "The Frontier in the History of New France," *ibid.*; G. F. G. Stanley, "Western Canada and the Frontier Thesis," *ibid.*

The importance of the opening up of new areas of economic exploitation in the economic history of Canada serves to justify the concern with the effects of such developments upon the development of social organization. If some of the older settled areas in Canada early reached a state of economic maturity, and if at times economic recession halted the pushing out into new areas, these developments did little more than punctuate the sweep of frontier economic expansion. The drying up of resources or the loss of markets resulted in a shift to new economic activities rather than in a prolonged economic regression; the succession of export staples provides evidence of the importance in the economy of Canada of new techniques of production rather than of techniques of conservation.[2] The establishment of the fishing industry in the Gulf of St. Lawrence led to the traffic in furs with the Indians and to the settlement of the Annapolis and St. Lawrence valleys. To fish and fur was later added the important staple of timber, opening up for agricultural exploitation the interior of New Brunswick and the new Province of Upper Canada. Expansion of the fur trade to the West brought about the sudden rush for gold in British Columbia, and eventually in the Yukon, and the settlement of the wheat lands of the prairies, and these developments hastened the growth of industrial capitalism in the East. The pushing out of the frontiers of manufacturing, and the exploitation of the mining and pulp and paper resources of the North, mark the final phases of the frontier expansion of economic life in Canada.

Social problems in Canada, accordingly, have been largely associated with frontier economic developments. The opening up of new areas or fields of economic exploitation made certain special kinds of demands upon social organization, and the failure to meet fully these demands resulted in disturbances in social relationships which may be described as social problems.[3] Centres of new economic activity became the points of origin of forces of

[2]Cf. H. A. Innis, *Problems of Staple Production in Canada* (Toronto, 1933); also, H. A. Innis, "Unused Capacity as a Factor in Canadian Economic History," *Canadian Journal of Economics and Political Science*, February, 1936.

[3]The classic statement of the theory of social disorganization and reorganization is to be found in W. I. Thomas and F. Znaniecki, *The Polish Peasant in Europe and America* (Boston, 1920), vol. IV. Because of what are considered serious shortcomings of the theory, it has been employed only in modified form in the discussion which follows.

disturbance, and these forces extended to the peripheries of such activity. The areas of greatest social disturbance were to be found where the impacts of the new techniques of production were most felt, and the intensity of the disturbance reached its peak during the interval in which the new economic developments were most rapidly taking place. As the economy became more mature, the social organization adjusted itself to the conditions of production, and an approximate state of equilibrium was attained by the time the economy passed beyond the frontier stage.

Frontier economic expansion involved the recruitment of capital and labour from outside and this growth of population made necessary the extension of institutional controls and often their establishment beyond customary boundaries.[4] Since institutions are essentially a body of trained functionaries performing specialized services, organization had to be widened and personnel enlarged if the needs of growing populations were to be adequately served. The considerable distance which often separated new areas of development from centres of control and supply made difficult the maintenance of effective supervision from the homeland in establishing institutional agencies and also imposed severe limitations upon the recruitment of personnel. In addition, conditions within such areas discouraged the financial support of institutions which did not directly promote economic exploitation and the immigration of professionally trained workers. The drain of capital into economic enterprise left little for community services while the demand for labour meant that even those who possessed specialized training of some sort were attracted into economic vocations. The failure of churches or educational institutions to secure adequate financial support, problems of public finance, and the lack of sufficient school-teachers, clergymen, and medical practitioners were characteristic features of Canadian frontier communities. The stronger pull of economic enterprise meant that capital and labour flowed beyond the boundaries of institutional systems. Where economic development took place rapidly and considerable additions to the labour force could be immediately absorbed, as in mining frontiers, the lag of such systems was most conspicuous, but even when development took place

[4]Cf. M. L. Hansen, *The Mingling of Canadian and American Peoples:* Vol. I. *Historical* (New Haven and Toronto, 1940).

slowly and the exploitative process did not require great numbers of workers there was a considerable interval before social organization could catch up with the movement of population.

When the economic exploitation was carried on by monopolies, controls of a political (and to some extent of a cultural) character were secured through the economic organization. Administrative obligations ordinarily accompanied the rights of monopoly, and, even when such obligations were not imposed, the monopolistic enterprise recognized the advantage of assuming considerable responsibility for at least the maintenance of law and order. The early trading companies of New France, and the Hudson's Bay Company, received extensive prerogatives of government, and even such semi-monopolistic enterprises as land colonization companies were endowed with a measure of political sovereignty. Though cultural obligations were less clearly defined, monopolistic organizations were expected to support the basic services of the community, and usually this support took the form of favours and financial assistance to an established church which in turn accepted the responsibility of such social services as education, relief, hospitalization, and recreation as well as religious teaching. For the most part, however, the economic development of frontier areas took place in terms of free enterprise rather than monopoly with the result that this agency for the transfer of social institutions was lacking. Monopoly tended to accompany the exploratory rather than expansionist phase of frontier development, or emerged later as a means of securing a greater conservation of resources. The development of new forms of economic exploitation implied the application of new techniques and skills, and this factor favoured individual enterprise. The very nature of monopoly discouraged efforts to expand the volume of production beyond an amount which the market would profitably absorb in terms of existing cost schedules, and, when abundant resources were available for exploitation as in frontiers, the restrictive policy of monopolistic enterprise led to the eventual triumph of free enterprise. As the expansion of the fur trade into the interior of the continent led to the collapse of trading companies in New France, the development of mining in British Columbia and of agriculture on the prairies marked the end of the western monopoly of the Hudson's

Bay Company; land colonization companies as a means of controlling agricultural settlement were generally even more short-lived.

To some extent, the failure of economic enterprise to provide an agency for the transfer of social institutions to frontier areas was offset by efforts put forth by the state. Imperial, or later, national forces promoted the extension of political agencies into new areas of development in Canada. Frontiers have always assumed considerable strategical importance in the political organization of the northern half of the continent, and, for this reason, never became unrestricted areas of economic exploitation. The presence to the south of a rapidly expanding nation served to emphasize the need of maintaining close political contacts with the frontier. The police force and courts of law, or at any rate the army, pushed out with the frontiersmen. The maintenance of military garrisons in New France and later in the British American colonies, the construction of roads and canals to serve as military routes, the despatch of a force of Royal Engineers to Victoria in 1859, and the organization of the North West Mounted Police in 1874 were instances of efforts to promote imperial or national interests in outlying areas of economic development. To some extent the political controls imposed by the state were paralleled by controls of a social or cultural character. Land grants to favoured individuals or organizations, financial subsidies, preferments in political appointments, or measures restricting the operation of competitive interests were means employed to build up privileged social institutions such as an aristocratic class or established church. The object was to assure the loyalty of frontier populations to the mother country, and such aids therefore served the same purpose as military garrisons or police forces. However, even when such supports of the state were extensive, there remained in new areas of development many needs not immediately taken care of by institutions. The coercive controls of the state, or of privileged social institutions, tended to be of a negative rather than positive character. The instruments of law provided no direction to behaviour outside of prohibitions, while institutions such as established churches supplied leadership only to those who were their adherents. For the large number of people who committed no infractions of the law or who did not owe allegiance to the formally constituted social institutions, authority was for the most part morally indifferent. The extension of social organization into all areas of social behaviour required the active participation of the population itself, and this involved more than simply the transfer of formal machinery.

The lack of institutional agencies securing the active participation of frontier populations increased the reliance upon individual resources, and the greater the lack the greater was this reliance. As frontier populations were left without leadership, they tended to become less dependent upon traditional institutions even after they were established. The weakened state of social organization thereby tended to perpetuate itself. Habits of independence were converted into attitudes of nonconformity, and what was first perhaps missed came later to be resented. New patterns of behaviour inevitably developed which did not fit into traditional systems of institutional control, and efforts of institutions to secure greater conformity led to a conflict of social values and to a condition which might be described as one of social disorganization. The difficulty faced by churches in reviving habits of worship after a considerable interval during which religious services were not provided and other ways of occupying the time on the sabbath day had developed illustrate the kind of problems resulting from the extension of social organization into new areas of development.

The character of the population which moved to frontier areas tended to strengthen nonconformist attitudes and to make more difficult the establishment of institutional systems. If the very fact of movement resulted in a considerable dislocation in habits and beliefs, this dislocation was greater when the population was recruited from a number of different cultural *milieus*. Conflicts emerged between opposing systems of control; the folkways, *mores*, and social codes of the various groups strove for supremacy. The efforts of some institutions to strengthen their position by privileges secured from the state were offset by the vigorous propaganda of less favoured organizations. The disturbances resulting from associations with strange people, in weakening traditional habits and beliefs, increased the area of cultural indifference and intensified as a result institutional competition. To the extent that segregation could not be achieved and long-established attachments preserved, frontier populations tended to be indifferent as to the particular institutions to which they gave their support.

The effects were evident in a large, culturally detached population in new areas of development which floated from one institution or group to another, their momentary attachments depending largely upon circumstances of convenience and waves of enthusiasm.

This tendency was accentuated when the population contained elements which had joined the movement to new areas as means of escape from restraining influences at home. In some respects, this was characteristic of all frontier populations in Canada. Those people migrated who were most exposed to economic, political, or cultural pressures.[5] New areas of economic development provided greater opportunities to realize potentialities of certain kinds. The worker, peasant, entrepreneur, and the religious or political heretic found there an outlet for their particular aptitudes or beliefs. These types of people made more difficult the establishment of certain forms of social organization. The extension of institutions is facilitated by the presence of a body of receptive attitudes and a favourable set of social customs, and, where these were lacking, dependence had to be placed upon the exercise of powers of coercion or upon propaganda. The weaknesses of economic monopolies, colonial class systems, established churches, or authoritarian systems of government, and the steady drain of the United States upon the population of Canada, were directly related to these characteristics of the settlers in Canadian frontier communities. When the nonconformist elements included those who sought escape from moral codes or agencies of law enforcement, the strains upon social organization in the newly settled areas were even greater. Habits of resistance of such groups to authority were carried over from the old to the new society and increased the general tendency of frontier populations to become independent of traditional institutions. The emigration of social misfits resulted partly from the social pressures applied to get them out of the way and partly from the opportunities of escape or freedom from restraint provided within rapidly growing and largely inaccessible communities. Though the nature of the frontier economy determined to a considerable extent the particular character of these people, in all of the newly developing Canadian communities there were outcasts of some sort from older societies.

[5]Cf. L. G. Reynolds, *The British Immigrant: His Social and Economic Adjustment in Canada* (Toronto, 1935).

Similarly, the presence in frontier areas of people who emigrated because they were failures at home, whether because of economic adversity, ill health, or some other reason, made more difficult the establishment of community organization. It is true that the rehabilitation of the individual's economic, physical, or mental condition often accompanied settlement in new areas, but this did not relieve the strain upon social organization in the interval before such rehabilitation was accomplished. The inability of such persons to provide for their needs meant that they could not fully participate in community life but were rather a burden upon frontier society. Numbers of such socially dependent persons have invariably accompanied the movement of population into Canadian frontier communities; if some found their way to such communities in the hope of bettering their state, others were sent there as a means of reducing the burdens of relief faced by local and national agencies in the home community. Efforts of France and later of Britain to secure through overseas colonization a solution to the problem of mounting poor-rates were paralleled by attempts on the part of Canadian cities to reduce burdens of relief by the promotion of settlement in 'the West and in recent years a back-to-the-land movement.

Other characteristics of the population served to make more difficult the establishment of orderly social relationships. Movements of people into new areas almost invariably involved disturbances in the equilibrium of age and sex groups. Though the nature of the economy largely determined the extent of these disturbances, migration ordinarily cut through the population structure to eliminate the very young and the very old and to secure a considerable predominance of males. Hazards of travel discouraged the immigration of women, children, and old people, while the frontier society placed an emphasis upon productive as distinguished from service occupations and favoured as a result adult males who could take part directly in the process of economic exploitation. The age and sex composition of the population had considerable significance with respect to the stability of social organization. The absence of the older age groups in frontier areas relieved the pressure upon health and welfare institutions but removed the steadying influence of tradition and deprived the communities of the leadership of those who were not strenuously engaged in making a living. With relatively few children among the early settlers, recreational and educational facilities were not required in the first years of development, but, where settlement of young persons of both sexes took place, problems of maternity and infant welfare quickly assumed considerable importance, and, in later years, an abnormally high proportion of school-age children imposed a heavy burden upon elementary educational institutions; it was not until after the passing of the first generation of settlers in frontier communities that a stable balance was secured between the school-age and total population. A predominance of males in the population raised problems of institutional adjustment of an even more critical character. Social organizations which depended upon the family unit, or which chiefly served the needs of the female or child sections of the population, failed to become established or remained largely ineffective. The result was that a large proportion of the normal controls of society were absent or greatly weakened. Apart from the *mores* of the family, religious and neighbourhood institutions were most affected. Devoutness tended to disappear when female influences were absent, while most of the niceties and refinements of social relationships depending upon companionship within the family group were disregarded or coarsened when such companionship was lacking. Where conditions were favourable, prostitution developed as a substitute for familial relationships, and the prevalence of drinking, gambling, and certain forms of crime in many frontier areas was indicative of general weaknesses of social organization resulting largely from the disproportionate number of males. In brief, the age and sex composition, like other characteristics, of the population intensified problems of institutional adjustment which resulted from the opening up and peopling of new frontier areas.

Such problems were still further accentuated by the contact of frontier populations with strange environmental influences, since adjustments to these influences were made much more quickly on the individual than on the institutional level. More strictly, adjustments took place most rapidly among that section of the population most exposed to strange environmental influences and were most resisted by that section least exposed, and it was those people least exposed who had chief voice in the direction of traditional institutional policies and activities. The dignitaries, priests, or official classes of the community were very largely sheltered from disturbing influences; the very nature of their roles meant that their employments were not directly related to frontier economic enterprise. It was the new occupational groups who faced the full force of new economic developments, and these groups had few claims upon the offices or emoluments of established social institutions. Individuals participating in frontier economic enterprise came in contact with new problems of life for which new solutions were necessary; the application of new techniques of production, and the development of new ways of living, involved a rational appraisal of the relation of means to desired ends and required the formulation of new habits of behaviour and thought. In a sense, such people moved out to the margins of society, and, while they carried with them some of the habits of thought and behaviour which had been implanted by previous forms of control, they had to leave behind, or cast off on the way, the great body of habits not fitted to the new conditions of life.[6] Habits, like tools, were abandoned through non-usage because they failed to work. Whether this represented a failure to maintain conditions of life which had been considered desirable, or a release from social obligations which had been felt as irksome, the effect was to emancipate the individual from controls to which he had been accustomed. He was left to work out by himself a code of conduct and philosophy of life which more nearly satisfied his present needs. The immediate reaction was one of uneasiness, relieved partly by a feeling of exhilaration. The ultimate result, if new group attachments failed to be forged, was complete personal disorganization. Problems of mental health and suicide, and to some extent of intemperance, in periods of rapid social development, were an indication of the failure of individuals to resolve the personal crisis in face of radically new conditions of living.

Usually, however, some sort of adjustment was brought about. New habits developed to take the place of those discarded. But such habits were not co-ordinated within any institutional system of social control. They represented individual responses to the new conditions of life. Since social institutions, by their very

[6]Cf. Robert E. Park, "Human Migration and the Marginal Man," *Personality and the Social Group*, ed. E. W. Burgess (Chicago, 1929); cf. also, F. J. Teggart, *Theory and Processes of History* (Berkeley, 1941).

nature, were established ways of doing things, cultural conflict emerged at the point of divergence between the new and old ways of life. The controls imposed by institutions had the object of making behaviour conform to socially-approved standards, while adjustments to new conditions implied the emergence of kinds of behaviour which had not yet secured such approval. Thus until new social standards were incorporated within institutional systems, there existed a condition of *anomie* which was characterized by a considerable reliance upon individual effort and upon individual solutions to pressing problems. It is true that problems shared by large numbers of people called forth identical or at least similar solutions, but behind these there was little sense of obligation. Certain ways proved better than others; their approval rested upon individual experience or at most upon the immediate experiences of the group as a whole. There was lacking any attempt to justify them within a traditional philosophy of the social good. Behaviour was in terms of a rational interpretation of the relationship of means to ends lying within the range of experiences of the individual members of the group rather than in terms of past loyalties and sentimental attachments. Reliance upon such criteria meant a relaxation of previously accepted standards and a freer expression of immediately felt wants; social considerations acted only slightly as forces inhibiting behaviour.

The emergence of deviate forms of behaviour in periods of rapid social development demonstrated the failure of large sections of the population to erect successfully group codes of conduct when freed from the controls of social institutions. The breakdown of the traditional institutional structure resulted in the emergence of random types of social action which, when proceeding along certain lines, came to be defined as social problems. Such definitions of social problems, however, were necessarily subjective in that unrestrained behaviour represented nothing more than deviations from generally prevalent social norms; the *mores* disintegrated, but the behaviour which took place through release from their control could be termed undesirable only when assessed in terms of some set of social standards. The existence of social institutions depended upon conformity, and that behaviour was condemned which did not conform.[7] In a sense, therefore, the emergence of social problems in periods of rapid development was a condition of the successful adjustment of individuals to the new environment. It indicated that while social institutions failed to meet new needs, solutions had been attained or at least were being sought on the individual level or within nonconformist groups.[8]

To some extent, even though resisting or failing to make adjustments, established institutions were able to maintain their controls among certain sections of the population. This was particularly the case if they had powerful means at their disposal of imposing their sanctions. By taboos and moral restraints which carried with them punitive means of securing conformity, deviations from established norms were held in check. The criminal law of the state was the most effective instrument in securing such conformity. It was the expression of the established institutional set-up, and, supported by authoritarian sanctions, it served to check the development of behaviour patterns damaging to prevailing *mores*. A number of other institutions possessed some power of coercion. The compulsive attributes of religious denominations, the family, and more general communal institutions, tended to assume considerable importance when behaviour became particularly refractory. Resort to coercive measures, however, was an indication of institutional weakness; the imposition of sanctions implied that the habitual behaviour of large numbers of the population was no longer in conformity with established norms. It is true that where the deviations were not too extensive, or the forces of disturbance not too compelling, institutions were to some extent successful in re-establishing normative behaviour. The taboo preserved certain habits which once fully accepted converted the taboo into a moral attitude. Generally, however, the forces of adjustment could not be checked by restraints imposed by external sanctions; even the controls of the state tended to break down when faced with conditions of far-reaching social disturbance.

[7]Efforts to use social pathological problems as indices of social disorganization fail because of the essentially subjective character of such problems.

[8]Cf. C. A. Dawson, *Group Settlement: Ethnic Communities in Western Canada* (Toronto, 1936); Robert E. Park and Herbert A. Miller, *Old World Traits Transplanted* (New York, 1921).

With the failure to maintain traditional controls, adjustments were made within the social organization, and those adjustments went furthest and proceeded most rapidly along lines which did not involve vested interests of some sort. Certain changes were readily permissible such as, for instance, in the case of churches, the building of places of worship with logs instead of with stones; that which proved of advantage to all the participants within an institution was ordinarily accepted without any prolonged delay. Rigidities entered at that point where certain groups, or officials, had something to lose by change. Opposition was greatest among those people furthest removed from new social conditions, while the dissatisfaction gathered greatest force among those most exposed to these conditions. Where flexibility was provided within the organization of the institution, successful accommodations often could be secured between these conflicting interests. Adjustments entered at the points of greatest disturbance even though disapproved of by those farther removed. Where such flexibility was lacking, however (and in all institutions it was lacking to some extent), attempts on the part of subordinate officials and dissatisfied members to bring about changes were promptly checked from above, and reform depended upon leadership from outside rather than within the organization.

This leadership came both from the ranks of specially trained persons dissatisfied with prevailing methods and from those who lacked any particular qualification to perform the services which they undertook to improve. The physician or judge who attempted to introduce changes at the risk of his professional reputation or employment by a public board was an example of the reformer drawn from the ranks of the technicians. Though reforms having to do with such matters as the practice of medicine or the administration of justice ordinarily were undertaken by those familiar with the techniques of these highly specialized services, in those situations where the need for improved methods was very pressing, leadership sometimes came from outside professional circles; the "quack" became a familiar figure during the cholera plagues in Upper Canada, and vigilante committees emerged (though not for long) in British Columbia and the Yukon when regularly constituted authorities of law enforcement were no longer able to maintain order. In other more legitimate ways people of non-professional status were able to make their influence felt in the advocacy of social reforms in fields where specialized training was required in the actual performance of the services. The royal commission emerged in Canada towards the middle of the nineteenth century and provided a means for the expression of opinion, although it was some time before its possibilities as an instrument of investigation and propaganda were fully appreciated.[9] About the same time the newspaper developed as a recognized channel for the dissemination of opinions, and reform editors came to assume an increasingly important role as critics of social services.[10] In the case of problems of a less technical nature, not only proposals for reform but participation could come from those who lacked any sort of specialized training, and, for this reason, there was a significant difference in the character of reform movements in, for instance, health and law on the one side, and morality and religion on the other. The guardians of public morals or the ministers of the gospel did not possess a body of skills which could not be quickly acquired by the layman. The temperance advocate needed to rely upon few of the findings of science to demonstrate to the satisfaction of many the evils of alcohol, while, if church bodies made efforts to establish standards of entrance to the ministry, few qualifications to preach could be insisted upon when the authority of the churches was called into question. The appointment and theological principles of the religious prophet depended upon no institutional intermediary since the truth of his version of the gospel and his charge to expound it came through special revelation; he answered an inner call, and God and his conscience were judges of the worth of his efforts.[11] If perhaps unusual in some respects, the unlicensed religious preacher was typical in many ways of the reform leader who emerged at a time when traditional leadership was proving unacceptable.

By the very nature of their role reform leaders tended to be people devoid of "respectable" attributes. The professional

[9]Cf. J. E. Hodgetts, "Royal Commissions of Inquiry in Canada," Master of Arts thesis, University of Toronto, 1940.

[10]Cf. W. S. Wallace, "The Journalist in Canadian Politics: A Retrospect," *Canadian Historical Review*, March, 1941.

[11]Cf. Talcott Parsons, *The Structure of Social Action* (New York, 1937), pp. 564-72.

person who practised unorthodox methods or advocated revolutionary changes was as likely to be denied "official" recognition as the person who lacked the qualifications required to serve within regularly constituted social institutions. Similarly, if the one type of reformer usually belonged to, the other was closely identified with, that class in the community which was without any acceptable social status. Reformers were social revolutionists in the sense that what they advocated involved an upsetting of traditional standards and very often traditional social distinctions. Thus they brought down upon themselves the full force of vested interests. In championing the cause of the unprivileged or unpopular, they challenged the privileges and accepted beliefs of the "respectable" leaders of the community. The influences which prompted people to break from established institutions and to take up the cause of reform often increased opposition against them. Desire to escape from the boredom of routine tasks, inability to secure a living or recognition in any other way, love of power which was experienced in swaying large audiences or large reading publics, and personal "grudges" against persons in authority, may have mingled, along with other motives, with the sincere conviction of doing good. But if their ideas caught on, it was because the underlying social consciousness provided a sympathetic response. The reformer differed from the "crank" in that he gave expression to genuine and persistent social needs and dissatisfactions; within programmes of reform, the vague and inarticulate feelings of large numbers of people were crystallized and identified with a clearly-defined goal. It was this need for social expression rather than the character or motives of reformers which gave rise to reform movements.

If the motives of reform leaders provide no explanation of the rise of reform movements, neither do the motives of the followers. Nothing inherent within a particular reform idea determined its success in meeting the personal needs of frontier populations. The enthusiasm aroused by inspiring leadership offered to the frontier settler, perplexed by strange surroundings, a means of escape from the task of determining by himself standards of thought and behaviour. In other words, from the point of view of the individual, the movement served as a means of reorganizing the personality in terms of a particular focus of group attention.

Joining or supporting the movement, particularly one of a moral or religious evangelical character but even one of health or prison reform, involved some sort of conversion which brought about a reformation of attitudes and established a set of standards depending upon group sanctions.[12]   Conversion involved the organization of habits in terms of a definite purpose and in this way it secured a stable personality.   But any one of many movements would have been equally effective in meeting such individual needs.   Different kinds of personal "crises," such as financial reverses, the death of a dearly loved one, or the loss of good health, caused people to endorse the cause of reform, but life histories which revealed the nature of these would throw little light upon the forces giving rise to particular reform movements.[13]   Movements developed because they provided machinery for the rationalization of individual wants on the basis of the common good.   They provided an interpretation of new phenomena, and in so doing developed habits in the individual which conformed to a general pattern of social behaviour.[14] The solution of individual "crises" was directed along channels securing the solution of social "crises"; in this way, movements became instruments of social as distinct from individual reorganization.

Similarly, cultural diffusion or environmental determinism provide no adequate explanation of the rise of reform movements. The reform movements which sprang up in Canadian frontier areas did not develop, of course, independently of outside influences. The close connection with Britain and the United States, or earlier with France, and the fact that economic developments in Canada were similar to those taking place in these other countries, meant that new ideas usually were derived from British, American, or

[12]Cf. E. Faris, "The Sect and the Sectarian," *Personality and the Social Group*, ed. E. W. Burgess (Chicago, 1929).

[13]The limitations of life histories as means of studying social as distinguished from individual disorganization are evident, for instance, in W. I. Thomas and F. Znaniecki, *The Polish Peasant in Europe and America*, 5 vols. (Boston, 1918-21); cf. Herbert Blumer, *Critiques of Research in the Social Sciences: An Appraisal of Thomas and Znaniecki's "The Polish Peasant in Europe and America"* (New York, 1939).

[14]Cf. E. C. Hughes, *The Growth of an Institution: The Chicago Real Estate Board* (Chicago, 1931); also, S. D. Clark, *The Canadian Manufacturers' Association: A Study in Collective Bargaining and Political Pressure* (Toronto, 1939).

in some cases French sources. Often local reform leaders identified their programmes with those of reform movements in outside countries; occasionally, the leaders actually came in from outside. That does not mean, however, that the development of these movements in Canada can be explained in terms of the relationship with outside movements since the fact that such a relationship became established (or, indeed, in many cases did not become established) requires explanation.[15] Though related to movements outside, reform movements in Canadian frontier communities were products of forces generated from within. On the other hand, the assumption of environmental determinism that the population within these new areas of development individually readjusted their habits of thought and behaviour, and that such random adjustments explain the character of new social developments, disregards the fact that environmental forces did not act equally and in the same way upon all the individuals of an area. These forces made adjustments necessary, but it was only through group leadership that general patterns of social adjustment were brought about. It does not matter whether that leadership was provided, as Walter Bagehot would have supposed,[16] by the intellectually élite, or, as Veblen would have argued,[17] by the members of that class most exposed to the full force of changing conditions, the point is that the adjustment in the first instance was peculiar to a few, and only became generally accepted through the unifying influence of reform movements. It is true that where needs were fairly well-defined, the nature of acceptable beliefs was reasonably predictable. The range of choice was confined to a limited number of solutions. In most cases, however, possible solutions were numerous and highly unpredictable as needs were ill-defined and variable in character, and here the process of reorganization, through the establishment of dominant and generally-accepted patterns of behaviour, was more halting and painful as competition between alternative solutions was more strenuous and drawn-out.

[15]Cf. Sidney Hook, "A Pragmatic Critique of the Historic-Genetic Method," *Essays in Honor of John Dewey* (New York, 1929); for a discussion of cultural transfer see Ralph Linton, ed., *Acculturation in Seven American Indian Tribes* (New York, 1940), chaps. VIII, IX and X.

[16]Walter Bagehot, *Physics and Politics* (New York, 1890).

[17]Thorsten Veblen, *Theory of the Leisure Class* (New York, 1899).

2

The ultimate form of social reorganization depended, in the final analysis, upon the strength of appeal of rival movements or institutions.

It was in those areas undergoing rapid change that competition in social appeals was most apparent and keen. The weakness of old-established forms of control meant that converts were easily won and the field was relatively open to a great variety of social doctrines. The "floating" character of frontier populations was indicative of the weaknesses of social organization and the tendency of individual grievances to find outlet in sporadic popular movements. Schisms within social institutions gave rise to new social movements, and schisms within these, in turn, intensified still further the disunities in the social structure. The break with old loyalties tended to create a disposition which discouraged stable loyalties of any sort. Sectarian religious groups, rebel trade-union organizations and new political parties constantly faced disaffections within their own ranks.[18] Offsetting these schismatic tendencies, however, there developed new stabilizing forces within reform movements. With institutionalization, the role of reformers was taken by that of officials, and programmes of reform became translated into group philosophies and sets of doctrines. Vested interests were accumulated which sought to perpetuate the organization of the reform movement by widening its area of control. In a sense, the organization became a repository of the attitudes and beliefs of the followers. That is to say, attitudes and beliefs, resulting from conversion, secured justification and a degree of security when officially accepted. In another sense, the organization became a repository of offices. The leaders, officials, and even the lay members were dependent upon it for their own welfare, whether it was a matter of making a living, obtaining prestige, or simply securing status in the local community. Denied leading roles in established or "respectable" institutions, nonconformists sought prestige through leadership or membership within reform organizations.

The increasing institutionalization of reform movements brought about significant changes in their role and personnel. Points of

[18]In this respect the recent experience of the Canadian Federation of Labour or of farmers' movements in Western Canada was much like that of Methodist movements in Upper Canada.

prestige tended to develop within such movements, and efforts were made to secure accommodations with older-established or traditional institutions.   The nonconformists came to accept, and consequently to be accepted by, the society in which they lived, and, in return for recognition, ceased warring upon the whole social front.   Greater attention was given to the qualification of officials, and even the recruitment of new followers tended to be much more selective.   While these changes may have indicated an abandonment of the more advanced claims of the earlier reformers, they meant on the other hand the attainment of many of their chief objectives.   With at least partial acceptance of their programmes, reform movements became incorporated within the social structure, and their controls became accepted as normative rather than revolutionary.   Such changes may be described as the final phase of social reorganization, when ordered and generally-recognized controls replaced those imposed, on the one hand, by authoritarian and unadjusted social institutions, or, on the other hand, by aggressive and non-accommodated social movements. The establishment of stable institutional systems, providing for such needs as those of law enforcement, health, destitution, education, recreation, cultural expression, and religion, marks the stage when the social organization had become fully adjusted to new social conditions, and *mores* had grown up to sustain its controls.   The cycle, it is true, was never completed as new disturbances threw up problems of social organization and adjustment, but if attention is focussed upon the broad stream of development in Canada, it is possible with respect to such frontier areas as those of the fur trade in the valley of the St. Lawrence, the fisheries in Nova Scotia, the timber trade and agriculture in New Brunswick, Prince Edward Island, and Upper Canada, mining in British Columbia, the Yukon, and northern Ontario, wheat-growing in the prairies, and industrial manufacturing in the central Canadian cities to describe the process by which controls became accommodated if not thoroughly integrated.

This process may be considered as a general *movement* bringing about the establishment of a new social equilibrium.[19]   Thus with respect to social developments in Canada, the large number of

[19]Cf. Vilfredo Pareto, *The Mind and Society* (New York, 1935), vol. I, pp. 65-70.

different efforts to secure reform, with respect to matters of crime, intemperance, education, the class system, and religion, together with the less conspicuous changes taking place in the nature of services of medical, social welfare, and other institutions, was closely related within a general movement of social reorganization. Further, this complex of reform efforts extended beyond the purely social to include the economic and political since problems within these fields as within the social grew out of conditions of disturbance which extended throughout the society. Demands for changes in the system of government or in economic policy were indicative ordinarily of states of unrest which found expression in a wide variety of social movements. An emphasis, consequently, upon the purely social or cultural, as distinguished from the economic or political, involves a limitation to but one aspect of a much more general social phenomenon. This limitation affords a means of distinguishing sociology from economics or political science; at the same time, however, it emphasizes the close connection between these social science disciplines.

I

THE FUR TRADE AND RURAL SOCIETY IN NEW FRANCE

THE most striking feature in the social development of New France was the conflict of two sets of frontier social values, the one promoting stability and the other expansion.[1] The rich resources of the St. Lawrence Valley favoured the development of agriculture while the extensive continental system of waterways favoured that of the fur trade, and the uneasy accommodation between these two forms of economic enterprise threatened the stability of the society of the colony until the fur-trade frontier pushed so far west as to be almost completely divorced from the agrarian community. If the effects of the clash of the opposing interests of agriculture and the fur trade were evident in the instability of economic and political organization and were in some measure responsible for the eventual fall of New France, they were no less pronounced in social organization. Most of the social problems of the community were the direct product of the pull of these two antagonistic sets of cultural values.

The character of settlement favoured the easy transition of the agricultural society from a frontier to a mature state. The establishment of monopoly control of the fur trade meant that early colonization was wholly in terms of agriculture and tended to take place slowly. Lack of interest if not hostility on the part of the trading companies, the ban upon the immigration of Huguenots, the policy of making large grants of land to individuals who made no effort to develop them, and the constant danger of attacks from the Indians checked rapid settlement. The state itself showed little interest in colonization. The revocation of the charters of successive trading companies when they failed to fulfil their engagements in bringing out colonists indicated the concern of the French government with matters of defence more than with problems of economic welfare. In 1663, only about two thousand people were

[1]For an early sociological study of New France, see W. A. Riddell, *The Rise of Ecclesiastical Control in Quebec* (New York, 1916).

to be found in the colony.[2] After this date, it is true, far-reaching
changes in the economic organization of the colony and in the
colonial relationship brought about more rapid settlement. So
long as the bonds of loyalty established with the Indians through
commercial ties could be maintained, reliance upon trading companies and a small number of settlers had incurred no great risk
to the state, but, with the alliance of the Dutch and the Iroquois,
the balance of power among the Indian tribes collapsed, and the
French were exposed to English competition and hostile attack.
At the same time, the depletion of the fur-bearing animals in the
area immediately adjacent the colony, and the loss of the Huron
Indians as middlemen in the western trade, cut the French off from
any secure supply of furs; if a supply was to be obtained, it was
necessary to penetrate into the distant hunting grounds of the
Indians, and this western extension of the fur-trade organization
and reliance upon individual traders not only imposed new strains
upon defence forces but made impossible the maintenance of
monopoly conditions in local trade.[3] Changes in defence needs,
and in the character of the fur trade, brought to an end company
rule in 1661 and resulted in the establishment of New France as a
royal colony, and the direct intervention of the state led to the
institution of a vigorous policy of colonization. The despatch of
the Carignan-Salières Regiment to make war upon the Iroquois,
and the settlement of the soldiers of the disbanded regiment along
the Richelieu River, were means of closing up the western line of
defence left exposed by the Huron defeat. The sending out of
girls to marry the disbanded soldier settlers, and the encouragement of the birth-rate by gifts to the heads of large families and
of marriage by gifts to married couples, were designed to further
the combined objects of settlement and defence. Subsidies to local
industries, the introduction of an apprenticeship system, and the
importation of skilled workers from France did something to widen
economic opportunities in the colony. Yet agricultural settlement
did not grow rapidly. Limitations in the very nature of the agricultural industry were reinforced by limitations in geography and

[2]M.Q. Innis, *An Economic History of Canada* (Toronto, 1935), chap. II; cf.
also H. A. Innis, ed., *Select Documents in Canadian Economic History, 1497-1783*
(Toronto, 1929).
    [3]Cf. H. A. Innis, *The Fur Trade in Canada* (New Haven, 1930).

in political and cultural controls.   The western extension of agricultural settlement was halted by the closing in of the St. Lawrence Valley, while the seigneurial tenure checked agricultural expansion. By 1673, 6,705 people had settled in the colony, and by the end of the century (1706), the number had increased to only 16,417.[4]   If the increase of population represented a gain upon the rate of settlement before 1660, it could scarcely be considered sufficiently great to impose serious strains upon social organization.

Moreover, the character of the colonists made for the development of stable social organization in the rural frontier.   Before 1660, the Jesuits carefully passed upon those intending to settle in the colony, and an effort was made to prevent any persons of immoral habits from embarking or to deport them if they arrived.[5]   What colonization took place during this period consisted chiefly of families rather than of detached individuals, and this meant that no serious break occurred in family attachments.   Settlement involved very largely the transfer of a peasant population, and peasant social institutions, to a new environment not strikingly different from the old.   After 1660, many of less desirable character did find their way to the colony in America.   The disbanded soldiers were not as likely to adapt themselves to farming conditions as peasant settlers; some of the destitute of relief-burdened French parishes were dumped down in the colony; absconded debtors and criminals escaping the restraints of justice were not entirely absent among incoming settlers; and young women of undesirable moral reputation were occasionally sent, or came out on their own accord, to marry unattached men in the colony.[6]   But the numbers of those who might have been described as disreputable were not considerable, while those who had little inclination to farm would have readily adjusted themselves if the fur trade had not discouraged such adjustment.   The agricultural industry, in itself, imposed severe demands upon the inhabitants and offered few opportunities to maintain habits of dissipation which the individual may have brought in with him.

[4]Innis, *An Economic History of Canada;* also, E. Salone, *La Colonisation de la Nouvelle France* (Paris, 1906).

[5]Mack Eastman, *Church and State in Early Canada* (Edinburgh, 1915), pp. 22-3.

[6]Cf. Francis Parkman, *The Old Regime in Canada* (London, 1909), pp. 276-86.

Finally, conditions within the rural frontier served to favour the establishment of traditional institutional controls. The danger of Indian attacks, the difficulties of carrying on agricultural operations, and the lack of available markets, made for a considerable dependence upon the state. The organization of the rural districts under militia captains, the development of an extensive system of economic controls, and the widening of the criminal law to cover almost all forms of undesirable behaviour were indicative of the part played by the state in the rural society of New France.[7] The establishment of the seigneurial system extended formal controls into the cultural realm, and the limited amount of good agricultural land secured the stability of this system in the rural society. The dues and acts of respect which the habitant owed to his seigneur, and political and social prerogatives of the seigneurs, such as that of holding court, made for a hierarchical social order in which the leadership of the privileged class was accepted by the rural population.[8]   Family attachments were also strengthened by the character of settlement in the colony. The extension of settlement along the river, and the failure, as a result, of vigorous village groups to emerge, enhanced the dependence of the individual upon the family unit. The low illegitimacy rate, before the development of the western fur trade, indicated the strength of the pioneer rural family. Only one of 674 children baptized between 1621 and 1661 was illegitimate.[9]   More important still, conditions within the rural frontier of New France favoured the establishment of religious controls upon a firm basis. Within the organization of the Catholic Church, and particularly of the Jesuit Order, there had developed techniques highly adapted to the needs of a rural frontier. The Jesuit missionaries, fired with the evangelical zeal of their first leader, Ignatius Loyola, and devoted to service in distant parts from the time their order was founded, quickly secured a strong position within rural New France.[10]   The other religious orders established in later years likewise readily fitted into the community

[7]Innis, *An Economic History of Canada*, chap. III; cf. also Parkman, *The Old Regime in Canada*.

[8]Cf. W. B. Munro, *The Seignorial System in Canada* (Cambridge, 1907); also, G. M. Wrong, *A Canadian Manor and Its Seigneurs* (Toronto, 1926).

[9]Eastman, *Church and State in Early Canada*, p. 23.

[10]Francis Parkman, *The Jesuits in North America* (London, 1909).

structure; the Sulpician Order of the seigneury of Montreal, the Hotel Dieu, the Ursuline Order, and the Congrégation de Notre Dame restricted themselves to fields of labour in which they were specially qualified. The episcopacy, itself, particularly during the incumbency of Bishop Laval, was well adapted to serve the needs of a frontier society; Laval had been trained in one of the schools of the Jesuits and his appointment was largely the result of their influence.[11] The geography of New France reinforced the position of the Catholic Church. The parish organization was unsuited to the needs of the extremely scattered rural population, and, until 1679, itinerant missionaries closely controlled by the Jesuit Superior, or later the Bishop, took the place of settled parish priests. Their preaching assignments required the missionaries to travel over large areas, holding mass in each place about once in six weeks, and this lack of any regular relationship between the priests and particular groups of inhabitants, and the absence of any strong feeling of local community solidarity, made for the dependence of the population upon the central authority of the church. The unifying influence of the river highway favoured centralization in the church as in the community generally.[12] The payment of all tithes into the Seminary in Quebec, and the retention by the Superior or Bishop of full control over the appointment and pay of the missionaries were forms of centralization within the organization of the church; the influence of the church in the choice of early governors, and the right of the Bishop to appoint members of the Sovereign Council, were indicative of the extension of such centralizing tendencies into the wider organization of the community.[13]

If the slow growth of settlement, the character of the colonists, and the nature of geographical conditions within the rural community made for the ready transition of New France from a frontier to a mature agricultural society, that is not to say that problems of social organization did not emerge as a result of frontier agrarian development. The distance of the colony from the homeland, the isolation of the settlers, the difficulty of establishing any sort of primary group life apart from the family because of the centralizing influences of geography, the dependence of the agricultural com-

[11]*Ibid.*
[12]Riddell, *The Rise of Ecclesiastical Control in Quebec*, chap. IV.
[13]Eastman, *Church and State in Early Canada*, pp. 16-19.

munity upon military protection, the failure of the French government to adapt its restrictive economic policies to the needs of a
frontier agricultural economy, and the generally paternalistic
attitude of both the state and the church had effects which were
evident in the inertia, extreme poverty, economic dependence, and
cultural indifference of many of the inhabitants.[14] Society in New
France inevitably felt the disorganizing influence of the agrarian
frontier.   But it was an influence not sufficiently great to lead to
any general breakdown of social organization.   Rigid limitations
of geography and also culture were imposed upon the expansion of
frontier agricultural enterprise; the agricultural community became
a closed rather than an open frontier.   Forces of social reorganization, as a result, quickly asserted themselves in establishing a considerable degree of equilibrium within the rural community and
in bringing about the transition from a frontier to a mature society.[15]
In terms, therefore, of the agrarian frontier in itself, problems of
social organization in New France were neither extensive nor of
long duration.

   The opening up of a new frontier of individual economic enterprise associated with the fur trade, however, introduced far-reaching problems of social organization which extended back into the
rural community and seriously disturbed society in New France
throughout the latter half of the seventeenth and early part of the
eighteenth century.   The collapse of economic monopoly in the
trade with the Indians, and the necessity of extending trading
operations further inland to tap supplies of beaver, led to the
increasing participation of the colonists in the fur trade, and such
participation resulted in weakening the restraints of the rural
society.   Those engaged in the trade came to constitute a large
proportion of the young men in the colony.   It is possible at the
peak that close to one thousand were fully employed in this occupation; Du Chesneau estimated the number as between five and six
hundred in 1679, not including those who made daily excursions
into nearby woods.[16]   Though there was in the life of the bush

   [14]Cf. Parkman, *The Old Regime in Canada.*

   [15]Cf. A. L. Burt, "The Frontier in the History of New France," *Report of
the Canadian Historical Association*, 1940; also, R. M. Saunders, "The Cultural
Development of New France before 1760," *Essays in Canadian History*, ed.
R. Flenley (Toronto, 1939).

   [16]Innis, *The Fur Trade in Canada*, pp. 62-3.

ranger much which was squalid and mean, and little which was as colourful as fire-side stories suggested, it made an irresistible appeal to the youth in the colony. Those traders who returned from the hazardous journey in the interior played freely upon their imaginations—like most travellers from distant lands—in recounting their experiences, and there developed as a result a romantic picture of the *coureurs de bois* which stirred the imaginations of the sons of every habitant and seigneur in the colony.[17] It is true, on the other hand, that the drabness and bleak poverty of rural life in New France provided little inducement to young men to remain at home. The hard work in clearing and cultivating the land, the lack of interesting diversions, and the puritanical restrictions of Jesuit priests, contrasted unfavourably with the fur trader's freedom from monotonous toil, his opportunities to experience new and exciting adventures, and his seclusion from the watchful eye of the cleric. Though bush ranging involved the sacrifice of modest comforts and a degree of security, there were few youths who did not feel that the many compensations offset the sacrifices.

By providing an outlet for the young men in the rural communities, the fur trade broke down the isolation of the scattered settlements, and quickened the tempo of social life. In this way, it probably exerted an invigorating influence in the colony. But it carried in its train social problems which seriously disturbed the rural frontier society. Those engaged in the trade came to lead a highly nomadic existence. Fur-trading parties setting out from the settlements journeyed into the upper reaches of the St. Lawrence waterways system, and were absent for as long as from one to three years. Among such groups the controls of the community broke down through the sheer impossibility of applying the sanctions upon which they rested. Always on the move, and returning to their homes for only short periods of time, the youthful traders could readily avoid the scrutiny or coercive controls of responsible community leaders. The emancipation secured through mobility was furthered by the adjustments made necessary by new conditions of life. The freedom of the woods developed in those engaged in the trade an irresponsibility which made it difficult for them to accept the discipline of rural life. The *coureurs de bois* lived recklessly, heedless of what the future held in store for them. Danger

[17]Cf. Willa Cather, *Shadows on the Rock* (New York, 1932).

was cheerfully faced, and privation grimly accepted. Few undertakings were too fatiguing or too perilous if they offered lucrative
returns from trade with the Indians.[18] These qualities were essential in the bush ranger as such; as early a governor as Champlain
had recognized the contribution which could be made by enterprising and courageous traders who found their way into the
territory of the Indian hunters.[19] But these same qualities unfitted
this group of young men to settle down in and accept the controls
of the rural society. A distaste for routine and steady labour and
an impatience of restraints of any sort became characteristic traits
of the hardened bush rangers. These traits were the product of
the conditions under which they lived. Their way of life required
adjustments which involved the abandonment of many old habits
and the forming of many new. The chief selective agency in this
process was the geographical environment of the interior of the
North American Continent. But in addition to a new geographical
environment, the *coureurs de bois* came in contact with a new
culture, that of the North American Indian, and the habits they
formed resulted to some extent from the accommodation of the
values of this new culture with those of an old. Sharing with the
Indians many experiences and problems, the *coureurs de bois*
readily adopted many of their ways of behaviour and with these
much of their philosophy of life.[20] Many of these acquisitions,
such as techniques of travel and manner of dressing, were essential
for survival under conditions faced by the traders. Even the adoption of the attitude of mind of the native, of not worrying about
the future, was necessary as a means of avoiding the nervous strain
of the trader's precarious way of life. But as many of the worse
features of western civilization were acquired by the Indians, so
many of their most dissolute habits were copied by the white
inhabitants. The presence within the neighbourhood of the
colony of Indian tribes who, as a result of the depletion of furs had
lost their economic security, intensified the disorganizing effects

[18]Cf. Philip Child, "Pierre Esprit Radisson and the *Coureurs de Bois*,"
University of Toronto Quarterly, July, 1940.

[19]R. M. Saunders, "The Emergence of the Coureur de Bois as a Social Type,"
Report of the Canadian Historical Association, 1939.

[20]A. G. Bailey, *The Conflict of European and Eastern Algonkian Cultures*
(Saint John, N.B., 1937), chap. x.

of the contact with Europeans. The demands made by the French fur-trading organization upon the native culture resulted in changes in the Indians' mode of life and increased their dependence upon their European neighbours.[21] The disorganization resulting from this loss of independence, in turn, contributed to the disorganization of the white culture through contact with these Indians. Even those habits of the Indian, however, which were not of a dissolute character took on that character when borrowed by the whites. Customs and attitudes which conformed to the Indian culture became forms of social disorganization when introduced into a different culture. Thus simple recreational and ceremonial activities indulged in by the natives tended to assume an immoral character when taken over by the *coureurs de bois*.

Through their contacts with the Indians, and because of their extreme mobility, the *coureurs de bois* came to constitute a distinct social group in the colony in which conformity to collective ways of behaviour and collective ways of thought was maintained by group loyalties. This emergence of new cultural patterns carried no threat to the traditional rural culture to the extent that the *coureurs de bois* were completely separated from the settled agricultural community. In such places as Michilimackinac, Green Bay, and Detroit, with populations consisting of western traders and transient Indians, social disorganization was wholly confined to the Indian society.[22] But the influence of the fur traders inevitably reached back into the settled community because it was from this community that they were recruited and it was there that they made their headquarters. Montreal became the chief centre of conflict between the settled rural and the mobile trading groups. Situated near the junction of the Ottawa and St. Lawrence rivers, it constituted the natural geographical centre for the western trade; on the other hand, situated at the point where the Laurentian and Appalachian ranges close together, it marked the western extremity of the settlements extending up the rich lowlands of the St. Lawrence Valley.[23] In Montreal consequently trader and habitant met.

[21]Cf. Innis, *The Fur Trade in Canada*.
[22]*Ibid.*, pp. 60-1.
[23]Cf. M. I. Newbigin, *Canada, The Great River, the Lands and the Men* (New York, 1926); also Ralph Flenley, *A History of Montreal, 1640-1672, from the French of Dollier De Casson* (Toronto, 1928), pp. 15-19.

Here the traders returned with their furs and secured the necessary goods to outfit another voyage. Although the importance of the fair in the town declined with the western extension of the trade, many Indians continued to frequent the place to sell their furs or for other purposes, and their presence was a further disorganizing influence in the community.[24]   The effects reached inevitably beyond the town to the rural society. Montreal provided an active labour market for farm youth. Young boys from the rural settlements, seeking an entry into the fur trade, found their way to the town; in the interval between western excursions, they often returned to their farm homes. The drift of this occupational group was the chief channel by which the values of the trading culture were transmitted to the rural. Although the truly floating population was largely confined to Montreal, the towns of Three Rivers and Quebec, and even the old-established rural settlements between, did not escape the pull of the fur-trade frontier upon their populations. The colony came increasingly to be made up of a body of traders continually on the move; the fur-trade party, in contrast to the rural neighbourhood group, exemplified the unsettled character of community life. Problems of social organization in the rural society were largely the result of the unsettlement which occurred.

Much of the destitution in the colony was indirectly if not directly related to the disturbing influence of the fur trade. The manner in which the *coureurs de bois* were paid when they returned to Montreal, and the example set them by the Indians of living from day to day, encouraged habits of extravagance which left numbers of those, too old to continue as traders, without means of livelihood. The periodical crop failures which occurred partly because of the neglect of farming through participation in the fur trade contributed further to problems of destitution.[25]   The practice of begging spread and assumed serious proportions in the town of Quebec, and, if many of the beggars were social dependents who had been shipped out by parishes in the homeland, their numbers were probably increased by the addition of persons

[24]Eastman, *Church and State in Early Canada*, pp. 224-5, 279-81; Parkman, *The Old Regime in Canada*, pp. 439-40.

[25]Cf. Parkman, *The Old Regime in Canada*.

demoralized by the fur trade.[26]   Within the Catholic Church there existed agencies adequate to deal with the wants resulting from genuine poverty as such, but the association of destitution with begging or vagrancy raised problems which required the exercise of powers of police.   The establishment of poor boards by the state, and state support of poor houses or hospitals, were prompted by the urgency of the problem of vagabondage attributed by the sponsors of these measures to the influence of the fur trade. More extensive controls involved the intervention of the formal authority of the criminal law.

Efforts were made by the French government or the local governmental authorities to suppress some of the worst evils emerging in the rural communities as a result of the fur trade. Trading in the woods was prohibited by law or subjected to regulation.[27]   Heavy penalties were provided for those selling brandy to the Indians.[28]   Taverns were licensed, drunkenness on occasion treated as a criminal offence, and prostitution rigorously suppressed. But such coercive measures of the state were largely ineffective in securing conformity of the fur traders to the norms of the rural society.   Constant violations of the law occurred among the inveterate rangers of the woods, and the ease with which they could hide in the forests, and the inclination of the inhabitants to assist them in escape, made it almost impossible to effect arrests. The influence of the traders resulted in an increasing problem of crime in the settled community as well as on the fur-trade frontier. Acts of violence, armed robberies and murders were not infrequently committed, while sex crimes were sufficiently widespread to attract attention and call forth measures of suppression.[29]   A number of taverns along the river front became hang-outs of robber gangs, and the existence of the open frontier to the West made difficult effective policing.   Criminals could readily escape into the interior, and, like the *coureurs de bois*, were often aided by local inhabitants, such as the tavern keepers, in making such escapes.   The lack of respect for authority which the conditions of the fur trade en-

[26]Raymond Du Bois Cahall, *The Sovereign Council of New France* (New York, 1915), pp. 248-59.

[27]Cf. Innis, *The Fur Trade in Canada.*

[28]Cf. Eastman, *Church and State in Early Canada.*

[29]Cf. Cahall, *The Sovereign Council of New France.*

couraged gave rise to some extent to attitudes of indifference on the part of the public to general problems of order and crime. The *coureurs de bois* who disregarded regulations of the fur trade became popular heroes in the eyes of many of the inhabitants, and this partiality for the outlaw traders asserted itself in a tendency to take the side of violators of the law in general. The fact that most forms of crime in the colony, apart from unlawful participation in the fur trade, involved little threat to the rights of private property but were rather acts of personal violence contributed further to the unconcern of many of the colonists with matters of law enforcement.

The fur trade not only encouraged attitudes of disrespect for the authority of the law, but introduced discordant interests into the councils of the state itself. There developed a set of problems respecting which there were serious conflicts between governmental and ecclesiastical officials, and even between the various governmental officials; and the divided jurisdiction, and the failure of the government to follow a consistent policy, weakened efforts to enforce the law. Some of the governors, and a number of the local councillors, under the influence of the ecclesiastical party, were prepared to go to considerable lengths in carrying out a policy of rigorous control of the fur trade, but their restrictions usually met with a cool reception from the Minister of Colonies in Versailles. The vacillation of official attitudes led to a policy wavering from stern oppression to mild tolerance. The failure of governmental controls, however, reflected more fundamental weaknesses of the colonial organization than simply that of the conflict between secular and ecclesiastical authorities. Efforts to suppress the evils of the fur trade by confining it to Quebec, Three Rivers, and Montreal failed in face of economic forces pushing it westward. Competition from the English in the south and north could be met by the French only through the extension of the fur-trade organization into the interior. The *coureurs de bois* played a vitally necessary role in the maintenance of French control over the western trade. The disorganizing effects of their activities were an inevitable result of the contradictions within the economic organization of the colony. The weakness of the state in controlling the *coureurs de bois* or checking the brandy trade lay in its dependence upon the fur trade as its chief source

of revenue. Expansion westward, in response to English competition, involved increasing governmental outlays, and the heavy
fixed costs of the trade made necessary a policy of promoting still
further expansion.[30] In the long run, expansion was economically
as well as socially disastrous to the colony, but the burdens of
overhead costs made impossible a policy of curtailment. Problems
of social disorganization were the immediate effects of economic
contradictions which led eventually to political collapse.

Expansion of the fur trade involved the weakening of the moral
and cultural controls of the local community and primary groups.
The effects upon the family were the most immediate, and, in the
eyes of those concerned with the welfare of the colony, the most
readily discernible. The opportunity of joining at a very early
age fur-trading parties going west gave to young boys a feeling
of independence of their parents. Sex *mores* as well suffered from
the participation of so many young men in the fur trade. The
domestic requirements of the fur traders encouraged the legitimate
employment of Indian squaws; but demoralization of the natives,
and impoverishment with the decline in returns from hunting and
increasing dependence upon European goods, led to a reliance
upon such employment as a means of subsistence. Such contacts
with the Indians resulted in sexual irregularities. Cohabitation
with Indian squaws was common among the single young men,
and even those who were married had often native mistresses.[31]
Illegitimacy, encouraged by the Indians as a means of establishing ties with the whites, increased in the Indian villages, and
prostitution developed in the chief centres of trade. The fact
that the economic relationships of the French with the Indians
were of a bargaining character favoured the commercialization of
sexual relationships. The traders possessed commodities readily
available to the natives, and the desire for these commodities
resulted in a willingness on the part of Indian females to engage
in prostitution. The small number of white prostitutes in the
colony increased the dependence of the traders upon the natives,
and there developed a regularized if not extensive trade of prostitution in Montreal and Michilimackinac in which Indian females

[30]Cf. Innis, *The Fur Trade in Canada.*

[31]Cf. E. B. O'Callaghan, ed., *Documents Relative to the Colonial History of
the State of New York* (Albany, 1856-87), vol. IX, pp. 278-9.

were employed. The effects of the fur trade extended back to weaken the family organization of the rural communities. Relationships with the Indians, and the free and easy life, made the *coureurs de bois* reluctant to accept the responsibilities of marriage. To acquire a wife meant settling down in the colony or at any rate making some provision for the wife's maintenance. Efforts of the colonial governors to encourage marriage largely failed with respect to this group, and many of the daughters of the habitants were left without husbands.[32] The prolonged absence of married men on excursions to the West further served to weaken the family and to give rise to problems such as adultery. Family disorganization, to the extent that it emerged, reflected the wider disorganizations in the rural *mores* of New France. The pull of the fur trade made more difficult the establishment of a stable community life, and the family suffered from the general unsettlement which obtained.

The weakening of family controls in the colony was not offset by the strengthening of other primary group attachments. Inherited cultural values associated with the ethnic background of the population had quickly weakened in face of forces of geography,[33] and the fur trade checked the development of new cultural attachments to take the place of those transmitted from the homeland. As a result of the influence of the traders, no group emerged with a strong sense of collective interest in, and a consciousness of, its obligations to the rural community. The attractions of the fur trade led to the neglect of agriculture and prevented the development of distinctions of social worth resting upon successes achieved in husbandry or rural public life. The enterprising but reckless *coureur de bois* tended to command, particularly among rural youth, more respect than the hard-working and patient habitant, while the swashbuckling leader of fur-trading parties won a position of prestige denied the public-spirited leader in the rural community. The agricultural class lacked definite social status so long as farming remained subordinate to the occupation of fur trading. Other social classes in the community were little more able to provide cultural leadership. The centralized character of the overseas trade in furs checked the growth of a well-to-do merchant

[32]Parkman, *The Old Regime in Canada*, p. 376.
[33]Riddell, *The Rise of Ecclesiastical Control in Quebec*, pp. 35-42.

class within the colony. The large merchants who reaped the really substantial profits from the fur trade by providing the necessary provisions for carrying on the trade with the Indians and by marketing the furs brought down to Montreal did not become settled inhabitants. Often they were represented in the colony by agents, and, if they personally transacted their business, they returned to France when their affairs were wound up.[34] This outside control of the fur trade resulted in a heavy cultural loss to New France. In effect, the only group which secured large material benefits from the fur trade made no contribution to the cultural life of the colony. The local *bourgeoisie*, petty traders, innkeepers, and others, did not acquire wealth and consequently failed to acquire attributes of social worth which would have separated them off from the great bulk of the inhabitants. Instead of providing leadership within the colony, they were subject with the rest of the population to the demoralizing influences of the western trade. The official class, likewise, failed to develop any strong sense of being a distinctive social *élite*. Though the members of this group were least exposed to the influence of the fur trade, their occupation was not sufficiently attractive to offset the prestige of the *coureurs de bois*. Salaries of the councillors were extremely small and did not induce the immigration of persons trained in jurisprudence; most of the local officials found it necessary to engage in petty trade to supplement their meagre incomes.[35]

If, of all classes in the colony, the seigneurs were the most securely established, a number of factors limited the effectiveness of their leadership in resisting the disorganizing influences of the fur trade. The crown, jealous of the royal prerogative, took care not to endow them with powers which would have made possible the erection of a genuine feudal order on the American frontier. They were deprived of privileges of a military character, and were not endowed with any real political power. Limitations imposed by the crown were reinforced by the forces of geography. Defence from Indian attacks required the centralization of the control of the army in the hands of the Governor, the building up of a mobile military force to wage war upon the Indians, and the appointment of militia captains throughout the rural districts who were directly

[34]Cf. Innis, *The Fur Trade in Canada*.
[35]Cahall, *The Sovereign Council in New France*, pp. 102-6, 134-7.

responsible to the chief executive. As a result, the patriotism which was aroused by the fear of the Indian enemy was directed towards the Governor rather than towards the local seigneurs, while the militia captain in many respects became the most important person in the local community. Furthermore, expansion of the fur trade westward resulted in the emergence of a distant frontier in which problems of criminal and civil jurisdiction could not be handled by the seigneurial courts. The heavy burden imposed upon the Sovereign Council with the increasing number of cases relating to trading matters or to the activities of western traders led to the erection of a system of royal courts throughout the colony and this development brought about a steady decline in the influence and prestige of the seigneurial courts.[36] The result of this combination of pressures of a political and geographical character was to divest the seigneurial system of New France of many of the attributes of feudalism.

The direct influence of the fur trade led to a further loss of such attributes. The interest of the seigneurs was wholly identified with the land since their economic welfare depended upon returns from agriculture, and the diversion of much of the resources and energies of the colony into the fur trade and the small returns from agriculture left them in a state often bordering on penury. At the same time, the little interest taken in rural problems, and lack of prestige attached to rural leadership, lowered their status in many cases to little more than that of debt-ridden farmers. The attempt to lead the life of gentlemen on incomes derived from feudal dues which from the circumstances of a new country could scarcely ever be profitable inevitably rendered the economic position of this class insecure. To reduce their standard of living to conform to their meagre incomes was as objectionable to their tastes as to increase their incomes by engaging in trade was disastrous to their social position. Some accepted the inevitable, and became little more than substantial farmers, working side by side with the habitants in the field; by such an adjustment the seigneurial institution was to survive and become an established feature of rural life in French Canada. Commercial vocations in the colony provided a more happy means of adjusting to economic demands, but petty trade offered little in the way of remuneration

[36]*Ibid.*, pp. 202-10.

or prestige, and the seigneurs were ill-qualified to engage in the
more lucrative exploits of commerce. They lacked the capacity
and financial resources to compete successfully with merchants
who came out from France; the *bourgeoisie* which attained a position
of supremacy after the British conquest recruited few from the
ranks of the seigneurial class. The participation of many of the
sons of seigneurs, and even of seigneurs themselves, in the fur
trade, to the extent of becoming *coureurs de bois*, was indicative
of the disintegration of the class rather than of its adjustment to
the conditions of a fur-trade-agrarian society. Some of the more
adventurous of the seigneurs, it is true, were able to place themselves in charge of fur-trading parties made up of their own
habitants, and thus achieved a position of leadership as fur lords
which they failed to achieve as lords of the land. For the most
part, however, the conditions of the fur trade favoured more
rugged qualities of leadership than those possessed by the seigneurs.
The fur trade gave rise to a type of hierarchical organization
which made no provision for such attributes of worth as those to
which the *gentilhommes* could lay claim. It was *coureurs de bois*
like Duluth who were able to assume charge of trading parties or military expeditions. The result was that the entry of seigneurs into the
fur trade meant the loss of those distinguishing marks of superiority
derived from the system of land holding.

Intendants and priests, in denouncing the *coureurs de bois*,
made little distinction between the sons of seigneurs and other
followers of this vocation. The social background of the former
made them if anything more difficult to control. They shared
with the common bush-rangers a dislike for discipline of any sort,
while their aristocratic ties gave them an exalted opinion of their
own worth. For this reason, the more spectacular forms of disorder
and dissipation of the *coureurs de bois* were likely to be indulged
in by these scions of the colonial nobility. The demoralization of
a large number of the sons of seigneurs, in combination with the
abject poverty of many of the seigneurs themselves, destroyed
the vestiges of aristocracy which the feudal system in the colony
was intended to create. A few of the seigneurs, it is true, with
more favourable holdings or other means of subsistence achieved
a position of influence and prestige in the community. A very
great number, however, fell hopelessly into debt, and were con-

stantly facing difficulties in relations with their creditors. Appearances were often kept up though it meant doing without the decencies of life.[37] In many cases the condition of their families was so critical as to make them objects of charity from the government. Appeals of the governors or intendants seeking assistance from the King for distressed seigneurs became increasingly frequent, and such appeals were usually accompanied by urgent pleas to bring to an end the creation of new seigneuries, or at any rate to give grants only to those who would not become a burden to the government. A variety of aids was designed to relieve the situation of hard-pressed seigneurs. Some secured political appointments, while others were granted the privilege of selling licences for the fur trade. Such expedients, however, offered little in the way of a solution to a problem, the existence of which was inherent in a social system torn between farming and fur trading. As the prestige of the class declined, a less desirable type of persons sought seigneurial grants. Originally intended to attract the lesser nobles of France, the seigneuries tended increasingly to be occupied by adventurers who had made money following other pursuits or by retired officers of the army who lacked other means of support. The seigneurial grants became for a certain class of persons a speculative venture and, for another class, a government sinecure. This disintegration of the colonial class structure would have been no great loss if conditions in the colony had given rise to a genuine rural social *élite*. But the attractions of the fur trade rendered this impossible until after the turn of the seventeenth century. The *coureurs de bois* came to constitute in the period 1660-1700 the aristocracy of the colonial society, and it was this class which set to some considerable extent the standards for the community as a whole.

The absence of any group able to assume a position of cultural leadership increased reliance upon the church. Vigorous efforts were made by the local bishops to check evils emerging in the colony as a result of the fur trade, and these efforts were ably supported by the Jesuit missionaries and by the Sulpicians in Montreal. Every opportunity was seized by the missionaries to denounce the trade in brandy, and *mandements* promulgated by

[37]Cf. Parkman, *The Old Regime in Canada*, pp. 315-25.

the Bishop carried the penalty of excommunication for this offence.[38]
Religious and moral prohibitions were widened to embrace a great
variety of evils associated with the fur trade. But these efforts
were largely ineffective so far as the *coureurs de bois* were concerned. Though Jesuit missionaries were stationed at the various
trading posts, and very often went along with the traders to and
from the settlements, this intercourse seldom led to the establishment of relationships such as ordinarily exist between priests and
their parishioners. The *coureurs de bois* could readily escape from
the watchful eye of the missionaries, and on occasion successfully
contrived to leave them behind when setting off on trading excursions. Once in the woods, the traders were too far removed from
the influence of the church to observe their religious duties seriously,
and tended to develop attitudes of careless indifference to things
sacred which were mitigated only by a fund of superstitious beliefs
made up of a mixture of Indian mythological and Catholic theological tenets.[39] The irreverence of the sceptic and the superstition
of the pagan became combined in the outlook of the bush rangers.

Consequently the Jesuits and the higher ecclesiastical authorities recognized that the secure establishment of the church in the
colony and of successful missionary enterprises among the Indians
depended upon checking the development of the western fur trade.
In their eyes, most of the evils in New France lay in the practice
of young men going off to the woods to engage in trade with the
Indians. The *coureurs de bois* sensed this threat to their economic
welfare; encroachments of the missionaries, and controls of the
church, as a result were met with suspicion and no little hostility.
This conflict between the church and the traders turned mostly
about the brandy trade. While the traders may have had no
strong religious feelings, they viewed with alarm the possibility of
excommunication; few of even the boldest *coureurs de bois* were
prepared to accept with equanimity the prospect of being turned
adrift from the church. Accordingly, many of them developed a
conscience which permitted their engaging in the brandy trade
without feeling the necessity of confession, and to meet this threat
to its control the church undertook to determine guilt outside the

[38]Cf. Eastman, *Church and State in Early Canada.*
[39]Bailey, *The Conflict of European and Eastern Algonkian Cultures*, chaps. x
and xi.

confessional, and upon such external evidence to apply its sanction of excommunication. Exercise of virtual police powers involved the ecclesiastical authorities in conflict with the secular, and gave rise to violent protests against any exercise of the power of excommunication in relation to the brandy trade. Early governors such as Argenson and Avaugour, though under the influence of the ecclesiastical party, found themselves opposed to the clergy in their treatment of the brandy trade as a crime, and Mesy, likewise, broke with the Bishop over this question.[40] But it was under the vigorous leadership of Talon and later Frontenac that the controversy was finally brought to a head.[41] The Recollets, absent from the colony from 1629, were brought back in 1672 to offset the influence of the Jesuits, and the protests of the governors to the home government forced the local Bishop to modify his policy. If the recall of Frontenac in 1682 and his succession first by Le Barre and then by the religiously minded Denonville represented a victory for the church, Frontenac's return in 1689 marked the failure of the church to put an end to the brandy trade.[42] This failure was a measure of the weakening of the controls of the church with respect to the activities in general of the fur traders.

The brandy trade, and the disorderly conduct of the bush rangers generally, were in themselves serious deviations from those norms which the church sought to uphold. But the influence of the fur trade upon religion to some extent extended back into the settled rural communities. The irreverent and superstitious attitudes of the *coureurs de bois* infected the thinking of a considerable number of the colonists. Church obligations ceased to be taken as seriously, particularly by the male members of the population, as they would otherwise have been, and there was evident throughout the colony a weakening of religious fervour. Though poverty provided a legitimate reason for the failure to contribute sufficiently to the support of the clergy, the opposition to increasing the tithes expressed, in slight measure at least, an underlying feeling of indifference to the welfare of the church. Sacred attitudes, fostered within the simple life of a

[40]Eastman, *Church and State in Early Canada*, pp. 26-31, 72-82.

[41]*Ibid.*, pp. 122-9, 179-201; cf. also Jean Delanglez, *Frontenac and the Jesuits* (Chicago, 1939).

[42]Eastman, *Church and State in Early Canada*, pp. 222-8, 243-54, 267-71.

peasant society, were weakening in face of the increasing importance of secular interests, represented in the fur trade. Such
a tendency did not involve any general resistance to Catholicism
—the habitants remained passionately attached to the church—
but it did mean an indulgence in forms of behaviour strenuously
opposed by ecclesiastical leaders. The concern shown by a zealous
priesthood for the morals of the inhabitants, and bitter denuncia-
tions by the bishops of immorality, drunkenness, impiety, and the
vain and immodest manner in which women dressed, may be
considered indicative of the attitudes of strict Catholic disciplina-
rians, but these efforts to secure reform found justification in the
prevalence of kinds of behaviour which represented deviations
from the strict code of a peasant society.[43] It was such tendencies
in the behaviour of many of the inhabitants of New France which
chiefly aroused the concern of the leaders of the church. If these
leaders represented the most evangelical of European movements
of Catholicism, this evangelism was increased by developments
within the colony. Though defining the issue in moral terms, the
church's emphasis upon the virtues of frugality and plain living
expressed a desire to maintain the conditions of a simple, peasant
society. So long as the fur trade flourished and exerted a strong
influence upon the rural communities that desire could not be
fully realized.

The challenge to the church's ideal of a peasant society was
simply a part of the larger challenge which involved the *mores* of
the rural family, the prestige of the seigneurial class, and (in so
far as it expressed rural rather than trading interests) the formal
law of the state, and to the extent that this challenge could not
be successfully met the colonial society was left without any single
focus of cultural values. What values emerged tended to relate
to the immediate needs of the inhabitants, and, in those areas
outside the province of individual self-interest, they were in some
degree morally indifferent. The confusion of values extended
furthest, of course, among those actively engaged in the fur trade,
and the *coureurs de bois* might be described as culturally marginal
in all respects, but to some extent this confusion was general
throughout the colonial population. Though no complete, nor
perhaps even considerable, break from the traditional rural culture

[43]Cf. Parkman, *The Old Regime in Canada*, chap. XXIII.

occurred, the increasing weakening of traditional cultural ties was apparent during the interval in which the pull of the fur trade was strongest.

The socially disorganizing influence of the fur trade was greatest in the years 1660-1700 during which period the *coureurs de bois* played the chief role in the trade. After the turn of the century, depletion in the supply of beavers in the Great Lakes region led to the extension of the fur-trade organization into the Saskatchewan area, and this change in the location of the trade involved a shift from individual economic enterprise represented by the *coureur de bois* to large commercial enterprise employing a steady labour force.[44] Those engaged in the trade became increasingly differentiated from those engaged in agriculture, and, seldom finding their way into the rural communities, they exerted no such disturbing influence as that which had been exerted by the *coureurs de bois*. Montreal remained the centre of the trade, but it became now a metropolitan centre independent to a considerable extent of the resources of the rural communities in so far as the actual carrying on of the fur trade was concerned. The break did not become complete until about 1783, but after 1720 the trend had become definitely marked. For the first time, there emerged a clear distinction between *urban* and *rural* society, and, as the urban became more sharply defined, the rural attained a greater degree of maturity. There developed a distinct agricultural group with its distinctive set of social *mores*. It was this development within the agrarian society which paved the way for the moral solidarity which became pronounced after the British conquest.

Immediately, however, after the turn of the century, new disturbing influences made themselves felt within the colony. As the organization of the fur trade became more complex and far flung, government came to play an increasingly important role and a greater dependence came to be placed upon military forces to defend the lines of trade and to resist the rapidly growing colonies to the south. A powerful bureaucracy emerged in Quebec, and the colony tended to be converted into something of an armed camp. The growth of a "smart set" in the capital, engaged in a round of dinners, balls, and theatrical entertainments (and in political corruption), carried threats to the simple virtues of a pioneer

[44]Cf. Innis, *The Fur Trade in Canada.*

rural society. Scepticism found its way into the colony through
the contacts of officials with liberal elements in Europe, and society
in New France after 1750 felt to some extent the effects of the
philosophes emerging in old France. These influences were confined
to small circles in the towns, but the increase of military forces
had much more general effects upon moral standards; the growth
of problems of adultery and illegitimacy in the colony was closely
related to the new demands being made by defence and war. In
the end, some sort of satisfactory accommodation would probably
have been made between interests identified with the rural society
and official and military interests; even before 1760 the seigneurial
class was becoming more closely identified with bureaucracy, and
the church was beginning to lose much of its evangelical pioneer
attitude—the Jesuits were coming into disrepute—and was tending
to adopt a more tolerant outlook. But other developments after
the turn of the century carried much more serious threats to the
rural way of life. The western extension of the fur trade served
to promote the growth of a group of local merchants,[45] and the
challenge of this class to the leadership of the seigneurial class
and of the church was beginning to make itself evident before
1760. Ultimately, the strengthening of commercial interests would
have meant a dominance of pecuniary values through the society
of New France. Such developments, however, were sharply
arrested by the British conquest. Both the tightening grip of
colonial officialdom and the growing power of local French commercial interests were destroyed by the Treaty of Paris which
transferred the administration and defence of the colony to British
officials and military forces and made possible the dominance in
commerce of American and Scottish merchants.[46] With political
and commercial control in the hands of a "foreign" group, the
seigneurial class and more particularly the church emerged as the
dominant institutions of the new social order of French Canada.[47]

In some ways the conquest and the assertion of supremacy of
the rural way of life were the inevitable consequences of develop-

[45]H. A. Innis, foreword to *Marketing Organization and Technique*, ed. Jane
McKee (Toronto, 1940).

[46]Cf. R. Flenley, "The French Revolution and French Canada," *Essays in
Canadian History*, ed. R. Flenley.

[47]Cf. A. L. Burt, *The Old Province of Quebec* (Toronto, 1933).

ments which had taken place throughout the French colonial period. If the growth of commercial interests before 1760 involved a threat to traditional authority, these interests did not become sufficiently powerful to bring about a modification of colonial policy and avert the disaster of military conquest. The dominance of the fur trade, and the highly centralized character of its organization, had led to the failure to develop a diversified economy, and this dependence upon a single staple made necessary increasing support from the state. The inevitable concentration of control checked the development of a powerful and independent commercial class as a support of the colonial system, and, involved in the contradictions of the economic order, the state collapsed with the decline of the fur trade upon which it depended. Traditional cultural institutions, such as the church, on the other hand, weakened during the long period when the fur trade was supreme, benefited when it declined and eventually passed under foreign control. Whereas the state, in the end, broke down because it lacked supports outside the interests of the fur trade, the church obtained a dominant position largely because of the lack of other strong interests in the colony.

1. SOCIAL WELFARE

Destitution from Lack of Trading Opportunities

Public Archives of Canada, *Series C¹¹A*, vol. 6, pp. 111-12: Quebec, November 12, 1682, de Meulles to the Minister.

There is so much corn, cattle and other commodities such as salmon, eels, fresh and dried cod, peas and other vegetables that the majority of the inhabitants cannot consume them. Not finding any market, they are obliged to keep them, without being able to make any money to buy necessities.

It would be desirable if trade could be established between Canada and the [West Indian] Islands. I know that that is the intention of the Court but it is very difficult to accomplish, since there is no one here good enough in these affairs to undertake it. It would bring about prosperity and would be extremely comforting to the people, and the sale they would have from that which they harvested would encourage them to enlarge their homes and even build new ones. They find themselves in great need of everything that comes from France, such as linen, cloth, serge, hats, shoes, etc. All these commodities are twice as expensive here as in France. They have the necessities of life but, everyone else having them also, they cannot make any money which prevents them from relieving their needs, and renders them so poor in winter, everyone has assured us, that the men and women are obliged to go almost nude.

Need for Provisions from France

Public Archives of Canada, *Series C¹¹A*, vol. 11, p. 158: Quebec, April 30, 1690, Frontenac to the Minister.

The apprehension which may develop here from being troubled during seeding and harvesting by new hostile invasions of the Iroquois caused M. the Intendant and myself to think it absolutely necessary to despatch to you a boat to advise you of the situation so that you would be pleased to provide for our great need, and send us as promptly as possible the flour necessary for the troops, according to the Memoir that the Intendant sent you, without which it would be impossible to find means of maintaining them.

Useless Servants Sent to the Colony

Public Archives of Canada, *Series C¹¹A*, vol. 6, pp. 142-5: Quebec, November 12, 1684, Memoir of de Meulles to the Minister.

Sixty indentured servants have been sent to this country again this year with the notion that they would be immediately useful. The oldest is not seventeen, and since I am certain that the majority are only twelve, thirteen, fourteen and fifteen, I believe that those who sent them are making a mockery of us, there being no one of an age to render service. If they had sent those like I requested, in three days they would have been all placed; but I find myself in the position of not being able to get rid of these children who are only good for herding cows and who have cost as much for their passage as big men in a useful state.

I have decided, in order to place them, to indenture them for five and seven years, and those who have done that I have scarcely any longer on my hands. As no one wished to pay the twenty *livres* they learn it cost to feed them at Rochelle, I have been obliged to reduce it for fear of losing everything. This expense amounted to eight hundred and eighty-four *livres* and two *sou;* besides that, I hope with care to cut down the other expenses such as the forty five *livres* for passage, and the eleven crowns which were advanced to them for their clothes and board at Quebec for fifteen days or three weeks.

There were sent besides six girls to teach the savage girls on the Mountain of Montreal to sew, knit and make lace. Six miserable girls were taken from the coast of Rochelle who had been found on the streets and whom it would be very agreeable to have returned to France, not having a good reputation. Sister Bourgeois, superior of the Sisters of the Congregation of Montreal, together with an ecclesiastic named Souart, a priest of the Sulpician Seminary, came here expressly to visit and take them away, but, after seeing these creatures and being informed of their life, they said they did not wish to take charge of them for fear they would corrupt everyone, in their community and also the savage girls whom the Sulpicians have raised in great piety and devotion, with the result that I was obliged to give them their freedom; Monsieur the General and Monseigneur the Bishop advised me to do that. They will not lack in finding someone to marry in this country; for this design, prudent, mature and very capable women are necessary and these are young, lively and very ignorant. But we have no great need of girls from France; there are girls in the country capable of executing the intention of His Majesty who will live at Montreal and teach the savage girls to spin, sew and knit, and to render this establishment perfectly useful, it is necessary to have two thousand *livres* a year and to oblige these women to live on the Mountain in Montreal among the savages which is the only way to civilize them since that places them in a state of gaining something which would make them envious of adopting our customs and dressing like us. And if His Majesty wished to make a small donation of one thousand *livres* paid at one time, would he have the goodness to send them thread to make lace and yarn to knit after which they could supply themselves.

Worthless Young People Sent Out by Parents

Public Archives of Canada, *Series* $C^{11}A$, vol. 69, pp. 167-8: Quebec, October 15, 1738, Beauharnois to the Minister.

I take the liberty of pointing out to you that there are several young people coming to this colony under the pretext of seeing the country and that the only object of their parents is to send them far away because of their faults which they hope will be corrected by the poverty they suffer.

Laziness of Inhabitants and Their Poverty

Public Archives of Canada, *Series* $C^{11}A$, vol. 9, p. 25: Quebec, November 6, 1687, Denonville and Champigny to the Minister.

The principal reasons for the poverty of the country, besides the wearing of extravagant clothes, are the laziness and bad conduct of most of the people. There is nothing so essential here as to accustom our colonists to raise and work hemp. That is the first manufacture which it is necessary to develop, and this will be the object of our future endeavours. Most of the women of this country are very lazy. In time all this must come to an end. The necessity of raising cattle will also be considered; sheep are difficult to raise because of the long winter.

Effects of the Fur Trade upon Industry of Inhabitants

F. X. de Charlevoix, *Journal of a Voyage to North America* (Chicago, 1923),
vol. I, pp. 131-2.

One part of our youth is continually rambling and roving about; and
though these disorders, which formerly so much disgraced this profession,
are no longer committed, at least not so openly, yet it infects them with a
habit of libertinism, of which they never entirely get rid; at least, it gives
them a distaste for labour, it exhausts their strength, they become incapable
of the least constraint, and when they are no longer able to undergo the
fatigues of travelling, which soon happens, for these fatigues are excessive,
they remain without the least resource, and are no longer good for anything.
Hence it comes to pass, that arts have been a long time neglected, and great
quantity of good land remains still uncultivated, and the country is but
very indifferently peopled.

Efforts to Check Desertion of Servants

*Arrêts et règlements du Conseil supérieur de Québec, et ordonnances et jugements des
intendants du Canada* (Quebec, 1855), p. 70.

*General Regulations of the Superior Council of Quebec for the Police,
May 11, 1676*

XXXI.   In order to remedy the abuses which increase every day through
the desertion of domestic servants from their masters to the great detriment
of the colony, all indentured servants are forbidden to leave or abandon
the service of their masters, under pain of being placed in the iron collar for
the first offence, and for the second to be beaten with rods and burnt with
the impression of the *fleur-de-lis*; all persons are also prohibited from giving
them refuge without written permission from their masters or a written
certificate from the commander, judge or parish priest that they are indentured to no one, under penalty of a fine of twenty *livres* and of paying for
each day of absence from the said service fifteen *sou*, as responsibility for
the acts of the fugitives.

Begging and Efforts to Control It

*Arrêts et règlements du Conseil supérieur de Québec, et ordonnances et jugements des
intendants du Canada* (Quebec, 1855), p. 102.

Order of the Superior Council of Quebec . . . Monday, April 26, 1683

On that which has been demonstrated by the Attorney-General that in
the year 1677, on the last day of August, the court had rendered an order
prohibiting all healthy beggars from begging in this town under pain of
punishment, enjoining them to remove themselves in the course of a week
and go to live on the places of abode which had been conceded to them in
order to cultivate and make them valuable, and making similar prohibitions

to all persons of whatever quality and condition from giving alms to them at the door of their dwelling under whatever pretext there may be, under pain of a fine of ten *livres*; that, nevertheless, the said order having been in force for some time, the same beggars who had left have returned, and burden the public, although they are able to earn their own living; even raising their children in idleness which leads them to all sorts of disorders and causing them to be unwilling to serve any inhabitant of the country although there is a very great need for domestics, besides that the huts which they build around the town become places of disorder and scandal for similar people without any honour, and attracting there all sorts of rabble, which it is very necessary to remedy immediately so that they will have time to remove themselves and become re-established in their places of abode, which lie in a state of waste, before the winter season.

Requesting the said Attorney-General that, conforming to the said order, it be expressly prohibited to all beggars in good health to beg in this town in the future under pain of punishment, to wit, for the first offence to be placed in the iron collar, and in case of repeated offences to be given the cat-o'-nine-tails; that they be required to remove themselves within a week and to go to dwell on their places of abode; as also to all persons of whatever quality and condition of giving or causing to be given alms at their doors, under penalty of ten *livres* fine. . . .

Signed: DE MEULLES

Establishment of Poor Boards

Arrêts et règlements du Conseil supérieur de Québec, et ordonnances et jugements des intendants du Canada (Quebec, 1855), pp. 119-20.

Order of the Superior Council of Quebec . . . Thursday, April 8, 1688

. . . On that which has been represented to the Council by the Attorney-General of the King that, notwithstanding prohibitions which have been heretofore made to all persons declaring themselves poor and in need, of collecting and begging without having a certificate of their poverty, signed by the parish priest or local judge, these persons, without consideration, do not cease to do it, maintaining themselves in idleness and laziness as also do their wives and children, instead of working or placing themselves in service to earn their living and maintenance, this being contrary to the well-being of the colony and a burden upon the public, it appears necessary to stop by some new regulation the continuation of this laziness by preventing the fathers and mothers from continuing this life and raising their children in it, and obliging both to enter into service; it is necessary to provide, however, that the unfortunate poor, aged and truly destitute invalids are known so that they can be supported, without which they are able to beg for any reason whatever, this which will be of benefit to the colony and to the truly poor; the matter placed in deliberation:

The Council, in order to provide means to the poor of Quebec, Three Rivers and Montreal, of subsisting, has ordered and orders that there be established in each of the said places a poor board, made up of the parish priest, who will take note of the unfortunate and miserable poor, of whom he will have knowledge, which he will seek with as much care as possible, without interfering with his other duties; of a director of the poor who will be charged with informing himself of the poor who are in need, and to whom those who will wish to receive public alms will address themselves, and whom he will examine as to the cause of their poverty in order to report to the other directors of the board; to seek work for those who are able to work, men as well as women; and if these people, in order to avoid working, demand too much so that they will be rejected, this director will fix the price which they ought to earn from those who will wish to employ them, with which the said poor will be obliged to content themselves; of another director who will have the responsibility and commission of treasurer to receive all sums which are given for the poor, as much from public collections as from the poor boxes which will be placed in the churches, which may be sent to the poor board in any manner whatsoever. Of all which alms the director will hold an exact daily account of that which will be delivered to him and the use which will be made of it, in conformity with the decisions of the board meetings, and everyone who will take public contributions will sign on the register of the treasurer the sums that they have delivered; and of another secretary-director who will keep a register of all the meetings with an exact statement of the poor who have been admitted to the alms and the day they will have received them; which parish priest and directors will have the power of deliberation. . . .

Signed: BOCHART CHAMPIGNY

Need of Support for Medical and Charitable Institutions

Public Archives of Canada, *Series C¹¹A*, vol. 9, pp. 3-5, 28-9: Quebec, November 6, 1687, Denonville and Champigny to the Minister.

So many soldiers and inhabitants have been sick throughout the colony this year that there is nothing so important for the good of the country as the support of the two hospitals of Quebec and Montreal without which the people and soldiers would have greatly suffered for lack of care. Although poor, the hospital of Quebec supports itself quite comfortably even if it is a burden to the charitable people and is in debt. But the one in Montreal is in extreme poverty and would be abandoned if it was not for our most charitable merchants who still lend to it, confident, Monseigneur, that you will not forsake them. It is the greatest pity in the world to see the lodging of these poor religious. We visited it in another connection; certainly they cannot remain there without running the risk of being crushed by a gale of wind, and besides that the rain and snow comes in from all sides since there is only some old rotten partition work. Yet without this house at the head of the colony I do not know what we would do for the soldiers and inhabitants. There are two surgeons whose only compensation is fifteen crowns each for serving every year for six months. This is given them by the poor hospital. They serve very well for so little. That is why we are obliged to ask you to give them some·more for their services and for the maintenance of their big families. We have sent you, Monseigneur, a memoir of the condition of this poor house for which we ask your protection in order to procure from him [the Prince] some gratuity to aid them in becoming established. . . .

We have been obliged to support this hospital in taking care of sick soldiers by a grant of three *sou* a day for each soldier beyond his pay. We felt, Monseigneur, that you would approve, and would you not approve that as much be done for those in Quebec where it is impossible to feed and lodge a soldier for four *sou* a day, which is charged to the hospital whose revenue is very small. A great number of inhabitants of all ages are dying in this country, and also many of our savages living in the colony. Our *curés* have not sent us a memoir about it because death is a daily occurrence from sickness beginning with the measles. There has been some typhoid fever and again some tuberculosis. . . .

Since our written letter, we have assembled the accounts of the deaths of this year which amount to 500 French, more than 400 within the last three months, and besides 300 savages of our village settlements. These deaths are of all ages. We sent to M. Fagon a memoir of our surgeons which informs him of the nature of the diseases and which was drawn up in order to be aided by his advice. It is a pity that we have only very poor surgeons to care for all these sick people. Happily we found a doctor last year on one of our merchant ships whom we retained for attendance upon the soldiers, and to whom the company was required to give something. He has made some very good cures, saved Father Anjalvan, and was of much use in the epidemic.

Establishment of Poor House in Quebec

Edits, ordonnances royaux, déclarations et arrêts du Conseil d'Etat du roi concernant le Canada (Quebec, 1854), pp. 271-4.

Permission of the King to Establish a General Hospital at Quebec

Louis, by the grace of God, King of France and of Navarre, to all present and to come, Greeting.

We have learnt by experience that there is nothing more useful than the general hospitals we have established in most of the towns of our kingdom for the police of our kingdom and for preventing the idleness of poor beggars who neglect to work, though able to do so, because of the facility of subsisting by alms and charities which are given them, and which would be much more usefully employed in relieving the destitute sick and invalids and those people not able to subsist by their own labour; and since our solicitude is not limited solely to the area within the ancient boundaries of France, and since we have always had particular concern for the conservation, increase and police of our colonies of New France in Canada, we have been informed that the hardships involved in clearing and cultivating the soil deter most of the inhabitants of the said colonies from this work, although they have sufficient strength and health to do it and they should make it their principal occupation, with the result that idleness reduces some to begging and others to throwing themselves into the woods to live there in libertinism with the savages, which hinders the said colonies from being as populated as they ought to be; and the disorders that that causes in Canada will become still worse if suitable remedies are not found, of which the best and most infallible is the establishment of a general hospital in which poor beggars, healthy and sick of both sexes will be confined to be employed at whatever work and labour they are able, even the cultivation of the land of those farms attached to the said hospital; and to facilitate the execution of a plan so pious and so salutary, our dear and good friend the Bishop of Quebec has represented to us that there are several business men of the town of Quebec and other inhabitants of New France who have offered to contribute, each according to his means, the sums necessary, as much for the building as for the foundation of the said general hospital.

With these reasons and others which move us, and with our certain knowledge, full power and royal authority, we have permitted and permit by these presents, signed by our hand, the establishment of a General Hospital in the town of Quebec. . . .

And since a single general hospital is not sufficient to confine all the beggars of the said country of Canada, because of the distance of the places, and since some charitable people of the said distant places would plan to contribute to the relief of the poor in their local communities, if they were certain that their benefices would be employed in perpetuity to the said relief of the poor, we permit to the said administrators [of the General Hospital] to establish, in places they judge suitable, houses of charity, and to receive all donations made for this purpose, and to leave to the founders during their life-time the direction and administration of this to which they will have contributed, save that the said administrators shall take over the administration after the death of the founders; and to govern the said houses of charity in the manner they will advise, which will continue attached to the said General Hospital until, with the passage of time, it will be judged necessary to establish as hospitals those of the said houses of charity which will be found sufficiently well supported, and if we judge it necessary. . . .

Given at Versailles in the month of March, in the year of grace 1692 and in the forty-ninth year of our reign.

LOUIS

Establishment of Poor House in Montreal

Edits, ordonnances royaux, déclarations et arrêts du Conseil d'Etat du roi concernant le Canada (Quebec, 1854), pp. 277-8.

Letters Patent for the Establishment of a General Hospital at Montreal, in the Island of Montreal

Louis, by the grace of God, King of France and of Navarre, to all present and to come, Greeting.

. . . We have permitted and permit by these presents, signed by our hand, those individuals who have presented themselves and those who will join with them, to establish a hospital at the said Montreal, where they will send poor children, orphans, cripples, old, infirm and other needy of their sex, to be lodged, nourished and supported by them and their successors, in their needs, to occupy them in suitable work, to teach trades to the said children, to give them the best education they are able, all for the greater glory of God and for the well-being and usefulness of the colony. . . .

Given at Versailles, the 15th day of April, the year of grace 1694, and in the fifty-first year of our reign.

LOUIS

Charitable Work of Hospital Brothers

Public Archives of Canada, *Series C¹¹A*, vol. 19, pp. 34-5: Quebec, October 5, 1701, Callières and Champigny to the Minister.

The hospital brothers are most grateful for the gratuity that you have accorded them. We earnestly pray you to continue it, as they are truly in great need of it, having many more poor charges than their funds enable them to feed, as you know by the state of the goods they possess and the use they make of them.

2. CRIME AND THE MORAL ORDER

Establishment of the Family in New France

(i)

Baron de Lahontan, *New Voyages to North America*, ed. R. G. Thwaites (Chicago, 1905), vol. I, pp. 36-8.

Several ships were sent hither from *France* [about 1665], with a Cargoe of Women of an ordinary Reputation, under the direction of some old stale Nuns, who rang'd 'em in three Classes. The Vestal Virgins were heap'd up, (if I may so speak) one above another, in three different Apartments, where the Bridegrooms singled out their Brides, just as a Butcher do's an Ewe from amongst a Flock of Sheep. In these three *Seraglios*, there was such variety and change of Diet, as could satisfy the most whimsical Appetites; for here was some big some little, some fair some brown, some fat and some meagre. In fine, there was such Accommodation, that every one might be fitted to his Mind: And indeed the market had such a run, that in fifteen days time, they were all dispos'd of. I am told, that the fattest went off best, upon the apprehension that these being less active, would keep truer to their Ingagements, and hold out better against the nipping cold of the Winter: But after all, a great many of the He-Adventurers found themselves mistaken in their measures. However, let that be as it will, it affords a very curious Remark; namely, That in some parts of the World, to which the vicious

European Women are transported, the Mob of those Countries do's seriously believe, that their Sins are so defac'd by the ridiculous Christening, I took notice of before, that they are look'd upon ever after as Ladies of Vertue, of Honour, and of an untarnish'd conduct of life. The Sparks that wanted to be married, made their Addresses to the above-mentioned Governesses, to whom they were oblig'd to give an account of their Goods and Estates, before they were allow'd to make their choice in the three *Seraglios*. After the choice was determin'd, the Marriage was conclud'd upon the spot, in the presence of a Priest, and a public Notary; and the next day the Governor-General bestow'd upon the married Couple, a Bull, a Cow, a Hog, a Sow, a Cock, a Hen, two Barrels of salt Meat, and eleven Crowns; together with a certain Coat of Arms call'd by the *Greeks* Kepara. The Officers having a nicer taste than the Soldiers, made their Application to the Daughters of the Ancient Gentlemen of the Country, or those of the richer sort of inhabitants.

(ii)

Baron de Lahontan, *New Voyages to North America*, ed. R. G. Thwaites (Chicago, 1905), vol. I, pp. 387-8.

Most of the Officers marry in this Country, but God knows what sort of marriages they make, in taking Girls with a Dowry, consisting of eleven Crowns, a Cock, a Hen, an Ox, a Cow, and sometimes a Calf. I knew several young Women, whose Lovers, after denying the fact, and proving before the Judges the scandalous Conversation of their Mistresses, were forc'd upon the perswasion of the *Ecclesiasticks* to swallow the bitter Pill, and take the very same Girls in marriage. Some Officers marry well, but these are few such. The occasion of their marrying so readily in that Country, proceeds from the difficulty of conversing with the soft Sex. After a Man has made four Visits to a young Woman, he is oblig'd to unfold his Mind to her Father and Mother; he must then either talk of Marriage, or break off all Correspondence; or if he do's not, both he and she lies under a Scandal. In this Country a Man can't visit another Man's Wife, without being censur'd, as if her husband was a Cuckold. In fine, a Man can meet with no diversion here, but that of reading, or eating, or drinking. Though after all, there are some Intrigues carry'd on, but with the same caution as in *Spain*, where the vertue of the Ladies consists in disguising the matter handsomely.

Growth of Vice in Montreal

R. Flenley, *History of Montreal, 1640-1672, from the French of Dollier de Casson* (London and Toronto, 1928), p. 301.

[From Autumn of 1664 to Autumn of 1665]. These rejoicings [at the arrival this year of a great body of people to Montreal] were mingled with a good deal of bitterness for the more clear-sighted when they saw their

father and most dear governor, M. de Maisonneuve, leave them this time
for good, and leave them in the hands of others from whom they could not
expect the same disinterestedness, the same affection and the same regard
for the exclusion of vices which have, in fact, risen and grown here since that
time, along with many other troubles and misfortunes which had not up
to that time made their appearance here.

Montreal the Rendezvous of Traders

Baron de Lahontan, *New Voyages to North America*, ed. R. G. Thwaites (Chicago, 1905), vol. I, p. 54.

The Pedlers call'd *Coureurs de Bois*, export from hence [Montreal] every
year several Canows full of Merchandise, which they dispose of among all
the Savage Nations of the Continent, by way of exchange for Beaver-Skins.
Seven or eight days ago, I saw twenty five or thirty of these Canows return
with heavy Cargoes; each Canow was manag'd by two or three Men, and
carry'd twenty hundred weight, i.e. forty packs of Beaver Skins, which are
worth an hundred Crowns a piece. These Canows had been a year and
eighteen Months out. You would be amaz'd if you saw how lewd these
Pedlers are when they return; how they Feast and Game, and how prodigal
they are, not only in their Cloaths, but upon Women. Such of 'em as are
married, have the wisdom to retire to their own Houses; but the Bachelors
act just as our *East-India-Men*, and Pirates are wont to do; for they Lavish,
Eat, Drink and Play all away as long as the Goods hold out; and when these
are gone, they e'en sell their Embroidery, their Lace, and their Cloaths.
This done, they are forc'd to go upon a new Voyage for Subsistence.

Character of Coureurs de Bois

Public Archives of Canada, *Series C¹¹A*, vol. 5, pp. 282-3: Quebec, November 13, 1681, Du Chesneau to the Minister.

And in order, Monseigneur, that you will be persuaded, permit me to
tell you that there are two types of *coureurs de bois*. The first go to the
source of the beaver in the country of the savage nations of Assinibouets,
Radoussieux, Miamis, Illinois and others. They are not able to make their
voyage in less than two or three years. The second type, who are not so
great in number, go only to meet the savages and French who come down
almost to Long-Sault, the small nation and sometimes almost to Michili-
makinac to sell their pelts, for whom they carry merchandise and more often
only brandy, in violation of the King's prohibition, with which they get
them drunk and ruin them. They are able to make their voyages almost
in the time which marks the summer or even in a shorter time. It is not
easy to arrest either the one type or the other.

Problems of Morality in the Trading Posts

R. G. Thwaites (ed.), *The Jesuit Relations and Allied Documents* (Cleveland, 1900), vol. LXV, pp. 219-41: Michilimakina, Aug. 30, 1702, Carheil to de Callières.

In whatever light we may consider the Commerce carried on, as regards either the Common interest of Canada, or the advancement of Christianity, It would be Infinitely more advantageous for both if the savages themselves went down annually for that purpose to montreal, than it would be to send the french here to trade, in the way in which they come every Year. I do not Consider it necessary to give the Reasons, so Manifest are they. For it is evident that the latter method serves but to depopulate the country of all its young men; to reduce the number of people in the houses; to deprive wives of their husbands, fathers and mothers of the aid of their children, and sisters of that of their brothers; to Expose those who undertake such journeys to a thousand dangers for both their Bodies and their souls. It also causes them to incur very many expenses, partly necessary, partly Useless, and partly Criminal; it accustoms them not to work, but to lose all taste for work, and to live in Continual idleness; it renders them incapable of learning any trade, and thereby makes them Useless to themselves, to their families, and to the entire country, through having made themselves unfit for the occupations that are most Common and most useful to man. But it is not only for these Reasons, which affect this Life,—it is still more on account of Those which concern the soul, that This Sending of the french among the savages must appear Infinitely harmful to them. It Takes them away from all the holy places; it separates them from all Ecclesiastical and religious persons; It abandons them to a total deprivation of all Instruction, both public and private, of all devotional Exercises, and, finally, of all the spiritual aids to Christianity. . . .

So long as all the young men devote themselves to no other occupation than That of Coming here for Beaver, There can be no hope that the Colony will Ever become flourishing; it will always be poor, for it will always lose thereby What would most enrich it,—I mean the labor of all the young men. Such, Monseigneur, is what I consider the most important step for the Temporal and spiritual welfare of the Colony, and what should, in Conscience, be most strongly represented to his majesty, by making him thoroughly Understand its necessity,—so that he may give orders to seek for and to find every possible means of restoring the Trade with the savages, and of establishing it at montreal, so as to keep all the young men in the country, and accustom them to work from early youth. . . .

They [the traders] have alleged various necessities for Establishing the Commerce with women, not Believing that we could reasonably oppose Such necessities; and, in fact, our opposition would not be just if they required only Certain outward and public services that can be rendered without any Fear of scandal, or any proximate danger or occasion for sin. But It is the very Bodies of the women that they desire; That is what their brutal passion makes their first necessity, under the apparent decency of other needs. . . .

Their first necessity consists in having women whom they Employ in pounding corn and doing their Cooking, and whom they detain under That pretext in their houses, when they wish and as long as they wish. The second consists in having some to Cut wood for them, and to carry it To their dwellings to Heat them. The third consists in having laundresses who, at the same time when, on the one Hand, they wash their linen, on the other defile their Bodies and blacken their souls by the most shameful brutishness. The 4th consists in having some women who make savage shoes, Garters (leggings?), and pouches, according to their fashion, and other similar articles. There are also some other necessities, less Common and less usual than Those 4 which are the chief ones, of which They make use to lure the women to their houses, and to give themselves a Pretext for going to theirs when It pleases them.

You see very well, Monseigneur, that even though it be true that they may sometimes need the services of women for Those four sorts of necessities, Still It is also true, on the other hand, that these give them at the same time both an easy means of obtaining the Commerce of the women's Bodies, And an apparently decent pretext for making them enter and for receiving them in their houses. . . . Those pretended necessities have been allowed to introduce themselves gradually, and to become a Custom; and Custom has made them Insurmountable to the missionaries who would Effectively oppose them, but whose opposition has had no other effect than that of being Useless. . . .

Moreover, lewdness has become Established not only through the liberty that the french have taken of admitting to their houses the savage women at all hours; but What has most Contributed to Establish it is the liberty, which they themselves have taken, of going to Seek those women in their villages. To such an extent is this carried that many of the most dissolute do not hesitate to leave the french houses, and to go to live with the women in their Cabins. . . . As a result of this, one of them has more than one child in The village. . . .

Here is another evil in connection with This matter, which is all the greater because it is Made more visible by trying to Hide it. It is that there are several who are addicted to such excessive and Continual lewdness that, as they cannot bear to have any other Company than That of the women who are necessary to their passions, They build separate houses for themselves alone—where, Remaining solitary as regards the french, They are Never so as regards the women, at the times suitable for their Commerce. You see very well that This is not an evil that can be tolerated, so scandalous is it. Traders—who are associated together, and have Common interests—should not live thus, separated from one another, lest while dwelling alone, accidents might happen to them which they Fear not, but which they should Fear, and which every one should Dread for them. May we therefore be delivered forever from Those solitaires and their Solitudes.

Finally, the most scandalous Evil of all, and that which needs to be most strenuously opposed, is that the traders have become so accustomed to have women for their Use in the trading-places, and these have become so necessary to them, that they cannot do without them even on their journeys. I do not refer to those who are taken with their husbands, because there is nothing in This that is not decent; and, consequently, Those are not the ones whose company is generally desired. I refer to single women, women without husbands, women who are mistresses of their own Bodies, women who can dispose of them to these men, and whom the latter know to be willing to do so,—in a word, They are all the prostitutes of Montreal, who are alternately brought here and taken back; and They are all the prostitutes of this place, who are carried in the same way from here to montreal, and from montreal here. At present this is the usual manner in which their journeys are carried on; and voyages are no longer performed without a continual flow and Ebb of That tide of prostitutes,—whom we see ascending and descending, going and coming from one mission to another, without cessation,—to the most Heinous and loathsome scandal of the people.

Demoralization of Youth through Contacts with Indians

Public Archives of Canada, *Series C11A*, vol. 7, pp. 44-9: Quebec, September 13, 1685, Denonville to the Minister.

This is the place, it seems to me Monseigneur, where it is necessary to render an account of the disorders which go on not only in the woods but in our villages. These disorders occur simply because of the laziness of children and the great liberty of long standing which the parents and Governors have given to the youth, permitting them to dally in the woods under the pretext of hunting or trading. This, Monseigneur, has reached such an excess that from the time children are able to carry a gun, fathers are not able to restrain them and dare not anger them. Judge, then, the evils which follow such a manner of life. These irregularities are greatest in the families of those who are, or would like to be gentlemen, either because of laziness or vanity, having no other resources of subsistence but the woods. Not being accustomed to hold the plough, pickax or hatchet, their only tool being the gun, they must spend their lives in the woods where they have no priests to restrain them, nor fathers, nor governors to compel them. There are, Monseigneur, some who distinguish themselves well above others in these disorders, and for these I have threatened to use the authority which the King has given me to chastise them very severely. I am convinced, Monseigneur, that you fully approve of this, and that you will approve that I do not amuse myself with the formality of justice which serves only to deceive by hiding vice and rendering disorders unpunished. Convincing proof has not always been easy to fully establish, and I believe, Monseigneur, that military justice in this instance is more suitable than any court order. M. de la Barre suppressed a certain order of cavaliers, but did not deprive it of its customs and disorders. A fashion of dressing nude like the savages is treated as a fine trick and joke, not only on carnival days but on all days of feasting and debauchery. All these practices tend only to attract the young people to the manner of life of the savages and to associate with them and become forever libertines among them.   I cannot tell you, Monseigneur, the attraction that all young people have for this life of the savage, which is to do nothing, be restrained in nothing, follow every whim and be removed from all control.

It was thought for some time that the visiting of the savages in our settlements was a very good thing to accustom them to live like us and become instructed in our religion.   I perceive, Monseigneur, that just the opposite has taken place.   Instead of becoming accustomed to our laws, I assure you, they have communicated to us very much everything they have which is most wicked and have acquired only that which is evil and vicious in us.   I have taken a great deal of time, Monseigneur, to give you the details of all these things so that you may adopt remedies through orders which you will give me.

I find that all those savages established in the small trading centres such as those at Sillery, Lorette, the Sault of the Prairie, and the Mountain of Montreal, Monseigneur, are in truth held in a discipline and rule which is a pleasure to see.   There is not, assuredly, a city or village in France so well regulated as all these places, so much so that there is none of the drunkenness which takes place in our settlements.   But, Monseigneur, in regard to those savages who are vagabonds and run about certain seigneuries without being assembled in marketing centres as the others, you could not believe the harm they do to the discipline of the colony.   The children of the seigneurs are not only accustomed to live in debauchery 'like them but even abuse the daughters and wives of the savages and take them on their hunts in the woods where they often suffer hunger almost to the point of eating their dogs.

Nothing is finer nor better conceived than the laws of this country, but I assure you, nothing is so badly observed with respect to discipline as the fur trade which ought to be carried on only in the towns of Quebec, Three Rivers and Montreal.   Everyone advances as far as he is able to secure the furs first although the orders of the Sovereign Council and ordinances of the Intendants prohibit trading with foreign savages elsewhere than in the above towns. . . .

There is, Monseigneur, besides that, another disorder which is that several individuals lend too much to the savages, and above all brandy, which they give at a much cheaper price than other merchandise.   Trade takes place with much fraud and deceit, especially when the savage has begun to drink heavily.   This trade on credit with deceit has obliged an entire village of savages, who were at Chambly, to desert this year and go to the English.   I am assured that they would like to return but their debts, which would have to be paid if they returned, prevents them.

I say nothing of the other disorders caused by the drinking of brandy in the savage settlements, which I learn about from all sides, as much in the distant country as takes place among the savages in the colony who create horror.

I must not forget here, Monseigneur, to tell you that orders of the King prohibit our French from carrying brandy to the savages in the woods, but I learn that there is so much trade of it with the savages that they desire, whenever they come, to fetch some of it.   In this way our French being in league with them elude entirely the execution of the King's order, doing by means of these savages that which they would not dare do by themselves. It would be well if I were informed of your intentions to remedy these disorders.

Prevalence of Drinking Habits

Public Archives of Canada, *Series C¹¹A*, vol. 10, pp. 123-7: Quebec, August 10, 1688, Memoir of Denonville to Seignelay.

In the memoir in which I render an account to Monseigneur of the present state of affairs in this country, there is an item to the effect that I must give an account of one of the greatest evils in Canada.   It is, Monseigneur, Brandy which is used to such an excess that I can only foresee as a result of it the loss of the country.   Until this point I had not believed it my duty to write you anything which I had learned for myself of the evils which have taken place and which may take place.

I learn from all the old inhabitants of the country that twenty years ago we had in our villages two thousand savages capable of making war, enemies forever of the Iroquois, who are now reduced to nothing, for of all these two thousand we would not be able to assemble thirty.   The use that I see made of brandy and those which I have seen die from it since I have come to this country convinces me, assuredly, that the great drinking of brandy is the principal cause of the destruction of all these savages who have lived among the French in the colony.   Besides that, I know that large debts as a result of brandy given to the Loups, who were at Chambly, caused these savages to desert the colony because of the persecution of creditors, who for ten *sols* of brandy charged a *pistolle*.   They ran off to the English during July of the year that I came to this country and abandoned the corn which they had sown.

I have seen in voyages that I have taken since I came here that drinking this liquor is so much in use among our habitant voyagers above all, and among others, that there is no cause to be astonished that the people of this country do not grow old.

I have noticed that from the weariness of running the rapids our Canadians, finding themselves fatigued, in order to recover strength take a barrel of brandy and, putting the neck to the mouth, drink almost a *chopin*, often taking a half measure before breakfast.   They feel better after that and pass the rapids, and afterwards sleep without eating, having no appetite until evening when the fumes are then dissipated.

Usually, Monseigneur, in the taverns, the heavy drinkers, who are very numerous and especially among the *coureurs de bois*, drink each a *chopin* or pint of brandy after having drunk well of wine.   What ravage, is there not, in a poor stomach with these mixtures, and since no man is able to withstand the least sickness after that, many have died this year.

Numbers of women drink constantly and several become intoxicated.
All the savages are fond of it and when they have drunk it become mad
and enraged, howling and biting like dogs and wanting to kill everyone.
Good regulations have been made but their execution is found every day
to be more and more difficult because of the deceit of the vendors and buyers.
The Intendant had some experience of the difficulty in the journey that he
made here last year.   With that, Monseigneur, it is pointless to speak of
discipline or police or of being able to live with the savages so long as it
can be sold or traded to them, especially when they are so numerous.

It is true, brandy is necessary within limits but in order to prevent these
disorders it is much to be desired that it be prohibited to sell or trade it
with the savages, still less to allow them to take it into the woods and into
their villages, and ways should be sought to chastise those who get the
habitants drunk on it.   It is still more certain that those who use much of
it do not grow old and all those whom we see who have drunk too much are
worn out before they are forty, especially the *coureurs de bois*.

The Tavern and Centres of Crime

Public Archives of Canada, *Series C¹¹A*, vol. 7, pp. 50-1: Quebec, September 13,
1685, Denonville to the Minister.

There is, Monseigneur, another great evil in the country, and that is
the unlimited number of taverns, which makes it almost impossible to
prevent the disorder which such places occasion.   The trade of tavern-
keeper has attracted all the rogues and lazy people who never think of
cultivating the land; far from that, they deter and ruin the other inhabitants.   I believe, Monseigneur, that in the villages the Seigneur should
hire and dismiss the tavern-keeper according to his good and bad conduct,
and the Seigneur would be responsible for him.   I know of seigneuries where
there are only twenty houses and more than half are taverns.   In Three
Rivers, there are twenty-five houses of which there are from eighteen to
twenty where a drink may be had.   Montreal and Quebec are on the same
footing.

Besides that, Monseigneur, there are houses of evil maintained in the
depths of the woods by individuals under the pretext of concessions given to
them of land where there is no thought of clearing and cultivating the soil.
These places are only retreats for robbers where all the crimes in the world
are committed.   I have no doubt that you will approve of making war on
these people and of forbidding these establishments.   The majority of these
places have been authorized by protection assuredly very contrary to your
intentions.   You will permit me, Monseigneur, to ask you to be good enough
to think of some way to occupy young people of the country in their early
years and in their more advanced ages, and consent that I render you an
account of my thoughts on the above since it is the thing most essential
to the colony.

Influence of the Army upon Morals

Public Archives of Canada, *Series C¹¹A*, vol. 47, p. 266: Quebec, October 4, 1725,
    Letter of Bishop of Quebec, enclosed in letter of October 19, 1725.

The financial difficulties and continual restraint under which the soldiers
are kept, a great number of whom cannot be given permission to marry,
fills the country with bad morals and illegitimate children.   One can only
express the need of remedying this situation.   A single view of the bad
results of what is taking place is convincing of the truth of what I claim.
One can only give permission to the soldiers to marry according as they are
dismissed to be replaced by newly arrived recruits, and the priests have to
be prohibited from marrying those who have not permission and to constantly keep a tight rein.

Immigration from France and Growth of Crime

(i)

Public Archives of Canada, *Series C¹¹A*, vol. 47, pp. 265-6: Quebec, October 4,
    1725, Letter of Bishop of Quebec, enclosed in letter of October 19, 1725.

Since there is nothing more important to this colony than to prevent
it from being lost and annihilated by sending and communicating to it
persons who are intemperate and guilty of almost every crime, as are those
you sent two years ago, who take pride not only in stealing in houses and
robbing on highways but even in poisoning people, of which the religious
and poor of the general hospital where I live have endured two terrible and
dreadful attempts, may I implore you, as the first pastor of souls here, not
to send us such people who are without faith and religion and capable of
the most hideous crimes and vices.   To continue to send such may cause
the colonists to lose their faith and make them like the English and even
the infidels.   Satisfy me, that you will prohibit and turn away these undesirables by not sending any more of them and that you will oblige the
magistrate here to treat these wretches as they do in France—the more
guilty when they fall into error.

(ii)

Public Archives of Canada, *Series C¹¹A*, vol. 52, pp. 68-72: Quebec, October 15,
    1730, Beauharnois and Hocquart to the Minister.

We entreat you, Monseigneur, to stop sending libertines to the colony.
There is already a very great number, and it is more difficult to restrain them
in this country than anywhere else because of the facility they have for
escaping and the difficulty of convicting them of robberies and assaults
which they commit often enough.   The inhabitants of this country are
naturally inclined to give shelter to the most guilty.   Crimes are constantly
committed and the criminals very difficult to discover. . . . The colony grows

every day and the crimes multiply. It will soon be necessary, Monseigneur, to increase the police by an officer and three or four constables in Montreal. The expense would be very small and this would serve to maintain good order. The Prevost and constables there are not sufficient.

Efforts to Encourage Marriage and Large Families

Edits, ordonnances royaux, déclarations et arrêts du Conseil d'Etat du roi concernant le Canada (Quebec, 1854), pp. 67-8.

Order of the Council of State of the King to Encourage the Marriage of Boys and Girls in Canada

. . . In order to multiply the number of children and encourage marriage, His said Majesty, in Council, has ordered and orders that in the future all the inhabitants of the said country [of New France] who have up to ten children living born in legitimate marriage and not priests or religious will be paid from the funds that His Majesty will send to the said country, a pension of three hundred *livres* for each one, and to those who will have twelve of them, four hundred *livres*; for this purpose, they are to represent to the Intendant of justice, police and finance, who will be established in the said country, the number of their children in the month of June or July each year, who after having verified it will order the payment of the said pension to them, one half immediately and the other half at the end of each year. His said Majesty wishes further that there be paid by the said Intendant to each boy of the age of twenty or younger and to each girl of sixteen or younger who marries twenty *livres* on the day of their wedding, which will be called a present from the King; that the Sovereign Council established at Quebec for the said country make a general division of all the inhabitants into parishes and market towns, that honours be given to the principal inhabitants who will take care of the affairs of each town and community, either according to their rank in the church or elsewhere; and that those inhabitants who have the greater number of children be always preferred to the others, if no reason prevents it; and that there be established some small financial levy, the proceeds to go to the local hospitals, upon fathers who have not their boys married at the age of twenty and girls at the age of sixteen. . . .

Made at the Council of State of the King, His Majesty being present, held at Paris the twelve day of April, 1660.

Signed: COLBERT

Prohibition of Trading in the Woods

Edits, ordonnances royaux, déclarations et arrêts du Conseil d'Etat du roi concernant le Canada (Quebec, 1854), p. 86.

Ordinance of the King which Prohibits Going to Trade Pelts in the Savage Villages

His Majesty being informed that the permission which formerly has been given to several inhabitants of his country of New France, to go to trade pelts in the villages of the savages and in the depths of the woods, among nations farthest distant, is very prejudicial to the well-being and advantage of the said country, not only because this permission causes the desertion of inhabitants, but prevents the trade and profit which the same inhabitants take away from the savages, when they come themselves to carry their pelts to the French villages, that it happens even that those to whom this sort of permission has been accorded are vagabonds and libertines, carrying their pelts to strangers, instead of bringing them to sell to the French; and since it is important to prevent in the future these disorders from occurring, His Majesty has made and makes very expressed prohibitions to all persons of whatever quality and state, from going to trade pelts in the villages of the savages and in the depth of the woods, and to his Governors and Lieutenant-Generals and private citizens of the said country of New France from delivering and despatching any permission under penalty against the private citizens for the first time they engage in the said trade, of confiscation of the merchandise which was seized in their possession, whether it was in going upon or returning from their voyages, and two thousand *livres* fine, applicable half to His Majesty and the other half to the poor of the hospital of Quebec, and in case of a second offence, to such corporal punishment as will be judged fit by Sieur Duchesneau, Intendant of the said country of New France. Written by His Majesty to Sieur Count de Frontenac, his Lieutenant-General to the said country to enforce the execution of the present ordinance, that he wishes to be read, published and affixed everywhere needed in order that no one pretends ignorance of it.

Made at Saint-Germain-en-Laye, the fifteenth of April, 1676.

Signed: Louis

and below

Signed: Colbert

Difficulty of Enforcing Fur-Trade Regulations

Public Archives of Canada, *Series C¹¹A*, vol. 5, pp. 7-8: Quebec, October 9, 1679, Frontenac to the Minister.

However, I must first tell you that whatever care I may have taken in Montreal to have the *coureurs de bois* apprehended, I would have been unable to accomplish it, either because of the contact they have with the inhabitants who warn them, of the inaccessibility of the places and the nature of the country open on all sides and thickly wooded, where they can hide themselves easily, or finally because of the connivance of those who, instead of pursuing them, favour them by buying their skins, furnishing them with supplies to return to the woods, and giving them shelter in their houses near Montreal, as is proven by information secured by the Prevost at my order.

And the one who went to Montreal six weeks or two months before me was no more fortunate than I in apprehending them. But the truth is, Monseigneur, he has a store there where he has more than forty or fifty thousand *francs* worth of merchandise, and he has tried so hard to sell it, without distinction as to persons, that he has found it necessary to cheat these libertines and vagabonds.

Unwillingness of Governor to Enforce Regulations

Public Archives of Canada, *Series C¹¹A*, vol. 5, pp. 47-56: Quebec, November 10, 1679, Du Chesneau to the Minister.

I return, Monseigneur, to the problem of the disobedience of the *coureurs de bois* and I must not hide from you the fact that it has finally reached such an excess that everybody boldly disobeys the ordinances of the King, that they no longer hide themselves, and that with surprising insolence they assemble to go to trade in the country of the savages.

I have done all in my power to prevent this evil which may cause the ruin of the colony. I have made ordinances against the *coureurs de bois*, against the merchants who furnish them with supplies, against the *gentilhommes* and others who give them shelter and even against those who know of their whereabouts and do not inform the local judges. . . .

It is thus, faithful Monseigneur, and everyone agrees that there is almost general disobedience in the country. The number in the woods has increased to almost five or six hundred not including those who go out every day. They are the ones most capable of doing good and defending the colony. They have Duluth at their head and are all ready to strike a bad blow and undertake not only to carry their skins to the English, as they are already doing, but even to shift there the trade of the savages. And all this misfortune has taken place because the Governor [Frontenac], who has the force at hand, has done nothing to prevent it and, on the contrary, favours them underhand. It is true, Monseigneur, that when it is a question of good faith nearly everyone obeys.

Please recall, Monseigneur, that the year before I arrived in this country there were complaints that the great number of people who went to trade skins in the villages of the savages were ruining the colony because those who were most useful, being young and having the strength to work, were abandoning their wives and children, the tilling of the soil and the raising of cattle, that they were debauching themselves and through their absence permitting the debauchery of their wives, which happened very often and is still happening every day, that they had become accustomed to a life of idleness and vagabondage which they were not able to give up, that they profited little by their work because they consumed in drunkenness and beautiful clothes the little that they earned which was very modest, those who gave them the *conges* taking the greater part of what was left beyond the price of the merchandise which they sold to them very dear, and that the savages no longer brought their skins in such great abundance to trade with the good inhabitants, since such a great number of young men had gone to establish themselves almost in the homes of the savages, who scorned us because of the great greed that we proved to have.

The next year was the one in which the King's farm was established. The farmers complained that the great freedom to run the woods ruined them because the pelts were being transported to strangers, that those which were brought did not fall into their hands to acquit debts they had contracted for the advancement of the colony because the *coureurs de bois* hid themselves from them and took their merchandise elsewhere so that they found themselves crushed by bills of exchange and defrauded of their rights.

In 1676 an ordinance of His Majesty prohibited the Governor from granting any more *conges* to trade in the depth of the woods and in the villages of the savages.

The Sovereign Council before whom I placed the King's ordinance made a decree which declared that, at the diligence of the farmers of the royal reserve, the ordinance would be communicated to the French who were trading with the savages in the more removed nations with the injunction that they return to their homes in the month of August of the next year under penalty provided in the said ordinance, posted up in the villages of Nipissingues, St. Marie du Sault, St. Ignace on Lake Huron, and St. Francis Xavier in Green Bay.

The Governor, although contending very loudly that this decree was made in his absence, when in Montreal on urgent business, could not avoid giving orders jointly with the Council for the return of the *coureurs de bois*, who in fact almost all were returning with the exception of three or four.

However, Monsieur the Governor, in order to elude the prohibitions carried by the ordinance of the King and at the same time not seem to contravene them, gave some hunting licences while serving the pretext of rendering them useless. As it was justified, His Majesty brought forward again the remedy and continued it by his last ordinances.

Since that time the Governor has done nothing to oppose the *coureurs de bois* and has contented himself with saying that the trouble was so great that it was beyond remedy, that this has happened simply because they have taken from him the power of giving *conges*, and that the only way to prevent the evil from continuing was by according amnesties. This has been done in the hope that everyone would abuse his liberty, and disobedience has become almost general!

The Prevost, who is a very honest man and very worried about doing his duty, has run around uselessly, and although he has often received good advice the disobedience has always had the better of him.

For myself, Monseigneur, I can only say that I have done that which my office required but without success, and all the care that I have taken has served only to augment the Governor's aversion to me and to cause my ordinances to be misinterpreted.

That is, Monseigneur, the true state of the disobedience of the *coureurs de bois*, of which I have had the honour to speak twice to the Governor and I cannot refrain from saying, with all the deference possible, that it would be fortunate for us and the colony if our Majesty . . . had the displeasure of learning that, in a country which has received so much evidence of his kindness and paternal tenderness, his orders were misinterpreted and violated and that a Governor and Intendant do nothing and content themselves with saying that the evil is without remedy, without using the garrisons that His Majesty maintains, the Prevost, nor any of his officers of the guard, nor any of the aids that can be drawn upon from the inhabitants to suppress the rebellion and make a memorable example which would live in the minds of the people, to preserve in their respect the fidelity and obedience that they owe to such a good and noble Prince.

In order to have these things represented to him [the Governor] again, I have drawn down upon myself words so full of spirit and outrage that I was constrained to leave his office to appease his anger. However, I went back the next morning and found there the farmers of the royal reserve with whom we continued to speak on the subject. I have, in the meantime, made public once again the order which I sent you a copy of, and have done everything possible to have it fully enforced, but as the Governor is interested with several of the *coureurs de bois* all that which will be done will be useless.

Land Concessions as Means of Evading Trade Regulations

Public Archives of Canada, *Series C¹¹A*, vol. 11, pp. 475-6: Quebec, May 10, 1691, Champigny to the Minister.

There will always be some people who will seek land concessions in distant places and in the neighbourhood of the savages for the sole purpose of going there to trade and even to carry brandy there without thought of settling. This causes the trade to go to certain individuals and the others are excluded. It is an abuse which must not be permitted, and it is necessary to prohibit the brandy trade with the savages in distant places and to only allow the trading of merchandise in the settlements.

Prohibition of Brandy Trade

Edits, ordonnances royaux, déclarations et arrêts du Conseil d'Etat du roi concernant le Canada (Quebec, 1854), pp. 235-6.

Ordinance of the King which Prohibits the Carrying of Brandy to the Marketing Centres of Savages Distant from the French Settlements, May 24, 1679

His Majesty having taken account of his ordinances of April 15, 1676, May 12, 1678, and April 25, 1679; the first prohibiting his subjects inhabiting the country of Canada from going to trade pelts in the villages of the savages and in the depth of the woods; the second, from hunting beyond the extent of the cleared and settled lands and a league all around; and the third permitting, by His Majesty, the giving of hunting licences from January 15 to April 15 in each year; together with all the memoirs from the said country concerning the sale of wine and brandy to the savages.

And wishing to terminate the difficulties which almost up to the present have occurred in the said country on the subject of the said trade, His Majesty has made very expressed prohibitions to all his subjects living in the said country, who will have permission to go to hunt in the depth of the woods from January 15 to April 15 in conformity with the said ordinance of April 25 last, from carrying or having caused to be carried brandy to the marketing centres of savages far distant from the French settlements, under penalty of a fine of a hundred *livres* for the first offence, of three hundred *livres* for the second, and of corporal punishment for the third. . . .

Made at Saint-Germain-en-Laye, the twenty-fourth day of May, 1679.

Signed: Louis

and below

Signed: Colbert

Regulation of Sale of Beer to the Indians

Public Archives of Canada, *Series C*¹¹*A*, vol. 32, pp. 189-90: Quebec, October 29, 1711, "Mémoire sur le Canada," not signed.

The excesses and horrible disorders that the use of brandy causes the savages to commit, since they are not able to drink without becoming drunk, made necessary rigorous prohibitions against its sale to them. These are executed punctually and those discovered selling it are punished.

In order to succeed more easily, M. Raudot appointed in the town of Montreal beer taverns for each nation, without, however, permitting the giving to them enough of this drink, which is not prohibited, to make them drunk. He has obliged, at the same time, the tavern-keepers to lodge these savages when they wish to remain in the town. This is the only expedient by which drunkenness can be prevented since it is possible to discover through the tavern-keepers any other persons who give drink to the savages. There have been very few who have been drunk since this precaution was taken.

Coercive Efforts to Suppress Intemperance and Immorality

Arrêts et règlements du Conseil supérieur de Québec, et ordonnances et jugements des intendants du Canada (Quebec, 1855), pp. 67-71.

General Regulations of the Superior Council of Quebec, for the Police, May 11, 1676

XVI. And because under the pretext of keeping a tavern, sometimes persons of bad life, in order to have a place to live and carry on their debaucheries, permit public scandals in their houses, it is prohibited to all persons to keep a tavern and serve the public with meals in their home, except to those whose honesty will be known and who will have permission by a written certificate of their good life and morals.

XVII.   Prohibits all tavern-keepers in this country from lending or giving credit to the sons of good families, soldiers, valets, servants and others, or taking any security from them, likewise also from serving drinks at night after nine o'clock, under penalty of an arbitrary fine and the loss of their pay; for whom the tavern-keepers will have no action against, whoever it be, for eating expenses, in conformity with ancient ordinances.

XVIII.   Prohibits all persons, of whatever quality and condition, from becoming drunk in the taverns and elsewhere, under penalty of an arbitrary fine and even of imprisonment, if the case occurs.

XIX.   Prohibits tavern-keepers from giving drink and food to masons, carpenters, joiners and other workmen during working days, if they know them for such, without permission from those for whom they work. . . .

XX.   All tavern-keepers are ordered to keep in every room in which they serve drink and food the articles of rules which have to do with morals, the punishment for swearing and blaspheming, and other disorders, and which prohibits the serving of drink and food in their establishments during the celebration of divine service, in order that by the sight of these ordinances everyone will continue in his duty and that no one transgresses under pain of an arbitrary fine; the tavern-keepers are enjoined to inform the said Lieutenant-General and Attorney of the King of those who will remain in their establishments in violation of the said ordinances under the same penalties.

XXXII.   Prohibits all persons from giving shelter or assisting prostitutes, panders or procuresses under pain of punishment, in conformity with the ordinances by which the said prostitutes, panders and procuresses will be chastised with the severity there set out.

XXXIV.   Prohibits also all vagabonds of one or the other sex from dwelling in and frequenting this city and its outskirts, without first having given a declaration of the reason of their residence, and having obtained permission from the said Lieutenant-General and Attorney of the King, on pain of being driven out and arbitrary fine, even of corporal punishment if the case requires it.

Efforts to Suppress Abortion

Public Archives of Canada, *Series C¹¹A*, vol. 60, pp. 45-6: Quebec, October 3, 1733, Hocquart to the Minister.

The parish priests of this colony have quite regularly published the ordinance of Henry the Second which concerns the punishment of persons of the fair sex who conceal their pregnancies and who kill their children. I will join myself with the Superior Council and Attorney-General of the King to enforce its execution in conformity with the declaration of August 2, 1717. I hope the example that the Council made in the cases of Marie Anne Gendron and Anne Segoin convicted of this crime will henceforth prevent similar disorders.

Lack of Prisons

Public Archives of Canada, *Series C¹¹A*, vol. 7, pp. 67-8: Quebec, September 13, 1685, Denonville to the Minister.

Nothing is so necessary to maintain discipline as the chastisement of evil living. I am surprised that there is no provision for such a purpose, there being neither prison nor dungeon. It is essential to have such places, at least at Montreal, Three Rivers and Quebec; those which are there are really not prisons. This is an expense which it is necessary to make, Monseigneur.

3. CULTURAL ORGANIZATION AND EDUCATION

Social Classes and Group Interests in the Colony

Public Archives of Canada, *Series C¹¹A*, vol. 5, pp. 60-4: Quebec, November 10, 1679, Du Chesneau to the Minister.

In order that you may know the country thoroughly, the true state in which it is and what goes on here, so that you may afterwards discover my views on those things which are advantageous and prejudicial to it, permit me to tell you of the interests of those who compose it.

There are some who have chosen to remain here for the rest of their lives and others who are interested only in the profits they endeavour to make here.

The first class may be separated into four groups, namely, secular and religious priests, officers of the Sovereign Council and inferior justices, gentlemen and officers retired on half-pay or land seigneurs, and, finally, merchants, artisans and labourers.

The second class are the foreign merchants.

The secular clergy of the Bishop's seminary, the Sulpician fathers, the Jesuits and the Recollets are, assuredly, very orderly and very pious. The secular clergy are concerned with making their establishments stable and assuring the foundation of parishes. The religious [Jesuits and Recollets], whom the Church does not allow to have parishes, are concerned necessarily with the general interest, and this unites them with the other clergy, although they regard their missions as their most proper work. They, alone, are occupied with the instruction of the savages with the single exception of the Sulpician mission on the Mountain of Montreal which has been established with great success, a small school having been founded to teach the children and accustom them in our ways. They [the Sulpicians] still have their mission at Kenté among the Iroquois but they have been obliged to recall their priests because of the lack of people and because they lost nearly all the provisions which were coming to them this year by the shipwreck of the vessel *St. Pierre*.

The Jesuits, besides the Iroquois mission, have established the mission of prairie of Magdeleine near Montreal which is very prosperous and well populated and where they carry out the will of His Majesty and the orders you have sent me. They have also established a school to instruct and Frenchify the savage children. They have still their missions among the Hurons of Lorette near Quebec and another commenced at Tillery for the Abenakis and all those for the nations of Algonkins, Hurons, Iroquois, Ottawas and Illinois, among whom they live. The Recollets are in Acadia, the Island of Perce and at Fort Frontenac. . . .

The greater part of the officers of the Sovereign Council and the inferior justices, although they ought to apply themselves principally to their vocation and to instructing themselves in it, are prevented by their poverty, the wages they are paid being very small, which makes them occupy themselves as much as possible with commerce and with improving their living.

Several of the *gentilhommes*, officers retired on half pay and owners of seigneuries, since they accustom themselves to what is called in France the life of a country gentleman which they have practised and wish to continue to practise, make their chief occupation that of hunting and fishing. Because their manner of life and clothing, and that of their wives and children, does not enable them to live on so little as the simple habitants, and since they do not apply themselves entirely to household work and to improving their lands, they mix themselves up in trade, running into debt on all sides, exciting young habitants to become *coureurs de bois*, and lastly sending their own children to trade in furs, in the Indian villages and in the depths of the forest, in spite of prohibitions of His Majesty, and yet nevertheless they are in great poverty.

The merchants living in the country, with the exception of five or six at the most, are poor. The artisans, if one excludes a small number who are inn-keepers, because of the social pretensions of the women among whom there is no class distinction here, and their own debauchery, spend everything they make. Consequently, their families are in great misery and are not settled down.

Whenever the labourers apply themselves assiduously to the land, they subsist not only more honestly but are without comparison happier than those who are called good peasants in France. But, in the spirit of this country of taking life easily, and having much of the savage temperament which is unsteady, fickle and opposed to hard work, seeing the liberty that is taken so boldly to run the woods, they debauch themselves with the others and go to look for furs as a means of living without working. This causes the land to be left uncleared and beasts not to multiply as they should and no industries can be established here.

To turn to those who come into the country for profits only with no intention of establishing themselves, and who are called foreign merchants, there is no doubt that their only interest is to fix up their affairs and afterwards return to live more comfortably in France with their families.

On all this you may observe, Monseigneur, if it pleases you, that among so many different interests, the chief and common interest of those who have chosen this country to live in, when they think seriously, must be to establish good order in the colony, to cultivate the soil, to raise and increase the number of livestock, to establish manufacturing and to attract the savages to trade in the French villages.

I have said nothing of the farmers of the King's Post because I do not regard them as inhabitants, all of them being in the royal reserve of Sieur De la Chesnaye. Their chief interest is that the *coureurs de bois* do not go to the country of the savages, diverting their furs to the commerce of strangers as they have already done most boldly this year, that the savages be attracted to come to trade in the French villages to sell their merchandise, that all the inhabitants share in such a trade and become enriched, and that, moreover, those who are most able to improve the land and increase the colony be kept at home because that would assure their paying their debts.

In truth, Monseigneur, it is deplorable to see this country in its present state, when this colony which could become so important because of its advantages, of which I have so often informed you, is so little established.

Social Demands upon Upper Classes

Baron de Lahontan, *New Voyages in North America*, ed. R. G. Thwaites (Chicago, 1905), vol. I, p. 97.

The Gentlemen that have a Charge of Children, especially Daughters, are oblig'd to be good Husbands, in order to bear the Expence of the magnificent Cloaths with which they are set off; for Pride, Vanity, and Luxury, reign as much in *New France* as in *Old France*. In my opinion, 'twould do well, if the King would order Commodities to be rated at a reasonable Price, and prohibit the selling of Gold or Silver Brocadoes, Fringes, and Ribbands, as well as Points and rich Laces.

Destitution of Seigneurs

Public Archives of Canada, *Series C¹¹A*, vol. 7, pp. 54-5: Quebec, September 13, 1685, Denonville to the Minister.

Before all, Monseigneur, you will permit me to tell you that the nobility of this new country is everything which is most beggarly and to increase their number is to increase the number of "do-nothings" in the place. A new country demands hard-working and industrious people who will handle the hatchet and pickax. The children of our Councillors are no more hard-working, and have as their only recourse the woods where they do some trading, and for the most part make all those disorders which I have had the honour to discuss with you. I will overlook nothing which can be done to engage them in commerce, but as our nobles and Councillors are all very poor and weighed down with debts, they would not be able to find credit for a crown-piece.

Efforts to Establish Sons of Seigneurs

Public Archives of Canada, *Series C¹¹A*, vol. 8, pp. 231-2, 236: Quebec, November 10, 1688, Denonville to the Minister.

I hope in time we shall have succeeded in suppressing the great disorders of our young people or at least in moderating them. However, Monseigneur, it is necessary to help them by giving them the means of relief and livelihood for, in truth, without that there is great fear that the children of our nobility, or of those living as such of whom there are a great number, will become bandits because of having nothing by which to live, not being able to apply themselves to labour on the soil since they are not accustomed to it. In truth, Monseigneur, it is an essential thing for this country to discipline all these young people and to keep them engaged in some companies. I would like to be able to do it without expense but that cannot be done for it is necessary that they live and not less than eight French *sou* could be given to the more sensible, six to the others. . . . I believe, however, that Monseigneur should not determine to cease to give letters of nobility but that it would be well to give them only to those who will be rich and who will enter into whatever commerce makes a noble in this country, for to be good neither in commerce nor in anything else is to increase the number of idlers.

Need for Education to Discipline Youth

Public Archives of Canada, *Series C¹¹A*, vol. 7, pp. 51-4: Quebec, November 13, 1685, Denonville to the Minister.

You will permit me, Monseigneur, to ask you the favour of making some reflections on means of occupying the youth of this country in their young and older years and consent that I render you an account of my thoughts on the above since it is a thing most essential to the colony.

To do that, Monseigneur, the first means to my mind is to multiply the number of parishes and to render them fixed. The Bishop is convinced of this by knowledge that he has gained of his diocese in his visits and in voyages that we have made together. There is no one more eager to be able to contribute to this undertaking which would be a sure means of establishing schools, with which the *curés* would occupy themselves and thus accustom the children at an early hour to control themselves and become useful. But, Monseigneur, in order to make this establishment effectual, it would be necessary to multiply the number of parishes to fifty-one. The memoir that I sent you shows you quite well that if one extends them, and makes it necessary for the *curés* to cross and recross the river as they do at present in order to carry out their duties, they will give up to strenuous work all the time that they would otherwise be able to devote to teaching the young, if their parishes were less extensive. Besides that, Monseigneur, at the beginning and end of winter there are almost two months during which the river cannot be crossed, which in many places is a league wide and much more in others, so that in these times the sick must remain without any spiritual succour. It is a pity, Monseigneur, to witness the ignorance in which the people live in this country who are far from the residence of the *curés*, and the trials that the Missionaries and *curés* endure to remedy it by travelling over their parishes on foot, as pointed out in the memoir that I sent you. You will realize, Monseigneur, from this the kind of roads the *curés* must take in order to visit their parishes in the depth of winter. . . .

I have found here in the Bishop's seminary the beginning of two establishments which would be admirable for the colony if one could enlarge them. These are, Monseigneur, two houses where children are taken to be instructed. In the one there are placed those who are found with a disposition to letters, for whom an attempt is made to provide a training for the Church, since these in the end can render more service than the French priests being more familiar than the others with the hardships and customs of the country. In the other house there are placed those suitable to be artisans, and these are taught trades. I believe that this would be an admirable means of commencing manufactures, which are absolutely necessary for the welfare of this country.

The Bishop is delighted with these establishments and would like to be in a position where he could support and enlarge them, but since that cannot be done without expense as much for increasing the number of parishes as for undertaking this kind of manufacture, I see only one assured means of bringing about his agreement to doing something substantial to make such an establishment succeed here and that is for the King to consent to give a large monastery to the Bishop without attaching it to the Bishopry since his spirit and heart are occupied solely with the cares of doing good for the poor and with increasing the faith and saving souls. It is certain that His Majesty would be pleased to see employed the revenue from this benefice in good and saintly works which would do marvels for the welfare of the colony in strengthening and enlarging it.

Limitations to Education

Public Archives of Canada, *Series C*[11]*A*, vol. 8, pp. 194-6: Quebec, November 10, 1686, Denonville to the Minister.

It is not possible to retain for a considerable time children at study if they are not ones who plan to become priests, and the number of these are small among the natives of the country who are light-headed.

In regard to the children whom we had planned to bring up in an establishment to improve their vocation and make them learn some trade, not having this year permission to give a contribution to their pension, our Bishop is not rich enough nor is our seminary to maintain these schools which have been well begun and which will end for lack of funds.

Problem of Recruiting Suitably Trained Teachers

Public Archives of Canada, *Series C¹¹A*, vol. 39, pp. 391-3: Paris, June 1, 1718,
Petition of Sieur Etienne Charon.

Etienne Charon represents very humbly to your Majesty that Louis XIV
by his letters patent of April 15, 1694, established in the Island of Montreal
under the administration of a community of school-masters a hospital to
maintain and assist the poor, the sick, the old and the crippled and to raise
and instruct young boys in religion and teach them some trades and that
Your Majesty, having been informed of the advantages that the colony
of Canada would receive from this establishment and of the great benefit
that the sisters of the congregation to the number of almost one hundred
are in the parishes of the country for the instruction of young girls, confirmed
by his letters patent of February, 1718, those of Louis XIV for the above
hospital and, in order to multiply the masters of the school who have charge
of it and put them in a position to instruct the young boys in the country
in our Holy Religion, deter them from joining the savages, discipline them
and render them more suitable for the service of the colony, there was
assigned in favour of the masters of the school 3,000 *livres* payable every
year by the farmers of your western domain. But the suppliant, having
informed himself fully that the good intentions that His Majesty proposes
by his letters patent will never have their execution, since the masters of
the school of Canada have no establishment in France where persons can
be found for this good work who are able to ·confine themselves during a
kind of novitiate in their vocation and in preparing themselves to instruct
young children, and since those who have come to Canada without this
test at considerable expense for the voyages and inland journeys, find
themselves often little suited, when they have arrived, to instruct the young,
and sometimes abandon with scandal their first assignment. The suppliant
offers to give a house valued at 9,000 *livres* and a sum of 8,000 *livres* which,
joined to that which would in addition be given the house by the City of
Rochelle as she formerly gave to charity schools for boys, would be sufficient
to establish a community of brothers of the school of Canada at Rochelle,
where they would be taken as needed, where they would make their novitiate,
would instruct the poor children of new converts in Rochelle in the principles
of the Roman Catholic and Apostolic religion and would be able to teach
the first elements of grammar to those children destined by their parents
to study at the college of the city.

Inability of Educational Institutions to Serve Country

Public Archives of Canada, *Series C¹¹A*, vol. 39, pp. 8-11: Quebec, October 4, 1718,
Vaudreuil and Bégon to the Minister.

Sieur Bégon has not paid and will not pay anything out of the 3,000
livres hitherto employed for the dowry of 60 girls that the King gave to the
General Hospital in Montreal for the maintenance of a ladies' school.

If the Council will permit us to explain to it our sentiment on this change, we would have the honour of representing to it that the instruction that is offered to the young boys of this colony is only a specious pretext inasmuch as in the towns there are some schools for them, kept by the Jesuits in Quebec and at Montreal by the Seminary, and in the country districts, the inhabitants not being gathered together in villages and being far from one another because of the extended character of settlement where land was granted in one long line, the school-masters are not in a position to instruct the young boys, who can come only to the Catechisms that the *curés* hold on feast days and Sundays.

If this gratuity was in the Extraordinary fund, the annual revenue, in furnishing to the General Hospital of Montreal the means of receiving the poor who are unable to earn their living, would be an advantage, but as the view of the Council is to contribute to the establishment of this country, which suffers from having so few inhabitants, it seems to us that the most useful employment of these 3,000 *livres* would be to leave them for the dowry of the 60 girls. It is a favour which the King has made since the country was returned to His Majesty by the last company and it was generally for all girls who married and qualified for the donation of the King in their contracts of marriage with inhabitants, and, although since that time it has been reduced to a dowry for 60 girls, this sum is distributed to the poorest, of which there are a great number in this country, and has done much good for them, enabling them to exist on land in uncleared woods, which is granted to them, which will not produce anything except by prolonged work, and on which they languish for want of having in the beginning some small advances.

Establishment of Free Education

Edits, ordonnances royaux, déclarations et arrêts du Conseil d'Etat du roi concernant le Canada (Quebec, 1854), pp. 465-6.

Order of the Council of State of the King . . . dated June 1, 1722

The King having seen, in Council, the order rendered here March 3, 1722, by which His Majesty ruled that he would support through the General Hospital established at Montreal, eight school-masters by means of a sum of three thousand *livres* accorded annually by His Majesty to the said hospital. . . .

His Majesty, wishing that the said school-masters founded by him, hold their schools gratuitously; having heard the report and considered everything, on the advice of the Duke of Orleans, regent, has decreed and decrees that the said eight school-masters founded hold free schools in the places and as it was decreed by the said order and without anything being required of the parents of the young boys whom they will instruct.

His Majesty does not, however, intend to restrict the charities that the inhabitants of Canada would wish to make to the said hospital for the instruction of their children.

His Majesty enjoins the Governor and Lieutenant-Governor in New France and the Intendant of the said country to enforce the execution of the present order which will be registered in the record office of the Superior Council of Quebec.

Made in the Council of State of the King, His Majesty present, held at Paris, June 1, 1722.

Dissatisfaction of Inhabitants with Support of School-Masters

Public Archives of Canada, *Series C¹¹A*, vol. 45, pp. 16-17: Quebec, October 14, 1723, Vaudreuil and Bégon to the Minister.

They will see that the hospital at Montreal always supports eight school-masters as it is obliged to do here. The inhabitants are disposed to furnish subsistence and lodging to those [masters] from country districts in consideration of the advantage that they will get back by the instruction of their children, and complain only that the General Hospital furnishes them nothing for their maintenance.

4. THE CHURCH AND RELIGIOUS CONTROLS

Coercive Efforts to Suppress Blasphemous Utterances

Arrêts et règlements du Conseil supérieur de Québec, et ordonnances et jugements des intendants du Canada (Quebec, 1855), pp. 71-2.

General Rules of the Superior Council of Quebec for the Police, May 11, 1676

XXXVI. It is very expressly prohibited to all our subjects of the King of whatever quality and station they be, to blaspheme, swear, and scorn the name of God, or to utter any words against the honour of the very Sacred Virgin, His Mother, and against the saints; and those who will be found convicted of having sworn and blasphemed the name of God, of his very Holy Mother and of the saints, will be condemned for the first offence to a pecuniary fine according to their means, the greatness and enormity of the swearing and blasphemy, two-thirds of the fine applicable to the local hospital, and where there is no hospital, to the church, and the other third to the informer; and if those who will have been thus punished fall again to making the said swearing, they will be for the second, third and fourth offences condemned to a fine doubled, tripled and quadrupled and, for the fifth offence, be placed in the iron collar on feast days, Sunday or others, and will be kept there from eight o'clock in the morning until an hour after noon-day, and be subject to all insults and shames, and in addition condemned to a large fine; and for the sixth offence, will be led and conducted to the pillory, and will have the lower lip cut, and if through obstinacy and inveterate evil habits, they continue after all these punishments to utter words of swearing and blasphemy, their tongue will be cut out entirely, so that in the future they will not be able to utter such words; and in case those who find themselves convicted have not the means of paying the said fines, they will be held in prison for a month on bread and water, or longer as the judges find more suitable, according to the enormity of the said blasphemies; and in order to know those who have committed more than one offence, the particulars of those who have been arrested and condemned will be registered; and those who have heard the blasphemies are enjoined to reveal the names of the offenders to the local judges within twenty-four hours under pain of a fine of sixteen *sou* and greater if not revealed at all; and among the oaths for which the above punishments have been given are not included the enormous blasphemies which express unbelief and detract from the goodness and greatness of God and from his other attributes, which crimes will be punished by greater penalties than those herein declared, according as it will be judged by the magistrates with respect to their enormity.

Religion and Brandy Trade

Public Archives of Canada, *Series C^{11}A*, vol. 11, pp. 370-2: Montreal, October 7, 1691, Letter of M. Dollier, Superior of the Seminary of Montreal, to one of his friends.

I would be aggrieved at your departure except that I hope for marvels from your voyage to France against the detestable misuse which is made here of drinking to the general perdition of all the savage missions where there is found without comparison more aptitude for becoming Christian saints than among the Europeans. There is only this single curse of drunkenness which is for them a damnable peril. Ah! my father, if you could be fortunate enough to make the truth known to our incomparable monarch. Ah! how happy we would then be, for the integrity of his intentions would no longer be deterred by so many emissaries of the devil who make out that without the brandy trade we would not be able to secure from the savages their furs. Whether that is true or not, we would be the delight of the savages if the sweetness of Christianity was not distempered by the hatred of drink. Within the twenty-six years that I have been in this country I have seen our Algonkin mission, which had been flourishing and well populated, completely destroyed by drunkenness. The Iroquois follow at the same rate. We would have had them all except that they see that when they quit their own country to live in our missions there is not less disorder here and, on this point, we even surpass the heretics [the English]. The drunkard gives in to the temptation to drink when liquor is available but when he sees after his drunkenness that he is nude and without arms, his profits spent and himself crippled and butchered from blows he is enraged against those who put him in this state, regardless of what one wishes the savages to believe and of what the interpreters say to content those who favour drinking. Indeed, I remember one Algonkin who seeing herself nude after drinking, cried with a hellish voice against the rulers of the savages. "They give to us and despoil us of all." "Ah! please God," she said, "that I am able to see them sunk in the middle of hell." After that she said to me a thousand frightful things without my being able to make her moderate her language. Finally, my father, knowing things as you do, I do not think that in conscience you can avoid using all resources and intrigues to obtain through the piety of our prince the abolition of this disorder which will be something greatly glorious to you in eternity.

Excommunication of Brandy Traders

Mandements, lettres pastorales et circulaires des Evêques de Québec, ed. H. Têtu et C. O. Gagnon (Quebec, 1887), vol. I, pp. 14-15.

MANDEMENT

To excommunicate those who sell intoxicating drink to the savages.

We, François de Laval by the grace of God and the Holy See, Bishop of Petree, Apostolic Vicar over all New France and adjacent countries.

Having recognized the great disorders that have come about by allowing intoxicating wine and brandy to be given to the savages and the still more fatal consequences which are feared from day to day; having seen, moreover, the orders of the King by which he has expressly prohibited all inhabitants of this country, merchants, artisans, captains, sailors, travellers, and all others from trading in any way or manner either wine or brandy with the savages under pain of corporal punishment; having seen, besides, the regulations of the Governors which have been made almost up to the present to arrest the course of these disorders, and that, notwithstanding, the evil increases from day to day, to such an excess that it is not only a public scandal but even places all missionary work in evident peril of total ruin, in the fear that we have that God, justly angered, will withdraw the flow of His graces and reserve his most rigorous punishments for this Church of which it has pleased His divine goodness to commit to us the care, although we are very unworthy of it; finally, seeing ourselves obliged to take the most ultimate remedies to meet these evils which have occurred in the most extreme form; to this effect we make a very expressed prohibition and forbid, under penalty of excommunication, incurred *ipso facto*, the giving in payment to the savages, selling, trading or giving gratuitously or for reward, either wine or brandy in any fashion and manner or under any pretext, from which excommunication we reserve to ourselves sole absolution. We declare, however, that in these prohibitions, under pain of excommuni-'cation, we do not intend to include some cases which occur only very rarely, where one can hardly avoid giving a little of this drink, as may happen on voyages and in extraordinary fatigue and similar necessities. But even in these cases one can fall under the aforesaid excommunication if one exceeds the small ordinary measure which persons of integrity and conscience

have the custom of serving among their domestics in this country, and
those who under this pretext would use fraud and deceit whenever they
can, should remember that nothing can be hidden from God and that
deceiving men will not prevent His malediction and just anger from falling
on them. But whenever it is a question of negotiating directly or indirectly
to trade skins, shoes or whatever it may be, one will not be permitted, in
any way, to give any drink to the savages, not even a small measure as in
the aforesaid cases, without falling under our prohibition and excommunication. And so that no one can pretend ignorance of our said prohibition
and censure, we desire that it be sent throughout the entire extent of our
jurisdiction and that publication of it be made for three consecutive Sundays,
or solemn feasts, if they occur, and that it be reread every three months,
on the first Sunday of the month, until otherwise ordered by us.

Given at Quebec in our ordinary residence under our seal and signature
and those of our secretary on this fifth day of May, 1660.

FRANÇOIS, Bishop of Petree.

Luxury and Frontier Religious Taboos

Mandements, lettres pastorales et circulaires des Evêques de Québec, ed. H. Têtu et
C. O. Gagnon (Quebec, 1887), vol. I, pp. 106-8.

MANDEMENT

Against the luxury and vanity of women and girls in church.

François, by the grace of God and the Holy See, first Bishop of Quebec.

If the fathers and doctors of the Church inveighed with so much force
against the luxury and vanity of women and girls who forget the promises
of their baptism, appearing dressed and ornamented in Satan's pomp which
they have so solemnly renounced, it is for us to make known the extreme
horror that God has for such a disorder, which renders those who are guilty
so much more criminal before him, that wishing to be pleasing in the eyes
of men they become the captives and instruments of the demon who uses this
luxury to make them, and those who see them in this state, commit an
infinity of sins. That is why God declares often in the Holy Scripture that
he will punish severely those worldly women who parade thus the marks
and livery of his enemy. . . . If these vain fineries displease God so strongly,
and if he takes such rude vengeance, of what crime are they not guilty
and what punishment must not attend those who carry this pompous
apparel even into our churches appearing in these consecrated places at
prayers and confession in indecent dress, showing scandalous nudity of
arms, shoulders, and throat, being content to cover them with a transparent
veil which serves more often to give greater lustre to these disgraceful
nudities, the head uncovered, or covered only with a transparent net and
the hair curled in a manner unworthy of a Christian, offending the holiness
of these places. . . .

The zeal we must have for the honour of the house of God and for the
salvation of the flock that it has pleased the Divine Providence to confide

to us, obliges us to employ every means within our jurisdiction and authority to drive out entirely from the churches of our diocese an abuse so pernicious and which was introduced there several years ago. . . .

In this cause we prohibit very expressly all girls and women of whatever quality and fortune from approaching the Sacraments, presenting the consecrated bread, going to the offering and making the collection in the churches in the indecent manner that we have just specified in our present *mandement*, and all the *curés* of our diocese from receiving them there in this state; instead we wish that when they come to church that they dress with the decency and modesty which is demanded by Christian holiness and humility. We forbid, likewise, all other priests of our diocese, seculars as well as regulars, from receiving at the sacraments the said girls and women in this state, and finally that no one pretends ignorance, we order that, at the diligence of our Grand Vicars, our present *mandement* will be immediately sent to all the *curés* of our diocese and everywhere it is needed, to be read there and published in the sermon and affixed to the door of the church.

Given at Quebec the 26th day of February, 1682.

FRANÇOIS, Bishop of Quebec.

Religious Efforts to Suppress Immorality

Mandements, lettres pastorales et circulaires des Evêques de Québec, ed. H. Têtu et C. O. Gagnon (Quebec, 1887), vol. I, pp. 267-70.

ORDINANCE

Concerning drunkenness and impurity.

Jean, by the mercy of God and the grace of the Holy Apostolic See, Bishop of Quebec. To all our dear Brothers, the *Curés*, Missionaries and Confessors of our Diocese, Greeting and Blessing.

God having inspired us to make a visit of our diocese with all the care of which we are capable, he also gave us the strength needed to execute this enterprise so difficult and perilous at a time when our enemies are attacking us on all sides. That which touched us most in the visits and missions we made in the towns and in the country was to see that our temporal miseries are nothing in comparison with the spiritual miseries with which our diocese is depressed. Having known perfectly our flock, we thought we would have no enemies to fear except the English and Iroquois; but God having opened our eyes to the disorders in our diocese, and having made us feel more than ever the weight of our charge, we are obliged to recognize and confess that our most redoubtable enemies are drunkenness, impurity, luxury and slander, and that we must employ all our forces to conquer them. After having prayed a long time before God to obtain from him the light and the suitable remedies for such great evils, it has come to us in our thinking that in order to stop drunkenness it would be proper that the confessors would not give absolution to those who intoxicate the savages or the French unless they give to the poor churches, the hospital or

other works of piety according to the advice of their confessor, all the gain
that they had made by this drink, leaving to them only the liberty of retaining
that which the drink cost them so that they might be able to satisfy their
merchants, it being quite easy through the obligation that we impose on
the confessors of giving this penance to those who wish to lose their souls
to satisfy their greed, to make known to the tavern-keepers and to others
who trade in drinks that they must use with moderation the liberty that
is accorded to them· to trade, which is only permitted to them to the extent
that they are able to guarantee the use that is made of it.

Regarding impurity which we consider as one of the principal causes
of the punishments that God sends us, we cannot exhort you too much to
take great care of the absolutions that you give when those who are in the
habit of sinning address themselves to you, realizing that there is nothing
which gives more occasion to impenitence for immoral acts than the facility
that they promise to find in the confessors, to be absolved of them as often
as they present themselves at confession, without placing themselves under
any penalty of reform.

Regarding luxury which touches so near lewdness, we desire that you
hold principally to three things: the first is, that you take great care to study
and eradicate in the persons in your charge the attachment that they have
for vanity, without regard to the pretexts that the ornaments which· they
wear to satisfy such vanity can be worn without mortal sin; for however
difficult it is to decide how far one can go in this matter without committing
mortal sin, there is nothing, however, more easy to lose oneself than the
disposition of wishing to be vain as much as one can without sinning mortally,
and nothing more certain for the confessor than to judge that a soul cannot
do anything for her salvation and for her protection when she is in such a
disposition.

The second thing is that you examine with attention if the attachment
which is found in the fair sex for the ornaments is not an occasion of impurity; for in this case, that which would otherwise be venial becomes mortal.
Now, it is very important to remark that there is hardly a person to whom
vanity is not an occasion for impure glances or words, and that there are
few of these vanities which do not expose one to hearing discourses against
honour, and to suffer even criminal liberties.   In a word, vanity opens all
the doors of the soul, that is to say, all the senses to the demon of impurity.
A vain woman finds herself daily in company where modesty is attacked by
the eyes, ears, touch, imagination and by all the senses, her vanity being a
signal for all lewdness to gather about her.   That is why we do not believe
that you should, nor that you can, give absolution to vain persons, to whom
their vanity is an occasion for mortal sin whether their ornaments are in
themselves criminal or not.

The third is that you do not content yourself that your penitents are
dressed modestly when in church or when they approach the sacraments;
but that you inform yourself further how they are dressed in their own homes;
for we have known that several women and girls do not scruple to have the

throat and shoulders uncovered when they are at home and we have even encountered them in this state. Now, in order to declare distinctly our intention on this matter, we forbid you expressly from absolving girls and women who have their necks and shoulders bare, whether inside or outside their homes, or who have them covered only with a transparent veil; and in regard to the communion, presenting the blessed bread, the offering and collections which are made by girls and women in the churches, we renew all that which has been ruled before by our predecessor in his *mandement* of February 26, 1682, and we desire that following the Apostle, the girls appear veiled, that is to say the head covered in church.

Regarding slander, although this sin is contrary to civil society and the peace of the colony, it is, however, almost universal in this diocese. The only remedy to prevent it would be to oblige those who commit this sin to retract and repair effectively the wrong that they have done to their neighbour, or if that was impossible to seek some other penance which would be at the same time satisfactory and a remedy for the past and future. It is to this we exhort the confessors of our diocese to give particular attention.

Given at Quebec in our Episcopal Residence, the last day of October, 1690.

JEAN, Bishop of Quebec.

Ecclesiastical Controls and the Governor's Circle

Mandements, lettres pastorales et circulaires des Evêques de Québec, ed. H. Têtu et C. O. Gagnon (Quebec, 1887), vol. I, pp. 169-74.

NOTICE

GIVEN TO THE GOVERNOR AND THE GOVERNESS ON THEIR
OBLIGATION OF GIVING A GOOD EXAMPLE TO
THE PEOPLE [1685]

In which Monseigneur the Bishop desires to have that which will be to the greater glory of God made known to M. the Governor and Madam the Governess concerning the following articles, herein afterwards set out, and, having asked the guidance of the Holy Spirit, that which one thought could be represented to them more justly in the knowledge that one has of their integrity and virtue.

I. Concerning feasts

1. When M. the Governor and Mme. the Governess honour some individual by going to dine with him, it is proper that this be for dinner and not for supper in order to avoid the long evening there, the dangerous pastimes and the other vexatious consequences which usually occur at feasts and night gatherings.

2. That they declare themselves discontented, disobliged and even dismissed forever, if it happens that the repast that is given to them is too sumptuous or magnificent; this is so that they will only find themselves at tables where frugality is observed, they will accustom little by little people

to retrench in their feasts this vexatious abundance which is opposed to the rules of temperance and injurious to modesty and Christian decency. This will not inconvenience the families.

3. That they will never permit these feasts to be accompanied by balls and dances and many other recreations and dangerous liberties; their presence at such diversions would be unfortunate, as experience has shown since a long time for one of the most notable persons in Quebec.

II.   Concerning the ball and dance

Although balls and dances are indifferent things in their nature, they are, nevertheless, so dangerous because of the circumstances which accompany them, the evil and almost inevitable consequences that one sees happening, that in the sentiment of St. Francois de Sales, it is necessary to say of them what the doctors say of toadstools, "the best of them have no value." . . . If avoiding the ball and dance is so important to private and individual persons, it is of greater consequence for public persons, and those who rank first, their example serving ordinarily as a rule for the others, above all when one sees them do or consent to the things which are pleasing to the senses, and, because of the esteem that one has of their virtue by their profession, they are given an occasion to approve and do the same things in imitation of them.

That being so, it is of great importance for the glory of God and the salvation of our neighbours that the Governor and Governess, on the conduct of whom the majority will not fail to form theirs, hold firm, not only from not going to homes where balls and dances are held but moreover to prohibit upon their entry these kinds of pastimes which, spreading afterwards to the homes of those everywhere else, will not be practised there without doubt with the same innocence that they can be, at least on the exterior, in their home when they are present there.

However, as the age and vivacity of Mademoiselle their daughter requires some diversion and recreation, one can condescend to permit her some modest and moderate dances, but with persons of her own sex only and in the presence of her mother, for fear of licence in speech and immodest songs, but not in the presence of men and boys, this mingling of sexes, speaking properly, is what causes the inconveniences and disorders of the ball and dance.

It is not always that dances practised between persons of the same sex have no great inconveniences, among which the one most to fear is the disposition that they give to admit persons of the opposite sex, which rarely fails to happen, either among the dances which are held at her home, or at other dances which are introduced elsewhere in imitation of the first, and it is for that reason that one may suggest to the Governor and Governess that they consider whether it would not be better that their daughter take another diversion for recreation.

III.   Concerning comedies and other theatrical performances

But one does not believe that it would be beneficial to the profession of Christianity to permit himself the liberty of taking the part of a person in a comedy, and of appearing before the public as an actor reciting verses, however holy the mat er may be; and much less still does one believe that one must permit boys to declaim with girls. This would revive here, without thinking, the customs of the theatre and comedy, as dangerous as and even more than balls and dances, and of which the disorders have given occasion to be inveighed against with much vehemence.

IV.   Concerning luxurious dress and nudities

As luxury and vanity of dress in girls and women are one of the principal disorders which have been noticed here for a long time and which have had the most troublesome consequences in every way, it is greatly to be desired that M. the Governor and Mme. the Governess exercise often their zeal on this point, testifying in gatherings by their words, as they do by their example, the indignation they feel against this abuse and caution and rebuke even in person those who affect to show themselves in fastidious and worldly clothes. . . .

Although the preachers have often inveighed against this disorder and it is believed that the confessors do their duty in regard to those who prove to be incorrigible, experience, nevertheless, shows that all that has served little up to the present, because the preachers and the confessors have had no support, one simple word from the governor has had more force to get the better of the spirits than all the right [reasoning] of the pulpit and confessional. Since interest, human respect or affection ordinarily has a greater impression on people, in making them act, it is easy to see what glory M. the Governor and Mme. the Governess will procure to God, by combatting strongly immodesty and pomp in dress and declaring haughtily in favour of those who will preserve in their dress the mediocrity of their state and their means, and who hold themselves to the rule of Christian modesty, and, on the contrary, testifying by their coolness, rebuke and even alienation against people affecting this worldly exterior entirely contrary to the solemn promises made in their baptism. It is thus that, not finding the applause that they seek by their luxury, they would be ashamed to continue it and would be obliged finally to renounce it.

V.   Concerning irreverences which are committed in church

There is only a word to say concerning this point which is that M. the Governor and Mme. the Governess, who edify everyone by the piety and modesty with which they appear in church, do one thing worthy of their zeal for the honour of God by obliging everyone in their suite and their court to hold themselves in restraint and respect there, to be in decent posture, to keep silence, and finally to comport themselves with the reverence demanded by the holiness of these places.

These are the things which one judges the most proper to be represented to M. the Governor and Mme. the Governess on the above articles and in which one has no doubt that they will enter willingly, following the zeal that they both show for everything which can contribute to the glory of God and the edification of their neighbour.

JEAN, Bishop of Quebec.

The Prohibition of Comedies

Mandements, lettres pastorales et circulaires des Evêques de Québec, ed. H. Têtu et C. O. Gagnon (Quebec, 1887), vol. I, pp. 302-4.

MANDEMENT
ON THE SUBJECT OF COMEDIES

Jean, by the grace of God and the Holy Apostolic See, Bishop of Quebec. To all the faithful of our diocese Salutations in our Lord.

The instruction which was given on Sunday, the 10th of this month, in the church of the Lower City for the enlightenment of the conscience concerning comedies which play in the world, has given us the occasion, by the discourses that it has caused in conversation, to discover the need that there is to support our authority in convincing the same conscience in the things which are said in this instruction that we have caused to be used.

And as it is our pastoral duty to turn away by all the means within our power the occasions of sins which can lose the souls which God has confided to us and to support people in doing good, We believe ourselves obliged to publish, by a *mandement*, our sentiments and intentions concerning the play-houses and comedies which are made in the world. This is why, after having approved as we do by the present *mandement* the above instruction, of which we judged it would be useful to have copies distributed, we exhort all the faithful of our diocese to pay serious attention to the unanimous sentiment of such illustrious persons in doctrine and holiness, who speak of the comedies in the world according as they are at present, instructing everyone that those even decent in their nature can be very dangerous by the circumstances of the time or place, or persons, or the end, or the things which are accustomed to precede, accompany and follow these sort of diversions and striving to impress upon all kinds of people a disgust and all possible aversion for them. We conjure them with all our heart for the love of our Lord to defer on this point by a docile acquiescence to the sentiments of the saints since in their proper light and natural inclination they ought to distrust [comedies].

But as regards the plays and comedies which are impious, impure or injurious to one's neighbour, tending only in themselves to inspire thoughts and affections in every way contrary to religion, to the purity of morals and charity towards one's fellow man, as are certain theatre pieces which turn piety and devotion to ridicule, which carry the flames of impurity into the heart, which seek to blacken and defame the reputation or which under the pretext of appearing to reform the customs only serve to corrupt them and under colour of reproving vice insinuate it adroitly and with artifice into the souls of the spectators, such as the comedy of *Tartuffe*, or of the impostor, or others similar, We declare that this sort of play and comedy are not only dangerous, but that they are absolutely evil and criminal in themselves and that one cannot assist at them without sinning, and as such We condemn them and expressly prohibit all persons of our diocese of whatever station or condition that they are from attending there.

And so that no one can pretend ignorance, we wish that our present *mandement* be read and published in Quebec and elsewhere needed in the sermon at mass and at other devotional gatherings that are held regularly in the said Quebec.   In faith of which we have signed our hand and had consigned by our secretary and affixed the seal of our arms.

Given at Quebec, January 16, 1694.

JEAN, Bishop of Quebec.

Opposition to Ecclesiastical Controls

Public Archives of Canada, *Series C¹¹A*, vol. 13, pp. 230-4, 262-3: Montreal, September 28, 1694, Memoir of Lamothe Cadillac.

The ecclesiastical state gets ready for battle.   There it is armed from top to toe, with its bows and arrows.   Sr. Glandelet began first, and gave two sermons, one on the 10th and the other on the 24th of January by which he strove to prove that one could not attend comedies without sinning mortally.   The Bishop on his part made public in prayer a *mandement* on the 16th of the same month in which he made mention of certain comedies impious, impure and injurious to men, and insinuated without doubt that those who played actually were such.   The credulous people, infatuated, seduced by this sort of sermon and *mandement* have begun already to regard M. the Count [Frontenac] as the corruptor of morals and the destroyer of religion.   The numerous party of false saints assembled in the streets, in the squares, and introduced themselves afterwards into the houses to confirm the weak ones in their error, or to try to inspire the stronger, forgetting nothing in breaking down those of neutral opinion.   But their schemes proving almost without success, they believed that it was necessary finally to vanquish or die, and persuaded the Bishop to such strange strategem as causing to be made public in church a *mandement* prohibiting Sieur de Mareuil, a retired Lieutenant, from the use of the sacraments.

If one believes an actor of the comedy, and it was apparent that he felt intimidated himself by this clap of thunder, the rest of the troupe were shaken by it, or at least, it having been rendered odious by a formidable pretense, hatred of the comedy became the lot of those who had formerly favoured it.

This officer felt injured and went to the Bishop but the Bishop did not wish to see him or hear him.   He went again a second and a third time. He was taken by the shoulders and driven out, being told that one did not wish to enter into conversation with an excommunicated person.   A procedure so injurious obliged Sieur de Mareuil to seek justice and address himself to a notary in order to make the Bishop give him a copy of his *mandement*. The notary refused. Mareuil addressed himself to the Intendant who ordered the notary to do his duty. This order had no effect. Mareuil obtained a second, and finally the notary obeyed. The Bishop perceived by this *démarche* that he was neither in Spain nor Portugal and that one could easily find means to obtain reparation for an injury so atrocious. It was this that made him consider a second strategem worse than the first, in every way opposed to episcopal charity, to the maxims of Christianity, and one which set a very bad example. The prelate played a very astonishing role. He went to the Sovereign Council on the 1st of February. He denounced Sieur de Mareuil and declared him guilty of an impious crime towards God, the Virgin and the saints and, forgetting nothing which would aid his beautiful scheme, he made a flowery discourse at this court in the absence of M. the Count, interrupted from time to time by outbursts from a heart armed with apparent charity, profound and infinite, but pushed finally by rebellion, he said, of an indocile child whom he had often warned and had had warned by persons of authority. All this, however, is to be supposed, I do not wish to tell any falsehoods.

There is Mareuil who changes from the theatre, from the comedy, and passes to these tragic affairs. The discourse of this prelate was well contrived, those of the Attorney-General in his decisions were part of the same counsel, and also the hasty sentence which was rendered upon this subject.

I am resolved to tell you of the crime of Sieur de Mareuil and I pray you to be persuaded that I hide nothing in this detail, having no end but to expose to you the truth in all its nudity. It is true that about two years ago on his arrival here, being found in a state of debauchery, Sieur de Mareuil sang a somewhat indecent song. M. the Count was warned of it and reprimanded him severely. This is the trial which is made today. Behold the pastoral zeal re-awakened after a silence of two years because of a comedy which they wished to abolish at all costs and about which the ecclesiastical authorities do not wish to be denied.

It is incontestable, and one cannot deny it without blushing, that Mareuil, since that time [two years ago] had had recourse to penance, had confessed and gone to communion several times, and had even become dangerously ill and received the sacraments and continued to do the duty of an upright and Christian man, and did nothing to re-awaken sleeping dogs, for even if it was true that the crime was as enormous as the Bishop pretended, was it not sufficient that it had escaped the memory of man and was buried in the sepulchre of oblivion, and only by a studied zeal was it produced today with all its attributes. I leave Sieur de Mareuil at the Sovereign Council appealing against the abuse of the *mandement* of the Bishop where he presented uselessly request upon request demanding justice. I leave him, I say, between the hands of M. de Villerai, his manager and those of his capital enemy. . . .

There remains nothing for me to tell you if it is only that the colony

is in such a very good state that one does not perceive poverty as it is in
Europe. We have fortunately a good, wise and very brilliant Governor,
a protector of the liberty that the King accords his subjects, an enemy of
odious and insupportable ecclesiastical domination. It is necessary to be
here to see the conspiracy which goes on every day in order to overthrow
the plans and projects of the Governor, and it is necessary to keep a firm
and level head with respect to what M. the Count does in order to support
oneself against the ambushes which are laid everywhere for him. If he
wishes peace, that is sufficient to be opposed here, and there is the cry that
all is lost; if he wishes to make war, he exposes himself to ruining the colony.
He would not have so many affairs on his shoulders if he had not abolished
a *hiericho* which was a house that the gentlemen of the seminary at Montreal
had built to confine, they said, bad living girls, if he had been willing
to permit them to take some soldiers and given them some officers to go
into the houses at midnight to drag away the women sleeping with their
husbands and have them flogged until they bled for having been to the ball
or masquerade, if he had said nothing against the *curés* who made
the rounds with the soldiers and who obliged the girls and women to confine
themselves to their homes at 9 o'clock in summer, if he had been willing
to prohibit the wearing of lace, if he had said nothing about the women of
quality being refused communion for having a topknot, if he had not also
opposed excommunications tossed at random, to the scandals which followed
them, if he had only made officers on the advice of the religious communities, if
he had been willing to prohibit wine and brandy for the savages, if he had not
uttered a word on the subject of fixed parishes and the rights of patronage,
if M. the Count had taken the above advice, he would assuredly be a man
without parallel and would soon be on the list of the greatest saints for they
canonize them cheaply in this country.

Ecclesiastical Dominance in the Colony

Baron de Lahontan, *New Voyages to North America*, ed. R. G. Thwaites (Chicago,
1905), vol. I, pp. 381-7.

In *Canada* the Politick, Ecclesiastical and Military Government, are all
in a manner one thing, in regard, that the wisest Governours have subjected
their Authority to that of the *Ecclesiasticks*; and such Governours as would
not embarque in that interest, have found their Poste so uneasie, that they
have been recall'd with disgrace. . . .

The Governour General that means to neglect no opportunity of advancing or enriching themselves, do commonly hear two Masses a day,
and are oblig'd to confess once in four and twenty hours. He has always
Clergy-men about him where-ever he goes, and indeed properly speaking,
they are his Counsellours. . . .

The people repose a great deal of confidence in the Clergy of this Country
as well as elsewhere. Here the outward shew of Devotion is strictly ob-
serv'd, for the People dare not absent from the great Masses and Sermons,

without a lawful Excuse. But after all, 'tis at the time of Divine Service, that the married Women and Maids give their humours a full loose, as being assur'd that their Husbands and Mothers are busie at Church. The Priests call People by their names in the Pulpit; they prohibit under the pain of Excommunication, the reading of Romances and Plays, as well as the use of Masks, and playing at Ombre or Lansquenet. The Jesuits and the Recollets agree as ill as the Milinists and the Jansenists. The former pretend that the latter have no right to confess. . . .

The Gentlemen of that Country, are oblig'd to be very cautious in carrying even with the *Ecclesiasticks*, in respect of the good or harm that the good Fathers can indirectly throw in their way. The Bishop and the Jesuits have such an influence over the Governours General, as is sufficient to procure places to the Children of the Noblemen or Gentlemen that are devoted to their Service, or to obtain the Licenses that I spoke of in my eighth letter. 'Tis likewise in their power to serve the Daughters of such Gentlemen, by finding 'em agreable and rich Husbands. The meanest curates must be managed cautiously, for they can either serve or disserve the Gentlemen, in whose Seigniories they are no more than Missionaries, there being no fix'd Cures in *Canada*, which indeed is a grievance which ought to be redress'd. The Officers of the Army are likewise oblig'd to keep up a good correspondence with the *Ecclesiasticks*, for without that 'tis impossible for 'em to keep their ground. They must not only take care that their own conduct be regular; but likewise look after that of the Soldiers, by preventing the Disorders they might commit in their Quarters.

Tyranny of Priests

Baron de Lahontan, *New Voyages to North America*, ed. R. G. Thwaites (Chicago, 1905), vol. I, pp. 88-9.

[Montreal, June 28, 1685]. I spent part of the Winter in hunting with the *Algonkins*, in order to a more perfect Knowledge of their Language; and the rest I spent in this Place, with a great deal of uneasiness: for, here we cannot enjoy ourselves, either at Play, or in visiting the Ladies, but 'tis presently carried to the Curate's ears, who takes publick notice of it in the Pulpit. His zeal goes so far, as even to name the Persons: and since he refuses the Sacrament of the Holy Supper to Ladies of Quality, upon the most slender Pretences, you may easily guess at the other steps of his Indiscretion. You cannot imagine to what a pitch these Ecclesiastical Lords have screw'd their Authority: They excommunicate all the Masks, and wherever they spy 'em, they run after 'em to uncover their Faces, and abuse 'em in a reproachful manner: In fine, they have a more watchful eye over the Conduct of the Girls and married Women, than their Fathers and Husbands have. They cry out against those that do not receive the Sacrament once a Month; and at *Easter* they oblige all sorts of Persons to give in Bills to their Confessors. They prohibit and burn all the Books that treat of any other Subject but Devotion. When I think of this Tyranny,

I cannot but be enrag'd at the impertinent Zeal of the Curate of this City. This inhumane Fellow came one day to my Lodging, and finding the Romance of the Adventures of *Petronius* upon my Table, he fell upon it with an unimaginable fury, and tore out almost all the Leaves. . . . These Animals cannot content themselves with the studying of Mens Actions, but they must likewise dive into their Thoughts.   By this Sketch, Sir, you may judge what a pleasant Life we lead here.

The Conflict between Frontenac and the Jesuits

Public Archives of Canada, *Series C¹¹A*, vol. 4, pp. 197-200: Quebec, November 14, 1674, Memorandum by Frontenac to the Minister.

I have discharged that which you prescribed to me to continue to encourage the Jesuits, the Seminary at Montreal and the Recollets to take young savages and instruct them in the faith and civilize them.   The latter ask nothing better and will strain themselves to do it in the mission of Katarakoui where they will assuredly make some progress.   For the others [the Jesuits] I have set them an example, and made them see that if they wish to serve their credit and extend the power that they have with the savages, they will civilize them and make of their children as I would have.

But it is one thing that they will never do unless absolutely forced for reasons which I have already written and which it is useless to repeat.

They make use of the same [reasons] in regard to the extension of their missions, on which I have spoken to them in the manner that you ordered me, but uselessly, they having declared to me very plainly that they were here only to seek to instruct the savages as quickly as possible and to attract beavers and not to be priests of the French.

They have even closed for eight days their habitation at Cap de la Magdelaine, and withdrawn two fathers who had always been there.   This mission is one of the most populous in this country and this act will presently cause fewer savages to come there.   Whenever I have wished to represent to Father Superior in a gentle manner the inconveniences in which the inhabitants find themselves without spiritual aids, he has not hesitated to tell me the reasons that I have remarked to you.

However, after having resolved not to permit any of their priests to accept the charitable warnings that I had made to them, they were obliged some days ago to change some resolutions, and the Superior has since come to me to say that one of them would be left, but I believe that that will only be for this winter and to let the great fuss which was made pass over.

If the Recollets were greater in number and one wished to employ them, they would assuredly do marvels in the missions.   But the two that you had the honour to tell me that you asked for last year have not come, nor the four for this year.   I believe that they are delayed by some underhand intrigue, feeling commencing to be very strong against them although on the face they appear friendly towards them.

They have need of good subjects in greater number . . . and that you prove to M. the Bishop that you desire that he will not let them become useless and will send them to missions near and far. The Superior who came last year is a great preacher and has overshadowed and given a little grief to the peaceful here, who are not assuredly so able.

In the belief that I had that some religious would be sent and because of the inconvenience that they have in erecting a lodging, I have had one built for them where they live comfortably, thinking that no charity would be more proper or would carry out better the intentions of His Majesty or you, for the accomplishment of which I desire nothing more.

Ecclesiastical Inquisitions

Public Archives of Canada, *Series C¹¹A*, vol. 11, pp. 420-1: Quebec, October 20, 1691, Frontenac to the Minister.

With respect to co-operating with the Bishop and Ecclesiastics as I am advised, there is nothing I have not done to accomplish such an object. They are all filled with much virtue and piety and, if their zeal was not so vehement and a little more moderate, they would succeed perhaps better in that which they undertake for the conversion of souls. But in order to attain their ends, they often use means so extraordinary and so little used in the Kingdom [of France] that they shock most people instead of persuading them and it is on that score that I have told them my sentiments with frankness and with as much gentleness as I am able, knowing the grumbling which their acts caused, and often receiving complaints of the constraint that they put on the conscience, especially the ecclesiastics of Montreal where there is a *curé* from Franche Comté who would like to establish a kind of inquisition, worse than in Spain, and all because of an excess of zeal.

Church and State

Public Archives of Canada, *Series C¹¹A*, vol. 22, pp. 120-4: Quebec, November 19, 1704, Ramezay to the Minister.

Eventually, the country being augmented and the King recovering the rights from the company, the Jesuits, being no longer the masters in the choice of Governors and Intendants, wished, however, always to preserve the empire that they had acquired for themselves in this country, the success of which depended on the softness or firmness of the Governors of the Canadas, and one has the expectation that those who have deferred to them too much have not succeeded for the service of the King in this colony.

The Count Frontenac, whose background and merit are known, having arrived in Canada, governed it with so much wisdom that he won the love and respect of all the people. One cannot imagine the cabal intrigues and calumny which the Jesuits have used in court in order to abuse his first government in which he never wished to have them take part, no more than in his last reign. I can advance ardently how very difficult it would be for anyone to do so much good for the country, and could so well govern it. The only fault which he had was to seek honours with too much forwardness.

Afterwards, Monseigneur le Chevalier de Callière who succeeded him had the same firmness in regard to the conservation of his authority, and, although he did not have the same vivacious spirit, one owes to his memory that he has very usefully served the King in this country as much as Governor of Montreal as in the capacity of Governor-General. . . .

When the ecclesiastical state wrote to you in his favour to demand from you, Monseigneur, your powerful patronage to obtain from His Majesty the governor-generalship of this country they did not realize that they made such bad use [of their influence], and I do not doubt Monseigneur that they complain to you unless the prejudice, that you have witnessed in his favour, prevents them, being anxious not to contradict themselves so promptly.

In the case of the Jesuits, although in the depth of their hearts they do not approve of him, there is no likelihood that they will complain about that which was their triumph. At present in place of distributing according to the will of His Majesty the two thousand *écus* which he had the kindness to give to the best families of this country, part of it is given at their instigation to the peasants, their creatures. They have the principal part in the government, one does not deliberate about anything without their councils, which often meet in their own homes where they find their particular interest as I have the honour to inform you Monseigneur.

Problems of Organization and Support of the Church

Public Archives of Canada, *Series C¹¹A*, vol. 5, pp. 272-3: Quebec, November 13, 1681, Du Chesneau to the Minister.

However, Monseigneur, the owners of the fiefs and seigneuries and the inhabitants have represented that if the boundaries [of the parishes] were extended the people would find themselves no more abandoned than in those which have already been assigned to each *curé*, the inhabitants who compose these having mass ordinarily only one Sunday in a month or in six weeks. They have represented, further, that even the tithes would not be greatly increased since the inhabitants, being served more rarely, would declare that it was their duty to pay tithes only in proportion to the service which would be given them. It is impossible to farm them out because of the difficulty of collecting them without great expense due to the location of the various settlements. It is necessary to rely on the people's good faith.

The priests, on the other hand, have claimed that they are already overburdened with work being obliged to travel incessantly, sometimes on snowshoes in the snow during winter, and sometimes by canoe during summer when they row all day, and that if the boundaries, which are already too wide, were extended they would find themselves incapable of keeping up such great toil.

However, Monseigneur, all these difficulties have not prevented me from making known the intention of His Majesty, you and of the Bishop of sending priests to places where they have been accustomed to attend and of ordering them to content themselves with the simple things of life, and the bare necessities for their livelihood. Some of the owners of the fiefs and of the seigneuries have offered to board them and they should be able to provide for their needs, but as that would be done voluntarily and independently of the tithes, one cannot be sure that it would be continued.

Problems of Conflict among Clergy of New France

Public Archives of Canada, *Series C¹¹A*, vol. 106, pp. 102-7: Quebec, October 16, 1727, Beauharnois to the Minister.

I have found, Monseigneur, in the Canadian ecclesiastics much haughti-ness and vivacity with little science and still less application to filling the duties of their ministry. The Foreign Mission Fathers in Paris in charge of the Seminary of this diocese have sent in the year past a superior and two ecclesiastics to train the young people. But those in the country, jealous that they had not been trusted with the government of this house, have excited the seminarians to revolt against their superior and even engaged on their side some seculars who assembled with them at the Seminary to obstruct his good designs. The Bishop and I have spoken, and I have taken into my office in particular those whom I believed to be able to listen to reason, which was partly successful. But I believe that there is need of more than talk to hold to duty those who are at the head of this cabal. They continue always to believe that it is to their honour not to suffer anyone whose ecclesiastical state does not accord to their liking.

A canon from here [M. Fornel] who had come from France triumphantly, they tell me, by having prevented the Fathers of the Foreign Missions from sending some subjects to join the three that came last year, had resolved to go again to continue, from appearances, the support of the cabal. . . . Only one such subject is a plague in a country so sane as are the country districts here. That reminds me, Monseigneur, that there is here one of grand name who came by arbitrary warrant in our vessel last year who would be better in France than here. It seems to me that he was accused of being a heretical preacher.

To return, Monseigneur, to M. Fornel, it seems from certain manœuvers on his part, of which I am informed, that without doubt he intends to make every effort to avenge himself against the superior. The conduct of these gentlemen (certain epithets would suit them better) makes me convinced of the necessity of having immediately a coadjutor provided with certain privileges as some arbitrary warrants in order to shift some of them about; an example would make all the others afraid and would set them right at their duty.

The Independent Spirit of the Canadian Clergy

Public Archives of Canada, *Series C¹¹A*, vol. 53, pp. 246-8: Quebec, October 13, 1730, Dosquet, Coadjutor to Quebec, to the Minister.

Knowing the bold and independent spirit of the Canadian priests, I did not think I ought to commence with them the reform of this diocese, which I have found in great disorder; I have reserved this undertaking until this year. . . . The ecclesiastics have become so insolent that they say that only three like them are necessary to become masters of the country and subdue all the bishops. . . .

The canons do not wish to recognize the laws, the statutes nor the superiors. They treat their Dean as their inferior and the Bishop as their equal, having undertaken to oppose themselves to everything that he desires, especially Messieurs Toruct and Hazeur who take pleasure in the division and who attract others to their party. Although the service is very short at the Cathedral, they assist hardly any, the latter has been found absent more than thirteen hundred times this year, and he claims to receive the reward as if he had been present, although he disputes with M. le Doyen whom I have employed for the affairs of the diocese and with Sieur Boulanger whom I have also occupied for six months according to the right granted to the bishops by the Councils.

I am obliged to close my eyes to many things until it appears that the court has the goodness to support me in establishing order among the clergy who scandalize the public by their independence, their division and their irregularity. If it is deferred any longer to correct them I fear that the evil may become incurable. . . .

I feel greatly how disagreeable it is to a bishop to be in this country if he is obliged to employ his time in responding to all that which idle and turbulent spirits can invent against him, as I know them to have done last autumn. Before finishing, I ask your pardon, Monseigneur, for having implored you to agree to the return to this country of Sieur Fornel. I confess my mistake, for as long as he remains here there is little hope of seeing peace reign.

II

THE FISHERIES AND RURAL SOCIETY IN THE MARITIME COLONIES

IF the disorganizing forces in the early social development of the Maritime region were less far-reaching than those evident in New France during the period of rapid expansion of the fur trade, they were considerably more diversified in character. The kind of socio-economic unity secured in New France by the St. Lawrence Valley was conspicuously lacking. Flexibility in economic organization resulted from the variety of resources and from the number of points of entry by which they could be exploited. Early development took place in terms of the fisheries, and the large number of different bases in the region and of centres of supply in Europe emphasized the diversity of economic interests. The result was the emergence of several widely separated settlements each of which gave rise to its own kinds of social problems. The different social heritages of the population and economic and technological conditions of life led to different sorts of social adjustments and different forms of cultural development. Only slowly did there emerge integrated social organizations for larger areas which became organized as provinces. The persistence of diversity made impossible any real cultural unity for the whole Maritime region.

Although the colonization of the Maritimes began about the same time as that of the St. Lawrence Valley, the character of economic development checked any considerable settlement. Exploitation of the Gulf fisheries by the French led to trade with the Indians and to the establishment of a settlement about the Bay of Fundy as well as along the banks of the St. Lawrence, but the hunting hinterland of the Maritime Indians was not sufficiently extensive to support any profitable trade in furs. The rapid destruction of the fur-bearing animals within the region, and the absence of any approaches to the interior of the continent, reduced the fur trade to a secondary interest of the inhabitants. Both the Indians and the whites found it necessary to depend very largely upon other means of livelihood. The raising of cattle became the chief in-

95

dustry of the French colonists about the Minas Basin. The Bank
and Newfoundland fisheries developed as the dominant interest
of French and English trading-capitalist organization.[1]

The nature of the fishing industry discouraged the promotion of
settlement.   Unlike the fur trade which came increasingly to depend
upon the participation of local colonists, the fisheries were exploited
by interests operating from a large number of European bases from
which the necessary labour and supplies were secured.[2] Attempts to
promote colonization met with the vigorous opposition of these
interests which feared the competition of local capitalists and labour.
The long struggle to prevent the establishment of fishing settlements
in Newfoundland was indicative of efforts to preserve the ship fisheries carried on from European bases.[3]   Settlement on the mainland,
accordingly, took place slowly, and was more in relation to the overseas-controlled fishing industry than in response to a genuine desire
for the development of colonies.   The retreat of France from most
of Newfoundland and from Acadia with the Treaty of Utrecht in
1713 led to the establishment of a fishing base in Cape Breton and
of an agricultural settlement in what later became known as Prince
Edward Island.   The British, in turn, established a military garrison
at Annapolis to police the rural Acadian settlements and to check
the considerable smuggling trade growing up with Louisbourg. Encroachments of the French upon the English base near the Strait of
Canso and upon the New England fisheries led to the capture of
Louisbourg by a party of New Englanders in 1745, and, when the
post was returned to France in 1748 and heavily fortified, Halifax
was founded to offset its military importance.[4] Growing concern on
the part of the British government with respect to the French settle-

[1]M.Q. Innis, *An Economic History of Canada* (Toronto, 1935), chaps. II
and III.

[2]H. A. Innis, *The Cod Fisheries: The History of an International Economy*
(Toronto, 1940).

[3]*Ibid.* The policy of carrying on the fisheries from home bases was favoured
particularly by the British who looked upon the development of this industry as
a means of strengthening the navy. In the French Empire, emphasis upon land
garrisons led to a greater interest in permanent colonization. Cf. G. S. Graham,
*Sea Power and British North America, 1783-1820: A Study in British Colonial
Policy* (Cambridge, 1941).

[4]H. A. Innis, ed., *Select Documents in Canadian Economic History, 1497-1783*
(Toronto, 1929).

ments in the Minas Basin gave rise to the project of establishing a number of German Protestant communities among them, and, when this failed through the danger of Indian attacks, and the Germans were settled at Lunenburg, the evacuation of the Acadians was undertaken.[5]

The subordination of the interest of these scattered communities to that of the fishing industry weakened their social organization. The rich marsh lands of the Minas Basin favoured the development of an agricultural industry in Acadia, and settlement spread down the Annapolis Valley and around the Bay of Fundy to the head of Cobequid Bay, but, though an uncertain market for live-stock was early secured in New England and a smuggling trade with Cape Breton later developed, the Acadians remained largely isolated and became increasingly dependent upon their own re-sources.[6] The lack of economic opportunities, and the ease with which agricultural operations could be carried on, destroyed any spirit of enterprise and made them content with their drab existence. To some extent this indolence was a protective device in resisting the demands of an aggressive commercialism. Security could be gained only through exerting a stubborn independence in face of governmental pressures. The hostile attitude of French and English officials was the price paid for the refusal to serve the needs of the fishing industry of either France or Britain. The reluctance of the settlers to move to French-controlled areas rendered their produc-tion of less value to the French fishing base of Cape Breton, while their opposition to taking the oath of allegiance made them a threat to the English fishing interests. If heavy cultural losses, and even-tual evacuation, were the prices paid, the Acadians were able to secure, by clinging to isolation, a degree of economic self-sufficiency and thus to avoid the immediate disaster of commercial exploitation.

Problems of social organization of the French settlement in Prince Edward Island, in contrast, reflected very clearly the effects of commercial exploitation and displayed the weaknesses of the precarious relationship between agricultural and fishing interests. The colonization of Prince Edward Island, in the end, contributed little to the economic organization of the French colonial empire. Frequent and disastrous raids by field mice and other misfortunes

[5]J. B. Brebner, *Acadia, New England's Outpost* (New York, 1927).
[6]*Ibid.*

7

rendered the colony of little value as a supply base for the fisheries of Cape Breton, while the prohibition by the French government of the right to fish prevented the inhabitants from seeking other means of livelihood.[7] Many of the colonists brought out to found the settlement were of an unenterprising character, while those Acadians induced to move to the island were unwilling to engage in the difficult task of clearing the land. The result was that the settlement remained largely dependent upon assistance from the home government. Supplying Cape Breton with such products as beef, this provisioning trade deprived the colony of sufficient livestock to establish the agricultural industry on a firm basis. The problems of the settlement were indicative of the failure to establish healthy relationships between agricultural and overseas-controlled fishing communities. The burden of military support for the fisheries imposed increasing strains upon the agricultural community, while the influence of military garrisons checked the development of stable social organization in the fishing community.

In the case of the British colonization ventures there was a similar failure to relate settlement to the dominant economic interest of the fisheries. Promotion came for the purpose of securing the strategic lines of empire and thereby removing any naval menace to the fishing industry. The choice of the site of Halifax emphasized considerations of strategy rather than of economic resources. Situated in an area of poor soil, a profitable agricultural industry could not be developed, and, until the province could support a considerable trade, the only source of wealth of the town was in its function as a governmental centre and naval base. Its economically dependent character was enhanced by the type of colonists brought out to found the settlement in 1749. While the influx during the winter of 1749-50 of a number of families from New England served to promote a local fishing industry, the German colonists after 1750 and the Acadian French who drifted into the town were useful only in providing labour in building fortifications. A system of municipal relief early developed to meet problems of destitution, and the presence of large numbers of physically unfit persons, vagrants, disorderly characters, and homeless children gave rise to institu-

[7]D. C. Harvey, *The French Regime in Prince Edward Island* (New Haven, 1926).

tional methods of treatment.[8] A hospital was erected in 1750 to care for the destitute ill, an orphanage established in 1752 to provide for the large number of homeless children among the German settlers, and a workhouse founded in 1759 for the confinement of vagrants and disorderly persons. The drinking of rum assumed major proportions in the habits of the population, while theft, smuggling, usury, and libel were common in the roll of crimes. The presence of naval garrisons gave rise to problems of illegitimacy and desertion. The economic and social dependence of the population upon institutions of the state checked the development of any vigorous cultural life. Governmental and military officials, and the few merchants, constituted something of a local aristocracy, but until the functions of government were broadened, and trade developed, there were lacking the supports of a true social *élite*. The large number of ethnic-religious groups within the town gave to it a cosmopolitan air, but the cultural effects were evident in the absence of a spirit of community or a pride in local undertakings. Although plans had been made for the recruitment of teachers, no schools were established before 1760.[9] The interests of religion were almost as neglected as those of cultural welfare. Two places of worship, St. Paul's Anglican and Mather's Congregationalist, were constructed, and a resident Church of England clergyman secured, but neither of these religious denominations exerted much immediate influence in the province. The Society for the Propagation of the Gospel provided missionaries to Annapolis and Lunenburg, but for the most part, with the exception of Catholicism, the formal organization of religion was confined to military and official circles and, in the case of Congregationalism, to the small merchant group in Halifax.

The German settlement in Lunenburg did little to strengthen the social organization of the colony. Though Lunenburg was favourably situated with respect to the fisheries, neither the policy of the colonial administration nor the inclination of the German colonists encouraged their prosecution. Farmers rather than fishermen

[8]K. R. Williams, "Poor Relief and Medicine in Nova Scotia, 1749-1783," *Collections of Nova Scotia Historical Society*, vol.XXI, 1938; also, H. L. Marguerite Grant, "Historical Sketches of Hospitals and Almhouses in Halifax, 1749 to 1859," *Nova Scotia Medical Bulletin*, April, May, August, 1938.

[9]K. R. Williams, "Social Conditions in Nova Scotia, 1749-1783," Master of Arts thesis, McGill University Library.

had been recruited with the intention of forming a number of agricultural settlements interspersed among the French Acadian population.   The abandonment of this plan and the final selection of Lunenburg as the site of the German settlement involved the heavy social costs of promoting an agricultural industry in an area more adapted to the fisheries. · In addition to the failure of selecting the occupational types suitable to settlement in such an area, there was a failure to discriminate properly between those able and unable to face the conditions of pioneer life.   The activities of the over-zealous colonization agent in Germany resulted in the recruitment of large numbers of persons hopelessly incapable of supporting themselves in the New World.[10]   The imperial government as a result found it necessary to make annual grants for the relief of the settlers, and efforts to discontinue these allowances were vigorously resisted by the colonial governors on the ground that in no other way could order and harmony be maintained.   Riots in Lunenburg, and the desertion of some of the Germans to join the French in the interior, indicated that the fears of the governors had foundation in fact. The German settlement remained on the cultural fringe of the English colony, and yet lacked sufficient means to develop any independent cultural life of its own.   Most of the settlers were Lutherans or Calvinists, and the failure to provide them with ministers of their own persuasion while supporting in the community an S.P.G. missionary did little to keep alive religious interests and much to antagonize the population to the Church of England.   The weaknesses of the social organization of Lunenburg, like that of the French agricultural settlement in Prince Edward Island, resulted from the tenuous ties between agricultural colonization and the overseas or New England controlled fishing industry.   Local industry and trade were alike discouraged, and this check to free economic enterprise not only reduced the agricultural communities to a state of economic self-sufficiency but prevented the rise of any towns but those which were the centres of government and military garrisons.   Thus the English like the French settlements in the Maritime region before 1760 failed to develop any secure cultural life. Intended primarily to supply fishing bases or to check foreign encroachments, they remained little more than outposts of empire or temporary bases of New England.

[10]Innis, ed., *Select Documents in Canadian Economic History, 1497-1783.*

Settlement in terms of free economic enterprise took place only after 1760 with the collapse of the French empire in America and the expansion of New England into Nova Scotia. A close relationship between settlement and the fisheries had emerged in New England with changes in the nature of the fishing industry involving the use of smaller units and the employment of local labour, and with the growth of trade which depended upon local bases of supply.[11] Though the decline of French interest in the Maritime region strengthened the hold of the west county interests of England upon the fisheries of eastern Nova Scotia, it made possible the extension of New England's control over the fisheries of western Nova Scotia, and the growth in importance of New England commercial interests resulted in the promotion of schemes of settlement. Anxiety in Britain respecting the danger of depopulation resulted in a policy of discouraging emigration, and settlement after 1760 was largely of people from the Atlantic seaboard. Nova Scotia shared in a general movement of population which greatly extended the frontiers of New England.[12]

The New England migration brought new sources of strength to the social organization of Nova Scotia. The settlements which grew up shared in the economic expansion of New England. The origin of the settlers, the advantages of the direct transportation route to Boston, and the character of economic production favoured the close relationship with the Atlantic sea-board colonies. The New Englanders were pioneers from a pioneer community, and they possessed all the advantages of familiarity with their environment. Fishing, farming, or, later, ship-building, was undertaken, and the products of their labour found a sale in the markets opened up by commercial interests in New England from which necessary manufactured goods, largely imported from England, were received in return. The result was the absence of any considerable problem of social dependency, though some of the settlers had to be given provisions during the first year or two in the province. Destitution was associated very largely with the individual hazards involved in

[11]Innis, *The Cod Fisheries.*

[12]M. L. Hansen, *The Mingling of Canadian and American Peoples*: vol. I. *Historical* (New Haven and Toronto, 1940); J. B. Brebner, *The Neutral Yankees of Nova Scotia* (New York, 1937); I. F. Mackinnon, *Settlements and Churches in Nova Scotia* (Montreal and Halifax, 1930).

fishing or farming, and those people who found themselves without means of support were readily assisted by local agencies of the community. The town meeting inherited from New England provided available machinery for poor relief.[13] The nature of problems of crime and morality likewise reflected the influence of the New England social heritage. Few of the settlers were without their vices, such as the drinking of rum, but these vices represented deviations from, rather than any general breakdown, of the *mores*. The New Englanders inherited the close village organization developed in the older colonies. The town meeting and the congregational organization of the church moved with the settlers, and the transfer of these institutions did not involve the intervention of secondary and thereby more rigid social agencies. Settlement in villages followed the pattern established in New England, and, to the extent that whole communities emigrated, there was no break in social continuity. Even movement of individual families involved little adjustment, as all the inhabitants were familiar with the form of community organization and readily participated in its erection in the new homeland. The result was that the New Englanders in Nova Scotia were not to any considerable extent emancipated from the moral controls of the communities from which they emigrated. The strict puritanical attitudes of the inhabitants of the older colonies were brought over without any serious impairment, and their preservation was secured through the sanctions imposed by the close village group and religious congregation.

The town meeting provided an effective agency of cultural leadership in the villages settled by New Englanders. Though many of the privileges claimed by the town proprietors such as the appointment of town officers, the levying of local taxes, and the surveying of land were assumed by the provincial government to the indignation of people highly jealous of the rights of local autonomy, these constitutional limitations upon their functions did not render them wholly unimportant in the pioneer communities.[14]

[13]A. W. H. Eaton, *A History of King's County, Nova Scotia* (Salem, Mass., 1910), pp. 161-2; Williams, "Social Conditions in Nova Scotia, 1749-1783."

[14]D. C. Harvey, "The Struggle for the New England Form of Township Government in Nova Scotia," *Report of the Canadian Historical Association*, 1933.

On the one hand, means of communication were not sufficiently developed to enable Halifax to maintain effective controls in out-lying areas, and, on the other hand, the feeling of local autonomy on the part of the New Englanders was too strong to be suppressed by administrative devices erected in the capital. The result was that many of the vestiges of the proprietary system persisted in the village organization of these settlements. The proprietors provided the nucleus of an upper social class. As substantial farmers and tradespeople or persons of superior education, they gained a position of influence in the local villages, and, when located in the larger towns such as Horton, Falmouth, and Cornwallis, their influence extended throughout the larger community.[15] The "Esquires" and "Gentlemen," such as Simeon Perkins in Liverpool, enjoyed a standard of life somewhat above that of the ordinary inhabitants, but in return they provided the leadership so necessary in the pioneer settlements. These settlements, consequently, were not exposed to levelling influences which led to a complete disregard of class distinctions, while at the same time their economic progress was not retarded by a rigid class system. Only in the failure to provide education were the cultural limitations of the village organization much in evidence. More extensive machinery than the town meeting was required for the erection of educational institutions and the recruitment of teachers. Many of the effects of inadequate educational institutions, however, were postponed until the neglected generation reached maturity, and in the mean-time local pride and a consciousness of the worth of the group's inheritance preserved those cultural values which did not depend upon such secondary services as those of education. Most of the demands of the pioneer society could be met within the village organization. It was only when this primary group relationship became insufficient, and the support of the tie with New England was lost, that the need for more effective agencies to preserve cultural values became acute.

Religious interests during the early period of settlement were likewise strong among the New Englanders. These settlers in-herited the attitudes of devoutness typical of the population of the older Atlantic colonies, and the persistence of these attitudes was secured through the strong link between the church and

[15]Cf. Eaton, *A History of King's County, Nova Scotia*, pp. 138-9.

the local community. The village settlement and town meeting provided the framework of the congregational organization. The prominent citizens of the community served as elders of the church, and the town meetings assumed the responsibility of erecting meeting houses. The result of this close tie between the church and the village was that devotional services were carried on even when ministers were not available, a situation which obtained in a large number of the early settlements.[16] That is not to say that Congregational clergymen were not eagerly sought and that their ministry was not essential for the ultimate survival of the church, but only that the character of Congregationalism made it possible to keep alive religious interests during the interval when regular services could not be provided. Eventually ministers were secured for the chief settlements of New Englanders with the conspicuous exception of Halifax where Mather's Congregationalist Church was left unsupplied.[17] If difficulties were still being faced in a number of communities, the church appeared to be firmly established in the province as a whole by 1775.

Though New Englanders comprised the great bulk of the population settling in Nova Scotia during the period 1760-75, a number of other groups found their way into the province. Ulster Irish from New Hampshire, Boston, and from overseas settled in Truro, Onslow, and Londonderry at the head of Cobequid Bay and a few along the banks of La Have River beyond Lunenburg. During the years 1773-5 a large number of Yorkshire English families came out and settled among New Englanders at Amherst, Cumberland, and Sackville in the Chignecto peninsula. The first group of Highland Scots arrived just before the American Revolution and joined a number of Pennsylvania settlers in Pictou. Irish Catholics from Newfoundland and French Acadians from the mainland located along with transient New England fishermen in Cape Breton.[18] Because of their isolation, however, these various settlements contributed little to integrating the social organization of the province.

[16]K. G. Sullivan, "New England Puritanism and Its Disintegration in Nova Scotia," Master of Arts thesis in Dalhousie University.

[17]Cf. Brebner, *The Neutral Yankees of Nova Scotia*, chap. VII.

[18]*Ibid.* For a bibliography of county histories of Nova Scotia see *Journal of Education, Being the Supplement to the Report of the Superintendent of Education for Nova Scotia,* January, 1941 (Halifax, 1941).

The Ulster Irish, most of whom were from the older American colonies, brought with them much the same heritage of village organization as the New Englanders, and they tended to accept the leadership of this larger group. The fact that the principles of church government of American Presbyterianism were very similar to those of Congregationalism strengthened the ties. The Yorkshire English, locating in communities containing numbers of New Englanders, were likewise influenced to some considerable extent by the cultural values of this group. Though followers of John Wesley, no missionaries came out before the Revolution, and the form of religious worship followed by the Yorkshiremen within their Methodist societies was not radically different from that followed by the New Englanders within their Congregationalist organizations. The Highland Scots of Pictou had no time to establish any sort of settled community life before the outbreak of revolution led to their recruitment in Highland military regiments. In the case of the settlements in Cape Breton, what cultural ties existed were mostly with New England, but for the most part the population of the island became detached from outside centres of influence almost entirely. Here Channel Island interests employing bilingual labour dominated in the control of the fisheries, and most of the local fishermen engaged in the industry without licences. In contrast with the South Shore, temporary stations took the place of settled villages, and the New England fishermen returned to their homes in the winter after spending the summer in Cape Breton. The isolation from Halifax made impossible effective policing, and when the British garrison was removed in 1768 the local authorities were left without support in maintaining law. The large number of inlets, and the proximity to Newfoundland, provided means by which the population could evade officers of the law sent to apprehend them, and a condition of almost general disorder prevailed along the coast-line.

The New England migration, and the smaller settlements in the interior and in Cape Breton, did little to strengthen the position of Halifax or extend her influence. The capital shared in few of the economic advantages from the extensive *entrepot* trade being developed with Nova Scotia as an important base. Lacking an immediate hinterland of her own, she did not possess the resources or organization to compete with the powerful commercial interests in New England in providing markets for the fishing and farming settlements along the South Shore, the Annapolis Valley and in the interior, while the costs of policing Cape Breton were offset by few economic gains. Some industries were established in the town—a brick factory, distillery, and sugar factory—but the government and military base continued as the chief means of support. When the strategy of imperial defence made necessary the stationing of a large military force in the province, the town prospered, but when it was withdrawn local trade declined and there were few alternative occupations to which the population could turn. The lack of economic opportunities, and the attractions of the town as the centre of governmental institutions and military forces, accentuated problems of destitution which had emerged before 1760. Hangers-on of the army fell on the relief roll when the army was withdrawn, while a continual influx of transient workers and indigent persons from outside added to the responsibilities of local authorities.[19] In 1759, and again in 1768, the Nova Scotia legislature attempted to check the immigration of socially dependent persons by means of legislation, but on both occasions the Act was disallowed by the British government. In 1770, chiefly as a means of relieving Halifax of the burden of supporting transient workers from the country districts, an Act of the provincial legislature introduced a residence qualification for relief. Efforts to check the influx of undesirable population elements, however, failed to provide any real solution to a problem which resulted from the weakness of the town's economic and social supports, and the result was a continuance and elaboration of the aids found necessary in the fifties.

Other forms of social life in the town were strengthened little more by the developments which took place in the province after 1760. The army and navy continued to set the moral standards of the community, and the puritanism of the New England settlements exerted no conspicuous influence. Similarly, the leavening effect of the New England migration upon cultural organization was not greatly felt within the capital. The exclusiveness of the colonial aristocracy tended to be maintained, and as a result the economic isolation of the capital found emphasis in its cultural

[19]Williams, "Poor Relief and Medicine in Nova Scotia, 1749-1783."

isolation. Intervention by the colonial administration in matters of local government in the out-settlements was indicative of the extension of political controls in the province, but these efforts found little support in the cultural influence of the governing classes. The predominant interests of these classes remained sharply divorced from the interests of the large fishing and farming population in the colony, and there was a failure to develop a social class equipped to provide leadership for the whole province. Ethnic differences increased the cultural particularism of the various settlements, and Halifax failed conspicuously to give a lead in establishing some sort of cultural integration. This failure was also conspicuous in the field of religion. Apart from the Congregationalists, a number of religious denominations became established in the province—Presbyterians, Methodists, Catholics, and a few Baptists and Quakers—which emphasized the autonomy of the out-settlements, and the established Church of England proved unable to provide leadership to offset their decentralizing influence. With the growth of settlement after 1760, the church, with the support of the government, undertook to win the adherence of the large nonconformist population lacking the services of regular ministers. The promotion of the interests of the church had the important object of securing more firmly the political allegiance of the new settlers in the colony. A corresponding society made up of prominent members of the government as well as of the church in the colony was organized to supervise missionary activities and to seize opportunities of extending Anglican influence, and, paid by the Society for the Propagation of the Gospel and the British government, missionaries were located at the chief centres of settlement, Annapolis, Windsor, Cumberland, Prince Edward Island, and Lunenburg. The record of achievement, however, was not noteworthy. In spite of efforts to make the church a truly provincial denomination, it remained representative of only the official and military interests in the colony, drawing its chief support from within the town of Halifax. The tie with the government proved in the end as much a weakness as a strength of the church. Identity with the ruling minority divorced the church from the great mass of the population. The bulk of the people were of religious persuasions other than that of Anglicanism, and, while the problems of the pioneer society made difficult the maintenance of their denominational connections, they showed little inclination to support a church almost completely lacking in an understanding of their needs.   The failure to develop an itinerant missionary organization, and its reliance upon holding services in the chief centres of population, contributed further to its lack of influence in the rural settlements.   The weakness of the Church of England in the society of Nova Scotia before 1776 was a measure of the weakness of the economic and cultural interests of Halifax. Efforts to extend the controls of the provincial capital met with the stiff resistance of the out-settlements, and the lack of support of the Church of England was simply one expression of these resistant attitudes.

The effects of the failure of Halifax to provide leadership did not result in any serious breakdown of controls in the provincial society so long as the local village organizations remained strong. The socially vigorous and community-conscious New England settlements provided an element of strength to the whole social organization of Nova Scotia before 1776.   It is true that the failure of Halifax to integrate the out-settlements within the provincial system of government weakened the colonial administration and institutions identified with this administration, but the effects of lack of leadership from the capital were offset by the strength of local organization and by the leadership provided from New England. The town meetings and Congregational churches derived sufficient support from the older colonies to function without the co-operation of the provincial government.   But this dependence upon outside aids and detachment from Halifax involved dangers which became conspicuous when the American Revolution cut these settlements off from their established lines of communication. Failure to retain cultural ties with New England was to reveal weaknesses in the organization of the local community while the aggressive feeling of local autonomy was not sufficient to withstand completely the centralizing influence of war and trade after 1776. Largely independent of the provincial capital before the outbreak of revolution, the New England settlements after 1776 were to become to some considerable extent an economic hinterland of the rapidly expanding metropolis.

The shift of trade routes and the growing importance of commercial interests in Nova Scotia resulting from the Revolution led to fundamental re-orientations in community organization. Whereas Halifax before 1776 had been divorced from the main stream of development, the Revolutionary War tended to emphasize her strategic position and thereby enhance her economic as well as political importance. She seized the trade with the out-settlements and with the British West Indies which formerly had been controlled by New England. But the activities of American privateers in raiding coastal towns and of American traders in smuggling commodities into and out of the province, during the Revolution, were an indication that economic integration in terms of the dominance of Halifax was not readily brought about; efforts of the provincial authorities to police the waters of Cape Breton were only partially successful in preventing contraband trade in this area, and little more success attended similar efforts to restrict the trade of the rural settlements with the revolutionary colonies.[20] After the Revolution, the aggressive commercialism of New England continued to provide a serious threat to the new *entrepot* trade being developed by Nova Scotian interests, and the advantages secured in the imperial Navigation System were offset by restrictions upon the trading operations of British vessels in American ports and by smuggling carried on by American ships in the Maritime and West Indian waters. Efforts to meet this competition by a policy of bounties to the fisheries when export took place in British boats led to conflict between Halifax and the outports which secured expression in the secession of Cape Breton from Nova Scotia in 1784 and in the increasing opposition of the Assembly to the Council in provincial politics.[21] This tendency towards centralization and increasing regional conflict was equally apparent with respect to social organization. Although the relief machinery developed in the early years of settlement continued, apart from Halifax, to meet problems of individual destitution as they occurred in the local communities,[22] the Revolution and movements of population after gave rise to problems of destitution for which local agencies were wholly inadequate. The influx of refugees with the evacuation of Boston in 1776, the large migration

[20]Innis, *The Cod Fisheries;* also W. B. Kerr, "The Merchants of Nova Scotia and the American Revolution," *Canadian Historical Review*, March, 1932.

[21]Innis, *The Cod Fisheries.*

[22]Cf. George Patterson, *History of the County of Pictou* (Toronto, 1877), p. 167.

of Loyalists at the conclusion of war, the periodical arrival of boat-loads of destitute colonists during the eighties and nineties, and the immigration of Highland Scots many of whom were poverty-stricken towards the end of the century, taxed the resources of local communities and led to efforts on the part of the provincial government (supported in the case of the war refugees and Loyalists by the imperial Parliament) to provide relief. The intervention of provincial authorities emphasized centralizing tendencies in the colonial society, and the shift of the function of relief brought with it a decline in the importance of local organizations. That is not to say that the colonial administration succeeded in building up any permanent organization of poor relief. Particular problems of destitution called forth some sort of action, but there was no attempt to regularize such activities within a general system of relief. The nearest approach to the development of institutional methods of action was the establishment of boards to determine among what Loyalists and disbanded soldiers assistance was required. Agencies of relief still remained institutions of the local community, and aids from the provincial authorities were in the way of emergency measures. But the increasing reliance upon such aids emphasized the inadequacies of the local machinery.

With respect to matters of order and morality, the immediate effects of the Revolutionary War and the expansion of trade were felt most fully by Halifax, but the developments of this period unloosed forces which extended throughout the rural society. The close group controls of the village settlements tended to disintegrate in face of the influences of war and trade, and these tendencies were considerably accentuated with the Loyalist migration.[23] The new population elements cut across established community lines and introduced habits of behaviour which had an unsettling effect upon moral standards and social order. The worst elements among the Loyalists settled at Shelburne and in the St. John Valley, and the difficulties of administration in the latter area resulting from its remoteness hastened the organization of the Province of New Brunswick.[24] Apart from these two settlements,

[23]M. Ells, "Settling the Loyalists in Nova Scotia," *Report of the Canadian Historical Association*, 1934.

[24]Marion Gilroy, "The Partition of Nova Scotia, 1784," *Canadian Historical Review*, December, 1933.

disorganization was greatest in those areas where a large number of the Loyalist settlers were disbanded soldiers. Long association in army camps had developed habits of heavy drinking and dissipation, and intemperance became increasingly prevalent in the rural districts. The importance of molasses and rum in the trade of Nova Scotia fostered the traffic in liquor and discouraged efforts of reform such as stringent licensing laws and temperance movements.[25] Crime increased as pecuniary relationships assumed greater importance, and the change in its character was evident in the shift from a reliance upon primary group controls to a reliance upon controls of a secondary and impersonal nature. Gaols were erected in the various towns, and the formal law came to play a greater part in the maintenance of order in the community.[26]

More far-reaching still were the adjustments which took place in cultural organization. The break with New England, the growth of commerce, and the war led to the disintegration of those ethnic and social bonds which had grown up in the local communities before the Revolution. Some of the more respectable members of the local communities, particularly those communities settled by New Englanders, identified themselves with the revolutionary cause of the American colonies, and, if they did not withdraw from the province, they lost considerably in prestige. The Loyalist migration served to weaken still further rural leadership in Nova Scotia. The Loyalists challenged established status relationships while they failed to achieve, except in New Brunswick, a privileged social position. These tendencies of disintegration of the rural class structure were accentuated by the expansion of trade which resulted to some extent in rural business men being overshadowed by those in large centres. The efforts of the new trading interests to integrate the economic life of the province in terms of the dominance of Halifax were paralleled by efforts to integrate the cultural life. But the resistance of the out-settlements to the controls of the metropolis evident in the economic sphere was even more evident in the cultural sphere. The tenuous commercial ties provided no solid cultural bond between the capital and the rest of the province. As the forces of centralization increased subordination to Halifax, forces of decentralization,

[25]Cf. Innis, *The Cod Fisheries.*
[26]Patterson, *History of the County of Pictou*, pp. 207-9.

together with the incapacity of the governing aristocracy to provide effective leadership, checked the establishment of a stable equilibrium in the relationships between Halifax and the hinterland.

The pull between forces of centralization and of local autonomy was even more apparent within religious movements. The developments resulting from the Revolution and expansion of trade had direct and far-reaching effects upon religious interests and attitudes, and led to fundamental adjustments in the organization and appeal of religious denominations. The period, indeed, was one of revolution within the churches which produced an almost completely new institutional structure by the time it had run its course. Old religious forms were swept aside, and new denominations arose and were accepted within the Nova Scotian society. These sweeping changes involved issues of control which extended throughout the organization of the provincial society. Efforts of Halifax to strengthen the controls of political and cultural institutions centred in the capital as a means of securing a position of metropolitan dominance were paralleled by efforts to strengthen the controls of the Church of England. The immediate effect of the Revolution was to weaken seriously religious leadership in the out-settlements. Before the Revolution, Congregationalism had been undergoing changes which greatly limited its spiritual influence. Schisms in New England resulting from the "Great Awakening" had enhanced the conservatism of the orthodox churches with effects evident in the increasing emphasis upon the form rather than upon the substance of religious services. Though the churches in Nova Scotia before 1776 escaped the direct influence of the evangelical movements, they felt the influence of the reactionary tendencies which had set in. Among the various Congregationalist organizations in the province at the time the Revolution broke out, there was lacking any vigorous spiritual life.[27] So long as there was no threat to the social influences of the churches, this lack was not seriously felt. What was lost in religious fervour was gained in social respectability; status in the community implied membership in the church. With the outbreak of the American Revolution, however, the social supports of the churches were greatly impaired. Many of the Congregationalist ministers identified themselves with

[27]Cf. Sullivan, "New England Puritanism and Its Disintegration in Nova Scotia."

the revolutionary cause and eventually withdrew to the American colonies, and, although the great body of members remained loyal, the churches became suspect in the eyes of colonial officials. As a result of the stigma of disloyalty, they lost the prestige and claim to respectability which had been the chief forces holding them together. Without a sufficient supply of ministers, many of the regularly constituted Congregationalist organizations found it increasingly difficult to maintain the controls of church government, and a spirit of acrimony tended to replace one of harmony among the general membership. The effect of the Revolution upon the Methodist societies of the Yorkshire English was almost as unfavourable. The strength of the Methodist societies depended upon the evangelical fervour of the members, and this led to a reliance upon vigorous evangelical leadership. The Revolution cut off a supply of Wesleyan missionaries and new additions to the population from Yorkshire, and, divorced from outside contacts, the evangelical enthusiasm which had been aroused by Wesley's preaching in England steadily cooled under pioneer conditions of life. The other nonconformist religious denominations were also weakened to some extent by the Revolution. The Presbyterians of Truro were cut off from a supply of ministers from the American colonies. The German Lutherans and French and Swiss Calvinists faced even greater official indifference than before 1776 to the problem of supplying them with clergymen of their own faith. The Catholic Church, though maintaining the attachments of the Micmac Indians, the French Acadians, and the Irish from Newfoundland continued to suffer under constitutional disabilities which the Revolution did not tend to ease. The Quakers, at no time influential, increasingly lost their identity as a religious sect when they became divorced from their fellow-brethren in the old colonies.

The Church of England, on the other hand, secured new supports as a result of the war. Advantages which the Congregationalist churches lost with the increasing emphasis upon loyalty the church gained. The colonial government vigorously promoted its interests as a means of strengthening the imperial connection. The greater importance of military interests enhanced the church's favourable position. Finally, the Loyalist migration brought new additions to membership and a considerable number of ministers to extend the constituency of the church throughout a large section of the province.[28] Yet, in spite of these favourable circumstances, the influence of the church was not greatly increased. The new economic ties being forged by Halifax with its hinterland failed to be reinforced by spiritual ties forged by the church. The reason, on the one side, lay in the lack of vigorous leadership within the church itself, and, on the other side, in the stiff cultural resistance of the out-settlements. Though an episcopacy was erected with a resident bishop in charge, the control of missionary activities remained in the hands of the Society for the Propagation of the Gospel and only slowly was there any improvement in the type of clergymen sent to the colony. Opportunities to extend the influence of the church were lost by the reluctance of missionaries to undertake strenuous preaching assignments and by their lack of a sympathetic understanding of the problems of the colonists. The result was that the church gained few if any new recruits from the ranks of those denominations disorganized by the Revolution, while it eventually was to lose a number of its own followers.

The failure of the Church of England to provide effective leadership secured emphasis by the success of new religious movements in the out-settlements. The evangelical preaching of Henry Alline among the New England settlers and of William Black among the Yorkshire English represented an effort to revive the religious feeling cooling within the Congregational churches and Methodist societies. The Newlight movement was a direct product of the disintegration of the Congregational churches, while Black's evangelical labours were undertaken to meet needs left unfilled by the Wesleyan Conference in England. But the implications of these movements extended much further. The spread of religious evangelism emphasized the cultural autonomy of the hinterland, and sharpened the divorce between the colonial aristocracy of Halifax identified with official and trading interests and the great mass of the population identified with fishing and farming interests. The conflict of economic interests, evident in the strained relationships between the Legislative Assembly and Council, found expression in the antagonism between the nonconformist churches and the Church of England, and that antagonism was brought into bold relief by the evangelical movements. The problem presented

[28]Cf. C. W. Vernon, *The Old Church in the New Dominion* (London, 1929).

in the out-settlements in maintaining their economic autonomy with the loss of their markets in New England found its counterpart in the problem of maintaining their cultural autonomy with the loss of New England leadership. The relief secured in the economic sphere through smuggling, privateering, and representation in the Legislative Assembly was secured in the cultural sphere through evangelical religious movements. Eventually there emerged powerful Baptist and Methodist churches out of the ferment aroused by Henry Alline and William Black.[29] With the turn of the century, two other religious denominations gained considerable accessions of strength and served to reinforce autonomous tendencies in the hinterland of the province. The shift to Baptist doctrines in the Newlight churches brought about the defection of the more orthodox Congregationalists and their eventual absorption into the Presbyterian Church, and with the Highland Scot migration to Pictou County and Cape Breton Presbyterianism became firmly established in eastern Nova Scotia.[30] Catholicism likewise grew rapidly in influence as Antigonish County and Cape Breton became populated largely by Highland Scot Catholics. The organization of these four denominations upon a provincial basis effectively isolated the Church of England in Halifax and Windsor and paved the way to the abandonment of her claim as the established colonial church. From Sydney to Yarmouth, along a line extending through Pictou, Truro, Cornwallis, and Annapolis, and back through Liverpool and Lunenburg, the church had been forced to retreat in face of rival religious denominations. The struggle was far from over at the end of the century, and continued particularly around the controversial issue of denominational colleges, but from it the church steadily emerged with fewer special privileges and with greatly reduced influence.

The migration of Highland Scots closed the last frontier in the settlement of Nova Scotia, and later movements of population largely passed by this province. Developments in the Maritime region after 1800 brought into prominence new forms of economic

[29]E. M. Saunders, *History of the Baptists of the Maritime Provinces* (Halifax, 1902); T. Watson Smith, *History of the Methodist Church of Eastern British America* (Halifax, 1877), 2 vols.

[30]George Patterson, *Memoir of the Rev. James MacGregor, Pictou, N.S., and of the Social and Religious Condition of the Early Settlers* (Philadelphia, 1859).

exploitation which shifted attention to New Brunswick. The rapid expansion of the timber trade was the chief note in the economic development of British North America during the early part of the nineteenth century, and the St. John, Miramichi, and Ottawa valleys became areas of dominant importance.[31] In New Brunswick, entrepreneurship from Maine and capital from overseas combined to set in motion the streams of squared timber destined for the overseas market. A ship-building industry developed to support the growing trade in timber, and ships as well as timber usually found a ready sale in Britain. The growing industrial structure gave rise to an increasing demand for labour, and waves of Irish immigrants populated the new towns and the frontier areas of settlement. Since the soft-timber lands bordered rich river valleys, the expansion of the timber trade was accompanied by the expansion of agriculture, in eastern Nova Scotia and Prince Edward Island as well as in New Brunswick. The economic and social effects of the timber trade were felt throughout New Brunswick and to some extent also in Prince Edward Island and Nova Scotia. Where the industry was dominant, other economic activities were subordinated to its interests, and there was a consequent failure to build up a diversified economy to meet the shocks of a rapidly shrinking market when British trade policy ceased to provide preferential protection for colonial timber.[32] The farmers and young men engaged in the trade developed habits which unfitted them for the conditions of rural life. The life of the lumbermen resembled in many ways that of the *coureurs de bois*. Neither completely detached from, nor completely a part of, the rural communities, they exerted a disturbing influence upon established social controls while failing to develop new controls adapted to their particular needs. Where there were regular camps there emerged something of a distinctive group life with its distinctive set of social *mores*, but the habits developed in this environment rendered more difficult the adjustment when the camps broke up and farm work commenced. Only slowly did there appear any sort of occupational demarcation between the lumbering and farm-

[31]A. R. M. Lower and H. A. Innis, *Settlement and the Forest and Mining Frontiers* (Toronto, 1936), part I, chap. III.

[32]H. A. Innis, "An Introduction to the Economic History of the Maritimes," *Report of the Canadian Historical Association*, 1931.

ing classes. This development awaited the pushing back of the timber frontier out of the reach of the farm communities, and the shift to industrial techniques requiring a full-time labour force. Until such economic specialization occurred, communities in close proximity to the timber trade felt the full force of its disorganizing effects.

The growth of an irregular labour force in the timber trade, and unemployment in the ship-building industry in times of depression, gave rise to problems of destitution particularly in such towns as that of Saint John. Crime emerged along the highways of trade and in the centres of industry, and intemperance increased throughout the rural society and assumed considerable proportions among those engaged in the timber industry. Growing debts, and a greater emphasis upon money values, weakened the moral as well as economic basis of the agricultural communities. The growth of commercial organization in the timber trade introduced new economic interests and had an unsettling effect upon the class structure, particularly of New Brunswick. The growing body of American and Scottish merchants assumed an increasingly important role in the economic and social life of the province and steadily challenged the pretensions to social superiority of the old landowning and professional aristocracy established after the Loyalist migration. On the other side, the large Irish immigrant group became sharply marked off from the more substantial elements of the population, and tended to become associated on the cultural fringe with the Acadian French. Religious differences, especially between Protestant and Catholic, hardened the social divisions forming along cultural lines. As industrial techniques became more elaborate and day labour more in demand, a social group approaching in character a proletariat made its appearance. These tendencies were most evident within the St. John Valley where capitalistic developments in the timber trade and ship-building industry had progressed furthest, but the hardening lines of class conflict extended out into the fringe settlements of New Brunswick. In Prince Edward Island, the system of absentee ownership introduced a different sort of rigidity in cultural organization. Disturbances in religious organization also accompanied the developments taking place in New Brunswick after 1800. The immigration of Americans, English, and Irish, and the intrusion of evangelical movements from outside, destroyed many of the supports which the Church of England had established in the province after the Loyalist migration. Catholicism gained in strength as the Irish immigration brought in great numbers of adherents, and the evangelical work of Baptist and Methodist missionaries, from Nova Scotia and the United States, won the allegiance of the considerable nonconformist population and gained numbers of recruits from the ranks of the Anglicans. The Baptist Church emerged here, as in Nova Scotia, as the chief religious denomination, and the growing influence of the Methodist, Presbyterian, and Catholic bodies emphasized still further the failure of the Church of England to maintain its position of dominance. In Prince Edward Island the predominant Scottish population secured the supremacy of the Presbyterian Church.[33]

With the development of the timber trade the continental pull upon the economy of the Maritime region became marked and this shift in emphasis introduced striking differences between the development of New Brunswick and that of Nova Scotia. The tightening bonds of American capital, and the increasing dependence upon the American market with the shrinking of the British market for timber, were powerful forces pulling New Brunswick into the American orbit. Railway projects designed to strengthen the links with the United States were only abandoned when Confederation provided a tie with the continental British colonies.[34] For this reason, the development of New Brunswick was in many ways more closely related to that of the Canadas than to that of Nova Scotia. It constituted something of a watershed between the development of the purely Maritime colony reaching out into the Atlantic and that of the St. Lawrence–Great Lakes colony reaching into the continent. By the early part of the nineteenth century the chief lines of development in Nova Scotia had become firmly established. The fishing industry and trade gave to the

[33]Rev. John MacLeod, *History of Presbyterianism on Prince Edward Island* (Chicago, 1904); Rev. John C. Macmillan, *The Early History of the Catholic Church in Prince Edward Island* (Quebec, 1905).

[34]A. G. Bailey, "Railways and the Confederation Issue in New Brunswick 1863-1865," *Canadian Historical Review*, December, 1940.

province its basic social character and not until those economic activities were severely dislocated by the industrial revolution in iron and steel was this character materially changed. In New Brunswick, the frontier phase of development had no more than set in by 1800. The developments which took place after were of a kind which involved expansion into the continent, into the Ottawa Valley and Great Lakes region as into the St. John and Miramichi valleys.

1. SOCIAL WELFARE

A. Character of the Population and Problems of Destitution

Indolence of Acadians

(i)

Public Archives of Canada, *Acadia C*[11], vol. 5, p. 317:   Port Royal, October 23, 1706, Subercase to the Minister.

The inhabitants of Acadia seem very lazy and not capable of undertaking anything by themselves. They have not the French manner although they are very healthy and physically fit. The only thing they like is litigation, and this colony will never be well established if means are not found of taking away the spirit of quarrelling and of establishing among them peace and unity.

(ii)

Public Archives of Canada, *N.S.A.*, vol. XXIII, p. 50:   Annapolis, August 3, 1734, Philipps to Lords Commissioners for Trade and Plantations.

As to the present inhabitants, they are rather a pest and encumbrance, than of an advantage to the Country, being a proud, lazy, obstinate and intractable People, unskilful in the methods of Agriculture, nor will be led or drove into a better way of thinking, and (what is still worse) greatly disaffected to the Government.   They raise (it is true) both Corn and Cattle on Marsh lands, that wants no clearing, but they have not in almost a Century clear'd the Quantity of 300 Acres of Wood Land.   From their Corn and Cattle they have plenty of Dung for manure, w'ch they make no use of, but when it increases so as to become troublesome, they instead of laying it on their Lands, they get rid of it by removing their barns to another Spot.

Destitution of Inhabitants of Prince Edward Island

Public Archives of Canada, C¹¹Ile Royale, vol. 20, pp. 97-8: Louisbourg, October 28, 1738, Lenormant to the Minister.

As the grain of all the inhabitants of this Island was entirely lost, even seed must be provided to them for next year, and since Acadia is the only place it can be procured, Monsieur Duchambau was engaged to send a schooner there and to take the necessary measures to get six hundred bushels of corn, wheat, peas and oats.   To enable him to meet the expense, I have advanced him six hundred *livres* from the treasurer.

I have written Sieur Dubuisson to distribute, conjointly with Monsieur Duchambau, the grain next spring to those inhabitants whose lands are worked and ready to receive the seed.   I have recommended to him at the same time to keep a detailed account of how this was distributed and the use made of that which was sent to the Ile St. Jean so that those who have received this help can be made pay for it in cases where they have the means and where you judge it proper.

I am assured the inhabitants of this Island had done much work to improve their land last spring, their grain had sprouted well and they would have harvested an abundant crop if it had not been for the last plague which afflicted them.   It must be hoped in the future they will be more fortunate and will get back from their labours the fruits which they should naturally harvest from them.   All the inhabitants have been very dejected.   The help procured for them and the measures taken to get them new seed has given them new courage.

Indolence of Inhabitants of Prince Edward Island

Public Archives of Canada, C¹¹Ile Royale, vol. 29, pp. 117-8: Louisbourg, November 25, 1750, Prevost to the Minister.

I have done everything that I can to engage the Acadians to settle here by preference, but this naturally indolent people are afraid of the clearing [of timber] which must be done and the distance from the town.   However there are some families who ought to leave next spring who promised me to settle and, if there are at that time some places, I hope they will be followed by others.   Those settled at Spanish Bay have harvested some beautiful cabbages and some good turnips, they will also be able to sow some peas if they break the land in the back of the bay and far from the sea.

I have done everything that depends upon me to engage them to work and establish themselves solidly, but it is inconceivable, Monseigneur, the cares and troubles that all these settlements give me.   The people are difficult to lead, lazy and require to be followed in everything they do without which nothing could be hoped for, and I have found some of them who spent the winter under a cabin of fir trees like the savages without taking the least trouble to lodge themselves, which determined me to render an account of the work of each family, and as soon as Sieur Prevost de la Croix, my brother, will be free from his inspection of the soldiers, I will send him to visit all the settlements to ascertain the progress of each family and oblige them to put to profit the kindnesses with which His Majesty favours them.

Venereal Disease among Soldiers in Louisbourg

Public Archives of Canada, *C¹¹ Ile Royale*, vol. 15, pp. 157-9: Louisbourg, November 5, 1734, St. Ovide and Lenormant to the Minister.

We shall continue to make certain that none of the troops are discharged whose time of engagement has not expired or who have not become absolutely invalid, and in order to assure ourselves of this we have visited those [seeking discharges] in person. We have the honour of addressing herewith to Monseigneur, the list of soldiers discharged this year. In no case has the time of engagement expired. He will receive at the same time an account of the new soldiers to whom M. de St. Ovide has accorded a holiday of six months to spend in France. There are four of these who have venereal disease which it is not possible to cure in the colony. As these are good and young subjects, we beseech, Monseigneur, to consent to give orders for their treatment at the hospital of Rochefort so that they can come back to join their companies next year. The others go back to put in order some family affairs they have in France and which they have made known to us.

We take the liberty of representing to Monseigneur that he agree to contract arrangements with the religious of the Charity to treat here similar diseases when they are found among soldiers of the garrison. Up until the present these religious have not had the means to treat these kinds of disease for which the expense is much higher than for other maladies.

Early Colonists of Halifax

Public Archives of Canada, *N.S.A.*, vol. XXV, pp. 202-4: Halifax, July 24, 1749, Cornwallis to Lords of Trade.

The number of Settlers, Men, Women and Children is 1400 but I beg leave to observe to your Lordships that amongst these the number of industrious active men proper to undertake and carry on a New Settlement is very small—of Soldiers there is only 100—of Tradesmen Sailors and others able and willing to work not above 200 more. The rest are poor idle worthless Vagabonds that embraced the opportunity to get provisions for one Year without labour, and Sailors who only wanted a passage to New England. Many have come as into a hospital to be cured, some of Venereal Diseases, some even incurables. I mention this particularly to your Lordships because I find by experience, that these idle abandon'd fellows are the most troublesome and mutinous and instead of helping hinder the rest as much as they can. As these men have cost the Government a great deal of money, I do all I can to make them useful, but I shall be obliged I believe, to send some of them away. . . . There are amongst the Settlers a few Swiss who are regular

honest industrious men, easily governed and work heartily.   I hope your
Lordships will think of a Method of encouraging Numbers of them to come
over.

Destitute German Settlers

Public Archives of Canada, *N.S.A.*, vol. XLIX, pp. 62-9:   Halifax, October 16,
    1752, P. T. Hopson to Lords Commissioners of Trade and Plantations.

Upon my examining into the State of Affairs of the Province, I found
Mr. Cornwallis extreamely distressed, by having on his hands, in and about
this Place, all the foreign Settlers who arrived in the years 1750 and 1751
whom he had not been able to send out from hence to make an Settlement
at a distance: this, not only through the want of Provisions, Arms, Tools,
Implements for clearing and cultivating the land and materials necessary
for building their habitations, proper to enable him for so doing, but also on
account of there being no place with any sufficient quantity of Land, near
them, proper for placing them upon agreable to the promises which had been
made them by Mr. Dick before they embarked.   As appears by a printed
paper I now enclose, and likewise because he had great reason to apprehend
they might have been molested by the Indians wherever they were sent, he
not having it in his power to protect them.   The great Expence was another
considerable objection.

He had likewise about three hundred of the foreign Settlers that arrived
this Year and was under the same dilemma with regard to them.   And since
I took the Government, the rest being arrived (which I must say I think
Mr. Dick contrived to be very late in the Season, for the purpose intended)
I imagine your Lordships cannot but think I must also be under the utmost
difficulties to know how to dispose of them, the sending them out being
impracticable for this Season and therefore all I could do was to build boarded
Barracks for them in the best and cheapest manner, yet so as that they
might be well covered and sheltered from the severity of the winter. . . .

I must observe to your Lordships that there was no possibility of sending
out the foreign Settlers this year to any places distant from Halifax there
being no Provisions for that purpose in Store, for as the Season is so far
advanced I could not do it without sending with them nine months Provisions
at the same time, and it is my sincere opinion that wherever they are sent
out, so far from nine months provision being sufficient for the purpose 'till
they get rightly settled and have raised something of their own, to be able
to subsist upon, that a further supply of fifteen Months more, will be absolutely necessary to be allowed them.   This I should think they cannot possibly do without, for as most of them are poor Wretches that have scarce a
farthing of Money among them, it is to be feared, little provisions or other
Necessarys would be carried to them from any of the neighbouring Colonys,
wherefore they must inevitably starve. . . .

I cannot omit acquainting your Lordships that the People in general
who were sent over this year by Mr. Dick complain of his having perswaded
them at their embarking to sell off every thing even the little Bedding they

had, by which means they have lain on the bare Decks and Platforms dureing their Voyage and are still destitute of all kind of bedding.   This has caused the death of many both on the Passage and here ashore since they were landed; what Mr. Dick could mean by persuading these poor wretches to dispose of all their Bedding and little Necessarys in the manner as they have represented to me, I really cannot say, but to me it looks as if it was done to give room for crowding in a greater number of People into the Ships that brought them, which I assure your Lordships, by the reports which were made to me, with regard to that Affair was done to a great degree, and thereby great sickness was occasioned, of which so many died.

I must further mention its being notorious to everybody here, that among the number of these Settlers which Mr. Dick has sent this year there were many, very many poor old decriped Creatures both men and Women who were objects fitter to have been kept in Almhouses than to be sent over here as Settlers to work for their Bread.   Several that are dead were reported to me by the persons that attended them to have been upwards of Eighty years of age.   And I have at this instant a report before me from one of our Surgeons, of two Swiss that came this year who are dying with old Age.

The 26th of last month, the last of these settlers were landed, when there were above thirty of them that could not stir off the Beach, eight of them Orphans who immediately had the best care taken of them, notwithstanding which, two of them dyed after being carried to the Hospital; within about twelve days time there were fourteen Orphans belonging to these Settlers that were taken in the Orphan house.   These are things which I do not doubt but your Lordships must think are very shocking, I can assure you my Lords, that I find them so, who am here on the spot, for no Mortal that has the least humanity can do otherways than feel to the very heart at the sight of such a scene of misery as it is, and the Prospect there is of its being a much more deplorable one before the severity of the Winter which now draws nigh, is got over.

Relief of German Settlers

Public Archives of Canada, *N.S.A.*, vol. LVIII, pp. 12-14:   Halifax, June 28, 1755, Chas. Lawrence to the Lords Commissioners of Trade and Plantations.

By Mr. Pownal's Letter of November 30th 1754 enclosing your Lordships observations on the Estimate for 1755, which I received by way of Boston April the 26th, I observe that you have disallowed the provisions that were Estimated for the Settlers here and at Lunenburg during the Rigour of the next Winter Months, and have ordered that these Settlers should not be victualled after the first of July 1755: In obedience to your Lordships directions I gave order for the Victualling to cease at Lunenburg, which produced a Memorial from the Inhabitants to the Council, praying some relief; which having been taken into Consideration, the Council in Compassion to their distresses, have granted (as your Lordships will see by the Minutes) a further allowance to a number not exceeding one thousand (of such as should be found the most industrious and deserving of this gratuity) of one pound of Beef and seven pounds of Bread each.

Economic Welfare of New England Settlers

Public Archives of Canada, *N.S.A.*, vol. LXIV, pp. 266-7: Halifax, December 12 1760, Jonathan Belcher to Lords Commissioners of Trade and Plantations.

Many of the inhabitants are rich and in good Circumstances, about one hundred have transported themselves and their Effects at their own expence and are very well able to support themselves, and as to the poor sort, there is provision made for them untill the month of next August.

Indolence of Settlers from New England

(i)

Public Archives of Canada, *N.S.A.*, vol. LXXXIX, p. 96: Halifax, October 23, 1773, Legge to Secretary of State.

From the best information I have, the progress of this Province is much retarded by Want of Industry among the People who came into the back part of it from New England. . . .
These people are decreasing by death, and the Sale of their Land to those who have been industrious.

(ii)

John Robinson and Thomas Rispin, *A Journey through Nova Scotia* (York, 1774), pp. 36-7.

Nothing can be said in favour of the inhabitants, as to their management in farming. They neither discover judgement or industry. Such of the New Englanders, into whose manners and characters, we particularly inspected, appeared to us to be a lazy, indolent people. In general, they continue in bed till seven or eight o'clock in the morning; and the first thing they do, after quitting it, is to get a glass of rum, after which they prepare for breakfast, before they go out to work, and return to dinner on eleven. They go out again about two, and at four return to tea. Sometimes they work, an hour or two after, and then return home.

Unfitness of Disbanded Soldiers as Settlers

Public Archives of Canada, *N.S.A.*, vol. LXIV, pp. 147-50: Halifax, May 11, 1760, Chas. Lawrence to Lords Commissioners of Trade and Plantations.

In having your Lordships Commands to do so, I have carefully and as well as I am able, considered what Lands may be fitt for accommodating disbanded Officers and Soldiers—and I now lay before you a paper containing the names of such places, as I conceive will be proper for such purpose. . . . But I fear the Difficulty of forming them into Societies will be great; That the Undertaking will be excessively expensive to the Crown, and that, after all, it will prove abortive for according to my Ideas of the Military which I offer with all possible deference and Submission, They are the least qualifyed from their occupation as Soldiers, of any men living to establish new Countrys, where they must encounter Difficulties, with which they are altogether unacquainted and I am the rather convinced of it, as every Soldier that has come into this Province since the establishment of Halifax, has either quitted it, or become a Dram Seller, upon the whole I am very much at a loss to point out to your Lordships, with any precision, any method of carrying such a design into effectual Execution, either with advantage to the Disbanded Military or with Security to the Province.

Indigent Irish Settlers

Public Archives of Canada, *N.S.A.*, vol. LXXVIII, pp. 16-22: Report of the Committee of the Council of Nova Scotia on the Memorial of Mr. McNutt; Enclosure in letter of Franklin to Lords of Trade, Sept. 2, 1766.

The Committee of His Majesty's Council Appointed to Examine into the facts stated in the Memorial of Colonel Alexander McNutt addressed to the Right Honorable the Lords Commissioners for Trade and Plantations . . . Having deliberately and Maturely considered the several Allegations and examined into the particular facts therein Asserted, do report Viz't. . . .

That in October 1761 Colonel McNutt arrived at Halifax from Ireland with about Two Hundred and Fifty Persons a very unseasonable time in this' Climate for Seating them on their Lands, and as most of them were indigent People without means of Subsistence they chiefly remained at Halifax the ensuing Winter, and were Supported by the Government, the Charitable Contribution of the Inhabitants, and some Provisions borrowed by Colonel McNutt from the Government for which He still stands indebted.

That early in the Spring 1762 a contribution was actually made by the Council and Principal Inhabitants of Halifax for the hire of a Vessel to transport those indigent People and their Families, to the District of Cobequid where the best Lands, and greatest quantities of Marsh in that Part of the Country were Assigned them also to furnish them with Provisions, Seed Corn, Tools and other Necessarys for Building, and being afterwards in great distress were further supplied with Provisions out of the Provincial Fund and without One Shilling expence to Colonel McNutt.

Problems of Contagious Disease

Public Archives of Canada, *N.S.A.*, vol. LXIV, pp. 300-1: Halifax, December 21, 1760, Jonathan Belcher to the Lords Commissioners of Trade and Plantations.

I think it necessary to apply to your Lordships for directions as to the powers of Government for preventing contagious Distempers in the Province: The reason of this application is founded on the very great danger that might have attended the New Settlements, the Troops, the Indian Commerce, as well as the utmost Calamity to the poorer sort of Inhabitants, in the rigours of this Season, from a Vessel arriving here with the infection of the small Pox on board: Immediate measures were taken with the Owners of the Vessell to persuade them to remove Her at some distance from the Town, with a promise of paying any damage which might arise: the arguments of the Government were not listen'd to, and what may be the Consequence the fact is too recent yet to conjecture. The Council foreseeing these dangers had prepar'd a Bill the Copy is inclos'd, which was rejected by the Assembly not on account of the form of the Bill, but on account of the matter; it is to be hoped that they will now see their error.

Nova Scotia a Refuge for Undesirables

Public Archives of Canada, *N.S.A.*, vol. LXXVII, pp. 223-4: Halifax, August 24, 1766, Green to the Lords Commissioners of Trade and Plantations.

I humbly hope your Lordships will pardon the mention of one thing more, which is done at the desire of the principal Inhabitants of this place, who esteem themselves greatly interested in obtaining your Lordship's favourable Regards for their Relief, which is, that the Repeal of the Act of the Legislature here for preventing the Scum of all the Colonies from being admitted into this Province without Restriction, has caused such an Inundation of persons, who are not only useless but very Bothersome to the Community, being not only those of the most dissolute manners, and void of all Sentiments of honest Industry, but also Infirm, Decrepit, and insane, as well as extremely indigent persons, who are unable to contribute anything towards their own maintenance, that the Industrious Inhabitants, especially of the Town of Halifax, esteem themselves subject to a grievous tax thereby, and are disabled from affording the Relief. They are willing to do to their own honest poor, the expence of whose support, especially in the Winter Season, is very considerable: and if I have not been misinformed, the passages of persons from Jails, Hospitals and Workhouses, in the neighbouring Colonies, have been paid for, and other Encouragement given them to embark for this place, since it has been known, that we were obliged to receive them.

Efforts to Prevent Influx of Undesirables

Public Archives of Canada, *N.S.A.*, vol. LXXXIII, pp. 84-5: Halifax, August 5, 1768, Franklin to Secretary of State.

Among the several Bills prepared this last Session there are two now sent to your Lordship for His Majesty's Approbation and permission to be passed one of them is intitled *an Act to prevent the Importing lame and infirm persons into this Province,* and the other Intitled *an Act for establishing the rate of Interest.*

The purport of these two Bills have formerly been provided for by Acts of the General Assembly and were repealed by His Majesty on the representations of the Lords Commissioners for Trade and Plantations.   But as these Bills are thought to be very necessary and the objections then made to them by their Lordships are removed it is hoped His Majesty will be graciously pleased to give directions for their being passed as Laws.

As to the Expediency of the first Law, I beg leave to remark to your Lordship that the frequent importation of such persons as the title of the Bill specifies from all parts of the other Colonies, And the many followers of the Army and Navy who become so, are so burthensome to this Town that the Inhabitants are very heavy taxed for their support and Maintenance through the Winters, and in addition to this heavy Tax the Government has been annually obliged to pay large sums towards Assisting the Poors' Rate which the present state of the Provincial Funds cannot afford.

Evacuation of Boston and Relief of Refugees

(i)

Public Archives of Canada, *N.S.A.*, vol. XCV, pp. 188-90: Halifax, March 18, 1776, Legge to Secretary of State.

The number of Families from the Continent hath been much fewer than I expected, it Seems the Rebels took every method to prevent their coming, by Stopping all their Vessels, and Seizing their Effects.   So that the Friends of Government among them, have in a manner been Totally ruin'd, those who came here, early took the opportunity, and bringing with them their Vessels and Effects, have most of them been Employ'd in the Fishery, and in Trade, so that their demands on Government have been trifling, not above three Families have applied for Relief, which I have order'd Agreeable to His Majesty's Instructions, and have not as yet drawn for more than One hundred pounds on the Treasury; but the last letters from General How, informs me, that two hundred Families will embark from Boston to this place, among whom are many necessitous, which will distress us greatly, as Provision is not to be, purchas'd on any account, the small Supplies we have had for the support of the Town, has been from Boston and the West Indies; I hope therefore the Provision I wrote for to be sent here in my Letter No. 52, wherein I have more fully explain'd the Circumstances of this Province, has been thought an essential measure, and that it will soon arrive, and relieve us from that Scene of Distress, which is likely to take place here.

(ii)

Public Archives of Canada, *N.S.A.*, vol. XCV, pp. 43-4: Halifax, June 27, 1776, Massey to Secretary of State.

I have sent to England and Ireland, a great number of poor distress'd Soldiers' wives and Children with the Invalids of the Army, under the care of Capt. Mountain of the 47 Regiment.

As I had application made to me from some Yorkshire families, to leave this Province and return home, who seemed heartily Sick of their jaunt, I thought it might have a proper Effect at home, to prevent the Old Country from loosing so many of her Subjects, I have therefore given some their Passage to England and others to Ireland if this Step meets your Lordship's approbation, I shall be happy.

I will do Everything in my power to Support the Distresses of the Vast number of woemen, as well as Children, still left here behind the Army, in as Cheap a manner as I possably can to Government.

(iii)

Public Archives of Canada, *N.S.A.*, vol. XCVI, p. 189: Halifax, October 6, 1776, Massey to Secretary of State.

Almost all the Refugees from Boston are leaving and, as they are frighted to death at the Cold already, as well as at the Expence of buying Provisions, I pitty the poor Subalterns, as till very lately Beef was one Shilling a pound, Mutton &c in Proportion, and three Shilling a piece for common Fowls: I have all the woemen of the Army and their Children still here, as they are almost naked, but I do Everything to Keep Peace and quietness, in my power, I hear the Soldiers with the Grand Army are vastly happy, that I have their poor Children at School, and Lt Governor Arbuthnot gives the woemen Work in the Dock yard to Pick Oakum.

Loyalist Migration and Relief of Destitution

Public Archives of Canada, *N.S.A.*, vol. CIII, pp. 184-5: Halifax, October 4, 1783, Parr to Nepean.

The increase of People to this Province is prodigious, about or near 20,000 Souls have already arriv'd from New York, and they are to be follow'd by many more, those who came early in the Year, have got under tolerable Shelter, and are doing very well, but those who have lately come, and are to come, must be miserable indeed, provided it is a severe Winter, you know what they are, several will be obliged to Hutt in the Woods, their case is truly distressing, many of them are obliged to quit their comfortable habitations and possessions.   I feel most sincerely for them, and have done everything in my Power to assist those unfortunate People, and have done it, at a very considerable expence to myself, much more than my present Income will bear, notwithstanding it is impossible to please some of them, who are most unreasonable in their demands and expectations.

Immigration of Destitute Persons

(i)

Public Archives of Canada, *N.S.A.*, vol. CV, pp. 175-6: Halifax, July 26, 1784, Parr to Secretary of State.

Since my last a Transport has arrived from St. Augustine with 260 Souls, the poorest and most distress'd of all Beings, without a Shilling, almost

Naked, and destitute of every necessary of life. Charity has made me ven
ture to give them warm Clothing, with other things to prevent them from
perishing by the Severity of this Climate, which I flatter myself will meet
His Majesty's Approbation.

(ii)

Public Archives of Canada, *N.S.A.*, vol. CV, pp. 216-18: Halifax, September 1,
1784, Parr to Secretary of State.

I beg leave to represent to your Lordship, that a Transport, the Ship
Sally, arrived in this Harbour about three weeks ago, with a number of
Persons on board, many of them in a sick and weak condition and without
Cloathing, thirty nine of them had died on their Passage, and 12 died in a
few days after their arrival. . . . (W. Tonge informed me) that these people,
amounting in number at the time of their Embarkation, to about three
hundred, had been sent out here by your Lordship's direction, and in consequence of this information, my Lord, I took the proper measures for the
Recovery of the Sick, by ordering them to be landed under Tents, and to
provide a reception for the others, and those who may recover; but, as many
of them are in want of Cloathing, and all of them are destitute of Provisions,
I am much at a loss to provide these articles for them . . . hoping I shall
soon be honor'd with some information from your Lordship on this Subject,
not knowing Whether as Refugees, or in what Quality I am to receive them.

(iii)

Public Archives of Canada, *N.S.A.*, vol. CVI, p. 44: Halifax, October 9, 1784,
Parr to Nepean.

I cannot let this opportunity slip, without requesting you to use your
good offices, in preventing the Lord Mayor of London from sending here any
more of the Canaille of the City, or sweepings of Jails, as he lately did in the
Sally Transport, by an application to Lord Sydney, they are unwelcome
Guests to Infant Settlements.

Deportation of Undesirables

Public Archives of Canada, *N.S.A.*, vol. CXI, pp. 214-15: Halifax, December 4,
1789, Parr to Nepean.

About Twenty poor Wretches have been here for some time past, they
are mostly old, and unable to earn their bread, from England, Scotland and
Ireland, this Town being unable to maintain so many transient poor, the
Inhabitants have contributed to send them home in the Ark Brig, in order
for their being removed to their several Parishes, as none of them have any
claim upon Government.

9

Destitution among Highland Immigrants

Public Archives of Canada, *N.S.A.*, vol. CXVI, pp. 279-80: Halifax, September 27, 1791, Parr to Secretary of State.

I have the honour of informing you, that lately Six hundred and fifty persons have arrived at Pictou, in the North East Part of this Province, from Glasgow—In general they are in a Wretched condition—The greatest part are at this time in want of Sustenance, and that number will daily increase.

As the Funds of this Province are so Assigned and Secured by Law, for several purposes, that I could not from thence procure them any Relief.   I have been oblig'd on my own Credit to furnish them with Provisions to save their Lives, and to prevent their Emigration to South Carolina. . . .

I have advis'd these People, to disperse themselves in different parts of the Province. . . . I request, Sir, to be inform'd what, or whether any allowance of Land shall be made to them.

Immigration of Destitute from Overseas after 1800

(i)

Acadian Recorder, Halifax, July 26, 1817.

To the Editor of the Recorder,
Sir,

I HAVE waited with an expectant confidence, that some of your numerous and intelligent correspondents would have noticed the late Emigration into this Province; none have I seen in the Recorder, or any thing more than the mere matter of fact, as a general remark, in any of the other Journals. . . .

Since the 1st of this month not less than nine Vessels have arrived from Europe, viz. 4 from Scotland, 4 from Ireland, and 1 from England, having on board 1254 passengers; the last arrival bringing advice that there are 5 Vessels taking in passengers for this Province, at Londonderry, and 4 others at Belfast; therefore, calculating they will bring a proportionate number of passengers, it is rational to consider, that in the course of a few weeks not less than *two thousand five hundred and eight* Strangers will arrive amongst us! What is to become of them, how are they to obtain a subsistence, is a question that not only concerns themselves but becomes our duty to consider as fellow Beings and friends of humanity.   A great proportion of these Emigrants are mechanics, viz. Carpenters, Taylors, Cordwainers and *Weavers*, and it is a fact too glaring to be disputed that there is scarce half employment in their respective professions, for those who have been born in the Province, or become long and established residents. . . . What Farmers there are, and of others *that would be Farmers*, the number is comparatively small, they have arrived at a season when it is almost too late to obtain employment as husbandmen, much less to take advantageous possession of that "Grant of Land" they were led to believe would be so easily obtained upon their arrival.—Thus situated, it is but rational to presume, nearly the whole must become, in the winter season, a burthen upon the community; for at present, scores are obliged to sleep on the wharves—without a home—without shelter —without a friend, and without money.   Is not this an humiliating admission? when hundreds of Negroes have palaces in comparison. . . .

A RESIDENT MECHANIC

Halifax, July 25th, 1817.

(ii)

T. C. Haliburton, The Old Judge; or, Life in a Colony (London, n.d.,
about 1840), p. 230.

We have two sorts of emigrants to this province, do you observe; droves of paupers from Europe, and shoals of fish from the sea: old Nick sends one, and the Lord sends the other; one we have to feed, and the other feeds us; one brings destitution, distress, and disease, and the other health, wealth, and happiness.

Unemployed Immigrants in Saint John, N.B.

British Colonist, Saint John, June 23, 1834.

LOUNGERS.—Our streets at this time are literally infested with this description of persons, chiefly Emigrants, hanging about in a listless and woebegotten manner.   Employment for such persons in the City is out of the question, and it is with difficulty they can be persuaded to go into the country, where they are much wanted; and where they would obtain a fair compensation for their labors.   It is a great pity that the authorities do not interest themselves in the condition of these poor creatures, a majority of whom would if properly directed, and partially assisted, be transferred from *impediments* to impellents to the "common weal."   The sections of the Province most in want of Laborers are Woodstock, Maugerville, Sheffield, and Sussex Vale.   These places alone would absorb some hundreds of servants of both sexes.

B. *Development of Social Service Institutions*

The Work of the Orphanage

(i)

Public Archives of Canada, *N.S.A.*, vol. LXVI, pp. 132-4: Halifax, November 3, 1761, Jonathan Belcher to the Lords Commissioners for Trade and Plantations.

I applied, My Lords, an immediate Attention upon receiving your Lordships Letter 3'd March, to the State and Expence of the Orphan house, and directed a return from the beginning of its institution, of the number and Ages of the Children admitted, their several Employments with the manner of placing them to service at the Ages assigned by the Government.

By this Return with Remarks annexed by Mr. Breynton the Guardian, now transmitted, it appears, that Two Hundred and Seventy five Children, mostly Orphans, have been graciously relieved in the Course of Nine Years, by this Royal Charity, who might otherwise have perished or been Useless to the Public. The Interval between their Admission and Indentures for Service, was from the Ages of Eight to twelve years, when they could not have been fit for any very Serviceable labor. The Guardian reports, that in such Employments as they were capable of, they were constantly at Work, and that the Profits were placed in Account to the Public. Children of the poorer Sort of Inhabitants, tho' not Orphans, have been admitted differently from the strict Institution, but with the same good intention, for relieving equally miserable Objects, and not to the Exclusion of any Orphans on the Extent of the Plan for admitting Forty Children. As this indulgence was only upon the past distresses and poverty of the Inhabitants, so it may be relied on, that the Charity will be hereafter confined to its Original Institution.

(ii)

Public Archives of Canada, *N.S.A.*, vol. LXVI, pp. 154-5: Enclosure in letter of
Jonathan Belcher to Lords of Trade &c., Halifax, November 3, 1761.

When any Children have been admitted into the Orphan House besides real Orphans it has always been by Express Order of the Governor or Commander in Chief and that upon extraordinary Occasions.

Such as when Children have been deserted by their Parents, of which more Instances have happened here than is common, from the great Concourse of dissolute abandoned Women, followers of the Camp, Army and Navy.

The Death of one parent and the Lameness Sickness or Inhability of their other to maintain the Children has been esteemed sufficient Cause for admitting Part and sometimes the whole of a Family so unhappily circumstanced.

It appears by the annexed Return that the Children are in general bound Apprentices so Very Young as to be unable to do any Serviceable Labour while in the Orphan House, the larger Girls however have been constantly employed in carding and Spinning Wool and knitting Stockings for the Use of the Orphans, And such Boys as were capable of doing anything have been preserved from Habits of Idleness (in the Intervals of Schools Hours) in attempting to pick Oakam during Winter, and in Summer in Weeding, gathering Stones and other little Offices in the Hospital and Orphan House Gardens.

State of the Hospital

Public Archives of Canada, *N.S.A.*, vol. LVII, pp. 26-33: Halifax, January 13,
1755, Memorial of John Grant, of Halifax, Nova Scotia, Surgeon, to the Lords of
Trade and Plantations.

. . . That the Patients of the Hospital, are Soldiers of the Governor's Regiment, who are supply'd with the Province Medicines, fire, and other Necessaries, as well as with the Province Surgeons, and the Inhabitants that are entertained, or that would Accept of the Hospital, are Venerials, and Miscreants that ought not to be supported or Countenanced by the Public, on any other terms, than their working for a Cure in Bridewell, when in this Hospital they are entertained from three Months, to twenty at great Expence to the Government, and to the great Advantage of the Surgeon, who is allowed one Shilling per day for each Patient Exclusive of his Sallery and Contingent Account.

That a Venerial Patient, upon a Moderate Calculation, costs the Government, when in the Hospital, for his, or her Cure, which they seldom obtain, twenty pounds Sterling, when by a Surgeon Practising for himself, he might be Cured for fourty Shillings, nor is the Hospital less crowded with Superannuated people, who, if they are supported by the Government, might be made useful to it, by doing what they are Capable of, in the poor House, where there would be no Surgeon to pay, nor Nurses, nor many other Attendants of an Hospital.

That the Sober, and the Industrious Settlers, from the Apprehensions of being among a Drunken, Profligate Set of Soldiers, a Miserable Tribe of Venerials, and from the many deaths that happen there, are obliged to apply for the Cure of any disease, to the Surgeons Practising for themselves, as the Surgeons employ'd by the Government have enough to do, to Attend the Gentlemen in office, by whoes Interest and Intercession, they are continued in their unnecessarie Sallarys. . . .

That the Hospital Patients, often Return upon the Town in the same miserable manner they went there, as will appear by the Affidavit Annexed, and that may well be supposed to Arise, from the liberty allowed the Patients, who are all day wandering about the Town, to procure Victuals, or when in the Hospital in Contact diseased with diseased and Drunkard with Drunkard, and this I can with great certainty Affirm, having seen Patients immediately discharged from the Province Hospital, taken into the Care of a Surgeon Practising for himself and put into a Salivation for their Cure, after being in the Hospital many Weeks to no Purpose, nor is this Case singular.

Provincial Aid to Halifax for Poor Relief

(i)

Public Archives of Canada, *N.S.D.*, vol. III, pp. 27-8: Journals of the House of Assembly of Nova Scotia, February 19, 1760.

A Memorial from the overseers of the Poor of this Town was Presented to the House, and read, Setting forth—"That they have no authority of themselves to send any Poor to the Workhouse, Either to be relieved or set to Work, nor to release them from thence.

"That there is no Provision made for relieving the Poor, other than being sent to the Workhouse, or by Voluntary Subscription, Which being unequal, is attended with very great Inconveniences, and is disagreable to the Publick; who Say, that Every one ought to pay their Equal Proportion towards relieving the said Poor. "That there are Many industrious Families with Children who only want temporary Relief, and are not proper objects for a Work House;" and that the "Vessells which come from different parts of the Continent frequently bring into this Port Lame, aged and Distressed people, who become a great Burthen to the place, and praying that the House would take the same into Consideration."

(ii)

Public Archives of Canada, *N.S.D.*, vol. VII, pp. 100-1: Journals of the House of Assembly of Nova Scotia, July 31, 1767.

A Memorial from the Overseers of the Poor of the Township of Halifax, was read, Setting forth, that by the great Increase of the Poor in the Province, the Sum granted by the Town of Halifax, last January, for the Support of the Poor the Current Year, is greatly insufficient to Answer that Purpose, and praying Relief.

Upon Consideration of which Memorial,

Voted, That there be paid by the Treasurer, out of the publick Monies in the Treasury, to the Overseers of the Poor, the sum of Sixty Pounds, towards discharging the Expence for Maintaining the Poor in the Poor house.

Establishment of Township Relief

The Statutes . . . of Nova Scotia from 1758 to 1804 (Halifax, 1805), p. 94.

An ACT to enable the Inhabitants of the several Townships within this Province, to maintain their Poor.   (1763)

Be it enacted by the Lieutenant-Governor, Council and Assembly, That from and after the publication hereof, it shall and may be lawful for the freeholders of any township within this province, where there are fifty or more families, freeholders, resident, to meet on the first Monday in January, annually, . . . at which meeting of the said freeholders then and there held, a chairman being first chosen, the freeholders shall proceed to choose twelve inhabitants of the said township, any nine of which to be a *quorum;* who are hereby impowered to assess the inhabitants of the said township for such sum, as shall be granted by the said freeholders for the relief of their poor.

II. *And be it further enacted,* That the said freeholders in such their annual meeting, shall be and are hereby impowered to vote such sums of money as they shall judge necessary for the current year to support and maintain their poor.

Attempt to Establish Residence of Relief Recipients

The Statutes . . . of Nova Scotia from 1758 to 1804 (Halifax, 1805), pp. 157-8.

An ACT for the settlement of the Poor in the several Townships within this Province.   (1770)

WHEREAS *it is necessary that the Poor in this province should have some fixed place of settlement, to prevent their wandering about the country, and that*

the towns to which they do not properly belong, should not be put to the expence
of supporting them; Be it enacted, by the Governor, Council and Assembly, That
from and after the publication hereof, no town or township within this province, shall be obliged to maintain any poor person or persons, unless such
person or persons be a native of such town or township, or have served an
apprenticeship, or have lived as an hired servant one whole year, next before
such persons application for relief, or have executed some public annual
office, or shall have been assessed and paid his or her share of the taxes for
the poor of such place, or any public taxes during one whole year, at one time.

II. *And it is hereby declared and enacted,* That every person within the
said descriptions shall be entitled to a settlement in the respective towns or
townships wherein such person or persons shall be so qualified as aforesaid.

The Town Meeting and Poor Relief

Public Archives of Canada, *Diary of Simeon Perkins, Liverpool, N.S.,* vol. I,
pp. 49-50; vol. II, p. 102.

Monday, April 9 [1781],—meeting for ye poor agrees to raise £40 for their
Support. . . .

Monday, April 4 [1785],— . . . a Town meeting to raise money for Support of the Poor, voted to raise £50.

Philanthropic Society in Halifax

Acadian Recorder, Halifax, February 15, 1817.

Mr. Holland,—
Sir,
From my knowledge of the general humane disposition of the Inhabitants
of this place, I am inclined to suppose that the principles which direct this
society are not publicly known, or I am satisfied Donations to it would be
more frequent, and few of the community would hesitate to join as Members,
so laudable an Institution. The Philanthropic Society was first established
in the year 1811. The annual expence of a subscriber is 12s. exclusive of
any voluntary addition his feelings may dictate. It is under the direction
of a President and Vice-President, who with a Secretary and Treasurer are
annually chosen by ballot; two members are also elected to serve monthly,
for the purpose of Visiting the Jail weekly, and relieving such of its miserable
inmates who are confined for Debt, without the means of procuring subsistence. This Committee supply these unfortunates with the most essential
articles of life, as far as the Funds of the Society will permit, and at every
Quarterly Meeting exhibit their Accounts with the names of the persons
relieved; at whose suit imprisoned, and for what amount; and such has been
the result of these charitable endeavours to alleviate human misery, that at
one period I am well assured not less than from twelve to fifteen Debtors
entirely destitute, were for many months supported from its funds. This

however, constant claim upon its limited means, has left little to spare at the present inclement season, when so materially required.   There are now by the last report of the society, Eight persons in confinement, almost totally dependent upon its fostering aid, and which is hardly sufficient to give them full provision for about half the week.

Any benevolent person inclined to further the views of this Institution, may have an opportunity of reading the Minutes, Rules, &c. by calling on Mr. THOMAS HOSTERMAN, the Secretary, who will receive any Donation which may be offered.

A Member of the Society.

Halifax, 14th Feb. 1817.

Efforts to Assist Immigrants

Acadian Recorder, Halifax, August 9, 1817.

EMIGRANTS

In consequence of the difficulties into which some of the Emigrants from the Mother Country have been thrown, upon their first landing in this place; and of repeated applications from different quarters, several individuals have undertaken to assist those Emigrants with information and advice—Their principal object will be to distribute them as generally as possible throughout the Province, that their labour may be more valuable to themselves and to the country.   In cases of extreme distress, it will also be the endeavour of these individuals to procure some small funds, from which a *Loan* may be made to those Emigrants who have no money, of as many shillings as may be sufficient to bear their expences to those parts of the country, in which they will be recommended to seek for employment.—It is confidently hoped, that every encouragement will be given by the Magistrates and other Land-holders throughout the Province, to the persons who will thus be distributed among them, and especially by assisting in procuring employment for them at fair and moderate wages—And with the happy prospects of an abundant harvest, with which this country is now blest, there can be no doubt that the persons lately arrived may soone be comfortably provided for, and eventually prove a valuable acquisition to the Province.

Any information from Gentlemen in the country respecting the number of persons whom it would be desirable, to receive in their respective counties and township, with a description of the persons most wanted, will be thankfully received—and all applications from individuals who wish to employ families, farmers, mechanics or labourers, will be attended to. —Application to be made to either of the Subscribers.

JAMES FRASER,
JOHN LIDDELL,
MICHAEL TOBIN,
SAMUEL CUNARD.

Halifax, 1st Aug. 1817

Efforts to Deal with Destitute Immigrants in Saint John

Acadian Recorder, Halifax, October 23, 1819.

St. John, N.B. October 6.

At a Meeting of several of the Inhabitants, at the City Hall on Wednesday the sixth inst. pursuant to a notice for the purpose of taking into consideration measures for the assistance of needy Emigrants during the ensuing winter.

His Worship, the Mayor, in the Chair.

Resolved, That it is the opinion of this meeting, that a Register Office be established, where all Emigrants may make known their circumstances, situation and objects; and Mr. Charles Parke having volunteered his services to open and keep such an Office, this offer is most gratefully accepted, and Mr. Parke is requested to open a Book of Registry for this purpose, without delay.

Resolved, That all Emigrants already arrived in this City, and all who may hereafter arrive during the present season with intention of remaining in the Province, be earnestly requested, without delay, to apply to Mr. Charles Parke, at his Office in Water-street, for the purpose of having their names entered on the Book of Registry.

Resolved, That it is the opinion of this meeting, that the most eligible method of assisting needy Emigrants, who cannot go upon lands to be allotted to them by Government, during the ensuing winter, will be to take measures, without delay, to have them hutted on some of the uncultivated lands in the neighbourhood of the City, where they may be enabled to provide their own fuel, and, if necessary, may be occasionally assisted with provisions. Some of the proprietors of these lands being present at the meeting, and giving their consent to any Emigrants being hutted on their lands, and supplying themselves with fuel for the winter, and taking a crop the ensuing season from any land they may clear, gratis.

Resolved, That this Meeting be adjourned to Monday next at 12 o'clock, at the City Hall, when all Persons friendly to the objects of the Meeting, are earnestly requested to attend, for the purpose of choosing a Committee of management, and making any modifications or alterations in the proposed plan that may be deemed expedient.

Development of Charitable Organization

Acadian Recorder, Halifax, January 26, 1822.

"Halifax, January 23, 1822.

The Annual General MEETING of the Halifax Poor Man's Friend Society, held on Monday evening, January 21st, 1822, in the Royal Acadian school—

The Hon. Judge Haliburton in the chair.

The report of the committee having been read, it was resolved unanimously . . .

On motion of J. G. Marshall, Esq. That the rules prepared to comport with the mode now adopted for the operation of the society be read.

The following were then read as the proposed rules:

1. This institution shall be designated "The Halifax Poor Man's Friend Society," the object of which shall be to relieve the distresses of the poor of the town of Halifax with a supply of *wood* and *potatoes* during the winter months, and such other relief, in extreme cases, as may in the judgement of the committee be deemed expedient; and a general meeting shall be held annually under the direction of the committee.

2. Twenty persons shall be annually chosen as a committee, also a treasurer and secretary, from among the members of this society, to conduct its business, and five of its members shall constitute a quorum.

3. The committee shall meet as often as business shall require—it shall be furnished with a map of the town to be divided into wards, and shall appoint from time to time as many and such persons as visitors in those wards, as it may judge expedient.

4. The acting visitors, donors of 20s. or subscribers of 12s. annually *paid in advance*, shall be considered the members of the society, and entitled to vote at the General Meeting.

5. It shall be the duty of the visitors of this charity in their several wards; 1st, to circulate extensively the society's annual Report; 2d, to solicit and collect as much as possible towards the funds of the society; 3d, to relieve the wants of those whose cases upon personal inspection are found to come within the spirit of the institution, agreeable to the instructions given them from time to time by the committee; 4th, to make correct returns of their expenditure and its amount to the committee, at such times as they may direct—and 5th; to furnish the secretary with any alphabetical list of subscribers when called for.

6. A subscription of one shilling per month to be collected in the different wards by the visitors, shall be solicited as extensively as possible, and any donations which the friends of this society may be inclined to bestow, shall be thankfully received.

7. As journeymen and servants who are now receiving wages, may through sickness or other causes be thrown out of employ and may become objects of attention from the society, they shall also be requested to contribute sixpence monthly.

8. Any sums remaining in the hands of the visitors at the meeting of the committee, shall be then paid in to the said committee, and by them paid over to the treasurer.

9. As this society is formed solely for benevolent purposes, none of its members shall receive the least remuneration for their services, and each subscriber shall at any time be at liberty to withdraw his name. . . .

Relief of Poor in Saint John

British Colonist, Saint John, February 13, 1829.

MR. EDITOR,

It is but a just tribute of respect to the CARMEN of this City, to record through the medium of your paper, their very praiseworthy liberality and personal exertion to relieve the sufferings of those unfortunate individuals at this inclement season of the year, who daily experience the complicated miseries of cold and hunger.   Those only, who visit the abodes of poverty can form a just idea of the miseries, which many hourly endure even in this City.—Our Carmen with a liberality and feeling which do them honor voluntarily gave a day for hauling wood for the poor: and a committee was appointed to distribute it to the most necessitous.—I do not extravagantly describe the miseries of the poor, when I say that many sickly mothers and half starved children have in this winter of severity crowded around a few expiring embers, assailed equally by the extremes of poverty and cold, until life has been nearly extinguished by their sufferings.   I do not mention this as a reflection upon our Poor Masters: their duties are fatiguing and distressing; and their public funds very unequal to the incessant demands upon them.   But in a town crowded with indigent strangers, it is difficult to discover every extreme of wretchedness, and still more difficult under the pressure of the times, to relieve it.   Aware of this, and of the heavy expences of supplying even the article of fuel to actual sufferers, I respectfully submit to the consideration of our Poor Masters the following suggestion, that a large and appropriate House be procured capable of accommodating a greater or less number of poor, and that it be warmed with two stoves, and that paupers be admitted. . . .

D.

Relief of Transient Paupers in Country Districts

Journal and Proceedings of the House of Assembly of Nova Scotia, 1839,
Appendix No. 45.

The Committee of Public Expenditure to whom were referred the Petitions of the Overseers of the Poor for the Townships of Pictou, Horton, Annapolis and Barrington, craving to be reimbursed sums expended by them respectively in the maintenance of Transient paupers—having maturely considered these subjects, beg leave to recommend that the accounts accompanying those Petitions be paid the applicants therein mentioned, excepting that of Pictou, which they have thought it right to reduce from £48 7s. to £36 10s. 11d.   The Committee have also had under their consideration, the Petition of William Adamson, a private individual of the Town of Pictou, praying the payment of an account incurred in the support of two Men, said to be Transient Paupers, which, under the circumstances of the case, the Committee also recommend should be paid.   But this Committee feel it to be their duty to state to the House, that the present diversified system adopted by individuals in applying to the House of Assembly to be refunded sums expended in the maintenance of Transient Paupers, and which appears to pervade the whole Province, is fraught with irregularity and doubt, and they therefore recommend that in future a better and more satisfactory method be devised; and that, when it may be necessary to apply to the Assembly in such cases, the clearest, most full and satisfactory statements shall accompany such appeals. . . .

Committee-Room, 25th February, 1839.

Poor Asylum in Halifax

Journals and Proceedings of the House of Assembly of Nova Scotia, 1848, Appendix No. 54.

The Committee to whom was referred the accounts of the Halifax Poor Asylum, beg leave to report:

That they have carefully examined the same, and found them correct. They have also had under consideration a Memorial signed by the Commissioners of the Poor for the City of Halifax, by which it appears that the number of Paupers received and maintained from time to time in the Poor Asylum at Halifax, during the past year, was nine hundred and twenty, of which number the larger proportion of seven hundred and fifteen were transient poor, and the comparatively small number of two hundred and five comprised these only who had a settlement in or were considered as belonging to the City of Halifax; that there are at present in this Asylum, in addition to the large number of Paupers, forty eight Lunatics admitted from different parts of the Province. The Memorialists further state, that the buildings of the establishment are unfit and insufficient for the reception of so large a number of insane persons, in addition to the present extensive number of Paupers, and consequently, that there is urgent necessity for erecting at the expence of the Province an Asylum for the sole reception of Lunatics. Your Committee in reference to this Memorial, beg leave to state, that however desirable it might be to many of them to see an Asylum erected in some part of the Province, to be solely appropriated to the reception of unfortunate Lunatics, yet in the present state of the Provincial funds they feel it would be improper at this time to recommend any appropriation of the public monies which would require so great an expenditure. If, however, the House should see fit, it might perhaps be desirable to vote a small sum to be expended in the erection of an additional building to accommodate the sane Paupers, so as to leave to the insane that portion of the buildings which was first apportioned to them exclusively, but which is now of necessity (as stated by the Memorialists) partly occupied by the sane Paupers. It is worthy of notice, that a great number of the insane inmates are natives of other countries. Only 26 out of 48, (the number at present in the Asylum) being from different Counties in this Province, and some of these not natives of Nova-Scotia.

Your Committee beg further to report, that notwithstanding the large number of Paupers which was received into the Asylum during the past year, only 320 now remain therein, which, together with 48 Lunatics, make the whole number now supported in the establishment 368.

Some of your Committee have visited the Poor Asylum, and are happy to bear testimony to the cleanliness of the establishment, and the good order of its unfortunate inmates.

All of which is respectfully submitted.

JAMES McLEOD, *Chairman*
JOSHUA SNOW,
STEPHEN FULTON,
JOHN McDOUGALL,
Committee Room, 8th March, 1848. PETER SMYTH.

Care of Destitute in Halifax

Annual Report of the Several Departments of the City Government of Halifax, Nova Scotia, 1861-2, Appendix No. 15: Report of City Medical Officer.

I cannot consistently, with what I consider to be my duty to the Board, close this report without making some suggestions which have forced themselves upon my mind in connection with the public health. The humane and enlightened treatment of poverty and disease is regarded as a matter of the highest importance in all well regulated communities. I do not think the treatment of either can be considered satisfactory in this city until a well-appointed Hospital is put in operation. At present the Asylum for the Poor is crowded indiscriminately with those who simply require food and clothing, and those who are suffering from the various forms of disease. A large proportion of the three hundred inmates of that establishment are undoubtedly subjects for Hospital treatment, and their removal to a purely medical institution, could not but be attended with highly beneficial results to themselves and to those left behind, whose only misfortunes are their poverty and helplessness.

Need of a Mental Asylum in New Brunswick

The Gleaner: And Northumberland, Kent and Gloucester Schediasma, Miramichi, January 12, 1836.

LUNATIC ASYLUM.
CIRCULAR.
St. John, N.B., October, 1835.

"The undersigned, a Committee appointed by the Court of General Sessions of the Peace for this City and County, to prepare a Petition to the Legislature for the passing of a Law for the better providing for and securing Lunatics within the Province, and to report the same at the sessions to be holden in December next, judging that they will best promote the object in view by giving every publicity to the subject and obtaining the opinions not only of men in public stations, but also of all others, as to the most advisable mode to be adopted for forming an Establishment, wherein Insane persons may be securely kept, and may receive such medical and other care and attendance, as the nature of their disease requires, beg leave to call your attention thereto.

"The rapid increase of the population of this Province, necessarily brings into it many unfortunate persons, whose cases imperatively demand the accommodation that would be afforded within an Asylum for Lunatics, and though at present, from the density of the population in this City, the want of it may here be more sensibly felt, yet when it is considered that cases of Insanity have already arisen in other parts of the Province, and must in the common course of events, increase in number, the importance of an establishment wherein such unfortunate persons may be properly secured and treated, must be acknowledged.

"By the Provincial Act 5, Geo. 4, cap. 9, two Justices of the Peace may cause any Lunatic or mad person to be apprehended and kept in some secure place, but it is notorious that there are no *secure* places fit for the safe keeping of such persons, except the *Common Gaols*, and when they are therein lodged, no proper attendance can be afforded them, and they are too often obliged to be placed in the same apartments with criminals, and subject to meet with treatment in the highest degree outrageous to humanity, and the natural consequence is, that there are now, at large, many persons who ought to be placed under restraint.

"The Committee having fully considered the matters thus referred to them, are persuaded that a Provincial Establishment will best answer the purpose, to which all Insane persons may be sent, and therein receive proper medical and other attendance. . . .

"The Committee feel confident that if an Asylum for the accommodation of those unfortunate persons who are deprived of the rational use of their medical faculties is established on the principles above set forth, it will be found a blessing to the whole Province, and will forever redound to the credit of those, through whose exertions it may be formed, and they respectfully suggest that petitions in favour of the measure may be forwarded to the Legislature at their next session.

W. H. STREET, *Mayor.*
R. F. HAZEN, *Recorder:*
CHARLES SIMONDS.
JOHN ROBERTSON.
GEO. D. ROBINSON.

The Lunatic Asylum

Journal of the House of Assembly of New Brunswick, 1841, Appendix, pp. clxxvi-clxxvii.

FIFTH ANNUAL REPORT OF THE PROVINCIAL TEMPORARY LUNATIC ASYLUM. MAY IT PLEASE YOUR EXCELLENCY,

During the first year of the establishment of this Institution, twenty four Patients were admitted, many of them taken from the Gaols throughout the

Province, and most of them from situations least likely to admit of their recovery. During the past year however no less than seventy two patients have enjoyed the benefit of this Establishment, fifteen of whom have been discharged cured, and eight dismissed very nearly recovered, but who nevertheless cannot with propriety be pronounced cured, as they had not gone through the usual test of six weeks probation. . . .

On the 31st December, 1839, twenty four Patients remained in the Asylum, of which number sixteen still continue inmates, and I have no hopes of the ultimate recovery of more than two of this number, being all cases of very long standing and of a hopeless character. At the end of the past year no less than forty remained, twenty three of which are improved, many of them much so, and three of them fit to be discharged in a few days. . . .

I have the honor to be

Your Excellency's most obedient humble servant,

GEORGE P. PETERS, M.D.

Unsanitary Condition of Saint John

British Colonist, Saint John, June 16, 1834.

Mr. HOOPER—Being a resident of King street, and a proprietor of property in Cooper's Alley, I would respectfully call the attention of the authorities to the filthy and unwholesome state of Cross street—the southern end of which is sufficient to produce fever or plague; as also to the filth that is daily thrown out from the Building owned and occupied by Mr. Bragg. I trust, Sir, although a member of the Corporate Board, you will do me the justice to insert the remark of

Yours, truly,

A SUBSCRIBER.

2. CRIME AND THE MORAL ORDER

A. Fishing and Rural Communities

Drinking in Cape Breton and Placentia

(i)

Public Archives of Canada, *C¹¹Ile Royale*, vol. 1, pp. 227-9: Louisbourg, November 5, 1715, Costebello to the Minister.

It is not possible here to take any more severe measures to repress the libertinism of these kinds of creatures [prostitutes] than to imprison them or put them in irons. . . .

I beseech Your Highness to be persuaded that this vice is not in any manner tolerated, nor do those who commit it go unpunished. With respect to those disorders which gather around excessive drinking and for which those persons who indulge without restraint are responsible, we can only severely chastise those who cause the disorders, not having it in our power to suppress the origins.   It is a dissipation attached to the different passions of men who are not all equally self-controlled, either because of faulty education or because of a temperament corrupted by bad habits.   Do not doubt, Monseigneur, that I shall avert as much as I am able the occasions which preserve this culpable license, but I do not permit myself to enlarge upon the questions with respect to this matter to Your Highness.

With respect to the ordinance published for the regulation of taverns, it was issued a little too quickly for the unfortunate situation in which one finds himself on his arrival in Ile Royale.   I have even been advised to have the proclamation delayed until the country is more solidly established and I have only had it in force at Plaisance from the time of the arrival of the merchant vessels until their return to France which would ordinarily be the fifteenth of May until the end of October.

(ii)

Public Archives of Canada, *C^11Ile Royale*, vol. 2, pp. 92-8:   March 27, 1716, Council of Marine.

The Question of Taverns

All the inhabitants of Plaisance and other foreigners are accustomed to sell wine and brandy which causes disorder and debauchery continually as much among the soldiers as among the fishing crews.   Messieurs de Costebello and Soubras were instructed to fix the number of taverns at least so that it would be in their power to prevent as much as possible the usual debauches of the soldiers and fishermen at Plaisance and to make the taverns pay a tax in favour of the hospital.   Consequently, they resolved to choose six of the more considerable merchants and more honest people to whom permission will be given to sell drinks to passing strangers and other inhabitants with the prohibition of selling to soldiers and fishermen without a written order from the captains of the companies and the masters of the fisheries on condition of paying each 20 quintals of cod per year to the hospital.

That was approved and they were instructed to place a tax of 25 quintals of cod per year instead of 20 quintals.

Monsieur de Soubras by his letter of October 8, 1715, remarked that it was not possible to repress in a short while the habits of debauchery and libertinism of ancient use in Plaisance.   Every care is taken by him and he does not blame himself for the capriciousness and unruliness of the inhabitants.   He read to them the intentions of the King on the privileges and rights to sell wine.   He offered them a reduction on the tax of 25 quintals of cod and he was still not able to make them see reason.

[In his letter, Soubras further remarked] that these people were badly disciplined and conformed little, that they confined themselves to saying that they did not wish to sell and sold more than ever, that he spied upon them and if he discovered anyone committing fraud he would send him to

France and would demand the favour that he be severely chastised as an example, that he had forcibly and without giving offence spoken of this affair to M. de Costebello at whose pleasure this establishment was suspended in 1714 which could do much harm here still in spite of the orders which were received on the subject; he would speak to him of it often and perhaps it would cause him to take a little more activity for the police of the bad subjects with whom the colony of Plaisance was filled. . . . By a letter of November 28, 1715, [Soubras] remarked that to him it was impossible to establish a law concerning taverns, because of the interest which the first people of the Colony had in the sale of drink which rendered them less disposed to maintain harmony and to increase the authority of the King's orders; the only means apparent to him of enforcing the regulations, if one judged it suitable, was to send him blank orders of the king to have placed in prison those inhabitants to whom he offered this privilege of selling [drinks] and who refused him under the pretext that they did not wish to sell anymore and had been bold enough to keep open taverns afterwards, with orders only to release those who would agree to it.   He proposed at the same time to reduce to 10 quintals the tax of 25 quintals of cod in order to remove all pretexts for complaint.

The inhabitants at Plaisance [Soubras remarked] would pay a higher tax per barrel than that proposed but this was a kind of intrigue which it would be well to chastise.

Monsieur de Costebello writes that he was advised to withhold the prohibitions to sell drinks until the place was more solidly established, that he had these prohibitions continued in Plaisance from May 15 until the end of October which would be the fishing season.

That the old inhabitants of importance would support no tax which would be imposed to keep together the *coureurs de bois* employed in ascertaining the movements of the enemy on the English side; that they would not pay it for the sale of drinks and other commodities and that there were only the new small inhabitants who lived only by the trade of their taverns on whom he imposed a duty of 5 *livres* per month to the profit of the hospital, that this restriction becoming general had, thus to speak, restricted so much the commerce of the inhabitants that the merchants suspended the sale of wines and other things on the principle of not wishing to agree to buy by a fixed tax permission to sell drinks to the public, which seemed to him to cause much discontent, and that if the thing was at his disposition he would allow the same liberty that there was at Plaisance, as a favour that one granted to people who bemoaned their poverty and he would make them understand that he had obtained this franchise on his own representations.

The Bailiffs and Aldermen of St. Jean de Luz [France].

Represent that these prohibitions were a vexation capable of destroying the Colony where nobody would voyage if liberty was curtailed and where one could sell drink only to the custom officers.

Beseeching permission for the ships to sell and retail wines and brandy without limiting the number of taverns.

10

Sieur Dela Motte representing himself as deputy of the inhabitants.

Demanded that all inhabitants be permitted to sell drinks, however selling to soldiers and fishing crews only with permission.

Observation.

It appears that it is necessary to make a distinction between ways of keeping taverns. It seems that if the inhabitants who fish are prevented from giving drink to their crews and to the captains of the ships to whom they can sell their cod and from whom they can buy their merchandise that would harm their trade.

It appears also that if the merchants who come to the colony are prohibited from giving drinks to the captains from whom they can buy and to the inhabitants to whom they can sell that would harm them also.

It seems also that those places must not be regarded strictly as taverns which are ordinarily kept by persons who having no other trade to live by except that, seek only to encourage debauchery in those who go to their places in order to take advantage of them.

These are the debaucheries which cause fishermen to find themselves in debt to the total of their fish instead of having something left over.

Disorder among French Fishermen

Public Archives of Canada, C^{11} Ile Royale, vol. 2, p. 208: Versailles, March 7, 1739, Memoir of M. Lenormant.

The little order that the inhabitants of Ile Royale have always observed in that which regards fishing, the custom they have adopted of enticing away fishing crews from one another and offering to them for that purpose wages and other advantages which they are not able to sustain, and the poor administration of their own affairs has contributed much, up until the present, to causing them to lose the profits they would be able to put away from the trade and fishing that is carried on in the Colony.

Almost all the fishermen inhabitants who are actually on Ile Royale came from Plaisance. They were ignorant there, without order in their affairs, susceptible to an ardent desire for gain, but little disposed to take measures suitable to make it, without industry but capable of deceit; such is still the character of these inhabitants without whom it has not been possible to get along up to the present.

Disorder among Germans in Lunenburg

Public Archives of Canada, N.S.A., vol. LIV, pp. 254-9: Halifax, December 29, 1753, Lawrence to the Lords Commissioners for Trade and Plantations.

I now enclose your Lordships a Copy of the Minutes of the only Council we have had since I wrote and beg leave to refer your Lordships thereto, for the particulars of an Insurrection among the Foreign Settlers at Lunenburg, who under the appearance of great tranquility (as I had the Honour to acquaint your Lordships in my last) have been long hatching this Mischief and I have reason to think only deferred the Execution of it till they were informed our Armed Sloops were laid up for the Winter which circumstance they thought would incapacitate us from sending any Troops thither from hence, however the Sloops were got ready in a few Hours. . . . I embarked two Hundred Soldiers under the Command of Lieutenant Colonel Monckton and they sailed as soon as the Wind would permit. . . .

The reason of my sending so many Troops on this Occasion was the Apprehension I was under that the Mutineers (being assembled in great Numbers with their Arms lodged in a Blockhouse of which they had the entire Possession, and having already Committed many Acts of Voilence) might have disputed by Force of Arms either the Landing or the Possession of the Blockhouse with a smaller Detachment which must have infallibly broke up the Settlement.

I have the pleasure to inform your Lordships that I have received a Letter from Lieutenant Col. Monckton, giving me an Account of the safe arrival of the Troops, and that he has taken Possession of the Militia Blockhouse which they immediately abandon'd on his Demanding it at Landing. He was endeavouring to discover the Ringleaders of the late Tumult in Order to bring them to Justice; but he acquaints me that he can get little information from them untill they are disarmed, as they threaten to rise again as soon as the Troops are gone and to Punish such as have given intelligence. The intention of disarming them has been kept very secret, Lieutenant Col. Monckton has concerted Measures with the Magistrates there for doing it which he proposed to Execute in Two days time, if possible without Voilence.

I hope your Lordships will approve of the reasons the Council have given for disarming these People, I was myself more strongly confirmed in this Measure from the knowledge I acquired of them during my stay among them, not only as I always found them inclined to Tumults on the most trifling occasions, but I observed a strong Disposition in them to throw off all Subjection to any Government and to affect the same sort of Independancy that the French Inhabitants have done, they have always insisted that the Indians would distinguish them from the English and never Interrupt them. . . .

I have just received another Letter from Lieutenant Col. Monckton giving me an Account that he has Succeeded in disarming them without using any Force, he seems to be of opinion that they were so universally concerned in this Affair that no other Measures can be conveniently taken with them but a general forgiveness, however I have pressed him if possible to discover some Ringleaders that may be made an Example of.

Drunken Brawls among Fishermen

Public Archives of Canada, *Diary of Simeon Perkins, Liverpool, N.S.*, vol. I, p. 33.

Friday, Aug. 21st [1767],—Jonathan Darling comes from Port Jolly wounded in a fray with Robert Roberts. The fishermen there, by bad weather, caught no fish. Now when good weather comes, and fish plenty, they must needs go to killing one another. The fatal effects of rum.

Problems of Order in Cape Breton

(i)

Public Archives of Canada, *N.S.A.*, vol. LXXXIII, pp. 123-4: Halifax, September 12, 1768, Campbell to Secretary of State.

Louisbourgh ever since the peace took place, has been chiefly the receptacle of adventurers in the Fishery, who found their account in settling there, and these sort of Peoples time being chiefly spent upon the Water they are very slightly acquainted with any form of Government, but whilst the Troops were there to afford assistance to the Execution of the Civic Power things were conducted with some sort of order, but that aid withdrawn leaves too much reason to dread Total Anarchy and Confusion, as the Civic Magistrate has no resource to fly to for protection in the Execution of His Office.

(ii)

Public Archives of Canada. *N.S.A.*, vol. XCI, pp. 100-2: Halifax, November 12, 1774, Legge to Secretary of State.

I have just received a Return of the State of the Settlement at the Isle Cape Breton and Isle Madame. . . . The number of Roman Catholics are Six Hundred and Eighty Six, which are more than double the number of Protestants who are no more than Three Hundred and Twenty Seven, who are not yet in General Settled, but many repair there in Summer to make Fish. The Justice of Peace appointed to keep up the Civil Police, is often interrupted in the exercise of his Duty, and they are in general such a lawless Rabble, that he is in continual apprehension of Danger whenever he puts the laws in execution. Few of these People have ever had licenses for Occupation in the Fishery, none of them any grant. The French Acadians, who are in number Five Hundred and Two Persons, have had no permission from Government but have taken up their Residence in such places as suited their Conveniency, the greatest number are Settled on the Isle Madame and St. Peters Western side of Cape Breton.

Law and Order in Outlying Fishing Settlements

Public Archives of Canada, *N.S.A.*, vol. LXXXVI, pp. 38-49: To the Lords of Trade and Plantations; Received March 3, 1770.

The Memorial of Mr. George Walker, of Nova Scotia:—

Humbly sheweth,

That your Memorialist, having about seven years ago carried a large cargo of salt and a quantity of fishing implements in his own Ships to America, to promote the fishing trade on the coasts of Nova Scotia Northward of St. John's and having largely enter'd into that branch of Trade & Commerce and establish'd settlements on shore, has had the opportunity & experience of making some observations thereon: which as he thinks them of publick utility, he has on purpose return'd to England to have the honour of laying them before your Lordships.

That from the Bay of Vert to the Bay of Chaleure is a tract of coast not less than fifty leagues, well known to the French, the most productive of fish of any part of all America; which large extent of country, Now in the legal possession of about Twenty British families only, is still inhabited by numbers of Indians & French Acadians; Which last, on account of the remoteness of the place from any other of our new Settlements, unawed by any authority, unite the former to them (tho' but very little their Superiors in any improv'd Knowledge) by ties of superstition; And by prepossessing their minds with a notion that they will be again reinstated under French Government, they hold them in an infatuated influence, equal to, a Total subjection; there being no person of proper authority among the British settlers to whom the Indians could on any 'occasion apply from French tyranny for redress, in case they should have an inclination so to do. Our whole authority there being but the single arm of one Justice of peace (who is the present Memorialist) whose power, destitute of means, is altogether insignificant to awe either the one or Support the other. Which Circumstance is further productive of another unhappiness, for it makes the residence of the British Settlers there dissagreable as dangerous; It being evidently foreseen, that the French wait only some fair opportunity to do an Act totally destructive of all British Establishment. . . .

That tho' the British Settlers might here find a happy & lucrative settlement under Providence, yet the want of proper authority, even among themselves, renders the situation precarious, as liable to Accidents, and all their good attempts almost abortive; For that our own fishermen in the midst of the fishing season frequently run away with their Master's boats and Vessells, in which they must necessarily be intrusted, full of their fish, to remote places in Newfoundland, where they cannot immediately be found out and there sell them, irrecoverable by the Owners, and with the Money enter into New and distant Service.

That others sell great part of their Masters fish on the very Banks to the New England Schooners for Spiritous Liquors; who come to fish on the same Banks or Rendezvous in some of the harbours along the Coast; and as long as the liquor lasts, Neglect the remainder of their work, often to the total loss of the whole season to their Masters.

That those very Schooners, while our Settlers and their Servants are out in the Bay, frequently thro' a pretence of wooding & watering, run into the infant settlements along the Coast & carry off the fish drying on the Flakes under the guard only of women & children; which they do knowing the weak call for Assistance on the Coast & the inability of any ship or Vessell to follow them with a force sufficient to recover their plunder. And in Case of any Vessel being stranded on the coast (which frequently happens) they embrace the opportunity of compleating the wreck, by immediately setting her on fire, tho' perhaps she may otherways have sustained little damage, in order to carry off the iron work.   And this they do unawed & unpunished for the reasons before mentioned. . . .

It is therefore most humbly submitted, Whether (if the whole Country should be thought at present too insignificant of being erected into a separate Government) the Appointment of some proper person in the Nature of Sub Governor under the Government of Nova Scotia, with power to make Constables & other Officers for the security of the Inhabitants, with a Sallary sufficient to pay & keep on foot such force & Assistance, would not effectually preserve the lives & tranquility of the British Settlers, by adjusting all differences between the Indians & our people & protect their property from all piratical invasions; And whether such person or some other person as Superintendant over the Fishery, having the Charge also given him of some cruizing Vessells in time of the fishing season, might not with that force & power of pursuing, keep & enforce good order and regulations among the fishing Vessells, and secure them, both from the piracies of Servants and depradations of others; and more especially prevent the illicit Trade carried on by the French with the Acadian Settlers. . . .

Character of the Loyalist Settlers

(i)

T. C. Haliburton, *The Old Judge; or Life in a Colony* (London, n.d., about 1840), p. 321.

Shortly after the termination of the American Rebellion, a number of the inhabitants of the old colonies emigrated to this province, the majority of whom were Loyalists, who, relinquishing their homes and possessions, followed the flag of their king into this cold and inhospitable country, while not a few belonged to the opposite side, which they had either disgraced or deserted.   Every county of Nova Scotia received great numbers of these "refugees," as they were called, and among others, Cumberland had a large proportion.   Driven from their homes and ordinary occupations, it was a long time before they settled themselves in the country of their adoption, and many preserved, during the remainder of their lives, the habits of idleness engendered by war and exile.   Taverns were then places of much greater resort than at the present day, when they are almost exclusively given up to travellers, and the voice of contention or merriment scarcely ever ceased within them, either by day or night.

(ii)

W. O. Raymond (ed.), *Winslow Papers* (Saint John, N.B., 1901), p. 337.

The new settlements made by the Loyalists [in Nova Scotia] are in a thriving way, although rum and idle habits contracted during the war are much against them.

Problem of Maintaining Order among Loyalists

(i)

Public Archives of Canada, *N.S.A.*, vol. CV, pp. 21-2: Halifax, May 12, 1784,
Parr to Sydney.

In my last letter to your Lordship, I mentioned the discontented conduct
of some of the Loyalists, I am sorry to say, that turbulent spirit has not
decreas'd, agreable to my wishes; upon the River St. John they are divided
into two violent abusive Partys, the one headed by an Attorney, whose
Faction opposes the Agents recommended to me by Sir Guy Carleton, the
Chief Justice has been there some time, doing every thing in his power by
gentle means to bring them to an agrement, but has not yet been able to
succeed.   At Shelburne the Magistrates are divided among themselves, and
also against the Surveyors, and the People are Enemical to the Magistrates.
I propose going there upon the Chief Justices return, or as soon as I can get
a proper conveyance by Sea, having not as yet had an Answer to my application upon that Subject.   I shall do every thing in my power, by a uniform
and impartial conduct to unite them, believe me my Lord, I have a most
arduous and difficult Task but shall persevere in doing my Duty.

The most liberal among the Loyalists are by themselves, in different parts
of the Province, I could not perswade them to mix with those who went to
Shelburne and the River St. John, and from this originates the disturbances
in those two new Settlements, it oblig'd me to make Magistrates of Men,
whom God Almighty never intended for that Office, but it was Hobson's
choice, either those or none, necessity obliged me to the former.

However, notwithstanding the above representation, I am happy to
inform your Lordship, that these complaints and disturbances do not hinder
them from cultivating their Lands and improving their Fisherys.

(ii)

Public Archives of Canada, *N.S.A.*, vol. CV, pp. 174-5: Halifax, July 26, 1784,
Parr to Sydney (Private).

For your Lordship's private information, I have the honor to inform you,
that the Loyalists in the several new Settlements of this Province, are settling
upon, and clearing their Lands with great industry and expedition, all seemingly happy and contented with the prospect that is before them, both as to
Fishing and Farming, except upon the River St. John, where Party and
Faction has prevented several Familys from geting upon their Lands as early
as otherwise they might, but I hope soon to surmount all difficultys, and that
in time they will be brought to think, they are one and the same people, in
which light the four Northern Colonies, have never looked upon those to the
Southward, and from this cause arrises a great part of their animosity.   There
shall be nothing wanting on my side to quiet their minds, it is an arduous
undertaking! but the great distance and difficulty of access, they being separated from this Peninsula by the Bay of Fundy, makes it often impracticable

for me to determine upon causes which daily occur, may I therefore take the liberty to offer my opinion to your Lordship, that it would contribute greatly to the welfare and prosperity of those unfortunate People, to have the part of this Province on that side the Bay of Fundy, form'd into a separate Government, it might make them more contented, and Business would be carried on with more expedition and accuracy, but this I submit entirely to your Lordship's superior judgement.   I have hitherto found them to be of a turbulent disposition, abounding with groundless complaints and false representations, and their Agents replete with gross partialitys.

Scarcity of Women in New Brunswick

P. Campbell, *Travels in the Interior Inhabited Parts of North America in the Years 1791 and 1792* (Toronto, Champlain Society, 1937), p. 55.

Having now got every thing ready for our journey to the Merimashee, we proceeded up the river Nashwack, through the settlements of the forty-second regiment, which is closely inhabited on beautiful spacious flats on each side of the river.

I found them happily situated, each on his own property, and glad to see one come so lately from their native country.   Their greatest want, and what they complained most of, was women for their young men; they begged of me to recommend some hundreds of them to come, and that they would engage that they should all get husbands, or masters, before they should be three weeks in the country, proportional to their rank and age.

Demoralization of Youth of Prince Edward Island

(i)

Walter Johnstone, *A Series of Letters Descriptive of Prince Edward Island* (Dumfries, 1822), pp. 53-4.

The uncommon juvenile vigour of both body and mind, if not well tutored in early life, and kept under due subordination and moral restraint, is in danger of engendering, in the minds of youth, great levity, pride, haughtiness, and indeed every juvenile vice, but especially in such as are allowed to become their own masters, before they have got sufficient skill to hold the reins.   A strong constitutional bias to these vices being very prevelant amongst the youth here, which is fostered greatly by the force of bad example around them, and often, on the part of their parents, there is a total deficiency of what can alone prove an antidote.   I must assert, though I do it with grief, that this has blasted the fairest prospects of many a family here.   Indeed, I may say, wherever Religion has not shed some of its benign and sacred influence, the prevailing features of their characters are those of levity and rompishness. . . .

They [the inhabitants] are remarkably fond of riding, roving about, frolicking, and drinking rum.   This last practice has been the ruin of many of the settlers, in a moral and financial point of view.

(ii)

J. McGregor, *Historical and Descriptive Sketches of the Maritime Colonies* (London, 1828), p. 73.

In Prince Edward Island among the young men, feats of running, leaping, and gymnastic exercises are common; but that which they most delight in is gallopping up and down the country on horseback. Indeed many of the farmers' sons who could make a certain livelihood by steady labour, acquire a spirit for bargain-making, dealing in horses, timber, old watches, etc. in order to become what they consider (by being idle) gentlemen: those who lead this course of life seldom do any good, and generally turn out lazy, drunken, dishonest vagabonds.

Idleness of Youth in Rural New Brunswick

J. F. W. Johnston, *Notes on North America* (Edinburgh, 1851), vol. II, p. 65.

[One thing] I am reminded of by the passages of this day's ride, which [has] frequently struck me as somewhat peculiar to this northern region . . . is the number of apparently idle boys who are seen almost everywhere lounging about, as if there was a want of work—a want of method on the part of those who would direct, or of willingness to work among those who ought to obey.

Social Life in the Lumber Communities

Isaac Stephenson, *Recollections of a Long Life, 1829-1915* (Chicago, 1915), pp. 31-2.

For those who were old enough life meant, at this time [about 1830], little more than hard work. My father gave his attention to the farm during the summer-time. In the winter and spring he was away in the woods, lumbering or logging. This routine was followed by most of the men on the upper St. John; and not a few of them, when the long day was over, came home to thresh grain and attend to the needs of their live stock. . . .

Our manner of living was simple. There was little leisure and the luxuries were few, but our activity in the woods and on the river kept us in bounding health and good spirits and we did not regard our lot as at all difficult. . . .

Public schools had not yet been established. The education of us children was committed to the charge of two Irish schoolmasters who taught with the aid of a birch rod and, as part compensation, were received as boarders and lodgers in the households of their pupils, going from one to another in succession. Even this rudimentary schooling was limited. As soon as a boy was old enough to share the pressing burden of labor his attention was absorbed by the farm or the forest, and the girls were called upon to perform some of the manifold household duties including carding, spinning, and weaving. . . .

The general diversion of the period was the "frolic," a neighbourhood affair combining industry with pleasure corresponding to the "bee" in New England. There were "frolics" for mowing and reaping, for carding wool, quilting, clearing the forest, and hauling and raising barns,—almost every kind of work that could be carried on collectively with one's neighbors. The host, as beneficiary of the concerted effort, provided refreshments as elaborate as the modest scale of living afforded, among which, for the men, was a generous supply of rum, the favorite beverage of the time.

Dissolute Character of Lumbermen

J. McGregor, *Historical and Descriptive Sketches of the Maritime Colonies* (London, 1828), pp. 167-8.

To stimulate the organs, in order to sustain the cold, these men [lumbermen on Miramichi, N.B.] swallow immoderate quantities of ardent spirits, and habits of drunkenness are the usual consequence. Their moral character, with few exceptions, is dishonest and worthless. I believe there are few people in the world, on whose promises less faith can be placed, than those of a lumberer. In Canada, where they are no longer bringing down their rafts, and have more idle time, their character, if possible, is of a still more struggling and rascally description. Premature old age, and shortness of days, form the inevitable fate of a lumberer. Should he even save a little money, which is very seldom the case, and be enabled for the last few years of life to exist without incessant labour, he becomes the victim of rheumatisms and all the miseries of a broken constitution.

But notwithstanding all the toils of such a pursuit, those who once adopt the life of a lumberer seem fond of it. They are in a great measure as independent, in their own way, as the Indians. In New Brunswick, and particularly in Canada, the epithet "lumberer" is considered synonymous with a character of spendthrift habits, and villainous and vagabond principles. After selling and delivering up their rafts, they pass some weeks in idle indulgence; drinking, smoaking, and *dashing off*, in a long coat, flashy waistcoat and trowsers, Wellington or hessian boots, a hankerchief of *many colours* round the neck, a watch with a long tinsel chain and numberless brass seals, and an *umbrella*. Before winter they return again to the woods, and resume the pursuits of the preceding year. Some exceptions, however, I have known to this generally true character of lumberers. Many young men of steady habits, who went from Prince Edward Island or other places, to Miramichi, for the express purpose of making money, have joined the lumbering parties for two or three years; and, after saving their earnings, returned and purchased lands, etc. on which they now live very comfortably.

Taverns and the Problem of Intemperance in New Brunswick

The Gleaner: And Northumberland, Kent and Gloucester Schediasma, Miramichi, January 5, 1836.

MR. PIERCE,

. . . I am not prepared to state correctly the number of Grog-Shops in the County, but to convey an idea of the facility with which liquor can be obtained in the village, I need only remark, that in the part which lies below the Court House, containing twenty-five dwelling houses, there are six licensed taverns, one selling without license, and four stores licensed to sell by the pint.

The consequence of the extensive system of licensing is—that notwithstanding the exertions of the friends of Temperance—intemperance continues on the increase. I will not pretend to estimate the amount of wretchedness, misery, poverty, and crime, which have followed in its train—but one fact is too glaring to be passed over in silence, and that is, that within a few miles from where I am sitting, in about eighteen months, no less than nine individuals have come to an untimely end in a state of intoxication. . . . Perhaps within that time an equal number of deaths were indirectly occasioned by the same means. . . .

A MEMBER OF THE TEMPERANCE SOCIETY.

Richibucto, December 30, 1835.

Drinking in the Rural Villages of Nova Scotia

T. C. Haliburton, *The Old Judge; or, Life in a Colony* (London, n.d., about 1840), pp. 9-12.

As an illustration of the condition of some of these County Courts in olden time, the Judge related to me the following extraordinary story that occurred to himself:—

Shortly after my return from Europe, about forty years ago, I attended the Western Circuit of the Supreme Court, which then terminated at Annapolis, and remained behind a few days, for the purpose of examining that most interesting place, which is the scene of the first effective settlement in North America.

While engaged in these investigations, a person called upon me, and told me he had ridden express from Plymouth, to obtain my assistance in a cause which was to be tried in a day or two in the county court at that place. . . .

In the afternoon we arrived at Plymouth. As we entered the village, I observed that the court-house as usual was surrounded by a noisy multitude, some detached groups of which appeared to be discussing the trials of the morning, or anticipating that which was to engross the attention of the public on the succeeding day. On the opposite side of the road was a large tavern, the hospitable door of which stood invitingly open, and permitted the escape of most agreeable and seducing odours of rum and tobacco. The crowd occupied and filled the space between the two buildings, and presented a moving and agitated surface; and yet a strong current was perceptible to a practised eye in this turbid mass, setting steadily out of the court-house, and passing slowly but constantly through the centre of this estuary into the tavern, and returning again in an eddy on either side.

Where every one was talking at the same time, no individual could be heard or understood at a distance, but the united vociferations of the assembled hundreds blended together, and formed the deep-toned but dissonant voice of that hydra-headed monster, the crowd. On a nearer approach, the sounds that composed this unceasing roar became more distinguishable. The drunken man might be heard rebuking the profane, and the profane overwhelming the hypocrite with opprobrium for his cant. Neighbours, rendered amiable by liquor, embraced as brothers, and loudly proclaimed their unchangeable friendship; while the memory of past injuries, awakened into fury by the liquid poison, placed others in hostile attitude, who hurled defiance and abuse at each other, to the full extent of their lungs or their vocabulary. The slow, measured, nasal talk of the degenerate settler from Puritanical New England was rendered unintelligible by the ceaseless and rapid utterance of the French fisherman; while poor Pat, bludgeon in hand, uproariously solicited his neighbours to fight or to drink, and generously gave them their option. Even the dogs caught the infection of the place, and far above their masters' voices might occasionally be heard the loud, sharp cry of triumph, or the more shrill howl of distress uttered by these animals, who, with as little cause as their senseless owners, had engaged in a stupid conflict.

A closer inspection revealed the groupings with more painful distinctness. Here might be seen the merry, active Negro, flapping his mimic wings and crowing like a cock in token of defiance to all his sable brethren, or dancing to the sound of his own musical voice, and terminating every evolution with a scream of delight. There, your attention was arrested by a ferocious-looking savage, who, induced by the promise of liquor, armed with a scalping knife in one hand and a tomahawk in the other, exhibited his terrific war-dance, and uttered his demoniac yells, to the horror of him who personated the victim, and suffered all the pangs of martyrdom in trembling apprehension that that which had begun in sport might end in reality, and to the infinite delight of a circle of boys, whose morals were thus improved and confirmed by the conversation and example of their fathers. At the outer edge of the throng might be seen a woman, endeavouring to persuade or to force her inebriated husband to leave this scene of sin and shame, and return to his neglected home, his family, and his duties.

B. The Town

Race Riots in Shelburne

Public Archives of Canada, *Diary of Simeon Perkins, Liverpool, N.S.*, vol. II, p. 70.

Thursday, July 29th [1784],—Pleasant day, & a Short Shower of Rain. Mr. Holmes works planking. Mr. Stephen Collins Arrives from Shelburn. a Fishing Schr. Arrives from there Also. they Report that an Extraordinary mobb, or Riot has happened at Shelburn. Some thousands of People Assembled with Clubbs, & Drove the Negroes out of the Town, and threatened Some people.

Disorder in Halifax

Acadian Recorder, Halifax, October 10, 1818.

To the Editor of the Recorder,
Sir,

It is much to be regretted, that the Police of Halifax have not taken active measures for preventing the disorders and riots that so frequently occur in our streets at night, which the patrole-law promised to remedy, but in fact rather increased the evil; it was little better than a nursery of mischief and dissipation for our youth, and its usefulness was attested by the vigilance of the patrole on the night the knockers were torn from our doors, and on many other occasions. Had a strict investigation taken place on the part of the Police, there is great reason to believe the knocker-breakers would have been discovered, and the great inclination for mischief nipped in the bud, but their being suffered to escape with impunity has rendered others bold; and now the smashing of windows, pulling down signs and spouts, &c has become so frequent, that it is regarded by some as a good joke, by many as nothing but sallies of juvenile indiscretion. But Mr. Editor, I view these acts in a far different light, it is my firm belief that if such things are suffered much longer, no property will be secure; many of my neighbours as well as myself, have lately had their windows broken, and been otherwise annoyed; and although I have not yet materially suffered, I have every reason to expect some greater violence. These nightly disturbers have taken a particular fancy to Lower Water Street, which they have chosen as their Rendezvous, and chief scene of action. . . .

PETER PAX.

Halifax, Oct. 7, 1818.

Prostitution in Halifax

Acadian Recorder, Halifax, September 26, 1818.

To the Editor of the Recorder,
Sir—

The very laudable interest which you have endeavoured to excite through the medium of your paper, on the subject of improper houses, no one possessed of the knowledge of themselves or of human nature will be so hardy as to condemn, indeed if report is to be credited, the evils of which the virtuous part of the community have to complain, call loudly for the interference of the Civil Power, and while the zeal which has been lately manifested in detecting and punishing two glaring offenders does the greatest credit to all concerned; it also intitles them to the gratitude of every honest man in the Province. Let us therefore unite all our talents, and all our influence, to check prostitution. . . . There can be no doubt but that one practical means of lessening the amount of this crying evil, is to shut up the avenues that lead to it, and by rendering the intercourse of lewd persons more difficult and less frequent, the profligate man will be constrained to relinquish his unhallowed attachment, while the income of the unhappy female will be rendered more precarious, and less competent to her support; and in the proportion that you can effect this, you strengthen her inducement to return to the paths of virtue, and to the habits of industry. As the matter stands at present, the facilities of licentious intercourse are as great as the most vicious and hardened of either sex could desire, but if the temperate and well-regulated zeal of the benevolent part of the inhabitants was put in motion, in order to discover and shut up those houses of ill fame, which have for so many years disgraced Halifax, what great things might soon be accomplished, and in order to prevent the wretched inmates from pursuing their vicious habits with impunity, it is to be hoped that suitable distinct apartments would be provided for them in Bridewell, or some other Building, by the Magistrates, and that such females might be employed in useful occupations—preserved from vicious company, and if possible, reformed and made good members of society, which has been happily the case in a variety of instances in the Mother Country, to the no small joy of their friends or benefactors.

Time will not permit me to point out several instances of sad misfortunes, which have befallen many once respectable families in this Town, by disorderly houses being permitted to carry on their illicit traffic, or the dreadful murders which have been repeatedly committed in them, but as it will doubtless be argued that the houses alluded to are a necessary evil, particularly in large towns, I shall give you an extract from Dr. Johnston, on that subject, which you will oblige me by inserting.

Yours, &c.
A Friend to decency and decorum.

Halifax, Sept. 18.

Liquor Traffic in Halifax

Acadian Recorder, Halifax, April 7, 1821.

PRESENTMENT
OF THE GRAND JURY TO THE COURT OF QUARTER SESSIONS, AT THEIR LAST MEETING

The Grand Jury for the county of Halifax respectfully present to the Worshipful Court, that, in considering the subject of Licenses, the vice of Intemperance in the use of ardent spirits in this town, forced itself upon their attention as one of the greatest magnitude, and wearing an aspect that may well inspire the deepest apprehensions. . . .

That this vice is not confined within the circle of those who have already arrived at years of maturity, but extends its baneful influence even to those who have scarcely yet arisen beyond the period of childhood, the Grand Jury are sorry to say the experience of every passing day renders but too evident.

From satisfactory observation it is clear that an enormous sum of money is annually expended for ardent spirits in the numerous licensed houses in this town, and that this fatal prodigality is mostly confined to that portion of our population whose daily existence is identified with poverty, want, and wretchedness, and who rely on manual labour for subsistence. . . .

The Grand Jury in making up their minds on this subject, have considered it of the first importance, and embracing in it the welfare of the community at large, as they are led to believe that very many paupers in the Poor-house, and by far the greater number of Culprits in Bridewell, have been brought to those unhappy situations, and the expences of those establishments, in a great measure, incurred, through the quantity of General Licenses; and the law of the province, under which *they* are permitted to be issued, they can view in no other light than that of a serious public calamity.

Under these impressions the Grand Jury cannot but consider the very great number of Tippling Houses of this town, as a source of incalculable mischief, and . . . they can only rely on the exertions of the Court to check an evil, the pernicious consequences of which are far beyond the utmost bound of calculation.

Halifax in the 1850's

Robert Everest, *A Journey through the United States and a Part of Canada* (London, 1855), p. 5.

The houses of Halifax appear slovenly kept and dirty; nor when in the suburbs did I see a trace of the neat little flower gardens I should have expected from people of English descent. Halifax is a great place for the army and navy; and whether the example of a life of idleness and amusement, balls and horse-races, parties and gossiping, be, or not, prejudicial to the sober and business habits of a mercantile community, it is impossible to say. Certain it is that the newspapers complain grievously of the quantity of drunkenness and prostitution; and in this respect the place probably resembles Portsmouth, Plymouth, Woolwich, and other garrison towns of England.

Gambling and Disorderly Houses in Saint John

The British Colonist, Saint John, December 9, 1831.

QUARTER SESSIONS OF THE PEACE.—The Court of Quarter Sessions of the Peace for December Term, was opened on Tuesday last by the Mayor and Recorder. His Honor the Recorder in charging the Grand Jury, directed their attention to the last return of the September Jury, wherein a number of disorderly houses had been presented, and many scenes of vice and wickedness brought to light and punished. His Honor entered minutely into an able detail of the evils arising from Gambling Houses being suffered to exist in a community, where from the want of other amusements, young men were induced to resort, and where the first lessons of intemperance were too often received. His Honor assured the Grand Jury, that all presentments or recommendations would be carefully attended to by the Court, in order that the exertions of the Jury should be met, by a corresponding activity on the part of the Justices, to carry those recommendations into effect.

Crime in Saint John

The British Colonist, Saint John, January 23, 1829.

SENTENCES, AT THE COURT OF OYER AND TERMINER ON SATURDAY THE 17TH INST.

Patrick Jollie—Convicted of keeping a disorderly house to pay a fine of ten pounds.

Patrick Mooney—Convicted of Forgery—to be imprisoned two months in Gaol.

John Holmes, and Arthur Mortimer—Convicted of Assault on a Magistrate in execution of his duty—*Holmes* fined Ten Pounds and imprisoned one month. —*Mortimer* imprisoned one month.

Duncan Smith—Convicted of Grand Larceny—to be imprisoned six months, and kept during that time at hard labour.

Pheby Carey—Convicted of keeping a disorderly house—to be imprisoned two months and kept during that time at hard labour.

C. Development of Social Controls

Moral Controls within Fishing Villages

Public Archives of Canada, *Diary of Simeon Perkins, Liverpool, N.S.*, vol. I, p. 13.

Thursday, Oct. 9th [1766],— . . . This evening an affair happened between one Ratchford, of Cornwallis, and some people here, and blows were exchanged. In the night the populace were enraged at the sin of adultery and fornication in Isaiah Thomas, of Kingston, New England, who lived here for some time with a woman of bad character. Thomas having a wife at Kingston. They took him and his miss out of bed, rode them through the streets, and ducked them in the dock at my wharf.

Justice in Fishing Villages

Public Archives of Canada, *Diary of Simeon Perkins, Liverpool, N.S.*, vol. I, pp. 33-4.

August 27 [1767]. Some fish are found on my wharf, under a hogshead, and some on board of a brig. They are supposed to be stolen by a Negro man on board. I give a warrant, and he is taken into custody.

August 28. The negro Sailor was brought before Elisha Freeman, Esq. and me. He was found guilty of taking fish out of Snow's yard, valued at one Shilling, (petite larceny). He was ordered to be stripped, whipped 20 stripes, set in stocks one hour, pay treble damage, and costs of prosecution. He was whipped at the new whipping post, and stocks. He was the first to suffer such punishment.

Formal Controls of Law

The Statutes ... of Nova Scotia from 1758 to 1804 (Halifax, 1805), pp. 28-31.

An ACT for punishing Criminal Offenders. (1758)

B E it enacted by his Excellency the Governor, Council, and Assembly, and by the authority of the same it is hereby enacted, That if any person shall presume wilfully to blaspheme the holy name of GOD, Father, Son, or Holy Ghost, or to deny, curse, or reproach the true GOD, his creation or government of the world, or to deny, curse, or reproach the holy word of GOD, that is, the canonical scriptures in the books of the old and new testament; every such offender, being thereof duly convicted at the Court of Assize and General Goal Delivery, or Sessions of the Peace, shall be set twice in the pillory, for the space of one hour each time, or be imprisoned for three months, at the discretion of the Court where such offender shall be convicted.

II. *And be it further enacted*, That if any person shall prophanely swear or curse in the presence or hearing of any Justice of the Peace, or shall be thereof convicted by the oath of one credible witness, or by the confession of the party, before any Justice of the Peace, every person offending shall forfeit to the use of the poor of the town where such offence shall be committed, for the first offence, two shillings, and in case such person shall, after conviction, offend a second time, such person shall forfeit double, and if a third time, treble the sum to be paid for the first offence; and upon neglect of payment, the Justice shall issue his warrant to a Constable, commanding him to levy the said forfeitures by distress and sale of the goods of such offender, and the forfeiture, when paid or levied, shall be delivered to the Overseers of the Poor, for the use of the Poor as aforesaid; and in case no distress can be had, such offender being above the age of sixteen years, shall by warrant of the Justice, be set in the public stocks for one hour for every single offence, and for any number of offences whereof he shall be convicted at one time, two hours; and if the party offending be under the age of sixteen years, and shall not pay the forfeitures, he shall, by warrant of the Justice, be whipped by the Constable, or by the Parent, Guardian, or Master of such offender, in presence of the Constable; *provided always*, that every such offence be proved or prosecuted within ten days after the offence committed.

III. *And be it further enacted*, That every person who shall by view of any Justice of the Peace, or confession of the party, or oath of one credible witness before any such Justice, be convicted of drunkenness, shall forfeit and pay for the use of the poor of the town where such offence is committed, the sum of five shillings, to be levied, on neglect or refusal to pay the same, by warrant of distress and sale of the offender's goods, and the said sum, when paid or levied, shall be delivered to the Overseers of the Poor for the use of the Poor as aforesaid, and for want of such distress, such offender shall be set in the stocks for any time not exceeding three hours, at the discretion of the Justice or Justices before whom such offender shall be convicted: and upon a second conviction of drunkenness in like manner as aforesaid, every such offender shall, over and above the penalty aforesaid, be bound with two sureties, in

11

the sum of ten pounds, with condition for the good behaviour, and for want of such sureties, such offender shall be committed to the common goal until he shall find the same; *provided*, That every such offence be proved or prosecuted within ten days after the offence committed.

Establishment of House of Correction or Work-House

The Statutes . . . of Nova Scotia from 1758 to 1804 (Halifax, 1805), pp. 41-3.

An ACT for regulating and maintaining an House of Correction or Work-House within the Town of Halifax, and for binding out Poor Children. (1759)

WHEREAS *by an Act of the General Assembly of this Province, entitled,* "An Act for erecting an House of Correction or Work-House within the town of Halifax, *made and passed at their Session begun and holden at Halifax the second day of October, one thousand seven hundred and fifty eight, the sum of five hundred pounds of the monies then in the treasury of the province, collected for the duties on spirituous liquors, was appropriated for erecting an House of Correction or Work-House within the town of Halifax; Be it enacted by his Excellency the Governor, Council and Assembly, and by the authority of the same it is hereby enacted,* That the overseers of the poor of the town of Halifax be, and accordingly they hereby are authorised and impowered, when and so soon as the said House of Correction shall be built and finished, to agree with some discreet and fit persons to be the master and keeper, and needful assistants for the care of the same; and to provide, as there shall be occasion, suitable materials, tools, and implements, necessary and convenient for keeping to work such persons as may be committed to the said House; and generally, to inspect and direct the affairs of the said house; and from time to time, to make such rules and orders as they shall judge best for the good government thereof.

II. *And be it further enacted,* That it shall and may be lawful for the Justices of the Peace in their General Sessions, or for any one Justice of the Peace out of court, to send and commit to the said house of correction, to be kept, governed, and punished according to the rules and orders thereof, all disorderly and idle persons, and such who shall be found begging, or practising any unlawful games, or pretending to fortune telling, common drunkards, persons of lewd behaviour, vagabonds, runaways, stubborn servants and children, and persons who notoriously mispend their time to the neglect and prejudice of their own or their family's support; upon due conviction of any of the said offences or disorders.

III. *And be it further enacted,* That the master or keeper of the said House of Correction, shall have power and authority to set all such persons as shall be duly sent or committed to his custody, to work and labour, if they be able, for such time as they shall continue and remain in the said house; and to punish them by putting fetters and shackles upon them, if necessary, and by moderate whipping, not exceeding ten stripes at once, which (unless the warrant of commitment shall otherwise direct) shall be inflicted at their first coming in, and from time to time afterwards at his discretion in case of their being stubborn or idle, and neglecting to perform such reasonable tasks as shall be assigned them, and to abridge them of their food, as the case may require, until they be reduced to better behaviour.

IV. *And be it further enacted*, That no person committed to the said House of Correction, shall be chargeable to the government, for any allowance, either at going in or coming out, or during the time of their abode there, but shall be maintained out of their earnings, and the remainder thereof shall be accounted for by the master or keeper of the said house, who shall keep an exact account thereof, and render the same upon oath, if required, to the said overseers, when demanded.

V. *And be it further enacted*, That if any person or persons committed to the said house of correction, be idiots, or lunatic, or sick and weak, and unable to work, they shall be taken care of and relieved by the master or keeper of the said house, who shall keep an exact account of what charges he shall necessarily be at therein; to be rendered to the said overseers, upon oath, if demanded.

Attempts to Check Desertion and Vagrancy

The Statutes . . . of Nova Scotia from 1758 to 1804 (Halifax, 1805), pp. 186-8.

An ACT for punishing Rogues, Vagabonds, and other Idle and Disorderly Persons. (1774)

B E *it enacted by the Governor, Council and Assembly*, That all soldiers belonging to His Majesty's Troops in this Province, or seamen or mariners belonging to any of His Majesty's Ships or Vessels, who shall be travelling or wandering within the said Province, and shall not have a pass from the commanding-officer of the regiment, company, or ship or vessel, to which they belong; and all idle and wandering persons, who shall not have a pass, or testimonial, from some Justice of the Peace, setting forth, the place from whence such soldier, seamen or mariner, or such other idle and wandering person, shall have come, and the place to which they are to pass; every such soldier, mariner or seamen, or other person, shall be deemed idle and disorderly persons, and shall be proceeded against as is herein after directed.

II. *And be it also enacted*, That all persons who run away, or threaten to run away, and leave their wives or children upon any township, and all persons who unlawfully return to such township, or place, from whence they have been legally removed by order of two Justices of the Peace, without bringing a certificate from the township whereunto they belong, and all persons who, not having wherewith to maintain themselves, live idle and refuse to work for the usual wages, and all persons going about to beg alms, shall be deemed idle and disorderly persons; and it shall be lawful for any Justice of Peace to commit such offenders (being convicted by his own view, or by confession, or by the oath of one credible witness) to prison, or to the house of correction, there to be kept to hard labour for any time, not exceeding one month.

Support of House of Correction in Halifax

Acadian Recorder, Halifax, March 21, 1818.

PROVINCIAL LEGISLATURE OF NOVA SCOTIA
HOUSE OF ASSEMBLY

Monday, March 16th

The petition of the Magistrates of Halifax, relating to Bridewell, was read. . . .

Mr. Speaker. It is out of the question that the expence of so large an establishment as Bridewell, should be borne by the people of Halifax exclusively. He should like to know what objections there can be, why it should not be a Provincial Establishment, he could see none. Will any one say, that all the criminals in Bridewell are exclusively criminals belonging to Halifax? It is true the Building is situated in this town, but does it follow on that account they should pay all the expence? certainly not. The fairest way, in his opinion, that the proportion should be borne, would be this— Take the proportion of the population of Halifax, to the proportion of the rest of the Province, and the respective proportion borne by each. . . .

Mr. Ritchie, would not allow the question to pass without his opinion. . . . He begged the indulgence of the House for a few moments—we were formerly told there was no Police in Halifax, and that the town was suffering much for the want of one. We were repeatedly called upon to remedy the evil, which was considered so great by the inhabitants, that they submitted the subject to the Executive, and it then came before them from that respectable quarter. When the Green-market was erected, it cost 600 *l.*;—when the Police was established they called for the market Rents to enable them to support the House of Correction, and we gave it them purposely, because they declared they had no intention to make it a Provincial establishment, and it should be recollected this money so granted, was not the property of Halifax, but of the Province. . . . Had they, he would ask, any right then to ask for more—Certainly not. They call it a House of Correction, but he called it their College; for they certainly took more pains to fill it than we do the College at Windsor, for instead of inflicting punishment at first, they send the persons to Bridewell to become Students there; and he was very well convinced that the present system was an injury to the town of Halifax, and it would in his opinion, have been much better to have withheld from them the means to make this House of Correction, and then the punishments would have been inflicted the same as they are in the country. He ever maintained and he would justify it, that if a Jury of the country does find a man guilty of *murder*, he *should* suffer the law, but we now find that such persons are sent to this House of Correction to receive their punishment there. . . . He was told this Bridewell was a very comfortable place, and that many wanted, and would be glad to go there: they had a good fire, plenty of associates, friends and companions in vice. He thought it was the duty of the House, rather than to encourage such a plan, to endeavour to suppress it. He hoped the time would come, when the house will see the impropriety of it;

do as they do in the country, inflict immediate punishment instead of initiating the prisoner in the principles of vice.

Mr. Archibald. . . . In examining the list of persons now in confinement, it would appear that a very small number of them belonged to the town of Halifax; they were transient vagabonds from all quarters, who resorted to the capital to carry on their depradations. . . . The town was open to persons of all characters, and with our other importations we must expect to import persons of desperate fortunes and dispositions; there was no proportion as respected crimes, between the town and the country, taking the aggregate of the population; the inhabitants of the country had homes and places of residence, and occupations which prevented their being led into the commission of crimes, as in the capital, where so many were transient and easily led astray, and this being the only institution in the Province, under fixed rules and rigid government, the public were bound to assist in its support, particularly as they had extended the law which added to its numbers—he had therefore, to propose the sum of 500 *l.* in aid of the sum to be raised from the town; he thought it should be an additional reason for the passing this vote, that the Magistrates had not resorted to an old law in force, by which the Governor was authorized to grant a warrant on the Treasury for any deficiency of funds, to support a Work house in the town of Halifax. . . .

Condition of House of Correction

Journal and Proceedings of the House of Assembly of Nova Scotia, 1839, Appendix No. 81.

THE Committee appointed to examine and enquire into the present state of the Bridewell in Halifax, and of the Prisoners confined therein; and also, touching various other subjects connected therewith, beg to report that they have visited and examined that Establishment, and find the same in a very delapidated and insecure state, and quite insufficient to contain any Prisoners disposed to make their escape. That there are confined within its walls 22 Culprits, viz: 7 men, 14 women, and 1 infant. Two of the men and one woman having been committed prior to 1838, and the term of their confinement not being yet expired. —That one of the men last mentioned was sent from Windsor—the remaining individuals being vagrants and persons committed during the present year by the Authorities of Halifax. Your Committee find that the expense of the Establishment exceeds the amount arising from the labour of its inmates; and that although the Establishment was originally intended, and may now be considered as almost exclusively, for the accommodation of the Town of Halifax, yet they, with surprise, learn that the Grand Jury and Court of General Sessions for the County of Halifax have contributed nothing from the County Funds towards its support since 1835. That no Criminals were sent to this Establishment from the several Counties of the Province previous to 1816, and such as have since that period been sent thereto have, either from the insufficiency of the Establishment or other causes, rarely remained therein their full term of confinement. . . . Your

Committee are of opinion that no further sum of Money should be granted by this House under any pretence whatever for the support of this Establishment, more especially as the several Counties in the Province have been instructed to provide for their own Criminals, until some efficient Provincial Establishment shall be erected.

Committee Room, House of Assembly, 2d April, 1839.

JOHN MORTON,
RICHARD J. FORRESTALL,
SAMUEL CHIPMAN,
W. F. DESBARRES,
THOS. DICKSON.

State of Halifax Gaol

Acadian Recorder, Halifax, April 17, 1819.

HOUSE OF ASSEMBLY

THURSDAY, 25th March.

... Mr. Lawson chairman of a Committee, appointed to report on the state of the Gaol, reported that the committee were of opinion too many persons were confined in one room, called the Long Room, and that in the rooms recently built in addition to the Gaol, there were no fire places which at the present inclement season of the year, was attended with consequences dangerous to the lives of the individuals—that they had ascertained that it was a prevalent practice to sell Spiritous Liquors to that Prison to such an alarming extent as to induce them to recommend to the House some measures to be adopted, to put an end to such pernicious practises.

Lack of a Juvenile Reformatory in Nova Scotia

Annual Report of the Several Departments of the City Government of Halifax, Nova Scotia, 1861-62: Report of the Mayor.

I cannot, however, conclude these remarks, without earnestly calling the attention of the Council and the citizens at large, to the crying necessity for the establishment of a Juvenile Reformatory in this city. Hardly a week or a day has elapsed since I was elected to the office of Mayor, that has not brought with it some urgent claim for such an institution; juvenile offenders of both sexes are constantly brought before the Police Court, charged with thefts and other similar offences, who ought not, either for their own sakes, or for that of justice, to be dismissed unpunished, and yet the only alternative is to send them to the City Prison, where at present it is impossible to separate them from a crowd of old and hardened offenders. The numbers of these youthful criminals are far greater than would be imagined. To pass over their offences unpunished is to lead them to think that the commission of a crime is not a matter of serious importance, and can be perpetrated with impunity, while to punish them in the only mode at present in our power, is but to harden them in crime. To allow the present state of things then to continue, is deliberately to allow a race of criminals to be growing up in the midst of a Christian community, without making the efforts due both to them and to ourselves, to rescue them from their unhappy condition. Were the Legislature to give the Council power to sentence such youthful offenders to longer terms of imprisonment than the period of 90 days, which now forms the limit, and which would be too short and utterly useless for educational purposes; and were the children carefully instructed in the various branches of a common, useful education, that which now is calculated to fill us with alarm for the future, might be made a blessing both to the community and to the objects of our solicitude.

Establishment of a Juvenile Reformatory in Nova Scotia

Annual Report of the Several Departments of the City Government of Halifax, Nova Scotia, 1864-5: Report of the Mayor.

In connexion with the City Prison, we have during the past year witnessed the commencement of a juvenile reformatory. The necessity for such an establishment has long been acknowledged; and although the funds at the disposal of the committee have not been sufficient to warrant them in placing it upon a proper foundation, there has been a firm impression produced on the minds of those who have witnessed its operation that it will prove serviceable in an eminent degree. It constitutes another specialty to which the attention of the Council might most usefully be directed.

The Temperance Advocate

T. C. Haliburton, *The Old Judge; or, Life in a Colony* (London, n.d., about 1840), p. 124.

Taking Barclay's arm, I now strolled to the other end of the glade [in which was being held a country picnic] previous to returning to Elmsdale. This portion of the company had also left the tables, and were scattered in detached groups; some packing up preparatory to leaving the place, and others listening attentively to a man who was denouncing those who had profaned the place with wine and dancing. He was a tall, thin, cadaverous-looking man, whose long black hair, falling wildly over his shoulders, gave his face a ghastly appearance, while his wild and wandering eye imparted to it a fearful expression. He appeared to be labouring both under great excitement and a considerable impediment of speech which effected his respiration, so as to contract and expand his cheeks and sides, and make the indraught and exit of his breath distressingly audible. Nothing could be more painful than to witness his convulsive utterance, unless it was to hear his dreadful language. He consigned all those who were not members of Temperance Societies to everlasting perdition, without the slightest compunction, and invoked an early fulfilment of his imprecations upon them. Occasionally, he would terminate a period with a long unmeaning alliteration, calling dancing a profanation of an ordination that led to damnation, or point his harangue against wine-drinkers, by observing, that they think it fine to drink wine like swine; but they'll repine, they'll repine.

Temperance Society in Miramichi

The Gleaner: And Northumberland Schediasma, Miramichi, May 12, 1835.

FOURTH ANNUAL REPORT OF THE MIRAMICHI TEMPERANCE SOCIETY

. . . The Miramichi Temperance Society has had to grapple with its share of opposition. . . .

Notwithstanding these discouragements, the Society has gradually extended; and now numbers 175 effective Members, 63 of whom have been added during the past year. Many have appended their names, who at first stood aloof with cold indifference, and some who raised their voice against the Institution, are now its active supporters. In proportion as knowledge, through the medium of Temperance publications, and the discussions at the regular annual and quarterly meetings, has been diffused on the subject, prejudices have given way: and many who have not enrolled their names, acknowledge the benefits which have already sprung from the Society, and concede the fact, that it is designed to accomplish still much greater good. The simplicity, benevolence, and grandeur of its design, are becoming more generally understood; and its members are ranked, in the estimation of many, among the benefactors of the community. —These facts are big with encouragement. They prove one great step in the advancement of the Society. It has been silently, yet irresistably, progressing. . . .

Besides a number of persons who, once mingling freely with society, and participating frequently in the poisonous and intoxicating draught, have avoided in time that dreadful crisis, when drinking becomes *habitual*, the Society holds in its ranks several individuals, who have been rescued from confirmed intemperance, who are now consistent members, and whose persons and families present an improved appearance, in comfort and respectability. These trophies alone, would be a sufficient reward for the exertions already made; but the Society confidently anticipates much more. It expects to *go on* "conquering and to conquer"; not, however, by physical force, but by *gentle persuasion, and the irresistable power of example*. Though, as heretofore, it hopes to effect considerable by *reforming* the intemperate, it expects to accomplish much more, by *preventing* in the young and others of a maturer age, the formation of that inveterate habit of tippling and drinking, which ruins so many for time and eternity.

The Society has been under the painful necessity of expelling some of its members, for a violation of its rules. But however keenly it has felt in the matter, however deeply it has sympathised with those fellow-members, who ran well so short a time, it has acted under the impression that its existence and usefulness depended on the severe remedy. . . .

These delinquencies ought not to be viewed as discouragements. They are only what the originators of the Society anticipated, and are occurrences incident to every similar Institution. It is not to be expected that every one, wedded to a vice so enslaving and debasing, will remain proof against temptation; especially when evil designing persons make it their business to ensnare them. But the instances of faithfulness to the pledge, and of triumph over deep-rooted habit, and the force of temptation, which still remain in the Society, inspire members with gratitude, lay a basis of encouragement, and are stimulants to increased perseverance and zeal. . . .

Character of Temperance Societies in New Brunswick

A. Gesner, *New Brunswick; with Notes for Emigrants* (London, 1847), p. 327.

Temperance Societies have been very generally introduced and encouraged. The chief objection raised against them is the political or sectarian character they sometimes assume; the resolutions of some Societies having been found to extend beyond their primary object, and to bear upon the freedom of elections, and even upon liberty of conscience. The teetotallers, or total abstinence men, and those who allow the moderate use of wine, have done no harm. The great objects of both parties being similar. Although objectionable rules have been adopted by some of these bodies, yet, it must be acknowledged that, taken altogether, Temperance Societies have done much good in the cause of moral reform. Since their introduction, the exhibition and drinking of strong liquors have become more and more unfashionable; many intemperate persons have been reclaimed, and intemperance is viewed with greater abhorrence than it was in former times: nor can there be a doubt, that as the simple object of absence from intoxicating liquors is steadily maintained, its salutary effect will appear still more manifest in the next and succeeding generations. But there is much reason to apprehend that these Societies will, in the course of time disappear. From their own influence, the necessity for active operations has been rendered less imperative, and the excitement created by their novelty has nearly disappeared: it therefore remains to be discovered whether the ordinary means of maintaining good morals, as taught by the Christian religion, are not more permanently efficacious in preventing any kind of crime than any system that can be devised by human agency.

3. CULTURAL ORGANIZATION AND EDUCATION

A. Social Classes and Cultural Leadership

Cultural Decadence of Fishing Communities

(i)

J. McGregor, *Historical and Descriptive Sketches of the Maritime Colonies of British America* (London, 1828), pp. 109-11.

For the want of roads, and the consequent difficulty of travelling, that intercourse which is so common in Canada, Nova Scotia and Prince Edward

Island, between the inhabitants of one settlement and another, does not exist in Cape Breton; nor is there yet the same facility of having children instructed in the rudiments of education, and Society is at the same time in a more simple state than in any of the other colonies. . . .

Contented however to exist as their progenitors did, they [the inhabitants] seem careless of living in a more cleanly and respectable style. . . .

The general character of the people is honest and hospitable; but not without exceptions, and many of the inhabitants about the Gut of Canso, and in the vicinity of the North Cape, are considered as infamous characters as any who exist unpunished. These were probably the most worthless people in the countries they came from, and living here until the last few years almost without the bounds of justice, their principles are not likely to have undergone any favourable change.

(ii)

Transactions of the London and Middlesex Historical Society, 1930, pp. 85-6: Diary of the Rev. Wm. Fraser.

October 28, 1834:—

That continued range of rock which extends with but very little interruption from Cape Canseau to Cape Sable forms an insurmountable obstacle to the progress of agricultural improvement.   Consequently the shores are uninhabited except in a few scattered spots which are occupied by the huts of Fishermen.   Their facilities for intellectual culture are equally bad with their agriculture.   And their dispersed situations render it impracticable for them to have either schools or churches.   Though then those whom I have seen of them are a quiet and peaceable people they must be brought up in a state bordering very near on Heathenish ignorance.   I by no means blame our christian people for their wishes to have the Heathen world enlightened. But it would be well if they first looked at home and tried to have a knowledge of pure religion and undefiled promoted among the destitute inhabitants of their native shores.

Cultural Inertia in French-Acadian Communities

W. S. Moorsom, *Letters from Nova Scotia* (London, 1830), pp. 256-60.

The settlement of Clare, of which the Roman Catholic chapel is the nucleus, extends for about thirty miles along the shores of Saint Mary's Bay. The population is almost entirely Acadian-French, and deserves particular mention not only from its origin, but for the distinct and peculiarly interesting features it displays.   The number of families comprising the pastor's immediate flock is about 330, giving a total of nearly 2500 souls; about 30 families also reside in the township of Digby; and at Tusket, below the town of Yarmouth, are nearly 200 families more; the whole being included in the cure of Abbe Segoigne.

. . . He is at once the priest, the lawyer, and the judge of his people; he has seen most of them rise up to manhood around him, or accompany his own decline in the vale of years: the unvarying steadiness of his conduct has gained equally their affections and respect: to him, therefore, it is that they apply in their mutual difficulties; from him they look for judgment to decide their little matters of dispute. . . [Since 11 years ago] there is no instance of a law-suit from Montaigan appearing on the records of the judicial circuit. The Abbe complains much of the indifference his parishioners manifest on the subject of education, with the exception of two or three young men who are under his own instruction, the rising generation of this settlement are wholly uneducated: his exertions to establish schools among them under the system framed by the legislature, have been attended with no effect: the parents are not willing to contribute the necessary quota, and consequently no schoolmasters can be appointed.   Probably this apathy may be attributable to the same source as that which renders these people so peculiar in the picture compared with those around them.   A feeling of isolated existence and separate interests, in the first instance, has been softened down into sacred reverence for the habits of their fathers.   Possessed of few ideas beyond those relating to their own immediate wants, they know not that active, perhaps I should say, that restless spirit of enterprise which ever urges forward to the acquirement of more: they are satisfied with their condition as it is: a competence sufficient for their simple mode of life is easily obtained; and beyond this they do not care to make any further exertion.   In practical traits of social morality, they shine pre-eminent.   Their community is in some respects like that of a large family.   Should one of their members be left a widow without any immediate protector or means of support, her neighbours unite their labours in tilling her land, securing the crops, and cutting her winter fuel.   Instances of a second marriage are rare among them. Children who may become orphans are always taken into the families of their relations or friends, who make no distinction between them and their own offspring.

Intermarriages between the Acadians and British settlers very seldom take place.

Lack of Leadership in Rural Areas of Nova Scotia

W. S. Moorsom, *Letters from Nova Scotia* (London, 1830), pp. 280-1.

In passing through the country, a stranger cannot fail to be struck with the small number of what we should call country-seats, and, consequently, with the comparative paucity of that class which corresponds to the country-gentlemen at home.   I do not take into account those worthies who, according to the definition of the term "Squire" given by the little American boy, "tend court and justice meetings," and on other days "help the mister there at the tavern."   I speak rather of persons of extended education, who, being possessed of some substance, have sufficient leisure to devote their intelligence to the general improvement of the country, and to diffuse, by personal example, a moral benefit through their own immediate neighbourhood.

This is of course one of the drawbacks naturally attendant on a young country; and the evil—for evil it must be deemed—will gradually correct itself, as population becomes more dense, and wealth more abundant; but, meanwhile, a species of interregnum must exist, which I would willingly see abbreviated.   The increase of this class of gentry would be the mildest, and, at the same time, the best antidote to those germs of wrangling and disputation, those petty jarring interests which rise up in the imaginations—for they are more imaginary than real—of the congregated villagers, and disturb the harmony and good-fellowship which would otherwise be universal.

Society in Halifax

W. O Raymond (ed.), *Winslow Papers* (Saint John, N.B., 1901), p. 288: Halifax, April 2, 1786, Penelope Winslow to Ward Chipman.

Your other friends are well, pursuing pleasure with ardour.   Feasting, card playing and dancing is the great business of life at Halifax, one eternal round—the votarys of pleasure complain of being fatigued and want variety of amusements.   The new Imported Ladies continue to be the Belles.   The Princes, Taylors and Halliburtons are totally eclipsed and the Millers, Betsy and Matty Matthews, are the admiration of all the Beaus.   The High Sheriff has been sighing at the feet of Miss Miller.   The world takes the liberty to condemn her as romantic for rejecting his hand.   The Newtonian race, who you know are connected with Mr. Green (the High Sheriff), are mortified and have advised and it is said have prevailed with him to transfer his affections to Harriet Matthews.   With this he readily complied and found her not reluctant.   The High Sheriff enjoys all the pomp of this pompous Town and you would, by the style and state he takes upon himself, swear he was born a Halifaxian—gives dinners two or three times a week and to-morrow evening all the noblesse are to be entertained at his house, a Ball and supper superb.   Charming doings is it not, don't you envy the gay circle?   Everybody here has independent fortunes—at least of this I am sure that there is not a family in this place, that figures at all, can spend less than five or six hundred [pounds] a year.   The Princes I am really distressed for—the House, the Coach, etc., is to be disposed of—the Ladies are going to New England, the Dr. to New Brunswick; what a cruel reverse.   The Attorney General and Lady are at the summit of this world's bliss; they dine with His Excellency one week and his Excellency and Chief Justice with them the next.

The Military Class in Halifax

W. S. Moorsom, *Letters from Nova Scotia* (London, 1830), pp. 29-30.

Since the settlement of the town on the present site, in the year 1749, its population has increased to nearly 14,000 souls.   The garrison forms about one-eighth of this population, and of course materially influences the tone of society.   A young officer, in whose head conceit has not previously effected a lodgment, from the specimen of military life he may have just tasted in

England, stands every chance of undergoing a regular investment, siege, and assault from this insidious enemy on joining his corps in Halifax. He finds himself raised at once to a level above that accorded to the scarlet cloth at home—society generally sought, frequently courted, and himself esteemed, as a personage whose opinions are regarded with no little degree of attention.

The Social Elite of Halifax

T. C. Haliburton, *The Old Judge; or, Life in a Colony* (London, n.d., about 1840), p. 74.

When I first knew Government House [the Judge recalled], the society to be met with there was always, as I have before said, the best in the place. In time, each succeeding Governor enlarged the extent of his circle; and, at last, as a corrective, two were formed for evening entertainments: one that was selected for small parties, and for frequent intercourse with the family; and a second, designed for public nights only and rare occasions, and so arranged as to embrace all within, as well as most people beyond, the limits of the other. The effect of this arrangement was, to draw the two classes apart, to create invidious distinctions, and to produce mutual dislike. Subsequently, the two have been merged into one, which has consequently become so diluted as to be excessively unpalatable. The best part have lost their flavour, without imparting it to others; and the inferior, being coarser and stronger, have imbued the rest with as much of their peculiarities as to neutralize their effect, while they have retained enough to be as disagreeable and repulsive as ever.

The evening to which I allude being a public one, the invitations were very numerous, and embraced the military, navy, and staff, the members of the legislature, which was then in session, and all the civilians whose names were to be found on the most extended list that had been formed at the time.

Gambling in Higher Circles of Halifax Society

Acadian Recorder, Halifax, December 20, 1817.

MR. HOLLAND,

... I assert boldly, and appeal to every man's experience, who mixes with the better classes of society in Halifax: That in their evening-parties, *cards* are almost always introduced: That playing for *Money*, more or less, is the universal practice; and that no young female is admissable, without her purse and a competent knowledge of loo. Gambling, therefore, lies at the very root of the social circle, and like the canker-worm, riots amid the corruption, which itself has created. In this general description are involved the aged Matron with her spectacles, and the Miss just entering on her teens, the honoured mother of a family and the old Maid left desolate and hopeless. —The character of the First Transgression, as given by Divines, is too applicable here: "It has passed upon All; and All have sinned.". . .

This passion for gambling, which in many, I may say, the most, is merely a source of amusement, becomes, in not a few, a morbid habit, and breaks out into moral distemper. The very ends of society are in some measure defeated by this eternal shuffling of cards; and more so to the female, than to the male part of the species. Men, from their more liberal education, and their contact with the world, have a thousand opportunities of improving their minds, from which women are necessarily debarred: and to them, therefore, conversation has always proved the great inlet of knowledge. A state of society, then, which excludes conversation, and chains down the mind to painted figures on bits of paper, is hostile to intellectual expansion, and dooms the fairer portion of Creation to frivolity and ignorance. . . .

MEMORATOR.

Halifax, Dec. 18, 1817.

Increase in Pretensions of Upper Class

Acadian Recorder, Halifax, August 18, 1821, and October 6, 1821.

On Present Customs and Manners

MESSRS. HOLLAND & CO.

GENTLEMEN,—It has now become a very general opinion among the reflecting part of the community, that the late American war, although it brought into our coffers such an immense flow of wealth, will eventually turn out a great and serious disadvantage, unless a thorough reform in the present style of society is accomplished. . . .

Before the commencement of the last European war, which has produced so many vast revolutions, and has added so much to the glory and honour of the present state, the commerce of Halifax was restricted within very narrow limits; and consisted more in our provincial than foreign trade. . . .

This state of commerce, which I have mentioned as existing about 28 years ago, was eminently conducive to simplicity of manners, and remote from anything like *style*. Little or no luxury prevailed, as the necessities and comforts of life were alone considered as the legitimate ends of expenditure. There were then no overgrown fortunes to cherish the introduction of luxurious and dissipated habits—no spare capital to waste in aping the costly and gaudy customs of fashionable life—no wish to excel in outward pomp and show. —All classes were more upon a level—the farmer with the lawyer—the lawyer with the merchant—the merchant with the mechanic. The component parts of society were balanced and harmonized:—and were nearly alike in the gifts of fortune, which alone are the causes of those nice divisions and differences—that separation of classes—those discriminating rules in the selection of friends that predominate so much throughout the arrangement of every old and rich country. . . .

This state of manners at once so remarkable and harmonized in itself, and which speaks to us such volumes, was swept away by the operation of certain political and fortuitous events. The French revolution produced throughout the world many great and lasting changes. . . .

This event, so great and unparalleled in the history of the old, could not but produce some sensible effects in the new world.   To us it was the origin of many important changes.   It gave rise to a new era in our commercial history—opened to our enterprise a wide and extensive field— and excavated a thousand channels in which to direct the stream of exertion. . . .

These circumstances so adventitious and unexpected, although in one point of view they were attended with such beneficial effects, at the same time undermined our simplicity of manners, and gradually levelled that structure so pleasing and grateful to contemplate.   The increase of wealth which, if placed under the guidance of a rigid parsimony, might have raised Nova Scotia to some rank and dignity in the colonial system, and might have conferred a commanding influence and weight on her representations, has been in a great measure lost, I fear, never again to be recalled.   A set of luxurious and expensive habits was introduced—society assumed a higher and more elevated situation—and that division of classes began to arise which an outlay of capital could only mark out and sustain.   Wealth seemed to inspire false ideas of its own innate and splendid attractions.   All seemed to have caught the prevailing contagion; and luxury—the usual concomitant of immense fortune—was here introduced by a transitory flow of riches.   In every article of expense this unjustifiable taste was displayed, and in a few short years a change in customs and manners was gradually establishing, which if left to the natural progress of improvement would have been the work of a century.   The causes which I have described laid the corner-stone; and a chain of fortunate events raised, completed and ornamented the present superstructure of social intercourse. . . .

If we look back for twenty years we will find that our government house was not then such a scene of splendour and show as now;—and even admitting that it were the case we could not ape its customs as we did not possess the means.   Luxury is not consistent with poverty; and that, and that alone was sufficient to preserve the admirable plainness of customs from being injured and infringed upon.   They continued so until we had acquired wealth. . . . Unquestionably we were led on by a bright and alluring example; and by the great increase in our circles of the military, who were stationed here at the determination of the war. —It was they who gave the tone to society; and who established that expensive and unfortunate state of customs, which has outlived the causes that gave it birth.   Would to God Nova Scotia had not yielded such ready and blind obedience, to the dictates of fashion and folly. It suits well the military life, where all its followers have fixed salaries from their country, and are entirely independent of fortuitous events; but it suits not the West India and importing merchant,—the ship owner and the mechanic,—whose capitals are invested in business, and are consequently exposed to all its difficulties and dangers.   I do not condemn the system if it be confined within its proper sphere; but when I see the mere man of business,—the man who should stick to his counter or desk, endeavour to imitate that, which he cannot reach, I feel all the pity and compassion which thorough contempt can do. . . .

ZENO.

A Landed Aristocracy of Half-Pay Officers in New Brunswick

P. Campbell, *Travels in the Interior Inhabited Parts of North America in the Years
1791 and 1792* (Toronto, The Champlain Society, 1937), pp. 281-4.

In this province and wintry cold climate, but fertile soil of New Brunswick,
I found the country flourish, and, the inhabitants do very well, excepting the
British half pay officers; who, it would seem, had neither foresight, industry,
nor prudence.   The first object of their care when they entered on the lands
granted them by government, was to build a genteel house, in which they
could entertain their friends in a becoming stile; before that conveniency was
finished, and a small garden cleared, their money was expended, and now,
as the only expedient, recourse must be had to the merchant for credit, to
whose shop they then became thralled, until the next term's half pay fell due.
The debt always increasing, and no possibility of paying it, a moon-light
flitting is thought of, put in execution, and away they set to Great Britain
or Ireland, damning the country, and in vindication of themselves, giving
out that the devil could not live in it.   Others of them judged the best thing
they could do, was to take to themselves a wife; never considering how they
and their children were to be maintained; therefore the most delicate American ladies were singled out as the only mates, and fit companions for their
beds, to pass the long winter nights with. . . . A match was thus made up;
the lady brought home, did the honours of the table with a becoming grace,
and showed away while the credit lasted; when that failed, the miserable
property, or rather wilderness, as there was nothing done on it of value, but
a house built, is mortgaged to the merchant: Away they set to the States,
saying, like those single men who went for Britain or Ireland, that the devil
could not live in it. . . .

Some of the gentlemen of the last description, who still continue on their
farms, and have had industry enough to make out two or three Milk Cows,
have now to milk them with their own hands, lay by the milk, make the
churn, muck the byre, sweep the kitchen, and do every menial but requisite
office that the family require.   My lady was not brought up to such drudgery,
and her nerves are too weak to milk the two or three Cows, which ever of
them it may happen to be, but rarely more; it is enough for her to take up
cream for the tea, rock the cradle, and look after the children; and as he
cannot get himself out of debt, so as to afford to keep a single servant, male
or female, old or young, he must do all the drudgery himself, or let it alone.
To this humiliating state, these dear creatures have brought themselves;
whereas the poor soldiers, that had not a shilling in the world when they
entered on their lands, have now in general from four to eight Milk Cows,
with their followers, and supply the markets with the produce of their farms,
live more comfortably than their officers, and as happy as they can wish.

The *gentlemen* of the American loyalists are of a very different description.
They are all men brought up either to the law, or to some mercantile or
mechanic business, or farming, to which they severally applied on their
entering into this country, and make out in general very well; yet there are
even some exceptions among them.

Influence of Military Class upon Society in New Brunswick

A. Gesner, *New Brunswick; with Notes for Emigrants* (London, 1847), p. 161.

If columns of British infantry are terrible on the fields of an enemy's country, they are also to be dreaded in a Provincial village among their friends and countrymen. It is true that their officers may impart a degree of taste, etiquette, and gentlemanly deportment to certain classes; but more frequently are their errors imitated, and habits introduced unfavourable to that industry by which alone a new Province can be redeemed from a wilderness state, or rendered a fit abode for a civilised people. The growth of the imperial moustache, or copious whisker is but too often cultivated by those whose better interest it would be to bring to perfection the nutritious and valuable productions of the country.

Patronage Class in New Brunswick

A. Gesner, *New Brunswick; with Notes for Emigrants* (London, 1847), p. 322.

The inhabitants of New Brunswick have heretofore been considered illiterate; that opinion having prevailed from the limited means of obtaining information enjoyed by the early inhabitants. It is a common remark in this Province and Nova Scotia, that it is vain to cultivate the higher branches of learning, so long as the Home Government bestows the principal offices and best pecuniary situations in the Colonies to persons from the Mother-country, who are sent out to fill them. That this feeling has operated against education, there can be no doubt; and the unfair distribution of patronage has the still farther evil effect of severing the affections of the Colonial subjects from the Parent state.

Lack of Class Distinctions in Prince Edward Island

Walter Johnstone, *A Series of Letters Descriptive of Prince Edward Island*
(Dumfries, 1822), p. 52.

They [the inhabitants] are a motley mixture of almost all nations; yet various as the countries are from whence they have emigrated, and the customs prevalent in each of them, they are remarkably assimilated here into one form of living, dress, general conduct, and manners. Some of them were driven from their native homes by their misfortunes, others by their vices, and a few were allured by the flattering hopes of obtaining great possessions, riches, and splendour; but whatever was the cause of drawing or driving them hither, they are all here placed on a level, and taught one lesson, namely, *that if they wish to eat, they must work.*

Upper Class in Prince Edward Island

The Englishwoman in America (London, 1856), p. 44.

The upper class of society in the Island is rather exclusive, but it is difficult to say what qualification entitles a man to be received into "society." The *entree* at Government House is not sufficient; but a uniform is powerful, and wealth is omnipotent.

B. Educational Institutions

Moral Failings of Early Schoolmasters

(i)

Public Archives of Canada, *S.P.G.*, *Nova Scotia*, B *25*, 1760-1786: Halifax, January 11, 1762, Rev. J. Breynton to Rev. Doctor Bearcroft, Master of the Charter House, London.

Mr. Wood and I jointly informed You of our appointing William Buchannan temporary schoolmaster to the Orphans and Other Poor Children at Halifax, his Moral Character not being clear prevented our recommending him for the Establishment, and what we Suspected is come to pass his Drunkenness and other Irregularities obliged us to dismiss him last Michaelmas.

(ii)

Public Archives of Canada, *S.P.G.*, *Nova Scotia*, B *25*, 1760-1786: Annapolis, July 9, 1768, Rev. Thomas Wood to Rev. Dr. D. Burton.

Mr. Wilkie the Society's late School Master Died, or rather, the poor Wretch (as there are too strong Reasons scarcely to admit a Doubt of it) Poisoned himself in May last; Soon after his Death, such a Scene of stupid Iniquity has appeared against him, as was ever heard of.   He Drew Bills in the Course of last Year on Persons in London who did not even know him; He also Forged Two Sets of Bills in a Gentleman's Name who lives here, & negotiated them, One of s.' Bills came back here a few Days before He Died, & the Day before, He writ a Letter to the Person who Bought the Bills from him, acquainting him that the Bill's were come back Protested thro' a Mistake, and that He & the Gentleman whose Name it appears He had Forged (& who knew nothing of the Matter) would Wait on him together & Satisfy him in Two Days. & the very next Day after supping w'th his Family he went into his Bedroom & took some small Beer with him & then tis imagined Took his fatal Dose for within Two hours after, He was a Corpse.

I was therefore not so much Surprized on Receiving your Account of his having Drawn so many Bills on the Society last year, as I should, had you Acquainted me of it sooner.   But I am now really much Surprized to Find that you have paid such of his Bills as Came home without my Signing, as you know I always Signed his Bills *"Approved Thomas Wood"*, as they became regularly Due, & consequently his Bills at Christmas w'ch I put my Name to, & were then Due, if they Come back Protested, will immediately Fall upon me with the Damage.   Therefore I hope, as my Name is to them you have not suffered them to be Protested.

I have neither approved or Signed any Bills for him since last Christmas, & the Society have no School Master here at present, nor can I get a proper Person; & when I Do Meet with One, I shall not appoint him untill I write you & Receive your Answer.

An Early Halifax Schoolmaster

Public Archives of Canada, *S.P.G.*, *Nova Scotia*, *B 25*, 1760-1786: Halifax,
August 1, 1768, Covering letter to Petition of John Collis, Clerk to the
Church at St. Paul's, Halifax, to S.P.G.

Dear Sur, be pleas'd, to Communicate to the Honerable Society, The
inclos'd [petition for assistance], for a poor Brother in Christ Jesus, I have
many things to Write, viz. from July, 1762, up to August 19, 1766, there was
no Schoolmarster, but myself, which was, to teach the Psalms, and Hymns,
for which I never Reciv'd no Consideration: I conclude your Humble Ob't
Servant, John Collis.

The School-Teacher

T. C. Haliburton, *The Old Judge; or Life in a Colony* (London, n.d.,
about 1840), pp. 128-9.

It is a melancholy condition of things [said the Judge]; and, so long as
education is so grievously neglected as it is at present, there appears to be no
hope for a change for the better.   The British Government, with that foresight and liberality which has always distinguished it in its treatment of the
colonies, founded, many years ago, a college at Windsor, an interior town,
situated about forty-five miles from Halifax, which has been of incalculable
advantage, not merely to Nova Scotia, but to British North America.   The
system of common school instruction, on the contrary, which depends upon
ourselves, is founded chiefly on the voluntary principle, which has proved as
defective in education as it always has in religion.   When a man fails in his
trade, or is too lazy to work, he resorts to teaching as a livelihood, and the
school-house, like the asylum for the poor, receives all those who are, from
misfortune or incapacity, unable to provide for themselves.   The wretched
teacher has no home; he makes the tour of the settlement, and resides, a
stipulated number of days, in every house—too short a time for his own
comfort, and too long for that of the family, who can but ill afford either the
tax or the accommodation.   His morning is passed in punishing the idleness
of others, his evening in being punished for his own; for all are too busy to
associate with him.   His engagement is generally for a short period.   He
looks forward to its termination with mingled feelings of hope and fear—in
alternate anticipations of a change for the better, or destitution from want
of employment.   His heart is not in his business, and his work prospers
indifferently.   He is then succeeded by another, who changes the entire
system, and spends his whole time in what he calls rectifying the errors of
his predecessor.   The school is then unhappily too often closed for want of
energy or union among the people; the house is deserted or neglected, the
glass is broken by the children, who regard it as a prison.   The door, after a
long but unsuccessful struggle with the wind, falls at last in the conflict; the
swine then enter, for protection from the violence or heat of the weather, and
retain possession until expelled by the falling roof, or the rod of a new master.
It is evident, therefore, that "the greatest, wisest, and best of mankind"

either do not need instruction, having the wonderful good fortune to possess knowledge intuitively, or else the rest of the human family, whom they are so often told they far excel, must indeed be in a state of hopeless and wretched ignorance.

Unsatisfactory Condition of Education

Acadian Recorder, Halifax, December 29, 1821.

To the Editors of the Recorder

GENTLEMEN—. . . The Legislature of Nova Scotia lately has done much, both by judicious regulations and pecuniary aid, to establish and maintain schools throughout the province: and many private individuals, likewise, actuated by similar motives, are making great efforts to continue and extend the utility of the schools. These laudable exertions, however, are not pro-ductive of that degree of improvement which might naturally be expected. What may be the general state of the province, I cannot pretend to say; but I need not hesitate to affirm, that in the district where I reside, the schools are yet in a very miserable condition. Though the government has, for a considerable time past, afforded liberal encouragement to qualified teachers, these till lately could seldom be found; and though they are now more numer-ous than formerly, yet, for other reasons the community is little benefitted. . . . A still greater barrier, however, in the way of improvement is the total indifference which many evince about educating their children. Though some are making strenuous exertions to provide instruction for their families, yet there are many possessing extensive land property and living in com-fortable independence, who cannot be prevailed upon to expend the smallest sum in providing the means of instruction for a numerous family. Others again in a similar condition have no children, or none fit to attend school. By this means it frequently happens, that in a flourishing community of four or five miles extent, there cannot be found more than three or four persons willing to contribute any sum annually to support a school. This being the case a teacher must be maintained by the exertions of these alone, though frequently in but mean circumstances. The difficulties under which such persons labour are great and numerous. Unassisted either by their neigh-bours or by government, they are forced to make many painful exertions, and even then to content themselves with teachers of mean capacity, merely because they cannot support a man of superior qualifications. Till some remedy for these evils is provided, little improvement can reasonably be expected. . . .

A SPECTATOR.

December 22, 1821.

Education in New Brunswick

A. Gesner, *New Brunswick; with Notes for Emigrants* (London, 1847), p. 326.

Formerly many of the teachers of common schools were very incom-petent, and not unfrequently men of dissolute habits were entrusted with the important office of instructing youth: this evil was permitted to exist until the consequences became apparent in the morals of the rising generation, and the energies of the well-informed were aroused by the introduction of abuses that could not be tolerated. The present Lieutenant-Governor, Sir William Colebrooke, has been active in the improvement of the parish school system, in which a reform is now manifest. By these schools education is carried to the door of the humblest villager, and instruction is placed within reach of the remotest settler.

High Cost of Education to the Poor

Acadian Recorder, Halifax, August 16, 1817.

To the Editor of the Acadian Recorder.
Sir—

... Through the medium of your paper, with *the utmost deference*, I beg the attention of the Committee, who superintend the concerns of the Lancastrian school, to the few following remarks on a part of its government, which I think is not exactly suited to the primary principles of the Institution: those are, to make education so easy to the poor, as to leave them totally without excuse,—if their children do not reap the benefit of it. What I refer to, is the terms on which pupils are admitted. The parent (or some one else) must advance a pound as one year's payment, before a child can receive admission to the school. Now Sir, although those are very reasonable terms, as it regards the sum,—yet in these hard times, the hardest *by far* that ever were seen in Halifax, how few among the poor are able with all the economy they can practice, to lay up twenty shillings, for that purpose, beforehand?—and if this is difficult in the case of one child, how is it to be accomplished where there are three, or four, of a family, equally in want of education?—add to this that there is a principle of *improvidence* in human nature, which often prevents mankind from providing, even for an occurrence that may be expected—in consequence, the day arrives when the school is to be re-opened, perhaps nothing is provided—the children are not sent, and perhaps may never be sent. It may be urged, this is the parent's fault, and that more perhaps has been spent on *spirits* in the course of a few weeks, (by many) than what the demand amounts to. —But should even this be allowed—it is quite inconsistent with the principle of the Lancastrian system to visit the sins of the parents upon their children—why punish the innocent for the guilty?

There are a great many among those visitors who have lately arrived amongst us, who, in whatever circumstances they may have been in their own country, are perhaps, not now in a situation to send their children, with *four dollars* each in their hand, to pay for an yearly "Ticket of admission to the school." —They will, therefore, be allowed to remain idle at home, and instead of becoming a blessing to the Province, are in danger of being its greatest curse.

Need for Higher Education

Acadian Recorder, Halifax, January 24, 1818.

To the Editor of the Recorder,
Sir,—

. . . The infant state of this country, has hitherto rendered an extensive attention to the business of education impracticable: men struggling for food, have little time to spend upon the pursuits of Literature. But there is a danger that the modes of thinking and habits, which arise out of such a state of society, may remain long after it is past; and imperceptibly enfeeble the community, amidst increasing means of energy. . . .

The rapidity of our improvement has been rarely equalled in a new country. Multitudes, by honest industry, have secured the comforts of life; and not a few can indulge themselves with its costly luxuries. Many conceive that they belong to what is termed polished society: yet, the degree of intelligence to be derived from a Grammar School, is all that the public system of education can communicate to the great body of inhabitants of this Province; and, with this preparation, many of them must enter into public offices, in which enlarged intelligence alone, will secure the general prosperity.

These remarks upon the present state of literature in the Province, ought, however, to be connected with a just tribute of praise to our Provincial Government. The Legislature has done much for the education of youth; and their general arrangement is evidently the result of enlightened policy. Nothing can be more important to the happiness of a country, and to the permanence of a good government, than the general diffusion of intelligence; and doubtless the aid which the Legislature has granted to the common schools of the Province, will be productive of excellent effects. . . .

But . . . it may be very easily shown, that this Province is really in great need of an open and general seminary for the higher branches of education. The learned professions are few; and comparatively few turn their attentions to these employments. But no man of sense will say, that, if any person wish to be a lawyer, physician, or clergyman, it does not concern the community whether he has within his reach the necessary means of excellence. . . .

A review of the state of any of the learned professions in this Province, will show ample room for improvement; and, surely, our rapid amelioration in other respects, ought not to be combined with the neglect of those persons and offices which are essential to our prosperity, and to which all civilized nations most carefully attend. . . .

Yours, &c.

Investigator.

C. *Instruments of Cultural Improvement*

Freemasons in Liverpool

Public Archives of Canada, *Diary of Simeon Perkins, Liverpool, N.S.*, vol. I, p. 16.

Friday, Dec. 5th [1766],—. . . I sup with a number of Freemasons, at Eben Doggett's, who, with Gilbert Malcolm, and Jesse Dodge, were introduced to that fraternity. The Lodge was formed two weeks ago, at which John Doggett, Esq., Samuel Doggett, and Robert Slocombe, besides the above mentioned, were entered. It causes much conjecture among the people.

Influence of the Newspaper

Acadian Recorder, Halifax, January 19, 1822: Editorial Comment.

Newspapers in the present age exert a mighty influence on the opinions of mankind. This remark applies to an eminent degree to our own population. Many persons read nothing else, connected with politics, literature, speculative doctrines, and the actual business of the world. The opinions which are maintained in the provincial newspapers become their's so naturally, that they are as it were grafted on the provincial intellect—they adopt without resistance such views, as are urged with strength or plausibility—they enter with a keen relish into the reasoning on which these are maintained—till at length the doctrine and argument become their own, and they propagate both with the devotion and zeal of proselytes. In the mother country public libraries are frequent—men of leisure and education abound—and books of general literature are of easy access, and divide with newspapers the power of modifying public sentiment. But in Nova-Scotia there are many houses where a book of general information is rarely, if ever, opened. The reading of the family is divided between the bible and the newspaper: and it follows inevitably that as they derive their religious hopes and opinions from the one, they must depend mainly on the other for their knowledge of events; the conclusions drawn from these—presented ready to their acceptance; and in short for all the materials of thinking. If any be inclined to condemn this statement as overcharged we would refer him to the experience of the last three years; and he will there find a mighty revolution in the agriculture, in the hopes and sentiments of this province accomplished in that short period through the agency of one paper—and that one, the Recorder. No man can reasonably doubt the vast and perpetual influence, with which a newspaper in Nova-Scotia does operate on the minds of its inhabitants, if he will only contemplate for a few seconds this singular, indisputable fact. On other subjects, it is true, the influence of our weekly journals is less perceptible—but on all subjects it is alike active and efficacious.—This paper is read every week, within the province, by from twelve to fifteen thousand persons; two thirds of these have not the time or the inclination to think deeply and for themselves; and the doctrines which are inculcated thus incorporate themselves with public feeling and propagate with rapidity.   The editors of a popular newspaper are thus armed with great power, and take upon themselves a task of great responsibility.

Public Libraries

Acadian Recorder, Halifax, May 26, 1821: Editorial Comment.

A library has been recently established in one of our most active and respectable townships—that of Newport; and we publish to-day an account of its origin with more than ordinary pleasure.   There are already several institutions of the same kind in country places within the province—particularly at Truro, where there is one connected with a society, which is producing, we understand, a very sensible effect on the habits and opinions of the young. . . . We consider these libraries as a decisive and gratifying proof of that excellent spirit and temper which is now so active throughout Nova Scotia, and we trust that by the efforts of our leading characters they will soon become general.   We respectfully and warmly recommend it to them, as the most essential benefit they can bestow upon a young country.

Library in the Backwoods

Mrs. F. Beavan, *Sketches and Tales Illustrative of Life in the Backwoods of New Brunswick* (London, 1845), p. 129.

As winter was now approaching, how to pass its long evenings agreeably and rationally was a question which was agitated.   The dwellers of America are more enlightened now than in those old times when dancing and feasting were the sole amusements, so a library was instituted and formed by the same means as the church had been—a load of potatoes, or a barrel of buckwheat, being given by each party to purchase books with.   The selection of these, to suit all tastes, was a matter of some difficulty, the grave and serious declaiming against light reading, and regarding a novel as the climax of human wickedness.

Travelling Lecturers in New Brunswick

J. F. W. Johnston, *Notes on North America* (Edinburgh, 1851), vol. I, p. 58.

There are wandering teachers, who supply with knowledge the thirsty cultivators in the humblest villages.   Notices are stuck up in the inns, or are printed in the newspapers, such as two I met with to-day—"Mr. Humphreys intends to lecture in this village, during the current week, on electricity and the electric telegraph."—"Mr. Dow intends to lecture on physiology and anatomy during the present week; we hope our friends will give him full houses during his stay among them."

4. RELIGIOUS INSTITUTIONS AND RELIGIOUS MOVEMENTS

A. Establishment of the Church of England in Nova Scotia

Support of Religious Worship by the State

The Statutes ... of Nova Scotia from 1758 to 1804 (Halifax, 1805), pp. 64-6.

An ACT for the better observation and keeping of the Lord's
Day. (1761)

B E *it enacted by the Honorable the Commander in Chief, the Council, and Assembly*, in order that all persons may, on the Lord's Day, apply themselves to duties of religion and piety, both publickly and privately, no tradesman, warehouse keeper, shopkeeper, or other person whatsoever shall, for the future, open his, her, or their shop or warehouse; or either by himself or herself, or by his or her servant or servants, child or children, sell, expose or offer to sale, upon any bulk, stall, or shed, or send or carry out, any manner of goods or merchandize, on the Lord's Day or any part thereof: *Provided nevertheless*, that this Act shall not extend to prohibit any persons from selling or exposing to sale, milk and fresh fish, before the hour of nine of the clock in the morning, and after five of the clock in the afternoon on the said day.

II. *And be it further enacted*, That no person, whatsoever, for the future, shall do, or exercise any labour, work or business, of his or their ordinary callings, or other worldly labour, or suffer the same to be done, by his or their servant or servants, child or children, either by land or by water, (works of necessity and charity only excepted) or use, or suffer to be used any sport, game, play or pastime on the Lord's day or any part thereof; upon pain, that every person or persons so offending in any of the particulars beforementioned, upon conviction thereof upon the oath of one credible witness, before any one of His Majesty's Justices of the Peace of this province, or upon view of any Justice of the Peace, for every such offence shall forfeit and pay the sum of ten shillings,

III. *And be it further enacted*, That no tavern keeper, retailer of spirituous liquors, vintner, or other person keeping a public house of entertainment within this province, shall, for the future, on any pretence whatsoever, entertain or suffer any of the inhabitants or town dwellers of Halifax, or any of the towns respectively where such tavern keepers, retailers of spirituous liquors, vintners, or other persons keeping public houses of entertainment, respectively dwell, or others, not being strangers or lodgers in such houses, or such as come thither for necessary dieting and victualling only, to abide or remain in their dwelling houses, out-houses or yards, drinking or idly spending their time on the Lord's Day; but shall keep their doors shut during the time of divine service, on penalty of forfeiting and paying the sum of ten shillings, for every person and persons respectively so found drinking or abiding in such public houses or dependencies thereof as aforesaid; and every such person or persons, who shall be found so drinking or abiding in any such public house or dependencies thereof as aforesaid, shall respectively forfeit and pay the sum of five shillings.

IV. *And be it further enacted*, That the church wardens and the constables, or any one or more of them, shall once in the forenoon, and once in the afternoon, in the time of divine service, walk through the town to observe and suppress all disorders, and apprehend all offenders whatsoever contrary to the true intent and meaning of this act: And they are hereby authorized and impowered to enter into any public house of entertainment, to search for any such offenders, and in case they are denied entrance, they are hereby impowered to break open, or cause to be broke open, any of the doors of the said house, and enter therein; and all persons whatsoever are strictly required and commanded to be aiding and assisting to any constables or other officers in their execution of this act, on the penalty of ten shillings current money for every neglect.

V. *And be it further enacted*, That if any person or persons whatsoever, being of the age of twelve years or upwards, being able of body, and not otherwise necessarily prevented by real sickness, or other unavoidable necessity, shall for the space of three months together, absent himself or herself from the public worship on the Lord's Day, shall be subject to a fine, that is to say, for every head of a family ten shillings, and for every child or servant five shillings, to be recovered, upon complaint, before any one of his Majesty's Justices of the peace, who is hereby impowered to cause the same to be levied.

Efforts to Capture Support of Dissenters

Public Archives of Canada, *N.S.A.*, vol. LXIV, pp. 208-9.

At a General Meeting of the Society for the Propagation of the Gospel in Foreign Parts

Held on the 15th day of August 1760. . . .

It was reported from the Committee, that they had read the following Letters to them referr'd viz.

A Letter from the Rev'd Mr. Breynton one of the Society's Missionaries in Nova Scotia dated Halifax June the 24th 1760, acquainting, that Governor Laurence had by that opportunity wrote to the Secretary of the Board of Trade, requesting, that application may be made to the Society for an Itinerant Missionary in that Province, there being at this time eight or ten Townships in that Colony, and all unprovided with Ministers of the Gospel of any Denomination: and pious and prudent Clergymen settled at the Governor's discretion at this time among them would go a great way to unite them in Religious opinions, and reconcile those who dissent from our Doctrines and Liturgy.

Official Support of the Church

(i)

Public Archives of Canada, *N.S.A.*, vol. LXXXIII, pp. 15-16: Halifax, July 11, 1768, Franklin to Secretary of State.

I think it my Duty to represent to your Lordship, that the Providing the Settlement, in their Infancy with Clergymen of the Church of England, is a measure that will be attended with many, and great good consequences— as the Settlers are generally of various Persuasions, some of whom are replete with Republickan Principles, and unless Government place proper Clergymen among them before they are able to support Teachers of their own, it will be difficult to Inculcate proper sentiments of Subordination to Government.

(ii)

Public Archives of Canada, *N.S.A.*, vol. LXXXIX, p. 99: Halifax, October 23, 1773, Legge to Secretary of State.

It is to be proposed to the Society [for the Propagation of the Gospel], by the Corresponding Members here, that a Missionary be provided who shall be itinerant to the Scattered Settlements, already, not only unprovided with any Person duly Qualified, but, open to the imposition of any Assuming, ignorant Wanderer, who shall come from any part of this Continent; with no other view than to gain a livelihood, which from the want of any good quality, he cannot obtain in any other manner.

The Church and Governing Classes

Public Archives of Canada, *S.P.G.*, *Nova Scotia*, *B 25*, 1760-1786: Halifax, October 23, 1767, Rev. J. Breynton to Secretary, S.P.G.

The principal officers of Government are members of the Church of England: Lord William Campbell has upon all occasions encouraged and supported the established Church.   Nor has Lieutenant Governor Franklin omitted any opportunity of shewing his zeal in the same cause.   Mr. Chief Justice Belcher is and always has been indefatigable, and Mr. Secretary Bulkely is our Constant Friend; by this joint Influence and Assiduity a Law has lately passed in Favor of St. Paul's Halifax and all other Parishes that may be hereafter settled.

Absentee Clergymen

Public Archives of Canada, *The Correspondence of Bishop Inglis:* To Archbishop of Canterbury, December 26, 1787.

The congregation of Halifax has considerably declined of late.   The causes which are assigned for this are—two popular preachers in town, one a Roman Catholic, the other a Presbyterian, each of which has had a

place of worship built; besides a Methodist meeting house lately erected—
the neglect of building another church about the year 1783, when a large
accession of church people came to Halifax.   Mr. Weeks, whom Dr. Breynton
left as his curate, though much liked as a man, is disliked as a preacher.
I have been repeatedly assured that if I had not come over in autumn,
half the remaining church people would have joined other communions. . . .
Certain it is that the Church here is in a disagreeable situation.   Mr.
Breynton is in England, and yet receives £100 from the Government and
the Society, as Missionary for Halifax, and upward of £100 a year from the
pew rents here, as Rector, according to my information.   Such I am assured
is his contract with the Vestry.   This cannot remain long so; and as it is a
point in which I do not wish to interfere, I must request that your Grace
would be pleased to admonish Dr. Breynton how improper it is that matters
should be in this state.   It is here understood that he means not to return.

Character of Clergymen

Public Archives of Canada, *The Correspondence of Bishop Inglis:*
To Archbishop of Canterbury, December 18, 1788.

In this province the Society now have *eleven* missionaries.   Of these,
four are diligent, useful clergymen—*three* are indifferent, neither doing
much good or harm, and as for the remaining *four*, it would be happy for
the Church, if they were not in their orders.   I mention no names, because
no injury is intended, and they have all shewed a proper attention to me.
The evil is the more to be lamented, as it scarcely admits of a remedy, but
from the slow hand of time.

This will account for the earnestness with which I entreated your Grace
in my last to prevent any Missionaries from being sent over, who are not
well known to the Society, and *known to be fit for the office*.   In this country
the address, persuasion, exemplary conduct and exertions of the clergy must
affect what in Europe is done through habit, usage and by virtue of established laws and supply their place.   Judge then what must be the condition
of religion in a congregation where the clergyman possesses none of those
qualities!   Yet the useless missionary, however unqualified, is as expensive
to the Society as the most diligent and best qualified; and although he
retards, instead of forwarding the growth of religion, yet he enjoys his portion
of the bounty which was given for propagating the Gospel. . . .

Were this Diocese once supplied with a set of respectable, active Clergymen, we should have few Dissenters in a little time.

Type of Clergyman Required

Public Archives of Canada, *The Correspondence of Bishop Inglis:*
To Archbishop of Canterbury, November 20, 1788.

I take the liberty to inform your Grace—that in this country more than
in any other, the support of religion and growth of the Church depend on
the personal qualities of the Clergy—that in Halifax, the capital of this

province, the rector will be connected with all descriptions of people from the highest to the lowest, strangers that resort here in great numbers, and therefore he should be affable, prudent, good tempered, and able to support the dignity of his office. He should have a good strong commanding voice, without which, and an exemplary pious life, the most shining talents would be lost. The Presbyterians have a popular preacher here. The Methodists have collected here their best speakers. We should also have a good preacher and an able man, to counteract the popularity of the former. . . .

As so much depends on the qualities of the Clergy here, I do most earnestly beseech your Grace to interpose for preventing any missionaries being sent out who are not *well known* to the Society, and *known to be fit for the office*. Your Grace would not be surprised at this earnest request, were you acquainted with all that has come to my knowledge to say nothing of foreigners, and others who were settled here before my appointment, some have been lately sent to Canada, who, I fear, will not much advance the interest of religion.

Incapacity of Clergymen from England

W. S. Moorsom, *Letters from Nova Scotia* (London, 1830), pp. 134-6.

In this country, the personal qualities of the minister have far greater effect upon the number and improvement of his congregation than is the case at home. A people accustomed from infancy to think for themselves, revelling in the freedom of moral and physical independence, and treating as old women's fables that host of reverential ideas, derived originally from the East, which in Europe compose a panoply to cover many a defect, political as well as ecclesiastical,—are not to be played with like children of a weaker age. How absurd, then, is the notion, that a lower standard of attainment may be marked for the Nova-Scotian missionary than for the English curate! A mind the most superior is, on the contrary, demanded; a mind endowed with sagacity to seize the peculiar points of a new people, and alike divested of clerical bigotry, and of the limited ideas incidental to a mere professional education. Yet we have found those whose qualifications do not admit of their entering into orders in England, receiving an episcopal benediction for this province: and again, we find the few who have regularly passed through the University courses, bringing with them, and maintaining, ideas, demeanour, and habits, but little calculated to conciliate their parishioners in this country. I repeat once more, brilliant exceptions exist among the latter; but how rare!— What is the effect produced by the repeated action of these events? Not merely that a congregation, in place of receiving its doctrine from a most legitimately constituted son of St. Peter, takes a fancy to receive the same (or one founded on the same broad basis) from the un-episcopal lips of Mr. So-and-So; but that a discredit is thrown upon religion; that the highway to immorality is opened still wider, and that the infinite blessings imparted by the revelation of the Most High, are perverted or treated with disregard. Among other facts to be deplored, I have witnessed one most flourishing district [Amherst, in county Cumberland]. . . . containing some thousand souls, provided with an excellent church, to the erection of which the then parishioners mainly contributed, and which, for some time past, has been left without an established minister. Why? "All the inhabitants are Dissenters." Is this the cause or the effect?—I am inclined to believe, the latter.

Falling off of Members

Public Archives of Canada, *S.P.G.*, *Nova Scotia*, B *25*, 1760-1786:
Lunenburg, November 28, 1771, Peter de la Roche to Secretary, S.P.G.

I am sorry to be obliged to say, that I have found the Church of England in a most deplorable situation here. Her followers are in general bound to her by no other ties than pecuniary interest. They are not obliged to defray the charges of keeping ministers, or to contribute in the least to necessary parochial expenses; and that consideration only supports their attachment to the Church of England: Time must strengthen it; and graft nobler motives on their self-interested hearts. I apprehend you have heard of the Separation of great numbers among the Germans from the Church: They have created two meeting houses; one for the Calvinists, the other for the Lutherans. The first have got a Minister ordained about a twelve month ago for that purpose at Halifax: he is a Hollander, was a mean artificer (a wool-comber) and being very illiterate has no other means for getting a reputation among his hearers than launching out upon the dangerous questions of Predestination, Newlight, etc. The Lutherans have no regular minister, and whether they will be able to get one at least is uncertain: meanwhile some among them take upon themselves to officiate and to preach. This behaviour howsoever illegal, is prudently winked at: the least attempt at putting a stop to their proceedings would be looked upon and cried up by them, as downright persecution. . . .
I apprehend that the old people who do not understand English and care not to learn the language, will never be reclaimed; unless they fall out among themselves, and grow dissatisfied with either their pastors or the heavy expenses their separation has involved them into. All our hopes must be in the rising generation, which is very numerous, and has been very much neglected. It is enough to make the heart bleed to see how ignorant, how idle and how wicked the young people are in this settlement.

Indifference to Church

Public Archives of Canada, *The Correspondence of Bishop Inglis:*
To Archbishop of Canterbury, March 1, 1788.

My residence here for four months, has enabled me to take a somewhat nearer and more accurate view of characters, and the state of things in this province, and to speak candidly, although I am far from being discouraged, the knowledge I have hereby gained, does not much tend to brighten my prospect, or flatter my hopes.   I find a general and deplorable lukewarmness prevailing—a strong attachment to former usages, however wrong; and that those who are most indifferent about the practice of religion, are the readiest to obstruct my measures for promoting it.

Rival Religious Sects

Public Archives of Canada, *S.P.G.*, *Nova Scotia*, B *25*, 1760-1786:
Windsor, September 14, 1776, W. Ellis to Secretary, S.P.G.

On my arrival [a year ago] I found the lower orders of the people, nearly to a man, Presbyterians or Fanatics, many of the better sort indifferent to all Religions, and a few Gentlemen's familys well affected to the church. The too extensive duty of my predecessor, had been in part the cause that things were not in a better condition, for the people living scattered up and down, and many of them, most of them indeed at a great distance from the church, they would not come at the hazard of not finding Divine Service, which must be often the case when the Minister was at the distance of Cornwallis, they therefore grew indifferent, or else indulged their own whims. . . . What we call the church here, was built by general subscription of the Township, some say for a Schoolhouse, others for a court house, but be that as it may, at present it serves for a church, Dissenting house, School house, Court house, and occasionally for a tipling house, on which occasion, the most indecent scenes, as I am informed, are acted in it; there was no Clerk, hardly anybody would take the trouble to make a response, indeed upon the whole, I believe Almighty God was never elsewhere worshipped, in so mean and slovenly a manner. . . .

In Falmouth and Newport fanaticism has taken strong hold of the inhabitants.   Labourers and mechanics turn preachers, and are much encouraged; many of our Magistrates, being themselves no better, to the reproach of Government, are their greatest favourers. . . . I am not for severe measures, being aware of the consequences, but discreet Magistrates might check this spirit without any appearance of persecution; the fanaticism of this country will never produce Heroes, like Barebones and his fellows, it is sly and selfish, and a piece of that levelling principle which pervades this whole Continent, as they are impatient of superiority in rank and condition, so they are offended that men should be sent on purpose to instruct them, who are all wise and learned in their own opinion.

Weakness of Church in Prince Edward Island

Walter Johnstone, *Travels in Prince Edward Island in the Years 1820-21*
(Edinburgh, 1823), p. 110.

When the Island was taken by the British, they designated it an Episcopal Settlement, regardless of where the people might emigrate from, or what profession they might be of who settled upon it.   The island was divided into counties, lots, and parishes, by government surveyors.   And one hundred acres of land in each parish was set apart for the clergyman, and fifty or sixty for a schoolmaster. But these lands are all lying unoccupied everywhere. And, however convenient they might be for accommodating a minister of the people's own choosing, if they do not belong to the Episcopal Church, they must not set a foot upon them nor put an axe into them. But so careless has the Church of England been to propagate even her own faith there, that, except the garrison chaplain, Mr. Desbrisay, no other clergyman has been sent till about three years ago. Indeed, I may affirm, that the Episcopal has succeeded the worst of any form of church order adopted upon the Island. Those who might be expected to be its warmest friends and supporters, I mean emigrants from England, are some of its worst enemies.

Weakness of Church in New Brunswick

J. F. W. Johnston, *Notes on North America* (Edinburgh, 1851), vol. II, p. 58.

The Church of England claims to be established in the colonies; but it has in reality no power, no peculiar influence, and no funds. It has, in fact, in these colonies less hold upon the people than either Presbyterians, Baptists, or Roman Catholics, because its clergy have hitherto been supported as missionaries, I believe, by the Propagation Society at home. Being independent of the people in pecuniary matters, they have not cultivated them as the other sects have; and till they are disengaged from home dependence, and are thrown upon the liberality of their own people, will not compete on equal terms with the rival denominations.

B. *The Evangelical Awakening*

Religious Inheritance of New England Settlers

John Robinson and Thomas Rispin, *A Journey through Nova Scotia* (York, 1774), pp. 34-5.

The Sabbath is most religiously observed; none of them will do any business, or travel on that day; and all kinds of sports, plays and revels are strictly prohibited. They take great care to educate their children in the fear of the Lord, and early to implant in them a right notion of religion, and the great duty they owe to God and their parents.

Beginnings of Newlight Church

Life and Journal of the Rev. Henry Alline (Boston, 1806), pp. 48-9, 67.

I rode with some of my Christian friends to Newport, in order to gather a visible church, to walk in the order of the Gospel; which had been some months in agitation. I was chosen to draw the articles, with the assistance of some brethren. Some articles were drawn, and the next day signed by some brethren. I preached a sermon, and the Lord seemed to own us. The reason that we called for no assistance from other churches was, because we did not think the churches in those parts were churches of Christ, but had only a dry form without religion.   The Church was gathered both of Baptists and Congregationals; for we did not think that such small non-essentials, as different opinions about water Baptism, were sufficient to break any fellowship, and to obstruct building together among the true citizens of Zion: and the Lord owned and answered us by increasing the gifts, graces and the numbers of the small, feeble band.   But the powers of darkness and church of antichrist rose against it from every quarter, both in public and private.

We then returned to Falmouth, where I remained preaching every Sabbath until the 27th of October, when we went over to Newport again, and set apart by ordination two elders: this was done without any assistance from any other church; and these elders came forward to lead the church, as far as their gifts and graces extended. . . .

Being requested, I attended now [October or November, 1778] a meeting of some of the Baptists in Horton, to advise about gathering a church there. O may the time come when Ephraim shall no more vex Judah, nor Judah envy Ephraim, and that there might never more be any disputes about such non-essentials, as water Baptism; the sprinkling of infants, or baptising of adults by immersion; but everyone enjoy liberty of conscience.   They gathered in church order, and made choice of one N. Peirson, (who was not endowed with a great gift in the word) for their elder; intending to put him forward, until God gave them some better one, or brought him out more in the liberty of the gospel; after which he was ordained.

New Religious Frontiers

Life and Journal of the Rev. Henry Alline (Boston, 1806),
pp. 73, 98, 117-19, 123, 159.

The next day [April, 1779] I went to Mahagony [up the St. John River], and preached there on Saturday; and Sabbath-day morning a boat came for me to go to the town and preach there, which I did, and although it was a dark place and the King's garrison; yet I must acknowledge there appeared some movings of the spirit among them; especially among some of the soldiers.   But O the darkness of the place.   The greatest part of the people conducted as if they were to die like beasts.   I suppose there were upwards of 200 people there come to the years of maturity, and I saw no signs of any christian excepting one soldier. . . .

[December 1, 1780].   I preached and conversed with [the Christians in Falmouth], and then went to Halifax to commit a small piece of my writings to the press.   O the trials I went through there to see the darkness and death of that great throng of people, and no door to proclaim the gospel, as my soul longed to do it. . . .

[March 20, 1781].   I set out for Halifax. . . .

21st.   This was an unhappy day to me; for although I had success in getting a book from the press, yet not seeing an opportunity to preach the gospel, as I longed to do; and having no religious society (though I found

13

two or three christians there) almost made ready to sink.   O that I could always live with God in the world.

22nd.   I remained in the town till the evening.   O what a land of darkness it is.   Who could believe by the conduct of the crowd, when passing through the place, that they were bound for an eternity, each one having an immortal soul of more value than millions of worlds.   O how it grieved my soul, when there appeared no desire no room for the gospel. . . .

April 1st [1781].   This day I preached in Windsor, where I never preached before.   There appeared something of an hearing ear; but at the same time the devil was raging, and the great men of the place very much opposing.   I trust God intends to begin a work of grace in that town. . . .

29th [April].   This day I preached in Windsor, where the gospel has long been shut out, and where unconverted ministers traded.   The Lord blessed his word by me and there appeared an attention with hunger here and there.   One began to make enquiry about that, which is so much undervalued by the generality of mankind.   O that God would carry on a work here.

30th.   Although many of the great men oppose the gospel, and my preaching here; yet there appeared more and more doors opened for me to preach.   I spent some time this day with some inquiring minds, and found by the grace of God, a great freedom to proclaim the name of Jesus, and the power of religion against whatever opposition there might be.

May 1st.   This day I preached again at Windsor; and the Lord was pleased to bless my labours to some souls: and although the evening raged to that degree that I was threatened by some of the leading men of the government to be silenced, and put on board a man of war; yet the Lord was kind to me, and gave me boldness in his name; and more doors were opened to receive the gospel. . . .

July 9, 1782.   I went on board a schooner for the island of St. John's, and we had a quick passage.   I found there very dark people, and indeed, most of them openly profane.   I preached four or five times in the principal towns, where some seemed to begin to be fond of hearing these strange things, and others opposed and blasphemed.

Revival in Liverpool and Break-up of Congregational Church

Public Archives of Canada, *Diary of Simeon Perkins, Liverpool, N.S.*,
vol. I, pp. 390-463, vol. II, pp. 2-105.

Wednesday, Dec. 5th [1781] . . . Mr. Henry Alline, a Seperate Preacher, belonging to King's County, Came here with Mr. Arnold.   Dined with me. he tells me he is an Itennerent Preacher, Ordained by the Seperate Church, & has been Preaching at Yarmouth, Argyle, Barrington, & Came to-wards Night. . . .

Sunday, February 3d [1782] . . . Several People, not being well Satisfied with Mr. Cheever [Congregational minister], & Some in the Church, etc., Meet at Mr. Stephen Smith's, & Carry on Worship, by reading, praying, Singing, etc.   Mr. Cheever preaches Very Strenuously against Seperation,

& Seems extremely Out of Humour with the People on Account of the Religious Stir there Seems to be.   he is Concerned that the people are going out of the way, & Says we are like to be broken up, etc., etc.   A Religious Meeting held at my House in the Evening, a large Concourse of People, I believe near 150 Attended, which is till of Late, a Very Strange thing in this Place. Such a meeting having Scarcely been Known in the Place Since the Settlement of it, till Since Mr. Alline was here.   what the Event will be God only Knows, but to Appearances many people who have not been remarkable for Religion heretofore, are now under great Concern, and making the Grand inquiry, what they Shall do to be saved. . . .

Thursday, Jany. 30th [1783],—a Meeting and Some Consultation about Renewing or Coming into a New Covenant. Nathan Tupper, Esq., and Samuel Hunt, Esq., are against it.   Stephen Smith, and Benjamin Parker are Leaders for it.   there was a great deal Said in the Meeting House upon it, but Nothing Decisive.   Mr. Smith Said he was Determined, and Sundry Others Went to his House, where I heard that himself, Benjamin Parker, Isaac Dexter, & Ephraim Hunt, Signed it.   there was a Covenant read over in the Meeting House, whether it was that they Signed, or not, I cannot determine.   Mr. Allen [Alline] preached a Sermon. . . .

Thursday, March 13th . . . the members of the Church Meet to Consult what measures to take Concerning the Members that have withdrawn from the Standing Church, & entered into a New Covenant. . . . The Standing Church Objects to the meathod of theirt wihdrawing, & to Some Articles in the New Covenant, one in particular Concerning Baptism, Said to be Non-Essential. . . .

Wednesday, March 17, [1784],—St. Patrick's day.   The Proprietors of the Meeting House meet to Consult whether Mr. Furmage Shall Preach any more, & whether the Seperate party Shall Come into the Meeting House . . . we then began Some discourse about the Seperate Party coming into the House.   my Self, for one Declared I would not agree that Mr. Alline, or any of his Adherants, Should ever Carry on the Publick Worship of the Place in that House, & gave my reasons for it, viz:—that Mr. Alline had denied the Fundamental Articles of the Christian Religion, and after some Altercation, we agreed to Adjorn the meeting to Next Tuesday. . . .

Friday, Jany. 7th [1785],—The Seperate Party begin to Cut Timber for Building a Meeting House, which they have determined to proceed upon, as I understand, Since the Congregation has refused to Receive them into the Meeting House, on their Terms, which Terms are that they Shall have the whole Rule.

Nature of the Newlight Movement

Public Archives of Canada, *The Correspondence of Bishop Inglis:*
To Secretary, S.P.G., August 16, 1799.

You have frequently heard of a sect in this Province called New Lights. They consist chiefly of people from New England, who emigrated to this country on the expulsion of the French neutrals; and the descendants of

those emigrants.   Their religion, as far as I can learn, is a strange jumble
of Independency and Bohemenism.   They always had a strong tincture of
enthusiasm; but this spirit greatly increased lately, and broke out with the
utmost violence.   Instantaneous conversion accompanied by strong bodily
agitations, divine and immediate inspiration and even prophecy, with the
impeccability of those who are once converted are among their favourite
doctrines and pretensions.   Formerly they were Paedobaptists; but they
have adopted the Anabaptist scheme, by which their numbers were increased
and their zeal inflamed.   They are all, without exception, very ignorant;
and their late self appointed teachers, whose number has much increased,
are among the most ignorant of the whole; consisting mostly of common
labourers and mechanics who are too lazy to work.   These people have been
very troublesome to the clergy; particularly in Granville, Annapolis and
Wilmot, where the Society's Missionaries have very laudably exerted themselves to check this enthusiastic and dangerous spirit—dangerous to all
rational and sober religion, and to the welfare of Society, for the New Lights
are, almost to a man, violent Republicans and Democrats. . . . A few church
people were at first drawn away.

A Revivalist Meeting in New Brunswick

P. Campbell, *Travels in the Interior Inhabited Parts of North America in the Years
    1791 and 1792* (Toronto, The Champlain Society, 1937), pp. 255-6.

I set out from Frederick Town on foot; and walking through Maugerville
along the river side, I fell in with a gentleman travelling the same way.   As
we were conversing along, I heard a great noise in a house at some distance,
on which I stopped to listen, and told the gentleman that there were some
people fighting in that house; at which he smiled and answered, "That he
knew the place well; that it was a house of worship, where a number of
religious fanatics assembled at all hours of the night and day; that no body
preached, every one prayed for himself, and the louder they roared, the more
sincere and devout they were supposed to be; so that the one vied with the
other who should bawl out loudest."   When we had come nearer, I was struck
with amazement at the hideous noise they made, and which could be heard
at a considerable distance; I asked him if he supposed they would permit me
to go in to see them; he said I might, provided I behaved properly, and did
not laugh, or offer to ridicule them in any shape; that they would not prevent
me, or give me the least trouble; thus encouraged, I went in, and found they
consisted of about three score persons, of both sexes, all on their knees, and
in tears, every one praying for himself, as already said, and bawling out, O
Lord! O Lord! which were the only expressions I understood of what they
said.   After standing for a few minutes in the house, my hair almost standing
on end at the horror of the scene these miserable people exhibited, I returned,
and just as I was passing the window of their apartment, some one called out,

that the devil was among them; upon which they all gave a yell, louder and more horrible than any Indian war hoop I had ever heard; and if the devil himself was to show his physiognomy in all the frightful grimaces ascribed to him in the middle of them, every door bolted, so that none possibly could escape his clutches, their screaming could not have been louder or more horrible.   I returned to the road with deep impressions of the deplorable effects of fanaticism on the human mind, where it gets a hold, and found the gentleman there waiting for me, and proceeded on my journey, and arrived in a few days at the city of St. Johns.

Ignorance of Self-Appointed Prophets

Acadian Recorder, Halifax, March 17, 1821.

MESSRS. HOLLAND & CO.
   . . . Many strange and surprising scenes take place among dissenters which cannot but excite the aversion and awaken the contempt of well educated men in the National Church.   The precincts of learning are daily invaded by the intrusions of ignorance; and the sacred functions of the Christian priesthood are usurped by self-appointed prophets, of the lowest intellectual form.   It has been said that in England it requires three things to make a new party in religion, "a cat, an old wife, and a minister".   But in this country the aid of a minister is not necessary.   It is the easiest thing in nature to put a new sect in motion.   A man with a leather apron will preach the gospel with as much popularity as the Bishop of Canterbury— If he would come from the gates of Egypt, or spring out of the foam of the sea, he would have for a season, a numerous and attentive auditory.   No wonder that the risible faculties of churchmen are awakened when they see a black-smith leaving his forge and bellows to blow the flame of party zeal; a cobbler leaving his stall to teach the mysteries of religion; and a knight of the thimble springing from the shop board to the pulpit, and preaching with as much popularity as if he had fallen down from Jupiter.   Such preachers are often a disgrace to the cause of dissent, and even to christianity itself.   Like Jonah's gourd in scripture, they often start up in a night; and it would be well for the repose of the community if they would disappear equally sudden. Some of them are bred in this province, and many of them are imported from Passmaquoddy along with contraband goods.   The evil is so alarming that all parties now complain of it.   The Presbyterians about Pictou, are united in a body, and have resisted the onset; but in less compact societies they have done a world of mischief.   Some baptist congregations have been scattered like feathers in the wind.   These gospel rangers cannot exist: but in a troubled state of society they rejoice in exciting confusion and in spreading disorder. Every intelligent dissenter will lament that such evils should exist.   A refor-mation in morals and manners cannot be effected by such instruments. . . .

(Not signed)

Missionary Work of Presbyterians

Acadian Recorder, Halifax, July 24, 1819.

PRESBYTERIAN CHURCH

The Synod of the Presbyterian Church of Nova-Scotia, met at Truro, June 29th. . . .

The Rev. Robert Blackwood, and Mr. John Sprott, Preachers of the Gospel, were appointed on a Mission to the Western part of the Province; the Rev. John Laidlaw and Robert Douglas, on a Mission to the Northern part of it, on the Gulf of St. Lawrence; and the Rev. Alexander Lewis, on a Mission to the country Eastward from St. Mary's. They were instructed, to go forth in the real spirit of Christian Missionaries, Preaching the Gospel peaceably to all who might be disposed to listen to them, and dispensing such other ordinances as prudence might warrant and circumstances require. They were charged to seek out the Presbyterians, in particular, who live in the districts which they should visit, and others also who stand in need of instruction; to mingle freely with Christians of every denomination and to Preach the Gospel, freely as from the lips of Jesus Christ, without money and without price.

Advantages of Locally Trained Ministry

Acadian Recorder, Halifax, August 18, 1821.

COMMUNICATION

A few Scottish Presbyterians at Shelburne have transmitted the sum of five pounds to the Pictou Academy, to purchase books for the use of students. This sum comes from a settlement where money has long ceased to be plentiful and of late has almost disappeared, but it seems that a good cause still finds in it money and friends. . . . They take a deep interest in the fortunes of this seminary and regard its divinity students as the rising hopes of the Presbyterian church in Nova Scotia.— This is the best and most legitimate source from which she is to be supplied with future Missionaries who would unite to other essential qualifications a more intimate knowledge of the dispositions and manners of the people.

It is confidently expected that young men of this description will form a more zealous and efficient body of preachers than ministers who are educated in the Mother Country, and who often cross the Atlantic in the decline of life, of settled habits, of unbending dispositions soured with the misfortunes of the old world, not aware of the difficulties to be encountered in the new; and ignorant of the best measures to be employed for enlightening the natives of the western wilderness. A young country thinly settled and consisting of people from different nations, of all creeds, and castes in religion, requires a particular class of ministers and a system of means and measures adapted to its circumstances and wants. Many ministers could do the duty of a parish kirk or a dissenting meeting house, or act as a chaplain in a particular station who would never make successful ministers in Nova Scotia. It is not every man that possesses that daring spirit of adventure, easy accommodation of manners suited to all varieties of character, and unconquerable patience and perseverance which are necessary to build up and enlarge the church of the Redeemer in this part of the world. Without the aid of native preachers our religion will make but little progress in this country. The European and native mind seem to be cast in different moulds,—the European sometimes finds it difficult to argue with the native, and he cannot fully enter into those misconceptions and prejudices which obstruct the reception of the truth. The native preacher is best acquainted with the habits and dispositions of his hearers, knows the avenues which lead directly to the heart, and may be supposed to make the deepest impression on their minds. But we cannot have native preachers without the means of intelligence. . . .

Evangelical Churches in Prince Edward Island

W. Johnstone, *Travels in Prince Edward Island in the Years 1820-21* (Edinburgh, 1823), pp. 115-16.

The Methodists maintain two regular preachers there [Prince Edward Island]. . . . They have so many excellent local preachers, that they seldom want sermon in all their regular places of worship; and it must be acknowledged that wherever the Methodists abound, vice and immorality is made to a great measure to hide their head, and every man and woman is taught to pray. The members of their churches are mostly from England, or the island of Guernsey, and their regular preachers have part of their support from home.

It only remains upon this subject that I take a little more notice of the Baptists. It has been observed already that they are the offspring of Mr. Haldane's connection in Scotland, and consequently have followed his views of church order and ordinances. There are eight different stations where they hold regular meetings for worship on the sabbath; and I was told there was about one hundred members in full communion altogether. At every one of these stations the life of religion is kept up.

A Methodist Revival in New Brunswick

Joshua Marsden, *The Narrative of a Mission, to Nova Scotia, New Brunswick, and the Somers Islands* (London, 1827, 2nd ed.), pp. 204-14.

During this fall [of 1806] my mind was deeply pained at the little prosperity attending the mission in New Brunswick, which being as it were, my own field, I felt a livelier interest in its welfare than if the labours had been divided among several. . . . I had been three years in the province without accomplishing any extensive good; though I ought not to omit, that a few had been brought to God. . . .

I requested several of my brethren to unite with me, in setting apart a day of fasting and prayer, that we might humble ourselves before God, and afflict our souls. We met in the chapel, to pour out our souls in intercessions and supplication, and the Blessed God was with us of a truth; he gave us a token for good; this was late in the fall, and before winter set in, he redeemed the pledge, and succeeded our poor intercessions, by a blessed and abundant out-pouring of his Holy Spirit. . . . A little after my departure [to another part of the mission], they held a watch-night, which was attended with some unusual tokens of a quickening and reviving nature; several old professors were powerfully wrought upon, and a spirit of mighty prayer pervaded the society. The flame kindled at their meeting was not a temporary flash, it continued and extended, and several children of professors became deeply affected with a concern for salvation. A few young people who had been drawn to attend the chapel prior to my going, manifested a more than ordinary interest in the work, and now decided to cast in their lot with us. . . . I arrived to witness what lay near my heart, the prosperity of his work and to adopt such regulations as this new state of things demanded. The brethren flocked to my house to inform me what the Lord had been doing, for this was the Lord's doing, no one seemed to have been made more than another, an especial instrument . . . probably about twenty young persons had been affected, and these were chiefly the children of praying parents. Some buddings of enthusiasm had begun to appear in the infant work, but in such a state of excitement everything cannot be measured with rule and line. . . . Such a stir in religion, was quite a new thing in St. John; some wondered whereunto it would grow; others condemned the whole as enthusiasm and delusion. A few respectable persons in the congregation took great offence, and requested that I would put a stop to the dangerous wild-fire that was spreading in the society. . . . The things that appeared most out of the ordinary way, were praising God aloud, crying for mercy, children exhorting, several praying at the same time, and holding the meetings till twelve o'clock at night, nay, upon a few occasions, till two or three in the morning: although I generally dismissed them myself about ten o'clock. These, with several other things, equally strange and unusual, and hence, forbidding in the eyes of unawakened persons, created a great outcry; but after weighing all sides, and comparing what was going forward, with all I had read and heard of the work of God, I did not hesitate to give its leading features, my unqualified approbation and support, and saw it my duty with as little of show, and as much tenderness and prudence as possible, to check anything that might assume so much of extravagance, as to bring the whole into odium and contempt. . . .

It is a fact that can neither be denied, nor well accounted for, that revivals of religion are more common in America than in most other countries. Nor are these revivals, mere human feelings, or excitements of animal passion; they are attended with such striking features, as must convince every true Christian, that the finger of God is employed. In the course of this year, several distinct works of this kind broke out in different parts of the two provinces; all resembling each other in their leading features: first, an unusual excitement to, and concern for religion; second, deep distress on account of sin; third, a more sensible and divine influence attending the word when preached; fourth, a visible change in the conduct of those wrought upon; fifth, a sudden transition from distress of soul to comfort and peace; sixth, a rapid acquisition of knowledge in the plan of salvation; seventh, the sudden attainment of spiritual gifts for prayer and exhortation. . . .

The subjects of the work [in Saint John], as observed above, were chiefly young people of both sexes, with about ten children from eight to twelve years of age. These had been in the habit of attending the chapel, and were more or less connected with the members of the Society. In its more general influence, however, the revival was felt by most of the old members, who were much quickened and stirred up, and an increase of love, simplicity, and zeal, was visible among them.

. . . The children were much and unusually wrought upon, they prayed much for their parents and relations, and several of them stood up, and at the prayer-meetings, they exhorted others, to the admiration of all that heard them. . . . The spectators were deeply affected with the novelty and fervency of these juvenile preachers, and the revival became the topic of the whole place. Though in the depth of winter, the meetings were attended by greater numbers than the places in which we held them would contain; and though intensely cold, the meetings were continued till midnight, and frequently much later. Some who before the revival were low and lukewarm in their souls, became much engaged. An uncommon earnestness in prayer and supplication was poured out upon those who exercised in the meetings: and with regard to myself I had great and unusual enlargement in my public ministrations. . . .

In this revival, none of the rich and great received the truth. . . . In this revival, there was little of what may be termed wild-fire, or extravagance in expression, although numbers cried aloud for mercy, there was no clapping of hands, and shouting; some irregularities could not be altogether prevented, but these were very few. The whole town, which is not small, felt the influence; an air of morality pervaded it, and the profaneness of the streets was greatly diminished. A great and visible change had taken place in many persons, and this even the proud opposers of the work could not deny; yet they thought, or affected to think, it was all sham and pretence, and would vanish into smoke. . . . Old bickerings were done away, and much love and harmony prevailed in the society. Upon the whole, there have been few revivals of religion, attended with less irregularity, or with more of those plain and decided marks, which plainly indicate a genuine and scriptural work of God. One hundred new members were added to the society in the space of a month; which in a place containing only about three thousand inhabitants, is no inconsiderable proportion; most of these afforded pleasing evidence of a change of heart, by the outward reformation which took place in their lives; as prior to this revival, many of them were both utterly ignorant, and outwardly wicked.

Baptists in New Brunswick

Mrs. F. Beavan, *Sketches and Tales Illustrative of Life in the Backwoods of New Brunswick* (London, 1845), pp. 60-3.

The greater number of the native population [of New Brunswick], I think, are baptists, and their ministers are either raised among themselves, or come from the United States or Nova Scotia. Once in every year a general association is convened of the members of the Society throughout the province, the attendance on which gives ample proof of the greatness of their numbers, as well as their fervency of feeling. The association is held in a different part of the province each season and generally lasts a week. Reports are here made of the progress of their religion, the state of funds, and of all other matters connected with the society. There is, generally, at these conventions a revival of religious feeling, and during the last days numerous converts are made and received by baptism into the church. This meeting is looked forward to by the colonists with many mingled feelings. By the grave and good it is hailed as an event of sacred importance, and by the gay and thoughtless as a season of sight-seeing and dress-displaying. Those in whose neighbourhood it was last year are glad it is not to be so this time; and those near the place it is to be held, are calculating the sheep and poultry, the molasses and flour it will take to supply the numerous guests they expect on the occasion—open tables being kept at taverns, and private houses are so no longer, but hospitably receive all who come. No harvest is reaped by exorbitant charges for lodging, and all that is expected in return, is the same clever treatment when their turn comes. This convocation, occurring in the leisure spell between the end of planting and the commencement of haying, is consequently no hindrance to the agricultural part of the community; and old and young "off they come" from Miramichi, from Acadia, and the Oromocto, in shay and wagon, steam-boat and Catamaran, on horseback or on foot, as best they can. This day, one towards the conclusion, the large frame building was crowded to excess, and outside were gathered groups, as may be seen in some countries around the catholic chapels. Within, the long tiers of benches display as fair an array of fashion as would be seen in any similar congregation in any country. The days of going to meeting in home-spun and raw hide moccasins are vanishing fast all through the province. . . . This morning [of which she wrote] was the time of transacting business, and the present subject one which had occupied much attention. It was the appropriation of certain funds—whether they should be applied towards increasing their seminary, so as to fit it for the proper education of ministers for their church, or whether they should not be applied to some other purpose, and their priesthood be still allowed to spring uncultured from the mass. The different opinions expressed regarding this, finely developed the progress of mind throughout the land. Some white-headed fathers of the sect, old refugees, who had left the bounds of civilization before they had received any education, yet who had been gifted in the primitive days of the colony to lead souls from sin, sternly declaimed against the education system, declaring that grace, and grace alone, was what formed the teachers. All else was of the earth earthy, and had nought to do with heavenly things. One said that when he commenced preaching he could not read the bible—he could do little more now, and yet throughout the country many a soul owned its sickness to have been healed through him. Another then rose and answered him—a native of the province, and of his own persuasion, but who had drank from the springing fountains of science and of holiness. . . . He pleaded, as such should, for extended education, and his mighty words had power, and won the day.

III

THE TIMBER TRADE AND RURAL SOCIETY IN UPPER CANADA

WITH the settlement of Upper Canada in the early nineteenth century, there emerged the first distinctively agricultural frontier in British North America. The agricultural industry assumed considerable importance in New France and the Maritime colonies, but other interests—the fur trade, fisheries, or timber trade—constituted the main drive of economic exploitation, and it was not until expansionist forces had been spent that agriculture began to assert itself as a primary industry. In Upper Canada a similar dualism appeared in the frontier economy to the extent that agricultural settlement was related to the development of the timber trade in the Ottawa Valley, but the relationship was one which did not extend beyond the recruitment of settlers as such. Once settled in the country, the farm population was considerably removed from the area in which the timber industry was being developed and thereby was sheltered from its disturbing influence. The social problems of Upper Canada were almost entirely those of a purely agrarian frontier, and consequently were in striking contrast to those of New France or the Maritime colonies.

Although the opening up of the agricultural resources of Upper Canada really began in the early years of the nineteenth century, some colonization was under way considerably earlier. The conclusion of the American Revolution released a large body of people who had favoured the British cause, and those in the up-country turned to Canada as a field for settlement.[1] The Loyalist migration hastened the organization of the Province of Upper Canada and led to the adoption of a policy encouraging colonization. Simcoe's vigorous programme of road building had in view the closely related needs of defence and settlement, and these early efforts to open up the country did much to divert to the province a

[1]W.S. Wallace, *The United Empire Loyalists* (Toronto, 1914); E. A. Cruik-shank, ed., *The Settlement of the United Empire Loyalists on the Upper St. Lawrence and Bay of Quinte in 1784* (Toronto, 1934).

part of the great western migration of American peoples which set in after 1790 with the end of the Indian wars.[2]   American frontier farmers poured across the St. Lawrence and Niagara, to join the Loyalists about the Bay of Quinte and in the Niagara district and to extend settlement along the whole north shore of Lake Ontario. Scattered overseas colonization ventures, chiefly of Scottish High-landers, served to push settlement into less accessible areas within the province.[3]

This influx of population, however, was unrelated to the acti-vities of any dominant set of economic interests within the colony. A large part of it represented a spilling over of the American frontier movement of people.   The fur-trade merchants located in Montreal thought in terms of a commercial empire reaching into the North-West, and agricultural settlement played little part in the erection of such an empire; the problems of Upper Canadian pioneer farmers did not enter into the politics of the Beaver Club.[4] Promotion of agricultural settlement in Upper Canada by the state arose largely from the interest in the strategical military value of the area.   Transportation facilities were geared to the needs of defence rather than markets, and the limitations of economic self-sufficiency sharply restricted settlement.   So long as the population remained small and hugged the lake and river shores no considerable problem of markets arose.   The chief concern of the settlers before 1812 was that of clearing the land and establishing homes, and the simple wants of the household could be met by domestic manufacture or through the sale of the readily transportable com-modity of potash.   The pioneer economy of Upper Canada during this period, as distinguished from the frontier economy which developed after 1814, was one based upon self-sufficiency, and the independence gained therefrom enabled the colony to escape problems associated with the price system.

A similar self-sufficiency obtained very largely with respect to social and cultural needs.[5]   The farm communities of Upper

[2]M.L. Hansen, *The Mingling of Canadian and American Peoples*. Vol. I, *Historical* (New Haven and Toronto, 1940).

[3]Helen I. Cowan, *British Immigration to British North America, 1783-1837* (University of Toronto Studies, Toronto, 1928).

[4]D. G. Creighton, *The Commercial Empire of the St. Lawrence* (Toronto, 1937).

[5]E. C. Guillet, *Early Life in Upper Canada* (Toronto, 1933).

Canada before 1812 inherited the simple, primary social institutions of the American frontier. The Loyalist and American settlers, for the most part, were thoroughly adjusted to the conditions of pioneer life. That is not to say that they accepted a completely orderly and settled mode of life in their new homes. The frontier was the habitat of the impatient and restless, and its very character implied an emancipation from social controls and a reliance upon individual effort and will. The people found in Upper Canada before 1812 were a product of the frontier heritage. However, though many of their habits and ways of life appeared distasteful to cultured observers from overseas, the early pioneer farmers drawn from the American frontier possessed a resourcefulness which enabled them to surmount the difficulties which they faced. The apparent absence of problems of destitution and mental disease might be taken as indicative of the capacity of these settlers to adjust their habits to new needs. Personal disorganization resulting from the sudden emancipation from all social control was avoided by the flexibility of social organization. Pioneer social institutions were for the most part closely adapted to the simple needs and wants of the population. The family constituted the basic institution in the economy and social structure, while strict codes of honesty and morality rested upon the sanctions of the neighbourhood group, and forms of mutual assistance and relief provided for the wants arising from misfortune. Distinctions of social class found little recognition in the pioneer communities where the demands of neighbourhood association pressed so heavily upon the inhabitants. Even with respect to religion, there was no great failure to meet the needs of the population. Itinerant Methodist preachers, already familiar with the pathways leading into the American frontier communities, found their way across the St. Lawrence River to carry the message of the gospel to the Upper Canadian farmers.[6] Most of the Loyalist and American settlers were Methodists, and the highly centralized missionary organization built up by the Methodist Episcopal Church in the United States made possible a ready supply of clergy. Quakers, Moravians, and members of other religious sects who

[6]John Carroll, *Case and His Contemporaries*, 3 vols. (Toronto, 1867-77).

settled in Upper Canada carried with them the simple organizations of their faith.[7]

What colonization from overseas took place in Upper Canada before 1812 did not introduce to any considerable extent disturbing influences into the rural society. Most of the overseas colonists were Highland Scots, and, if they lacked the experience and resourcefulness of the American settlers, they inherited the traditional close group controls of the clan organization. Their tendency to settle together enabled them to resist many of the disorganizing effects of new social conditions. Adjustments of the individual came about with the support of the group, and too radical deviations from traditional *mores* were strictly checked. This group or clan authoritarianism was reinforced by the authoritarianism of the Catholic priest or Presbyterian minister. Though few clergy were available, the ecclesiastical system of government was preserved as part of the group organization. The inevitable conservatism of such leadership within the Scottish communities had the effect of arresting economic progress and cultural advancement, but during the early years of settlement the strain upon the individual in adjusting himself was considerably eased and any general breakdown of the social organization avoided.

Only in the small towns growing up along the shore of Lake Ontario did the simplicity of pioneer life give way to the greater complexity of a pecuniary civilization. Here the erection of gaols indicated the approach of problems of social welfare which were to bear more heavily upon the society in a later period. The tavern and retail store emerged as the chief centres of contact between the town and the country. The army, church, and, in the capital, governmental services introduced a hierarchy of social classes which became more pronounced as the towns grew in size. The establishment of schools indicated a growing concern for education, and emphasized more sharply still the distinction between this privileged group in the towns and the mass of pioneer farmers without.[8] The inhabitants of the towns tended to be attached to the Church of England, and the colonial government sought to

[7]A. G. Dorland, *A History of the Society of Friends in Canada* (Toronto, 1927).

[8]Adam Shortt, "Life of the Settler in Western Canada before the War of 1812," *Bulletin of the Departments of History and Political and Economic Science in Queen's University*, no. 12, July, 1914.

vest this church with the privileges of establishment.[9] The erection
of places of worship and parsonages in the chief centres of population indicated the church's anxiety to identify itself with official
and military interests in the province and provided something of
a forecast of its later incapacity to serve the rural communities.
For the most part, the towns exerted little influence beyond their
immediate surroundings. They were garrison centres of the
Empire in Upper Canada, and, if they provided the rural society
with little leadership, their contacts with the country were so few
that they introduced no disturbing influences.

The society of Upper Canada before the War of 1812, of course,
was far from stable, but the absence of serious problems of
social organization stands out in striking contrast to the later
period. In 1812, the population of Upper Canada was 33,000
after thirty years of settlement; in 1851 it had grown to 952,000.[10]
The contrast between the rate of increase of population in these two
periods provides in itself sufficient reason to consider the interval
1812-20 as the watershed between two sharply separated phases
of development. After the war, a set of forces were unloosed which
brought about far-reaching changes in the character of society in
Upper Canada.

If the war appeared to re-emphasize the strategic military
position of Upper Canada, the developments after asserted her
importance as an economic frontier within the British colonial
system. Restrictions upon alien land holdings which stopped up
the flow of American settlers coincided with a newly awakened
fear in Britain of over-population which gave rise to schemes for
encouraging emigration to the colonies.[11] The settlement of disbanded soldiers in strategically if not agriculturally favourable
areas of the province served the purpose of defence while at the
same time relieving the home exchequer. Government- and parish-
assisted emigration was undertaken to lessen the burden of poor-
rates and to strengthen the loyalty of the colonial population.
The real impetus to settlement, however, came from the development of the timber trade. The shift from a reliance upon furs to

[9]D.B. Read, *Life and Times of Sir John Simcoe* (Toronto, 1890).
[10]M.Q. Innis, *The Economic History of Canada* (Toronto, 1935).
[11]Norman Macdonald, *Canada, 1763-1841: Immigration and Settlement*
(London, 1939).

timber involved the transportation of a bulky rather than compact cargo to the British market and raised the problem of a return cargo. The desire of ship-owners to secure a profitable return load for their timber vessels resulted in unloosing upon Upper Canada a swelling tide of immigration.[12] The port of Quebec developed as the poor man's route to Upper Canada, and the large numbers coming in this way were sharply differentiated from the more fortunate arriving by way of New York. Cheap ocean rates and a more liberal policy of granting land made possible the unassisted movement of population to Upper Canada during the twenties and thirties.[13] Settlers pushed into the interior of the province, and backwoods communities separated by many miles from the lake shore came into being. The growth of settlement about Perth, Peterborough, in the heart of the western peninsula, and on Lake Huron marked the widening belt of population stretching across the province.[14]

Economic expansion and the rapid growth of population imposed heavy strains upon the pioneer social organization which had been established before 1812. The opening up of the Ottawa Valley gave rise to a society of unattached male workers who spent the winters in camp and the summers in floating timber down to the market in Quebec City.[15] But the disorganizing effects of this society were little felt by the rural frontier pushing westward into Upper Canada. The Precambrian Shield sharply separated the soft timber lands of the Ottawa Valley from the hard timber lands of the Great Lakes region, and those engaged in the timber industry were chiefly recruited in the cities of Montreal and Quebec from the surplus labour force of the mature French-Canadian farming community or, later, from the bodies of Irish immigrants. The timber trade, as a result, did not noticeably increase the mobility

---

[12]H. A. Innis, "An Introduction to the Economic History of Ontario from Outpost to Empire," *Papers and Records, Ontario Historical Society*, vol. XXX.

[13]Gilbert Patterson, *Land Settlement in Upper Canada, 1783-1840* (Sixteenth Report of Department of Archives for the Province of Ontario, 1920).

[14]A.R.M. Lower, "Immigration and Settlement in Canada, 1812-1820," *Canadian Historical Review*, March, 1922; C. Armstrong, "A Typical Example of Immigration into Upper Canada in 1819," *Papers and Records, Ontario Historical Society*, vol. XXV.

[15]A.R.M. Lower and H.A. Innis, *Settlement and the Forest and Mining Frontiers* (Toronto, 1936).

of the population of the frontier rural areas. It was a metropolitan industry, involving large capital outlays—the timber merchant— and a regular labour force which increasingly became differentiated from the rural population and came to constitute rather a part of an urban proletariat.

Problems of the rural frontier of Upper Canada derived largely from the character of colonists and of settlement in the period after 1814. The great bulk of overseas settlers came in as single individuals or families, and lacked the group supports enjoyed by the Highland Scots. Complete strangers to the conditions of pioneer life, their adjustments were slowly and painfully made. The large number of failures was evidence of the trials faced by the overseas settlers. The disbanded soldiers and commuted pensioners were the least able to adapt themselves to the demands of pioneer farm life, and contributed most heavily to the ranks of habitual drunkards and vagrants, but among the whole body of overseas colonists the incidence of failure was high. The considerable number of pauper immigrants added to the difficulties of social adjustment while it increased the strains upon the inadequate social services of the colony. The lack of agencies to provide assistance and advice to recently arrived immigrants shifted heavy burdens upon the local community; an absence of leadership in the location of settlement involved severe personal hardships when a reckless land policy made the individual selection of location an extremely hazardous undertaking. Though the local communities assumed extensive functions of relief and assistance, such agencies proved less effective when settlement tended to become dispersed and needy families were separated by considerable distances from neighbours. The accumulation of distressed persons in the small towns, the result of failure on the land or the lack of capital to begin farming, gave rise to a growing need for such agencies as houses of refuge, hospitals, and mental homes.[16] The establishment of a house of industry in Toronto was a recognition of the new demands pressing upon the social organization. For the most part, where indiscriminate charity failed to provide for the needs of the unfortunate classes, the gaols served as a means of removing them from the local communities.

The increasing mobility of population, and the growing numbers

[16]C.H. Clarke, *A History of the Toronto General Hospital* (Toronto, 1913).

of those drifting into the towns, added to the tasks of law enforcement authorities. The rural society as such produced no serious problem of crime.[17] The modest equipment of the pioneer farm homes offered little temptation to commit burglary, and the capital of the backwoodsman could not readily be removed or disposed of. Breaches of the criminal law, however, became more prevalent as the simplicity of early pioneer life tended to disappear. The presence in the country of ne'er-do-weels shipped out from respectable English middle-class homes, the influx of Irish workers and female domestics, and the construction of canals in various parts of the province introduced new disturbing influences in the society of Upper Canada which were reflected in the pressure upon gaol accommodation and in the establishment of a provincial penitentiary. The growing problem of classification of penal inmates, and the lack of institutions to care for juvenile offenders, were indicative of the increasing diversity in the character of crime and criminals.

The increasing strains upon social organization were more evident with respect to the primary and cultural institutions of the local pioneer communities. Though the family retained many important economic and social functions, it proved a far less effective social institution among the overseas colonists than among the early Loyalist and American settlers. The long frontier tradition in America had produced a type of family closely adapted to the needs of rural pioneer conditions. The overseas colonists did not share in this tradition, and the individual, accustomed to look outside for the satisfaction of many of those needs which in a pioneer society could be taken care of only within the family, found himself frustrated and dependent upon his own resources. The considerable nervous strain imposed upon overseas farm women in the country as a result of isolation, and the prevalence of drinking habits among the males, were indications of the failure of the family to satisfy such needs as that of companionship when other social supports were absent.[18] Though limitations of the family were not wholly responsible, the personal disorganization

[17]J.E. Jones, *Pioneer Crime and Punishments in Toronto and the Home District* (Toronto, 1924); J. H. Elliott, "Crime and Punishment in Early Upper Canada," *Papers and Records, Ontario Historical Society*, vol. XXVII.

[18]F. Landon, "The Common Man in the Era of the Rebellion in Upper Canada," *Report of the Canadian Historical Association*, 1937.

of so many overseas colonists revealed, at least in part, the failure of this primary institution to assume functions ordinarily performed in mature societies by secondary organizations.

If human companionship was the want most keenly felt by recent overseas settlers in Upper Canada, the lack of vigorous cultural leadership left marks more deeply impressed upon the rural communities. The poverty, hard work, and deadening routine of pioneer farming discouraged efforts to maintain social or cultural standards. Superior educational attainments, certainly, were of little advantage in wringing a livelihood from the soil, while the preservation of the refinements or impedimenta of "polite society" served only to divert much needed labour or capital from the farm. This ceaseless pressure of the pioneer economy involved sacrifices which in the end impoverished the cultural life of the community. A disregard for precautions with respect to health and physical welfare imposed eventually heavy costs upon both the individual and the society. If the neglect of such things as the teeth and eyesight of children transmitted physical handicaps to the new generation, the neglect of elementary principles of sanitation imperilled the health of whole communities. The pioneer began unable to afford the decencies of life; he often ended by losing an appreciation of their worth. This was true of educational institutions.[19] The isolation of farm homes, and the urgent requirements for farm labour, made school attendance difficult in the rural districts. Even where country schools were established, the teaching was so bad that little learning was imparted. The emphasis in the frontier upon economic exploitation discouraged entry into service occupations such as teaching, and the scattered teachers in Upper Canada were largely recruited from the ranks of those who had failed in other occupations. These obstacles to the establishment of an effective educational system were largely unavoidable in the early years of pioneer settlement, but they contributed to the growth of an attitude of indifference to education which provided little preparation to meet the more exacting demands of society when pioneer conditions had disappeared. The social costs of some of this negligence tended to be postponed, but the pioneer society did not escape certain immediate

[19]J.G. Hodgins, *Documentary History of Education in Upper Canada*, 2 vols. (Toronto, 1894).

effects. Observations made by British travellers in the country were coloured by their class bias, but they do suggest serious shortcomings in the cultural life of the communities of Upper Canada. The influence of the frontier upon a population unequipped to deal with its demands tended to a general lowering rather than raising of standards, and this tendency became more pronounced when standards became increasingly diversified.

The large overseas immigration introduced new ethnic and cultural distinctions between groups in the rural communities of Upper Canada. The lines forming to mark off the Loyalist from the American settlers, largely as a result of prejudices arising out of the War of 1812, were extended when the English colonists held themselves aloof from the Americans. The Scots, Irish, and other ethnic groups, in turn, tended to form cultural islands in the larger community.[20] This ethnic segregation weakened relationships of co-operation and mutual assistance in the pioneer society. On the other hand, to the extent that assimilation did occur, it tended to take the form of accepting American habits of thought without acquiring the Americans' pioneer way of life. The doctrine of equality went to the heads of the overseas immigrants, and they exerted their emancipation from traditional controls before they had fully learned the lessons from their new experiences. Assimilation, or Americanization, consequently, had something of a disorganizing effect in destroying the inherited culture of the overseas colonists before they had become a part of the pioneer culture.

The class distinctions among the overseas immigrants served even further to weaken the social organization of the rural communities of Upper Canada. The two ports of entry, Quebec and New York, symbolized the new social division which was transposed from the homeland to the Canadian backwoods. The attempt to maintain this division made more difficult the task of erecting new social controls in communities which could not afford the luxury of segregation. For the most part, the attempt ended eventually in failure. Only in a few instances, such as in that of the settlement north of Peterborough, were members of the socially superior class able to segregate themselves in some degree from the common folk, and then only at a price which was socially painful.

[20]W. H. Breithaupt, "First Settlements of Pennsylvania Mennonites in Upper Canada," *Papers and Records, Ontario Historical Society*, vol. XXIII.

Throughout rural Upper Canada class distinctions tended to disappear. Efforts to erect a colonial aristocracy through making large grants of land to favoured individuals failed to produce more than a class of speculators as greater profits could be made by dealing in, than by working, the land. Apart from a few isolated cases, such as Talbot and MacNab,[21] land-holders did not seek to secure social position by establishing themselves on large estates. The economic laws which discouraged the growth of a landed gentry operated equally effectively in reducing the farm class to a common social level. The capital, educational attainments, and refined tastes which some of the overseas colonists brought with them were little if any advantage in achieving success in agriculture, and distinctions arising out of inherited wealth disappeared when those who began with the least worldly goods often ended by acquiring the most. Furthermore, the frontier did not produce a labour group which became distinguished from the body of farm employers, and attempts to maintain traditional master-servant relationships soon had to be abandoned. The social demands of the pioneer society reinforced the economic demands, and select social circles disappeared in face of the need among neighbours for mutual help and sympathy. Only in the towns, where governmental and military officials, Anglican clergymen, and well-to-do merchants congregated, did there emerge anything approaching a socially superior class.

This disintegration of class distinctions served to release the expansionist forces of an agrarian frontier. Economic resources were not diverted into wasteful channels to support the vestiges of aristocracy; nor was the development of new techniques and methods of farming retarded by influences of tradition. Whatever course of action appeared to promise the greatest pecuniary returns was followed regardless of standards of respectability or social worth. But, while the economic gains from the disintegration of class distinctions were immediate and direct, some of the social gains were more remote and were offset by immediate cultural losses. Emancipation of the lower-class overseas immigrants from the obligations imposed upon them by the traditional class structure encouraged the display of vulgar pretensions of equality which

[21]Andrew Haydon, *Pioneer Sketches in the District of Bathurst* (Toronto, 1925); C. O. Ermatinger, *The Talbot Regime, 1791-1840* (St. Thomas, 1904).

had little relationship to pioneer standards of social worth. On the other hand, the loss by the socially superior class of their hereditary prerogatives discouraged the preservation of values of social leadership accepted within the traditional class structure. A disregard on the part of both classes for standards of respectability and social worth meant, to some extent at least, a disregard for standards of moral decency. Much of the cultural heritage of the overseas immigrants consisted of rules of conduct governing relationships between the privileged and unprivileged, and the breakdown of these relationships weakened considerably the *mores*. The effects were evident in a general lowering of standards, among the emancipated "gentry" as well as among the common folk. The latter lacked the cultural and moral leadership of a true social *élite*, the former felt no obligation to provide such leadership.

The sharp division between town and country meant that the leadership lacking in the rural communities was not supplied by the urban centres. Among a considerable section of the population of the towns the chief concern was that of securing political or military preferments, and those with more ambitious prospects sought gain from the speculation in land. The economic welfare of the farmers was of little consequence. Even the retail merchants, who apparently sought a livelihood by trade with the rural inhabitants, were often more interested in acquiring land in payment for debts than in building up a healthy cash business. The pecuniary and cultural interests of the town inhabitants divorced them from the rural communities. The political organization of the colony reinforced the exclusiveness of these groups and accentuated the isolation of the rural communities. The state was closely identified with urban interests in the colony, and responded slowly to the feelings and demands of the farm population. The irresponsibility of the executive, and the lack of popularly organized parties, deprived the common citizens of an avenue of political expression. The failure of the rural inhabitants to secure cultural status combined with their failure to secure political status. Demands for responsible government were closely related to the social needs of the farm communities.[22] Political unrest was symptomatic of disturbances extending through the entire range of the pioneer society of Upper Canada.

[22]A. Dunham, *Political Unrest in Upper Canada, 1815-36* (London, 1927).

The disturbing effects of overseas settlement in Upper Canada after the War of 1812 were as apparent in religious as in cultural and political organization. A large number of the overseas colonists were members of the Church of England, and it was upon this church as a result that the heaviest strain was placed in meeting the needs of rapidly growing rural communities. Before 1812, the church could fairly adequately serve the colony through its establishments in the chief centres of population; its lack of an effective missionary organization occasioned little loss since it was in the towns that most of its supporters resided and those settled in the country were usually sufficiently near the towns to attend services of worship. But the rapid increase after 1820 of rural adherents of the Church of England in Upper Canada, and the pushing of settlement into the inaccessible backwoods, revealed the inadequacies of the church's policies and methods. Attitudes of religious indifference attributed to the inhabitants of Upper Canada by outside observers probably were confined chiefly to those people belonging to the national church. Certainly, evidence of rural inhabitants failing to support religious services was most pronounced in the case of this religious denomination. It is true that the very character of pioneer society discouraged acts of religious devotion on the part of the population. The isolation and hard work of pioneer farm life made impossible the observance of many religious practices, and this unsettlement of old habits tended to the neglect of even those practices which could have been observed. Profanity appeared an inevitable ingredient in the habits of pioneer farm work, while Sabbath days provided the only occasions for such recreational activities as hunting or fishing. The lack of opportunities of worshipping collectively discouraged, in the end, private worship among individuals. Pioneer rural conditions, furthermore, tended to weaken those habits of thought which supported devout attitudes. Life in the backwoods of Upper Canada emphasized the ruthlessness of materialistic forces, and the struggle to gain a livelihood forced obedience to them. The atmosphere—and neighbours—were uncongenial to the religious mystic as to the poet. Yet the reality of the want felt by large numbers of the inhabitants to join in religious worship was made evident by the success achieved by the evangelical sects. Where the neglect of religious habits occurred among the population, therefore, the reason would seem to lie largely in the failure of the Church of England to adapt itself to the conditions of the pioneer society. The reluctance of hard-working farmers to drive many miles over bad roads to attend a brief devotional service which offered little in the way of emotional stimulation could rarely be overcome by appeals to the feeling of loyalty to the church. With its dependence upon services in regularly appointed places of worship, and its reliance upon a ritual attractive to a sophisticated population, the church found itself unable to maintain the support of rural parishioners scattered over large areas. Its class and political bias served to divorce it even further from the rural communities. The concern to establish exclusive educational institutions,[23] the partiality shown by many of the clergymen for the company of "polite society," and the anxiety of the ecclesiastical authorities to court the favour of a government upon which it depended for its privileged position, won for the church a claim to respectability but only at the price of losing its title to spiritual leadership. The shift of the allegiance of a large number of the rural inhabitants from the church to the more evangelical denominations provided concrete evidence of its weakening influence in the community. Efforts to bring about reforms within the organization of the church and to build up a competent staff of missionaries suited to the type of work required[24] came too late to arrest its decline in leadership.

The other denominations did not wholly escape the disturbing effects of rapid settlement after the War of 1812. The great advantage of Presbyterianism in the early years of settlement lay in its reliance upon congregational principles of church government. To a very considerable extent, the people made the church, and, wherever the people moved, the organization of the church followed. The fact that most of the early Presbyterians in Upper Canada were Scots had simplified the task of organizing the church. Clan and congregational loyalties combined to favour the preservation of habits of religious worship. With the increase in the number of Presbyterian adherents in Upper Canada in the twenties and thirties, however, the strengths of congregational principles

[23]See, however, George W. Spragge, "John Strachan's Contribution to Education, 1800-1823," *Canadian Historical Review*, June, 1941.

[24]J. J. Talman, "Church of England Missionary Effort in Upper Canada, 1815-1840," *Papers and Records, Ontario Historical Society*, vol. XXV.

became less apparent and the weaknesses of a lack of strong centralized organization more evident. The strict Presbyterian discipline required trained clergymen, and with increasing population a sufficient supply was not readily available. The jealousy with which congregations preserved the right to appoint and dismiss those who served them discouraged ministers from emigrating from Scotland when they were uncertain of obtaining or retaining a position. The trials incurred by the Reverend William Proudfoot in Upper Canada before he received a favourable call were illustrative of the weaknesses of congregational principles of church government. The development in Scotland of missionary organizations did something to meet the difficulties.[25] Schisms within the church produced liberal denominations more alive to the possibilities of missionary work than was the Church of Scotland. Nevertheless, the supply of clergy remained for some considerable time insufficient to meet the demand. Other weaknesses in Presbyterianism in a rural frontier became apparent. The obstinacy with which ministers conformed to the Presbyterian discipline tended to confine their influence to the faithful adherents. So long as Presbyterians were settled in compact communities, the refusal of the minister to dispense the sacraments to non-members of the church occasioned no great hardship, but as population became more scattered, and members of other religious denominations became interspersed among Presbyterians, the rigidity of the church's discipline made itself more felt. In sparsely settled communities, where a minister for each denomination was a luxury which could not be afforded, a degree of co-operation between the churches was highly necessary, and the Presbyterian Church failed to avail itself of the opportunities which such co-operation offered.

A shift in the attachments of a number of Presbyterians to the Methodist or Baptist denominations indicated weaknesses of the church as well as the aggressiveness of the evangelical sects. More striking still was the challenge to the Scottish leadership within the church itself and the growing strength of evangelical Presbyterianism. This movement, it is true, derived its support chiefly from the American-born settlers in the border communities

[25]Harry E. Parker, "Early Presbyterianism in Western Ontario," *Transactions of the London and Middlesex Historical Society,* 1930; W. Gregg, *History of the Presbyterian Church in Canada* (Toronto, 1885).

where ministers, thoroughly schooled in the religious evangelism of the American West, introduced such practices as the protracted meeting and temperance pledges, but it had the effect of restricting the influence of the Scottish churches to the immigrants from overseas. The stern and uncompromising theological doctrines and scholarly erudition of the Scottish pastors made little appeal to those who had not been reared in a strictly Calvinist society. Evangelical Presbyterianism spread as the demand for a more sympathetic religion made itself felt in the rural settlements of Upper Canada.

For the most part, the developments in Upper Canada served to emphasize the strengths of Methodism as a frontier religious movement, but, even with respect to this denomination, the War of 1812 and its aftermath brought disturbing influences to bear. The cutting off of the supply of Methodist Episcopal preachers during 1812-14, the outburst of ill-feeling against the United States, and the immigration after 1814 of Methodists from Great Britain, encouraged the intrusion of Wesleyan missionaries into Upper Canada, and the internecine struggle for ecclesiastical sovereignty which ensued darkened the pages of the history of Methodism during the next two decades and embittered relationships within the church particularly in those areas where the rivalry was most keen.[26] The conflict, however, was not wholly disadvantageous to the Methodist cause as the number of missionaries in Upper Canada was actually increased thereby. Moreover, to the extent that the field was successfully divided between the Wesleyans and the Episcopal Methodists, the one group of missionaries tended to maintain the support of the overseas immigrants and the other group the support of the American-born settlers.

In other respects, the organization and practices of the Methodist Church proved extremely well adapted to the conditions which developed in Upper Canada with the rapid growth of settlement.[27] The retention by the central Methodist conferences of the right of making appointments saved Methodism from the damaging effects

[26]G.W. Brown, "The Early Methodist Church and the Canadian Point of View," *Report of the Canadian Historical Association*, 1938.

[27]C.B. Sissons, *Egerton Ryerson: His Life and Letters* (Toronto, 1937); G.F. Playter, *History of Methodism in Canada* (Toronto, 1862); T. Webster, *History of the Methodist Episcopal Church in Canada* (Hamilton, 1870); A. Sutherland, *Methodism in Canada* (London, 1903).

of long-drawn-out negotiations between congregations and ministers such as was evident in the case of Presbyterianism. In a community where the population was extremely scattered, the Methodists did not wait until congregations could be formed, but rather relied upon the itinerant preacher who travelled from one settlement to another, and from one household to another, holding devotional services wherever people could be got together. The division of the province into a number of circuits, and the shift of preachers to different circuits at the end of each year, not only assured that no section would be overlooked but provided the inhabitants with a wide variety of talent. The local preachers in the more settled communities performed those day-by-day tasks of a regular clergy which could not be taken care of by itinerants. The enterprising character of both the itinerant and local preachers of the Methodist Church was in striking contrast to the more leisurely manners of the clergy of the Church of England. The fact that many of them possessed scarcely the rudiments of learning was little disadvantage in a community which set no high value upon knowledge. The fervour and earnestness with which they performed their duty, and the highly emotional content of their preaching, appealed to a population which knew few of the comforts of life. No intellectual or social chasm separated the Methodist preachers from their followers, and they were able to meet them on a common basis of experience and understanding. The development of such techniques as the protracted and camp meetings enabled the Methodists to overcome even more successfully the obstacles to religious services in the backwoods.[28] While the itinerant preacher sought out the household of the pioneer, the camp meeting, in turn, provided the pioneer with sufficient occasion to search out the religious service. It offered an opportunity, in communities where such opportunities occurred only infrequently, for numbers of people to participate in social gatherings. If the distance travelled was considerable, the attractions of the week-long camp meeting afforded ample compensation.

The fanaticism loosed by the Methodist evangelical movement proved something of a disturbing force in the society of Upper Canada. Work and domestic duties were often neglected to attend

[28]M. A. Garland, "Pioneer Religious Life in Upper Canada before 1850," *Papers and Records, Ontario Historical Society*, vol. XXV.

religious services, and the highly emotional reaction resulting from conversion occasionally led to personal disorganization. In addition, the aggressiveness of the evangelical sects contributed to a growing intolerance of different religious faiths. There was lacking in Methodism the deeply imbedded liberal philosophy evident in the secessionist Presbyterianism of such people as Proudfoot. The mass appeal of the Methodist preachers did much to strengthen the popular will but less perhaps to increase public intelligence. There emerged a type of leadership which, as exemplified in Egerton Ryerson, might be described in some respects as "boss" rule; a not wholly satisfactory substitute for the rule of the Family Compact. But these undesirable features of the Methodist movement were largely the inevitable by-products of a far-reaching social revolution taking place in Upper Canadian society. Evangelical Methodism was an expression of social dissatisfactions with an order of privilege; it provided, at a time when secular means of communication were still largely ineffective, a means of outlet for democratic feelings being generated on the frontier.[29] This political appeal of Methodism was closely related to its religious and moral appeals. The spread of a belief in temperance, a quickening of the cultural life of farm communities, and a strengthening of religious sentiments, followed in the wake of revivals, and the group rapport developed through such religious association provided a basis for the erection of the democratic party system.

Other religious sects, particularly the Baptists, tended to support the evangelical movement set under way by the Methodists. As the spirit of revival gained force, an increasing number of churches felt to some degree its influence. On the other hand, the unity of the Protestant body was considerably weakened by denominational schisms which resulted in the emergence of a great variety of religious sects. The bitter conflicts between the different branches of the Protestant churches evident during the thirties and forties were symptomatic of the passing of the simplicity and co-operative spirit of pioneer social conditions. Other influences tended to widen and deepen the roots of such conflicts. The immigration of Irish peoples which began in the 1820's and continued throughout the next two decades considerably increased the

[29]J.J. Talman, "The Newspapers of Upper Canada a Century Ago," *Canadian Historical Review*, March, 1938.

Catholic population in the province, and the hostile attitudes to the Irish, derived largely from economic and social sources, found expression in movements directed at the Catholic Church. It is true that the earliest formed lodges of the Orange Order, emerging in those sections of the province where the population was predominantly Protestant, performed chiefly social functions; they provided the one means of social intercourse familiar to the early settlers from overseas. A much more aggressive set of lodges, however, were organized in the 1830's, almost wholly within the triangular area formed by the towns of Kingston, Bytown (Ottawa), and Peterborough, and these arose directly in response to the growing threat of the large Irish-Catholic population. The bitterness of religious conflict immediately made itself apparent in the local communities, and its effects upon colonial politics became increasingly felt with the union of Lower and Upper Canada and the extension of the democratic process.

The growth of religious conflict was indicative of the emergence of new disturbances in the society of Central Canada. The focal points of Protestant-Catholic antagonism were to be found very largely in areas where public works were undertaken and in towns growing rapidly from the influx of workers, and this was true also of sectarian conflict within Protestantism and of more general forms of social conflict. The increase in the number of people dependent upon wages for a livelihood, and the growth of towns, introduced new kinds of tensions in the society. The large Irish immigration, and seasonal unemployment associated with the construction industry imposed heavy strains upon the inadequate social services of local communities,[30] and still greater burdens had to be assumed during those intervals when the railway "booms" of the forties and fifties collapsed. The business cycle was essentially a new phenomenon in the economy of Upper Canada, and few supports had been erected to relieve the effects of its downward swing. The apprehension resulting from the increase in the numbers of those people who were not satisfactorily provided for within the economic structure found expression in attitudes of hostility, apparent in the bitter feelings towards the Irish Catholics,

[30]Gilbert Tucker, "The Famine Immigration to Canada, 1847," *American Historical Review*, April, 1931; F. Morehouse, "Canadian Migration in the Forties," *Canadian Historical Review*, December, 1928.

and in the development of new economic philosophies some of which, as propounded for instance within one or two religious sects, had definite socialistic tendencies. The increase in the number of Irish inmates in the gaols and penitentiary, and the emergence of a problem of prostitution, indicative of the wider social effects of commercial expansion and the growth of towns, reinforced attitudes of hostility which had their basis in fear or dissatisfaction. Social alignments emerged in terms of new social divisions. The increase in the numbers of the wealthy class paralleled the growth of an urban proletariat, and the segregation which had proved impossible in the rural communities became conspicuous in the urban centres when the rise of real estate values produced exclusive residential areas. The extension in the influence of select social and cultural institutions was only partly offset by the establishment of organizations serving the needs of the working population—trade-unionism awaited the development of industrial capitalism after 1870— and this cultural disfranchisement of a large section of the urban population was accompanied by an increasing divorce between religious leadership and the unfortunate classes. Such disturbances in social organization, if little more than a warning of the kind of social problems which were to be thrown up by the expansion of industrial capitalism in the latter part of the century, had already become apparent in Central Canada in the fifties and sixties.

Actually, however, the problems of social organization which emerged after 1850 had little to do with adjustments which had been set under way with the frontier expansion of agriculture after the turn of the century. The growing trade in wheat, and railway-building, increased the importance of commercial interests, and it was commercial expansion which produced the town and the resulting problems of social organization. Within the rural communities, by 1850, cultural stability had become established to a very considerable extent. Social welfare institutions had grown up to meet the simple needs of a farm population; the family had become fully adapted to a rural environment; strains within the class structure had been eased by the growing preponderance of second-generation settlers and by the ceaseless pressure of the rural agricultural economy; a provincial system of education had been established; and rural religious sects and denominations were becoming accommodated to one another and satisfactorily meeting the needs of the population. A complete integration of the culture was not accomplished—the rise of the city and opening of the West resulted in new pulls upon the population of the rural communities —but by 1850 the frontier expansionist phase of agriculture in Central Canada had run its course, and social reorganization in terms of a mature agricultural economy had proceeded a considerable distance. Later forces of social disorganization emerged outside of rather than within the rural communities of this region.

1. SOCIAL WELFARE

A. *The Rural Community*

Destitute Immigrants

John Howison, *Sketches of Upper Canada* (Edinburgh, 1821), pp. 61-4.

On my way back to the village, I was occupied with reflections upon the helpless condition of most of the emigrants who come to Canada, and the indifference which the supreme government have ever manifested about the welfare and prosperity of the colony. Those people, who came to the province with an intention of settling in it, are totally destitute of the means of obtaining authentic information respecting the place to which they should proceed, or where or in what manner they should apply for a grant of land. Inexperienced, ignorant of the country, and often disappointed with it at *first*, it cannot be expected that they should resolutely struggle with the difficulties that present themselves on every side. The slaves of vague reports, and false and exaggerated descriptions, they know not where to direct their steps; and, after being alternately encouraged, depressed, and deceived, they perhaps prematurely determine to return to their native country, wretched as the asylum is which it at present affords to the poor and unfortunate of all classes. When I was in Quebec and Montreal, I had opportunities of knowing, that many of the hovels of these cities contained crowds of British emigrants, who were struggling with those complicated horrors of poverty and disease, whom the hope of being exempted from such evils had induced to abandon the clime of their birth. The greater number of these people, when they first landed, had funds enough to carry them to the Upper Province, and even settle them comfortably on their locations; but they knew not where the "promised land" lay, and were detained in Lower Canada, by anxious and unavailing efforts to obtain correct information upon the subject. All the misery occasioned by this circumstance, and various others of a similar nature, might be easily prevented, and thousands of active settlers annually added to the province, if the supreme government would bestow a moment's attention upon the matter, and place in Quebec, Montreal, and the other towns, an agent, to whom the emigrants could apply for advice and information. . . .

Some years ago, government gave liberal encouragement to those who were disposed to emigrate to Canada.   Besides paying their passage across the Atlantic, it provided them with rations and farming utensils, during one year subsequent to their arrival in the country.   But this plan apparently did not answer; the lower and most worthless members of society immediately took advantage of the facilities which it afforded to emigration, and lived in idleness as long as they received rations; and at last sold their agricultural utensils and went to the United States.   The conduct of these people made government abandon all idea of assisting emigrants farther, than by granting them a certain quantity of land.   At first there was too much done for them— *now* there is too little.

Commuted Pensioners and Destitution

Anna Jameson, *Winter Studies and Summer Rambles* (new ed., Toronto, 1923), pp. 436-8.

At Penetanguishene there is a hamlet, consisting of twenty or thirty log-houses, where a small remnant of the poor commuted pensioners (in all a hundred and twenty-six persons) now reside, receiving daily rations of food, and some little clothing, just sufficient to sustain life.

From some particular circumstances the case of these commuted pensioners were frequently brought under my observation while I was in Canada, and excited my strongest interest and compassion. . . .

The commuted pensioners were veteran soldiers, entitled to a small yearly pension for wounds or length of service, and who accepted the offer made to them by our government in 1832, to commute their pensions for four years' purchase, and a grant of one hundred acres of land in Canada.

The *intention* of the government seems to have been to send out able-bodied men, who would thus cease, after a few years, to be a burthen on the country. . . . Of those who came out, one half were described to me as presenting a list of all the miseries and diseases incident to humanity—some with one arm, some with one leg, bent with old age or rheumatism, lame, halt, and even, will it be believed, blind.   (One of these men, stone-blind, was begging in the streets of Toronto).   And such were the men to be set down in the midst of the swamp and forest, there to live as they could. . . .

Those who were located were sent far up into the bush (there being no disposable government lands nearer,) where there were no roads, no markets for their produce if they *did* raise it; and in this new position, if their hearts did not sink, and their limbs fail at once, their ignorance of farming, their improvidence and helplessness, arising from the want of self-dependence, and the mechanical docility of military service, were moral obstacles stronger than any physical ones.   The forest-trees they had to contend with were not more deeply rooted than the adverse habits and prejudices and infirmities they had brought with them.

According to the commissary, the number of those who commuted their pensions was about twelve hundred.   Of these it is calculated that eight hundred reached Upper Canada: of these eight hundred, not more than four hundred and fifty are now living [1837]; and of these, some are begging through the townships, living on public charity: some are at Penetanguishene: and the greater part of those located on their land have received from time to time rations of food, in order to avert "impending starvation". To bring them up from Quebec during the dreadful cholera season of 1832, was a heavy expense to the colony, and now they are likely to become a permanent burthen upon the colonial funds, there being no military funds to which they can be charged.

Poverty and Relief in Rural Communities

(i)

Views of Canada and the Colonists, By a Four Years' Resident (Edinburgh, 1844), pp. 41-3.

I will now give you an important statement, more illustrative of what we are than anything I have as yet perhaps told you—that is, the number of persons subsisting on alms, which is ten [in the district of London]! Ten persons only in a population of 30,000—one pauper only for every 3,000! And even this amount of pauperism not real perhaps; at least, I should say, of a different nature, arising from other causes, than yours—chiefly from four causes, I should suppose: first, extreme intemperate habits; old age distant from relations; physical disability in like circumstances; and lastly, it may be a depraved choice, attended sometimes by some one or more of the three other causes. . . . During the four years I have been in Western Canada, I have scarcely met a case of the low beggary which is so pitifully prominent with you. . . .

There are instances of subscription papers being presented by the neighbours of some family or individuals who have met with a calamity, as fire or long sickness; and these are ever attended to with prompt liberality. The societies so general throughout Canada, under the names of St. George's, St. Andrew's, and St. Patrick's, composed of individuals immediately or remotely connected with the three kingdoms, have done much good by relieving accidental suffering, or assisting the emigrant whose means may have become exhausted in the search for employment. There is another class of cases where assistance is required, and which occurs in the towns during long and severe winters among the families of labourers out of work, with means run short, and many, from being strangers, wanting also credit, or confidence to ask it. A supply of labour greater than the demand collecting at a certain place, would easily account for this were other as likely causes awanting, as sickness, accidents, or unfrugal or worse habits. Generally throughout Western Canada these cases prevail to no great extent, and are usually promptly and liberally relieved. At Quebec and Montreal, the first landing points of emigration, and where the winters are so much longer and severer, the case is very different, and attention to such destitution becomes a subject of considerable public importance.

(ii)

Susanna Moodie, *Roughing It in the Bush* (new ed., Toronto, 1913), pp. 252-4.

To the benevolent philanthropist, whose heart has bled over the misery and pauperism of the lower classes in Great Britain, the almost entire absence of mendicity from Canada would be highly gratifying. Canada has few, if any, native beggars; her objects of charity are generally imported from the mother country, and these are never suffered to want food or clothing. The Canadian are a truly charitable people; no person in distress is driven with harsh and cruel language from their doors; they not only generously relieve the wants of suffering strangers cast upon their bounty, but they nurse them in sickness, and use every means in their power to procure them employment. The number of orphan children yearly adopted by wealthy Canadians, and treated in every respect as their own, is almost incredible.

It is a glorious country for the labouring classes, for while blessed with health, they are always certain of employment, and certain also to derive from it ample means of support for their families. . . .

It has often been remarked to me by people long resident in the colony, that those who come to the country destitute of means, but able and willing to work, invariably improve their condition and become independent; while the gentleman who brings out with him a small capital is too often tricked and cheated out of his property, and drawn into rash and dangerous speculation which terminate in his ruin. His children, neglected and uneducated, but brought up with ideas far beyond their means, and suffered to waste their time in idleness, seldom take to work, and not infrequently sink down to the lowest class.

Lack of Medical Facilities

(i)

T. W. Magrath, *Authentic Letters from Upper Canada*, edited by the Rev. T. Radcliffe (Dublin, 1833), p. 109.

Physicians are very much wanting here, and apothecaries still more. Ignorant persons act in that capacity, who scarcely know the names of the drugs they sell. At Niagara that most necessary branch is solely conducted by a female, who compounds medicines and puddings, with equal confidence, but not with equal skill. . . .

Nurse-tenders are in great demand. They might make their own terms.

(ii)

Transactions of the London and Middlesex Historical Society, 1914, pp. 69-70; 1922, p. 6: Journal of the Rev. Wm. Proudfoot.

Dec. 2, 1832. Scarborough:—

Females, when confined, do not call the assistance of either midwife or surgeon; the reason is they charge too high. So the neighbours assist, and all goes well enough. . . .

Dec. 4, Home [York)]:—
Have heard of many females dying in child bed these two weeks. The season appears to be unfriendly to those in that way. . . .
Dec. 6, 1832, York:—
Heard of nine females dying in child bed.

Prejudice against Doctors

Papers and Records, Ontario Historical Society, vol. XXVII, 1931, p. 464:
Proudfoot Papers.

Feb. 23, 1834, Home:—
. . . The people are very ignorant and very full of prejudice against doctors.

Co-operative Medical Services

E. S. Dunlop (ed.), *Our Forest Home: Being Extracts from the Correspondence of the late Frances Stewart* (Montreal, 1902), p. 33.

April 5, 1823 . . . There is a most skilful doctor who lives about fourteen miles off. He visits every family in the neighbourhood once a fortnight, and appoints places where he can receive messages. Our names are down on his lists; every one he visits in this manner pays him *three dollars a year*! He is a Scotchman, young but clever.

B. Rise of the Town

Canal Workers and Poverty in Kingston

Public Archives of Canada, *Upper Canada Sundries:* Kingston, October 24, 1827, R. W. Tunney to Hillier.

There is scarcely a Hut or log-house here but is filled with sick and needy, who are suffering, not only from Disease, but also from Hunger, and from almost every other misery concomitant upon the want of the common necessaries of life. . . .
I do not recollect ever to have seen before so much distress as now presents itself under almost every form, and principally occasioned, I understand, by the numerous labourers returning from the Rideau Canal, where they have fallen victims of disease.

The Irish Immigration

J. J. Bigsby, *The Shoe and Canoe or Pictures of Travel in the Canadas* (London, 1850), vol. I, p. 23-4.

I hope there are few towns in Christendom where such an amount of disease and destitution exists as in Quebec. . . . This misery does not touch the native poor, but the fever-stricken, naked, and friendless Irish—a people truly "scattered and peeled"—who year after year are thrown in shoals upon the wharfs of Quebec from ships which ought to be called "itinerant pest-houses."

These poor creatures, on landing, creep into any hovel they can, with all their foul things about them. When they are so numerous as to figure in the streets, they are put, I believe by the Colonial Government, into dilapidated houses, with something like rations, of which latter the worthier portion of the emigrants are apt to see but little: they are clutched by the clamorous.

The filthy and crowded state of the houses, the disgusting scenes going on in them, can only be guessed by a very bold imagination. I have trod the floor of one of such houses, almost over shoes in churned and sodden garbage, animal and vegetable. It required dissecting-room nerves to bear it.

After starving about Quebec for months, the helpless Irishman and his family begin to creep up the country on charity or government aid, and thus strew the colony with beggary and disease. At Quebec winter does not allow of lazzaronism. Some perish, some are absorbed into the general population, and many more go into the United States.

Poverty and Drunkenness in Quebec City

J. S. Buckingham, *Canada, Nova Scotia, New Brunswick* (London, 1843), p. 231.

From Wolfe's Cove we returned to the town, by the lower road as it is called, coming through a long, narrow, and straggling suburb, called Champlain Street, which extends itself for two or three miles, at the foot of the Heights of Abraham, the breadth between the cliffs and the river being rarely more than fifty feet. As this quarter is the resort of sailors, lumber-men, and newly-arrived emigrants, it presents a fearful scene of disorder, filth, and intemperance; and we thought that in this comparatively short drive of less than an hour, we saw more of poverty, raggedness, dirty and disorderly dwellings, and taverns and spirit shops with drunken inmates, than we had witnessed in all our three years' journey through the United States. There could not have been less than a hundred openly licensed houses of this description in this single street. We were assured that the number of places at which spirits are sold illicitly, exceed even the licensed houses; and these, as might be expected, are the most mischievous and disorderly of the two, being kept by the most reckless characters, and without the slightest check or responsibility. Everyone here complains of this, but no one sets about its reform, who has the power to effect it. The Temperance Societies, of which there are two in Quebec, call the public attention to the subject from time to time, but the government are indifferent to the matter; and the municipal authorities seem to think the paltry revenue afforded by the sale of spirits and licenses, of more importance than the misery which it brings in its train; accordingly, no one who desires a license and will pay for it, is refused.

Poverty and Disease in Montreal

C. P. Traill, *The Backwoods of Canada* (London, 1836), pp. 55-7.

We were struck by the dirty, narrow, ill-paved or unpaved streets of the suburbs, and overpowered by the noisome vapour arising from a deep open fosse that ran along the street behind the wharf. This ditch seemed the receptacle for every abomination, and sufficient in itself to infect a whole town with malignant fevers.

I was greatly disappointed in my first acquaintance with the interior of Montreal; a place of which travellers had said so much. I could compare it only to the fruits of the Dead Sea, which are said to be fair and tempting to look upon, but yield only ashes and bitterness when tasted by the thirsty traveller. . . .

Every house of public resort was crowded from the top to the bottom with emigrants of all ages, English, Irish, and Scotch. The sounds of riotous merriment that burst from them seemed but ill-assorted with the haggard, care-worn faces of many of the thoughtless revellers.

The contrast was only too apparent and too painful a subject to those that looked upon this show of outward gaiety and inward misery.

The cholera had made awful ravages, and its devastating effects were to be seen in the darkened dwellings and the mourning habiliments of all classes. An expression of dejection and anxiety appeared in the faces of the few persons we encountered in our walk to the hotel, which plainly indicated the state of their minds.

In some situations whole streets had been nearly depopulated; those that were able flew panic stricken to the country villages, while others remained to die in the bosom of their families.

To no class, I am told, has the disease proved so fatal as to the poorer sort of emigrants. Many of these, debilitated by the privations and fatigue of a long voyage, on reaching Quebec or Montreal indulged in every sort of excess, especially the dangerous one of intoxication; and, as if purposely paving the way to certain destruction, they fell immediate victims to the complaint.

C. *Development of Welfare Institutions*

Support of Orphans

The Statutes of the Province of Upper Canada (Kingston, 1831), p. 85.

An Act to provide for the education and support of orphan children. [Passed June 29, 1779].

Whereas it is expedient to provide for the education and support of orphan children, or children who may be deserted by their parents; be it enacted. . . .

That when the father and mother of any infant child shall die, or shall abandon their infant child or children, it shall and may be lawful for the town wardens of any township where such child or children shall be, by and with the approbation and consent of two of his Majesty's justices of the peace, to bind the said child or children as apprentices, until he, she, or they, shall have attained the age of twenty-one years, in the case of males, and eighteen, in the case of females; and an indenture to this effect, under their hands and seals, and countersigned by two justices of the peace, shall be good and valid in law.

Provision for Destitute

Public Archives of Canada, *Upper Canada Sundries:* Memorandum respecting
York Hospital, 1831.

Within the last ten days my attention has been called to the wretched condition of several families; and although it may be thought imprudent, or absurd, to create any Institution at York that may attract the destitute, and idle to this part of the Province, I am persuaded that greater evils will result from persons of this description being allowed to enter the Town, without notice, than from searching them out, and bringing them to a well regulated establishment supported by the exertions of a few active individuals, and public collections.

If the Hospital be declared open for all the sick of the Province, under the present regulations, I am induced to believe that the Legislature will grant the sum required to extend its use; and that we have the means sufficient to enable a committee, that may be appointed, to carry into execution the arrangements proposed for conducting the Institution.

Poor Relief in the Small Towns

(i)

The Brockville Recorder, December 13, 1833.

RELIEF OF THE POOR IN BROCKVILLE.—At a Meeting held in the Court House on Monday, the 25th of November, 1833, for the purpose of affording relief to the poor of the town of Brockville, Jonas Jones, Esq. was called to the Chair, and the following resolutions were carried:—

1st. Resolved—That a Society be formed for the relief of the poor to be called "The Brockville Poor-Relief Society."

2d. Resolved—That the said Society shall consist of a President, Vice-President, Secretary, Treasurer, and twenty-four Managers.

3d. Resolved—That the following persons fill the offices of the Society for the present year. . . .

4th. Resolved—That the objects of the Said Society shall be first to dispense the necessaries of life to such as are destitute and unable to provide them. 2d—to procure medical aid for the indigent sick. 3d—to provide employment for the destitute and able-bodied who cannot themselves procure it.

5th. Resolved—That an Annual Subscription be now entered into for the support of the objects of the Society, and that Messrs. Grant and Venor be a Committee to circulate the same, and that a Subscription of 5s. constitute a member.

6th. Resolved—That the Ministers of the Gospel resident in town be requested to afford a generous supervision of the Society under such regulations as shall be arranged between them and the officers of the Society.

7th. Resolved—That the Ministers of the gospel and Medical gentlemen affording aid to the objects of the Society, shall be ex-officio members thereof.

(ii)

The Brockville Recorder, November 25, 1836.

To His Excellency Sir Francis Bond Head, Lieutenant Governor of the Province of Upper Canada, &c. &c.

The petition of the undersigned inhabitants of Brockville, humbly sheweth:—

That pauperism and vagrancy are increasing to an alarming extent, in some of the Districts of Canada, and believing, that all those persons who are walking from door to door, begging food and clothing, might on a farm or in a House of Industry support themselves. Therefore we your Excellency's petitioners, do most respectfully solicit your Excellency, to recommend such a plan for the relief and instruction of all in want, as may be thought best calculated to free this country, from a great and growing evil. We would not presume to dictate; yet would humbly suggest that the voluntary plan of subscription aided by a grant from government of a lot, of land and a part of the funds for erecting the necessary buildings would be a good plan.

The poor law system has been found a great burden, and if by means of a Relief Union in every District, the destitute could be fed, clothed and instructed by their own labour. This would be better than a tax which has become very burdensom in England.

Establishment of Houses of Industry

The Statutes of the Province of Upper Canada (Toronto, 1837), pp. 80-2.

An Act to authorize the Erection, and provide for the Maintenance of Houses of Industry, in the several Districts of this Province. (Passed March 4, 1837).

Whereas it is expedient and necessary to provide a House of Industry in the several Districts of this Province, and to provide employment for the Indigent and Idle: *Be it therefore enacted* . . . That the Court of General Quarter Sessions of the Peace, to be holden in each District, after the presentment of three successive Grand Juries recommending the same, it shall be the duty of the Justices of the said District, to procure Plans and Estimates for the erection of suitable Buildings for the reception of the Poor and Indigent, and of the Idle and Dissolute, and to procure and purchase a suitable Site whereon to erect the same, and to contract for the erection thereof: *Provided* the expense thereof shall not exceed the sum of One Thousand Pounds; and also to appoint five Inspectors, who shall have the Inspection and Government of the said House, with full power to appoint a Master, Mistress, and such needful assistance for the immediate care and oversight of the persons received into, or employed in that House. . . .

II. *And be it further enacted by the authority aforesaid,* That the Monies requisite and necessary for the building, erecting, keeping and maintaining the said Houses of Industry, in the several Districts of this Province, shall be paid by the several Districts; and all the rateable property of the District shall be taxed in the same way, for this purpose, as it is for the purpose of erecting Gaols and Courthouses. . . .

III. *And be it further enacted by the authority aforesaid,* That two of His Majesty's Justices of the Peace, or the Inspectors appointed as aforesaid, are hereby authorised, empowered and directed, to commit to such House, by writing under their hands and seals, to be employed and governed according to the Rules, Regulations and Orders of said House, any person or persons residing in the District that are by this Act declared liable to be sent thither.

IV. *And be it further enacted by the authority aforesaid,* That the persons who shall be liable to be sent into, employed and governed in the said House, to be erected in pursuance of this Act, are all Poor and Indigent Persons, who are incapable of supporting themselves; all persons able of body to work and without any means of maintaining themselves, who refuse or neglect so to do; all persons living a lewd dissolute vagrant life, or exercising no ordinary calling, or lawful business, sufficient to gain or procure an honest living; all such as spend their time and property in Public Houses, to the neglect of their lawful calling. . . .

VI. *And be it further enacted by the authority aforesaid,* That all and every person committed to such House, if fit and able, shall be kept diligently employed in labour, during his or her continuance there; and in case the person so committed or continued shall be idle and not perform such reasonable task or labour as shall be assigned, or shall be stubborn, disobedient or disorderly, he, she or they, shall be punished according to the Rules and Regulations made or to be made, for ruling, governing and punishing persons there committed.

Relief of Distressed in Toronto

The Statutes of the Province of Upper Canada (Toronto, 1838), pp. 182-3.

An Act to afford relief to the Sick and Destitute Poor of the City of Toronto (Passed March 6, 1838).

Whereas the high price of provisions, and the increased number of paupers, arising from various causes, has rendered the efforts of private charity insufficient for the relief of the sick and destitute poor in the City of Toronto: *And Whereas* it is therefore expedient to afford some public aid: May it therefore please Your Majesty, that it may be enacted, *And be it enacted....* That from and out of the rates, duties and assessments, now raised levied and collected, or hereafter to be raised, levied and collected, and remaining in the hands of the Receiver General, unappropriated, there be granted to Her Majesty the sum of three hundred and fifty pounds, to enable her Majesty to advance the like sum in aid of the means already adopted, during this season, for the relief of the poor and distressed of the City of Toronto.

The Gaol as a House of Refuge

Journals of the Legislative Assembly of Canada, 1852, Appendix H H, pp. 17-18:
Report of Dr. Wolfred Nelson ... on the Present State ... of the District and other Prisons in Canada East (Communication of Gaoler of Montreal, April 16, 1852).

It appears to me that little or no saving can be actually effected in this department, either as regards the rate per head or the aggregate expenditure, which is certainly small, when the number and character of the prisoners is taken into account; the Gaol at present being in some sense an asylum for homeless and friendless persons, who from age, decrepitude, blindness, or other infirmity, are unable to maintain themselves, and these, not only from the different parts of the District, but not unfrequently from the other side of the Atlantic by emigration. These require nourishment—not punishment; nursing, not hard labour. But again the Gaol is made an Hospital for incurables, who have been discharged from other Hospitals, a lying-in Hospital, and a receptacle for children whose vagrant parents are sent to the House of Correction. The drunkard too, both male and female, instinctively fly to the Gaol for care and treatment, warned by the premonitions of *delirium tremens*. The wretched prostitute artfully turns laws ostensibly made to suppress her vice, into timely and efficient auxiliary to her sad career. A sentence to hard labour in her case practically means medicine and nourishment, the one to arrest if not to cure a loathsome disease, the other to recruit the wasted frame and flagging energies. This description will apply to three-fourths of the females who enter the Gaol.... Lunatics too are frequently

found in the Gaol during long periods, thereby rendering their cure less probable, and materially adding to the annual expense.

Provision for Mentally Ill

The Statutes of the Province of Upper Canada (Kingston, 1831), p. 534.

*An Act to Authorize the Quarter Sessions of the Home District to Provide for
the Relief of Insane Destitute Persons in that District.* (Passed March 6, 1830.)
Whereas it appears by the petition of the Chairman of the Quarter Sessions
in and for the Home district, and also by presentment of the Grand Jury of
the said district, that several insane persons, destitute of any provision for
their maintenance, have been charitably received into the gaol of the Home
district, and that there being no funds for their support provided by law, a
charge has been incurred from necessity, and paid from the funds of the
District, without any legal authority for the same; . . . *Be it therefore enacted*
. . . That at the next ensuing Quarter Sessions of the Peace in the Home District, it shall and may be lawful for the Clerk of the Peace, and he is hereby
required, to lay before the Grand Jury of the said Quarter Sessions, an account in detail of all sum and sums of money advanced, or which shall be
necessary to advance until the said Sessions, for the purpose of maintaining
and supporting insane destitute persons, as aforesaid. . . .

Conditions of Toronto Asylum

Journals of the Legislative Assembly of Canada, 1849, Appendix M: George H.
Park, Superintendent, to Hon. R. B. Sullivan, Provincial Secretary,
September 13, 1848.

When the Superintendent first entered upon the duties of his office, he
found, as might be readily supposed from what occurred previous to his
appointment, the Institution in a very bad state; there was not clothing
enough of any, or all kinds, for a change: there were several patients that
had been naked for several months, constantly confined in cells, or, if quiet,
lying on the floor of the attic ward, a place where from sixty to seventy
patients were constantly kept in a very filthy condition; as they were the
worst class patients, they were not let out at all into the yard, or open air.
The stench of this ward was scarcely bearable, from the great amount of filth
that had been allowed to accumulate in different parts of it. The other wards
are not quite so bad, but there was no part of the whole establishment, but
what was dirty, and otherwise badly attended to. There were no baths, or
proper arrangements for cleansing the patients; the cells and sleeping appointments were confined, and filthy; the beds and bed-steads full of vermin;
the noisy and restless patients were kept for days and nights together, locked
in cells, as an easy mode of getting rid of taking care of them; the keepers

and servants were in the habit of going in and out of the asylum without permission; the clothing and other articles belonging to the Institution had no marks upon them, by which they could be distinguished from other articles of a similar kind, for the want of which, no doubt, the Institution has suffered much loss.   The lunatics received their meals, if such they could be called in a careless, uncomfortable, and disorderly manner, accompanied with a great waste of provision; a large amount of intoxicating drinks used, said to be for the benefit of the patients, far too much of which they actually received.

2. CRIME AND THE MORAL ORDER

A. The Rural Community

Horse Racing among Early American Settlers

Public Archives of Canada, *Journal of William Bentinck*, 1800-1, pp. 13-14.

Williamsburg [Eastern Townships] consists of Six or eight houses, widely dispersed.   The race course lay along the road about half a mile long: All the farmers and poor, for many miles round, were collected to see this favorite diversion, for which the Americans will sacrifice anything. —There was only one Public house, but that deficiency was amply supplied by a large waggon loaded with beer, rum, whiskey, bread and cheese.   About 1 O'clock, a shower drove us into the house of an old German soldier, who had left his residence on the Mohawk, that he might live under the Government of Great Britain: his Wife deplored the change, being disgusted with the manners of the people. The banks of the Mohawk are settled by peacable Germans, while the Neighbourhood of Williamsburg is inhabited by Americans, who have imported with them their love of Gambling and drinking.   Five hundred came over this Winter: their attachment to our Government, is the reason they give out for the change; but the cheapness of Land, and their not having any Taxes to pay, are the real causes.

We had some specimens of their manners before the race began, many were drunk, bets began to run high, and we should most likely have seen more, if it had not rained violently.

The Neighbourhood Bee and Pioneer Recreations

Major Samuel Strickland, *Twenty-Seven Years in Canada West* (London, 1853), vol. I, pp. 35-7.

Soon after my arrival at Darlington, one of my neighbours residing on the lake-shore invited me to a mowing and cradling Bee.   As I had never seen anything of the kind, I accepted the invitation.   On my arrival at the farm on the appointed day, I found assembled about forty men and boys.   A man with a pail of spring water with a wooden cup floating on the surface in one hand, and a bottle of whiskey and glass in the other, now approached the swarm, every one helping himself as he pleased. This man is the most important personage at the "Bee," and is known by the appellation of the "Grog-boss." On this occasion his office was anything but a sinecure. The heat of the weather, I suppose, had made our party very thirsty. There were thirty-five bees cutting hay, among whom I was a rather awkward volunteer, and ten cradlers employed in cutting rye.

At eleven o'clock, cakes and pailfuls of tea were served round. At one, we were summoned by the sound of a tin bugle to dinner, which we found laid out in the barn. Some long pine-boards resting on tressels served for a table, which almost groaned with the good things of this earth, in the shape of roast lamb and green peas, roast sucking-pig, shoulder of mutton, apple-sauce, and pies, puddings, and preserves in abundance, with plenty of beer and Canadian whiskey. Our bees proved so industrious, that before six o'clock all Mr. Burke's hay and rye were finished cutting. Supper was then served on the same scale of profusion, with the addition of tea. After supper a variety of games and gymnastics were introduced, various trials of strength, wrestling, running, jumping, putting the stone, throwing the hammer, etc.

About nine o'clock our party broke up, and returned to their respective homes, well pleased with their day's entertainment, leaving their host perfectly satisfied with their voluntary labour. One word about bees and their attendant frolic. I confess I do not like the system. I acknowledge, that in raising a log-house or barn it is absolutely necessary, especially in the Bush, but the general practice is bad. Some people can do nothing without a bee, and as the work has to be returned in the same manner, it causes a continual round of dissipation—if not of something worse. I have known several cases of manslaughter arising out of quarrels produced by intoxication at these every-day gatherings. As population increases, and labour becomes cheaper, of course there will be less occasion for them.

Logging-Bees and Drinking

(i)

Susanna Moodie, *Roughing It in the Bush* (new ed., Toronto, 1913), pp. 341-2,352.

A logging-bee followed the burning of the fallow as a matter of course. In the bush, where hands are few and labour commands an enormous rate of wages, these gatherings are considered indispensable, and much has been written in their praise; but to me, they present the most disgusting picture of bush life. They are noisy, riotous, drunken meetings, often terminating in violent quarrels, sometimes even in bloodshed. Accidents of the most serious nature often occur, and very little work is done when we consider the number of hands employed, and the great consumption of food and liquor.

I am certain, in our case, had we hired with the money expended in providing for the bee, two or three industrious, hard-working men, we should have got through twice as much work, and have had it done well, and have been the gainers in the end.

People in the woods have a craze for giving and going to bees, and run to them with as much eagerness as a peasant runs to a race-course or a fair; plenty of strong drink and excitement making the chief attraction of the bee. . . .

The conduct of many of the settlers, who considered themselves gentlemen, and would have been very much affronted to have been called otherwise, was often more reprehensible than that of the poor Irish emigrants, to whom they should have set an example of order and sobriety. The behaviour of these young men drew upon them the severe but just censures of the poorer class, whom they regarded in every way as their inferiors.

(ii)

Transactions of the London and Middlesex Historical Society, 1914, p. 68: Journal of the Rev. William Proudfoot.

Dec. 1 (Saturday), 1832:—

Mr. Craig came into York to-day to take me out on horseback to Scarborough. . . . Intended to lodge this evening with Mr. David Thomson, but when we got to his house we found them all tipsy. Mr. Thomson had had a bee on Wednesday, and they had been drinking ever since. Scarborough folks are noted drinkers.

Drinking and Gambling

E. A. Talbot, *Five Years' Residence in the Canadas* (London, 1824), vol. II, pp. 57-8.

The Canadian are very much addicted to drinking; and, on account of the cheapness of liquor, are very frequently under its influence. Card-playing, horse-racing, wrestling, and dancing, are their favourite amusements; and as the jingle of a dollar is a rarer sound in the ear of a Canadian, than the voice of liberty is in that of an Algerine, their bets are usually made in stock, and are sometimes exceedingly extravagant. The fate of a cow, a yoke of oxen, or a pair of horses, is often determined by the colour of a card; and an hour's gambling has deprived many a Canadian farmer of the hard-earned fruits of twenty years' industry.

The Tavern

Views of Canada and the Colonists, By a Four Years' Resident (Edinburgh, 1844), pp. 43-5.

The number of 100 taverns above stated, as existing within this district of London in Upper Canada, may be partly accounted for by explaining, that owing to the great deal of travelling in waggons and on horseback in Canada, taverns are situated every seven or eight miles, perhaps throughout the country generally on an average of every six miles or so, along the roads for the accommodation of feeding and watering horses, and rest and food for the traveller.

Not infrequently, however, many of them are the resort of the least industrious individuals residing in the vicinity, who, in hours through the day, as well as during the evenings, seek the grosser excitements which intoxicating liquors, party politics, and gaming, all too temptingly furnish. Yet these roadside taverns may be said to be harmless compared with those so prevalent in many of the villages and towns, the number of which, one is constrained to observe, is noways complimentary to the discretion, to say the least, of the majority of the bench of magistracy licensing them. . . .

Canada, though provided from an early period with some kind of national schools, yet with a widely scattered and comparatively poor population, though abundantly possessed of the material necessaries of life, has never been completely able to extend a beneficial, solid education over its far-stretched and thinly-peopled territory. And the mass of the population were thus left to seek from other sources the gratification naturally required to lighten and relieve their monotonous round of toil, and their isolated dwellings in the bush. . . .

But perhaps not among the least numerous portion of the population who have had immoderate recourse to drinking usages, and from partly similar circumstances, were a class of colonists chiefly from among the middle classes of home society, who, entering this country with a little money, though in many cases with an assumption of no little consequence in their manners and intercourse, affecting superiority among a people unused to allow such to mere assumption or rank—these people, finding their position so altered in this country, too frequently and readily seek, among a restricted circle, the gratification of the over-social board. Individuals, too, from among every class, may be found to whom the above applies, who, from contracted notions of some fancied superiority to most people around them, prejudices of country, and such like, make their settlement in any new country necessarily disagreable to themselves, as it is offensive to others and comparatively useless, if not prejudicial, to the social and general well-being of their adopted abode.

Prevalence of Drinking Habits

(i)

J. R. Godley, *Letters from America* (London, 1834), vol. I, p. 171.

The bane of this province is "brandy and water"; at least half of the young settlers fall into the habit of drinking, more or less, and many have been pointed out to me who came from England with the most gentlemanlike habits, and apparently good principles, but from bad company and *ennui* have been led to excess, and have finally gone to utter ruin from habitual intemperance.

(ii)

Susanna Moodie, *Life in the Clearings versus the Bush* (London, 1853), pp. 63-4.

Alas! this frightful vice of drinking prevails throughout the colony to an alarming extent. Professional gentlemen are not ashamed of being seen issuing from the bar-room of a tavern early in the morning, or of being caught reeling home from the same sink of iniquity late at night. No sense of shame seems to deter them from the pursuit of their darling sin. I have heard that some of these regular topers place brandy beside their beds that, should they awake during the night, they may have within their reach the fiery potion for which they are bartering body and soul. Some of these persons, after having been warned of their danger by repeated fits of delirium tremens, have joined the tee-totallers; but their abstinence only lasted until the re-establishment of their health enabled them to return to their old haunts, and become more hardened in their vile habits than before.

Disbanded Soldier Settlers and Intemperance

Eliot Warburton (ed.), *Hochelaga; or, England in the New World* (London, 3rd ed, 1847), vol. I, pp. 296-7.

At one time the misuse of ardent spirits, with all its melancholy and disastrous consequences, was very general in Upper Canada; it cannot be said that the evil is cured, but it is, certainly, much mitigated, and the consumption, proportionately to the population, has been diminishing for some years past. At one time, settlements were given to a number of disbanded soldiers, with a small commuted allowance for their pensions; this scheme proved eminently unsuccessful: when so many of these veterans were in the same neighbourhood, their old idle, and, in some cases, dissipated habits, were not likely to be at once abandoned, and the dram-shop became the only prosperous place; their farms were carelessly and unskilfully cleared and tilled; their capital soon wasted; and, in a very short time, the great majority of them had sold out their lands for next to nothing, and were wandering about as beggars, thoroughly demoralized and discontented.

Crime in Rural Communities

J. B. Brown, *Views of Canada and the Colonists* (Edinburgh, 1851), pp. 162-3.

Serious criminal offences, especially against property, may be said to be comparatively rare in Canada. The large amount of material comfort afforded to the widely-spread population of the colony—with exceptions, mostly in large towns—allows, of course, fewer temptations to commit offences against property than among the overdense and too frequently starving masses of the parent country.

Much of the old severity of the English laws against property are still in force in Canada. . . . Offences against the person, originating in quarrels or assaults, are perhaps the more common class of offences in Canada, and these may not infrequently be traced to the agency of intoxicating drinks.

Drinking and Crime

Journal of the House of Assembly of Upper Canada, 1836, Appendix No. 44:
Report of the Grand Jury of the Niagara District on the Gaol, September 8, 1835.

In closing the responsible duties which the Laws have conferred upon
the Grand Jurors, they feel impressed with the conviction that much the
greater portion of crime which has come under their cognizance has been
occasioned by the intemperate use of ardent spirits, which the vast number
of Taverns and Tippling Houses in every part of the District, and more particularly in the Towns and Villages cause to be but too easily procured.
They are fully aware that the Law vests the practical right of granting
Licenses in the majority of the Magistrates in sessions, but from the Houses
having been long kept as places of resort, and the proprietors in many cases
not having any other apparent means of supporting their families, the evil
has been suffered to continue.

B. *The Timber Trade and Public Works*

Disorder among Raftsmen in Bytown

(i)

The Brockville Recorder, October 23, 1835.

A correspondent asks of us, what we mean by "the blood thirsty scenes
of Bytown," and we answer him.   That in Bytown, there is a band of about
150 desperadoes, who entirely swarm the place, a Canadian is not allowed
to live there, if he is caught on the bridge, he is thrown into what is called
the kettle, (a whirlpool,) and that terminates his miseries, but if caught in
the woods or towns, these 150 Shiners, as they are denominated, beat and
injure them so that few recover.   If any of this band enter a shop, and
demand any particular goods or ware, the shopkeeper dares not refuse, for
should he his life is instantly sought, and failing to get which, his property
is sure to be destroyed by fire.   In fact, the law is there a dead letter, and
before so many of our journalists, exult in the continued riots in the States,
and deprecate as severely as they do, the recourse to Lynch law, they should
look nearer home and call the attention of the Government to these facts.
If the arm of the civil authorities cannot restrain the scenes such as are daily
reacted in Bytown, let the aid of the military be called in and let no more
quarter, or mercy be shown to these demons in human shape than they have
shown to them they have sacrificed.   His Excellency Sir John Colborne,
ought to be made acquainted with these circumstances without delay.—
Belleville Int.

(ii)

The Brockville Recorder, February 23, 1837.

State of Society at By-town.—We learn by a gentleman who has recently
visited By-town that outrages of a most brutal nature are of frequent occur-

16

rence in that place and its neighbourhood;—the work of a set of men called "Shiners." A few weeks since a poor Indian was taken into a house and after being most inhumanely mutilated thrown out at a window. —He was taken up by some humane individuals who endeavoured to preserve his life, but it was useless, he expired in a few hours.

On Saturday week, a man named Scarf was dragged from his sleigh in Lower By-town, his shoulder dislocated, his head cut open in three places by a stake taken from his sleigh, and his body otherwise badly beaten. Another man named Hobbs, had his horses taken from him their ears and tails cut off, the side of one cut open, and his harness cut to pieces. Two others were attacked that afternoon;—and a man named Isabell was the same evening robbed of Thirty dollars, within two miles of Richmond. Notwithstanding the frequent occurrence of such outrages on society, no means seem to be adopted to put the laws in force. The men in authority either want the *power* or the *will* to discharge their duties. If the former, their hands should be strengthened, if the latter, dismissed from office. As matters appear to stand, the inhabitants in and about By-town must live in a wretched state of apprehension; which is likely to be much enhanced by the high prices of the necessaries of life.

Social Controls and Morality in Lumber Communities

Joshua Fraser, *Shanty, Forest and River Life in the Backwoods of Canada* (Montreal, 1883), pp. 26-8, 32-7, 112-13, 329-32, 347, 349-51, 353, 359-60.

In a community of men, so isolated and far removed from the ordinary restraints of social and judicial influence, it may be supposed that absolute lawlessness, and reckless independence will reign supreme, that each man of these hardy, rough-and-ready sons of the forest will think and act as if he were a law to himself. But such is very far from being the case. There is government and discipline in shanty life, just as pronounced and strictly carried out as in the most exemplary and well-regulated village, town, or city corporation of the Dominion. . . .

Conditions and mutual obligations are generally very clearly understood between foreman and men, and, as a rule, there is very little disturbance of the peace, or absence of harmony in the general working of both inside and out-door shanty life. . . .

There is rather a new phase of shanty government being developed within the last few years, and that is the appointment of general managers over the business. Those lumber-merchants who carry on an extensive business, say of three or more shanties, and perhaps have other large interests to attend to, are now in the habit of appointing a "manager" who has full oversight and charge of all the foremen and men, and is directly responsible to the proprietors for the general "running" of the concern. These gentlemen, however, are very chary how they interfere between the foreman and his men; though if any difficulty does arise they are the referees who arbitrate upon it. . . .

Of course, the fact that they can discharge men when they please, without detriment to the business—being so near the settlements that they can quickly replace them—gives the manager and foreman the whip-hand over the men in maintaining the order and general efficiency of the shanty. . . .

A great mistake is entertained by many people regarding the general character of shantymen: they are commonly looked upon as a wild harum-scarum class of men who have no right sense of the decencies and proprieties of ordinary respectable life, who when they go to the woods leave behind them their good manners and morals, along with their Sunday clothes. That the shanty itself is a city of refuge for the abandoned and profligate of the earth, and resounds continually with oaths and profanities of the vilest nature is a common error. . . .

Now there is no doubt that this low estimate of character is tolerably correct as applied to the average shantyman of many years ago. But it does not hold true now in any sense whatsoever. A great change for the better has been wrought in the character and conduct of these men. . . .

I account for this great change in the morals and habits of this class on two grounds:

First, there is a different class seeking work and being engaged by the employers from what used to be. A few years ago the great bulk of the men were hired at Ottawa and Quebec, and were principally French Canadians, of the lowest class. Now, since the sawn lumber business has assumed such large proportions, the drive on the river is comparatively short, generally over by the first of June, consequently a much larger number of the farmers' sons in the vicinity of the works are seeking employment, as they generally can get home in time for sowing the crop; and as they are a much more steady and reliable class, and just as able-bodied and skilful workmen, they are more readily engaged than any others. The number of men who engage in the fall to go through to Quebec is but a fraction of what it used to be, and the number of French Canadians who work in the woods is now reduced to a minimum.

Hence the *personnel* of the shanty is greatly changed, and that vastly for the better, within the last few years.

Another reason, and one that is a mighty factor in this improved state of things, is that the foremen, as a rule, are exerting themselves more strongly in favor of sobriety and morality. The foremen themselves are a better class of men. The old bullying, brute-force principle of governing is now almost entirely done away with. . . .

A foreman now-a-days never thinks of taking a handspike and knocking a man down if he neglects his duty, or is in any way refractory. If the man will not listen to remonstrance or reproof, he orders the clerk to "give him his time," and then quietly tells him to leave. The dread of this has a far more powerful effect upon the men in keeping them up to the mark than handspikes or fisticuffs. . . .

There is no honester class of men living than shantymen, and the dwellers in the backwoods generally. Trunks and boxes lie about for the most part unlocked, and socks, moccasins, boots, and underclothing are scattered about, or hanging from nails and pegs in every nook and corner of the shanty; and yet every man can always find his own, and seldom or never appropriates the property of another. There is one article, however, which is a notable exception to this honest rule of conduct, and that is liquor of any kind. The shantyman has no conscience in the matter of whiskey. It is considered fair plunder, wherever he can lay his hands on it. If, therefore, you go to the backwoods with a supply of liquor for your private use, you must keep it constantly under lock and key, otherwise it is certain to be pilfered from you before you are a day in the shanty. In the matter of scenting out and appropriating whiskey, the thirsty shantyman is as keen as a weasel, as cunning as a fox, and as unscrupulous as a wolf.

With this exception, however, the general character of the shantymen is one of the strictest probity. A thief is the unknown quantity among them. . . .

Notwithstanding what I have written about the greatly improved morality, and general tone of character, and habit of shantymen now, compared with what it used to be, still it can be readily understood by those who know human life and nature that there necessarily must be much that is rough, coarse and even brutal among this class of men.

I deny most emphatically that the general influence of shanty life in the woods during winter is prejudicial in itself to a good, fair tone of character and morals. . . .

But I must confess that a certain change takes place in these aspects of character when the drive commences in the spring. The river life is more calculated to unsettle good resolutions and habits, and to develop the harum-scarum propensities of human nature than that of the winter. It is a life of irregular, unsettled and changeful interest, and is beset with new and peculiar temptations to the ex-hibernated shantyman.

If he is groggily inclined, he has now frequent opportunities of gratifying his appetite. Every few miles on the river side there are low taverns, or shebeen shops, licensed and unlicensed, where rank vitriolized poison, under the name of good-whiskey, is sold by the glass or bottle to the thirsty drivers.

These places are hot-beds of abominations. They awaken and revive in full force the long repressed devil of strong drink which has been lying dormant, perhaps almost extinguished, by the lengthy winter sojourn amid the pure bracing influences of the forest. Now it is that, upon occasion at least, the river-man can, if he pleases, give full fling to all that is sensuous, low, and debasing within him. On Saturday nights especially, when the week's work is finished, and he can sleep off the effects of a debauch on the Sunday, these river-side shabeens are often the scenes of frightful orgies, and of most inhuman and brutal "fights" between individuals of the same drive, or free fights between rival gangs of other "drives."

These encounters in their ferocity, bloodshed, and often serious and even fatal consequences, beggar all description. When the devilish passions of those rough and powerful men are thoroughly roused by the demons of whiskey, then they become more like wild beasts, and infuriated madmen than human beings.

I have never seen the terribly demoralizing effect of strong drink in completely changing the character and disposition of a man more strongly exemplified than among those men, and especially on such occasions. You would not know them to be the same men. . . .

The "settling up" in Quebec is an anxious time for both the lumber merchant and the shantyman. . . .

As soon as the raft is "snubbed" within the booms at Quebec, and put in its most presentable shape for the inspection of the buyers, then the "boss" comes aboard with a bag of money, and with his clerk pays to each man the amount coming to him. . . .

Like Jack Tar when he gets into port, the poor shantyman has now to run the gauntlet of the very worst and vilest temptations that can assail a man. For the past ten months or more he has toiled, take it all in all, as no other class of working men have to do; during that time he has led, as a rule, a careful, abstemious, saving life, twenty-five dollars would probably cover all his necessary personal expenses. . . . In the revulsion of their position from restraint and abstemiousness, there is also a revulsion of their feelings as to indulgence and licentiousness. In the first burst of his absolute freedom and idleness the thoughtless shantyman is too apt to go headlong into every indulgence that presents itself, and you may be very sure the devil is at his elbow to help him on. As he leaps with a light heart and a heavy pocket from the raft on to the shore he is at once beset with a host of hell-runners in the shape of calash drivers, boarding-house agents, brothel sirens, and crimps and sharpers of the blackest stamp. . . .

These open-hearted, free-handed men, flush with money and the self-confidence of redundant health and spirits, are like children in the hands of these cunning pitiless crimps that dog their steps from the moment they set foot in Quebec until their last cent is gone, when they are remorsely kicked into the street and sent about their business. . . .

Ottawa is the great "hiring depot" of the lumbering region. To this city the merchants or their agents come to engage men for the next season's work.

Work in the woods generally commences about the middle of September—up to this time, therefore, after being discharged at Quebec a month or six weeks previously, and having their "spree" over, if they will have one, the men are either at their homes in the country or, if they have none, boarding in Ottawa until they are hired again.

This period is, of course, a harvest time for boarding-houses and low grog shops in Lower Town, and, consequently, with too many of the shantymen, a time of rioting, and spending what money may be left after their Quebec escapades. Even though a man may not have a cent of money when he comes to Ottawa, those boarding-house sharks will receive him with open arms, and give him all he asks for, knowing right well that when re-engaged all his bills will be paid by the merchant, who, of course, in turn deducts the amount out of the man's pay as the season goes on. Many a man while idling away his time at these places spends beforehand his whole winter's wages. In fact, in numberless cases, the Quebec experience, both on the part of the shantyman and his despoilers, is here re-enacted.

Disorder among Irish on Public Works

(i)

Public Archives of Canada, *Upper Canada Sundries:* Bytown, May 18, 1827, A. Wilson to Hillier.

It is with deep regret, that I have the honour to acquaint you,—for the information of His Excellency the Lieutenant-Governor, that the public peace is most dreadfully disturbed—and the lives and property of the inhabitants in danger day and night in this new Town, by drunken, riotous, persons employed on the works of the Rideau Canal: —as there is not an evening passes—not even the Sabbath day excepted—wherein there is not a riot and general fight.

(ii)

J. R. Godley, *Letters from America* (London, 1844), vol. I, pp. 156, 165-6.

A good deal of fighting has been going on among the Irish labourers, of whom 600 or 700 are employed on the Welland canal; two lives were lost, and many are now in prison, charged with having been engaged in the disturbance, the cause of which was merely anxiety to monopolise the work on the part of the first comers.   It is to these government works that all the Irish emigrants of the labouring class crowd upon landing, so that there always appears to be a super-abundant supply of labour near them, while, perhaps, fifty miles farther up the country far better wages may be obtained, and there may be an ample demand for hands. . . .

In the evening we returned to Brantford, where we found a good deal of alarm prevailing, and the magistrates swearing in special constables, in consequence of a riot which has taken place among the Irish labourers upon the Grand River canal, about three miles from hence.   Wherever these countrymen of mine are, they must and will fight.

Efforts to Check Disorders on Public Works

Provincial Statutes of Canada (Montreal, 1845), pp. 45-50.

An Act for the better preservation of the Peace and the prevention of Riots and violent Outrages at or near Public Works while in progress of construction. [Passed March 7, 1845.]

Whereas it is necessary to make further provision for the preservation of the peace, and for the protection of the lives, persons and property of Her Majesty's subjects, in the neighbourhood of public works on which large bodies of laborers are congregated and employed: Be it therefore enacted. . . . That it shall be lawful for the Governor in Council, from time to time, and as often as occasion shall require, to declare by Proclamation the several places in this Province, within the limits whereof any Canal or other public work whatsoever shall be in progress of construction, or such places as shall be in the vicinity of any such Canal or other public work, within which it shall be found necessary that this Act shall come into force and effect. . . .

II. And be it enacted, That upon and after the day to be fixed in such Proclamation for that purpose, no person employed in or upon any such Canal or other public work within the limits specified in such Proclamation, shall have or keep in his possession or under his care or control, within such limits, any gun, blunderbuss, pistol, or other fire-arm, or any stock, lock, barrel, or any other part of such gun, blunderbuss, pistol, or other fire-arm, or any bullets, sword, sword blade, bayonet, pike, pikehead, spear, spearhead, dirk, dagger, or other instrument intended for cutting or stabbing, or other arms, ammunition, or weapon of war, under a penalty of not less than ten shillings, nor more than twenty shillings for every such weapon found in his possession. . . .

XIII. And for better carrying this Act into effect and more effectually ensuring the preservation of the peace, and that safety to the lives and property of Her Majesty's Subjects which it is the object of the Act to attain; Be it enacted, That it shall be lawful for the Governor in Council to cause a body of men not exceeding in number one hundred inclusive of officers, to be called *The Mounted Police Force*, to be raised, mounted, armed and equipped . . . and to cause such Police Force or any portion thereof, to be employed in any place in this Province in which this Act shall be in force. . . .

XVI. And be it enacted, That the expenses to be incurred in carrying this Act into effect, shall be paid through the Board of Works out of the monies appropriated for the work on which such expences shall be respectively incurred, and shall be charged and accounted as part of the cost of such work.

Irish Immigration and Problem of Crime

Journals of the Legislative Assembly of Canada, 1852-3, Appendix III: Report of the Roman Catholic Chaplain of the Provincial Penitentiary, January 24, 1853.

Persons may be startled at seeing that the great majority of the Catholic convicts are either Irish or of Irish extraction, whereas the Irish Catholics do not form much over one-fourth of the whole Catholic population of Canada; but this ought only to surprise a very superficial observer, and should lead no one to conclude that there is any more natural vicious disposition in the Irish character, than in that of any other people; for virtue, honesty, and absence from crime, the Irish farmers in this Country can bear a very fair comparison with either the Scotch or English, and Irish women are admitted on all hands, to be more virtuous than those of any other nation. A great allowance ought to be made for the early education and prejudices of the Irish; for centuries back they have been a persecuted and trodden down people in the land of their nativity; their forefathers have been plundered of their property, and until very late it was a capital crime for an Irish Catholic to teach even an Elementary School—under such rule, ignorance and poverty were the only inheritance to the Irish to hand down to their posterity, with this was mixed a pretty fair dose of hatred towards their persecutors. Place any nation in the world in the same position in which the Irish had to live for the last three hundred years, and I am convinced that after such an ordeal, it would not be half so virtuous as the Irish are; persons must not also judge of the Irish character from that of many of those we see in this Country, nor from the lying accounts with which the English Press generally teem. The great majority of the Irish who have selected Canada for the land of their adoption, arrive pennyless in it; they must for many a year depend upon employment in the Public Works, to obtain the means of keeping body and soul together; men of every description and disposition congregated together in large numbers have never been the best school of morality, and they must be more than men, if this has not a most deteriorating effect upon their conduct. Few of those employed in the mines of California are Irish, and yet, if we believe the daily accounts we receive from that country, there are more crimes committed in it in one week than there is in this country for years. I will be told that in this free Country, the Irish enjoy the same advantages as those of every other country, but generally speaking this is not the case. Few of the German settlers arrive in this country without being the possessors of some hundred dollars or pounds; large numbers of them, the moment they make up their minds to emigrate to Canada or the United States, send out Agents to procure large tracts of land, where numbers from the same locality can settle together. On their arrival they know where to direct their course, and they have means not only to pay for the land, but also to stock it, and support their families for two or three years. The first European settlers after the Conquest, received large tracts of land gratis, which enabled them to provide for the future settlement of their children and grand children; among these there were few or no Irish. The first Irish emigrants who came to Canada, were those brought out by the late Mr. Peter Robinson, and every one knows that, instead of being a proper selection, they were the very worst characters, of whom the people of the south of Ireland wanted to rid themselves. With all the advantages imaginable, persons of this description could not succeed; but the misfortune was, that from their idle and dissipated habits, they were the cause of creating very unfavorable prejudices against the whole Irish Nation; this prejudice was really carried so far, that I have known a certain Judge for whom the knowledge of one being an Irishman, and particularly an Irish Roman Catholic, was a sufficient evidence to obtain conviction. Thus poor Paddy, Esopus like, whether he saw many or few birds, whether they appeared to the right or to the left, was sure of going off with a sound flogging.

C. Rise of the Town

Crime with the Growth of the Town

R. H. Bonnycastle, *Canada and the Canadians in 1846* (London, 1846), vol. II, pp. 194-200.

It will surprise my readers to state that, in an agricultural country, where the manners of the people are still very primitive, where education is still backward, and civilization slowly advancing, out of a population of about 1,200,000, scattered widely in the woods, there should be so large a proportion as twenty women, and five hundred men, in the Kingston Penitentiary. . . .

Recent discoveries of the police in Montreal have shown that *hells* of the most atrocious character, and one in imitation of Crockford's, as far as its inferior means would go, have been found out.

At Kingston a most wretched establishment of the same nature has recently been broken up, and at Toronto great incentives to vice in the very young exist.

Clerks in banks have gambled away the property of their employers in these places to the amount of several thousands. . . .

Border population is usually of a low character, and I cannot think it can be worse anywhere than where the maritime, or rather *laculine*, if such a word is admissable, preponderates, and where that race is unemployed for at least five months of the Boreal winters of Canada. It is only a wonder that serious crime is so infrequent. Burglary was almost unknown, as well as highway robbery, until last year; but instances of both occurred near Toronto, and the former twice at Kingston.

Crime in Toronto

Public Archives of Canada, *Upper Canada Sundries:* Toronto, January 21, 1835, Mackenzie to Rowan.

The cheapness of intoxicating liquor, the violent passions of the individuals, the vast number of taverns and pothouses, the want of education in many persons, the prejudices of persons meeting here from different countries and of conflicting creeds, present difficulties of a formidable nature to the civil magistrate—if to these is added a belief that premeditated crime of an aggravated nature can be committed with impunity, or meet with but slight punishment, I think that an increase of crime will be the consequence and that the state of Society will be less tranquil.

Crime in the Cities

Sessional Papers of the Province of Canada, 1860, No. 32: Preliminary Report of the Board of Inspectors of Asylums, Prisons, Etc., 1859, p. 15.

In Lower Canada, the Districts of Three Rivers, of Ottawa, and of Gaspe, have not sent a convict [to the Provincial Penitentiary]. Kamouraska and St. Francis, have sent one each, and the District and City of Quebec only two.

In Upper Canada, the County of Grey, and the United Counties of Stormont, Dundas, and Glengarry, and of Prescott and Russell, have not furnished any convicts, and the County of Prince Edward but one.

As a melancholy reverse to this picture, take the following cities and environs which seem to monopolize great crimes: Hamilton has sent 35 convicts, Toronto 34, and Montreal 26, to the Penitentiary.

Larger Proportion of Criminals from Canada West

Sessional Papers of the Province of Canada, 1860, No. 32, pp. 66-7: Report of the Inspectors of the Provincial Penitentiary, 1860.

Nativity of Convicts received in the Provincial Penitentiary.

| | From Canada West | | | | | From Canada East | | | | |
	1856	1857	1858	1859	Total	1856	1857	1858	1859	Total
Canada...	51	45	81	60	237	42	25	33	19	122
England ..	34	20	34	32	120	8	6	10	..	24
Ireland...	48	64	63	51	226	18	12	13	6	49
Scotland..	10	10	9	16	45	3	1	1	1	6
U.S.A.....	45	30	45	55	175	..	2	4	1	7
Elsewhere.	6	6	6	12	30	6	3	6	3	18
Totals....	194	179	238	226	833	80	49	67	30	226

It may be sufficient, on the present occasion, to make the following remarks: If Canada West has any just cause to boast of the increase of its inhabitants, it has, on the other hand, but too good cause to deplore the depravity and crime that abounds among them. It is, however, just to suppose that the criminals are not a correct representation of its population. Perhaps, in a greater degree than its sister below, it receives a large number of bad persons from the United States; it must also be admitted that emigration is directing its steps in that quarter in an increased ratio, bringing with it very many good and respectable citizens, but at the same time not a few poor destitute individuals who "at Home" were incapable of gaining an honest livelihood, and there is yet another element which contributes its full share of penal subjects, and that is the large number of escaped slaves— unfortunate creatures whose minds have been little or not at all cultivated; who are not taught the advantages of self-reliance, self-respect, and provident habits. . . . Their advent is no acquisition to the real wealth and prosperity of a northern climate; they are not adapted for agricultural pursuits in such a climate; they only aspire to be menials, and not always of the most docile or useful disposition. It must be admitted, however, that we occasionally meet a coloured man who is really an acquisition, but this is a striking exception.

In the Lower Province, the population is essentially agricultural, besides being naturally of mild and retiring habits; they are not by any means addicted to the brutalizing vice of drinking. . . . And this favourable condition of Lower Canadian Society, it is but fair to say, is mainly due to the incessant efforts of the Parochial Clergy, who not satisfied with denouncing the accursed habit from the pulpit, battle with it elsewhere; they form and head associations throughout their parishes, and by precept, example, and the most energetic appeals, they contend against this dread enemy of mankind, and their efforts are blessed; the admirable social and domestic habits of the kind-hearted people are thus preserved and ameliorated.

Prostitution in Toronto

Public Archives of Canada, *Upper Canada Sundries:* Toronto, November 23, 1834, W. L. McKenzie, Mayor of Toronto, to Secretary of Lieutenant-Governor.

Frequent complaints have been made to me by the people living in Front street, against two houses of bad fame, the inmates of which had scandalized the reputable neighbours, and the frequenters of which by their riotous and disorderly conduct had made it unsafe to walk the streets after nightfall. W. Leslie and myself examined a number of persons on oath, and after proving by their own testimony (in the most ample manner) the lewd, disorderly conduct of two young women from the States, residing in these bad houses, we sent the two women to the jail, which is by law made the House of Correction for the City. The sentence was to be kept a fortnight at labour in that part of the prison which is set apart for female convicts, away from the male prisoners—so that their confinement might not be a pleasure instead of a punishment. We further required them to give security for decent conduct at the close of the term.

As I doubted whether the sentence would be carried into effect, so far as related to the confinement of the women in such a way as would not turn the jail into a brothel, I went in the evening to see what had been done, and in requesting to be shown to the place where they were, the gaoler and his turnkey went with me, and I found the women *walking at large among the debtors in their (the debtors') rooms!* The jailer said he had given strict instructions to the turnkey in conforming to the sentence. How that was I know not but when I visited the prison the night previous about eight o'clock, I found the turnkey so much intoxicated that he could hardly stand. . . .

I admit readily that the jailer's situation is one which few would envy—it is a very troublesome one. But unless the worthless drunkards and prostitutes who lead the unwary into the snares of vice can be punished in a more effectual way than hitherto, they will increase in number, daring and wickedness.

Crime and Prostitution among Females

Journals of the Legislative Assembly of Canada, 1852-53.   Appendix III: Report of the Roman Catholic Chaplain of the Provincial Penitentiary, January 24, 1853.

Of the female convicts who led a life of prostitution before they were sent to the Penitentiary, and I am sorry to say that too many of them have been persons of this description, little can be said in respect to their religious feelings or impressions. Sometimes, judging only from outward appearance and their general conduct, an inexperienced person would be led to pass a favorable opinion upon them. But, unfortunately, from the conduct of the majority of them, the very moment they are discharged from the Penitentiary, a more experienced person would be led to judge that their abstinence from indulging in certain irregularities, arises from the impossibility of doing so, rather than from a real change of heart. To this general rule there may be, and there are exceptions, but the number is so very small, that it is hardly worth mentioning; of the other description of female convicts, many are unfortunate rather than vicious. Some of them are Emigrants sent out from the poor-houses of Ireland, and land upon our shores without a friend or relative to receive them, and without a penny to support them. They have not been brought up to habits of cleanliness or industry; as servants, they are for a long time, useless; and yet, from foolish ideas imbibed from stories about the imaginary facilities of earning high wages in this Country, they will not be contented with receiving even more than their services are really worth. After a few days seeking shelter, food and employment, from door to door, they find themselves in a complete state of destitution; necessity compels them, in order to support wasted nature, to commit some petty larceny, and for this, probably their first offence, they are sent to one of our common Gaols, where, for months, they are compelled to live in daily communication and contact with the most depraved and profligate characters. In every large City, there are a certain number of irreligious and profligate Lawyers, hawkers of their legal advice, and assistance about our Gaols, and who take a certain number of those ignorant and inexperienced young females under their patronage, in order to seduce them. Such monsters, in human shape, should never be allowed to speak to any of those females, except in presence of respectable witnesses. This is not an imaginary case; it occurs oftener than the public could suspect, sometimes with the connivance, and always by the indifference of some of our Gaolers. Generally these novices in crime can be reclaimed; however, this becomes more difficult from the absence of any classification among the female convicts. . . . There is another description of female convicts; that is, those who have had the misfortune of having been united to dissipated and drunken husbands, and have, after having long resisted the evil example daily before their eye, at last yielded to the temptation, and in a fit of intoxication, have committed some petty theft, for which they were sent to the Penitentiary. . . . There are at present about twenty Catholic female convicts in the Penitentiary; of this number, two only are of French Canadian extraction, one black woman, and all the others are either Irish or of Irish extraction.

D. Development of Social Controls

Effort to Curb Intemperance

Papers and Records, Ontario Historical Society, vol. XXVI, 1930, p. 567: Proudfoot Papers.

August 7, 1833, Home:—
    Called on Mr. Cottar to-day, the person who has leased the "King's Arms" and suggested to him the propriety of shutting his bar on the Sabbath. He thanked me for my good advice and although I did not extract any promise from him (I wished him to think of it). I hope he will follow my advice and if he does much good will be done to London.

Methodists and Temperance Reform

(i)

Minutes of the Annual Conferences of the Wesleyan-Methodist Church of Canada, from 1824 to 1845 inclusive (Toronto, 1846), p. 39.

We would also recommend *Temperance Societies* to your attention and zealous patronage. These associations are designed to place ardent spirits where they ought to be placed—among the drugs of the apothecary; and to confine their use (if they may be used at all) to cases of *extreme* necessity, or when the use or application of them may be prescribed by a temperate physician: and we fervently hope, that not one member of our Church will either be so attached to the use of ardent spirits, or so indifferent to the sobriety and welfare of his fellow-creatures, as to withhold his name or support from an association which is so admirably adapted to accomplish the object it avowedly contemplates—the banishing of the use of ardent spirits from among us. Temperate persons should join a Temperance Society, for the same reason that religious persons should join a society of religious people; and that intemperate persons ought to reform and become temperate, is not disputed by any. It is the design of our Discipline, and it has ever been our aim, to make our Church emphatically a Temperance Society; and it is devoutly to be wished, that every member of our Church should be a member of a Temperance Society, as he thereby unites his co-operating example and influence with the temperate of every name and creed, to accomplish a common object and promote a common interest. [Pastoral Address of the Conference of August 30, 1830].

(ii)

Life and Times of the Rev. Anson Green, Written by Himself (Toronto, 1877), p. 141.

1830—The Temperance Movement is progressing finely, and the Conference has gone in for its full share of the work and of the glory connected with it. Drunkenness and tippling are crying evils in the land, and that man is a benefactor of our race who can and will contribute, in any degree, to stay this torrent of evil, and dry up this river of poison and death. Much has already been accomplished by sermons, addresses, and the formation of societies; but still there are thousands who are not ashamed to brawl in our streets and stagger in the presence of the sun!

A Temperance Meeting

The Brockville Recorder, March 21, 1834.

TEMPERANCE MEETING

The second Anniversary of the Elizabethtown Union Temperance Society took place on Thursday the 4th inst. in the School House near Eri Hays's.

The meeting was opened with prayer by the President, who gave a short Address, after which the Secretary read the following:

REPORT.

In submitting the Annual Report of this Society, the Secretary congratulates its members on the success that has attended their benevolent exertions. Although there are some circumstances to be regretted, the cause is far from declining, and the institution is prospering in a manner highly gratifying to every friend of Temperance.

During the year past, 101 have enlisted under the banner of this Society; one has removed; six expelled; one death; making the present actual number of the Society 331. The Society is exerting a powerful and moralizing influence, and many who yet oppose its objects, and refuse to acknowledge its utility, cannot but feel they are hindering a work which is calculated to produce the most beneficial effects on the moral condition of man.

Instead of being disheartened, we have every encouragement to proceed: and the wonder is, not that so little has been effected, but that so much has been done in so short a time; and from the unhappy consequences that are daily produced by intemperance, it is hoped that the time is not far distant when not one will be found to advocate the baleful vice—drunkenness.

An opportunity was then given for such as felt disposed to give in their names, when 23 signed the pledge of abstinence; which, deducting four afterwards expelled, increased our number to 350.

The Society then proceeded to appoint its officers for the present year. . . .

The special business of the meeting being concluded, the following resolutions were severally put and carried.

Resolved—That the success which has attended the Temperance Enterprize in this and other countries, affords ample encouragement to its friends to persevere in the good cause.

Resolved—That this Society deplore the yet wretched condition of many individuals and families within the sphere of its operations and the sad effects of intemperate drinking; and the members feel it their duty to persevere in the endeavors to rescue their fellow men from this most cruel bondage.

Resolved—That in order the more effectually to promote the cause of Temperance, this Society would recommend to the friends of abstinence the propriety of being particularly guarded in the use of wines.

Resolved—That this Society deem it the duty of every member of the temperance cause to make the owner of a public house a direct compensation for the accommodation of his house and fire, instead of an indirect one by purchasing an article they do not want.

This meeting, on the whole, was an interesting one, and conducted in a manner calculated to enlist more warmly the feelings and zeal of its members, and give a new impetus to the cause of temperance in this part.

H. W. BLANCHARD, Sec.

Elizabethtown, March 10, 1834.

Orange Lodge and Temperance

Report of the Proceedings of the 26th Session of the Grand Lodge of the Loyal Orange Institution of British America, Brockville, U.C., June 17-19, 1856 (Toronto, 1856), p. 25.

It has afforded me, my dear brethren, the most sincere gratification to find, that amongst the other reforms and improvements so rapidly going on in the Institution during the last year or two, none has progressed with a more steady hand, or produced more excellent fruit, than the introduction of Temperance into the private Lodges. [Speech of the Grand Master].

Temperance Society in Toronto

J. S. Buckingham, *Canada, Nova Scotia, New Brunswick* (London, 1843), p. 26.

There is a Temperance Society here, on the principle of total abstinence from all that can intoxicate; but their numbers are few, the higher classes of society, and the Episcopal clergy, withholding their patronage and support. During one of the evenings of my stay here, I delivered a public address on the subject of Temperance in the Wesleyan Methodist Church, but though it was very numerously attended, there were very few of the leading families among the auditory; and the only members of the clergy present were a Congregational minister and a Roman Catholic priest. The absence of all the heads of the community on this occasion could not be attributed to any other cause than their indifference or unwillingness to countenance or uphold the Temperance cause; for when my lectures on Egypt and Palestine were given in the same building, one course before and one after the Temperance address, the church was crowded to excess, and there was scarcely a family of any note or influence absent. The Lieutenant-Governor, the Chief Justice, and the other official dignitaries of the province and city, attended with their families regularly for three nights in succession at each course, and in several instances put aside other engagements, to enable them to be present; but the Temperance Reformation was to them evidently an unpopular and unattractive subject; . . .

Effect of the Temperance Movement

Letters from Settlers in Upper Canada (London, 1834), p. 7.

Whisky is very cheap, it is about $7\frac{1}{2}$ d a quart, and many drink it to the ruin of their health and circumstances, not that the expense ruins them, but the loss of time. But since the establishment of Temperance Societies this evil has very considerably abated. [Thomas Drury, York, U.C., June 27, 1833, to G. Thompson, Bethnal Green].

Undesirable Features of Temperance Movement

R. H. Bonnycastle, *The Canadas in 1841* (London, 1841), vol. I, pp. 128-9.

It is unfortunately the case, that in a state of society so new as that of Upper Canada, there are never wanting motives to incite obscure individuals to the attainment of a pseudo celebrity, without the previous acquirements of education, observation, and research. Hence, perhaps, as much evil arises from the meddling of these persons with temperance societies, as the good they achieve. Farragos of voluminous temperance tracts issue in clouds from the presses, under the auspices, frequently, of the most inadequate people, and of people, too, whose previous career has convinced the thinking that the desire to become known is the prime mover. The temperance doctors are as innumerable as the religious schisms in this new country; the result is the same in both; fewer are really convinced; for where everybody is right nobody can be wrong. Thus you will find, that political quacks, whose sole dependence and livelihood depend on keeping up a scurrilous, agitating, unprincipled newspaper, are generally the firmest and most untiring temperance advocates.

Houses of Correction

The Statutes of the Province of Upper Canada (Kingston, 1831), p. 161.

An Act to declare the common gaols in the several districts of this province to be houses of correction for certain purposes. [Passed March 12, 1810].

Whereas it is expedient that until houses of correction shall be erected in the several districts of this province, that the common gaol in each and every of the said districts shall be held and taken to be for certain purposes, a house of correction; be it therefore enacted . . . That until such houses of correction shall be erected as aforesaid, the common gaol in each of the said several districts respectively shall be, and the same is hereby constituted a house of correction; and that all and every idle and disorderly person or persons who may by law be subject to be committed to a house of correction, shall be committed to the said common gaols in the said districts respectively, any law or usage to the contrary in any wise notwithstanding.

Increase of Population and Gaol Accommodation

Journals of the House of Assembly of Upper Canada, 1836, Appendix No. 44: Report of the chairman of the Quarter Sessions Home District, on the state of the Gaol, March 9, 1836.

Having given to the whole matter their most attentive consideration, the magistrates in adjourned Quarter Sessions beg leave most respectfully to report for your Excellency's information:

That in the early settlement of the Province, and from the thin and scattered state of the population of this district, as well as the comparative absence of crime, and the unfrequent detention of persons in custody on civil process for debt, the means for the safe-keeping of criminals and others, was, perhaps, but a secondary consideration—a known place for their reception under the proper officers, was, at such period, all that was found to be indispensably necessary, and for many years without any serious inconvenience being found to result from such an arrangement, an ordinary building, constructed in almost the rudest manner, with a common enclosure marking its precincts, was found sufficient for the existing wants of the district.

As the population increased and with it the inmates of the prison began to be more numerous, the necessity for a building better adapted for their safe custody became apparent. . . . After various suggestions for providing the necessary accommodation and convenience for the then increasing wants of the district, and with a view of it being afforded without causing any additional burthen upon the inhabitants by additional assessments of taxes—the result of these deliberations was an application to the Legislature in the year 1823, for authority under the sanction of law, to loan an amount for the purpose of erecting adequate buildings for a Court House and Gaol. . . .

At the period of the erection of those buildings it is also proper to observe, that in the proposed accommodation considered as necessary, at a time when though the population had considerably increased it was yet comparatively limited in amount, that accommodation was estimated for, and made rather with a regard to the ordinary increase of inhabitants than with any reference to the rapid growth of numbers, the result of an unexpected emigration from the Mother Country, which has of late years brought to the province so great an increase of population, and in the benefits of which the Home District has had the good fortune to partake, in, perhaps, a larger proportion, than any other district in the province. . . .

The buildings which were erected without any additional tax having been imposed, at a period when the accommodation required was regulated with a view to the ordinary increase of a population of 21,329 have within the short period of eight years [1827-1835] been found inefficient in consequence of the rapid and extraordinary growth of numbers by emigration for a population of more than 56,000. . . .

Independent of the ordinary expenses incurred for the safe keeping of prisoners within the Gaol, and for which purpose it was more expressly designed from the necessity of the case, and in the absence of other provision for such an object an additional item of expenditure of no inconsiderable amount has been incurred in the care and maintenance of insane persons. . . .

It is with great satisfaction that the magistrates have in prospect the relief which may be expected in this respect from its having attracted the attention of the Legislature, where measures they understand are in progress, which they have no doubt will have the effect of providing more ample means than can be expected within the walls of a gaol, for the care and support of a portion of the community labouring under the severest of all dispensations. . . .

As regards the inefficient state of the building, it is beyond all doubt that for the present population increasing as it is, this cannot be denied, and that it must be apparent to general observation that for the purpose to which it is now by law rendered applicable in the safe keeping of ordinary offenders and those under sentence of imprisonment—in the asylum it is made to

17

afford to the insane—in being rendered applicable for all city purposes, serving as it does as a lock up house for disorderly persons and night brawlers—and when the maintenance of any of these classes cannot be compensated for in any way by useful labor—it is perfectly inadequate; and that the period has arrived when the means for erecting proper and commodious buildings, applicable to the district purposes is loudly called for.

State of the Gaols

The Brockville Recorder, September 20, 1832.

To the Editor of the Brockville Recorder
Sir,
    I have much pleasure in stating that two successive Grand Juries have visited this prison since I have been confined, and that the gentlemen composing both those Juries have presented the Debtors' Wards unwholesome in their present state, for the health of prisoners; yet those presentments do not remedy the evil. What is to be done? Are we to be couched up in this jail with a nuisance in one corner, without a stove or fuel at this season of the year? Please inform me. If this is to be the case, I will first petition Sir John Colborne to give us a new set of Magistrates, and if that fails, petition His Majesty on the throne. Nothing is better protected by British law than men's lives. If these laws are not put in execution in this Province, it is high time they should be. My life is in danger in this prison.
                                                    JAMES BREAKENRIDGE.
    Mr. Buell, as an independent conductor of a public journal give this an insertion, and oblige him who is freezing in this prison.
                                                                J. B.

16th Sept. 1832.

Crowded State of Toronto Gaol

The Daily Globe, Toronto, August 8, 1856.

    On Saturday last, at the Police Court, Mr. Allen brought under the notice of the sitting magistrates the difficulty in which he was placed, from the over-crowded state of the prison. He said that the prison had been constructed to accommodate only eighty-two persons, whilst on that day he had under his charge no fewer than *one hundred and fifty*, all proper attempts to classify the prisoners are, on account of this anomaly, almost impossible; and he was compelled to mingle all classes together, the only separation being that of sexes. . . . He need not remind their worships of the fatal results such association must have, ruining, perhaps, many for life. Nor can ordinary cleanliness be carried out, for no less than 24 prisoners had no sleeping accommodation for the last fortnight.

State of the Gaols in 1860.

Sessional Papers, Canada, 1860, No. 32: Preliminary Report of the Board of
Inspectors of Asylums, Prisons, Etc., 1859, pp. 9-10.

An examination of the documents (upwards of one hundred in number)
which have resulted from the preceding enquiry, presents a mass of facts of
the most deplorable kind.   Facts, which, it is important to state, generally
at least, in order that society may feel the responsibility which rests upon it,
and the dangers with which it is threatened.

Let us then state at once (and here we merely echo the opinion of the
great majority of the officers of our Prisons), that our common Gaols are
schools of vice, to which the novices in crime repair to receive, in an atmosphere of idleness and debauchery, lessons in villainy from hardened adepts,
older than themselves in crime, who become at once their models and their
guides.

The defects of our prisons are of every possible kind, and, although they
differ in degree, it is not the less true that there is not a single one which
answers the triple objects for which they are intended,—namely, to punish,
to deter, and to reform.

Defects in superintendence, defects in discipline, defects in construction,
in the internal and external distribution of the buildings, defects in the sanitary arrangements, defects, above all, in the means of reforming; defects
everywhere.

In the majority of Gaols, and especially in those which constantly contain
a large number of prisoners, the superintendence is necessarily nugatory,
owing to the inadequacy of the prison staff. . . .

So neglected are the Prisons, that in at least thirteen of them there are no
rules of any kind—things go on as they best can, and the unfortunate Gaoler
is forced to get on as he may, and to shield himself under the authority of
the Sheriff, who, in this respect, is not much better off.

. . . With the exception of a separation, more or less perfect, of the sexes,
it may be said that all ages, ranks and crimes, form, in these establishments,
an indescribable medley, in the midst of which are found unfortunate lunatics, miserable idiots, and those, more unhappy still, whom a first (often
comparatively slight) fault condemns almost inevitably to complete ruin,
in condemning them to gaol.

The present system of our Gaols (which is in fact an utter absence of all
system) fails entirely in effecting the objects of penal institutions. We do
not punish, or we punish improperly. We do not deter from crime, and we
do not reform the criminal.

The majority of our residents in Gaols (we use the word *residents* design-
edly,) are not in the slightest degree punished by their repeated temporary
sojournings in these places, which, for a certain class of offenders, are a sort
of harbour of refuge.

For this class of persons a few weeks in the *Government boarding-house*
forms a pleasant change in their street life; here they are treated gratuitously
for the ailments contracted by excesses in intemperance or vice.   Here they

meet freely old or new friends, here they repose in the *far niente* of vice; here they plot against society, organize their next campaigns, and enrol fresh recruits into their ranks.

If prisonment as it stands is a punishment for any, there is no kind of proportion in the punishment, and, in spite of the letter of the Law and of the sentence of the Court, the amount of punishment inflicted depends on the accident of the locality where the sentence is carried out. . . .

No provision is made for the religious wants of the prisoners, and yet, without religion, reformation is impossible. The religious ministrations (scanty and inadequate as they are) which the inmates of our common gaols receive, are attributable to the zeal of a few clergymen here and there; but even they, feeling how little influence they can exercise from their false positions and absence of all authority in the prison, and sensible of the almost utter uselessness of their efforts, in the existing state of things, afford their services reluctantly, and often abandon the field in absolute despair.

By reason of the inadequacy of the material appliances, the Magistrates, the Ministers, and the Medical Attendants are absolutely prevented from co-operating, in the discharge of their respective duties, in preventing the repetition of crimes, and in bringing about the reformation of prisoners.

Gaols as Refuges for Prostitutes

Sessional Papers, Canada, 1860, No. 32: Preliminary Report of the Board of Inspectors of Asylums, Prisons, Etc., 1859, pp. 11-12.

Number of women in prison during the year 1859	3,503
Boys under 16 years of age	414
Girls	171
Total	4,088
Total of all prisoners	11,131

Almost all the female prisoners in our gaols are prostitutes, for whom our prisons serve as boarding houses and places of shelter. The gaol is for them a resource in distress, a refuge during the inclement season, and a sort of common rendezvous. Our Canadian Legislation has not (as others have) placed the prostitute in an exceptional position. She can follow her infamous trade with just the same facilities as any honest tradesman. The public street is open to her as to others; and she can plant her den of infamy in front of a church, or beside the doors of a school, and no one can interfere. When they have reached the lowest depths of degradation, they wander, during the summer months, in the fields in the immediate neighbourhood of our large towns, and in the winter find shelter in the gaol. They know exactly what misdemeanor or breach of the police regulations will secure their admission into the *public boarding-house*, with the certainty of getting out within a few days of what ever time may suit them.

It is well to be able to state, as an agreeable contrast to this sad picture, that in our rural districts and counties this class of prisoners is almost unknown.   The towns are, almost exclusively, tainted with this moral leprosy; and in some of our city prisons the number of prisoners of this class is increasing in a frightful ratio.

State of the Penitentiary

Journals of the Legislative Assembly of Canada, 1849, Appendix BBBBB: Second Report of the Commissioners of the Penitentiary Inquiry.

In Canada, while the history of our prisons does not furnish the tales of horror, which those of Europe have so often unfolded, little progress has been made towards introducing the ameliorations and improvements which the wisdom and philanthropy of other countries have tested and approved.   The juvenile offender is yet confined with the hoary-headed evil-doer—we have as yet no asylum by which the child of vice and ignorance may be stopped and rescued on his first entry upon the path of crime—in our common gaols the erring youth and the hardened offender, the innocent and the guilty, those committed for trial and those actually convicted, are too often found herded together in one apartment.   We have but one penal Institution of which the aim is reformation, and the little success which has as yet attended its operations, it has been our painful duty to disclose. . . .

At every step of our proceedings we have felt keenly that the entire penal system of the Province demands a thorough reform; and that so long as our Common Gaol system remains as at present, no satisfactory moral results can be expected from the higher institution.   The District Gaols are the nurseries of crime and vice, and ere the prisoner is transferred from them to the Penitentiary, he is too often thoroughly contaminated and hardened. Men do not sink at once into the depths of crime—the descent is gradual and imperceptible—and while considering how to reform the criminal, we have constantly felt how much more desirable it would be to prevent the crime, and how much more hopeful would be the labor of leading the young offender into a good course, and inspire him with better feelings, than to eradicate habits which have been the growth of years.

Though the scope of our instructions did not extend beyond the Penitentiary, we have felt that the success of that Institution depends so much upon the Common Gaol system, that it was our duty to call Your Excellency's attention to the evils arising from it; and in considering the improvement of the Penitentiary system, we could not avoid associating with it, to some extent, the reform of gaol discipline throughout the Province.   We cannot refrain from suggesting to Your Excellency whether the discipline of all the County Gaols might not, with advantage, be placed under the control of Government Inspectors, from whom periodical reports of their condition would emanate.

Of scarcely less urgency than the reform of the gaols, is the necessity of some immediate action on behalf of the youthful delinquent.   It is distressing to think that no distinction is now made between the child who has strayed for the first time from the path of honesty, or who perhaps has never been taught the meaning of sin, and the hardened offender of mature years.   All are consigned together to the unutterable contamination of the common gaol; and by the lessons there learnt, soon become inmates of the Penitentiary.

We recommend to Your Excellency the immediate erection of one or two more Houses of Refuge for the reformation of juvenile delinquents. . . .

The task of governing well such an Institution as the Kingston Penitentiary, is evidently one of no ordinary difficulty.   It is true that so far as mere bodily coercion is concerned, the security is ample.   The walls of the Prison Buildings are of massive thickness; locks and bolts and bars are there in profusion; the outer enclosure is so high as to defy escalade, and in short effectual precautions have been adopted to baffle any attempt at escape from within its precincts.

Whatever other objections may be offered to the plan on which this edifice has been erected, so far as regards the safe-keeping of the prisoners it is unobjectionable.

Our former Report has abundantly shown that, as in the construction of the Prison, in its internal economy and management, the idea of physical force alone has been kept in view; whilst the milder, but it is to be hoped the not less powerful influence of moral suasion, has been altogether lost sight of. Here indeed the Penitentiary system has been presented in its sternest aspect, and if the cat-o-nine-tails, the raw-hide, the box, the solitary cell, deprivation of food, or of the light of heaven, could ever have deterred the criminal from again preying on society, or violating its laws, here, at all events, the salutary effect would have been produced; but we cannot say that the experiment has proved successful, or that the torture which the inmates endured within the walls of the Penitentiary, have rendered their returns to it a matter of less frequent occurrence than in similar Institutions, where a milder influence has prevailed.   Have the frequency and severity of punishment conduced even to the maintenance of the discipline of the Prison?   The tables which we furnished under this head in our former report clearly show, that the only effect has been to render callous and to harden the offenders, and that each addition to the weight of punishment has increased the number of infractions of the Prison rules.

Need for a Reformatory Institution

Journals of the Legislative Assembly of Canada, 1852-3, Appendix III: Report on Houses of Reformation for Juvenile Offenders by Andrew Dickson, Inspector of Gaols and I.P.P., Canada West, March 10, 1853.

Defective as the Common Gaols or County Prisons in Canada West are in many respects, his inspection, hurried as it was, convinced him that their effect upon young persons must be most pernicious and even ruinous, and that in nine cases out of ten, the youthful delinquent, whether innocent or guilty, at the time he was therein confined, would leave the Gaol, more conversant with crime than when he entered, a greater adept in acts of villainy, with less regard for the claims of society upon him, with less terror of prison restraint, with less reverence for the laws of God and man, and more hardened and determined in criminal pursuits.   This result arises from the fact, that no pains are taken to separate the young from the old, from the contaminating influence of an experienced villain upon the youthful culprit, and from the almost entire absence of reformatory means.   Shut out from communion with his relations and virtuous friends, already degraded in his own eyes, alternately pitied and jeered by his seniors in crime, now excited by some story of the rapid gains of fraud, now thrilled with the perils and exploits of some heroic son of iniquity, and then taught that hundreds of the best men in society are more criminal than himself, coupled at the same time with the total want of instruction and the ordinary means of reform, it is in no way extraordinary that the youthful transgressor should leave the prison more corrupted than he found it, with less prospect of making a useful member of society, and two-thirds more a child of iniquity than before. . . .

For let it be borne in mind, it is not for the veteran in crime, one who has lost all respect for the rights of others, who is vicious in spite of experience and criminal in defiance of law, one who is not only morally loathsome himself, but who has corrupted and is still corrupting others; one, in short, who totally disregards his fellow creatures and seeks to invade their rights, violate their property and contaminate their morals with impunity; it is not for such, but for those, in many cases, who are more or less imbecile in mind, whose parents have left them in many ways impaired, many of whom were orphans at an early age, and others, victims of nefarious men; for those, in some instances, who were schooled in nothing else than crime, who never had any teaching than how to defraud; and of others who from intemperate parents, depraved associations, want and poverty, or innate depravity require seclusion and instruction, for those who have no means of providing for themselves, who, often wander about from place to place without knowing what they shall do, or where they shall rest at night; who are sometimes reduced to the awful alternatives of starving or stealing, and who are nevertheless children of the civil state and for its own safety, as well as their usefulness must not be overlooked; for these and various others, for their safe-keeping, and instruction, for their right thinking and right acting, some provision is most urgently required. . . .

The numbers of young persons who need some place of refuge, instruction and isolation from the evils and temptations of society, and especially of the dangers attending youths in Cities and large Towns, are far more numerous than at the first glance they might seem to be.   Considering how many persons under twenty years are now in our Provincial Penitentiary and Prisons, the many crimes which escape so severe punishment, the numbers of vagrant, idle, ignorant, quarrelsome, obstinate, drunken children; how many paupers who must steal or starve; how many, especially of young females, who ought to be rescued from destruction before it is too late: and when it is also added that for many years the Public Works of Canada will produce a vast influx of the poorer and more criminal classes into the country, it is unquestionable that the number to be provided for, if society is to be saved, is very considerable.

3. CULTURAL ORGANIZATION AND EDUCATION

A. Ethnic Heritages and Social Groups

Segregation of National Groups

S. P. Day, *English America* (London, 1864), vol. II, pp. 80-1.

There is a strong and natural tendency in immigrants of various nationalities to amalgamate in new settlements. Perhaps this peculiarity is more strikingly exemplified in Canada than anywhere else. Of the 22 townships comprising the county of Simcoe, five are composed principally of Protestants from the north of Ireland; four are chiefly or largely inhabited by Irish Roman Catholics; another is almost entirely settled by Highlanders; while the natives of the Island of Islay form the majority of one particular township. In extent of population the Irish take precedence; the Scotch next, and the English last.

The Highland Scots

Papers and Records, Ontario Historical Society, vol. XXVI, 1930, p. 566 and vol. XXVII, 1931, p. 445: Proudfoot Papers.

Aug. 6, 1833, Home:—

These Highlanders are a stiff-necked race. They will not understand anything that is not spoken in the Gaelic and they will not understand anything that requires thought. I felt very little interest in them to-day, chiefly because of their obstinate refusal to hear the Gospel because it is not in Gaelic. . . .

Oct. 26, 1833, Home:—

Matters do not wear so promising an appearance in the Proof Line as they did a while ago. The cause is that the Scotch and Irish do not like one another. The Irish would be the most active and the Scotch, who will do nothing, are jealous of them. . . .

The Dutch Mennonites

Joseph Pickering, *Inquiries of an Immigrant* (London, 1832), p. 127.

The Dutch in general are in pretty good circumstances, living in large substantial, though plain-built houses; built with a stoop, that is, the roof projecting considerably over for shade in front of the house; this is rather common in America; the Dutch hang the horses' harness and ox-yokes, and other implements of husbandry, under them, on pegs driven into the wall of the house; and having very large barns, and generally good yards and other convenient out-buildings for cattle, etc. In this house, and in that in which I slept last night, they had large log fires on the hearth, besides a large stove in the sitting rooms of each, placed on the opposite side, so when sitting at the fire you had the stove at your back! Another custom peculiar to the Dutch is, instead of lying upon a feather bed, to have it for a covering in lieu of a sheet and blankets, having a straw or chaff one underneath! It is certainly a warm, but to me not pleasant, method of lying.

The Negroes

J. B. Brown, *Views of Canada and the Colonists* (Edinburgh, 1851), pp. 62-3, 289.

The number of coloured persons of African descent in Upper Canada was, in 1848, 5,400; 3,000 of whom were males. . . . These people are usually employed in the towns as waiters in hotels, barbers, and generally in performing the most burdensome and lowest descriptions of labour, such as cutting up and preparing wood for fuel. They have, as labourers, usually great powers of endurance; and when their dispositions have not been soured by ill usage, they are most generally civil and attached servants. There are also some educated coloured persons whose qualifications and general conduct have assisted much to remove those prejudices against the race that exist less or more all over America. . . .

Generally speaking, this coloured portion of the population, both in the country parts and in the towns and villages of Canada, live apart from the white inhabitants. They are very usually to be found collected together in the least valuable corners of the towns—their houses and style of living most frequently denoting a scale of civilization greatly inferior to the mass of the population surrounding them; among whom, it can scarcely be doubted, they too bitterly feel themselves to be merely "the hewers of wood and drawers of water."

British Immigrants

Major Samuel Strickland, *Twenty-Seven Years in Canada West* (London, 1853), vol. I, pp. 134-40.

There is no colony belonging to the British Crown better adapted for the poor industrious emigrant than the Canadas, particularly the Upper Province, which is essentially the poor man's country. Twenty-five years ago, the expense of the voyage out to Quebec, and the difficulty, delay, and additional outlay of the inland journey put it completely out of the power of the needy agriculturist or artizan to emigrate; the very classes, however, who, from their having been brought up from their infancy to hard labour, and used to all sorts of privations, were the best fitted to cope with the dangers and hardships attending the settlement of a new country. The impossibility of the working hand raising funds for emigration, confined the colonists to a set of men less calculated to contend with difficulties— namely, half-pay officers and gentlemen of better family than income, who were almost invariably the pioneers of every new settlement. . . .

Eighteen or twenty years ago a number of gentlemen located themselves in the township of Harvey. The spot chosen by them was one of great natural beauty; it possessed no other advantages, except an abundance of game, which was no small inducement to them. They spent several thousand pounds in building fancy log-houses and making large clearings which they had neither the ability nor industry to cultivate. But, even if they had possessed sufficient perseverance, their great distance from a market, bad roads, want of knowledge in cropping after they had cleared the land, lack of bridges, and poor soil, would have been a great drawback to the chance of effecting a prosperous settlement. In a few years not a settler remained of this little colony. Some stayed till their means were thoroughly exhausted; others, more wise, purchased ready-cleared farms in the settlements, or followed some profession more congenial to their taste, or more suited to their abilities. . . .

Since 1826, a steady influx of the working classes from Great Britain and Ireland has taken place. This has tended much to the prosperity of the country, by cheapening labour, and the settlement of vast tracts of wild land.

Several experiments have been made by Government in sending out pauper emigration: that from the south of Ireland, under the superintendence of the Late Hon. Peter Robinson in 1824, was the most extensive, and came more immediately under my own observation. I have understood that some most obnoxious and dangerous characters were shipped off in this expedition—no doubt to the great comfort of landlords, agents, and tithe-proctors.

The Government behaved very liberally to these settlers. A grant of a hundred acres of good land was given to each head of a family, and to every son above twenty-one years of age.

A good milch cow, and rations of pork and flour were assigned to each emigrant family. These provisions they continued to receive for upwards of eighteen months, besides a variety of stores, such as axes, hammers, saws, nails, grindstones, &c. A good log-shanty was also built on each settler's lot. These people have done as well as could be expected, considering the material of which they were composed. It has been observed that, whenever these people were located amongst the Protestant population, they made much better settlers than when remaining with Catholics.

In fact, a great improvement is perceptible in the morality, industry and education of the rising generation, who grow up more virtuous and less bigoted to their exclusive religious opinions.

As a general rule, the English, Scotch, and north of Ireland men make much better and more independent colonists than emigrants from the south of Ireland.

Seven years after the location of Robinson's emigrants, a colony of Wiltshire people settled in the township of Dummer under many more disadvantages than those placed by Government in the township of Douro.

The Dummer people had no shanties built for them, no cows, and were given much worse land; and yet they have done much more in a shorter time. An air of comfort and cleanliness pervades their dwellings, and there is a neatness about their farms and homesteads which is generally wanted in the former.

It must, however, be borne in mind that paupers sent out by the Government, or by their own parishes, are not a fair specimen by which to judge the working classes, who emigrated at their own expense. Of the latter, I know hundreds who, upon their arrival in the Upper Province, had spent their last shilling, and who, by persevering industry, are now worth hundreds of pounds. No person need starve in Canada, where there is plenty of work and good wages for every man who is willing of labour, and who keeps himself sober. The working man with a family of grown children, when fairly established on his farm, is fully on a par, as regards his prospects, with the gentleman, the owner of a similar farm, and possessing an income of 100£ per annum. The reason is obvious. The gentleman and his family have been used to wear finer clothes, keep better company, and maintain a more respectable appearance, and if he has children, to give them a more expensive education.

Disintegration of Ethnic Distinctions

E. A. Talbot, *Five Years' Residence in the Canadas* (London, 1824), vol. II, pp. 9-11.

It is very remarkable, that although the present population of this fine Province is composed of emigrants from almost every European nation, and from every state of North America, there should be so little difference in their manners, customs, and habits of life. Germans, Hollanders, French, English, Scotch, and Irish, after a few years' residence in Canada, forget their national customs and peculiarities, and become, in almost every particular, entirely assimilated to the people of America.

These emigrants, having generally been of the lowest class of society in their respective countries,—and consequently mere cyphers except in their own immediate sphere,—as soon as they arrive in Canada, begin to assume an appearance of importance, and to be quite ashamed of their former unassuming manners and native customs. The most absurd notions of equality and independence take instant possession of their vestiginous and unreflecting minds. As they travel through the Province and mingle with its inhabitants, they hear the dialects and peculiarities of their respective nations derided and ridiculed, while those of America, both Republican and Monarchical, are invariably defended and extolled. The first, and, as they conceive it, the most essential study in which they can engage in this new state of existence, is therefore to imitate everything American; and so successful are they in their endeavors to copy the example of those by whom they are surrounded, that, before they have spent a single season in the Province, they exhibit the most ludicrous specimens of ignorance and affectation that this or any other country can produce. Not a single trace of native simplicity or of native manners remains. Everything must give place to the influence of example; and American variety must be engrafted on the stock of foreign diffidence. No magpie was ever more assiduous in mimicking his *music-master*, than those imported work-birds are in copying the fashionable slang of their immaculate neighbors.   They are indefatigable in acquiring a knowledge of the Rights of Man, the First Principles of Equality, and the True Nature of Independence, and, in a word, of every thing which characterises an American; and thus they quickly become divested of common manners, and common civility, and not infrequently of common honesty too.

B. Social Classes in the Rural Community

Disbanded Soldiers and Half-Pay Officers

Rev. Wm. Bell, *Hints to Emigrants, in a Series of Letters from Upper Canada*
(Edinburgh, 1824), pp. 144-5.

You will perceive by what I have already said, that when I first settled here, [Perth] the majority of the population consisted of discharged soldiers. This, however, is not the case now.   The number of emigrants has increased, while that of the soldiers has decreased.   Few discharged soldiers make good cultivators, they have not in general acquired the habits of industry and application necessary for farmers.   They were allowed rations by government for one year, and while these lasted they seldom deserted their land, except to earn wages; but when their rations were eaten up, a great part of them left the settlement.   Those that remain are hard working industrious people, and seem to make good settlers.

A few of the half-pay officers reside upon their lands in the country, but most of them remain in the villages—the majority in Perth.   The whole number amounts to between thirty or forty, and most of them are justices of the peace.   This gives them a greater influence in the settlement, than is perhaps agreeable to the civilians, few of whom hold commissions of the peace, or any other office under government.

Trials of the British Gentry on the Frontier

Patrick Shirreff, *A Tour through North America* (Edinburgh, 1835), pp. 362-3.

The greater portion of British emigrants, arriving in Canada without funds and the most exalted ideas of the value and productiveness of land, purchase extensively on credit, and take up their abode in the midst of the forest, with the proudest feelings of independence, and in the confident hope of meeting their engagements, and becoming fine gentlemen at the end of a few years.   Every thing goes on well for a short time.   A log-house is erected with the assistance of old settlers, and the clearing of forest is commenced. Credit is obtained at a neighbouring store, and at length it is found necessary to work a day or two in the week for hire to obtain food for the family.   The few garden stuffs and field crops, grown the first year, produce little for want of a free circulation of air, and the imperfect manner in which they had been sown.   Should fever and ague now visit the emigrant, which is frequently the case, the situation of himself and family, enfeebled by disease, is truly wretched. Hope, is however, still bright, and he struggles through the second year, with better crops and prospects than the preceding one. The third year brings him good crops, which furnish a supply of food for his establishment. During this period he has led a life of toil and privation, being poorly fed and most uncomfortably lodged. But the thought of owning so many fair acres has been a never-failing source of joy and sweetener of life. On arrival of the fourth harvest, he is reminded by the storekeeper to pay his account with cash, or discharge part of it with his disposable produce, for which he gets a very small price. He is also informed that the purchase-money of the land has been accumulating with interest. The phantom of prosperity, conjured up by his imagination, is now dispelled, and, on calmly looking into his affairs, he finds himself poorer than when he commenced operations. Disappointment preys on his spirits, and the aid of whisky is perhaps sought to raise them. The hopelessness of his situation renders him indolent and immoral. The land ultimately reverts to the former proprietor, or a new purchaser is found.

Education and Leadership in Rural Communities

Major Samuel Strickland, *Twenty-Seven Years in Canada West* (London, 1853), vol. I, p. 81.

The employments of a respectable Canadian settler are certainly of a very multifarious character, and he may be said to combine, in his own person, several professions, if not trades. A man of education will always possess an influence, even in bush society: he may be poor, but his value will not be tested by the low standard of money, and notwithstanding his want of the current coin of the realm, he will be appealed to for his judgment in many matters, and will be inducted into several offices, infinitely more honourable than lucrative. My friend and father-in-law, being mild in manners, good-natured, and very sensible, was speedily promoted to the bench, and was given the colonelcy of the second battalion of the Durham Militia.

Privileges of Educated English Immigrants

Susanna Moodie, *Life in the Clearings versus the Bush* (London, 1853), pp. 49-50.

The native-born Canadian regarded with a jealous feeling men of talent and respectability who emigrated from the mother country, as most offices of consequence and emolument were given to such persons. The Canadian, naturally enough, considered such preference unjust, and an infringement upon his rights as a native of the colony, and that he had a greater claim, on that account, upon the government, than men who were perfect strangers. This, owing to his limited education, was not always the case; but the preference shown to the British emigrant proved an active source of ill-will and discontent. The favoured occupant of place and power was not at all inclined to conciliate his Canadian rival, or to give up the title to mental superiority which he derived from birth and education; and he too often treated his illiterate, but sagacious political opponent, with a contempt which his practical knowledge and experience did not merit.

The English Refined Family on the Frontier

Six Years in the Bush; or Extracts from the Journal of a Settler in Upper Canada (London, 1838), pp. 16-17.

During our necessary detention on the lake [Erie], we became acquainted with an English settler's family; they were well connected in England, and had been long enough in the province to have mastered the *"Res augusta domi,"* which originally drove them from home, and assembled about them several English comforts, and even refinements; the lady, nevertheless, spoke feelingly of the privations and hardships she had endured in the first years of her exile: some of which, though softened by habit and bettered circumstances, still remained; one grievance she particularly dwelt upon, was the difficulty of procuring respectable servants, unless she would consent to treat them as equals, and admit them to sit at table with her husband and children; at the time of our visit, she was combining in her own person all the domestic offices, and I believe retired from the dining table to wash up the dishes and boil the tea kettle.

Occupation and Loneliness of Pioneer Women

E. S. Dunlop (editor), *Our Forest Home: Being Extracts from the Correspondence of the Late Frances Stewart* (Montreal, 1902), pp. 38-131.

(Douro, June, 1823) My time is very completely filled up here so that I never feel the want of visitors, though I do not like giving up society too much.   I have numberless things to attend to and a great and never ending store of needlework going on, but I make a little time every day for reading that my mind may be employed while my fingers are the same.   I often wish for a pianoforte; in the evening I have some spare time and I often look over my old music books now piled in a corner; but I hope in a few years I shall be able to have this delightful amusement again. . . .

(July)   This place is so lonely that in spite of all my efforts to keep them off, clouds of dismal thoughts fly and lower over me.   I have not seen a woman except those in our party for over five months, and only three times any one in the shape of a companion.

Our friend Mr. Faulkner paid us one visit and I am in hopes of seeing him again. He is a very pleasing, agreeable, well informed man, whose conversation improves as well as pleases.   But alas! till sleighing comes we cannot hope to see this friend or anyone, for we have no roads fit for wagons, and boating is too tedious for the ladies of this housekeeping country.

Every hour of the day I feel gratitude to my dear Harriet who gave me tastes which in a great measure make me independent of society. . . .

(August)   My occupations in this country are not of a kind to interest the *mind,* and, alas for my perverseness, I am fonder than ever of reading—the greatest indulgence I can give myself is to devote half an hour to a book or writing home.   There are so many calls on my time—the superintending of the household, the care of the three children, and the everlasting, always-increasing piles of needlework.   This last I sometimes think I can never hope to get through; a year of wear and tear and no shops from which to procure anything obliges me to plan most carefully.   I continue, however, to read a chapter or two in 'Mont's Bible' with the notes every day, and am also enjoying the 'Lights and Shadows of Scottish Life,' and looking forward to refresh my memory by the perusal of 'Bigland's Letters on English History.'   And though I can read but very little at a time, yet even these scraps give me something to think about as I sit at my little south window plying my needle.   As T—— is out almost all day I have abundant time for thinking, and constantly in spite of every effort my mind will turn to 'home' and former times, and occasionally take a far stretch forward.   In this silent solitude you cannot fancy what a feast the dear home-letters afford me.   Our posts occur so seldom that I generally receive letters from Ireland and England all together.   These letters come to Mr. Bethune's care and when opportunity offers he sends them to us.   Papers, though old, are a great treat. . . .

(July, 1824)   I have often in my days of affluence said that I disliked house-keeping mistresses and mammas who could think of *nothing* but the care of their children; but I have found it necessary of late to become *both,* entirely and completely, and to give up all my former favorite employments, walking, gardening, reading, writing, and even the more agreeable parts of sewing. . . .

(1830)   Peterborough is increasing most rapidly and will soon be a fine flourishing town; every time I go there I see new houses being put up.   There are now two mills, a tannery and distillery; all sorts of tradespeople are settling there, but as yet no gentle-people have come, so that in point of society we are not much better off than we were four years ago.   I never see anybody but the Reids and Armors; the latter do not come here oftener than once in two months, and I only meet the former on Sundays unless I go there, which I cannot do easily, as I have nobody to leave in charge of house and children.   But when we do meet we enjoy ourselves very much. . . .

We have been too much interrupted of late by strangers coming at all hours, it is a great change after being so long almost entirely deprived of society, but everything is changed, we are now in the midst of a populous country.   Some of our new neighbours are very pleasing, but none what we could call agreeable; their conversation consists of chit-chat concerning local occurrences in our village. . . .

(April, 1833)   Alas! my present mode of living does not afford anything in the least entertaining for I do not think I ever was so dead, my whole time is occupied by family duties, which, although pleasing when they go on smoothly, become tiresome when there are so many little annoying circumstances as I meet with constantly.   All I want is a little rest sometimes for mind and body, for I have quite as much to think of and do as is agreeable, and rather more than is pleasant. I find it impossible to attend to the improvement of the children with that quietness and regularity which alone can bring success. It harasses me greatly and disheartens me when I find how very backward my poor little dears are in common learning; as for accomplishments, though I should like very much to have my daughters taught any of those pursuits which would certainly make them more pleasing to others, yet I never expected I could do so. Nor will this be a loss, as after marriage I find that these things are always laid aside in this country in its present state, indeed it can scarcely be avoided.

Disintegration of Class Distinctions

Susanna Moodie, *Roughing It in the Bush* (new ed., Toronto, 1913), pp. 245-50.

Many a hard battle had we to fight with old prejudices, and many proud swellings of the heart to subdue, before we could feel the least interest in the land of our adoption, or look upon it as our home.

All was new, strange, and distasteful to us; we shrank from the rude, coarse familiarity of the uneducated people among whom we were thrown; and they in turn viewed us as innovators, who wished to curtail their independence by expecting from them the kindly civilities and gentle courtesies of a more refined community. The semi-barbarous Yankee squatters, who had "left their country for their country's good", and by whom we were surrounded in our first settlement, detested us, and with them we could have no feeling in common. We could neither lie nor cheat in our dealings with them; and they despised us for our ignorance in trading and our want of smartness.

The utter want of that common courtesy with which a well-brought-up European addresses the poorest of his brethren, is severely felt at first by settlers in Canada. At the period of which I am now speaking, the titles of "sir," or "madam," were very rarely applied by inferiors. . . .

Why they treated our claims to their respect with marked insult and rudeness, I never could satisfactorily determine, in any way that could reflect honour on the species, or even plead an excuse for its brutality, until I found that this insolence was more generally practised by the low, uneducated emigrants from Britain, who better understood your claims to their civility, than by the natives themselves. Then I discovered the secret.

The unnatural restraint which society imposes upon these people at home forces them to treat their more fortunate brethren with a servile deference which is repugnant to their feelings, and is thrust upon them by the dependent circumstances in which they are placed. This homage to rank and education is not sincere. Hatred and envy lie rankling at their heart, although hidden by outward obsequiousness. Necessity compels their obedience; they fawn, and cringe, and flatter the wealth on which they depend for bread. But let them once emigrate, the clog which fettered them is suddenly removed; they are free; and the dearest privilege of this freedom is to wreak upon their superiors the long-locked-up hatred of their hearts.   They think they can debase you to their level by disallowing all your claims to distinction; while they hope to exalt themselves and their fellows into ladies and gentlemen by sinking you back to the only title you received from Nature—plain "man" and "woman." . . .

But from this folly the native-born Canadian is exempt; it is only practised by the low-born Yankee, or the Yankeefied British peasantry and mechanics.   It originates in the enormous reaction springing out of sudden emancipation from a state of utter dependence into one of unrestrained liberty. . . .

And here I would observe, before quitting this subject, that of all follies, that of taking out servants from the old country is one of the greatest, and is sure to end in the loss of the money expended in their passage, and to become cause of deep disappointment and mortification to yourself.

They no sooner set foot upon the Canadian shores than they become possessed with this ultra-republican spirit.   All respect for their employers, all subordination is at an end; the very air of Canada severs the tie of mutual obligation which bound you together.   They fancy themselves not only equal to you in rank, but that ignorance and vulgarity give them superior claims to notice.   They demand the highest wages, and grumble at doing half the work, in return, which they cheerfully performed at home.   They demand to eat at your table, and to sit in your company, and if you refuse to listen to their dishonest and extravagant claims, they tell you that "they are free"; that no contract signed in the old country is binding in 'Meriky'; that you may look out for another person to fill their place as soon as you like; and that you may get the money expended in their passage and outfit in the best manner you can. . . .

When we consider the different position in which servants are placed in the old and new world, this conduct, ungrateful as it then appeared to me, ought not to create the least surprise. . . . The serving class, comparatively speaking, is small, and admits of little competition.   Servants that understand the work of the country are not easily procured, and such always can command the highest wages.

Demoralization of the Immigrant

Six Years in the Bush; or Extracts from the Journal of a Settler in Upper Canada, 1832-1838 (London, 1838), pp. 20-1.

At an inn on the road side [Yonge St.], I met with a young farmer who had lately emigrated from my own county in England; he was altogether hopeless and desponding, a thing in itself by no means uncommon with settlers of his station in life during the first two or three years, their minds being generally too contracted to look far into the future, or to bear with patience present hardships, that good may come: but from what little I saw of my co-patriot, there was no room to hope that his prospects would brighten as time advanced; for instead of business, he had evidently turned all his attention, since his arrival in the province, to the study of Yankee manners and idioms, which, disagreeable as they are, he certainly continued to render more offensive by his unmeant caricature; cool impertinence he mistook for independence; and a swaggering jaunty air for an easy manner; of course he "guessed and calculated;" but to my enquiries respecting his prospects, and what information he had gained, and where he meant to settle, he was utterly unable to give a straight forward reply:—doubtless he will soon be a bankrupt here, as he probably has been already in England, where, if he has friends or credit left, he will return "seven times" more worthless than he came out.

Demoralization of Servant Class

T. W. Magrath, *Authentic Letters from Upper Canada*, edited by T. Radcliffe (Dublin, 1833), p. 226.

Without any matter of doubt the servants are great plagues; they think of nothing but bettering themselves, and they that come out hardly puts their foot on the land when they get's roaring thoughts in their sculls, as if the air of this country gave them a rambling way with them. [Letter of Bridget Lary, a servant of Upper Canada, December, 1832].

Social Effects of Disintegration of Classes

J. J. Bigsby, *The Shoe and Canoe or Pictures of Travel in the Canadas* (London, 1850), vol. I, pp. 130-1.

The great defect in colonial life is the lower civilization which characterizes it; where the inferior appetites, the animal instincts, prevail, and are exclusively gratified; where a man's thoughts seldom go further than himself, his shop, farm, bottle, horse, and rifle.

In the country parts of Canada few young men get above the class of "gents," and the elders seldom rise higher in their notions than the second-rate retired tradesmen at home. There are here and there some few loftier minds, driven into hiding-places by misfortune; but they only mark, and so thicken, the general gloom. There is not enough of the fine gold of English Society to make a public impression.

Low Social Status of Farm Class

J. F. W. Johnston, *Notes on North America* (Edinburgh, 1851), p. 272.

Little knowledge of improved agriculture has hitherto been diffused in Upper Canada; and it is, as yet, among practical men, held in little esteem. In revenge, the farming class are not, as a body, regarded with much estimation by the other classes of society. They do not assume their proper position among a community where, if they only knew how to use it, all political power is, in reality, in their hands.

Cultural Destitution and Country Merchants

Patrick Shirreff, *A Tour through North America* (Edinburgh, 1835), pp. 387-9.

The merchants and storekeepers are said to be the most wealthy and influential people in the province, and owe the position they have attained to the situation and character of the inhabitants. The settlers being thinly scattered over an immense and almost inaccessible territory, are necessarily unacquainted with traffic and the price of commodities. Their limited produce does not spur them into active exertion to dispose of it; and the state of the roads only admitting of transport for a part of the year, confines the time of sale to the winter months. During this season, the St. Lawrence, which is the only channel of trade, being closed by ice, limits the number of merchants, and drives all out of the market but capitalists. The necessities of farmers do not enable them to hold produce from year to year, and they appear to be at the mercy of the merchants, who obtain thousands and tens of thousands of bushels of wheat, at the head of Lake Ontario, in exchange for shoes and other necessaries, without a fraction of cash being paid on either side. The inland store-keeper has still greater advantages over the farmer, and their profits are said to be excessive; 300 per cent on dry goods having been currently obtained at one time. The merchant and storekeeper are however, distant from the market of Britain, which regulates the price of Canadian wheat; and the navigation of the St. Lawrence, and transport of goods, are so expensive, that profits may not be so great as is reported. Of their influence in the country, there is, however, no doubt; and that it arises from the pecuniary difficulties of landowners is universally admitted, who, in numerous instances, are irretrievably burdened with debt.

The first settlers, at the close of the war with the colonies, being at too great a distance to admit of much intercourse with each other, and having no outlet for their produce, soon sank into listless inactivity. Many Germans and Dutch afterwards followed, who commonly settled near each other, and although quiet and industrious people, were altogether without enterprise. The greater portion of British emigrants, who first settled in the province, having little capital or education, and obtaining grants of forest in isolated situations, made small progress in a mode of farming so new to them. Having been nurtured in poverty, they had few wants and were not ambitious to improve their condition. From a people so situated, and composed of such materials, little could be expected. Individuals connected with government seem to have been more solicitous about their own than the people's welfare, and little was done to call forth the resources of the country, or to rouse the slumbering energies of the inhabitants. The people, however, formed good subjects for active traders, who still gather a plentiful harvest. How long this state of things may last with traders will depend on competition. Their profits will fall with the opening of communication throughout the country, but capital employed in trade is likely to yield a good return, so long as the necessities of the agricultural population continue urgent.

Every inhabitant of Britain, contemplating the commencement of trade in Upper Canada, must be prepared to do so in a new mode, and, while he views high profits, he ought not to lose sight of transacting business on a limited scale, and in an expensive and disagreeable manner.

If the early inhabitants of Upper Canada sank into indolence, some of the succeeding settlers were ill fitted to improve them, being blended with the scum and refuse of mankind. For many years the bankrupts in character and fortune, the poor, the idle, and the dissipated, departed from Britain. From the United States the knavish whites, and the runaway blacks found shelter, and after having cheated the Canadians again set off. Such a population receiving grants of forest, separated from each other by clergy reserves and large absentee estates, could not be expected to exert themselves amidst the difficulties of first settlement. People of enterprise, who reached the province, soon made a fortune and retired again.

I found some of the oldest settlers treading out their wheat crop with horses; living in miserable houses, and without a particle of sugar to sweeten their tea. This state of things arose from laziness, their possessions being large, their time unoccupied, and the juice of the maple might have been collected a few yards from their residence for the making of sugar.

At the time of my visit nine-tenths of the hotel-keepers and stage-drivers, and most of the active business people, had originally come from the United States. Every horse and ox of size or fatness could be traced to have come from the same territory, and the Canadians appear to me to be much indebted to the people of the United States for any activity and refinement that is to be met with in the province.

The first settlers, the people of business, and almost all travellers for pleasure or health, having come from the United States, their manners and customs have been impressed on the inhabitants of Upper Canada, and I do not think the large influx of British emigrants which has taken place of late years will efface them. I found much less refinement than in the lower province or in the United States, while the coarse manners of the people, and their habits of intemperance, were so prominent, that I heard more oaths and witnessed more drunk people the first few days I was in Canada, than I had met with during my previous wanderings in the States. I must do Upper Canada, however, the justice to say, that such characters appeared to be late importations from Britain and Ireland, and I was sorry to observe intoxication was by no means confined to the lowest class of emigrants.

C. The Town and Social Classes

Parasitical Character of the Gentry

T. R. Preston, *Three Years' Residence in Canada* (London, 1840), vol. II, pp. 46-8.

Among that class of the community termed by courtesy the gentry, there is creeping up a false state of things, which, unless it soon find a corrective, is calculated to retard very materially—if, indeed, it has not already retarded,—the prosperity of the province, and consequently of its young society.

I allude to the disinclination evinced by far too large a portion of the Canadian youth of the class designated, to engage in those pursuits which the primitive condition of the country they inhabit, no less than their own well-being, imperatively requires that they should follow.   In lieu of devoting themselves to agricultural and commercial occupations, they blindly seek, in an undue ratio, to qualify themselves for those of a professional nature; because, from the fallacious notions in which they have been reared, they conceive, or affect to consider, the two first to be beneath them. . . .

Another mischief arising from this pernicious practice, is that many of the young aspirants in question, being disappointed in their expectations, and possessing interest in influential quarters, become applicants for office in the public service, and are promoted to vacancies in district appointments, perchance, to the exclusion of persons more entitled to fill them, or else wait the chance of some new post being created, for which they may compete.

The Upper Class of Toronto

R. H. Bonnycastle, *The Canadas in 1841* (London, 1841), vol. I, pp. 168-70.

The public amusements in Toronto are not of a nature to attract much attention.   There have been various attempts to get up respectable races, and to establish a theatre, and a winter assembly for dancing; but owing to the peculiar state of society, these attempts have always proved nearly abortive, as well as those of a much higher and more useful kind, which have been made by persons attached to science and the arts.   A national Literary and Philosophical Society was by great exertion established; but, after being in a wavering state for about a year, it dropped.   The United Service Club met with the same fate; and there is now only a Mechanics' Institute, and a commercial news-room, which can fairly be mentioned, although some young men, under the patronage of the Vice-Chancellor, have recently got up a literary club.

In Toronto, which has only advanced rapidly within the last five years, the original settlers were chiefly persons holding public appointments, whose duty obliged them to reside at the seat of government. Tradesmen, mechanics, and labourers came to the village by very slow degrees; and, as they were chiefly concerned in supplying the wants of the gentry, were not until recently, enabled to amass much money.   Thus, a very clear and defined line was drawn in the society of York; and, as the families of the office-holders became connected by marriage (for York was not sought as a place of residence by general settlers in the country, and was chiefly visited by them on public business), a close and impenetrable bond of union arose among these public servants; and the aristocracy of Little York was able to carve out at will the destinies of the town, naturally endeavoring to retain in the family compact all situations of honour and profit.   They were, however, too few to establish, however willing, any useful public institutions;

and hence, when the place became a city, and wealth and intellect flowed into it from foreign sources, a little jealousy would obviously, for some time, prevent these self-constituted leaders from patronizing efforts made by strangers.

Lack of Community Spirit

Anna Jameson, *Winter Studies and Summer Rambles*
(new ed., Toronto, 1923), pp. 50-1.

Toronto is like a fourth or fifth rate provincial town, with the pretensions of a capital city.   We have here a petty colonial oligarchy, a self-constituted aristocracy, based upon nothing real, nor even upon anything imaginary; and we have all the mutual jealousy and fear, and petty gossip, and mutual meddling and mean rivalship, which are common in a small society of which the numbers are well known to each other, a society composed, like all societies, of many heterogeneous particles; but as these circulate within very confined limits, there is no getting out of the way of what one most dislikes: we must necessarily hear, see, and passively endure much that annoys and disgusts any one accustomed to the independence of a large and liberal society, or the ease of continental life.   It is curious enough to see how quickly a new fashion, or a new folly, is imported from the old country, and with what difficulty and delay a new idea finds its way into the heads of the people, or a new book into their hands. . . .

There reigns here a hateful factious spirit in political matters, but for the present no public or patriotic feeling, no recognition of general or generous principles of policy: as yet I have met with none of these.

Growth of Social Classes in the Towns

(i)

Transactions of the London and Middlesex Historical Society, 1911-12, p. 66:
"Reminiscences of Mrs. Gilbert Porte."

The town [of London] was growing rapidly; the rebellion was quelled. The military occupied the barracks and social distinctions were being marked by the time.   I became a pupil of Mrs. Pringle's Young Ladies' School, and I remember so well when Mrs. Richardson, mother of Mrs. Judge Hughes and Mrs. Judge Horton, started in opposition a more fashionable and expensive establishment, and took away quite a number of pupils.   This, of course, raised some feeling of resentment.

(ii)

Ontario Historical Society, Papers and Records, vol. XXX, 1934, p. 136: Proudfoot
Papers.

Aug. 25, 1836 [London]:—
Every time I go into the village I meet with something to make me think meanly of the people, i.e., those who think themselves the leading people.

The Tory party have become insolent since the late elections, and seem determined to take vengeance on all who are not their way of thinking, and they are at best a sorry set. . . .
Sept. 9:—

The society of the village is now very little to be desired. The influence of the political strife has eradicated everything amiable that was in it. It could ill afford this as it never had much of it.

D. *Educational Institutions*

Low State of Cultural Life and Education

Anna Jameson, *Winter Studies and Summer Rambles in Canada*
(new ed. Toronto, 1923), pp. 182-4.

I know it has been laid down as a principle, that the more and the closer men are congregated together, the more prevalent is vice of every kind; and that an isolated or scattered population is favourable to virtue and simplicity. It may be so, if you are satisfied with negative virtues and the simplicity of ignorance. But here, where a small population is scattered over a wide extent of fruitful country, where there is not a village or a hamlet for twenty or thirty or forty miles together—where there are no manufactories—where there is almost entire equality of condition—where the means of subsistence are abundant—where there is no landed aristocracy—no poor laws, nor poor rates, to grind the souls and the substance of the people between them, till nothing remains but chaff,—to what shall we attribute the gross vices, the profligacy, the stupidity, and basely vulgar habits of a great part of the people, who know not even how to enjoy or to turn to profit the inestimable advantages around them? —And, alas for them! there seems to be no one as yet to take an interest about them, or at least infuse a new spirit into the next generation. In one log-hut in the very heart of the wilderness, where I might well have expected primitive manners and simplicity, I found vulgar finery, vanity, affectation, under the most absurd and disgusting forms, combined with a want of the commonest physical comforts of life, and the total absence of even elementary knowledge. In another I have seen drunkenness, profligacy, stolid indifference to all religion; and in another, the most senseless fanaticism. There are people, I know, who think—who fear, that the advancement of knowledge and civilization must be the increase of vice and insubordination; who deem that a scattered agricultural population, where there is a sufficiency of daily food for the body; where no schoolmaster interferes to infuse ambition and discontent into the abject, self-satisfied mind; where the labourer reads not, writes not, thinks not—only loves, hates, prays, and toils—that such a state must be a sort of Arcadia. Let them come here!—there is no march of intellect here!—there is no "schoolmaster abroad" here! And what are the consequences? Not the most agreeable to contemplate, believe me.

I passed in these journeys some school-houses built by the wayside: of these, several were shut up for want of schoolmasters; and who that could earn a subsistence in any other way, would be a schoolmaster in the wilds of Upper Canada?   Ill fed, ill clothed, ill paid, or not paid at all—boarded at the houses of the different farmers in turn, I found indeed some few men, poor creatures! always either Scotch or Americans, and totally unfit for the office they had undertaken.   Of female teachers I found none whatever, except in the towns.   Among all the excellent societies in London for the advancement of religion and education, are there none to send missionaries here?—such missionaries as we want, be it understood—not sectarian fanatics.   Here, without means of instruction, of social amusement, of healthy and innocent excitements—can we wonder that whiskey and camp meetings assume their place, and "season toil" which is unseasoned by anything better.

Lack of Educational Facilities in Pioneer Communities

(i)

Robert Gourlay, *Statistical Account of Upper Canada* (London, 1822), vol. I, pp. 245-6.

The first inhabitants, as was stated in the historical sketch, were generally poor, in consequence of the revolution.   They had also to struggle with the labours and privations incident to new settlements.   As their habitations were sparse, it was difficult for them to unite in sufficient numbers to form good schools; and they could neither afford much expense for instructors, nor allow their children much time for receiving instruction.   From such inevitable causes, education was neglected among them, until the neglect almost became habitual.   The want of books, at the same time, relaxed their taste for reading.

A sense of these disadvantages excited desires for surmounting them, which have at length produced some corresponding exertion.   Books are procured in considerable numbers.   In addition to those with which particular persons and families are supplied, social libraries are introduced in various places; and subscribers at a small expence thus enjoy the benefit of many more volumes than they could individually afford to purchase.

A spirit of improvement is evidently spreading.   The value of education, as well as the want of it, is felt.   The practicability of obtaining it is considered.   Gentlemen of competent means appear to be sensible of the importance of giving their children academical learning, and ambitious to do it without sending them abroad for the purpose.

(ii)

E. A. Talbot, *Five Years' Residence in the Canadas* (London, 1824), vol. II, pp. 116-19.

The inestimable advantages resulting from a well-educated and enlightened population, cannot be experienced in Canada for many years to come. The great mass of people are at present completely ignorant even of the rudiments of the most common learning.   Very few can either read or write; and parents, who are ignorant themselves, possess so slight a relish for literature, and are so little acquainted with its advantages, that they feel scarcely any anxiety to have the minds of their children cultivated. . . .

Many circumstances concur to make it impracticable for the Canadians, even if they were capable, to educate their own children.   In consequence of the difficulty of procuring labour, which I have already mentioned, the farmer is not only compelled to devote himself entirely to the cultivation of his ground, but also to call in the aid of his sons, as soon as they are able to assist him.   Boys of seven or eight years old are put to work, in Canada, and are kept at it during the remainder of their lives,—unless they acquire those habits of indolence which, I have before observed, are so general, as to preclude the devotion of much care and attention to any honest or equitable sort of trade.

Parental Responsibility for Education

E. S. Dunlop (editor), *Our Forest Home: Being Extracts from the Correspondence of the Late Frances Stewart* (Montreal, 1902), pp. 152-3.

I feel the responsibility of my situation as a parent.   Heaven has blessed me with a very large family.   I have now ten children, four boys and six girls, all healthy and sound in body and mind, well disposed and amiable, but sadly deficient in education, from want of time on my part to attend to them.   It is impossible for me with such a set of little ones and so much to do for them to attend to teaching sufficiently to bring them on as well as I could wish.   The constant call on the elder ones for help is another difficulty.

The School-Teacher

Robert Gourlay, *Statistical Account of Upper Canada* (London, 1822), vol. I, pp. 433-4.

The state of education is also at a very low ebb, not only in this township [of Grimsby], but generally throughout the district; although the liberality of the legislature has been great in support of the district schools, (giving to the teachers of each 100 *l.* per annum), yet they have been productive of little or no good hitherto, for this obvious cause, they are looked upon as seminaries exclusively instituted for the education of the children of the more wealthy classes of society, and to which the poor man's child is considered as unfit to be admitted.   From such causes, instead of their being a benefit to the province, they are sunk into obscurity, and the heads of most of them at this moment are enjoying their situations as comfortable sinecures.   Another class of schools has within a short time been likewise founded upon the liberality of the legislative purse, denominated common or parish schools, but like the preceding, the anxiety of the teacher employed, seems more alive to his stipend than the advancement of the education of those placed under his care: from the pecuniary advantages thus held out, we have been inundated with the worthless scum, under the character of schoolmasters, not only of this, but of every other country where the knowledge has been promulgated, of the easy means our laws afford of getting a living here, by obtaining a parish school, which is done upon the recommendation of some few freeholders, getting his salary from the public, and making his employers contribute handsomely besides.

It is true, rules are laid down for their government, and the proper books prescribed for their use; but scarcely in one case in ten are they adhered to, for in the same class you will frequently see one child with Noah Webster's spelling book in his hand, and the next with Lindley Murray's.   However prone the teachers are to variety in their schools, much blame is to be attributed to the trustees, who are in many instances too careless, and I might also add too ignorant to discriminate right from wrong, in the trust they have undertaken for the public benefit.   It is therefore not to be wondered at why the parish school system should meet with almost universal reprobation from most discerning men.   [Report from Grimsby to Mr. Gourlay].

State of Education in 1840's

Views of Canada and the Colonists, By a Four Years' Resident (Edinburgh, 1844), pp. 55-6.

Education, notwithstanding legislative efforts which have existed from an early period in the settlement of Western Canada to the present time, continues still in a very unsatisfactory state.   This is no doubt much owing to the great stretch of country, thinly populated, and without sufficient means to plant and support the large number of schools required in a country so situated during its early stages of existence.   Among a great proportion of the population, too, comprising chiefly a class of the older settlers, and the humbler class of emigrants from Britain, the benefits of education are but indifferently appreciated; and where there is found, as is the case in the country parts, joined with this apathy, some foundation for indulging it, on account of long and bad roads for the children, and also the early value of their services in the work of the farm, it is not much matter of surprise to see the roadside school-house thinly attended and the schoolmaster not at all an individual the best qualified for his duties.   I do not remember an instance of having journeyed through the country without witnessing evidences of this depressed state of education.

Text-Books from the United States

Public Archives of Canada, *Upper Canada Sundries:* Port Hope, June 2, 1828, A. Davidson to Major Hillier.

Nine tenths of the books in use [in schools], as far as I have had an opportunity of observing, are from the United States, which is scarcely consistent with prudence, not to speak of their defects.   The Board of Education indeed does not approve of their use, and the Europeans object to them, but it is in vain to contend with the imperious dictates of necessity.

For several years past no English Books could be procured in this neigh-bourhood, so that I am led to believe that the supply from England is precarious, and not at all equal to the growing demands of the Province.

E. *Newspapers and Libraries*

Books and Bookstores

Anna Jameson, *Winter Studies and Summer Rambles* (new ed., Toronto, 1923), pp. 67, 119.

Two years ago [in Toronto] we bought our books at the same shop where we bought our shoes, our spades, our sugar, and salt pork; now we have two good book-sellers' shops, and at one of these a circulating library of two or three hundred volumes of common novels. . . . Archdeacon Strachan and Chief Justice Robinson have very pretty libraries, but in general it is about two years before a new work of any importance finds its way here; the American reprints of the English reviews and magazines, and the Albion Newspaper, seem to supply amply our literary wants. . . .

I saw no bookseller's shop [in Hamilton], but a few books on the shelves of a growing store, of the most common and coarse description.

Libraries in the Backwoods

C. P. Traill, *The Backwoods of Canada* (London, 1836), p. 293.

I could hardly help smiling at your notion that we in the backwoods can have easy access to a circulating library. In one sense, indeed, you are not so far from the truth, for every settler's library may be called a circulating one, as their books are sure to pass from friend to friend in due rotation; and, fortunately for us, we happen to have several excellently furnished ones in our neighbourhood, which are always open to us. There is a public library at York, and a small circulating library at Cobourg, but they might just as well be on the other side of the Atlantic for any access we can have to them.

Influence of Newspapers

(i)

J. B. Brown, *Views of Canada and the Colonists* (Edinburgh, 1851), pp. 161-2.

There being neither stamp, advertisement, nor any paper duty in Canada whatever, the press has every opportunity to diffuse its influence. The smallest farmer in the neighbourhood of his town or village, or even in the backwoods, if he is able to bring in his load or two of firewood to the printer during sleighing time, may very easily enjoy the newspaper suitable to his politics.

. . . The leading newspapers in most of the large towns, such as Quebec,

Montreal, Kingston, Toronto, and Hamilton, are generally well supported. Being usually conducted with ability and intelligence, they have circles of readers much beyond their local influence.

(ii)

J. S. Buckingham, *Canada, Nova Scotia, New Brunswick* (London, 1843), pp. 22-3.

These [Toronto papers] are all conducted with more moderation, and in a more subdued tone, than party papers in the United States; but their influence on public opinion did not appear to me to be great; few persons ever adverting to their articles or opinions in general conversation; and none of them being so extensively read as newspapers are even in England.

4. RELIGIOUS INSTITUTIONS AND RELIGIOUS MOVEMENTS

A. *Religious Destitution of Frontier Communities*

Lack of Religious Instruction

J. R. Godley, *Letters from America* (London, 1844), vol. I, p. 174.

There is much to lament in the religious condition of most of the rural districts, as must always be the case where the population is much scattered, and allowed to outgrow the supply of ecclesiastical ministration. From never having the subject forced upon them, they begin to forget it, gradually neglect the observance of the Lord's Day, or else employ it as a day simply of bodily relaxation and amusement, omit to have their children baptized, and end by living as though they had no religion at all.

Irreligion of Immigrant Population

W. Bell, *Hints to Emigrants, in a Series of Letters from Upper Canada* (Edinburgh, 1824), pp. 89, 103-4.

New countries are generally settled by adventurers, with whom religion is not a primary consideration. Pious persons are seldom found willing to break off their former connexions, and forsake the land where both they and their fathers have worshipped God. Persons coming from a country where religious institutions are observed, into one where they are neglected, unless they have known something of the power of godliness, will feel themselves set free from restraints which were far from being pleasant. They will find the profanation of the Sabbath, and the neglect of religion, quite congenial to their unrenewed minds; and, if this is the case when they first settle in the woods, what can we expect when they have lived a number of years without religious instruction? May we not expect that depraved passions will be indulged, that vices will be practiced with avidity, and that the future world will be neglected amidst the clamorous demands of the present? This we

find to be actually the case in the backwoods of America.   It is true, there
are few new colonies in which some persons are not to be found who feel the
power of religion, but even *they* discover how soon evil communications
corrupt good manners.   Professing Christians themselves, when they are
placed where no Sabbaths are observed, and no religious ordinances administered, soon become lamentably deficient in the discharge of Christian
duties.

On looking around me [1817], however, I saw a moral as well as a natural
wildness, requiring cultivation.   With regard to a great majority of the
settlers, religion seemed to occupy no part of their attention.   The Sabbath
was awfully profaned; and drunkenness, swearing, and other vices, were
thought matters of course.   The number of those inclined to attend public
worship was small, and of those possessing real piety still smaller.

Indifference of Inhabitants to Providing Religious Instruction

Views of Canada and the Colonists, By a Four Years' Resident (Edinburgh, 1844),
pp. 243-4.

With the exception of the very thinly-peopled parts of the colony, there
are not the wants [for means of religious worship] experienced which many
in this country are led to suppose; and when these wants exist, it would seem
in many instances to result more from the apathy of the colonists themselves,
in not coming forward with the same hearty zeal to the support of religious
ordinances, which is shown in England or Scotland.   Colonies, however favourable they may be to the inhabitants maintaining themselves in comfort,
or acquiring wealth, appear rather to be prejudicial than otherwise to the
interests of religion.   Colonists do not experience the same restraints which
in old and compact communities are found to exercise so powerful an influence
in causing individuals to wear professions at least, and as a means to other
than the professed ends.   One is most forcibly struck with such views in
surveying the state of religion in new settlements of colonies especially.
Individuals who have never felt the power of genuine religion, finding themselves removed from a state of society, which influenced them so far as to
cause them to pay outward observance to its forms and interests, and thrown
into a somewhat disjointed and scattered population, composed of stranger
people of various countries and sorts, who exercise upon them no such influence—do usually become indifferent, more or less, to religious interests, and
their indifference constantly reaching a state of torpor rather predominates,
and genuine attachment to Christianity may thus readily be conceived to be
the exception.   In new and rising villages, it is more difficult to distinguish
the points of difference, and in the towns the shades have again further
blended, and the influences of home in the older countries are more felt.

This is rather a disheartening and gloomy view, but it has forced itself on
the observation of many as the most truthful one—and it goes in a great
measure to explain why so much missionary aid is required for colonists who
possess so substantially the means of worldly comfort.   No doubt in quite

new settlements, having a scattered population, this aid is essentially necessary, and the want of it is frequently severely experienced; but the cases are more frequent, I would say, throughout Canada, where a healthy state of religious feeling among certain bodies is more wanted than the necessary worldly means to support Gospel ordinances. One great evil which is observable in all the churches of Canada, and mostly, I feel in truth constrained to observe, in the Church of Scotland as it existed—has been that men of indifferent abilities have usually fallen to the lot of the colonists. This is, without question, the effect of the natural principle (from the influence of which not even ministers of the Gospel are exempted), that the lower the rate of worldly encouragement the more indifferent the description of ability presents itself in the field which calls for occupation. This state of affairs has been greatly aggravated by reason of the imperfect knowledge possessed at home of the actual condition of our colonies. We have greatly erred in estimating them as so outlandish and uncomfortable abodes as we have done; at least, the case is so with respect to Canada; and the consequence has been that, where it was of material importance the labourers should be powerful and skilful, the field has been all too much occupied in a manner most unfortunately calculated to aggravate evils.

B. The Church of England

Recruitment of Clergymen

Public Archives of Canada, *Q Series*, LXXXV: Quebec, August 20, 1800, Bishop of Quebec to Duke of Portland.

But your Grace will permit me to observe that although I have been so happy as to have acted thus far in coincidence with the plan you have marked out for me, yet I see no immediate prospect of supplying the wants of the Church by a further selection of persons at all fitted, by their situation, or character, for the sacred office.

Of the persons born in the country, I need not inform your Grace that few indeed have been so educated as to give them any decent pretension to instruct others, and among the persons who come to settle here, there is still less probability of finding proper subjects—Your Grace, I am sure, would be very far from recommending it to me to open the Sacred Profession for the reception of such adventurers, as disappointed speculations may have disposed to enter it.

I acquiesce, with as much sincerity as respect, in all that Your Grace has suggested with regard to the advantages to be derived from holding out an inducement to the best disposed of the inhabitants to give such an education to their children as may tend to qualify them for the Holy Calling;—but here again, I would beg permission to observe, that nothing effectual to this purpose can be done, till better means of education are obtained, than this country at present possesses.

State of Established Church

Public Archives of Canada, *Q Series*, XCII: Quebec, June 6, 1803, Bishop
Mountain to Lieutenant-Governor Milnes.

Compared with the respectable Establishments, the substantial revenues,
and the extensive powers and privileges, of the Church of Rome, the Church
of England sinks into a merely tolerated sect; possessing at the present
moment, not one shilling of revenue which it can properly call its own; without laws to control the conduct of its members, or even to regulate the
ordinary proceedings of Vestries and Church-Wardens; without any provision for organizing or conducting the necessary proceedings of an Ecclesiastical Court, or power to enforce their execution.   And what is worst of all,
and what cannot but alarm and afflict the mind of every serious and reflecting man, without a body of clergy, either by their number sufficient for the
exigencies of the State, or by any acknowledged right, or legitimate authority,
capable of maintaining their own usefulness or supporting the dignity of a
Church Establishment.

. . . In both Provinces the majority of His Majesty's Protestant subjects
are Dissenters; and of these there is a great variety of Sects: I speak not only
my own opinion (sir), but that of many of the best informed persons in both
Provinces when I say that an effectual and respectable *Establishment* of the
Church of England would go near to unite the whole body of Dissenters,
within its pale.

Laxity of the Church

Robert Gourlay, *Statistical Account of Upper Canada* (London, 1822), vol. I,
pp. 432-3.

Religion, I am sorry to say, has hitherto been but of secondary consideration.   This, however, is not to be ascribed to the general immoral character
of the people, who are naturally of pious and orderly habits; but is to be
attributed more to the seeming disregard of the head of the established
church in the Canadas, under whose immediate care and protection it more
especially belongs; and although this parish is one of the few which can boast
of a church of England, we have the mortification to say, that in twenty
years we have had but one solitary visit from the lord bishop of the diocese.
While such apathy prevailed for the advancement of the interest of the
mother church, other sects and denominations were not idle, and the result
has proved, that their labours have been but too successful; as our church
congregation, which was once respectable, is now almost dwindled to nought.
One good thing, however, has resulted to us from his lordship's visit.   A
representation was drawn up to him by the parishioners, requesting a clergyman; upon which one was sent us from England last spring; and although
his efforts have not hitherto added to the number of the congregation, yet
he has served to keep the remnant of the flock from the jaws of the all-
devouring wolf; and if proper perseverance is shewn, the good cause may yet
ultimately prevail. [Second Report from Grimsby to Mr. Gourlay].

Unsuitability of Anglican Clergymen

J. J. Bigsby, *The Shoe and Canoe or Pictures of Travel in the Canadas* (London, 1850), vol. I, pp. 28, 343-5.

I have little to say respecting the Quebec [Anglican] clergy. They were personally amiable. They worked the outward machinery of the Church of England with professional accuracy, but I fear they did little more than visit and relieve the sick when called upon. The archdeacon, Dr. Mountain, however, . . . was a priest of another and a better order. . . .

It seems to me that the Episcopal clergy are taken from too high a class for colonial service. They are usually so dissimilar from their flocks in tastes, habits, and prejudices, that they might come from another planet. Their early nurture has been too nice, and their education too academic, to admit of that familiarity, combined with true respect on the part of their people, which gives such well-earned influence to the Roman Catholic clergy in certain parts of Europe, and to the Wesleyan in Great Britain,—an influence which pervades both civil and spiritual life. . . .

The colonial bishops are more active [than those in England]. Many of them are laborious and useful men, but others again are deeply tainted with Puseyism (so worshipful of bishops), and are doing no little harm by frowning down evangelical religion—oppressing it, I ought to say—and encouraging formalism, which is sure to end in Popery.

Greatly as I prefer the constitution and formularies of the Church of England, I am not sorry to see a considerable share of evangelical dissent in Canada West. It shows, that thought is active in the woods upon subjects of extreme importance, and also that many of the settlers are from the meditative and independent classes.

Weakness of Establishment as Pioneer Church

T. W. Magrath, *Authentic Letters from Upper Canada*, edited by T. Radcliffe (Dublin, 1833), pp. 190-205.

Episcopalian, as I am, it grieves me to observe, that our number of Church of England Ministers is lamentably insufficient; and that unless prompt and energetic arrangements be made, to meet the wants and desires of our rapidly increasing colonists, there will be, with the absence of sound religious principle, a proportional accession of sects, or total indifference to, and ignorance of, any religion. Many districts are in a deplorable state in this respect, and, what is the worst feature, some of the settlers themselves seem careless about it. . . .

I much fear the government of the parent country has let the time pass by, when good might have been effected through the instrumentality of our clergy. The Methodist dissenters have obtained an ascendancy over our infant population. Their habits of domiciliary visitation, their acquaintance with the tastes and peculiarities of the Canadians, their readiness to take long and fatiguing rides, in the discharge of their self-imposed labours, render them formidable rivals to our more *easy going* clergy. . . .

The Sabbath is shamefully desecrated in many places, even by those who might be expected to observe it. A clergyman in a certain township, finding that drinking and sabbath-breaking were prevailing offences in his district, had a petition drawn up, and signed by the respectable inhabitants about him, to have fishing on Sunday prohibited by law: a point which happily has been accomplished, and in that neighbourhood, one remarkable for the most disrespectful negligence of the Lord's day, there is now a strict observance of it.

C. The Presbyterian Church

Weakness of Presbyterianism

Transactions of the London and Middlesex Historical Society, 1914, pp. 70-2: Journal of the Rev. Wm. Proudfoot.

In order to leave a just idea of Canada as a field of missionary labour under the superintendence of the United Associate Synod (of Scotland), it is necessary to divide the country into the townships within the limits of the United Synod of Upper Canada, and those that are beyond them. The Synod has congregations at wide intervals from Cornwall, fifty miles below Prescott, to London, in the Western Territory; and from York to Lake Simcoe. The number of ministers is fifteen, but some of these have as many as six congregations under their charge. Indeed, I know of only two or three ministers who preach statedly on Sabbath in one place. Many of these congregations, which were nice missionary stations, and perhaps are so still, have so grown in numbers and worldly circumstances as to be able to support each a minister at a moderate stipend. But the Synod has not ministers to send to them; and consequently there is reason to fear that some of these congregations will go over to those churches that can afford them a regular ministry, if the Synod receive not help from the United Associate Synod, or from Ireland, whence they have hitherto drawn their chief supply of preachers. Within the bounds of the Synod there are very many townships where small congregations might be collected, which the ministers have never visited, and which they cannot visit. These might be formed into excellent stations for missionary labor. . . .

That part of the country that is without the limits of the United Synod is very extensive, and very destitute of preaching. There are places in which the people have not heard a sermon for a year. . . . The evil is in part remedied now by Methodist preachers, who have spread themselves over all the province, and who, owing to the efficiency of their mode of operation, have penetrated into almost every township. [Letter from Proudfoot to Synod in Scotland, written about 1832].

19

Presbyterians Turn to Methodism

Transactions of the London and Middlesex Historical Society, 1930, p. 125: Diary of the Rev. Wm. Fraser.

March 30, 1835:—

If the people of West Gwillimbury, Tecumseth and Essa can be united in their sentiments and exertions I have not the least hesitation in saying that in the course of a very little time they would have a good congregation. Immediate attention to their spiritual wants is very necessary for the Methodists are making inroads in the place. I have understood that among some Scotch folk to the west of the Nottawasaga river in the township of Essa they had established a sufficient footing to have a class formed. Were the people in these places however supplied with the stated dispensation of Gospel ordinances I am well persuaded that the evil would not proceed much further.

A Presbyterian Revival Meeting

Transactions of the London and Middlesex Historical Society, 1922, pp. 34-45: Proudfoot Papers.

Jan. 15, 1833:—

Shortly after my arrival at Hamilton, Mr. Leonard's sleigh was proceeding to Barton Church to bring him down, so I stepped into it and was conveyed to the church where was being held a four days' meeting, or in other words a revival. I got hither about six o'clock p.m....

When I went into the meeting house there were present, I suppose, from 150 to 160 persons, the males on one side of the church and the females on the other, as is usual in all the churches in country places in the Province. The meeting for evening service had not commenced. Very shortly after I entered, the congregation sang a hymn. In this country amongst the churches where ministers from the States labour, the congregation sings and prays until the minister comes in....

After the hymn the whole congregation kneeled to pray. The minister, kneeling, began and was succeeded by Mr. Goodal (probationer) and by several of the congregation, to the number I think of seven. There were nine prayers. The people, I now understood, were holding a-prayer meeting before the evening service....

In these prayer meetings any one who wishes may pray, and he strikes in as soon as the person praying has pronounced amen. Sometimes there is a pause of a few seconds....

After the prayers were over Mr. Marsh made a very short address to the people, saying a very few simple and plain things, and then read out a hymn which the people of themselves sing. Mr. Eastman then entered the pulpit, gave out a hymn, prayed, sung, and preached from the text; "Come unto me all ye that labour and are heavy laden and I will give you rest." The sermon was intended to awaken the people to induce them to come to Christ immediately. The method was, 1, The invitation: 2, The characters addressed: 3, The Command: 4, The blessings promised. This wretched method was as wretchedly illustrated. Grammar, taste, logic, were all set by while he was making a push, firing (as he said) red hot balls at the conscience: though I could not exactly see the reason why these trifling ingredients in a sermon were left out. . . .

After the sermon Mr. Marsh made a few remarks, telling sinners that Christ did by him invite them, that if they would comply with the invitation in the text they should find rest, but if they did not that they must go down to Hell to bewail their crimes and their folly in unending misery. . . . He then bade the anxious seat be cleared. Mr. Searle then began a hymn to a most sweet, light, stirring tune. Every eye was now eager, the deepest interest prevailed in the assembly. In the midst of all this solemnity there were heard sobbings and weepings in different places in the house, there were many little knots of two or three persons talking and weeping with those who wept. After a little pause there came out from different places five men and a woman and weeping aloud, with hankerchiefs on their faces, threw themselves on their knees on the anxious seat. There was then a pause, sobbings were heard in different parts of the house. There seemed to be a movement amongst the people. Mr. Searle struck up a hymn to the same tune as before and during the singing of it a woman and four men came forward and knelt at the anxious seat. The singing continued, but no more seemed disposed to come. Mr. Eastman then spoke. . . . Still no more came. Mr. Marsh then spoke. . . . None came. Mr. Marsh then sang a verse of a suitable hymn to the same tune. All was still. . . . Mr. Marsh and Mr. Eastman prayed, and I think Mr. Goodal. The meeting was now over, a hymn was sung and the blessing pronounced at half-past nine p.m.

After the blessing there seemed a little gathering of the people about the stove in the middle of the church. Mr. Marsh hinted to them that they had better go home so they might be able to be here at 9 in the morning. They did not disperse rapidly. Mr. Eastman whispered to Mr. Marsh, we must disperse them, for if we leave them, they will go a praying in a crack and nobody knows when they will break up, they may remain the greater part of the night. . . .

All who came to the anxious seat, both men and women, were in tears, and many of them crying aloud. Their eyes were red with weeping. Their first step was to throw themselves down on their knees: they did not solemnly and gravely kneel, they threw themselves down like children when violently agitated, and it was not till Mr. Marsh told them to rise and sit on the seat that they got up. . . .

I could not say what was the occasion of their grief, their tears, their agitation. It was believed by all present to be the work of the Holy Ghost, but while I would not wish to oppose so good a sentiment in the remotest degree, I thought I saw in their manner what was not the evidence of the spirits working. All of them continued to manifest a strong feeling while they were in church, but when the prayer was over the agitation ceased, and they were moved no more. I thought it strange that peace had come so soon.

In the sentiments uttered by the preacher, I saw nothing remarkable. . . .

It appeared very forcibly to me that there was a feeling pervading the congregation which went a great deal farther than anything said by the minister to produce the result.   Every one in the church seemed to take so hearty an interest in what was going on, every one seemed to look upon those who had come to the anxious seat with a look of such benignant entreaty, that was scarcely resistable, and when they came forward there beamed in the countenances of the congregation such satisfaction and there was such a cordial shaking of hands with those who had come forward as must have had a very great share in producing the so-much desired demonstration of turning unto God.   And indeed, I suppose that in those cases where great revivals have taken place the general tone of feeling in the church has contributed a great deal. . . :

Jan. 16:—

Went to Bartón meeting house to-day at 9 o'clock a.m.   When I entered the church there were a good many people collected, say 70 or 80.   [After prayers for a woman unable to repent, there was sung a hymn].   Mr. Marsh stated to the audience that there were still many who had not felt the power of the Holy Spirit, and he invited all present to unite in prayer to God that he send down His Holy Spirit.   The address was very simple, nothing in it remarkable except that I thought it too feeble for the occasion. . . . The object which he and the people aimed at was to fill the anxious seat, but neither at this time nor any other time could I certainly make out whether all who came to the anxious seat were converted or not, but I fancy often that the people were made to believe so.   And from the way in which I heard those conversing who had been at the anxious seat, I am satisfied that they did consider their conversion as having taken place at that time.

Mr. Marsh then led the way and was followed by the church people to the number of nine, the whole church during this time being on their knees. The burden of their prayers was that God would break the heart of sinners. . . .

The looks of those on the anxious seat indicated that struggle was now over, that they had taken their ground, that they had got through the fiery ordeal and were now safe.   Something of the above might be read on their countenances.   I did not like the smirk on their faces.

After conversing with the converted, Mr. Marsh directed the attention of the meeting to the case of those who were still under the power of sin and far off from God. . . .   The whole congregation kneeled for prayer, Mr. Marsh, Eastman, Wm. Eastman, Goodall, Leonard, and another to the number of six prayed. . . .

There was after prayer, a hymn sung and then an interval of half an hour, during which time the people drew from their pockets, some a piece of cake and some an apple, and ate, all crowding around the stove. . . .

After the interval had elapsed, the church held a prayer-meeting for the success of the Gospel which was to be preached to them and for the Minister who was to preach it.   There were ten prayers by members of the church, the whole congregation kneeling during the whole time.   The prayers were, as usual, very deficient in scripture phraseology, but there was great apparent earnestness.   The burden of their supplications was that God would have mercy upon sinners. . . .

Mr. Marsh, after praise and prayer, preached. . . . The ideas were all of the same kind, and there were not many of them.   But there was very considerable feeling of expression, and they were very well delivered.   In speaking to sinners there was a bitterness which I did not like.

At the conclusion of the sermon there was a call to sinners who were willing this day to choose whom they would serve, to come forward to the anxious seat.   No one came.   Mr. Seyle then commenced a hymn and sung it all—no one moved, no commotion, no sobbing, no gathering in little knots. Mr. Marsh then said that there were three or four sinners in the house; that he had his eye upon them; that they were well known to be sinners; that if they continued in their present state they must go to hell; that they might die this night, this hour, this minute.   Still none came. . . .

We met again at six o'clock. . . . After service a call was made to those who were willing to be Christians to come forward to the anxious seat, but after every means of persuasion were exhausted, there came forward only one man.   In trying to persuade the concerned to come forward to the anxious seat, Mr. Marsh spoke to sinners in a way that gave me a good deal of pain.   He spoke like a disappointed man and his address partook sometimes of a taunt and sometimes of a scold.   He was evidently nettled. . . .

The people are to meet to-morrow to eat the Lord's Supper.   The anxious will be examined and if found possessed of knowledge, they will be admitted. Their examination must be very superficial.   There have been nearly fifty persons at the anxious seat and these must be examined in two hours at the most. . . .

Upon the whole I was not greatly reconciled to a revival meeting by what I saw.   I thought, however, I could improve the whole system.

D. The Methodist Church and the Evangelical Awakening

Methodists Provide Evangelical Leadership

(i)

C. Stuart, *The Emigrant's Guide to Upper Canada* (London, 1820), pp. 110-14.

Although some recent improvements have been made, the church of Christ has deplorably languished, and still deplorably languishes in Upper Canada. . . .

There are at present in Upper Canada, twelve or fifteen clergymen of the established church, and not quite so many churches.   These are supported partly by the government and partly by the Society for Propagating the Gospel.   I need not add (stationary as they are, or at least confined to narrow circuits) how totally insufficient such a provision must be, for the spiritual wants of a secluded population, scattered over a frontier of nearly one thousand miles. To the mass of the people, it is almost as nothing.

Yet the province has not been left entirely thus destitute. The spirit of the establishment seems improving; and the Baptists, Methodists, and Presbyterians, have concurred, in keeping alive in it, the worship of God. Of these, the most active and the most successful, are the Methodists.

. . . The fruits of the labours of the Methodists are striking in Upper Canada. I have, indeed, there as elsewhere, heard the most absurd and most disgusting stories concerning them; but my own observation is that on which I judge. I am not of their persuasion; and think several of their principles decidedly erroneous; but I believe them, in the most essential particulars, to be correct; and with respect to the results of their efforts, I cannot deny the clearest evidence of my senses. Where drunkenness, Sabbath-breaking, and profaneness reigned, sobriety, attention to the holy day, and seriousness have arisen. Little congregations have been formed, and exist extensively, where holiness and devotion (however abused by false professors) grace the exterior, at least, with propriety, and I doubt not, flourish sweetly in many a regenerate bosom. They have evidently been (and in a very extensive degree) the ministers of God to the people for good. They pervade, more or less, almost every part of the province; and they are going on, I trust, to thrive in the power and spirit of the Lord.

The Baptist ministry is more confined, and far less energetic; but in their narrower sphere, they appear to me more spiritual and more scriptural; and the tone of character, produced under their preaching, is more interesting to me, and as far as I can judge, more sound. I can only lament the contracted circuit of their means and of their efforts.

It has not come within my sphere to observe the course of the Presbyterian branch.

(ii)

Rev. Isaac Fidler, *Observations on Professions, Literature, Manners and Emigration in the United States and Canada* (New York, 1833), pp. 318-19.

The Methodists are very numerous throughout all the country, and use every possible exertion to thwart the views of the Established Church. I was informed by an episcopal minister, of some years' residence in Canada, that nothing gives greater annoyance to the Methodists, than the establishment in any district of a new mission, and the appointment of an efficient minister. Where this takes place, their efforts are redoubled. . . . Where a church establishment has been formed, the Methodists gain no respectable converts. In extensive districts, where there are no churches, they bear unlimited sway. I do not deny that good is produced by them in several ways. They prevent the people from being altogether without religious instruction; they establish Sunday Schools in different places; they stimulate clergymen of the established church to greater exertions; and they point out the good effects of well-concerted measures unanimously pursued. There is, perhaps, no body of ministers so systematic as those of the Methodist persuasion, as well in their modes of declamation, as in their plans of church government.   They are the same in every place, and with the same hostility to establishments of all kinds.

Evangelization in Port Hope

The Life and Times of the Rev. Anson Green, written by Himself (Toronto, 1877), pp. 57-8.

November 30, 1824—This afternoon, by previous arrangement, I delivered what I was informed was the *first sermon* preached in Port Hope by a Wesleyan minister—it was certainly the first appointment in our circuit work there.   I had a shoemaker's shop for my church, his shoe-bench for a pulpit, and six persons for a congregation.   Port Hope is the largest village on the circuit.   It is situated at the mouth of Smith's Creek, from which our circuit takes its name.   It is full of enterprise and spirit, but so full of whiskey and sin that it bears the name of "Sodom."

Fanatical Character of Methodism

John Howison, *Sketches of Upper Canada* (Edinburgh, 1821), p. 150.

Although there has long been an established presbyterian church at St. Catharine's, yet a large number of the people in its vicinity profess Methodism, and carry their religious mania to an immoderate height.   Meetings are held at different houses, three or four times a week.   At some of these I have seen degrees of fanaticism and extravagance exhibited, both by the preachers and congregation, which were degrading to human nature.

A Methodist Meeting

Transactions of the London and Middlesex Historical Society, 1930, p. 103:   Diary of the Rev. William Fraser.

London, Jan. 6, 1835: —
Last evening I attended a Methodist meeting.   The manner in which the exercises were conducted and the exhibition of feeling real or pretended which was made reminded me forcibly of the account which the inspired penman gives of the worshippers of Baal.   We first had a sermon in which neither sense nor connection were much observed.   And in the delivery of which the preacher exerted his powers of vociferation to the very utmost, while the audience at short intervals or whenever anything striking was said interrupted the speaker with their plaudits and amens.   After bawling for nearly an hour the first orator concluded when a second sprung up on his legs, and appeared determined that he should not be outdone by the first.   Possessed of a voice set to a pretty high key and of pulmonary capacity of no ordinary description his scream absolutely terrified.   And I greatly felt apprehensions for the safety of the functions of his life.   Besides, too, his speaking was

accompanied with stamping of the foot and with the most wild and extravagant gesticulation I ever beheld.

The people were afterwards exhorted to engage in prayer when any person who was desirous of having the prayers of the congregation was to kneel at the altar.   It was at this point of the proceedings that the confusion became general.   Two or three of the preachers and a considerable number of the people engaged in prayer at the top of their voices.   It was impossible for me at least, to catch a single sentence of what was said by any of the speakers, there was such a babel stirred up.   After about 10 minutes the tumult became less violent and only a few voices could be heard.   I observed one man in particular who got within the altar and who continued in a perfectly screaming tone to vociferate for fully half an hour if not more.   A little old woman too, I observed who made a ludicrous exhibition of her devotions. She walked backward and forward about the altar clapping and wringing her hands and occasionally throwing her arms heavenward and dancing on tiptoe.   After a little time two of the preachers travelled among the audiences to examine into their experiences—while a number of persons about the altar were still engaged in prayer.

The Camp Meeting

Patrick Shirreff, *A Tour through North America* (Edinburgh, 1835), pp. 183-8.

In travelling from London to St. Thomas, we were told of a Methodist camp-meeting in the neighbourhood; and as I had long been anxious to see one, we agreed to attend on the Sunday, when the meeting would be fullest. Early in the morning, people, in waggons and on horseback, were streaming in crowds through St. Thomas towards the meeting, and as I was afraid of losing patience before evening, when the richest scene is said to take place, we embraced an offer of going to Colonel Talbot's in the forenoon, distant about twelve miles west from St. Thomas. . . .

We returned to St. Thomas, which we left at half-past four, in a waggon, for the camp-meeting, and on our way met multitudes of people on their return home.   It now became evident we had been too late in visiting the meeting, to see the greatest assemblage, but consoled ourselves that the most fervent worshippers would be more readily distinguished.   Our waggon was left within a mile of the meeting, and we proceeded on foot through the forest.   The ground in the midst of the forest had been prepared for the occasion, having had the brush or underwood removed, and trees laid in parallel rows, by way of seats, for five or six hundred people.   On entering a square, formed by tents, in which the people reside for four or five days together, I was disappointed at the smallness of the assemblage, which did not exceed three hundred souls.   Many people were walking up and down, engaged in mirthful conversation, and five or six small groups were standing in different parts, singing hymns in a low tone.   At this moment I observed a comely young woman in front of a tent, laughing and nodding familiarly to a numerous acquaintance, which induced me to think she might be engaged in attending a tent for entertaining the company. She bore a striking likeness to a valued friend in Scotland; and while engaged in tracing the resemblance, feature by feature, she and a younger companion jumped into a waggon, and seated themselves in a conspicuous situation, as if wishing to attract attention. On walking round the square, I was riveted to the spot by the sweetness of a young lady's voice, dressed in white, with a very broad gipsy straw-bonnet, and black veil hanging over her shoulder. Her figure was above the middle size, slender and graceful, her features expressive and handsome. She was accompanied by another lady, wearing a bonnet and veil of the same description, and a gentleman, seemingly her sister and brother, and all were engaged in singing. From the appearance of things, I concluded the people had a short time before been engaged in taking tea.

A little while after entering the square, five or six old men placed themselves in front of a rude platform erected for the preachers, and commenced singing in a loud strain, on hearing which the different small parties came and joined the old men. The singing lasted about ten minutes, when praying succeeded, and each individual pronounced a different prayer aloud. At this time a minister placed himself on the platform or pulpit, and in a stentorian voice, ejaculated an impassioned prayer, which, by degrees, excited the feelings of the people below him, and when they reached what he, perhaps, considered the proper key, he descended and joined them on his knees.

I was standing close beside the worshippers, on a trough used for collecting the juice of the maple in spring, leaning my back against a tree, and gazing on the extraordinary scene. Many individuals of both sexes were bellowing at the utmost pitch of their voice, and clapping their hands in seeming transport; others were whining supplicatory strains, and wringing their hands in despair. The comely young woman and her companion, formerly noticed, joined the group in a standing position in the first instance; they soon became bathed in tears, and ultimately joined in prayer in a state of high excitement. A very emaciated old woman, with dishevelled locks of silvery whiteness, shrieked so loud and piteously, that the minister's voice became unheard, and something like a thrill of uneasiness vibrated on my nerves. Such was the confusion and discord, that I was unable to collect two connecting sentences from the prayer of any individual. When the devotees had seemingly reached the highest pitch to which their feelings would strain, the lady with the gipsy bonnet stepped forward near to where I was standing, and commenced singing in the most soothing and melodious tone. She was joined by her sister and brother, and soon afterwards by all the sect. In this manner prayer and praise succeeded each other, during which the feelings of the worshippers were alternately excited and lulled by minister and nymph, like ocean by tempest and calm.

Many bystanders were laughing at the exclamations and postures of the worshippers; others were reading newspapers, or carelessly engaged in conversation. One individual, more prominent in his ridicule than the rest, was rebuked for his conduct by one of the sect, when a controversy ensued between the parties, who were listened to by a crowd collected around them.

On approaching the disputants, one was openly avowing his unbelief in the Bible, and the other, without meekness, condemning his sentiments and conduct; but neither possessing the power of arranging an argument, I left them engaged in the hopeless task of trying to convince each other.

There was something so different in the impassioned supplications of the minister, whose aim seemed to be to rouse the feelings, without impressing the minds, of his audience—in the time, place, and manner of addressing the Supreme Being, so different to what I had been accustomed to in the Presbyterian worship of Scotland, that at first I could not believe the sect was addressing the same Deity. The earnest, excited, I may say hysterical, devotions of one party, the indifference and unrestrained scoffing of the other, gave rise to such conflicting emotions, that I arranged to meet my friend in half an hour, and retired from the multitude.

In the meantime, fires had been lighted up on the ground in different parts of the square, one six feet high near the platform, and a few candles were glimmering in the tents. The foliage of the maple and oak, so remarkable for richness and variety of autumnal tints, formed a beautiful canopy over the heads of the people, and, when gilded by the flames of blazing fagots, and intermingled by rising sparks, had a supernatural and solemn effect. Could I have alone contemplated nature unconnected with the part humanity was acting, my enjoyment might have been great, but the wailings of fellow beings, and the shouts of boys on reaching the ground, disturbed returning repose.

On again approaching my friend, a preacher was thanking the Almighty for the manifestations of his goodness since they had met together, and concluded by requesting all who desired to be released from their sins, to accompany him to another place, and a procession to the place ensued. This consisted of a small enclosure, formed by a single rail of saplings, nailed to the standing trees, in the centre of which were two branchless trunks lying parallel to each other, and was perhaps what is termed the pen. Here the preacher again requested all who earnestly desired to be relieved from their sins, to come within the lines which had been prepared for them.

The whole devotees then prayed promiscuously aloud, and when at the height of excitement, the nymph of the gipsy bonnet commenced singing, standing on the outside of the enclosure, and was joined by the people within.

When the singing ceased, it was announced that Brother Fraiser was to preach, and the people assembled around the shade on the seats prepared for them, after being repeatedly requested to do so. At the conclusion of praise and prayer, a text was given out, and sermon commenced. Mr. Fraiser now discovered that he was hoarse, perhaps from previous exertion, and in the midst of his apology to the audience, I took my leave at half-past eight o'clock.

The devotees were few in number, perhaps not more than sixty, and almost either old men or young women, the Irish brogue being conspicuous amongst the former. They seemed of the lowest class, not more than half-a-dozen of well-dressed people being amongst them. There were four ministers.

I could not divine why the pretty creature with the gipsy bonnet did not join in prayer, and commenced singing at the proper time.   Could her bonnet and clothes be too fine for kneeling and tossing on the ground like others, or had she a part to act?

At the time of my departure, there might be nearly three hundred people on the ground, including all descriptions, amongst whom were fifteen or twenty females, unconnected with the sect, and a great many boys.   On walking from the meeting, many youth were met on their way to it.

It is but justice for me to say, that I did not witness any act of impropriety or indecency by the attenders of the camp-meeting; but whether this arose from the character of the people, the time of night, or my want of discernment, others may determine.   The meeting was, however, a small one, and in a part of the country not likely to have furnished many examples of disregardless profligacy.   Whether camp-meetings are favourable to the cause of genuine religion, is matter of dispute, and the greater part of those whom I heard speak on the subject, supported the negative side of the question.   Perhaps the matter is oftener determined by feeling than reason.   It would be presumption to give a decided opinion on so serious a subject, with such limited opportunity of judging; but something extraordinary will occur to induce me again to visit a camp-meeting.   This may be prejudice.

The Backwoods Preacher

Susanna Moodie, *Roughing It in the Bush* (new ed., Toronto, 1913), p. 345.

Old Thomas was a very ambitious man in his way.   Though he did not know A from B, he took it into his head that he had received a call from Heaven to convert the heathen in the wilderness; and every Sunday he held a meeting in our loggers' shanty, for the purpose of awakening sinners, and bringing over "Injun pagans" to the true faith.   His method of accomplishing this object was very ingenious.   He got his wife, Peggy—or "my Paggy", as he called her—to read aloud to him a text from the Bible, until he knew it by heart; and he had, as he said truly, "a good remembrancer", and never heard a striking sermon but he retained the most important passages, and retailed them second-hand to his bush audience.

I must say that I was not a little surprised at the old man's eloquence when I went one Sunday over to the shanty to hear him preach.

Growing Concern for Education of Ministers

The Minutes of the Annual Conferences of the Wesleyan-Methodist Church of Canada, from 1824 to 1845 Inclusive (Toronto, 1846), pp. 8-9.

That the Conference [of September 14, 1825] view with concern the want of intellectual improvement among our young preachers generally,—that it is expedient and necessary, in order to meet the wants of society, now improving in literary acquirements, that our young men should have more advantages for the improvement of their minds; therefore, resolved further, that the Presiding Elders, and other of our senior brethren, be requested to pay special attention to this matter; taking the oversight of, and affording to, our young men all the aid in their power for the attainment of this object.

Progress and Influence of Methodism

Egerton Ryerson, *Wesleyan Methodism in Upper Canada* (Toronto, 1837), pp. 21-5.

[In 1791] one Episcopal Clergyman at Kingston, another in Bath, and a third in Niagara, constituted the sole religious instructors of the country. As for Methodism, it was only known by hear-say to the dispersed inhabitants, as a subject of ridicule and scorn. Its principles were deemed absurd; its services and society meetings were ridiculed as enthusiastic; its Ministers were viewed as ignorant, idle, hypocritical adventurers, and political spies; some of them fell victims to Magisterial persecution; up to a very recent period, Methodism has been regarded by many leading Magistrates and other civil officers throughout the Province, and by the most prominent members of the Executive Government, as dangerous to the supremacy of British power; and the combined influence of men of wealth and learning, together with the Civil Government itself, from the Representative of the King (with few exceptions) down to the Church Sexton, has been arrayed against the progress of Methodism, and bent, as far as the spirit of the age would permit, upon its extermination.

Such were the circumstances under which the standard of Methodism was raised in this Province; and such are the formidable obstacles which have opposed its progress. It had no pecuniary resources but the voluntary liberality of those who embraced its principles. Its doctrines and precepts waged war with the prevalent vices and popular prejudices of the country. Its teachers were men of humble rank, as well as of humble literary or educational pretensions. . . . In the spirit of primitive Christianity those devoted men went forth, not counting their lives dear unto them, but in weariness and poverty, in the extremes of heat and cold, at all seasons and in all kinds of weather—sometimes whole nights in the wilderness, surrounded by the wild beasts of the desert,—they traced their way by blazed trees and Indian bye-paths, and forded creeks and rivers—in some instances at the risk of their lives—to testify to the pioneer settlers of the country "the glorious Gospel of God our Saviour,". . .

Viewing the progress of Methodism *numerically*, I will add nothing to the following statistical statement:

In 1792, there were 2 Preachers and 165 members; in 1800, there were 6 Preachers and 933 members; in 1810, there were 12 Preachers and 2,597 members; in 1820, there were 24 Preachers and 5,383 members; in 1830, there were 62 Preachers and 11,348 members; at present there are 101 Preachers and 15,453 members, besides regular and occasional hearers.

The progress of Methodism in a *civil* and *social* point of view is equal to its numerical increase. It has trampled over widespread and deep-rooted prejudices, by practical proofs that it is not a congeries of enthusiastic impulses, but a consistent system of scriptural truth, rational experience, and sound morality. It has silenced a double-tongued calumny, by a scriptural adherence to the principles of civil and religious liberty in the hard days of bigotted exclusion and despotic invasion; and by a scriptural support of the constituted civil compact and authorities of the land, in a season of anarchical encroachment. It has levelled to the very ground the inquisitorial walls of political proscription, by obtaining, after many an arduous struggle, the enactment of laws for the security of its chapel property and legal celebration of its marriage and other religious ceremonies, by its own ministers and according to its own forms. It has refuted in the face of the world the oft-repeated imputation that it honoured "ignorance as the mother of devotion," by unprecedented efforts to promote the general education of the youth of the country upon the principles of the Bible. . . .

But there is another and a higher view in which we are to survey the success of Methodism in Upper Canada. It is in the *moral* transformations of which it has been the divinely owned instrument,—in the spiritual achievements it has effected, that its appropriate office and character are seen in their true light. . . .

Follow it in its progress from place to place, and the path of its *success* will be traced by a visible and essential improvement in piety and virtue, public order and individual happiness; in the enlargement of that kingdom which is "righteousness, and peace, and joy in the Holy Ghost."

E. Other Religious Sects

The Baptists in Upper Canada

(i)

Transactions of the London and Middlesex Historical Society, 1922, pp. 5-6: Proudfoot Papers.

Dec. 5, 1832, York:—

Was considerably disappointed to-day in Mr. Stewart [the Baptist preacher]. I have been now several times in his house, but never heard anything that could indicate his possessing a literary turn. He is always working as a labourer, covered with mud or lime. His manners are the manners of a man of work, and forwardness and conceit supply in him the place of ease. He piques himself upon being one of those converted by the instrumentality of Mr. Stewart, Mowlin, Perthshire, and taking his stand upon that vantage ground he looks down upon almost all others, not of his own denomination, as hardly Christians, if they be Christians at all. Were I to be much about York I should not choose to cultivate his acquaintance. . . .

In speaking of the people of Lobo, Mr. Stewart complained that they were so full of prejudices that they would not come to hear the Gospel. I understand that they are so resolute Presbyterians that they would not flock after a Baptist. Had they been Baptists, and had a Presbyterian complained that they would not come to hear him, it is likely Mr. Stewart would have praised them for their consistency, and would have exultingly said that Presbyterians need not go amongst them, they are too well rooted in the faith to follow such.   And yet, when I was in the West, I heard of the people of Lobo that there are many Methodists and Baptists amongst them, and that the Baptists are throughout the community as wild as the Methodists, a piece of information for which I was not prepared, as I had been accustomed to think the Baptists a very excellent class of Christians.   I must enquire further about these Baptists before I just take it as a settled point that they are wilder than Methodists, or even as wild.

(ii)

Papers and Records, Ontario Historical Society, vol. XXVII, 1931, p. 455: Proudfoot Papers.

Jan. 4, 1834, Mr. Bryce's:—
In the evening Asa Ditton, Mr. Bryce's son-in-law came to talk with me about baptism.   He has been hard pressed to become a Baptist and so has his wife.   I stated to him views about baptism at which he was much surprised saying that hitherto he understood nothing about (it).   I succeeded in driving Baptists out of his mind but I fear that these low fellows who go about from house to house imposing upon silly and ignorant persons may after all drive out of his head all that I have said.   If he turn Baptist now he must do so with the consciousness of sinning against light.   The Baptists in this neighbourhood are of the Free will order and maintain the most absurd notions.   The leader of them is one Huckins, a joiner, who seems to be an artful, vulgar person.   The Baptists are in the habit of holding class meetings in the neighbourhood of those they wish to gain over to their way of thinking and then invite them to attend and this they do till they gain their point.   It is impossible to resist these people for their work is all done in secret and they hang on till they have taken the victims of their delusions across the Rubicon and then they set out upon some other poor ignorant victims.

The Davidites

Transactions of the London and Middlesex Historical Society, 1930, pp. 116-18: Diary of the Rev. Wm. Fraser.

N. Gwillingbury Tuesday 24th.
Truly this is a land of marvels.   This seems to be an age of extravagance and fanaticism, & this country one of those which abounds with delusion. The infatuated ravings of the monomaniac are taken for the dictates of inspiration . . . the unsubstantial phantoms of bewildered fancy are regarded as heavenly visions . . . and the blinded zeal of ignorant and foolish men held in utmost veneration.   Indeed the experience of all past times as well as the present age goes to establish the conclusion that no system of religion however absurd, that no fanaticism however wild, that no fancies however impalpable

if propounded with sufficient arrogance and with an air of sanctity can fail of attracting the attention of the volatile & ignorant or of securing a certain number of deluded followers. The uncultivated mind is naturally disposed to superstition and it is not therefore astonishing that in the present day pretentions to inspiration should meet with so much countenance or so many deluded mortals should be led away by blind guides into the inextricable mazes of frenzied enthusiasm.— These remarks I have thought proper to premise as introductory to some brief account of a sect of Religionists whose settlement I have this day visited.

In the town ship of East Gwillimsbury, on Union Street about 2½ miles to the Eastward end of the Holland Landing on Yonge Street & about 34 miles distant from Toronto is situated the village of Hope. This place is remarkable as being inhabited by the Davidites or Children of Peace as they style themselves. The village itself has nothing extraordinary in its appearance. It contains probably about 300 inhabitants. When I say that the village has nothing unusual about it I must except a splendid edifice which is situated near one of its extremities and which is called the Temple. Before however I attempt to give any description of the building let me take a glance at the history of its founder and indeed of the whole village.

David Willson the leader of the Children of Peace appears—(for I have seen him) to be a man about 60 years of age of a heavy and solemn cast of countenance with small squinting eyes and demure carriage. He appears well adapted to be the leader of those who are disposed to enthusiasm. He is now beginning to exhibit the marks of age in his bended form and scattered locks, his dress was of the plainest description. Inexpressibles of brown homespun scarcely meeting the short boot which ascended only to the top of the ankle and quite tattered at the lower part of the legs,—a vest of blue or black homespun with a single row of brass buttons—a coat of mixed blue and white of quite a homely cut and a slouched half Quaker hat composed the clothing of this singular man. He appeared to have disciplined his features into eremitical gloom and though I succeeded in inducing a slight curl of the lip he instantly resumed his former gravity.

It is now upwards of 15 years since the sect of David has been in existence. This man I am told once belonged to the Society of Friends. It appears that either from some suspicion of his growing influence or other causes he had been restrained in the free exercise of the gifts of utterance. His ambitious Spirit could not brook the insult thus offered to his importance and his wounded pride it seems determined him to strike into quite a new path. He separated from his Quaker brethren on Yonge St. and retired to the place which he has called Hope. And such was the veneration in which he was held that many of his acquaintances sold their farms on Yonge St. and retired along with him. The settlement has been gradually on the increase since its formation so that now the population of the village (all Davidites) may very probably amount to nearly 300 souls. Besides these there (are) not a few of his disciples who occupy farms in the neighborhood.

Of the peculiar principles held by this man I can say little or nothing.

He is so extremely shy that it is no easy matter to get him in conversation and even when this has been effected he exhibits the most extreme caution. I have consoled myself for the want of conversation with him by the opportunity which was afforded me of purchasing ½ a dozen of his discourses. These I had made myself sure would afford me some clue to his system. I was completely disappointed. It would be difficult to convey any idea of those publications. They are truly of the most nondescript character of anything which I have ever seen issue from the Press. Such a mass of heterogeneous disjointed ungrammatical absurd nonsense I am persuaded has seldom been inflicted on a deluded community. If any sense at all can be collected from such a mass of confusion the burden of the story to which every description of text must bend consists in the most splenetic railings against learned priests and those who receive pay for their ministrations. Some of his uncouth remarks on government paid parsons are very appropos. But regarding the compositions as a whole, I would venture to defy any person whose intellect was not equally obtuse with that of this author to learn from them a single theological tenet which he holds. Truly the men who allow themselves to be duped by such an imposter must be under strong delusion. Yet so it is and this poor crazed being has collected about a large society and has now a regular appointment and obtains hearers in the city of Toronto. But I must now proceed to attempt some description of the public buildings of Hope & first of the Temple.

The Moravians

P. Campbell, *Travels in the Interior Inhabited Parts of North America in the Years 1791 and 1792* (Toronto: The Champlain Society, 1937), pp. 153-4.

In this neighbourhood [Niagara] live a set of religionists called *Moravians*, with long beards, originally from Germany; they emigrated to this place from Pennsylvania. They are a very innocent, inoffensive, and industrious people, that have many peculiarities in their manner of worship and mode of living, though of the Lutheran persuasion. In one settlement in that province they have all sorts of trades and manufactures, and have every thing in common. There is a large house or hall for the young women, apart, in which they work, and another for the young men in which they do the same. The sexes are never allowed to see one another. When a young man signifies a desire to marry, he and the first girl on the list are put into a private room together, and continue in it for an hour. If he agrees to marry her after this meeting, good and well; if not, he will not get another, and she is put the last on the list; so that all before her must go off before she gets any other offer. And though the parties had never seen one another before this meeting, which is rarely otherwise, they have no alternative, and must make up their minds and acquaintances in that short intercourse. If the parties are satisfied, and they marry, a house is built for them in the village where they live, and carry on business for the good of the community at large. There are as yet not above a score of them in this neighbourhood, but many more are expected;

I have heard several people say that they would like them well as neighbours, and the Quakers are particularly fond of them on account of their mild and inoffensive dispositions.

The Mennonites

Papers and Records, Ontario Historical Society, vol. XXVIII, 1932, p. 88:
Proudfoot Papers.

Jan. 30, 1835, Guelph:—

In Wilmot where the farmers are all Dutch and in Waterloo the same we could do nothing because we cannot preach in Dutch.   Most of these Dutchmen belong to the sect of the Aumish of whom I could learn nothing but that as an important article of their religion they cultivate long beards. The rest of the people are mostly Menees (Mennonites) which I do not yet understand.   There are some Presbyterians amongst them.   These Dutchmen have noble farms; . . . yet it is said they are quite against giving anything to ministers.   They will hold no man a preacher who is not inspired by the Spirit and if he gets his preaching talents so easily he needs no pay. The Dutch in Waterloo are said to be a wild race, carried off by the wildest enthusiasm and there was something spoken about bad living which I had not time to enquire into.

The Millerites

C. H. C., *It Blows, It Snows: A Winter's Rambles through Canada* (Dublin, 1846)
pp. 39-43.

On our return expedition up stream [on a hunting trip], we found ourselves necessitated, for lack of sufficient physical force to prosecute our journey, to accept the voluntary assistance of a solitary stranger, whom we accidentally picked up, wending his way along the bank of the river towards Bytown, for the express purpose, he afterwards contended, of propagating the undeniable doctrines of the true faith.   This benign promulgator of the gospel (who very quickly discovered himself to be no less a personage than an American citizen fresh from Cape Cod, Mass., where, he was proud to acknowledge, he had been both born and raised) gave us to understand, that he was an independent Millerite, or true believer in the proximate appearance of the second advent. . . .

Having received rather a cordial invitation to attend a course of lectures which he proposed giving, for the particular benefit of the good people of Bytown, indiscriminately, I made it a duty of especial importance, to present myself in person the first evening of his spiritual outpourings, and was not a little surprised to find, after having listened attentively to him for five and twenty minutes, that there was not less than a congregation of four hundred people. . . .

In the estimation of many then present, I do firmly believe, he brought his arguments to bear with such force, as to make very considerable pro-

20

gress. . . . In the tender minds of the rising generation, his convincing proofs were altogether successful. . . . His lecture lasted for about one hour, and might have continued for double that space of time, had not some of the more rational tradesmen of the neighbourhood . . . come in a body consonant, and threatened instant destruction upon the head of the false prophet, if he did not immediately close his discourse and leave the town.

F. Roman Catholicism and Religious Conflict

Growth of Religious Animosity on the Frontier

C. H. C., *It Blows, It Snows: A Winter's Rambles through Canada* (Dublin, 1846), pp. 180-1.

It is much to be deplored that religious animosities have at length been effectual in winding their way, from the contaminating differences which seem ever to beset European spiritual institutions, to the once peaceful retirements of Canada. A few years back, and whatever the professed creed of the Backwoodsman might have been, he was seldom or never known to have been so unmindful of his Heavenly interests, as to call down dread anathemas upon the heads of that individual whose means of seeking salvation were not exactly in strict accordance with his own: at present a course of diametrically opposite principles seems to pervade the minds of the majority of every rank and persuasion in this country; and I have not the slightest hesitation in saying, that there exists amongst the present condition of Society in Canada, as much hatred and bad feeling towards each other, on the score of religious differences, as the sixpenny adventurer in search of knowledge is likely to hear vociferated in the Conciliation Hall, or round room of the Rotunda in Dublin.

Irish Immigration and Rise of Orange Lodges

(i)

Public Archives of Canada, *Upper Canada Sundries:* York, February 14, 1827, W. Morris to Major Hillier.

About 18 months since I acquainted His Excellency the Lieutenant-Governor by letter addressed to you, that an Orange Association which exists in the District of Bathurst was in active operation, to the great annoyance of the Catholic part of the community. . . .

The lodge still continues to be conducted with zeal on the part of many individuals, and some of those who give it countenance being persons of respectability in the District the mortification to the Catholics is that more vexatious.

I look forward to the consequences which will follow this institution with very serious apprehension. . . .

(ii)

Public Archives of Canada, *Upper Canada Sundries:* Kingston, January 21, 1828,
W. Fraser to Major Hillier.

I cannot help expressing my grief at seeing that instead of the last unfortunate affray that took place in this Town between the Orange party and the Catholics producing reconciliation has to all intents and purposes been the cause of very different effects. The Orange party have concluded from the success they met with in every stage of the trials that there is a decided partiality in their favour; the consequence is, that there is a new Lodge formed in Kingston, regularly attended twice a week: headed by a gentleman that arrived a few months ago from Ireland for the express purpose of organising Orange Lodges in this country.

(iii)

Public Archives of Canada, *Upper Canada Sundries:* Peterborough, January 26,
1831, To His Excellency Sir John Colborne.

We the Committee of the Peterborough General Society take the liberty of addressing your Excellency on the recent attempts which have been made, and, we understand, continue to be made to extend Orange Societies in this neighbourhood. . . .

That men emigrating from Ireland to this province should bring with them their early principles and prejudices is natural, and we feel disposed to respect them, so long as no offensive display takes place; but that attempts should be made to induce the rising generation to join in these Societies, we think decidedly injurious to the internal peace and best interests of the Province.

IV

MINING SOCIETY IN BRITISH COLUMBIA AND THE YUKON

D EVELOPMENT of placer gold mining on the Pacific Coast in
what was to become the Province of British Columbia gave
rise to a type of society very different from any which had grown
up in the eastern regions of Canada. The phenomenal rate of growth,
the character of the population attracted by a gold rush, the high
mobility of those engaged in mining, and the isolation of the area
from the outside world gave to the gold-mining society a distinctive
character.[1] The long streams of eager miners reaching into the
interior in search of gold, and the sudden accumulation by the
fortunate few of substantial fortunes, struck the imaginations of
those both within and outside the area in a way that scarcely any
other kind of social phenomenon did. The unsettling effects of the
gold rush reached back into older societies thousands of miles
removed, and forward into a distant interior inhabited by natives
and fur traders.

The development of the Fraser and Cariboo mining regions
took place in terms of "rushes." Placer gold mining made heavy
demands upon labour and provided a field of endeavour in which
returns, occasionally fabulous in size, could be secured without any
lengthy period of outlay or preparation. In spite, therefore, of
restrictions imposed by the Hudson's Bay Company, hostile to the
mining industry, and the lack of adequate transportation facilities,
the movement of population into the two colonies of Vancouver
Island and British Columbia from 1858 to 1862 was phenomenal.
The influx began in the early spring of 1858. In the four months
of April, May, June, and July of this year, something like twenty-
five thousand persons arrived in Victoria or found their way over-
land to the Fraser River.[2] Though the next year the movement
abated, and, indeed, many returned to California disappointed
with the findings, a steady stream of miners during the years 1860,

[1]Cf. W. P. Morrell, *The Gold Rushes* (London, 1940).

[2]E. O. S. Scholefield and F. W. Howay, *British Columbia* (Vancouver, 1914),
vol. II, pp. 17-18; W. N. Sage, *Sir James Douglas and British Columbia* (Toronto,
1930), p. 204.

1861, and 1862 pushed into the mining areas. In the latter year the influx of population once more assumed the character of a rush, several thousands leaving England, Canada, Australia, and New Zealand to seek their fortunes mining gold.

The extremely rapid growth of population in such a short time imposed strains upon social organization which were intensified by the character of the people who joined in the rush. Before 1860 the lower Fraser constituted a frontier of California and almost the whole of its population was drawn from this older mining area; but as the fame of the Fraser River diggings became more widespread, people poured in from various parts of the world and many of these had had no previous mining experience. If many of the problems of the new society resulted from the undisciplined character of the California miners, others resulted from the inexperience of adventurers from outside.[3] These two layers of population remained sharply distinct during the early years of development, and each set its distinctive imprint upon the society. Other characteristics of the population carried threats to the new social order. The gold rush involved, as scarcely any other movement of population, a complete tearing away from old ties and traditional controls, and this emancipation was more thorough because it extended to such large numbers of people at the same time. Joining the rush to the mining frontier was something in the nature of a "grand spree" for the individual. The engagement in mining was not intended to be of long duration, and this feeling that the return to a settled mode of life was not far off encouraged an attitude of making the most of a brief period of freedom. The seasoned miners looked upon their occupation as of a more permanent character, but even among them the dominant urge was to strike it rich and then get out of the country. The result was that the temptation to enjoy life to the full tended to be overwhelming, and defeated any desire to establish enduring social relationships and institutions for the future. Finally, the absence of family settlers made for unstable conditions in the mining frontier. The hazards accompanying the journey to the Pacific Coast, and the nature of the mining occupation, discouraged female immigration, and the society became almost wholly made up of males. Only in the towns, more especially Victoria, did anything approaching

[3]Cf. Sage, *Sir James Douglas and British Columbia*, chap. VII.

normal family life appear. Some alliances between the Indians and whites took place within the mining interior, but most of these were between retired Scottish fur traders turned hostel-keepers and squaws presumably gifted in the culinary art. The miners had little desire to settle down to home life and particularly in a country in which they intended to stay for only a short time. Little promise of matrimony accordingly was held out to girls immigrating to the colony, and their opportunities for employment were confined to domestic work in Victoria. Some females were sent to the country by charitable organizations in Great Britain, but the movement never assumed more than trifling dimensions.

In addition to the rapid growth and composition of the population, the nature of the mining industry itself made difficult the establishment of stable social organization. A considerable mobility was characteristic of the total population. Exhaustion of the bars on the lower Fraser led to the pushing of miners farther up the river and eventually into the Cariboo country, and this shift of population came about by a series of sudden rushes after the circulation of reports of new findings.[4] New mining camps grew up overnight; old mining towns vanished almost as suddenly. There was little in the mining community which possessed the character of permanency. The seasonal nature of the mining industry intensified the mobility of the population. Large numbers of miners returned to Victoria to spend the winter, and this influx and exodus of people weakened community organization in the capital as in the mining interior. The summer tended to be a period of feverish activity and the winter a period of complete idleness. The sharp separation of work from leisure meant that when working the miners neglected interests other than the purely economic while during periods of leisure they tended to give themselves up wholly to play. Placer gold mining was fatiguing and was carried on largely in isolation from fellow-men, but, when the season came to an end and the miners returned to the city, the rigorous tasks of the summer gave way to the more pleasant pursuits of the winter. Emotional urges long held in restraint through the lack of leisure and human companionship suddenly found release, and, with the proceeds of the

[4]Cf. M. Q. Innis, *An Economic History of Canada* (Toronto, 1935); also, H. A. Innis, ed., *Select Documents in Canadian Economic History, 1497-1783* (Toronto, 1932).

year's labour, the miners enjoyed an interval of complete relaxation. It was in the mining towns, accordingly, that some of the most serious problems of the mining society emerged. Here miners returning from the interior joined recent arrivals, and the total population tended to be of a floating character. Problems of destitution, crime, morality, cultural organization, and religion, though extending into the interior, centred very largely in the town of Victoria.

Problems of destitution were associated with the influx of people unsuited to the life of a mining community, the highly speculative character of gold mining, and the long period of idleness during winter months. The familiarity of the Californians with mining techniques, and their willingness to accept the trials and discomforts of mining life, gave them a great advantage over others in making the personal adjustments necessary for success on the new frontier. Failure recorded in terms of destitution or personal disorganization had a much higher incidence among those who lacked experience in mining. The inexperienced miners were less prepared to face reverses, hardships, and strenuous toil than those with a disciplined schooling in mining, and consequently their over-optimism when they arrived in the country quickly gave way to despondency and despair when the first efforts to locate gold ended in failure. On the other hand, if they chanced to stumble upon a rich find they seldom considered the possibility of their luck coming to an end. As a result, a large proportion of the destitute and personally disorganized individuals found in Victoria during winter months was made up of those who had entered upon the occupation of mining from other walks of life; even in adversity, many of the panhandlers and casual labourers who frequented the pool-rooms and taverns of the town were people who boasted of their family connections and educational attainments. Not all the failures in Victoria, however, were drawn from the ranks of those unsuited to the conditions of mining life. The highly speculative character of mining meant that even some of the most seasoned miners failed to secure returns from their labour and capital. The miner often had to be "staked," and he faced the risk of not being able to pay off his debts or to accumulate sufficient to carry him over the winter months. Even when the season had been a suc-cessful one in the way of returns, the miners often spent everything they had during the early part of the winter and were left with nothing to live on for the rest of the year. In gambling, drinking, and other forms of dissipation, men of wealth sometimes became paupers in a single evening.

The mining population, for the most part, treated none too kindly those unprepared to pass the severe tests imposed by the rigours of work and manner of life. Few had time or inclination to show concern for the failure. The claims of friendship operated within small groups, and a helping hand was readily given out to the needy "pal"; but there was no strong sense of community obligation, and collective efforts to provide charity met with the resistance of a stubborn individualism. The lack of alternative occupations accentuated the difficulties of those who had failed in mining. Within Victoria, organizations made up particularly of philanthropic-minded ladies undertook to provide aid to some of those in need; the unfortunate miner, however, was likely to be too proud to accept assistance proffered in this way. A form of begging grew up as a regularized system of taking care of those without means. For those with Oxford degrees or with other attributes which secured the favourable attention of colonial officials, employment by the government provided a welcome shelter from the harsh penalties imposed upon the unsuccessful by the frontier mining society.

The influx, into Victoria and the mining interior, of criminal elements from California, the isolation of the colony from the outside world, and the considerable mobility of the population, gave rise to immediate and pressing problems of law and order. The danger of disastrous clashes between the American miners and the Indians was only narrowly averted by decisive action on the part of the authorities, and the gangster rule which such leaders as Ned McGowan sought to establish threatened to remove policing powers entirely out of the hands of the government.[5] Though no complete breakdown occurred in the administration of justice, the limitations of the policing power were evident in the failure to prevent criminals escaping across the border or evading arrest in the interior. Even after criminals had been arrested it proved difficult to bring them to a place of trial and to keep them under confinement. The frequent escape of prisoners on the way to trial

[5]Cf. Scholefield and Howay, *British Columbia.*

or after they had been sentenced to gaol discouraged arrest on the part of the police, and, if punitive measures could not be immediately applied, the offenders were often permitted to remain at large. Instances of miners taking the law into their own hands were not absent in the distant interior, and these efforts to secure justice probably met with little disapproval from the few police on patrol. Even more difficult in many ways was the task of maintaining order in the rapidly growing town of Victoria. Here, particularly during winter months, large numbers of professional crooks, gamblers, and confidence men mingled with the miners recently returned from the summer's toil and with the local inhabitants. Petty crimes, street and dance-hall brawls and barroom fights were frequent occurrences in the town. In addition, the highly lucrative but illegitimate trade in whiskey with the Indians constituted a serious threat to order. The proximity to Victoria of the demoralized tribes of Songish Indians increased very considerably the tasks of policing and law enforcement. The apprehension of the whiskey traders was extremely difficult because of the lack of reliable witnesses willing to testify and the corruption of police officials, while the sale of liquor to the Indians introduced new problems of order when fights broke out between the intoxicated natives or between them and the white men. The increase of the penalties imposed upon conviction was offset by the high profits from the trade and the comparative immunity from arrest. The trade continued to flourish in spite of efforts to suppress it, and its demoralizing effects upon the white community were as great as upon the native.   ·

To meet the problem of crime, agencies of law enforcement were created and improved. The administrative officials in Victoria profited by their long experience in the service of the Hudson's Bay Company, and to the tradition of law and order secured through the Company was added the prestige and power of the British Empire. A contingent of Royal Engineers was dispatched to the colonies, and it combined policing functions with such other duties as that of building roads.[6] The number of regular police was increased, gaols were established in Victoria and New Westminster, and a system of law courts was erected for the whole area. As a result of such measures, an uncontrolled frontier dependent en-

[6]*Ibid.*

tirely upon vigilante committees for the maintenance of law and order never emerged in British Columbia. The presence of a large number of Californians in the area constituted a serious threat to the formal institutions of law. With the experiences of the 1849's still fresh in their minds, the Californians placed little reliance upon the police and courts of law to preserve order, and, while this suspicion of state institutions gave to the informal organization of the mining frontier a flexibility which enabled it to withstand the social strains of the early stages of the mining rush, the failure to admit the supremacy of the formal law carried ultimate threats to the whole system of justice. As the society became more complex, direct action in the maintenance of law would have become increasingly ineffectual and would eventually have taken on the character of gangster as opposed to collective rule. But this development was successfully checked by the colonial authorities supported by British elements in the population. That is not to say that problems of crime were not of a serious character within the mining frontier of British Columbia. But the existence of such problems did not lead to a breakdown of the authority of law. The tradition of British justice secured respect for the institutions of judicial administration even when those institutions failed to maintain complete order.

In the wider sphere of morality, the major problems of the mining society were drinking, gambling, and prostitution. These problems were largely confined to the towns and particularly to Victoria. Drinking was prevalent within the mining camps as within the towns, but in the mining camps liquor constituted more an item of diet than a means of dissipation. The same was true, though to a lesser extent, of the liquor served by the hostels along the road reaching into the interior. Here drinking was heavy but it took place among miners who lingered only long enough to secure food and rest before continuing their journey. In the towns, however, drinking became associated with idleness, and during the winter the numerous taverns of Victoria were thronged with miners returned from the interior. The sale of liquor constituted one of the chief business interests of the capital, and heavy drinking in the town contributed to rowdyism, petty crime, and personal demoralization. Gambling was likewise common in the mining society and particularly in the mining towns. The playing of cards or the participation in other gambling games provided a means of passing the time and satisfied the needs of the miners for human companionship.   The very nature of the mining occupation favoured a gambling spirit.   Chance played a great part in the finding of gold, and considerable risks were taken with the uncertain prospects of high returns.   Broke on one day and rich on the next was a familiar experience of many miners, and there was a tendency as a result to assume a careless and, at the same time, sporting attitude to the making of money.   Gambling during the winter in the towns was little more than a continuation of the gambling carried on during the summer in the search for gold.   Confined to the miners themselves, the recreation of gambling, though at times involving high stakes, was generally harmless, but professional gamblers quickly took up positions at strategic points and much of the fruits of the miners' toil was drained into these parasitic channels.   Almost every pool-room, bar, and barber shop in Victoria combined gambling with its legitimate function, and, wherever any concentration of miners took place, small knots of earnest gamblers were to be found.   Prostitution emerged inevitably out of a situation in which the population was predominantly male and was engaged in an occupation which brought in ready cash.   The inaccessibility of the area to prostitutes from outside was offset by the proximity to Victoria of a large demoralized Indian population, and a regular trade grew up between the town and the native encampments.   Squaws plied the streets of Victoria, and brothels, under the management of white men, were established in the town and along the road leading to the Indian villages.   The survival of practices of slavery among the Indians promoted prostitution as girls were virtually sold to white managers.   The traffic in Indian females became closely linked with the liquor traffic, and the trade in the one promoted the trade in the other.   Prostitutes served as go-betweens in the sale of whiskey to the Indians, and the demoralization resulting from the drinking of whiskey increased reliance upon prostitution.   At the height of the mining boom, the traffic assumed considerable proportions.   As the community became older, and links with the outside world closer, professional prostitutes began to replace those secured from the Indian tribes.

Within the community, movements emerged to raise moral standards.   The small but substantial group of respectable heads of families in Victoria became increasingly alarmed as the widespread immorality of the society began to threaten their own security. Efforts to establish healthy recreational facilities and to promote reforms such as temperance were indicative of the growing moral consciousness of the community, and more stringent police regulations were secured to support these informal controls. But such measures of reform were more in the way of guarding against the moral contamination of contacts with the mining masses than in the way of raising the moral standards of the miners themselves. The temperance reformers and youth leaders played heavily upon their claims to respectability, and their usefulness was confined very largely to those who belonged to the exclusive circles of Victoria society. Moral reform among the mining population awaited leadership which relied upon appeals to their distinctive interests, and such leadership developed slowly without the aid of the family group.

Like problems of morality, those of cultural organization revealed in striking fashion the effects of the rapid growth and instability of the mining society. The population was made up of a great number of nationalities suddenly thrown together in a community where no sort of segregation was possible. Canadians, Americans, Australians, New Zealanders, English, Irish, Scots, and various national groups from Europe jostled together along the trails into the mining interior or within the mining towns. To some extent the English, and particularly those who boasted university degrees or aristocratic ancestry, kept themselves apart from the rest of the population, but such distinctions tended to be artificial and aroused no recognition on the part of the general population. The cultural heritages of the various groups were largely lost in the general mixture of nationalities. Social divisions did appear along economic or political lines, but they tended to emphasize the lack of distinctive features within the mining population. The older inhabitants in the colony had been traders in the Hudson's Bay Company, and, identified with government employments, they considered themselves something of an aristocracy apart from the great mass of miners.[7] The struggle for responsible government hardened the lines marking off this privileged group, and the prerogatives of class superiority became caught up in

[7]R. H. Coats and R. E. Gosnell, *Sir James Douglas* (Toronto, 1911).

political issues. The acrimonious relationships between newspapers in the colony reflected underlying animosities between economic and cultural groups. Other social divisions quickly developed in the colony along racial lines. The inherited antagonism of the Americans to Negroes came to the fore when large numbers of the dark race, many of them escaped slaves, found their way into Victoria and some of the smaller mining towns. Displays of racial tolerance on the part of the British peoples served only to aggravate the strained relationships by giving the Negroes an undue sense of their importance and thereby irritating even more the American populace. Riots in the theatre of Victoria and bitter controversies over the issue of attendance of Negroes at religious worship were indicative of the intensity of the racial conflict. Besides the Negroes, the Chinese constituted something of a despised race in the mining society, though their general inoffensiveness provided little occasion for acts of vituperation. The Chinese worked the diggings abandoned by the whites, and, so long as apparently inexhaustible supplies of gold were to be found further inland, their presence aroused little resentment by the miners. It was when the supplies began to be exhausted, and opportunities for employment scarce, that feelings of racial antagonism towards the Chinese became widespread among the population. Economic recession and eventual industrialization finally crystallized the extremely bitter issue of Oriental immigration.

Institutions developed to provide cultural leadership, but little support was secured from the great mass of gold-hungry miners. Newspapers played the chief role in arousing opinion about public issues and in developing a community consciousness. The reform editor who boldly challenged the vested privileges of party, class, and church won a position of influence equal to that attained by the evangelical religious leaders in the older Canadian colonies. But the newspapers of the time, and particularly those appealing to a somewhat crude and preoccupied mining population, set no high standards of propriety in manners of expression or questions of discussion, and accordingly took no conspicuous lead in the raising of the cultural level of the mining community. Fraternal societies and clubs made their appearance in Victoria and New Westminster where there was a concentration of persons of wealth and leisure, and libraries were established to serve the needs of the reading public, but few of the large body of miners profited from these cultural agencies. Similarly, education remained an insignificant cultural force, though institutions grew up under the direction largely of the church or private individuals to provide instruction to children found in the larger centres. The absence of the family accounted for much of the weakness of cultural organization, as the effects of its absence extended into every sphere of social life. Cultural values were forgotten in the mad search for gold. The character of the mining society emphasized the present at the expense of the past and future. The community inherited no rich cultural life and it built up no tradition to be passed on to new generations.

Concentration upon the present became still more conspicuous in the weakness of religious organization. If the miners gave little attention to the future, they were likely to prepare even less for life in the hereafter. The nature of their occupation discouraged attitudes of devoutness, and carelessness towards matters of religion was enhanced by the absence of female companionship. There is little evidence that the miners, cut off from any sort of religious service, felt the lack of means of worship as, for instance, did many of the pioneers of Upper Canada. Some of them, it is true, carried with them to the mining frontier habits of devoutness which persisted within the highly materialistic social *milieu*. But most of them quite cheerfully accepted a state in which the minister of the gospel did not enter to disturb the customary disregard of the Sabbath or the indulgence in playful vices.

Vigorous efforts were made by the various churches to propagate the faith on the mining frontier, and some success was achieved by the more enterprising of the missionaries. Roman Catholic, Church of England, Congregational, Presbyterian and Wesleyan denominations were represented, and the first two quickly became organized into bishoprics. Proselytization among the native populations gave to the churches a vast constituency in which to work, and, for the most part, the same missionary organization was employed in serving the mining communities. The Roman Catholic Church had become most deeply entrenched in the work with the Indians, but the Church of England secured the advantages of official recognition and enjoyed a privileged position. The bitterly controversial issues in the politics of the colony were closely identified with the issue of Church of England supremacy, and attacks upon the governing clique were indistinguishable from attacks upon the hierarchy of the church. Much of the attention directed towards religious matters in the colony, as a result, was concerned with questions of privilege rather than with those of spiritual leadership. The Church of England, as so often in colonial possessions, sacrificed the goodwill of the great mass of the people in return for the uncertain advantage of securing official favour. The bitter attacks made upon it in the press and on the platform lowered the tone of political life and served to bring religion into discredit.

These controversies, of course, were largely confined to Victoria and New Westminster. Within the mining interior the various missionaries carried on their work with less regard to matters of politics or denominational rivalry. The highly mobile character of the mining population made the task of holding religious services an extremely difficult one. Towns or mining camps suddenly grew up and then as suddenly disappeared, and efforts, particularly of the Church of England, to build places of worship were largely wasted when depopulation left church buildings without congregations. Even itinerant missionary activities proved largely ineffectual as miners were often isolated in groups of two or three and few of them showed any inclination to go long distances to a religious service on the only day in the week in which they could rest and attend to such menial tasks as cooking and mending. In a frontier mining community such as British Columbia there was no great concentration of miners settled in village communities with their wives and families, and opportunities of evangelization like those seized by Wesley among the miners in England did not occur. Religious evangelism made no conspicuous headway among the population. The highly individualistic character of placer gold mining may have been in part responsible, but even more the absence of a female population left religion without its chief support. Social reorganization on any sort of permanent foundation awaited the establishment of the family, and the slowness with which this basic institution was introduced checked reorganizing movements such as religious evangelism.

In a sense, the reorganization of the mining society never became complete. As the community became older, and the rapid influx of population into the area came to an end, the institutional structure was able to embrace a greater number of the needs of the population. The administration of government underwent improvement, systems of police and courts of law were extended and made more effective, charitable organizations and recreational facilities developed, the moral sense of the community became more alive to the dangers of intemperance and vice, the basis of a system of elementary public schools was laid, and churches gained prestige with the erection of permanent and imposing places of worship. But these gains were being made at the very time when exhaustion of gold was bringing near to collapse the whole economic structure erected upon the foundation of mining. In British Columbia there was no easy transition from a frontier to a diversified economy. In many respects, the mining society was swept aside before a new society could be erected. Other industries, such as farming and lumbering, grew up around mining and eventually came to supplant it in large part, but the labour force and capital structure fostered by the mining boom could not be supported by these secondary economic activities, and adjustment involved the painful processes of depopulation and economic recession. To some extent development after 1870 took place upon the economic wreckage left behind with the passing of the mining period. Eventually the potentialities of the area were sufficiently attractive to promote new economic activities and the erection of a society upon a more secure basis. By the latter part of the century the sweep of industrial-capitalist forces generated in Eastern Canada was wide enough to embrace the Pacific region. Economic growth took place in terms of the links forged by the Canadian Pacific Railway, and British Columbia became now a frontier of industrialism.

The opening up and exploitation of the mining resources of the Kootenay were part of the process of industrialization which included the development of the lumbering industry, the fisheries, fruit-growing and canning.[8] While industrialism in British Columbia, however, led to an increasing emphasis upon capital in mining as in other activities, a new frontier emerged in the

[8]A. R. M. Lower and H. A. Innis, *Settlement and the Forest and Mining Frontiers* (Toronto, 1936), part II, chaps. V and VI.

Yukon where individual miners once more took the lead. The Yukon inherited many of the economic techniques of the Fraser River and Cariboo mining areas, and developments during the period 1897-1905 resembled in many respects those which had taken place in British Columbia forty years earlier.[9] The undoubted richness in gold of the Klondike River bed, and the subsidiary streams of the Yukon, quickly attracted a large body of experienced prospectors and miners once the first discoveries had been made. But very soon fabulous stories of enormous wealth spread, and there followed a mad rush into the area of people from all walks of life. Reports of the hardships of the trip, and lurid descriptions of society in the mining camps, served only to fire the imagination of those seeking release from the boredom of life in settled communities. Something like 40,000 people found their way into the area during the period of the rush; the police estimated the population on January 10, 1899, as 28,018.[10]

Of these the great majority were people who lacked any previous experience in mining. The Yukon made an appeal which attracted an overwhelming number of raw recruits who were only painfully organized into a disciplined army of miners. It was this body of gold-seekers, composed of men of all ages and of a great variety of occupations and social backgrounds, who proved so difficult to absorb during the period of rapid development from 1898 to 1902. In contrast, the seasoned American and Australian miners, like the Californians in British Columbia, readily adapted themselves to life in the diggings. On the other hand, the Americans and Australians, by the very fact that they had previous experience in mining, carried with them habits of thought which clashed with inherited British cultural values, and this conflict of authority was to prove a seriously disturbing factor in the political and social life of the Yukon. Problems of law enforcement, morality, cultural organization, and religion reflected the pull of these two opposing systems of thought, and, if the stubborn individualism of the seasoned miners checked the establishment of order through constituted authority, the intolerance of the Canadian official class prevented the easy working of the informal controls of the miners' code.

[9]Cf. Morrell, *The Gold Rushes.*

[10]Lower and Innis, *Settlement and the Forest and Mining Frontiers*, pp. 191, 207.

These problems were complicated by the influx along with Americans and Australians of numerous other ethnic and racial groups. The diversified cultural heritages of the Yukon population made difficult the establishment of any set of social values either through constituted authority or voluntary association.   The large number of professional criminals, gamblers, whiskey-runners, and prostitutes who arrived in Dawson during the period of the rush added to the problem of erecting a stable social organization.   In many respects, the activities of these parasitical groups were subject to the control of the code of the seasoned miners and suitable sanctions had evolved, but such activities were not recognized, except within the criminal code, in the system of Canadian cultural values which had been imported from without.   The formal machinery of the state proved highly effective in dealing with the depradations of the criminal, but efforts to treat the activities of gamblers and prostitutes as crimes resulted in releasing such people from the more effective controls of the informal community.   Though unrecognized by authority, the gamblers and prostitutes in Dawson City constituted an unavoidable element within the population. The predominance of males in the mining population enhanced the disorganizing influence of parasitical social groups.   Some women came in with, or later joined, their husbands, but the female population for the most part consisted of public entertainers, dance-hall girls, and prostitutes.   The free flow of gold in the community encouraged such occupations, while other occupations were lacking to attract more respectable women.   Dawson with its mining hinterland was a male society, and it was the needs of the men which determined very largely the kind of services and social institutions found in the community.

The nature of placer gold mining in the Yukon added to the difficulty of erecting stable social institutions.   Even more speculative in character than the gold mining in the Fraser and Cariboo had been, the population of the Yukon was kept continually on the alert, waiting to hear of new finds richer than anything which had already been discovered.   Dawson City was something of a nerve centre of the whole area, and here newcomers and returned miners congregated, ready to dash off at the first whisperings of a strike.   Rumour came to play a dominant part in setting in motion the springs of collective action, and sudden rushes punctuated the constant milling around of the aimless mass of gold-seekers. The tempo of the society of Dawson as a result was kept at feverish pitch. While one part of the population was anxiously waiting opportunities to stake profitable claims, another part was recklessly spending the returns from previous operations. The seasonal nature of the mining occupation intensified the unsettled character of society in Dawson. While the long days of the Arctic summer led to a period of strenuous activity in the diggings, the long nights of the Arctic winter led to a period of relative inactivity in Dawson. There was little time during the summer for such menial tasks as the cooking of proper foods; there was a great deal of time in winter for loafing and dissipation. Dance halls and saloons thrived in a climate where warmth and cheerful illumination were not easy to find.

The geography of the Yukon basin tended to concentrate the population in and about Dawson.[11] The richest of the creeks were not far distant, and all the creeks upon which mining took place were tributaries of the Yukon or Klondike rivers which joined at the site of the town. Other mining centres—Circle City, Rampart, Nome, Sunrise, and Fairbanks—grew up in the Alaska territory, but the Yukon developed largely in isolation from these areas. There was not, as in British Columbia, a string of mining towns or camps reaching far into the interior, each serving the more immediate needs of the population though depending upon larger centres to supply a number of secondary services. Centralization within the one town of Dawson intensified very considerably the problem of community organization. Here the task was faced of converting a huge mining camp into a stable community. A complete lack of sewerage facilities, side-walks, and zoning restrictions was an inevitable accompaniment of conditions where the first residents simply pitched tents or built rude shacks preparatory to engaging in prospecting and mining operations. The cabins of the mining creeks reached back into the town, and there was virtually no distinction between the mining population and town residents.

Other factors enhanced the dominance of the mining population within the town of Dawson itself. Unlike Victoria, which had grown up as a fur-trading post and which continued to support a local aristocracy of officials sharply divorced from mining inter-

[11]*Ibid.*, part II, chap. I.

ests, Dawson lacked any tradition of past greatness and contained no population identified with rival interests to mining. The erection of the miners' tents or shacks marked the beginnings of the town's history, and the few government officials who later came in never became socially differentiated from the great mass of inhabitants. Business and social services emphasized the absence of needs other than those of a mining population. Dawson was completely exposed to the influences of the frontier which surrounded it on all sides. Within the town as a result the disorganizing features of the mining society were sharply focussed.

The disorganization of the society was more complete because of the short time within which the gold rush took place. Though miners had come into the Yukon in the early eighteen-nineties and there were many new arrivals after 1900, the mass movement of gold-seekers occupied little more than eighteen months. The influx of population did not occur in terms of a number of waves between which there were periods of adjustment but rather took place in terms of one mighty wave which was only checked through the lack of winter transportation facilities. The whole community was populated by newcomers at the same time, and the result was an almost complete absence of experience within the community upon which to erect stable social institutions. Few societies of comparable population were ever so completely unorganized as that of the Yukon in the early summer of 1898. Orderly social relationships and social controls were almost entirely lacking where all the members of the community had been suddenly brought together for the first time.

Yet the very factors which accentuated the early disorganization of the mining society promoted the establishment of a new social order. The growth of a community consciousness and the erection of a network of social institutions and controls proceeded rapidly in an environment where all the people had equally few ties with the past, experienced much the same kind of problems of livelihood, and were engaged in the same occupation of gold mining. The completeness of the break with the society of the outside world and the concentration upon a single economic interest meant that new adjustments came about readily and tended to proceed at the same rate among all the members of the group.

Cultural conflict as a result did not seriously delay the creation of a new social order. It is true that the old miners disliked the new-comers and that bitter controversies raged about issues of government and the regulation of mining, but these conflicts were not a reflection of deeply imbedded interests which set up barriers between social groups and made effective collective action difficult. The absence of privilege and vested interest as means of establishing authority in the Yukon allowed freer expression to the natural impulses of the population, and, if those impulses tended immediately to an unrestrained licence, they favoured eventually the establishment of orderly conditions in the community.

Outside aids, of course, were of considerable importance in establishing a stable organization. The chief of such agencies was the Royal North West Mounted Police which quickly took up strategic positions in the Yukon territory and not only succeeded in maintaining a state of law and order but, by means of checking the supplies people had before setting out on the inland journey to Dawson and by constant patrols along the routes of travel and the mining creeks, served as something of a social welfare institution. Behind the Police rested the authority of the Canadian government, and, although many of the local officials were accused of corruption and the officials in Ottawa were often ignorant of conditions in the mining frontier, the introduction of British traditions and practices of justice arrested the development of popular methods of law enforcement such as those secured within miners' meetings and associations. Fraternal societies and lodges, and even to some extent trade-union organizations, reached out from older communities to assist in establishing institutions within the distant mining frontier. Finally, religious denominations vigorously promoted the spiritual and social interests of the mining population. Among the older denominations, the Roman Catholic, Church of England, Presbyterian, and Methodist churches were most active. Of evangelical religious organizations, the work of the Salvation Army was conspicuously successful, and here, as in the rapidly growing urban communities, the methods employed by the Army were closely adapted to the needs of the population.

Institutional controls derived from outside, however, were

effective only as a result of the development of an underlying social consciousness favourable to the establishment of order within the community. This was true even of the work performed by the Mounted Police. That is to say that processes of social reorganization were generated from within rather than from outside the society. Lacking external aids the establishment of social order would have come about more slowly as the experience of mining communities in Alaska amply demonstrates, but these aids in themselves provided no solid basis upon which to erect a stable society. Collective efforts were canalized and provided a more permanent goal of achievement; they sprang, however, from the urge of the people themselves to better their conditions.

New accommodations and the establishment of order did not proceed unhampered by forces of disturbance within the society. Institutional rivalries particularly between religious denominations, increasing racial bitterness with the growth of feelings of self-consciousness on the part of certain groups, and problems of capital and labour as the operation of mining passed into the hands of large corporations and the miners found themselves becoming day labourers, gave rise to new points of conflict within the community. For the most part, however, these disturbances were associated with the developments of a society which had already passed beyond the frontier stage. Like British Columbia, the Yukon very soon faced problems of economic recession and depopulation when exhaustion of resources began to take place. The development of secondary economic activities, and the shift to machine methods of production and large capital organization in mining, were indicative of the passing of the earlier frontier of individual enterprise.[12] The Yukon became caught up, if somewhat remotely, in the wider structure of industrial-capitalism in Canada. But these new adjustments came about very largely after the boom society of 1898-1902 had disappeared. Within this four-year period the development of the Yukon passed through the full cycle of social disorganization and reorganization; for study of these social processes, few social laboratories could be more revealing.

[12]*Ibid.*, part II, chap. III.

1. SOCIAL WELFARE

A. British Columbia

Floating Character of Mining Population

The British Colonist, Victoria, July 17, 1860.

Caribou Lake, June 28, 1860.

Editor British Colonist:—

To any one at all conversant with life in the diggings, it would appear that the miner is never to profit by past experience, in order to guide him in future operations. He is just as ready to pack up his blankets, together with a pick, pan and shovel, and a week's provisions, and start out on a tour of prospecting, or to go in pursuit of some fabulous yarn that has been privately circulated with regard to the golden fleece existing in some secret gulch, as he was in the days of Gold Lake, Kern River, Pike's Peak, and lastly that of the Argenauts and Queen Charlotte's Island.

Although he may have permanent diggings, and be realizing good wages, yet his mind is always on the *qui vive* to learn if any one is out prospecting, and if rich discoveries are not being made at some distant point, difficult of access and no trail leading thereto. . . .

Such is the state of affairs at the point I am now writing from at the present time. Some are rushing to Salmon River and the streams emptying into Fraser River above Fort George; others to Swift Creek and streams below Fort George. A great excitement has been created lately with regard to the richness of this locality, termed the Caribou Country, which is situated above the lakes forming the north branch of the Quesnelle, of which there is little knowledge yet; and thus the miners go floating about, so that the season, from present appearances, is likely to be trifled away like many others, resulting in injury to the mines at present, and no benefit to the country hereafter. . . .

Yours, etc.

JUVERNA

Dissipation of Earnings

W. W. F. Milton and W. B. Cheadle, *The North-west Passage by Land* (London, 1865), pp. 362-3.

The wealth thus rapidly obtained is generally dissipated almost as quickly. The lucky miner hastens down to Victoria or San Francisco, and sows his gold broadcast. No luxury is too costly for him, no extravagance too great for the magnitude of his ideas. His love of display leads him into a thousand follies, and he proclaims his disregard for money by numberless eccentricities.

Mental Strain of Miner's Life

Matthew MacFie, *Vancouver Island and British Columbia* (London, 1865), p. 410.

The intense pitch to which the feelings of people are strung in a gold-producing country is a frequent cause of insanity. Whether that malady exists in a greater degree in this community than in one of a more settled description, I am not sufficiently versed in the statistics of the subject to aver. But certainly a much larger proportion of cases have been personally known to me here than in the same period I ever saw in the much denser populations of England. I can reckon up eight persons—all of whom I have been on speaking terms with, and most of whom I knew intimately, who, in four years and a half, have become lunatics, and as such are either living or dead.

Society for Relief of Poor

The British Colonist, Victoria, August 22, 1859.

Editor British Colonist:—

I have to inform you that a number of the ladies of Victoria, have formed themselves into a Society for relieving the sick and clothing the naked. I believe that Mrs. Cridge is President; Mrs. Nagle, Treasurer; and Mrs. Col. Moody, Mrs. Gladwin, Mrs. McCrea, Mrs. Spaulding, Mrs. Guild, and several other ladies, whose names I do not remember, belong to the Society.

Any person making application for relief will be assisted as far as the limited means of the committee will permit.

PHILANTHROPIST

No Provision for Insane

The British Colonist, Victoria, February 16, 1860.

Poor "Scotty."—This miserable lunatic perambulates our streets day and night, reciting his insane gibberish to all who will lend an ear. What a pity we have not an Asylum where all such might be properly cared for.

The Gaol as a House of Refuge

Matthew MacFie, *Vancouver Island and British Columbia* (London, 1865), p. 79.

The Police Barracks [of Victoria] are situated inconveniently near the main street. They contain the Court rooms and offices of the Police Commissioner, chamber of the Government Assessor and Sheriff, rooms belonging to the police force, the cells of prisoners, and a prison yard. It is not to the honour of the city, however, that lunatics should be placed under the same roof with felons. It is to be hoped that this reproach will soon be wiped out, and a suitable asylum provided for these unhappy creatures. The ladies of the town are exceedingly attentive to the wants of the sick and destitute of their own sex.

B. The Yukon

Early Miners and Mining Life in Yukon

Sessional Papers, Canada, 1896, no. 15A: Report of Assistant Surgeon to Officer Commanding Yukon Detachment North-West Mounted Police, Fort Constantine, January 20, 1896.

Miners are a very mixed class of people. They represent many nationalities and come from all climates. Their lives are certainly not enviable. The regulation "miners' cabin" is 12 feet by 14 feet with walls 6 feet and gables 8 feet in height. The roof is heavily earthed and the cabin is generally very warm. Two, and sometimes three or four men will occupy a house of this size. The ventilation is usually bad. Those miners who do not work their claims during the winter confine themselves in these small huts most of the time.

Very often they become indolent and careless, only eating those things which are most easily cooked or prepared. During the busy time in summer when they are "shovelling in," they work hard and for long hours, sparing little time for eating and much less for cooking.

This manner of living is quite common amongst beginners and soon leads to debility and sometimes to scurvy. Old miners have learned from experience to value health more than gold and they therefore spare no expense in procuring the best and most varied outfit of food that can be obtained.

In a cold climate such as this, where it is impossible to get fresh vegetables and fruits, it is most important that the best substitutes for these should be provided. Nature helps to supply these wants by growing cranberries and other wild fruits in abundance, but men in summer are usually too busy to avail themselves of these.

The diseases met with in this country are dyspepsia, anaemia, scurvy caused by improperly cooked food, sameness of diet, overwork, want of fresh vegetables, overheated and badly ventilated houses; rheumatism, pneumonia, bronchitis, enteritis, cystitis and other acute diseases, from exposure to wet and cold; debility and chronic diseases, due to excesses. Venereal diseases are not uncommon. One case of typhoid fever occurred in "Forty mile" last fall probably due to drinking water polluted with decayed vegetable matter.

The Gold-Rush Population

Jeremiah Lynch, *Three Years in the Klondike* (London, 1904), pp. 1-4.

On June 11, 1898, the new steamship *St. Paul* left San Francisco for St. Michaels with 275 passengers, bound for the Klondike *via* the mouth of the Yukon River. . . .

In a week we came to Dutch Harbour, in the Aleutian Islands, where the *St. Paul* anchored three days to coal. Other steamers and sailing-vessels were there and at Unalaska, three miles distant, all laden with passengers for the Klondike. Three thousand people, including scores of women, were of the number; we made a strangely assorted assemblage with our motley costumes. . . .

I looked over our 3,000 very carefully, for it was my interest to know the manner of people who were to be both my rivals and companions in exploiting the new land of gold. None seemed very rich, few very poor. There were neither capitalists nor paupers. None were very old, none were very young. Perhaps two-thirds were from the United States, largely from the Pacific coast. Of the remaining third a goodly proportion were Swedes. Those who are born in cold climes preferably seek the same in other lands; and the reverse seems to be true. For there were very few Italians, Mexicans, or Spaniards, and a scant number of French; and the same rule I found to hold afterwards during my sojourn in the Klondike, with the exception, of course, of the French-Canadians, the *Canayens*, who are the *voyageurs* of all this Northern world of ice and snow.

Of the 3,000, very few were in ill health, and if they were poor in everything else, they were rich in good constitutions and robust frames. Even the women seemed to expect all kinds of physical difficulties up north, and were stoically prepared. But withal I gleaned in conversations that not many of the men had ever lived or laboured in a mining country, and while possessing fortitude were yet very ignorant, both of what had to be done and if they could do it. . . .

The men adventurers [aboard] were an epitome of the multitude assembled in the harbour of St. Michaels. There were some who had lost fortunes and hoped to regain them; some who never possessed means, and therefore were full of ardour; and a few whom the tide of life had cast as flotsam upon this mighty river, and for whom the future had neither hopes nor fears. A large proportion were miners who had come from South Africa, Montana, British Columbia, and other mining localities—young, healthy, stalwart.

Stampedes within the Mining Community

Stratford Tollemache, *Reminiscences of the Yukon* (Toronto, 1912), pp. 116-19.

Among the crowds who arrived at Dawson in 1898, only a very small proportion were able to secure claims which appeared from their positions likely to become valuable, as the ground in the vicinity of Bonanza, Eldorado, and neighbouring creeks had already been taken up. A certain number of the inhabitants had migrated to Dawson for the purpose of establishing stores or engaging in trade; but these constituted only a small minority. By far the greater proportion of the population had become fascinated with the glamour of digging up gold, and had started for the Klondike purely for that purpose, so that having now reached their destination, after considerable trials and expense, their main ambition was to acquire a claim and become the owners of gold-mines. People were loitering about, constantly on the *qui vive*, in the hope of obtaining information of some fresh locality where gold had been discovered; and whenever a report was circulated of a new gold strike in some remote spot, a fever of excitement would ensue, and a rush or stampede would promptly occur to the vicinity, which might be situated a hundred miles or more from Dawson.

Stampeding is not a particularly enjoyable occupation; and as the number of people engaged was usually far in excess of the claims available, the stampede would devolve into a race, each striving to be amongst the foremost to secure a claim in the most favourable locality. Supplies for double the distance would generally have to be transported, as provisions would probably be unobtainable before returning to Dawson. A few people might be able to employ pack-horses during the summer, but the majority would have to convey the supplies on their backs. Only the barest necessities could by this means be taken, as the loads must necessarily be reduced to the smallest possible dimensions; and engaging in a race under such conditions, packing supplies day after day, up hill and down dale, through thick brush or marshy ground, clambering over fallen timber, and tormented all the time by swarms of mosquitoes, involved a considerable amount of endurance and determination. During the winter the circumstances, of course, would be different. Blankets or a fur robe would be necessary, and supplies would probably be conveyed by means of dog teams; but freshly broken winter trails are not often easy to travel over, while the temperature may be 50° or more below zero.

During the first two or three years of Dawson's existence any report, however vague or unreliable, would be sufficient to start a crowd of people rushing off to the locality, so that stampedes were constantly occurring, of which only a very small proportion proved ultimately of any value. By far the majority of stampedes resulted in a row of claims being staked which would turn out to be utterly useless, and were, consequently, soon abandoned. In the earlier years, when supplies were so expensive, only very rich ground would prove remunerative, and therefore numbers of claims were staked and abandoned, which in later years, when mining operations became cheaper, were re-staked by other people and worked at a profit.

Many of these stampedes were arrant swindles, some of them being termed road-house stampedes and steamboat stampedes. In the former instance, a road-house keeper situated in some remote locality, perhaps several days' journey from Dawson, on finding trade rather dull, would bribe somebody in Dawson to circulate a report that a rich gold strike had been recently discovered in the vicinity of his road-house. This report would be invented and circulated during the cold winter months, while the road-house keeper would be careful to procure an extra stock of supplies, so as to be ready for the excited crowd which he knew would shortly arrive. . . .

Steamboat stampedes, which occur during the summer, are started on much the same principle. The mines are worked principally during the summer months, so that a large number of people leave Dawson late in the autumn, and spend the winter at their homes on the outside, returning to Dawson in the spring when the Yukon is clear of ice. The middle of the summer, therefore, constitutes the slack period for passenger traffic on the Yukon, and by way of compensating for the deficiency, a report would be spread about Dawson that a man had just arrived from some place far away up the Yukon, or probably one of its tributaries, and had reported a rich discovery of gold.   A special steamer would undertake to convey passengers to the locality, and although the report would probably be a pure invention, a large crowd of excited people would promptly engage passages, to the great advantage of the owner of the steamer.

Paupers in Yukon

Sessional Papers, Canada, 1899, no. 15:   Report of Superintendent S. B. Steele, Commanding North-West Mounted Police, Yukon Territory, January 10, 1899.

I recommend that legislation be passed to prevent indigent and feeble people from coming into the country.

The steamboat companies should be held responsible, and if they bring them in should be forced to take them back from whence they came.   If the steamboat owners are warned in time against carrying that class of people there would be no difficulty in enforcing such a law.

Should no steps be taken to keep useless people out of the country, I am convinced that the government will be forced to spend a great deal of money to keep them from starvation and transport them hence.

Relief of Destitute in Yukon

Sessional Papers, Canada, 1900, no. 15:   Report of Superintendent A. B. Perry, Commanding North-West Mounted Police, Yukon Territory, November 30, 1899.

There is nothing which has so established the high reputation which the force has among the inhabitants of this territory as the assistance invariably given to any person in distress, from accident, sickness or want of food.   No case is ever neglected.   Long journeys are undertaken in midwinter under trying conditions of travel, and relief carried, or the suffering person trans-ported to a place of safety.

The government of the Territory has dealt with all cases of distress with the greatest generosity and during the past year has spent upwards of $100,000 in the care of the sick and the relief of the poor.

Early Benevolent Institutions

Tappan Adney, *The Klondike Stampede* (New York and London, 1900),
pp. 356, 429.

The Yukon Order of Pioneers was organized by "Jack" McQuesten, at Circle City, for the purpose of furthering the interests of its members, caring for them when sick, burying them when dead.   No one is eligible who came into the Yukon since 1895.   It numbers seventy or eighty active members, and one honorary member, Captain Constantine.   The badge of the society is of gold—a carpenter's rule partly folded, the two arms being crossed with a spray of laurel, with the letters Y.O.O.P. inside. . . .

The benevolent societies, such as the Masons, Odd-Fellows, etc., were organized by Colonel O. V. Davis, of Tacoma, Washington, and the government presented them with a plot of ground upon which they built a 40x40-foot "Society Hall" of logs.   Many destitute men were cared for by these societies.

Sanitary Condition of Dawson

(i)
Tappan Adney, *The Klondike Stampede* (New York and London, 1900), pp. 429-30.

As had been predicted, the town was in a terrible sanitary condition. There was no drainage, and, except by giving warning about cesspools, the government did nothing but provide *two* public conveniences, entirely inadequate for a town of nearly 20,000.   Fortunately good drinking-water was had at several springs.   Still, as could not be otherwise in a city built upon a bog, by midsummer the hospital was filled to overflowing, men were lying on the floor, and there were many in cabins, suffering from typhoid fever, typhoid-malaria, and dysentry.   The number of deaths was three to four a day, in one day reaching a total of nine.   At this juncture, when the amount of sickness had become a cause for general alarm, the Canadian doctors, who were greatly outnumbered by American, began prosecutions against the latter, and several of the highest standing, but who had come unprovided with licences to practice in Canada, were haled before the magistrate, jailed, and fined.   While Americans should have expected this, it was admitted by most persons that a more unfortunate moment for the prosecutions could hardly have been chosen.   The American physicians continued practising, however, without signs or asking fees.   In all there were about seventy physicians in the camp, only a few of whom, however, found lucrative practice. In August another hospital, "The Good Samaritan," was established, with a local board of directors, the government contributing $5000 towards its maintenance.

(ii)

Robert C. Kirk, *Twelve Months in the Klondike* (London, 1899), pp. 115-16.

Dawson has never found time to build a sewerage system, and the filth that accumulates during the long winters and then lies exposed to the decomposing effect of the warm sun in summer is, in great measure, the cause of the prevalence of malarial-typhoid fevers that are epidemic in June, July, August, and even September and October.   The gases that arise from the swamps and marshes which occupy a large part of the town-site are equally unhealthy, and an attempt has lately been made to drain the surface-water from these by means of trenches; but the experience of almost every mining camp has been that it is extremely difficult, almost impossible, to interest a floating population in public improvements, and the one desire of the inhabitants is always to work energetically for themselves while they are in camp and to retain every crown or dollar they can save to take to their homes. The ones who have greatly interested themselves in proper sewerage and the establishment of a fire-department have, of course, been the representatives of the larger companies and property-holders, whose investments have been such that improvements of this character are almost imperative to secure the safety of the property and to avoid a shrinkage in values.

The epidemic of fever during the summer of 1898 carried away several hundred people, and the death-list of the summer of 1899 will be proportionately large to the increase in population.

Physicians and Hospitals in Yukon

Tappan Adney, *The Klondike Stampede* (New York and London, 1900), pp. 350-1.

Physicians did uncommonly well. The charge for a visit in town was never less than $5, while a visit to the mines was sometimes as high as $500, the charge being regulated according to the "victim's" ability to pay; and the price of drugs was proportionately high. One young doctor was said to have earned $1200 to $1500 a month, while another who invested his earnings judiciously in mines was reputed to have made $200,000. The hospital, although a sectarian institution, was maintained by local subscriptions. Three ounces of gold-dust ($51) entitled a person to a ticket for treatment during one year, and a certain number of weeks in the hospital, with board and nursing free. To non-subscribers the charge was $5 a day, and $5 extra for the doctor's usually daily visit. From its establishment in the fall of 1897 up to April 1st, 1898, the number of deaths was twenty-four, of which seven or eight were from typhoid fever. The hospital was a godsend, and many a man came out from under the tender care of the venerable Father Judge and the little band of Sisters with a broader view of religious work and a better personal understanding of what it meant to devote one's life to doing good for his fellow-men.

Public Support of Hospitals

Sessional Papers, Canada, 1899, no. 13: Report of Major J. M. Walsh on the Yukon District.

Some time after my arrival at Dawson the Rev. Father Judge, priest of this district, informed me that the St. Mary's Hospital under his charge had reached a state of financial embarrassment, and that if no assistance was forthcoming he should have to discontinue receiving patients. He also informed me that some provision would have to be made for the patients already in the hospital. This institution has been one of great mercy to the district, and up to last year had received sufficient support from the mining population to meet all its expenses, but the scarcity of food last fall and the large number of persons who were left in the district without money or labour to provide it, threw upon the hospital a great number of sick who were unable to pay for attendance. . . . Owing to the condition of affairs here, institutions of this kind are far more required than in any other district I have ever known, and it was quite apparent that we would have to come to the assistance of St. Mary's Hospital; otherwise, should it be forced to close, the care of the sick would surely fall upon the Government. This would entail an expenditure of not less than forty or fifty thousand dollars. Under these circumstances, I sanctioned a grant of $5000 to aid in the liquidation of the debt of St. Mary's Hospital, which grant was cordially approved by the clergymen of other churches resident in the city. Messrs. Wade and Davis collected a similar amount by private subscription, and a committee was formed for the purpose of raising the balance necessary to clear the hospital of debt.

A general hospital was also under construction by the Presbyterians, and I authorized a grant to them of $2,500 to enable them to open the hospital as soon as possible. These institutions are absolutely essential to Dawson. A large population of men living alone in cabins or tents, with nobody to assist them in case of illness, have but one place to go to and that is the hospital, and I therefore recommend that the matter of future assistance for such institutions be given consideration.

Problem of Mentally Ill

Sessional Papers, Canada, 1901, no. 28a: Annual Report of Acting Assistant Surgeon H. H. Hurdman, North-West Mounted Police, Dawson, Yukon Territory, 1900.

During the year, eight lunatics have come under the Assistant Surgeon's care, and all of them, after an average detention here of 81.61 days, have been transferred to New Westminster asylum. The longest time any of these were in custody here was 136 days, and the shortest was 11 days. Besides these, seven other persons have been arrested, charged with insanity, and discharged after an average detention of 9.71 days. The necessity for an asylum for the proper care of these poor unfortunates is great. At present they have to be confined in the guard room, where the surroundings tend to make them worse instead of better; and where they prevent the prisoners, who have to work all day, from sleeping. I believe the necessity for an asylum was pointed out to the Yukon Council nearly two years ago, but as yet nothing seems to have been done.

2. CRIME AND THE MORAL ORDER

A. British Columbia

Character of Mining Population

J. Despart Pemberton, *Facts and Figures Relating to Vancouver Island and British Columbia* (London, 1860), p. 130.

As a class, the miners of British Columbia have a much worse character than they deserve. Generally speaking, they are not only civil and sober in their habits, but well-read and intelligent. On their first arrival in the country, however, they were accompanied with the usual proportion of gamblers and "Rowdies"; but for these, the place was soon made anything but a desirable residence by the firm and uncompromising attitude of the British authorities.

Few Females in Rush to Gold-Mines

R. Byron Johnson, *Very Far West Indeed: A Few Rough Experiences on the North-West Pacific Coast* (London, 1872), pp. 59-60.

All the passengers [on the river steamer] were bound for the mines in different capacities; three parts of them were *bona fide* miners in the roughest of attire; the remaining fourth were storekeepers and gamblers, and two members of the other sex; one of the latter a washerwoman, who afterwards made a large fortune I heard, and the other a courageous lady about to join her husband.   Ladies bound for the upper country were rare birds, indeed, at that time, and as such were regarded with much wondering curiosity, and some amount of chivalric respect by the miners, who, with the greatest self-denial, actually refrained from swearing within ear-shot, or squirting tobacco-juice within a yard of them.   Even the homely laundress was raised by the scarcity of her sex into a goddess for the nonce.

Women in Mining Interior

The Daily British Colonist, Victoria, May 2, 1861:   Letter from Correspondent, Cayoosh, April 24, 1861.

White females are rarely met with on this portion of the river.   The philanthropists of Victoria should bestir themselves and by bringing their mighty influence to bear in the proper quarter, would probably induce Miss Burdett Coutts to export a cargo or two of young women for these benighted colonies.

Female Emigration to British Columbia

Public Archives of Canada, *B.C. Archives, Correspondence of Sir James Douglas, 1839-1864.*

Christ Church Parsonage,
Victoria, V.I., 11th July, 1862.
Madam,
At the request of His Excellency the Governor I have the honor to reply to your letter of the —— commending to his Excellency's protection a party of twenty females emigrating under your auspices to this colony in the Tynemouth.

The Governor begs to assure you that he will do all in his power to comply with your request in promoting the safety and welfare of these emigrants, believing in so doing he will be aiding the cause of humanity, as well as serving the interests of these Colonies.

A Committee will be formed at Victoria for the reception of these females on their arrival, for the disposition of them afterwards, and also for communicating further with you on the subject of any further Emigration of a similar character should you still continue to have an eye to this Country in your benevolent exertions.

The classes of females, permit me to say, most needed in this Country are those who are willing to take positions as domestic servants. A considerable number of this class would I believe obtain situations without difficulty at from £20 to £30 a year. Several would doubtless soon find husbands although the immediate wants of the Country in this respect are perhaps somewhat over-estimated. A considerable proportion of the population consisting of Miners, traders and others who are either not yet in a position to marry, or whose views it does not suit to settle in the country, a large number of a superior class of females, I mean in point of position and education would find it difficult to obtain suitable situations or connexions. With the working class of females there is I think no fear in view of the large immigration at present setting in of soon over-stocking our Colony. . . .

I have, etc.,
(signed) EDWD. CRIDGE,
Rector of Christ Church.

Lack of Leisure in Mining Interior

R. Byron Johnson, *Very Far West Indeed: A Few Rough Experiences on the North-West Pacific Coast* (London, 1872), p. 115.

The town [William's Creek] comprised the ordinary series of rough wooden shanties, stores, restaurants, grog shops, and gambling saloons; and, on a little eminence, the official residence, tenanted by the Gold Commissioner and his assistants and one policeman, with the British flag permanently displayed in front of it, looked over the whole.

In and out of this nest the human ants poured all day and night, for in wet-sinking the labour must be kept up without ceasing all through the twenty-four hours, Sundays included. It was a curious sight to look down the Creek at night, and see each shaft with its little fire, and its lantern, and the dim ghostly figures gliding about from darkness into light, like the demons at a Drury Lane pantomime, while an occasional hut was illuminated by some weary labourer returning from his nightly toil.

The word here seemed to be *work*, and nothing else; only round the barrooms and the gambling-tables were a few loafers and gamblers to be seen. Idling was too expensive a luxury in a place where wages were from two to three pounds per day, and flour sold at six shillings a pound.

Demoralization of Youth in Mining Society

Matthew MacFie, *Vancouver Island and British Columbia* (London, 1865), pp. 406-8.

Single young men, many of them well connected and possessing a good education, form a large portion of the population. The habits of some

22

indicate them to have been "black sheep", in the domestic fold at home; others of good reputation are sometimes to be found, who fail in success for want of the tact, energy, and endurance requisite to conquer the difficulties peculiar to colonial life.   Others are distinguished by an indomitable spirit that smilingly breasts the passing wave of misfortune; they never lose an affable and modest bearing, or a regard for integrity, under the most trying disappointments, but pursue their aims in the unfaltering assurance that victory, though delayed, will eventually reward their struggles.   The beams of a prosperous future are reflected in the glance of such men, and the community instinctively makes way for their promotion.

If, however, there be any vulnerable point in the character of the young and inexperienced colonist, it is certain to be hit by the arrow of temptation. It is impossible for the imaginative youth, surrounded with the blandishments of fashionable English life, the associations of the Church, the proprieties of the debating club, or the restraints of fond relationship, to overestimate the fiery trial that awaits him, when thrown like a fledged bird from the maternal nest into the society of strangers, for the most part selfish, and interested in the "greenhorn" only as far as they can profit by the attentions they pay him.   Should his concern for speedily entering on a money-making career outweigh that better judgment which compasses its end by cautious measures and slow degrees, and looks out first for a right start, nothing is more probable than that he will be pounced upon by those disguised falcons that are ever on the watch for such a quarry. . . . Over the mortal remains of how many promising characters, wrecked on the shoals and reefs against which friendly warning has been given above, have I been called to perform sad offices!   Many still meet one's observation in the streets of Victoria, who, unless a merciful Providence interpose, are doomed to the drunkard's grave.   Frequently have I been delighted to see the beneficial change effected by marriage, in arresting the progress of dissipation. It is only to be regretted that the paucity of respectable females in Vancouver Island and British Columbia limits so much the opportunities of single men who desire to cultivate domestic virtues, and lead sober lives.   From a volunteer rifle corps which has been organised under encouraging auspices, I anticipate much good, in affording the class referred to amusing occupation for part of their leisure.   Happy will it be, too, for the comfort and morals of young men, when the "shanty" life, involving the inconvenience of cooking with their own hands, and the restaurant, which fosters home feelings to even a smaller extent, are more generally displaced by lodging-houses, kept by private families, at moderate rates, and in the style familiar to clerks and warehousemen in England.

Prevalence of Gambling

R. Byron Johnson, *Very Far West Indeed: A Few Rough Experiences on the North-West Pacific Coast* (London, 1872), pp. 60-1.

When dinner was over [on the river steamer]—it didn't take long at the rate everyone gobbled—and the cloth was removed from the long table, it was soon occupied by the gamblers, professional and otherwise. Gold and notes began to appear freely, and to change hands rapidly. Great piles of twenty-dollar pieces lay about the tables in tempting confusion, and the clattering and chinking were incessant. As the players became warmed to their work the excitement increased, and shouts and oaths rang through the place. Everyone who, from want of inclination or money, did not play, looked on, almost equally interested with the players in the different games, of which "poker" seemed to be the favourite. This game is founded on our English one of "brag," and affords great facilities for rash speculation, as well as for the light arts of the *chevaliers d'industrie.*

At one end of the board, where two of these gentlemen appeared to have a couple of foolish fellows in their clutches, a dispute soon arose, owing to one of the pigeons seeing his neighbour pick a card from his lap. A revolver and a knife were drawn in an instant, but luckily the adversaries were separated before any harm happened. A duel on shore was threatened; but as I didn't hear afterwards of any catastrophe, I suppose our friends thought better of it when their blood was cooled.

Rowdy Dance Halls

The British Colonist, Victoria, July 5, 1860.

The Dance House.—This institution was re-opened on Tuesday night. A few minutes after the doors were opened, a row commenced; and the regular and special police were called in and cleared the establishment.

Drinking in Mining Communities

(i)

W. W. F. Milton and W. B. Cheadle, *The North-west Passage by Land* (London, 1865), p. 349.

The town of Lillooet is situated on a grand plateau, one of the terraces of the Fraser, which are here more than ordinarily extensive and well-marked. The place was full of miners, on their way down to Victoria for the winter. Drinking and card-playing went on until long after midnight, amid a constant string of oaths and miners' slang.

(ii)

The Daily British Colonist, Victoria, November 7, 1860 : Letter from Correspondent, Fort Hope, Nov. 1, 1860.

There are now about seventy-five men on the river [Similkameen], and strange to say three taverns—a train which we met on our way home being almost entirely laden with spirits destined to enrich a "new house." Is the question of licensing left entirely to the local magistrate—and if so, ought it to continue? The men on the river are mostly of a superior class, and comfortable log houses are being erected for the winter—as mining will be carried on during the next five months.

Great Number of Acts of Violence

D. G. F. Macdonald, *British Columbia and Vancouver Island* (London, 1862), pp. 328-30.

The public Journal of Victoria is literally teeming with records of the lawlessness of the people of these unhappy colonies. In a single copy of the paper referred to, the following unparalleled black list is given—black, indeed, considering the scanty population: one murder, two attempts at murder, three cases of burglary, four of theft, one of stabbing, one of indecency, and numerous other minor offences. . . .

As in all new colonies, there is in British Columbia a set of gambling low fellows, who are utterly unsusceptible of any of those impressions which virtue, honour, sensibility, and friendship should excite. Gambling is frightfully common among the miners and others. . . . Duelling, too, although not common, nevertheless exists; and the man who never was prone to take offence under the salutary eye of good English law, here becomes the football of passion, and suddenly blows his friend's brains out.

Highway Robbery

Matthew MacFie, *Vancouver Island and British Columbia* (London, 1865), p. 418.

In a country where so many are governed by impulse, and rendered desperate by losses sustained in speculation, it is not surprising that instances of highway robbery and murder should occasionally happen. The commission of these crimes, however, as in California and Australia, has been hitherto confined to solitary intervals, between the towns of British Columbia, on the way to the mines. The proportion of crime, at present, is decidedly small, considering the character and number of the population.

Law and Order in Mining Interior

The Daily British Colonist, Victoria, April 8, 1861: Letter from a regular correspondent, Cayoosh, March 23, 1861.

Since my last there have been stormy times here, caused by returning trains from up country with exciting news; and, as some facetious wags here say, the "Cayoosh spring fights have commenced." On Monday last there was a row over the river, in which one man broke another's head with a decanter. . . . In the evening of the same day two others got at it on this side of the river, and one finally broke a bottle of lager beer on the head of the other. . . .

The next row I am sorry to say, proved a far more serious affair, as it terminated in the death, of a fellow creature. . . .

The fearful result of the above was thought to be enough to cause peace for some little time; but the very next day two Spaniards were found drawing their knives and pistols on each other, and were arrested and fined fifty dollars each.

The morality of B.C. is no longer anything to boast of; and if vigorous steps are not taken by the authorities, life will be no safer here than in the worst regions of California in '49. It is a sad state of affairs when men, for the slightest offence, draw knives and pistols on each other. Nevertheless, it is a matter of daily occurrence, and cowardly bullies do not scruple to draw their weapons when they know that the only penalty is a few dollars fine.

Liquor Traffic with Indians

(i)

The British Colonist, Victoria, March 8, 1860: Editorial.

This infamous business has become one of the most profitable occupations in Victoria. As many as six scamps are notoriously engaged in the manufacture and sale of the deleterious compound, and although arrests are frequently made, it is almost impossible to fasten the crime upon the guilty parties.

We yesterday paid a visit to the Northern Indian encampment, about half a mile across the Esquimalt bridge, and there beheld about twenty poor wretches, who were more or less under the influence of the fire-water. Some were wandering about in a state of hopeless idiocy, while others lay upon the ground, unable to rise, foaming at the mouth, and muttering over some outlandish gibberish; others again were making frantic exertions to escape from the clutches of their friends, who were evidently restraining them from avenging some real or fancied grievance upon some one of their neighbours. The place was a perfect Bedlam. On every side could be heard the raving, moaning, and shrieking of the poor beings who had fallen victims to the avarice and heartlessness of white brutes. . . . Never, in all our lives, have we gazed upon a scene of more utter wretchedness or hopeless debauchery. The mortality, from this cause, among the natives, is estimated at one per day for the last year.

Some of the manufacturers have amassed considerable sums of money, and whenever they get into trouble, are fully able to buy all the evidence necessary to ensure their escape. As an inducement to the police to ferret out these men and bring them to justice, one-half of the fine goes to the officer making the arrest; but so cunningly is the whole affair managed, that spies or sentries are always out watching the every movement of the police. As a consequence, but little can be done under the present arrangement, owing to the inadmissability of Indian testimony.

(ii)

The British Colonist, Victoria, August 15, 1860: Report of the Grand Jury, Victoria, August 14, 1860.

The grand jury would further direct the attention of the honourable Court to the fact that the penalties for the crime of selling intoxicating liquors to the Indians are not sufficiently onerous to suppress the practice.

The crime in their opinion should be declared little short of capital, since through its commission murder and maiming are frequently committed, whilst violence and disorder are the constant result.   The attention of the Grand Jury has been painfully drawn to the importance of the suggestion now made by the flagrant nature of several cases which have during this session been presented before them; and they earnestly trust that the Legislature will speedily adopt stringent measures to stop effectually a practice so seriously affecting the peace and security of the colony.

Adventurous Females and Emergence of Social Evil

Matthew MacFie, *Vancouver Island and British Columbia* (London, 1865), pp. 401, 406.

A number of females have found their way into the country who give themselves out as *widows*, without being entitled to that sad but honourable designation. . . .

"The social evil," if it does not prevail in greater ratio than it does in the parent country, at least rears its head more unblushingly, and prostitutes are reputed to be the richest of their sex.   Nor is scandal confined to unmarried or obscure circles in the community.

Growth of Immorality

Public Archives of Canada, *S.P.G. in F.P.*, *Canada 1860-7:* Nanaimo, January 6, 1861, the Rev. J. B. Good to Secretary, Society for the Propagation of the Gospel.

This community must be reformed: unblushing vice which now lifts itself on high and stalks abroad must be made to cower and hide its hideous head from the gaze of the public eye and eventually be crushed out of our midst.

Slave Traffic in Indian Prostitutes

The Daily British Colonist, Victoria, October 11, 1860: Occasional Papers; Letter from the Bishop of British Columbia to Commissary Garrett, London, January 13, 1860.

The [Indian] tribes have much decreased since 1846.   More than half the Songish are gone—these live here—their destruction is occasioned principally by drink and dissolute habits.   Those nearest the whites are worst.   Slavery has increased.   Female slaves are in demand. . . . You will hardly credit it, but it is strictly true, women are purchased as slaves to let them out for immoral purposes. . . .

re is a white man, we trust not an Englishman, near Langley, who
h slaves, and hangs out a sign over his door to signify the horrible
ere pursued.   An Indian named Bear's-Skin makes large profits
in female slaves.

Indian Prostitutes

(i)

The British Colonist, Victoria, May 8, 1860.

Arrest of Street-Walkers—Mary, Sumox, Ca-at, Kate, Emelie, and Mush, squaws belonging to the northern tribes, were arrested on Saturday night charged with loitering in the public streets. They were locked up for the night, and discharged in the morning with a warning that if caught again in the streets after dark they would be punished. These squaws presented a queer sight in the prisoner's dock; some of their hoops being so large that they could scarcely get inside the railing. On Sunday and last night not a squaw was to be seen on the street.

(ii)

The British Colonist, Victoria, August 22, 1860.

A Street-Walker—"Kitty, the Gay Deceiver," a Hydah woman, was found patrolling the streets at a late hour on Monday night by the police, and was taken to the station-house. Yesterday morning she was convicted of being a common street-walker, and was ordered to give bonds in the sum of £2 to be of good behavior for the space of two months.

Indian Brothels

The British Colonist, Victoria, July 7, 1860.

The Grand Jury Respectfully Present:
. . . That the Indian brothel, where a robbery is alleged to have been committed by Jones [a member of the police force], is a nuisance, that the Indian brothels on Stone Street and its vicinity, and in other parts of the town, used as they are for the still worse purpose of selling liquor to the Indians are nuisances, and we hope that the squaws will be ordered off to the camps of their respective tribes, and that means will be found to punish white men who harbor squaws for such vile purposes.

Rise of Temperance Movements

The British Colonist, Victoria, July 22, 1859.

We are pleased to learn that a division of the Sons of Temperance has been organized in Victoria. It is undeniable evidence of our progress; and shows that we have those amongst us who deplore the lamentable consequences which are felt in our small community from intemperance; and that they are willing to deny themselves, by setting an example of total-abstinence, in order to reclaim, by moral suasion and fraternal kindnesses, their erring brethren.

Organization of Y.M.C.A.'s

The British Colonist, Victoria, September 5, 1859.

Pursuant to public notice the Supreme Court room was filled on Saturday evening by a large and respectable audience for the purpose of organizing a Young Men's Christian Association.

Col. Moody R.E., on taking the chair, requested the Rev. E. Evans, Superintendent of the Wesleyan Mission, to open the meeting by prayer; after which the chairman explained the object of the Association, and urged with great cogency the importance of scientific and historical knowledge to young men, and the immense advantages they would derive from Divine assistance in pursuing those various branches of study which were essential to the good citizen and Christian.

The Rev. E. Cridge, pastor of the Victoria Established Church, then moved the following resolution: "That this meeting, recognizing the usefulness of Young Men's Christian Associations, is gratified to find that steps have been taken to establish one in this town." He supported it at some length with many pertinent illustrations, and expressed himself warmly in favor of the institution.

T. J. Pidwell, Esq., seconded the motion. He adverted to the good results from similar institutions elsewhere; passed some strictures upon the alarming increase of saloons, and concluded that the organization of a Christian Association with its library, and the opportunity which it would afford for the discussion of general theological and political questions would have a powerful tendency to guard the young men of this colony from falling into habits destructive of good morals.

The Rev. Dr. Evans, with an eloquent and forcible speech, then moved: "That this meeting pledge itself to encourage and support by every means in its power this the first Young Men's Christian Association established in Vancouver Island." His remarks exhibited the greatest degree of tolerance. . . . The moral and spiritual advantages to the young men of the colony arising from the Association he was satisfied would be very great. . . .

The Rev. W. F. Clarke, Congregational Missionary, with great pleasure seconded the motion, and supported it with a speech of considerable length, replete with argument and illustration, portraying the advantages of the Association in a community like this, where there was so little public opinion to influence and direct young men; whilst there were so many things incident to the love of money in a gold country to induce youth to contract habits adverse to the progress of morals and religion.

B. The Yukon

Social Code of Old-time Miners

Tappan Adney, *The Klondike Stampede* (New York and London, 1900), pp. 267-73.

The miners, most of whom were old-timers, lived comfortably in their cabins, which were overheated rather than cold.

In the evening, after work is done, they visit around or remain indoors reading papers and books.   One finds all sorts of books, from a cheap novel to Gibbon's *Roman Empire* and Shakespeare, in the cabins of Bonanza and Eldorado. . . .

The old-timer is punctilious in the matter of washing dishes and clothes as far as that is practicable.   Every cabin has its wash-tub and wash-board, and once a week the woollens are changed and scrubbed.   He gives more care to the quality of his food and to its preparation than the new-comer, for he has learned by experience that it pays to do so.

Although the trading companies agree between themselves on prices— the highest that the miner can pay—still the competition is so keen that the quality of the food is the very best.   The old-timer never speculates in food. One who is better supplied lets his neighbor have flour at the price it cost him in the store.

The old-timer is often bitter against the new-comers.   He wonders what will become of the country and of them.   What a change!   Four years ago, if you told a man in Seattle you were going into the Yukon, he would set you down as a crazy fool.

The trouble seems to be that the old-timer has come to regard the country as his own, and naturally resents innovations, particularly those just now associated with "government," which they may well do, as "government" had small use for the country until they, the old-timers, by their own hands proved it to be rich.   The greatest number of the old miners are Americans, or have imbibed American ideas. . . .

He has his own strict ideas of morality.   Theft was as great a crime as murder, and when either happened, which was rarely, a miners' meeting was called, the accused was given a chance to be heard, and then by a vote the decision was rendered swiftly but surely.   If guilty, he had to leave the country at once.   *How* he left was a matter of no concern.   *He had to leave!* Gambling was regarded as a legitimate amusement, but it did not mean that they all gambled.   They considered that anyone who chose to spend his money that way was as free to do so as in any other.   But if he could, but would not, pay his debts, the recalcitrant was requested by a miners' meeting to settle—and he did.   The professional gambler is respected as any other man who behaves himself, only he is considered in the light of a non-producer, and not in the same class or entitled to the same consideration as a prospector or miner.   A man who thoroughly knows the spirit of his fellow-miners says: "Here the man who patronizes a saloon and the man who goes to church are on the same footing."   A startling statement, but none the less true.

There is a dearth of blood-curdling tales that are expected to be the stock of every mining-camp.   The Yukon has been too law-abiding for many stories of violence.   The rigors of the country and the broadening effect of the life have made men behave themselves.   The police have not, as is claimed, brought about this condition.   It existed before there were any police here. The cold weather, the poor grub and little of it, incidents of a hard trip with dogs, the time there was no butter in Circle City—these constitute about the whole stock of conversation. . . .

Their sense of honor in the matter of debts is most strict, but, as unbusiness-like people often are, they are "touchy" about the presentation of a bill. . . .

But with all his whims and prejudices, the old-timer might serve as a model for courage and manliness and honor to some who pretend more. At the mines he is industrious and hard-working. It is only when he occasionally goes to town with a sack that he relaxes into often reckless dissipation. But when one has lived the dreary life, he has little blame in his heart for him who returns with empty "poke" and no apparent increase of wisdom.

The old-timers have been called "nondescripts." The new-comers are more distinguishable—photographers, newspaper men, physicians, mining engineers, farmers, lumbermen, and clerks. On one claim not far below Discovery, on Bonanza, a Salvation Army captain worked down in the hole, an ex-missionary turned the windlass and dumped the bucket, an archdeacon of the Church of England worked the rocker in the cabin, while the cook was a young man who had dealt faro.

The "Spree" after the Season's Work

Tappan Adney, *The Klondike Stampede* (New York and London, 1900), pp. 312-15.

Wild scenes followed the clean-up. Men with never a penny to spare in their lives were suddenly made rich. There was no real disorder, there were no shootings, no hold-ups, none of the things associated with a real live mining-camp. Something in the Yukon air discourages all that. It could not be the presence of the police, for there were no police at Circle City, and only a baker's dozen at Dawson. Gold flowed, and when it would not flow it was sowed, literally sowed, broadcast in drunken debauch over the sawdust floors of the saloons as if there were no end to the supply. Gold was panned out of the sawdust—whole saloonfuls of men would be asked up to drink, at half a dollar a drink. Sometimes orders were given to call in the town, and then the bartender would go out into the street and call everybody in, and all would have to drink. Whenever one of the new "millionaires" was backward in treating, which was not often, the crowd—always a good-natured one—would pick him up by the legs and arms and swing him like a battering-ram against the side of the house until he cried out "Enough!" There had never been seen anything like it before, nor will anything quite to equal it ever be seen again.

Demoralization of Men

Mary Lee Davis, *Sourdough Gold: The Log of a Yukon Adventure* (Boston, 1933), pp. 194-7.

One of the sad things was to see men go to pieces, in body or in spirit. I told you that women did not "go to the bad" in Dawson, unless they had already been there. I cannot say the same for men, many of whom slid rapidly down hill. I knew a fellow on the early part of the Chilkoot Trail who looked and felt rather a "swell." Imagine my surprise, on reaching Dawson, to see him standing before a saloon, playing a cheap wind-instrument with might and main. He got fifteen dollars a day for this, to attract customers inside. He was no musician, but just made a noise. There were many who did the same thing. It was of course inevitable that a' large proportion of the too venturous and too unprepared cheechakos, who had paid dollars by the hundred thousand to the touting steamship lines and outfitted for the north unwarily, should, after failing in the search for gold, seek means of gaining a miserable existence in some—in any—wage-paid occupation. . . .

I knew another, decent sort of chap, on the early trail. When I reached Dawson I found him cleaning out the spittoons in a saloon, which seemed to me about the lowest of all callings. . . . Another of my early acquaintances on the trail had been a gentlemanly bank-clerk from Chicago. He said that his forbears were men of adventuresome spirit and that he had inherited their spunk. He was decidedly uppish, a flyer to the Sun. Before the river closed in '98 he left Dawson as a waiter on a boat, a broken man. . . .

Another trail companion we had met got a job running the ferry-boat across the Klondike river, and was paid an ounce a day. . . .

Miners who struck even richest pockets on the fabulous fractions of the Klondike, and took out fortunes, acquired (the most of them) that treacherous, too easy philosophy of all "good times." They thought they could surely turn the trick again. Consequently, they spent it gloriously (ingloriously, if you prefer) and then—the inevitable morning after, with its black taste of failure and frustration. . . .

There were some true gentlemen here, some true ladies, judged even by the strictest standards; but the Yukon was a terrible test of character and personality. That sudden break and loss of a whole tradition, of which I have already spoken, was an inescapable phenomenon in social and personal experience. No organized group was any longer compelling us to anything; there was nothing, outside our own inner compulsion, to live up to. It was our task to build up a new ethic. The genuine pioneer has standards, decidedly. He has honor and he has virtue. He has a certain tough unformulated faith, but his standards are not the standards of home.

The Saloon the Centre of Dawson Social Life

Tappan Adney, *The Klondike Stampede* (New York and London, 1900), pp. 336-42.

In a new mining-camp the saloon is the centre of social life. At Dawson, shut out from the world, under conditions that tried the very souls of men, it was less wonder that men were drawn together into the only public places where a friendly fire burned by day and night, and where, in the dim light of a kerosene lamp, they might see one another's faces. The Yukon saloon was a peculiar institution (I feel that I am describing something that passed away when the horde of new-comers came later). Most of the proprietors were old-timers who had been miners, men of honor and character, respected in a community where a man was valued, not according to his pretensions or position in "society," but in proportion to his manliness and intrinsic worth. Class lines are not drawn sharply in a mining-camp, and the freedom from the restraint of society and home makes temptation greater than many can withstand. Taken as a whole, the experience of a year in the Klondike is such as to search out the flaw in the weak but to strengthen the character of the strong. . . .

"Pete's" was a two-story log building, the upper story being the living-rooms of the proprietor. One entered from the street, in a whisk of steam that coated the door-jamb with snowy frost, into a low-ceiled room some thirty by forty feet in dimensions. The bar, a pine counter stained red, with a large mirror and bottles and glasses behind, was on the left hand. A lunch-counter stood on the right, while in the rear, and fenced off by a low wooden railing, but leaving a way clear to the bar, was the space reserved for dancing. Here, in the glow of three or four dim, smoky kerosene lamps, around a great sheet-iron "ram-down" stove, kept always red-hot, would always be found a motley crowd—miners, government officials, mounted policemen in uniform, gamblers, both amateur and professional, in "citified" clothes and boiled shirts, old-timers and new-comers, claim-brokers and men with claims to sell, busted men and millionaires—they elbowed each other, talking and laughing, or silently looking on, all in friendly good nature.

Pete himself, one of the few saloon-keepers who had not been miners in the "lower country," served the drinks behind the bar in shirt-sleeves, with his round head and bull-dog expression, hair carefully oiled and parted, and dark, curled mustache, smiling, courteous, and ignorant—a typical "outside" bar-tender. . . .

The whiskey [in the Yukon] varied greatly in quality, some being very bad, while the best, by the time it reached the consumer, was apt to be diluted to the last degree.

Whenever whiskey runs short the Yukoner falls back upon a villainous decoction made of sour dough, or dough and brown sugar, and known as "hootchinoo," or "hootch." The still is made of coal-oil cans, the worm of pieces of India-rubber boot-tops cemented together. This crude still is heated over an ordinary Yukon stove. The liquor obtained is clear white, and is flavored with blueberries or dried peaches, to suit the taste. It must be very bad, for its manufacture is forbidden by law; they say it will drive a man crazy; but there were persons willing to take their oath that the regular whiskey served over some of the bars was worse than "hootch." A home-brewed beer, or ale, was also served, a whiskey glassful costing 50 cents. Cigars were mostly a poor five-cent grade.

An example of the better class of Dawson saloon was the "Pioneer," or "Moosehorn," a favorite resort of old-timers. The proprietors, Messrs. Densmore, Spencer and McPhee, were types of the early Yukon pioneer. Frank Densmore, in fact, was among the first who crossed the pass, and rocked for gold on the bars of the upper Yukon a dozen years before the Klondike was known. I recall the "Pioneer" as a large, comfortable room, with the usual bar on one side, having a massive mirror behind, and several large moose and caribou antlers on the walls, a number of unpainted tables and benches and chairs, the latter always filled with men talking over their pipes, reading much-worn newspapers (six months out of date), a few engaged in games of poker, and nine-tenths "dead broke," but as welcome, apparently, as the most reckless rounder who spilled his dust over the bar. It struck the outsider with wonder, the seeming indifference of the proprietors whether one patronized the bar or not, for what other interpretation can one place on a water-barrel at the end of the bar? Then, too, the "busted" man of to-day might be the "millionaire" of to-morrow; but the reason lay deeper than that. There were men destined not to have fortunes. Very late at night, when Dawson had turned in for a snatch of sleep, one might see them lying on benches and tables, homeless, stranded men, half-sick and dependent from day to day on the charity of strangers, and who, but for this welcome bench or table, had no place to lay their heads. Something of the generous spirit of the old Yukon life made these men welcome.

Amusements

Sessional Papers, Canada, 1899, no. 15:   Annual Report of Inspector F. Harper, North-West Mounted Police, Fort Herchmer, Dawson, Yukon Territory, December 29, 1898.

The principal public amusements in Dawson, consist of music halls, of which there are two, where dancing takes place after the entertainment, two or three dance halls, and several places where gambling takes place. During the past year I have on several occasions visited these places. I consider, taking into consideration the kind of town Dawson is, and the very respectable way in which the music halls are conducted, that they are no worse than some of the entertainments I have seen in the music halls in some parts of London. With the exception of one man who was summoned before me under section 177 of the Criminal Code and fined $50 and cost, there have been no complaints whatever regarding the morality of the entertainments. The dance halls and gambling places are also conducted in a very orderly manner, the proprietors of the same being very quick to stop any row or disturbance that may commence in their establishment, knowing that they will be punished, should they allow such a state of affairs to exist. These are the only public amusements, if they can be classed as such, that I know to exist in Dawson.

Public Entertainments

Mrs. George Black, *My Seventy Years: As told to Elizabeth Bailey Price* (London and Toronto, 1938), pp. 121, 133-6.

Almost every other building was either a dance hall, saloon, hotel, or restaurant, with such names as the Floradora, Aurora, Northern, Monte Carlo, M. and N. (the name derived from the initials of the owners' names), Sourdough, Can Can, and Chisholm's Saloon, nicknamed the "Bucket of Blood," where the first drink was accompanied by a whisk. (What for? To brush you off when you came to.) One or the other told the world by painted signs and printed notices that "crap, chuck, and draw poker, black jack, roulette wheels, and faro banks were run by the management; that every known fluid—water excepted—was for sale at the bar; that there were special rates for the 'gambling perfesh'."...

It was a wild winter in Dawson that winter of '98. As I look back to it I have an infinite pity for the men of those days, many of superior breeding and education. They were lonely, disillusioned, and discouraged. There were so few places to go where it was bright and cheerful. They gathered with the others in the saloons and dance halls. They joined the party with the "first round," and then they drank to drown their woes. The continued Arctic darkness contributed to the debauchery. Revellers lost all sense of time as to day and night periods, and attuned themselves to the ever-present night until they passed out from sheer exhaustion....

The dance-saloon-gambling-variety halls were built on the same order, the bars usually to the left of the entrance. They were backed with plate glass mirrors on the upper wall, and the lower was lined with bottle-laden shelves. On the hardwood counters rested several finely-balanced gold scales for weighing "dust," as there was practically no currency in the country. (An ounce of dust was worth fifteen dollars).

To the right were the gambling rooms, usually furnished with poker and crap tables and chairs, faro banks, and roulette wheels. Although there was generally a house limit on the bets, sometimes the games were "wide open," as high as twenty thousand dollars being lost in a single whirl of the roulette wheel, five thousand at stud poker, and a thousand dollars a throw in a crap game. (Speaking of bets, I knew two old Sourdoughs who bet each other ten thousand dollars on their respective spitting accuracy—the mark being a crack in the wall.)

Dance and variety halls had fine floors and were lighted by large oil lamps. There was always good music, some of the musicians having played in the best orchestras in America. The larger halls had stages and galleries, with curtained boxes, where patrons might have a certain privacy for entertaining their girl friends or watching shows and dances. Drinks served here cost double.

Dances were a dollar apiece, and each was concluded with a "promenade all" to the bar, where the male dancer would buy two drinks, ginger ale for his girl partner, and generally hard liquor for himself. If he fancied champagne, he paid thirty dollars a pint.

Gambling in a Mining Society

Robert C. Kirk, *Twelve Months in the Klondike* (London, 1899), pp. 93-5.

The games that found most favour with the miners were faro, roulette, craps, black-jack, and poker, but faro was more universally played. These gambling places were often crowded even when the dance-halls were deserted, and the faro tables in particular were always surrounded by men busily watching the successive turns of the cards. Around the walls of these places could be seen numerous roulette wheels and crap tables, but these games were not so heavily patronised as faro. . . .

When the miners play against the games they hand their gold sacks to the dealer, who gives them as many stacks of chips as they want, charging the amount against the sack. When the player quits the game he "cashes in" by giving back whatever chips he has, and then, if he has won, subtracts the amount originally advanced him. His winnings, or losses, are marked down on a piece of paper by the dealer, and then the miner takes this and his gold sack to the cashier, who either takes out or weighs in dust according to whether the player has won or lost.

The gamblers in Dawson have led lives of varying success, and many of them have made and lost fortunes. I knew of one instance that occurred during one of Dawson's earlier winters, of where a gambler, who had sold a claim for three thousand pounds (or fifteen thousand dollars), lost it all at the faro tables in a few nights' play. A story is told of a gambler who borrowed forty pounds (or two hundred dollars), and, after playing all night, won eight hundred pounds (or four thousand dollars). He repaid the amount he had borrowed, returned to the tables, and then lost all his winnings. Two miners once played a game of poker for a claim worth about two thousand pounds (or ten thousand dollars), and when one had lost and the other had won, the loser made out the papers as he had previously agreed to do, and seemed to consider the matter of very little moment.

Gambling is carried on more extensively in Dawson than it would be if the camp were not so wholly isolated from the civilised world. But under the existing conditions, where the men are shut in from all outside communication, without daily newspapers, theatres, and other things to attract their attention, they patronise the gambling tables merely to occupy their mental faculties, rather than for the sake of the small financial gains they may make. The games are always quiet and orderly, and there is seldom any trouble between the dealer and the player; and there are certainly no instances where shooting affrays have occurred, as they commonly have in other places.

A Movement to Stop Gambling

The Klondike Miner, Dawson, Saturday, May 31, 1902.

FROM A YUKON DUNGEON CELL

. . . .

Greeting All:

... The object of the present communication is not to deal with generalities, but to inform my fellow Canadians of the true reasons why I, one of yourselves, for no crime, but being a true Canadian, for no injustice, but a determination to stop crooked gambling, and as editor of a Canadian paper which does not happen to agree with all the present government and its servants, am forcibly detained in the Common Gaol of Dawson, the Penitentiary of the Yukon.

For four or five years, or since the discovery of the Yukon Canadian Gold Fields known as "The Klondike" it has been the custom and practice of the federal officials of Canada, in the Yukon, to tolerate public, open, downstairs, gambling throughout the Territory, and such games as Faro, Roulette, Craps, Black Jack and Poker have until about a year ago, run without interruption within this Territory publicly and openly, with the knowledge, consent and toleration of the Federal Officials of Canada.

About one year ago or more public indignation at this notorious disregard of the breaking of our Criminal Code became so great that our local officer commanding the N.W.M.P. closed all public gambling; this was about March or April, 1901.

Great efforts were made to secure a reopening of the gambling, by the gamblers interested, and some of the merchants whose business was assisted by reason of the games being permitted. So great was the selfishly inspired power of these people, that in a few days after Major Wood had ordered the games closed, a telegram was alleged to have been received from Deputy Minister of the Interior Jas. A. Smart, which was immediately published and never contradicted, which telegram gave instructions that the order to close the gambling houses should be suspended from operation until June 1st, 1901; that is to say until after the season of Yukon plenty, after most of the workingmen had received their wages for their winter's work and had an opportunity to spend the same over the gambling tables.

On June 1st the games closed, but in a very short time black jack and poker were opened upon the people again, set in public places to catch with the "decoys" or "boosters" the unsuspecting traveller, like Soapy's nut shell men on the Skagway trail.

These short-marked-card-decoy games as operated in the Yukon give an unskilled card player far less opportunity to win than do faro, roulette or craps.

Many complaints were made against these games, that they were crooked; that they run wide open on Sunday, etc.; and at that time, September, 1901, I, personally, on behalf of a man who alleged he had been robbed in a gaming house on the first Sunday in September, 1901, wrote a full account and complaint of same to the Trades and Labor Council, then in session at Brantford, Ont., which communication was duly received, acknowledged, and nothing more heard of it. The crooked games continued to run however, Sunday and all, until the hold up and robbery of the Dominion saloon gambling house by Tomerlin, Brophy, both, either or another, so drew public attention to the notorious character of the then existing gambling hells, that they could no longer be winked at by the authorities. This series was by far the most notoriously crooked, cheating and robbing games ever run except under Soapy Smith's personal protection.

During all of last winter the games remained closed and the condition of the workingmen, road-house keepers, small merchants and hotels has been greatly benefited thereby, and the above majority of our people are by far more prosperous and happy than at any time in the history of the Yukon.

But there was no GRAFT for anyone in a continuation of this condition of affairs.

Now that our wash up season of plenty has once more arrived, however, the gamblers once more arrange for the final swoop, and made use of their peculiar pressure or power to secure a grand final liberty, licence, and protection to rob, pillage and plunder the workingmen of the Yukon of their winter's earnings.

This peculiar pressure or power finally culminated on the evening of May 2nd inst., when the Madden house gambling room opened up full blast, wide open, upstairs gambling, faro, roulette, craps, poker and black jack being in full swing and crowded with players. . . .

as ever,

JOSEPH A. CLARKE.

Problems of Government in First Stage of Rush

Tappan Adney, The Klondike Stampede (New York and London, 1900), pp. 432-3.

During the winter of 1897-8 only ten per cent of the population of Dawson were Canadians; a considerable percentage were of English birth, but the overwhelming majority were Americans, or foreigners who had lingered in the United States long enough to imbibe American ideas. In the crowd which poured in later the percentage of Canadian citizens, or British subjects, was probably still smaller. These people under United States law would have had the making of their own laws, subject only to broad statutory limitations. Indeed, with reference to Alaska, non-interference with liberty by the central government has been but another name for neglect.

In the Klondike, those who best knew the country's needs had no voice whatever in its government; all laws were made at Ottawa, and those sent out to enforce them were responsible only to the home government, or to the officials to whom they owed their appointment. Dawson was an "alien" camp, where, if the position of the majority of the residents was different from the "Ouitlander" at Johannesburg, it was only that the laws were *in intent* more liberal. Distant weeks and months from the seat of responsibility, it is not difficult to understand how, even if government intended well, the condition of the miner might be scarcely better than that of his unfortunate *confrère* in the Boer republic. In fact, conditions which actually prevailed at Dawson were likened by British citizens direct from the Transvaal as even worse than what they left.

The natural difficulties that stood in the way of putting into immediate operation an effective government were so great that one should not judge the Klondikers too harshly. On the other hand, if there were not serious disorders it was due less to the quality of government than to the orderly character of the population, and to the fact that men were there enduring the privations of an Arctic climate to make their fortunes and get away, not to help set in order the political house-holds of their Canadian friends.

23

Diversified Nationalities and Government

Sessional Papers, Canada, 1899, no. 13: Report of Major J. M. Walsh on the
Yukon District.

I wish to call your attention to the reports which have been published
accusing officials of the Yukon District of corruption. These reports are
absolutely false. . . .

Officials of any Government entering into a new and isolated district
where the people are not closely restricted by law and are free from taxation
have almost invariably met with just such an experience as we have had.
The introduction and enforcement of law and taxation naturally made us
unpopular with the older residents, who were unaccustomed to that sort of
thing. Added to this, some twenty thousand people had flocked into the
district in a few weeks. They did not find things as they were in their own
country and, as might be expected, in a few weeks everyone was dissatisfied
with everything around him. The Englishman from South Africa wanted
things carried on as he had been accustomed to having them carried on there;
the New Zealander, as they had been carried on in New Zealand; the Germans and Swedes as in their motherlands. Those who came from the United
States wanted the mining laws and regulations adopted which are in force in
that country, and the British Columbian called out for the regulations of his
province, with this exception, that in his case he preferred the 500-foot claim
of the Yukon to the 100-foot claim of British Columbia. When regulations
could not be made to suit all these varied elements of population, the officials
and the law had to be abused and, therefore, the crusade that was started
against both.

Gateway to Yukon—Law and Order in Skagway

Sessional Papers, Canada, 1899, no. 15: Report of Superintendent S. B. Steele,
Commanding North-West Mounted Police, Yukon Territory,
January 10, 1899.

The town of Skagway at this time [the spring of 1898], and for some
months later, was little better than a hell upon earth. The desperado commonly called "Soapy Smith" and a numerous gang of ruffians ran the town.
Murder and robbery were daily occurrences, hundreds came there with plenty
of money and the next morning had not sufficient to buy a meal, having been
robbed or cheated out of their money. Men were seen frequently exchanging
shots in the streets. On one occasion, half a dozen in the vicinity, and around
the North-west Mounted Police Offices, were firing upon one another, bullets
passing through the buildings. There was a United States deputy marshal
at Skagway at the time for the purpose of maintaining law and order, but no
protection was expected from him.

Crime

Sessional Papers, Canada, 1899, no. 15: Report of Superintendent S. B. Steele,
Commanding North-West Mounted Police, Yukon Territory,
January 10, 1899.

I am glad to be able to report that in proportion to the population, crime is not very prevalent, and in fact the crime sheets of the Yukon Territory would compare very favourably with those of any part of the British Empire.

The most serious are two cases of murder and one of manslaughter. . . .

During the summer a number of cases of robbery with violence and assault were reported from up the creeks, and although no arrests were made directly, increased vigilance and examples made of the men caught in town, seem to have had a wholesome effect, as no such cases have occurred of late.

Theft is, and has been, one of the most frequent charges and there are now three serving five years—one, one year and eleven months, all convicted of theft or receiving stolen goods, etc.   There are many cases of petty theft, but this I think is on the decrease, prompt punishment having a very salutary influence among this class of people.

The commoner offences usual in mining communities, *i.e.* non-payment of wages, nuisances, drunkenness, prostitution, gambling, are easily dealt with by the Police Magistrates, Inspectors Harper and Belcher, assisted by the other officers. . . .

Although the majority of the population are honest people, hardworking and anxious to make money to enable them to start in life elsewhere, there are at the present time at many points in the Yukon Territory, but particularly in Dawson, a very large number of desperate characters.   Many of them have committed murders, "held up" trains, stage coaches, and committed burglary and theft in the United States.

These men are at present giving us very little trouble, but as times are getting hard in the town of Dawson, work difficult to obtain and the clean-up still distant, when gold will be plentiful, I expect that some serious crimes may be committed if immediate action is not taken.

I have therefore given orders that such characters might be arrested immediately and brought before a magistrate for examination.   The patrols are directed to seek out any on the creeks or in the different mining camps.

When I arrived here in September, I took action which received earnest support, setting detectives to work to obtain the names and modes of life of such characters as those to whom I refer.   Many were arrested and fined, and steps were taken with such satisfactory results as to make this large mining camp tolerable for respectable people; particularly the wives and families of those who have settled down in the country.

In the music and concert halls and on the stage, improprieties of any character are forbidden.

Acts of indecency are severely punished and it can safely be said that any man, woman or child, may walk at any time of the night to any portion of this large camp with as perfect safety from insult as on Sparks street, Ottawa.   This in the midst of a population which has been for some time without the softening influences of older civilization.

Law and Order in Dawson

Sessional Papers, Canada, 1901, no. 28a: Annual Report of Inspector C. Starnes, Commanding 'B' Division, North-West Mounted Police, Dawson, 1900.

The police duties in the town of Dawson are in the hands of the town squad, which consists of one non-commissioned officer and eight selected men, with a special constable, who acts as cook for the detachment. Four men are detailed for day duty, being relieved at seven p.m., and a similar number for night duty. The town is frequently patrolled both by day and by night, dance halls, theatres, saloons, hotels, &c., visited, and I think I am safe in saying that so far as the maintenance of law and order is concerned, Dawson will compare favourably with any outside city.

With the extent of ground to be covered, the many places requiring police visitation, the absence of serious crimes, the mixed population—all nations being represented—it seems to me that our town squad perform their duties efficiently and satisfactorily.

Regulations have been made respecting dance halls which prevent the evil which prevailed while "box rustling" was permitted. Women are not allowed to drink at any bar or to gamble. Remarks of persons just arriving from the outside would lead us to believe that they had never visited a mining camp, or were not familiar with them, and they either cannot or will not, realize that conditions generally are different from the old settled towns and cities of the east.

The Law and Prostitution

The Daily Klondike Nugget, Dawson, September 29, 1902.

POLICE COURT

. . . Lottie Devine, charged with keeping a disorderly house on Third Avenue near King street, pleaded guilty. She has before been in court on a similar charge but not recently. The magistrate asked if she had not been warned to leave town, to which she replied in the negative. It appeared, however, that she had been warned when engaged in such business on King street, and had then removed to her present quarters. She was fined $25 and costs, which she paid, and warned not to offend again.

"Red-Light" District in Dawson City

(i)

R. A. Bankson, *The Klondike Nugget* (Caldwell, Idaho, 1935), p. 273: From issue of *Klondike Nugget,* autumn, 1898.

Second Avenue is now becoming one of Dawson's most prominent and important thoroughfares. Before this city had assumed its present and growing commercial importance the maisons de joie were located as they now are on Paradise Alley and Second Avenue. Of late the number has been increased on Second Avenue until the street is prominent in its display of red curtains between First and Third Streets.

Whatever may be the opinion concerning the locations, there can certainly be no excuse for permitting the advertising so vulgarly displayed of the "off society" of the city as may be seen there today. Business houses are now locating on Second Avenue rapidly, and naturally ladies alone and children are and will be more or less passing to and fro on errands of shopping. It is certainly a most discreditable thing to see glaring signs of "Jennie and Babe," and wanton use of names of places and respectable business houses to attract the attention of passers-by to these houses of ill fame. Why shouldn't the police department order down all such signs?

(ii)

R. A. Bankson, *The Klondike Nugget* (Caldwell, Idaho, 1935), pp. 292-3: From issue of *Klondike Nugget*, April 12, 1899.

The thread which has so long held the official ax over the famous "tenderloin district" has snapped asunder, the inexorable demands of progress have won the day. No longer may the woman in scarlet occupy the choicest of city lots and flaunt her crimson colors on Dawson's crowded streets; no longer may the seductive window tap beguile the innocent prospector or hurrying man of business. The reign of the scarlet letter is on the wane, and one of the institutions most cherished and nourished in the halcyon days of yore is about to be degraded.

"Second Street," or that which Second Avenue most means, must go— not out of existence, not swept from earth by an iron hand—but transplanted, severed from its old relations of intimacy with everything material in Dawson, and placed in splendid isolation, to work out its own destiny alone, to stand or fall as fortune shall decree.

It had to come. The clearing of the waterfront, the growing population, the increasing business interests, the demand for better public morals. These and other influences had been long pressing upon the powers that be, and on Saturday the first step was taken. The 300 or so representatives of the demi-monde have been notified that they will not longer be tolerated, on the prominent business streets and in the alleys; after May 1st they must occupy quarters less conspicuous and convenient.

It is understood to be the desire of the authorities to confine the sisterhood to that section of the city lying between Fourth Avenue and the base of the hill east of the town, and an effort in that direction will be made. It cannot be done at once, of course, for the people must have new buildings erected for their accommodation, and that will take time as none now exist there. It is also understood that the authorities have approved the plan of a well-known business firm to erect a huge tenement house for the accommodation of such as prefer the economy which goes with that class of structure.

Establishment of Family through Marriage with Indians

Tappan Adney, *The Klondike Stampede* (New York and London, 1900), pp. 355-6.

The number of women in camp was a continual subject of comment; and there were a few children. Dawson was, in the main, a city composed of grown people and dogs. Four years ago there were four white women in the Yukon. Two years later a theatrical troupe increased the number. This winter there were probably two hundred, most of whom were the wives of fortunate miners, and all of whom were as intent as the men upon earning, or helping to earn, a fortune.

Nearly all the first old-timers married Indian women, who have shared the good fortunes of their husbands in the Klondike strike, and are treated with the same respect that would be accorded a white woman. At Pioneer Hall, on New Year's eve, the "Yukon Order of Pioneers" gave a grand ball, at which, it is needless to say, "boiled" shirts were not *de rigueur*, but several were in evidence, in which their wearers, more accustomed to flannels, looked extremely uncomfortable. They brought their Indian wives, who in turn brought their children, and it made a quaint sight, the men, some in fur *parkas*, others in black broad-cloth, and all in moccasins; the women decked out in their best and newest "store" clothes, not much behind the fashion either; the babies in odd little *parkas*, playing on the floor under the feet of the dancers; and, as a final touch to the picture, here and there a lost dog looking for its owner. Tickets to this, the swell event of the season, were $12.50, which included an excellent supper.

Shift from Commercial to Matrimonial Relationships

Jeremiah Lynch, *Three Years in the Klondike* (London, 1904), pp. 56-7.

There was no honest occupation for women. Many went professedly as housekeepers to miners who were rich enough to employ one; but it was only another name. A very few found precarious and unremunerative employment in the stores, and the others drifted into houses kept for dancing, with gambling at faro and roulette as a principal adjunct. Those who could, danced and played; those who could not, assisted as *claqueuses*. But, withal, prizes were distributed quite impartially by fortune in the shape of rich mining husbands, and more than a dozen of these same dancing-hall girls are to-day enjoying married happiness at London, Paris, New York, and other places. And I make no doubt that they are quite as moral as the traditional Becky Sharpe. I know more than one case where the lady has reformed her dissipated husband, and keeps him in good strong leading-strings, to the edification of everyone who had witnessed a glimpse of the Klondike past. Those who have lived and are not altogether lost make excellent exemplars of virtue. Of good women there were few; of bad women plenty. So your lucky miner with cans of gold in his dilapidated ·abin, pining in the cold winter days for women's society, dropped down to

Dawson, into the music-halls, and engaged—a housekeeper. The house-keeper soon became a wife if she handled the gentleman rightly.

Public Recreational Facilities for the Family

The Klondike Nugget, Dawson, September 7, 1898.

THE FAMILY MATINEE

Mr. F. E. Simons, the popular manager of the Combination theatre, has undertaken to furnish Dawson theater-goers with a first-class entertainment devoid of any feature that might offend the most sensitive. There are a great many ladies and children in Dawson by whom such an innovation will be hailed with the greatest pleasure. It is the intention of the management to give a family matinee every Saturday afternoon. A private entrance to the theater has been arranged, so that the patrons of the entertainment need not pass through the saloon. No liquors are sold, and, in fact every objectionable feature has been removed so that ladies may attend the matinee and enjoy a pleasant afternoon.

Increase in Number of Women and Children

Sessional Papers, Canada, 1900, no. 15:   Report of Superintendent A. B. Perry, Commanding North-West Mounted Police, Yukon Territory, November 30, 1899.

I cannot give accurate information as to the population of the Yukon Territory. A conservative estimate would be 20,000. Nearly all are men, there being very few women and children in comparison. However, this is changing rapidly, and many men are bringing in their wives and families, finding that the social conditions and the climate though vigorous, still very healthy, and not inimical to their comfort and health. There are at least 160 children of school age now in Dawson, and the necessity of establishing schools has become very pressing.

3. CULTURAL ORGANIZATION AND EDUCATION

A. British Columbia

Diversity of Racial and National Groups

Matthew MacFie, *Vancouver Island and British Columbia* (London, 1865), pp. 378-9.

It was remarked by an intelligent shipmaster, whom I met in Victoria, that he had not found in any of the numerous ports he had visited during a long sea-faring career, so mixed a population as existed in that city. Though containing at present an average of only 5,000 or 6,000 inhabitants, one cannot pass along the principal thoroughfares without meeting representatives of almost every tribe and nationality under heaven. Within a limited space may be seen—of Europeans, Russians, Austrians, Poles, Hungarians, Italians, Danes, Swedes, French, Germans, Spaniards, Swiss, Scotch, English and Irish; of Africans, Negroes from the United States and the West Indies; of Asiatics, Lascars and Chinamen; of Americans, Indians, Mexicans, Chilanos, and citizens of the North American Republic; and of Polynesians, Malays from the Sandwich Islands.

Negroes and Racial Prejudice

Matthew MacFie, *Vancouver Island and British Columbia* (London, 1865), pp. 388-91.

The descendants of the African race resident in the colonies are entitled to some notice. About 300 of them inhabit Victoria, and upwards of 100 are scattered throughout the farming settlements of the island and British Columbia. The chief part came to the country some time previous to the immigration of '58, driven from California by social taboo and civil disabilities. They invested the sums they brought with them in land, and by the sudden advance in the value of real estate which followed the influx of gold seekers, most of them immediately found themselves possessed of a competency. It was not surprising, under these circumstances, that some, formerly habituated to servitude or reproached as representatives of a barbarous race, should, on being delivered from the yoke of social oppression, fail to show much consideration for the indurated prejudices of the whites, most of whom at that period were either Americans or British subjects, who sympathised with the ideas prevailing in the United States respecting the social *status* of the coloured people.

Whereas they had been restricted in California to worship Almighty God in their own churches or in a part of those frequented by whites, designed for the exclusive accommodation of persons of colour, they were permitted on coming to Vancouver Island free range of unoccupied pews, in the only church then erected in the colony. The church-going immigrants in the mass wafted to our shores in '58 were at once brought into a proximity with coloured worshippers which was repugnant to past associations. . . .

The same prejudice of race continues, unfortunately, to interfere with harmony in social gatherings for the purposes of amusement. More than once has the presence of coloured persons in the pit of the theatre occasioned scenes of violence and bloodshed, followed by litigation. When, a few years since, a literary institute was attempted to be formed, and the signatures of one or two respectable negroes appeared in the list of subscribers, the movement came to an untimely close. A white member of a temperance society, which was eminently useful in the community, proposed the name of a coloured man for admission, intentionally avoiding to disclose at the time any information as to his race, and when it was discovered that the society had been beguiled, ignorantly, into accepting a negro as a brother teetotaller, it broke up.

Negroes and Overt Conflict

The British Colonist, Victoria, July 31, 1860.

Rotten Egged.—A negro forced his way into the parquette of the Colonial Theatre last evening, and was pelted with rotten eggs by some men in the gallery. Several white people were also struck with the missiles. The affair was very disgusting and highly reprehensible.

Chinese Immigration

The British Colonist, Victoria, July 10, 1860.

Chinamen.—Our streets are crowded with Celestials bound for the British Columbia mines. From China and from California, they continue to pour in at the rate of 500 weekly, and lose no time in making arrangements for transportation to the gold regions. Large numbers are said to be still on the way. From all along the river we hear accounts of the Chinese having paid large sums of money for bars already worked over by white miners, and in some instances settling down upon new ground. The sale of hardware and big boots to these new comers is immense; but with other articles they are generally well supplied. Taken all in all, the Chinese have really been of great benefit to the mercantile classes generally this season. Whether mining interests will receive a corresponding benefit, remains to be seen.

Opposition to Chinese Intrusion

The British Colonist, Victoria, August 31, 1860: Letter from W. T. Ballon, Fort Hope, August 27, 1860.

A few more miners have returned this (Tuesday) morning, and say the diggings east of Hope, Similkameen and Rock Creek, are not as good as reported.

The white miners out there have driven away a company of Chinamen who went out to Similkameen, and would not let them work. In my opinion, much trouble will ensue, and I would not be surprised to hear that the officials who went out there first, fare roughly.

Social Classes

Matthew MacFie, *Vancouver Island and British Columbia* (London, 1865), pp. 392-7.

The manners of the white residents toward each other strike one accustomed to the taciturnity for which society in England is proverbial, as remarkably free and hearty. This rule, however, is not without exceptions.

The Government officials constitute the centre of the social system (still in a formative state), and around it multitudes of broken-down gentlemen and certain needy tradespeople rotate. The most wealthy members of the community have, in general, more money than culture—a condition of things always incident to the early stage of colonial development. Many of them owe their improved circumstances simply to being the lucky possessors of real estate at a time when it could be bought for a nominal amount. Some who eight years ago were journeymen smiths, carpenters, butchers, bakers, public-house keepers, or proprietors of small curiosity shops in San Francisco or Victoria, are now in the receipt of thousands of pounds a year. Among this class there are those who bear their prosperity with moderation, while others indicate the limited extent of their acquaintance with the world by an air of amusing assumption. . . .

A certain description of immigrants fresh from England, imagine in their verdant simplicity that their recent arrival from that great centre of knowledge and civilisation gives them a right to patronise colonists whose condition they deem benighted from long exile. The class I refer to have a weakness for manufacturing stories of better days, departed greatness, and rich relations. One person whom I knew professed to be a University man; to have been familiar with a European prince; heir of a large estate and ward of a gentleman of influence in England. The curiosity of a friend being excited to learn particulars respecting the mysterious history he supposed to attach to this hero, wrote home to parties claimed by him as former associates. On investigation, it appeared that he was a bankrupt draper and an outlaw, who had changed his name.

Amusing disclosures are sometimes made about certain ladies who are anxious to impress the public by exaggerated representations of their former position in society at home. These elegant specimens of affectation entertain visitors, languidly, with narratives, intended to set forth the contrast asserted to exist between present hardships and former affluence. But, by an unhappy coincidence, some one usually turns up who knows all about their antecedents; and then the truth comes out, assigning them a very different place in society from what they pretended to. . . .

Refugees from bankruptcy, disgrace, or family strife, suffered in some other part of the world, are to be met with in Victoria every few years. But among the unfortunate are some of the most estimable men I have ever seen.

The tone of society has become decidedly more British since 1859; but still, as then, the American element prevails.

Change in Fortunes in a Mining Society

R. Byron Johnson, *Very Far West Indeed: A Few Rough Experiences on the North-West Pacific Coast* (London, 1872), pp. 160-3.

Victoria was wonderfully changed for the better since we had last left it. The pretty little town was now filled with some ten thousand or more inhabitants, and was beginning to grow into an extensive place. Huge hotels were springing up to feed and house the roving hordes of gold-seekers.

Banks, assaying offices, warehouses, and even churches, appeared in unexpected locations. . . .

But I saw other sights which did not please me, and filled me with some trepidation. Thousands of men, without means or work to do, were hanging about the bar-rooms or their little one-roomed shanties, sponging on the first acquaintance any better off than themselves for a meal. In my walk down Government Street I was "tapped" on no less than four separate occasions for "half a dollar." This made me look at my own slender finances with troubled thoughts, for, without the chance of earning anything, I could not hold out very long.

I met lots of my old shipmates and acquaintances, and the changes of fortune that had befallen them were strange indeed, varying from the ludicrous to the sad. My original partner I found "keeping bar" in a whiskey saloon of decidedly second-rate character; his person adorned with a "biled" shirt of questionable cleanliness, and many sham diamonds. He had not much of interest to narrate. His first experience in the labour market had been the common one of road-making. His next employment was to dig potatoes for a wealthy "gentleman of colour," who had amassed his riches as a drayman, aided by judicious speculation in town lots. This occupation I thought (with my social ideas becoming fast Americanized) to be very low down indeed; but my friend appeased my disgust by stating that nothing less than impending starvation had driven him into it. Finally, he had happened upon his present berth, which seemed to suit him sufficiently well.

Going into a restaurant of humble character to obtain a "square feed" at fifty cents, I was waited upon (deuced badly too) by a young man of gentlemanly appearance, in whom I recognized a quondam associate and first-class through passenger, who had taken his degree at Oxford the year before, but had been allured from his intended profession, the Church, by the British Columbia excitement. The poor fellow seemed dreadfully down, and did not recognise me until I made myself known, when we had a talk together, and he informed me that his employer was a sort of steward's mate, who had worked his way out, and whom we had all kicked and cuffed about the steamer.

In the evening, visiting for an hour a place of entertainment, which was a dim reflection of a London Music Hall, I was filled with surprise to see in the person of a singer a lady of the most superior attainments and connections, who had accompanied her husband with the view on his part, as we all understood, of taking up a large tract of land and raising stock. But the husband had taken to drink instead, and squandered his money, and the wife was what I saw her; and that, alas! was only a cloak for a viler life. It was no pleasant spectacle to see this poor creature—who, whatever she might be now, had once been a lady, and a virtuous wife—drinking champagne, after her singing was concluded, at a public bar, with ruffians in mufti, whose ordinary conversation was blasphemy, and whose assumed manners fitted them as ill as the "store clothes" they wore.

Unemployed "Intellectuals"

The British Colonist, Victoria, January 28, 1860: Editorial.

Already the mischievous working of fake views in regard to labour has begun to show itself in our midst. We have strutting about among us, vain, empty-headed, conceited apologies for men, waiting for a "situation," which to *them* signifies, a chance to live without work. They are incapable of doing anything toward developing the resources of the country. Other and better men must do that, and virtually carry these drones on their shoulders through the world. As one of the unavoidable circumstances connected with the history of a new country like this, certain professions are overstocked, and some branches of business overdone. Hence many who came to make a living by these professions and branches of business, must turn to other channels of activity, or if they have not independent resources, starve. Mechanics and labourers, have been in demand, but a *gentleman* to touch tools and earn his bread by the use of such vulgar things as the spade or jack-plane, would be a terrible degradation, and subject him to a general *cutting* by his class. This is not a fancy picture. Some have literally *starved* at the bidding of this ridiculous and cruel sentiment. Unable to find hope for engagement in the profession or business to which they were accustomed, and not daring to face the absurd prejudice against work, they have gone on short allowance. Genteelly-dressed young men have picked their teeth around the precincts of the Colonial and other respectable hotels, barely keeping body and soul together on a meal a day. Some few, having moral courage enough to despise the prejudice we are combatting, or victims of the stern maxim, "necessity knows no law," have actually *gone to work*. Surveyors and physicians have especially abounded in this and the sister colony. It was very natural that the over-wrought accounts of our teeming population should attract a large number of these classes. But our government being in no hurry to have the public lands surveyed, and our population being neither very dense nor very sickly, it was impossible that all should find spheres of professional activity.

Lack of Class Distinction in Mining Interior

The Daily British Colonist, Victoria, April 23, 1861: Letter from Correspondent, Yale, April 15, 1861.

The Robinson troupe are performing here and draw good houses. After the performance yesterday evening a few gentlemen got up a dance and supper, to which I received an invitation, and spent one of the most pleasant evening (or rather morning) since I have been in these colonies. Thirteen ladies were present and I must say the Yaleites may be justly proud of having such ornaments to their town.

I hear that these social meetings are of frequent occurrence, and I was much struck with the friendship and good feeling which seem to exist

throughout the town.   There appears to be a total absence of any envy
or hostility among business men, which I take to be a good sign that everyone
is satisfied with his prospects.   Political faction does not show its head here
as in some places, and I do not believe there is a single specimen of the
"codfish aristocracy" extant in the neighborhood.

Society in Mining Interior

The Daily British Colonist, January 8, 1861: Letter from Hope, January 2, 1861.

We of this town have passed the holidays peacefully and pleasantly.
Some of the "boys" got up some *tall* performances in the terpsichorean line
on Christmas Eve.   Great harmony and unbounded good humor prevailed,
although the sport was rather "fast," and the liquids were of a variety
known as *skookum.*

Messrs Browning and Pringle have delivered some interesting lectures
to our citizens on historical and miscellaneous subjects.   It is hoped that
the reverend gentlemen will continue in their laudable efforts during the
remainder of the winter months.   The lectures were able and listened to
with attention; and listening to them is a pleasant and useful manner in
which to pass long evenings.

Educational Institutions

Matthew MacFie, *Vancouver Island and British Columbia* (London, 1865), p. 84.

The city is abundantly supplied with schools, in which is taught every
branch of a superior English education.   "The Collegiate School," conducted
by a principal, vice-principal, and assistant masters, is patronised and
aided by Bishop Hills, and is connected with his denomination.   Besides
the elements of a plain education, instruction is given in the ancient classics,
French, German, mathematics, music, and drawing; all these departments
being under the supervision of competent masters.

Under the auspices of the same Church there is also a Ladies' College,
in which several governesses labour with great assiduity.   The fees in both
these establishments are 1£. per month and upwards, according to the
number of subjects in which teaching is imparted.

"The Colonial School," under a master salaried by the Local Government,
is designed for families unequal to the expense of a first-class education.
There are not less than six private Protestant day-schools, kept by ladies
and gentlemen respectively, most of which are carefully superintended.

It is expected that in a short time a bill will pass the Legislature for the
establishment of what is known in Canada as a "Common-School System."
Under this desirable measure a tax will be levied upon the inhabitants for
the erection and support of schools, in which the children of all bona fide
settlers will be taught free of charge.

B. The Yukon

Ethnic Groups

Sessional Papers, Canada, 1900, no. 15: Report of Superintendent P. C. H. Primrose, North-West Mounted Police, Dawson District, November 30, 1899.

A census of the town, including West Dawson (on the opposite side of the river) and Klondike City, was taken, and Corporal Smith reports as follows: Total population, 4,445, composed of the following nationalities:

Arabia	1	Germany	46
Australia	25	Holland	1
Austria	4	Ireland	48
America, U.S.A.	3,205	Italy	9
Belgium	4	Indians	11
Canada	645	Japan	19
Denmark	3	Norway	25
China	1	Russia	4
England	208	Sweden	39
Finland	7	Scotland	69
France	65	Spain	5
Greece	1		

There are in Dawson 3,569 males and 786 females, including 163 children under fourteen years of age. This census includes West Dawson, Klondike City, and as far as the upper Ferry.

All persons having taken out first or second naturalization papers are shown as Americans.

Of these figures I have not much to say, except that they must be very much under the real numbers for the reason that the occupants of the hundreds of cabins are constantly going and coming. Men are pouring in and out of town from early morning until late at night, so that it would be next to impossible to get a correct census.

Communication with Outside World

Jeremiah Lynch, *Three Years in the Klondike* (London, 1904), pp. 37-40.

A week after my arrival I saw a great crowd at the principal street corner as I came down in the morning. A man clad in a dirty red shirt and high rubber boots stood on a waggon, and in loud, clear, and penetrating tones read, from a newspaper that had just arrived from up-river, an account of the battle and capture of Santiago. The throng cheered and cheered, and men whose faces had suffered no smile to be visible on days clasped hands with those standing near, while someone struck up "Marching through Georgia." To my surprise, the Britishers present, who were quite as demonstrative as the Americans, joined in the song, and appeared to know its music quite as well as my own countrymen. Afterwards I knew that the melody is an old English refrain.

The reader of the war extract, after finishing its perusal, announced that the rest of the paper would be read aloud in a hall nearby—admittance 1 dollar! In fifteen minutes the place was thronged at that price with 500 men, who patiently stood for over an hour while the enterprising owner read to them accidents, suicides, telegrams, advertisements, and all that go to make up the life of a Vancouver daily newspaper. For three weeks not one recent paper had appeared in Dawson, and in our sudden isolation the craving for news was as the craving for food. We had something besides mines to talk about for the rest of the day.

The next morning the mail, of which the paper had been the private precursor, arrived from the States and Canada. A line was formed in the afternoon extending 100 yards down the dusty street from the log-cabin post-office. The line was kept at an unvarying length by the constant arrival of miners who, hearing on the creeks that a mail had arrived, dropped pick and shovel, and hastened to Dawson with the hope of receiving letters from the loved ones at home. The post-office arrangements for delivery and distribution were abominable in those days. Ignorant and incompetent clerks delivered letters to the eager, anxious applicants from the two little windows in a slow and exasperating manner. . . .

There were no papers—only letters were brought down by the mail contractors; but newspapers, carried on the boats by private passengers, sold readily in Dawson for a dollar each. In two or three days they were collected again, sent up the creeks, and resold for 50 cents each, because they were a few days old in the Klondike. All were disposed of, and the bringing in of newspapers became quite an enterprise that fall and winter. When I bought a San Francisco paper for a dollar it was a delightful revelry for the whole evening. I began at the first page, and read every line, advertisements and all, and so on to the last word of the last line of the last page. Nothing escaped me, and I was therefore better informed of the doings of the world, for that day at least, than anyone in Frisco. I learned of businesses and affairs that I never knew before to have existed.

Newspapers

Tappan Adney, *The Klondike Stampede* (New York and London, 1900), pp. 422-5.

The first number of the *Yukon Midnight Sun* was issued on the 11th of June [1898]. It was a four-page, three-column (9 x 12 inch form) weekly, but was subsequently enlarged to a four-page paper of seven columns each. The subscription price was 50 cents per copy, or $15 per year. Its first Yukon number was published in the late winter at Caribou Crossing, its single issue there being the *Caribou Sun*. On the 16th of June appeared the *Klondike Nugget*, a particularly well-printed, four-page, four-column folio, issued semi-weekly, at 50 cents per copy, or $16 a year. Early in September appeared *The Klondike Miner*, a weekly. . . .

The first newspapers with war news [Spanish-American] brought whatever was asked. As it was known the news was for public reading, their owners did not make exorbitant demands, the highest price I knew of being $1. In April sixteen hundred newspapers, all several months old, were brought in by dog teams and sold for a $1 each. The new-comers brought boatloads of all the prominent daily, weekly, and monthly periodicals; magazines sold for a $1 and newspapers for 25 cents.

It sounded strangely out of place, in this erstwhile wilderness, to hear the newsboy, walking up and down the street, with a bunch of papers in his arms, shouting at the top of his voice, "Springfield *Republican*, Detroit *Free Press*, Chicago *Times-Herald*, Omaha *Bee*, Kansas City *Star*—all the daily papers!" even though they were from three weeks to a month old.

Establishment of a Social Club

The Klondike Nugget, Dawson, September 7, 1898.

A Club to be Organized

The leading business and professional men in Dawson are organizing a club. It is intended to erect a large and commodious building which will be equipped with everything requisite to the comfort and convenience of members. The gentlemen having the matter in charge at the present time are Messrs. Capt. Galpin, P. R. Ritchie and Dr. Dunn.

Organization of a Miners' Association

The Klondike Nugget, Dawson, September 7, 1898.

On Monday evening the Miners' Association of the Yukon Territory held a meeting and completed its organization by the adoption of a constitution and by-laws and the election of officers for the ensuing term ending June 30, 1899 . . . .

The constitution and by-laws as adopted appear in full below:

Name of Organization.—Miners' Association of Yukon Territory, headquarters, Dawson City.

Objects.—The objects of the Association shall be to provide for the welfare of the mining community and attend to the interests of its members, and to enlighten the government as to the needs of the district from the miners' point of view.

It shall endeavor to protect its members from any injustice of legislation.

It shall become an authentic source of reliable information concerning the country, so that mining laws for the future may be framed from intelligent knowledge.

It shall investigate any matter that is reported to it as being detrimental to the members as a body, or the mining industry, and extend its protection to members who may suffer loss through negligence, error or incompetence of the mining officials . . . .

Emergence of Educational Institutions

The Klondike Nugget, Dawson, September 7, 1898.

Miss Lulu Alice Craig desires the announcement made through the Nugget that she has opened a private school at the Church of England building.   All the elementary and grammar branches will be taught.

Changing Character of Society in Dawson

Jeremiah Lynch, *Three Years in the Klondike* (London, 1904), pp. 166-7, 179-83.

Dawson [by the autumn of 1899] was full of men and women.   To promenade Front Street on the river-front was like walking for a block or two in the Strand.   The street was sewered, macadamized, and side-walked. Shops with full stocks and plate-glass windows occupied the east side.   The west side consisted of wharves fronting the river.   Scores of handsome women sauntered up and down dressed in most appropriate costumes.   But one could see from their overbright eyes and carmine cheeks that they had been late overnights.   The number of modest and refined women was still scanty.   Wives and daughters were coming slowly.   Homes had to be provided, and the future of the husband fairly well assured, before he dared to send for his family.   Besides, people outside had such odd notions, both of Klondikers and the way they lived, that it took love and persuasion combined to induce women to come to the Far North.   These imaginary terrors were ultimately dispelled, and the next year Dawson supported two schools and three churches.   Still, it was not so bad as the winter of 1898, when an entertainment had been given at which an effort was made to exclude the undesirables.   One of the two papers in Dawson observed that, if this purpose was successfully accomplished, not enough would remain to form two quadrille sets, which, though a gross falsehood, and contemptible in its origin and author, nevertheless effected its malicious design in making us out worse than we were to the "outside." . . .

I had come to Dawson to enjoy a pleasant winter.   I knew that my mines were good, and would be quite productive next summer.   I was content with my coming to the country, and was resolved to have a good time. As I had lived at the mines all summer, I knew few women, and not many more men of the town.   But gradually I made acquaintances, and after a while gave a dinner to a few of my new friends. . . .

Other dinners followed, and a little later St. Andrew's ball.   There were more Scotsmen in Dawson that winter than all other British nationalities combined except the Canadians.   Scots and Swedes have always predominated in these Northern regions.   Everyone that could get the proper habiliments attended.   The town was ransacked for materials to make dresses and coats of the proper hue and cut.   Any woman who could cut and sew was employed either for herself or her friend, usually for both. Tailors sprang up like the men of Cadmus, and received preposterous sums for suits "made to order."

24

Dawson became suddenly a "society" city. Nothing but rubber boots, moccasins, and felt shoes, with accompaniments of flannel shirts and fur coats, had been in evidence since its foundation; but lo! it was "in the air" that those who did not go to the ball were out of the pale, and not among the elect and select. The committee in charge found themselves, indeed, on the horns of a dilemma in selecting the ladies, for there were those who wanted to go, and there were those who wouldn't go if the others went.

Now, in Dawson lived half a dozen women whose position and reputation were unassailable. These quietly assembled and constituted themselves a Vigilance Committee. All applications for ball tickets by ladies had to be submitted to them, or they would not go. If they did not go—well, the heavens might not fall, but the ball would fail. They did censor those applications mercilessly. No Grand Chamberlain of a Queen's levee scrutinized names more closely and made more inquiries—searching, remorseless inquiries—than did this Council of Six. . . .

Nevertheless, when the fateful night came, the number of ladies present at the entertainment was largely over a hundred, and Dawson plumed itself on possessing, in spite of the sifting process, so many beautiful and unexceptionable goddesses.

Quickly thereafter came the dinner of the ex-cadets of the Canadian Military School, which was a most finished and charming affair. Speeches were made, toasts drunk with good wine and plenty of it, and the table, with officers in military dress, looked like a banquet at the Hôtel Cecil.

We were becoming quite metropolitan. Meanwhile the telegraph wire was for ever breaking, the letter mail was exasperatingly slow and uncertain, and there was no newspaper mail. Some people went out over the ice, but very few came in, and, take it all in all, we were very nearly as completely isolated from the "outside" as in the preceding winter, despite the apparent progress in comfort and conveniences we had made. So we turned with energy to our local sports and pleasures, for we were, as we sometimes felt, banished from the world.

4. RELIGION AND RELIGIOUS INSTITUTIONS

A. British Columbia

Mining Population and Religion

R. C. Mayne, *Four Years in British Columbia and Vancouver Island* (London, 1862), p. 350.

By far the larger portion of the colonists are miners, who, though as yet their conduct since they arrived in British territory has been very praiseworthy, had previously been living for years in California, where the "Almighty Dollar" is the only object of worship. Apart from this, the very nature of the miner's life tends to ungodliness: he is perpetually roving about, in the morning rich, at sunset poor; to-day a gentleman—in the American sense of the term—to-morrow a labourer. For a few years some perhaps work with the notion of returning as rich men to their native land; but during that time the many fluctuations of the struggle, and the hard, wild life they lead, so unfit them for domestic existence, that, if they are fortunate enough to have made money and leave the country, they probably spend it all in the first large town they come to; or, reaching home, tire of it in a few months, and return to the life which has become second-nature to them. These miners, as I have said before, are by no means always uneducated; many men of good parentage and education are to be found among them, and this very fact renders the inculcation of religion more difficult than it otherwise would be.

Religious Institutions in Mining Interior

Matthew MacFie, *Vancouver Island and British Columbia* (London, 1865), pp. 414-15.

Society in the interior is very depraved. In Yale, Douglas, Lytton, Lillooet, Forks of Quesnelle, and the mining towns, little trace of Sunday is at present visible, except in the resort of miners on that day to market for provisions, washing of dirty clothes, repairing machinery, gambling, and dissipation. Out of the 5,000 souls in Victoria, a few may be found who respect the ordinances of religion. But at the mines, adherents of religious bodies have hitherto been numbered by scores and units.

Up to the present there have been but two places of worship in Cariboo —one connected with the Church of England, and the other with the Wesleyan Methodists. Till the fall of 1863, when these were built, the services of public worship were conducted in a bar-room and billiard-saloon. At one end of the apartment was the clergyman, with his small congregation, and at the other were desperadoes, collected unblushingly around the *faro* or *pokah* table, staking the earnings of the preceding week.

Profane language is almost universal, and is employed with diabolical ingenuity. The names of "Jesus Christ" and the "Almighty" are introduced in most blasphemous connections. Going to church is known among many as "the religious dodge," which is said to be "played out," or, in other words, a superstition which has ceased to have any interest for enlightened members of society.

Population Mobility and Problems of Church

Public Archives of Canada, *S.P.G. in F.P., Canada 1860-7:* Account of the Mission to Cariboo, 1862, by the Rev. C. Knipe.

The population of British Columbia and Vancouver Island, comparatively stationary during the winter months, becomes floating with the opening of the mining season. The movement commences with the Spring; and during April and May the towns lose more than half their population, while large arrivals from California and other places swell the tide of travel moving all in the one direction of Cariboo. Besides the actual miners, the number is of course considerably increased by traders, packers, cattle dealers, etc., not to mention less reputable and defined occupations. It thus becomes necessary that some of the clergy whose cures in the lower country have been in this manner thinned out, should follow the exodus, and do their best to keep up and enlarge the influence of the church amongst the people. . . .

Of course there are a good many material difficulties in the way. No church edifice and the consequent change of building is one of these. Not being able to have service in the same place, persons have sometimes a difficulty in learning the locality. . . . The want of Prayer books and Hymn books has been very successfully met by service cards and Hymn Cards, which can easily be brought up in sufficient number to supply the congregation. . . . We have hitherto been obliged to acquiesce in a state of things which limits our efforts chiefly to Sunday duty. It must however be remembered that at the mines Sunday Services are as much a novelty and an improvement for the better as additional week day services are in a more standing community. The evening weariness, and the evening occupations of cooking, mending clothes, preparing the tent or shanty for the night's rest, etc., are likely to be continuing obstructions. A building for worship, of decent and characteristic appearance, would be a very great advantage and probably the cost of erecting it might without difficulty be obtained by subscription on the spot. The argument, which has hitherto precluded such a step, is that the tide of mining may rapidly go on to another place and leave the church deserted: and in a place where there are no regular roads to travel by and no church going habits formed, the church service to be successful must be held in the very heart of the population.

In considering the work done at the mines this season, any one supposing that Cariboo could be worked like an English parish, would certainly be disappointed. Those however who were engaged in it have a happy conviction that their labour was not in vain, and feel that in the reception which they met with from the mixed population among which they moved, their success was greater than could have been expected. Men were not left to themselves; many were reminded of things forgotten; not a few heard the sounds of that Gospel from which in a life of wandering they had been banished for years. A precedent was established, so that we may hope that henceforth the Church's work and her services will be received not as a novelty or an intrusion but as a settled and expected order of things. The means of grace were afforded to men in the midst of all the temptation of an unsettled society; the sick were visited, the dying instructed and are comforted and the christian dead christianly buried.

Diversity of Nationalities

Public Archives of Canada, *S.P.G. in F.P., Canada 1860-7*: Victoria, May 8, 1860, Bishop of Columbia to Secretary, Society for the Propagation of the Gospel.

The population consists for the most part of emigrants from California, a strange mixture of all nations, most difficult to reach. A large proportion have been long unused to religious opportunities, although amongst them are those who will welcome the minister of Christ.

An idea of the mixture may be afforded by one instance, that of the Town of Douglas in British Columbia; out of 200, 35 only are British subjects. The rest are Germans, French, Italians, Africans, Chinese, Spaniards, Mexicans and Americans. . . .

The African settlers at present are not numerous. I have visited some. They are destitute entirely of the means of grace. Many men are living unmarried with Indian women.

Predominance of Males and Religious Destitution

The Daily British Colonist, March 14, 1861: Copy of letter written by the Bishop of Columbia to Miss Burdett Coutts from Cayoosh, B.C., July 14, 1860.

The miners are a fine hardy race of men; they are of all nations—Germans, Americans, French, Italians, Swedes, Norwegian, Chinese, as well as English. The latter are the fewest of all. There is an utter absence of religion, and much awful vice and profanity abounds.

I make a practice of speaking to everybody I meet, and I am often, alas! compelled to hear in common talk the most profane language. This I always reprove, and have generally found my remarks taken well.

Whenever I have had services the miners have attended, and several here have told me that they had not for 10 or 14 years attended a religious service. How thankful one is to have the privilege of first bearing to these our fellow-men the renewed opportunities of grace! . . .

The great drawback to the wholesome progress of society is the dearth of female population. I suppose there is not one to every 200 of the other sex. I came upon a pleasing exception the other day at Hill's Bar. I was visiting the miners. One log hut seemed more neat than the rest. As we approached, a modest-looking young woman asked us to come in. She was from the North of Ireland, a Protestant, and had married in Australia. There was something simple and touching in her manner. I entered upon the subject of religion; she loved to attend church, and had been piously brought up by her parents, whose custom was to have family prayer night and morning. Her father was still living. She was very lonely, and had no female society. One other there was, but her character was such she could not associate with her.

Religious Indifference of Miners

(i)

Public Archives of Canada, *S.P.G. in F.P.*, *Canada 1860-7:* Douglas, July 3, 1863, the Rev. James Gammage to Secretary, Society for the Propagation of the Gospel.

The resident population of the parish of Douglas remains much the same, in most respects, as it was last year: there is but little response made to the efforts of the Clergyman to kindle and keep alive a spirit of devotion among the people: our Sunday services are but scantily attended, and the administration of the Lord's Supper is impracticable. Hitherto I have been sustained in my work by the hope that in time I should succeed in gathering to the Church in this remote colony a congregation of sincere Christian worshippers, but the obstacles are very great, opposing prejudices are deeply rooted, and above all, the prevailing immorality is so fearful, that but for reliance upon the Divine promise that God's word "shall not return unto Him void, but it shall accomplish that which He pleases" the attempt might be abandoned, as altogether hopeless.

(ii)

Public Archives of Canada, *S.P.G. in F.P., Canada 1860-7:* Victoria, November 5, 1863, the Rev. James Gammage to Secretary, Society for the Propagation of the Gospel.

In reference to religion, affairs in my parish are not cheering: the utmost that I could do on this occasion was to hold three public services at different points of the route [to the outlying districts], the attendance at each of them being but scanty, and an occasional domestic service.

Type of Clergymen Required

The Daily British Colonist, Victoria, October 11, 1860: Occasional Papers; Letter from the Bishop of British Columbia to Commissary Garrett, London, January 13, 1860.

How important is our work. The Church of England here is in a feeble state. Had it been left long so, it would almost have been trampled out. Mr. Cridge, Chaplain under the Hudson's Bay Company, the only Clergyman, previous to the endowment of this Bishopric, is an excellent good man, but has been burdened overmuch with work. Consequently, Dissenting Chapels are rising up. There is a Methodist Church, ecclesiastical, with a tower and spire, nearly completed, built, I understand mainly by subscription of Church people! There are also two other Chapels, being the fruits of a split already between two Congregationalists. There is a Roman Catholic Church, with a bishop, priests, and nuns. . . . There is no use having any man out here who is not an effective preacher; better without him unless so gifted. The class of men required are those of forcible character, gifted in the same way; each one must also be, without mistake, an earnest man, a soul-loving man. Too many, alas! seek the colonies because they do not get on in England. They have much less prospect of getting on here. The class attracted as colonists to a country like this is remarkable for shrewdness and special abilities. The congregation I am preaching to every Sunday here contains a larger proportion of shrewd, thinking, intelligent, educated gentlemen than any in England out of London. It is a remarkable sight; five-sixths are men. The Church holds 400 and is quite full. If the proper proportions of women and children were filled up, it would be utterly too small. I am most thankful we are here so early in the field.

Need for Increased Assistance

Public Archives of Canada, *S.P.G. in F.P.*, *Canada 1860-7:* Victoria, July 7, 1865,
Bishop of Columbia to Secretary, Society for the Propagation of the Gospel.

I hope earnestly the Society will be able to increase our Grant.

These two colonies are in that Infant stage of a mining district subject to great fluctuations. The chief part of the white population are of a different nationality from that of the Motherland, and just now we are passing through a period of commercial depression.

Such circumstances give an unsettled character to the people and render it difficult if not impossible to get assistance.

No less than three towns where churches, and in two cases where Parsonages were built are now deserted.

Other places spring up suddenly into prominence. Cariboo, Koutenais, the Columbia and Leach mining districts—the three former from 300 to 500 miles away and most expensive to live in have no regular ministrations and yet thousands move to and fro in those localities whose souls should have the spiritual care of our Church.

Inroads of Wesleyans upon Church of England

Public Archives of Canada, *S.P.G. in F.P.*, *Canada 1860-7:* Nanaimo, B.C.,
January 6, 1861, the Rev. J. B. Good to Secretary, Society for the
Propagation of the Gospel.

Formerly a large proportion of the white population belonged nominally to the church, but some three years ago the Wesleyans obtained a footing here: considerable grants of land etc. were made them and by energetic labours they gathered many of these neglected wanderers into their fold: whilst many others alas! have been allowed to sink into a state of complete heathenism.

Since however the church has been established the attendance has been steadily increasing and the good effects of her teaching and Pastoral care are freely acknowledged on every side.

During the winter I have been carrying on a series of cottage services, carrying the Gospel of the Church, so to speak, into the very Household of many who frequent not the House of God—they appear to have been greatly blessed.

Competition between Wesleyans and Anglicans

(i)

The Daily British Colonist, Victoria, March 14, 1861: Copy of letter written by the Bishop of Columbia to Miss Burdett Coutts from Cayoosh, B.C., July 14, 1860.

The Church of England is alone in the field. Not a representative of any other religious body is yet among the miners. At two places, Hope and Yale, there was a Methodist minister, but he has been withdrawn. We have two clergymen in those towns, both of whom are working well.

(ii)

The Daily British Colonist, Victoria, March 20, 1861: The Rev. E. Evans, Superintendent of Wesleyan Missions in Vancouver Island and British Columbia, to Editor, March 16, 1861.

It is utterly incorrect to state that the Methodist Minister "has been withdrawn" from Hope and Yale. Nor was the statement justifiable at the date of his letter. He knows that the economy of Methodism occasions periodical exchange of stations by its ministers; and if, as was the fact, those places were unsupplied for a somewhat longer period than usual, because my own health required the temporary assistance of the appointed and now resident Minister, prior to his proceeding to his new appointment, his Lordship had no right to lay hold of that fact to aim a blow in England at Methodism. . . .

Were I disposed to retort, I might furnish the English public with *facts* concerning his Lordship's diocese, which he has thought it politic to conceal. He surely knows that there has been no minister "withdrawn" in British Columbia, *except one of his own clergy,* although, at the expense of the Crown a commodious church and parsonage had been built for him, and are still standing at the deserted post. Nor can he be unaware, if he has truthful informants, that the Methodist Missionaries were the first Protestant Clergy who visited Hope and Yale,—that a Methodist Parsonage was erected and occupied at Hope, prior to the advent of "Anglican Priests,"—that the congregations of the Methodist Clergymen there have been from the beginning, and are still much larger than those of the Preachers under his jurisdiction,—that the Methodist Missionaries have been indefatigable in their labors among the miners on the river,—and that one of them has visited and preached at the Similkameen mines, a point not yet reached by any of his agents.

I have not drawn invidious comparisons in my correspondence with England or Canada, and would have been spared from doing it now. I have not informed the British public that his Lordship's sympathy for the miners of the upper country has a strange mode of displaying itself. That while he mourns over their destitution, he retains *five* of his clergy in Victoria, keeps *two* at New Westminster, and that *three* others are stationed at places supplied by Methodist Ministers previously to their arrival.

Conflict between Catholic and Anglican Churches

The Daily British Colonist, Victoria, October 11, 1860: Occasional Papers; Letter from the Bishop of British Columbia to Commissary Garrett, London, March 14, 1860.

The Roman Catholic Bishop Demas has not seemed pleased at the cordial reception I have met with, and in consequence voted against the Government at the election. I imagine he has incensed his people against me. I have had to endure little inconveniences, in the stoppage of my supply of milk, and other trivial matters. I think it likely I may have trouble with the Romanists.   At present they are not strong.   They are, however, forward in the matter of education, both in the cases of boys and girls.

Local Hostility to Church of England

The Daily British Colonist, Victoria, April 10, 1861:   Editorial.

There is no disguising the fact; there is a sore place in this community, created by Dr. Hill's squatting on the Church Reserve.   The irritation is not caused generally by any feeling of sectarian hostility nor any desire to humiliate the Episcopal Church; but from a firm conviction that the reserve was public property, was set apart for public uses, was intended for a public square, was to be kept for a public breathing-place; and finding that it has been surreptitiously appropriated for a private garden and private residence for the local head of the Anglican Church, it need be no matter of surprise that the smothered indignation of the populace should occasionally be heard.

Social Status and Religious Affiliation

(i)

Public Archives of Canada, *S.P.G. in F.P.*, *Canada 1860-7:* Victoria, November 5, 1863, the Rev. J. Gammage to Secretary, Society for the Propagation of the Gospel.

There are two excellent congregations [here], comprehending the wealthy and educated of the colony.

(ii)

Matthew MacFie, *Vancouver Island and British Columbia* (London, 1865), p. 417.

The sentiment of "pure and undefiled religion" does not flourish at present in the colonies.   In the Protestant world on the Pacific coast, the religious sect to which a man is attached may commonly be determined by the extent of his business.   Small retailers and mechanics swarm among the Methodists; jobbers, who break packages, and the larger class of store-keepers, frequent the Presbyterian and Congregational chapels; and the bankers, lawyers, and wholesale dealers prefer the Church of England. Just as with their augmented resources they erect comfortable houses, so they seek to provide themselves with a church suited to their advanced social position.   The utilitarian tendencies of the people are such, that eloquent or spiritual preaching by itself will not attract worshippers.   Their comfort must be consulted, as it respects the place of worship erected, and their emotions must be appealed to through the medium of an organ and an efficient choir.

Religious scepticism prevails to a remarkable extent, as it does in all new countries.   I have known cases in which Christian pastors have been turned away from the bedside of the dying colonist, and forbidden by him either to offer prayer to Almighty God for his restoration to health, or administer the consolations of the Gospel.   But I trust such cases of extreme obduracy are not common.

Racial Prejudice and Religion

The Daily British Colonist, Victoria, October 11, 1860: Occasional Papers; Letter from the Bishop of British Columbia to Commissary Garrett, London, March 14, 1860.

There has been a sharp contention on the question of colour; the Americans, requiring that the coloured people should not be allowed to occupy the same place with them in worship. One Independent Minister, a Mr. McFye, favored their unchristian narrowness; another maintained the English principle, that there should be no difference in the house of God. He has, however, been overthrown by the Society in London who maintained him, the "British Colonial Missionary Society." Mr. Clark nobly upheld the Christian and English sentiment, but his patrons have decided against him, and he has to leave the place; he seems a very respectable man, too good for his employers.

B. The Yukon

Sabbath Observance on Mining Creeks

Stratford Tollemache, *Reminiscences of the Yukon* (Toronto, 1912), p. 69.

The law of observing the Sabbath was not enforced during the earlier years in the Klondike, as the mine-owners were much too busy scooping in gold to enable them to afford a weekly day of rest to the labourers, so the work continued on Sundays exactly the same as on week-days.

The Law and Sabbath Observance

Sessional Papers, Canada, 1899, no. 13: Report of Major J. M. Walsh on the Yukon District.

It has been a matter of gratification to me to note the law-abiding and orderly character of the permanent and transient residents of Dawson and the district generally. All have evinced an earnest desire to obey and uphold the law. I found, however, on the first Sunday after my arrival at Dawson that while order was preserved as usual, the general week-day business was continued. I deemed it highly improper that the Sabbath should be desecrated, and at once gave orders for its due observance in accordance with the statutes in that behalf, and since that time the Sabbath has been quite as well observed as it is in the older towns east.

Salvation Army

R. A. Bankson, *The Klondike Nugget* (Caldwell, Idaho, 1935), p. 155: News item in *Klondike Nugget*, June 28, 1898.

SALVATION FREE

Adjutant Dowell and party of seven of the Salvation Army reached Dawson Saturday, at 12 o'clock. It made the Nugget man think of home to see the well known uniforms, and there are probably few in Dawson but who felt the same way.   In the number were two ladies, and, though looking tired with the journey, their faces were quite cheerful.

Religious Institutions in Dawson

(i)

Mary Lee Davis, *Sourdough Gold: The Log of a Yukon Adventure* (Boston, 1933), pp. 121-2.

I suppose that to any gently reared person, Dawson in '98 and '99 would seem a city horribly wicked and depraved, probably more so than any spot on earth inhabited by white men at that moment.   Morality was set at defiance and shame was generally lacking.   It's true that shooting, fighting, stealing, and rowdyism were not tolerated, even where there were no officers of the law; but the governing powers had set their seal of approval upon vice. And yet religion flourished side by side with vice, almost every denomination being represented.   The Roman Catholics had a really splendid log church, lined inside with snow-white canvas, with well-made pews and altar, and with a chime of bells, an organ, and a good choir.   The Presbyterians, Church of England, Methodists, and Salvation Army were also comfortably housed in log-cabin structures.   The Salvation Army were a fine lot of men. I knew their captain and esteemed him highly.   Their main work was in being charitable, and they seemed never to rest from their labors.   I never heard them adversely criticized and they were praised by the whole community.   They were even welcome at the saloons and often knelt for prayer in the coldest weather, out in the open.   They provided work for the needy, food for the destitute.   They had no ulterior motives and won a tribute of high commendation from a crowd of men in whom sympathy for good works might not have been expected.

(ii)

Tappan Adney, *The Klondike Stampede* (New York and London, 1900), pp. 428-9.

Besides the Jesuits already spoken of, several religious bodies established missions for work among the miners.   The Presbyterians, under Rev. Hall Young, built a church in the fall of 1897, the upper story of which was cut into rooms and rented to lodgers, but it was destroyed early in the winter by fire.   The Church of England, under Rev. R. G. Bowen, built a church in the summer of 1898.   The Christian-Endeavorers and the familiar Salvation Army held daily meetings in the open during summer.   The attendance at the missions seemed so small in so large a population as that of Dawson as to incline one to the prevailing opinion that among miners of the class of whom prospectors are made religious work finds not much place, unless accompanied by work for their physical as well as moral well-being.

V

TRANSCONTINENTAL RAILWAYS AND INDUSTRIAL-
CAPITALIST SOCIETY

THE construction of the Canadian Pacific Railway, the exploitation of the mineral resources of the Kootenay, and the gold rush to the Yukon paved the way for the rapid economic expansion in Canada after 1900. Manufacturing industries which had survived the long depression of the seventies and eighties by means of protection secured through the National Policy and by combination and price control responded quickly to new developments taking place after the turn of the century. The enormous demands made by gold mining in the Yukon for capital and consumers' goods promoted industrial expansion and the establishment of new manufacturing plants, while the considerable movement of population into the North West resulting from the gold rush contributed to the settlement of the prairies, and the expansion of wheat-farming in turn led to still greater demands for manufactured commodities. The building of two new transcontinental railways reflected the buoyant prospects of manufacturing and wheat-farming, and metal mining in Northern Ontario developed largely as a by-product of these railway undertakings. The emergence of the pulp and paper industry emphasized the importance of the new northern frontier, while the daily newspaper which this industry made possible increased the extent of urban concentration and metropolitan control.[1] Expansion into new frontiers in Canada after 1900 took place through the leadership of dominant industrial and financial centres, particularly Montreal and Toronto. The enlarged scope of financial organizations, improved techniques of transportation and production, and new sources of power made possible a diversity in the nature of economic activities and in the kind of resources brought under exploitation. The great number of new frontiers—manufacturing, agricultural, mining, lumbering, pulp and paper, and fishing—which emerged after the turn of the

[1]H. A. Innis, "Economic Nationalism," *Papers and Proceedings of the Canadian Political Science Association*, vol. VI, 1934.

century was indicative of the wide sweep of industrial-capitalist expansion. Problems of social organization in various Canadian communities were evidence of the disturbing effects of such expansion.

To the extent that these problems were associated with the development of industrial manufacturing and the rise of cities they were not strikingly different from those found in such older industrialized countries as Great Britain, Germany, and the United States. Canada shared in technological improvements in the use of iron and steel which led to far-reaching changes in processes of production and in methods of transportation, and the effects of such developments upon social organization tended to be much the same throughout the western world. The fact that industrial entrepreneurship and organization extended into Canada from Britain and the United States gave her the advantage of the experiences of these countries. A considerable familiarity with the nature of the problems of industrialism was secured even before these problems had appeared in Canadian communities. But if Canada profited some from the experiences of her neighbours, vested interests operated as an effectual check to the easy diffusion of ideas from outside. The claim, as made for instance by manufacturers with respect to problems of labour, that conditions were different in Canada retarded the acceptance of social policies successful elsewhere. The result was that problems even when not distinctive to Canada required solutions which could only be fashioned out of the raw materials of Canadian experience. However, the most crucial problems were distinctive to Canada in that the particular character they assumed resulted from a great variety of economic developments rather than from the development of industrial manufacturing by itself. The opening of the West and the exploitation of the pulp and mineral resources of the Precambrian Shield accompanied the growth of manufacturing in the Central Provinces, and it was this combination of economic developments which gave to the industrial-capitalist society of Canada its distinctive character. A purely urban society did not emerge in Central Canada; nor did a purely agricultural society grow up in Western Canada. Metropolitanism became a dominant feature of Canadian community organization, but it was a metropolitanism in terms not of one economic interest but of a great variety of such interests, and the way in which these interests were related to one another determined the distinctive pattern of social development.

It was this fact, furthermore, which sharply set off developments in Canada after the turn of the century from developments which had taken place before. Urbanization as such was not something which began at any particular time; Montreal, Quebec, Halifax, and Toronto grew into substantial cities during the nineteenth century, and, if Montreal and Toronto (together with Hamilton and Winnipeg) forged ahead more rapidly after 1900, the growth of the twentieth century was a continuation of that of the nineteenth. Similarly manufacturing had grown up throughout the whole of the nineteenth century, and by 1870 many of the towns along the Grand Trunk Railway from Montreal to Sarnia had become important industrial centres. But it was not until the end of the century that urbanization and industrialization joined forces, and industrial concentration—and industrial cities— became a dominant feature of Canadian life.[2] This development was made possible by the sudden opening up of new resources of industrial-capitalism—in the West and the North—which called for large-scale organization and mass production in manufacturing. The new industrial-capitalist society was one associated with the extension of metropolitan organization into fields of economic exploitation stretching across the whole of Canada. Thus the problems of Canadian communities after 1900 were not simply the problems of the preceding century on a grander scale. New forces combined to give rise to distinctively new social developments, in urban and rural communities alike; an examination of problems of social welfare, crime, morality, cultural organization, and religion serves to emphasize this fact.

Immigration in large numbers from overseas, expansion of manufacturing enterprises, and the rapid growth of urban communities after 1900 resulted in new problems of social welfare associated with the slum, overcrowding, and poverty. The opening up of new farming, mining, and lumbering frontiers made possible the absorption of that surplus labour which possessed the character of mobility, but within the recesses of the cities there accumulated

[2]S. D. Clark, *The Canadian Manufacturers' Association: A Study in Collective Bargaining and Political Pressure* (Toronto, 1939); W. J. A. Donald, *A History of the Iron and Steel Industry* (Boston, 1915).

a growing number of people who possessed neither the desire nor the ability to move. The city selected the failures out of the streams of overseas immigrants and out of the armies of industrial workers recruited by, and often ill-paid within, the factory.[3] Even the extractive frontier industries, though absorbing increasing numbers of workers, contributed to social dependency, overcrowding, and the development of slums when seasonal unemployment resulted in the drifting of unattached and homeless men to the city to spend the winter. The rural background of a large section of the urban population, and the exaggerated view of the potentialities of western expansion, led to a failure to appreciate the nature and extent of the social effects of industrialization and urban growth. It is true that the period before 1913 was one of unbounded prosperity, and the demands made upon social welfare agencies were not overwhelming, but the feeling of security to which these buoyant prospects gave rise accounted for the failure to do anything about those very real problems which emerged independently of, and in some cases conditioned by, prosperity. Straitened financial resources, a reliance upon obsolete techniques of charity, and an almost complete lack of trained workers were characteristics of institutions of social welfare before the Great War.

Similar factors gave rise to new forms of crime and explain the failure of law enforcement agencies to deal adequately with this problem. Crime inevitably accompanied the process of assimilation of immigrant groups and infractions of the criminal code were particularly evident among second-generation immigrants where social and personal disorganization extended furthest. It was within the community structure, however, that the chief factors determining the extent and nature of crime were to be found. In some respects, Canadian institutions of law and order escaped disorganizing forces evident in the United States. The influence of the West in regard to crime was very different in the two countries. Though an interval of general disorder occurred between the passing of the control of the Hudson's Bay Company in 1871 and the organization of the North West Mounted Police in 1874, and immigration and railway-building provided points of disturbance throughout the period of development before 1914, the vigi-

[3]*Annals of the American Academy of Political and Social Science*, Philadelphia, May, 1923.

lance of the Mounted Police and the predominantly British background of the population checked the growth of crime in the Canadian West, and the habit of carrying fire-arms evident in many western American communities never developed; here neither the Indian nor the desperado was a continual threat to the life of the settler. Again, the larger Canadian cities were more sheltered than were the American cities from any undesirable influence the West might have exerted; the Great Lakes and Precambrian Shield provided an effective barrier to close and constant intercourse. The result was that organized crime in Canada emerged almost wholly out of conditions within local urban communities and from the influence of the larger American cities. If this meant a slower growth of the more elaborate forms of crime, the development of improved techniques of dealing with the criminal was similarly retarded. Though the British heritage, and the dominantly rural background of the population in the cities, had the effect of making law enforcement agencies highly effective in the apprehension and conviction of criminal offenders, the nature of the problem of urban crime required new tools of reformation and, in the forging of these, judicial agencies in Canada lagged behind those of other countries. The necessity of paying greater attention to the character of the criminal and less attention to the nature of the crime, and of devising improved methods of treating criminal offenders, was only slowly realized by Canadian judicial authorities. The effects of this lag were evident with respect to crime in general, but it was most seriously felt with respect to the particular problem of juvenile delinquency. Juvenile delinquency was almost wholly peculiar to the city. Conditions of urban life greatly restricted the scope of parental controls while increasing immensely the variety of activities indulged in by children, and only slowly did there arise agencies to meet the needs of the juvenile population and new methods of treatment in dealing with juvenile criminal offenders. To the extent that public recreational facilities failed to be developed to offset the loss of those means of recreation which had been provided within the rural environment, the child was forced to place dependence upon street play-groups and gangs. On the other side, to the extent that there was a failure to distinguish between juvenile delinquents and adult criminals, within the police-court and penal institutions, the child was subjected to the demoralizing influence of traditional methods in the treatment of crime. The establishment of reformatory institutions after 1860 was a recognition of the desirability of classifying prisoners, but such institutions did little in the way of improving methods of punishing or reforming juvenile offenders. The distinction between the juvenile and adult in methods of determining guilt and of reformation came only with the establishment of juvenile courts and with legislation dealing with juvenile delinquency; the next logical step of abandoning the distinction between socially dependent and delinquent children, though increasingly made within social welfare institutions, was retarded by the constitutional rigidities of a federal system where social dependency was a provincial and crime a Dominion matter. In the field of prevention, reform efforts consisted largely of the public playground movement and the establishment of juvenile and youth organizations chiefly under church leadership. Distinct advances were made in both directions, but vested interests, particularly of old established institutions, and public indifference checked the introduction of fundamental changes. Ultimately, attacks upon methods of dealing with juvenile delinquency involved an attack upon methods of dealing with crime in general, and here traditional interests offered more determined resistance. Though the work of voluntary associations such as the Salvation Army, and the appointment of royal commissions to enquire into penal methods, were indicative of the growing appreciation of the nature of the problem among certain sections of the community, eventual reform awaited more wide-spread changes in public attitudes.[4]

Developments in Canada after 1900 provided new points of disturbance to the moral order. As in most rural frontiers, no serious problems of morality emerged in the rapidly expanding wheat-growing communities of Western Canada, but in other areas which came into prominence after the turn of the century such problems tended to become wide-spread. Extractive industries grew up along the Precambrian Shield or within the mountain valleys of British Columbia, and here the predominance of males led to a weakening of *mores* associated with family life. The disintegration of moral standards which resulted from adjustments of such a large, purely male, population was not confined to these

[4]C. W. Topping, *Canadian Penal Institutions* (Toronto, 1929).

25

frontier communities. The chief centres of mining, lumbering, or of the pulp and paper industry were to be found in areas which skirted the thickly-populated communities of Central Canada or which reached back from the urban communities on the Pacific Coast. The presence of these male-populated centres within short railway distance of Montreal, Toronto, Winnipeg, or Vancouver constituted one of the most distinctive features of urban society in Canada and accounted in large part for the particular character of moral problems. Workers engaged in the outlying industries found their way readily into one of the cities, particularly during winter months; professional prostitutes serving the needs of a purely male population passed backwards and forwards between cities and centres in the hinterland. Vice suppression in the cities intensified the moral problems of the hinterland, while suppression in the hinterland intensified the problems of the cities. In addition to such influences, moral standards in Canadian cities were subject to the various disorganizing effects of rapid urban growth. The strains upon family organization, particularly of immigrant groups, resulting from the new conditions of life, the greater opportunities for sexual licence made possible by the breakdown of neighbour-hood controls, and the demoralizing effects of starvation wages in marginal industries and service occupations, were evident in the increase of desertion, illegitimacy, and prostitution.

The predominantly rural background of the Canadian urban population checked effective movements of reform. Most of the immigration to Canada after 1900 came from European peasant districts, and, by segregation, the immigrants who settled in the city clung tenaciously to the strict *mores* which they brought with them. The rural-urban movement of population within Canada resulted in a similar transference of *mores* from an environment to which they were adapted to one to which they were not. The recruitment by Canadian cities of a peasant or rural population secured strong supports for traditional moral standards, but it retarded the adjustment of those standards to the new conditions of urban life. Puritanical moral controls within the family and com-munity involved the heavy price of failing to meet some of the most crucial social problems of urban society. Prostitution, venereal disease, and illegitimacy taxed the resources of welfare and medical agencies so long as the first was treated as a crime and the other two as just punishments for sin. Reliance upon police controls and social ostracism served only to drive prostitution underground and to shroud the whole subject of sex under a veil of ignorance; commercialized vice, venereal disease, and illegitimacy rapidly increased in situations where even the discussion of sexual problems was strictly tabooed. These particular forms of social disorganization were part of the much larger problem of adjustment of moral standards in the urban community. The law, custom, and formal organization of Canadian cities were only slowly adapted to meet the new demands of urban life upon the individual and family group.

The development of industrial-capitalism, urban growth, and the appearance of new outlying frontiers imposed heavy strains upon cultural organization. A Canadian proletariat grew rapidly as manufacturing extended throughout Central Canada, and for a considerable interval agencies such as trade-union organizations were lacking to secure the social status of this class in the community.[5] Conflicts of interest between employers and workers were typical of strains in cultural organization resulting from social divisions along economic, regional, ethnic, or religious lines. The increase in value of real-estate property in certain sections of the city, and building restrictions secured by property owners jealous of the advantages of exclusiveness, made possible a segregation of social classes which had been impossible in rural communities. The settlement of immigrant peoples in isolated groups accentuated the tendency for a number of cultural islands to develop in the city sharply separated from one another. Natural areas emerged in terms of processes of urban growth, and the boundaries of these areas coincided with cultural boundaries imposing strict limitations upon social intercourse.[6] Consciousness of community lagged behind the erection of the urban physical structure, and community services rested upon no solid basis of collective sentiment. Efforts of those institutions which sought to develop a realization of common interests were offset by the activities of those institutions which emphasized cultural differences within the population.

[5]H. A. Logan, *The History of Trade-Union Organization in Canada* (Chicago, 1928).

[6]L. G. Reynolds, *The British Immigrant: His Social and Economic Adjustment in Canada* (Toronto, 1935).

Even those institutions which presumably existed to serve the total community—churches, fraternal societies, and certain welfare organizations—recognized the reality of social divisions, and, indeed, tended to maintain such divisions, by organizing along class or ethnic lines. Cultural conflicts secured accommodation within the institutional structure, but these conflicts made impossible any sort of real integration in the total social organization of the urban community.

Cultural strains resulting from metropolitan expansion and urban growth extended into the rural hinterland of Central and Eastern Canada. The movement of population from the country to the city presented rural districts with problems of depopulation and a serious lack of leadership. There was no longer felt the invigorating influence of new population elements, and in some communities isolation led to a degree of inbreeding dangerous to the physical and cultural welfare of the inhabitants.[7] To some extent, closer contacts with the city, made possible by the automobile and the radio, served to offset the effects of the drain of the city upon the rural population. Rural organizations developed to capitalize upon the advantages of increased communication with the outside world and, at the same time, to assert the distinctiveness of the rural way of life. There was implied in the rise of such movements a realization of the threat of metropolitan expansion (in the form, for instance, of the tourist trade) to the rural culture. In areas where vigorous leadership was lacking, the rural culture suffered either through isolation or through the dominance of the nearby urban centres.

In the northern and western frontier areas of development, problems of cultural organization were very different. The absence of family life, and a concentration upon a single economic interest, had the effect of weakening cultural interests in the mining, pulp and paper, and lumbering communities of northern Quebec, Ontario, and the interior of British Columbia. Trade-union organizations made little headway, and the most active form of cultural association was to be found in nationalist groups. Fraternal societies, libraries, and educational institutions were erected only with the establishment of family life. In Western Canada, the

[7] G. A. Kidd, "A Sociological Survey of an Ontario Rural Community," Master of Arts thesis, University of Toronto, 1936.

rapid growth of population, the settlement of large blocks of land by immigrants unacquainted with the English language and Canadian customs, and the concentration of people upon the task of making a living from wheat-growing made difficult the creation of cultural institutions adequate to serve the needs of the community.[8] The segregation of ethnic groups, in particular, limited social intercourse and weakened organizations depending upon the active participation of the members of the whole community.[9] Social clubs, libraries, and other cultural institutions grew up slowly in the prairie towns and rural districts. More serious still was the problem of providing elementary education to the large school-age population. The scattered nature of settlement, the lack of trained teachers, and the indifference to education of the foreign and of some of the English-speaking settlers were obstacles to the establishment of educational institutions.[10] The considerable use of cash, however, in an agricultural region where wheat was the chief staple made possible the rapid accumulation of financial resources to support public schools, and an increasing number of trained teachers were recruited from Eastern Canada as large salaries made teaching an attractive profession. Problems of education, and of cultural leadership generally, persisted in those areas where poor soil made farming a marginal industry or where foreign groups remained isolated from the English-speaking community. Throughout the prairies, the occurrence of drought seasons or sharp declines in the price of wheat resulted in placing heavy strains upon cultural institutions.[11]

Other cultural problems evident in Canada since the Great War had already become apparent before 1914. The shift of the flow of the surplus labour force of rural Quebec from industrial centres in the United States to industrial centres within the province itself involved far-reaching adjustments in the cultural institutions

[8]Cf. C. A. Dawson and Eva R. Younge, *Pioneering in the Prairie Provinces: The Social Side of the Settlement Process* (Toronto, 1940).

[9]C. A. Dawson, *Group Settlement: Ethnic Communities in Western Canada* (Toronto, 1936); Robert England, *The Colonization of Western Canada* (London, 1936).

[10]Marion Deverell, "The Ukrainian Teacher as an Agent in the Assimilation Process," Master of Arts thesis, University of Toronto, 1941; J. T. M. Anderson, *The Education of the New Canadian* (Toronto, 1918).

[11]G. E. Britnell, *The Wheat Economy* (Toronto, 1939).

of French Canada and raised new problems of conflict in the relationship of French and English peoples.[12] The growing importance
of the northern mining and pulp and paper frontiers in the economy
and politics of Central Canada hardened tendencies of regionalism
in Canadian national life.   The development of manufacturing in
western Canadian cities, and rural-urban migration, had effects
upon the older settled rural prairie districts, particularly Manitoba, similar to those which had become pronounced in Central and
Eastern Canada.   These and other problems were evidence of the
continual emergence of new points of disturbance in Canadian
cultural life.   On the other hand, much had been accomplished by
1914 in the way of adjustment to conditions thrown up by industrial-
capitalist expansion after the turn of the century.   Trade-union
movements in Central Canada and farm movements in Western
Canada were typical of the sort of solutions being attained on the
cultural level.   More significantly still, the strengthening of
national sentiment was indicative of far-reaching adjustments to
the metropolitan organization of industrial-capitalism.   The
nation emerged as something of a cultural focus in Canadian
community life; national associations with headquarters in one of
the larger cities and regional offices across the country provided a
type of leadership in keeping with the demands of the new
metropolitan economy.[13]

Industrialization and expansion into the West and North
widened the field of religious institutions and called for the development of radically new methods of organization and of new sorts
of appeals.   Churches organized on a national basis had grown up
by the turn of the century and were much better equipped as a
result than the earlier colonial denominations to meet the needs of
rapidly growing and distant communities.   The establishment of
mission stations in Western Canada was evidence of efforts to
extend the field of religious ministrations.[14]   By 1900 leaders of

[12]Cf. E. C. Hughes, "Industry and the Rural System in Quebec," *Canadian
Journal of Economics and Political Science*, August, 1938; also, E. C. Hughes and
Margaret L. McDonald, "French and English in the Economic Structure of
Montreal," *ibid.*, November, 1941.

[13]H. F. Angus, ed., *Canada and Her Great Neighbour* (Toronto, 1938), chap. x.

[14]C. C. McLaurin, *Pioneering in Western Canada: A Story of the Baptists*
(1939); E. H. Oliver, *The Winning of the Frontier* (Toronto, 1930); Dawson and
Younge, *Pioneering in the Prairie Provinces*.

most of the religious denominations had been thoroughly schooled in the needs of a rural society, and lessons learnt from experiences in older agricultural communities proved useful when the church moved into the western rural frontier.   Yet many shortcomings in religious organization and appeal quickly became apparent in efforts to serve the scattered prairie settlements devoted to the raising of wheat.   Denominational rivalry prevented effective co-operation, and centres of population were provided with far more churches than they required while isolated areas were left without regular services of any sort.[15] Dominance by eastern interests in the councils of the churches, moreover, checked the development of an aggressive policy of championing the interests of western farmers.   Unlike the evangelical sects of earlier Canadian rural frontiers which owed no close allegiance to any outside body and which could therefore crystallize in their religious appeal the political dissatisfactions of the population, the churches in Western Canada found it necessary to avoid any close identification with economic or political interests.   The failure to associate with powerful farm movements involved an immediate loss of influence in the western prairie communities and, in some instances, ultimately led to the emergence of new religious movements which combined their religious appeal with an appeal to economic and political dissatisfactions.

The failure of the church to align itself with new occupational interests and marginal social groups was even more conspicuous in the growing Canadian cities and their industrial hinterlands.   The fact that urban communities in Canada inherited a culture largely agrarian in its origin enabled the churches to maintain an appearance of strength.   But many of their most faithful followers were people who had moved from rural areas, and participation in religious activities represented a survival of habits of an older culture. · Problems of an essentially urban or industrial-capitalist society lay largely outside the province of interest of the churches. The failure to develop a social philosophy offering any solution to the pressing problems of industrial workers—in the factory or in mining communities—had the effect of lessening the dependence of this section of the population upon religion.   Successful business people tended to dominate in church politics, and the middle and

[15]Cf. C. E. Silcox, *Church Union in Canada* (New York, 1933).

upper classes came to form the chief body of church supporters, while skilled workers and the industrial proletariat turned increasingly to other agencies for leadership. When the church took the side of employers on issues such as strikes, as it sometimes did in the early years of the century, the loss of goodwill among the labouring population became still more pronounced, but even efforts to assume a neutral position did not keep the support of workers who felt the need of a positive policy on the part of the church. Among some of the leaders of the church, even before the Great War, there was a realization of the necessity of developing a more sympathetic and understanding approach to the problems of labour, but the defections from the church among working-class people indicated that such adjustments were not sufficiently extensive to maintain unimpaired the influence of religion. The churches failed even more to meet the needs of that large section of the population upon the cultural fringe of the urban community: slum-dwellers, transient workers, petty crooks, prostitutes, and others. These "outcasts" of polite society found no recognition within religious denominations. Respectability was a condition of membership in the church, and respectability was maintained by ignoring undesirable members of the population. Charitable contributions to the poor and sermons denouncing vice were means of preserving the isolation of these contaminating elements within the urban community. The psychological and philosophical assumptions of most of the leaders of the church, and the orthodox techniques of evangelization, made almost impossible the adoption of effective methods of dealing with problems such as the slum, crime, and prostitution. Some of the more enterprising of the churches undertook programmes of an experimental character, but early activities for the most part were confined to pious declarations from the pulpit. Religious leadership among such marginal groups in the urban community came from new evangelical sects, particularly the Salvation Army. The rapid growth of this movement in Canada, with the immigration from Britain in the 1890's, paralleled the successes of the Methodist and Baptist revivalist sects in the early part of the century. The Army was a product of the industrial revolution, and its organization, techniques of preaching, and appeal were thoroughly adapted to the conditions of the urban environment. By 1900, it had made considerable inroads into the followings of the established denominations, and, if the rate of its growth fell off after 1914, it was because the traditional churches learnt valuable lessons from its experience. The securer establishment of the foundations of religion in urban society came with the recognition of the possibilities of evangelism among the newer sections of the population. In the pushing of religious influences into these frontier urban areas, the Salvation Army played a highly important role.

The Great War marked something of a transition in developments in Canada since the turn of the century. Social problems which had arisen in the period before the war had by no means secured complete solution, and new social problems emerged, but in many respects there was established some sort of equilibrium in social structure. Industrial-urban communities by 1914 had attained some degree of maturity, and most sections of the western prairies and the older established centres of the pulp and paper industry and of mining in the North had passed out of the raw frontier stage. If new areas still were being opened up, as in the Peace River district,[16] and if industrialization was being extended beyond its former limits (into Quebec and the West), these developments did not become the dominant note in Canadian social life. Financial concentration, rather than the concentration of industrial plants, was the most marked economic tendency after the Great War.[17] Social problems associated with industrial-urbanism and metropolitan expansion in the 1920's were not essentially different from those social problems which had emerged during the early years of the century, and developments in the early period consequently provided a wealth of experience to meet the needs which arose in the later period. The elaboration of social welfare agencies, the growth of a familiarity with improved techniques in dealing with problems of crime and juvenile delinquency, the rise of a more realistic attitude to questions of morality, the establishment of organizations providing more vigorous cultural and educational leadership, and the broadening of religious programmes were an indication that reorganization had advanced considerably in the

[16]C. A. Dawson assisted by R. W. Murchie, *The Settlement of the Peace River Country: A Study of a Pioneer Area* (Toronto, 1934).

[17]H. A. Innis, "The Penetrative Powers of the Price System," *Canadian Journal of Economics and Political Science*, August, 1938.

chief social institutions of the community. Much remained to be done it is true, but the most critical problems of Canadian communities after 1918 were no longer associated with the development of new economic enterprise and the opening up of new areas of economic exploitation.

War and depression imposed new and heavy strains upon institutions of social life, and adjustment to the conditions which arose from these developments became the chief problem of social organization. The sudden collapse after the inflationary boom in 1919 and the much more prolonged depression which followed the stock-market boom of 1929 were accompanied by wide-spread unemployment and acute economic dislocations in exposed areas. To some extent the problems of Canada were problems of the western world resulting from the Great War and national policies of economic autarchy. To a very considerable extent, however, the Canadian depressions represented the backwash of forces of frontier economic expansion which had run their course. Depletion of resources and loss of markets for staples were not something new in Canadian experience. Earlier frontier economic enterprises—the fur trade, fisheries, timber trade, wheat-growing in Central Canada, and gold mining in British Columbia—eventually encountered either or both of these limitations to expansion. But the decline of one frontier economic enterprise led quickly to the promotion of another. Expansion in new directions made possible the avoidance of general economic depression resulting from the economic recession of older industries. After 1920 no conspicuous new development took place to offset the depletion of the resources or the drying up of the markets of those frontier enterprises which expanded rapidly in the early years of the century. The exhaustion of gold in the Yukon, the emergence of a dry belt in the western prairies, the disappearance of timber stands in northern lumber communities, the increasing overhead costs of and declining returns from the coal industry in Nova Scotia were problems of exposed areas which reached back into the whole Canadian economy. The social maladjustments resulting directly or indirectly from these economic dislocations became the major note in the social development of Canada after 1920. They indicate the passing of the frontier stage of economic expansion; on the other hand, they emphasize the importance of such expansion in the building of the Canadian community structure.

1. SOCIAL WELFARE

Conditions of Factory Work

Sessional Papers, Canada, 1882, no. 42:   Report of the Commissioners Appointed to Enquire into the Working of Mills and Factories of the Dominion, and the Labor Employed therein.

There is very little attention paid to the question of ventilation, and, as a consequence, no provision whatever is made, other than the doors and windows, the latter, of course, being always closed in cold weather. While this question of such vital importance to humanity is being treated with indifference by the authorities of churches, halls, and our public schools, it certainly cannot be a matter of surprise that manufacturers do not take the lead of equally responsible parties on this question, or that they should be forced to an expenditure which the State, under similar circumstances, does not provide for its subjects.

The subject of over-crowding of factories has also received our attention, and undoubtedly exists in some instances, prejudicially to the health and comfort of those engaged. This must be taken as an opinion formed from common-sense observations rather than by a scientific basis of how many cubic feet is necessary for each occupant of a room. The rule, apparently, which is observed by employers, is, not how many hands should occupy a certain room or building, but how many can be got into it. The practice is common also, of crowding too much machinery into a given space; this applies not only to old and inefficient buildings, but likewise some built more recently, and causes much inconvenience and more liability of accident to the operator. . . .

We have noticed a few buildings where manufacturing is carried on, that those parts which are below the ground surface are utilized as work-rooms, the walls being damp all the time, and water being allowed to remain under the floors; this is, however, exceptional. . . .

A question which demands the immediate attention of the authorities is the inadequate and unsatisfactory provision made to meet the conveniences and common necessities of humanity. That insufficient closet accommodation exists, as a rule, in factories and workshops employing over twenty-five hands, is beyond dispute. The evils arising from such inconveniences are not only superficial and temporary, but it is to be feared, are serious and permanent in their nature. We feel great reluctance in informing the Government of two or three cases coming under our notice, where girls or women were employed, of no provision whatever being made for closet accommodation. This we believe to be very limited in its extent, although closely allied in its results to insufficiency. The closets that are provided are in many cases very objectionable and unsatisfactory:

1st.—On account of publicity of location, they are not sufficiently protected from the public.

2nd.—When located in the building, are too often public for the operatives of both sexes; in some cases we have found only one closet for the accommodation of from fifteen to fifty hands, and located in the basement, with very little light and no ventilation; in one case access was obtained by a common ladder fixed in the hoist well.

3rd.—When an attempt of separation of closets has been made, they lie in too close proximity, and the divisions in some cases are only inch boards six feet high. The pernicious tendency of this need not be enlarged on by us.

4th.—Very often, on entering a mill or factory, our senses have been convincingly informed of imperfect ventilation and drainage of closets, the only ventilation in many instances being a door opening directly into the factory. The above facts in relation to the imperfect sanitary arrangements of some factories cannot be too harshly commented on, and show a callous indifference on the part of the employer toward the physical and moral interests of those under his charge.

Pauper Immigration from Overseas

Debates of the House of Commons, Canada, Session 1888, vol. II, p. 1595.

Sir RICHARD CARTWRIGHT. I am not going to make a motion, but I have a few words to say before we separate on a question which I have twice brought to the notice of the Minister of Agriculture, a question that is attracting a good deal of attention in my Province at any rate, and especially in the chief cities. Hon. gentlemen will, I daresay, recollect that I interrogated the Minister of Agriculture some weeks ago, almost a month ago, on the question whether the Government had seen fit to take precautions to prevent unfit persons settling in Canada, in view of the large immigration which was expected. After that I brought the subject a second time under his consideration with respect to certain resolutions passed by the city council of Toronto, which declared on their authority as municipal officers that a considerable number of such persons had in the past been made chargeable on the public rates. I do not know whether the Minister's attention has been directed to the subject, but since that time there have been a considerable number of complaints in the newspapers pointing out that a large number, or, at all events, an appreciable percentage of these persons who were coming out, were persons who had been apparently shipped to this country by divers charitable institutions and municipal bodies in England, for the purpose of getting rid of weakly and infirm persons who were apt to become a charge on their parish rates. Now, I happen to know that is a practice which has been had recourse to more or less by English parish authorities on several occasions. . . . There appears to be a likelihood that this evil to which I have alluded may assume considerable proportions. I have received private despatches from one or two quarters, in which the parties intimate that the statements made in some of the newspapers, notably in the *Mail* newspaper, are not exaggerated, and that a certain percentage, how large I cannot say, but that a certain number of persons, who are unfit to become good and useful settlers, are now being landed in Canada. . . . And I would add this, that I have myself over and over again interrogated persons who were brought to this country by the representations of different immigration agents. I am unwilling to believe that the regularly authorised agents of the country could have made such representations as those poor persons alleged to have been made to them, but I have no doubt whatever that a great many of the agents of the railways and steamship companies are utterly unscrupulous in inducing persons to come to this country either as assisted immigrants or in any other way. . . . I have many times, as I have said, conversed with those persons who came here, and I think that inducements were held, which were impossible of fulfilment, and they are brought here sometimes under circumstances of extreme hardship, and very often have to make their way back again.

The Chinese and Living Standards

Sessional Papers, Canada, 1885, no. 54a: Report of Mr. Justice Gray, Member of the Royal Commission on Chinese Immigration.

There can be no doubt of the truth of the charge, that about their residences and in their mode of living in their own domiciles the habits of the lower classes of Chinese, as a rule, are most objectionable and filthy. The air is polluted by the disgusting offal with which they are surrounded, and the vile accumulations are apt to spread fever and sickness in the neighbourhood, which in the end may affect extensive districts. . . .

In British Columbia there has never been a density of population, or pauperism sufficient to render such scenes possible among the whites, and it is, therefore, that the mere probability of their approach is regarded with such justifiable horror.

In Canada they can be prevented under effective existing legislation, without expense to the Government of the Dominion; and so far as the Chinese are concerned, their obedience and submission to authority, the peculiar characteristic of the people of their country, resulting from the long training, and despotic nature of their Government, its assumed divine origin, and absolute arbitrary will, render the carrying out of measures by the local authorities to that end, a remedy of simple means.

It is difficult to conceive upon what principle such charges are made. Where the local authorities have power to remove or abate the evil, it is a waste of time to abuse it. Where they can punish the offender, and do not, it is a premium to offend.

Chinese Immigration and Destitution

Sessional Papers, Canada, 1885, no. 54a: Return of Sir Matthew Begbie, Chief Justice of British Columbia, before the Royal Commission on Chinese Immigration.

I am sorry to say we have no system of public poor relief, or of public relief of any kind, except the hospitals and the asylum. Chinamen do not much trouble the hospitals. I never heard of Chinamen becoming a burden on the private charity of whites. I have an indistinct remembrance of having been once asked to contribute to the cost of removing a disabled Chinaman; I am not sure. Such cases must be extremely rare. Nothing is more common than to be called on to relieve whites by private charity.

Urban Mobility

Proceedings Twelfth Canadian Conference of Charities and Correction, Held in Hamilton, Ont., Sept. 22-25, 1911, pp. 63-4.

RUFUS D. SMITH, Secretary of the Charity Organization Society, Montreal: . . . Canada at present is in a peculiar position in regard to its social work. We have a population of nearly 8,000,000 now; and it is probable that the cities of Canada will grow at a more rapid rate than the cities of even the United States. The small city of to-day, in Canada, in one generation will be a large city. The problem has got ahead of us and we are trying to catch up. . . . After it has got ahead of you there is confusion and you have to deal with many petty jealousies connected with charitable work. One of the hard things to do is to secure co-ordination when you get a large number of organizations doing indiscriminate relief work. . . . In Canada we have these problems on our hands. I would like to see better organized charity, and the Charity Organization Societies properly supported in doing the work that has to be done. It is hard in Montreal. The problem there in some ways has got ahead of us. On the relief side of the question right principles now will mean efficient work; later—a saving of life and expense. There is one peculiar problem, so interwoven and mixed up that I don't know just where to begin on it. In my Organization we have a great deal to do with transportation and the population is moving rapidly from one place to another. It is coming from England, from all over; it stops at Montreal for a day or two, then moves on to different places. In some cases families coming from England have not enough money to take them to their destination, and the man goes to some place in the West, leaving his wife and children in Montreal. This might come under the head of desertion. The man never thought of desertion when he left Montreal, but left to get work, perhaps in a lumber camp, or anywhere to get work. In many such cases we never hear of the man again, although I don't believe he left with any intention of deserting his family. He found it easier to get on alone, perhaps, and forgot them. Many letters come from England asking us to look up a man and see if we can get him to support his family. He has left home with good intentions, but circumstances have caused the bonds to be broken. . . .

As to the question of transportation, we are going to have the tramp problem sooner or later and ought to work out a better system of co-operation in transporting people from one place to another.

The question of seasonal labour in Canada is a difficult problem. We have the short summer of about four months, and then employment has to be found for the winter. If some of you gentlemen in this audience had to find a job twice a year perhaps you would be up to my office to see me. It is a hard thing when a man has to find a job twice a year or oftener. That break in the Fall and Spring is enough to put a number of men and families under. . . . If that question of seasonal labour were studied we would find it has much to do with the desertion problem. Don't blame the man altogether; blame society or business a little. We are not meeting our problems as we should. We leave undone what we ought to have done, and do what we ought not to have done.

Seasonal Unemployment

Proceedings Ninth Canadian Conference of Charities and Correction, Held at Toronto, Nov. 25th and 26th, 1908, pp. 80-1.

Mr. John Keane, of Ottawa, said he agreed with a good deal of what had been said by Rev. Father Minehan [the previous speaker]. We are all aware of the underlying causes of a good deal of the poverty and distress that occurred in cities were mostly caused by drink and waste during the earning season of the year, the amount spent in sports and pleasure and, probably as important as any, the lack of continuous work in the winter season, when large numbers of the working class, owing to the exigencies of our rigorous climate, cannot find employment. He referred particularly to the difficulties encountered by the labouring class, that so many of our industries are shut down during that season. It throws large numbers out of employment, who thus have to betake themselves to other avocations if they can find them.

It is, of course, very easy to say that no man who really wants work but would be able to find it. That is true only in a limited sense, because it is found in actual experience that just as soon as work begins to be plentiful, applications for relief or help diminish in exact proportion. This was as sure as the rise and fall of a barometer. . . .

A great number of manufacturing concerns here have to shut down owing to the rigours of the Canadian winter, with the result that the numerous hands thus engaged are thrown out of employment. These have to depend upon the precarious chance of odd jobs between that and spring, and this during a period of the year when the cost of living is considerably higher than during the working season.

It was formerly the case that a large number of the able-bodied men were absorbed in the lumbering operations during the winter, but now, owing to the restricted output and the greater desire to have only more or less skilled labour at the work, immigrants and other inexperienced persons find it impossible to maintain themselves or make an ordinary livelihood.

Poverty and Overcrowding

Proceedings Seventh Canadian Conference of Charities and Correction, Held at London, Ontario, October 5-7th, 1904, p. 48: Statement of Mr. Walsh, Assistant Relief Officer of Toronto.

Of the many problems that are agitating the public mind at the present time, there are none in my opinion of greater importance than the proper housing of the poor. If the conditions that exist in the City of Toronto are a fair example of what exists in other places, and I believe that such is the case, then it is time that political and municipal reformers and social and charitable workers rise up and grapple with this most important subject, before the poor get in such conditions as exist in some of the larger cities of Great Britain and Ireland. In our city at the present time there is scarcely a vacant house fit to live in that is not inhabited, and in many cases by numerous families; in fact cases have come under my personal notice where respectable people have had to live in stables, tents, old cars, sheds (others in damp cellars), where we would not place a valued animal, let alone a human being; but when there are no houses to rent, people cannot live on the street, and hence are forced (because of this house famine) to live in such places.

Feeble-Mindedness and Mental Disease

Proceedings Eighth Canadian Conference of Charities and Correction, Held at Toronto, November 15th to 17th, 1905, pp. 22-4: Statement of Dr. Bruce Smith, Inspector of Hospitals and Charities.

In every Refuge, Rescue Home and Orphanage may be found deplorable evidence of the necessity of some action being taken that will check the ever-increasing number of mental degenerates that are being brought into the world. There are hundreds of feeble-minded girls in this Province that should be cared for in some institution specially set apart and conducted as an Industrial Refuge. Only last week in one of the smaller cities of Ontario I counted a dozen young women who could be classed only as high-grade imbeciles, and who had either just become or were about to be mothers. The probable destiny of their offspring need be little questioned. Then when I looked about and saw the marks of degeneracy so evident in many of the other children I could only wonder how long it will take to awaken public conscience to a proper comprehension of the importance of this great question. Every few years this great Province adds, with commendable liberality, to the institutions established for the care and custody of its unfortunates. The time has surely come when as much attention should be given to prevention of insanity as to the care and custody of its unfortunate victims.

There is another point that must not be lost sight of and that is that we are altogether too lax in regard to allowing undesirable emigrants to find a shelter in this Province. Too often of late years by the pernicious system of bonusing emigration agencies abroad, mental and physical degenerates have been landed on our shores and have finally drifted, either through mental, physical or moral deficiencies into one or other of our great public Charities. The majority of the feeble-minded girls, who having fallen an easy prey to some designing villain, are sent to our Rescue Homes, have only been a short while in this country. . . .

There is no doubt that fifty per cent. of the inmates of Canadian asylums are drawn from the farming community. This must be accounted for largely by the mode of living which obtains in many farm houses. Socially they are isolated from the world, especially in the newer districts. Imperfect hygienic surroundings, the monotony of their daily lives, a dietary that seldom varies, often the entire absence of bathing facilities, and we might draw a picture that reveals a state of domestic life that no wonder often ends in despair. The human brain demands diversity, and we must teach the farming community that they owe it as a duty to themselves as well as to the nation to cultivate a higher ideal of home life.

The class of literature which people read has a marked influence in moulding thought. Are there not many books published, which we, as physicians, know are not conducive to soundness as well as purity of mind? If the literary tastes of the people may be judged by the class of trashy literature that is most popular, degeneration is surely manifesting itself.

Gaols as Refuges for Destitute

Report of the Commissioners Appointed to Enquire into the Prison and Reformatory System of Ontario, 1891 (Toronto, 1891), pp. 145-6.

The evidence shows that in a large majority of the counties the gaols are used as poorhouses, and that those, classed in the returns as vagrants, who are committed twice a year or oftener are really old, infirm, helpless people whose poverty and infirmity are their only crimes. In some counties such old and infirm people as do not belong to the county are sent to the gaols, but in several counties all the aged and helpless poor for whom the municipalities cannot or will not otherwise provide are committed to the gaols as vagrants. . . .

The insane, too, occupy in the gaols much of the room intended for criminals. The Inspector's report states that 437 persons were committed as lunatics during the year 1889. The evidence shows that of the persons so committed a large proportion are merely imbeciles who should be cared for in a poor house, and that these generally remain a long time in the gaols because they are not regarded as fit subjects for a lunatic asylum. Of those who should be sent to an asylum some, when the accommodation in the lunatic asylums was insufficient, remained in the gaols for months; and in some instances lunatics still remain in the gaols longer than they should because the proper means for procuring their removal are neglected.

Provision for Destitute in Toronto

Report of the Commissioners Appointed to Enquire into the Prison and Reformatory System of Ontario, 1891 (Toronto, 1891), Appendix, p. 613: Evidence of John Edward Pell, Secretary of the St. George's Society and Associated Charities, Toronto.

During the winter seasons for many years I was engaged in managing various kinds of work here in Toronto, work which was started for keeping people of this kind employed. I found, as a rule, that of the people who applied for assistance during the winter season, from one-half to two-thirds would be willing to work if they had an opportunity of getting it. According to my experience, extending to over 50 years in Canada, there is in winter seasons, owing to climatic influences, and so forth, a large section of the people thrown out of employment. Many of them are improvident, but some are really unable to provide for themselves. I question whether it is reasonable and right, that people who are simply in necessitous circumstances should have to go to the police magistrate and be sent to gaol for periods of from three to six months. We have in Toronto two poorhouses, both good institutions. They are maintained chiefly by means obtained through a grant from the city and a grant from the government, but they are managed as private institutions, and consequently the police magistrate has no authority to send anybody to these charities and as a matter of fact, never does so. One is the House of Industry and the other the House of Providence. . . . I object most strongly to people being sent indiscriminately to gaol simply because they are needy and unable to maintain themselves.

Need for a Social Welfare Officer in Toronto

Social Problems: An Address Delivered to the Conference of Combined City Charities of Toronto, May 20th, 1889, by Goldwin Smith, President of the Conference (Toronto, 1889), pp. 3-5.

In the department of charity, as in all other departments of municipal life and administration, questions are raised by the marvellous growth of Toronto. What sufficed for a population of twenty, or even of fifty, thousand will not suffice for a population of a hundred and eighty thousand, with a prospect of further increase. These cities of the New World have traversed in half a century the distance in the race of progress which it has taken the cities of the Old World ten centuries to traverse; young in years they are old in magnitude, and the liabilities and cares of maturity have already fully come upon them. When I first settled in Toronto, a little more than twenty years ago, cows wandered in the streets of my quarter, where land is now selling at a high price per foot. The need of a more regular and skilled administration is felt in the department of health and in that of engineering: the time can hardly be far distant when it will be felt in regard to the relief of destitution, of which a certain portion unhappily has its seat even amidst the pleasant and stately homes of the fairest, proudest and most prosperous city. We must all sympathize with the unwillingness to introduce a poor law, though it is a great mistake to suppose that public charity regularly and justly administered demoralizes or degrades more than private charity. . . . On voluntary effort, in the main, we may still rely. . . . To voluntary effort, and especially to that of the churches, we must look for the relief of the indigence which shrinks from sight and would never ask for public relief, yet is often accompanied by the keenest suffering. But though you may rely mainly on these agencies, you cannot, in such a city as this, rely entirely upon them. Responsibility in the last resort must rest somewhere, and it can scarcely be thrown even on the most devoted volunteers. Volunteers cannot give all their time, be always ready at a moment's notice, or be always in the city. Cases of emergency may occur, particularly in the depth of winter, and if no one is responsible for their relief the community may one day be awakened to the necessity of a change by something that would shock its humanity. The treatment of tramps and vagrants is in some measure a matter of police, and police authority is necessary to maintain the proper rules and discipline in a casual ward. Cases of wayfarers in need of passes to help them to their destination often occur, and the Mayor of such a city as Toronto has not the leisure to attend to them; indeed the Mayor already finds it necessary to have special assistance in this part of his work, and it may be said that the principle of a regular relief officer has been adopted. There are also cases with which volunteers or private associations, from want of authority, are unable to deal. What is to be done, for example, where chronic destitution is the consequence of mental disease or infirmity, and where a private individual or charity can have no right to interfere? Besides, a centre of guidance, information and observation is needed, and this nothing but a public office can supply.

One use of a centre of information would be the prevention of imposture, against which, in the absence of the means which such a record office affords of ascertaining the identity and verifying the stories of applicants, it is very hard, at least for those whose hearts are not fenced with the steel of experience, to guard.

Care of Destitute in Urban Centres—1900

Proceedings Third Canadian Conference of Charities and Correction, Toronto, September 27th and 28th, 1900, pp. 46-50: Paper Presented by the Secretary of the National Council of Women.

It is a most encouraging fact that the important subject of the care of the aged and infirm seems to be attracting more of the attention of thinking people, besides the workers connected with charitable institutions, than was formerly the case. . . .

The National Council of Women of Canada have felt for several years past that . . . that class of the community which may be designated as "the aged and infirm poor" should especially claim their attention.

For this reason one of the standing committees of the Council is that of "the care of the aged and infirm poor"; and in each local council throughout the Dominion a sub-committee of ladies assists the standing committee by furnishing them with any particulars bearing on the subject.

By this means a great deal of valuable information has been gathered, some of which, as briefly as possible, I will try to outline.

Province of Ontario.—There are in Ontario 40 houses of refuge and 18 county homes for the poor; but the number must be largely increased to make provision for those who are now in the jails.

Toronto.—The number of aged and infirm poor who last June were in the 5 institutions into which they are received is as follows: House of Industry, 243; House of Providence, 691; Aged Women's Home, 57; the Church Home, 35; Old Folk's Home, 23.   Total, 1,049.   At the same time the number of aged and infirm poor who have been committed to the city jail as vagrants averages 25. . . . The poor in the neighboring counties are cared for in the county poorhouse.   Out-door relief is given by the House of Industry, the City Relief, and directly by the Municipal Council through a paid agent. . . .

Hamilton.—In the House of Refuge the poor are housed by the municipality and receive the usual government grant.   Poor from the neighborhood are frequently sent to the Refuge, and are paid for by the municipality wherein they resided.   In the jail the aged and infirm vagrants are treated as to food and dress as are the other prisoners.   Many prefer to be committed to the jail for the winter, so as to have their liberty during the summer months, as it is sometimes difficult for those who have left of their own desire to re-enter the Refuge.

London.—An aged people's home receives both men and women.   It has a government grant, and is under the supervision of the Young Women's Christian Association.   The city has a Poor Relief Officer and Inspector, whose duties are to inspect and relieve deserving cases from the City Poor Fund.   Many charitably disposed citizens help poor men through giving them coupons to the Salvation Army Workman's Hotel.   Through the Charities Organization, the Young Men's Christian Association, and the King's Daughters, also, the poor are relieved. . . .

Kingston.—The municipality gives a yearly grant of $700, and the use of a building, for the House of Industry, which is aided by a grant from the provincial government and private subscriptions.   During the past eighteen months several men and women were committed to jail as vagrants without any charge against them of law-breaking.   An effort has been made to establish a poorhouse for Kingston and the adjoining counties.

Manitoba.—Winnipeg.—No poorhouses exist, as the charitable institutions are able to deal with all cases that require relief. . . .

Mrs. Bryce, Convener of the Winnipeg sub-committee, says: "Quite a number of old people, particularly old women, are gathering into our city; and it is becoming a problem to know what to do with them, for they object so strongly to going into an institution.   When they are infirm, they are sent to the Home for Incurables. . . ."

Province of Quebec.—Montreal.—Montreal reports that, while no provision for the care of the aged poor is made by the municipality, the Roman

Catholic Church provides the Grey Nunnery, the St. Bridget's House of Refuge, the Hospital St. Vincent de Paul, and numerous other institutions, and, also, in some cases provides a kind of insurance by which the poor help to provide beforehand for such a shelter. The Jewish community, through the Hebrew Young Men's and Ladies' Societies, provide by private subscription for the support of their aged poor, who, for the most part, are boarded out. The principal Protestant institutions are the House of Industry and Refuge, the Ladies' Benevolent Society, which takes in old women; and the churches often support their poor in these institutions. The various national societies also look after their own poor. The boarding-out system, except in the case of the Jewish poor, is not adopted in Montreal, as it is almost exclusively in the rest of the province of Quebec. In the Montreal jail were found poor people placed there under the vagrancy act. . . .

In the other parts of the province of Quebec the boarding-out system is so generally provided that to the enquiry made of thirteen of the sheriffs of county jails only two cases of the aged poor in these penal institutions were reported. . . .

Quebec.—There is no municipality poorhouse in that city, but four institutions belong to the Roman Catholic Church and to other philanthropic societies. In that province the legislature gives grants of from $200 to $300, to assist the institutes named. . . .

Prince Edward Island.—Charlottetown.—No provision is made by the municipality for the care of the class named. Two small houses, the gift of a private individual, are used for that purpose, but are quite inadequate. There is a government poorhouse for the province, but it is inadequate for the purpose. . . .

Nova Scotia.—Halifax.—In the city of Halifax a well-managed municipal poor asylum, and in the county of Halifax a farm for the poor, provide good accommodation for the aged and infirm poor who by the law of Nova Scotia are never committed to jail as vagrants. The provincial legislature does not give grants for the erection of poorhouses. Out-door relief is supplied by voluntary subscriptions,—voluntary in the fullest sense, because they are unsolicited,—and the fund so supplied is administered by a city official.

New Brunswick.—St. John.—There are county poorhouses, charitable institutions, and the poor are also farmed out by auction to the lowest bidder. . . . Overseers of the poor are appointed; and outside relief is given, when needed, from public funds by the Almhouse Commission, after strict investigation. The legislature gives no financial assistance to the poorhouses in this province.

British Columbia.—Victoria.—There is a Municipal Old Men's Home for those over sixty years of age who have lived a certain number of years in the city. A home for old women is partially supported by the municipality. The Friendly Help Society and the Benevolent Society also care for the aged poor. . . .

Vancouver.—In this comparatively new city there has been no occasion as yet for the erection of a poorhouse, as the isolated cases of aged poor people are cared for by the charitably disposed.

Mrs. Hill, on behalf of the New Westminster sub-committee, makes the following report: "As far as we know, there is no provision made on the mainland of British Columbia for our poor, aged, and infirm women. At Kamloops there is a home for men, and at the Royal Columbian Hospital in our city there is provision made for them; but for the poor women there is nothing. The local council have cared for those cases that we have known of; and, fortunately, they were few."

2. CRIME AND THE MORAL ORDER

A. Crime and Institutions of Law Enforcement

Disorder Associated with Railway-Building

Sessional Papers, Canada, 1899, no. 15: Report of Inspector G. E. Sanders on the Crow's Nest Railway Construction, North-West Mounted Police, Macleod, November 2, 1898.

I have the honour to submit my report in connection with my work on the construction of the Crow's Nest Branch of the Canadian Pacific Railway from Crow's Nest Lake to Kootenay Lake, a distance of about 200 miles. . . .

Contractors' camps were established every three or four miles, and probably no less than 3,500 men were employed for a time. At Crow's Nest Lake a thriving village sprang up and flourished during the months of December, January and February. Its inhabitants, outside of the Canadian Pacific Railway officials and contractors, being composed of illicit whiskey vendors, gamblers, thieves and prostitutes, are all bent upon fleecing the poor railway man of his hard earned gains.

The main work of the police was to keep these people within bounds, and it was done in an effective manner. Heavy fines were imposed in all cases brought before the magistrates, and the lesson learned at Crow's Nest Lake had a wholesome influence on all the towns, permanent and otherwise, which sprang up in quick succession as the work progressed west. By the end of February Crow's Nest Lake was a deserted village, and Fernie (on Coal Creek), forty miles further west, became the centre of attraction, and it was certainly for a time the hottest town on the road. Elk River Crossing, Wardner, Cranbrook and Moyie City in turn became points where a large number of men congregated and where a lucrative business was done in the dispensing of ardent spirits, and by the sharks and adventurers who moved up and down the line seeking whom they might devour.

At the beginning of the year it was suggested that the Public Works Act be proclaimed, but I asked that it should not, as it would have been impossible for me to have enforced the Act properly, with the few men that could be spared me for the work, and on account of the great distances to be covered. Subsequently a number of retail licences for the sale of liquor were granted by the provincial authorities along the line. Had there been only one at each place it would, to a certain extent, have helped to keep down drunkenness, but when two or three of these licences were granted at the same point, a rivalry for the trade was created and it was more difficult in every way to control them. The work, however, was never noticeably interfered with owing to the presence of liquor. . . .

The duties devolving on the men under my command, were varied and in many instances new to them.

Responsibilities were thrust upon them which they, in the ordinary course of events, would not assume; the unorganized district traversed by the railroad, the few magistrates and other officials to act, obliged them, however, to do so.

Every grievance was referred to the police, and the diversity of matters which we attended to in order to maintain peace and quietness and to enable the work to progress, would open the eyes of the ordinary constable with nothing but his routine duties to attend to.

The police acted as sanitary inspectors, settled, where practicable, small disputes between master and employee, complaints about food, medical attendance, mail, got employment for men, wrote letters for them, and generally outside their ordinary duties, had an insight and control of everything which would assist and help to maintain the object desired, viz., the maintenance of peace. . . .

The presence of our men had always a quieting effect on the rowdiest crowd, and it was seldom that they met with even a semblance of resistance. Whenever any one had temerity enough to offer opposition, they were speedily shown the futility of their doing so. On one or two occasions, however, things did not go so smoothly. . . .

As I have already stated, the principal offence we had to deal with was the illicit sale of liquor. The profits to be made out of this business had a great attraction, and tempted many. It was of the utmost importance that liquor should be kept out of the Construction Camps and the work not interfered with. We therefore, paid special attention to this matter, and the British Columbia government derived quite a revenue from the fines imposed for infractions of the License Act.

Between $2,500 and $3,000 were inflicted for this offence alone.

The most serious crimes which came under our notice were four cases of homicide and one of horse stealing. . . .

The Crow's Nest road became notorious by reason of the numerous complaints on the part of the men; to one who was constantly on the work, as I was, the hardships and ill-treatment spoken of, seemed exaggerated to a degree. That there were cases of hardship was to be expected, but it appeared to me that the condition of a few was applied to the whole, that it was taken for granted that what one suffered, all endured.

A great deal of the trouble was due to men being deceived by employment agents in the east, and to the fact that a very large number were totally unfitted to perform the work for which they engaged. . . .

We did the utmost to have real grievances rectified, and my representations to the general manager of construction always met with prompt attention. The medical attention was the cause of most complaints during the winter; the haste and suddenness with which the line was covered with men west of Crow's Nest Lake made it well-nigh impossible to put up hospitals at once. A great deal of sickness occurred, perhaps more than might be expected, owing to the inferior physique of many of the labourers, and the doctors certainly had more than they could attend to for a short period. These matters have been thoroughly gone into by two Royal Commissions, and I will therefore, refrain from going into particulars. . . .

As to the amount of wages received by the men and their not having money to send to their families in the east, it was very noticeable to me that the men who complained most, drank most. I think I am coming pretty close to the mark when I say that during one month (April) nearly $10,000 worth of liquor went into the Crow's Nest Pass for licensed houses and others. Supposing this was only retailed at twice what it cost, which is putting it down very low, one can form a fair idea of where part of the wages went. It must be borne in mind that the Public Works Act was not in force, and we could not prevent the introduction of liquor upon the work, all we could do was to confine the sale to the licensed houses. Besides his love of liquor the Crow's Nest navvy was an inveterate wanderer, change of scene seemed an absolute necessity for him; and the "Tote" road during winter was covered with men travelling from one camp to another.

Liquor Traffic on the Prairies

Sessional Papers, Canada, 1893, no. 15: Annual Report of Commissioner L. W. Herchmer, North-West Mounted Police, 1892.

On the 1st of May the License Act was introduced in the Territories, and great improvements in the state of the country were confidently expected by many people dissatisfied with the working of the "permit" system, as only a certain number of licences were to be granted, and an efficient staff of commissioners and inspectors were to see that the provisions of the Act were strictly carried out. While these expectations have been partially realized in some districts, in others the law has not been carefully administered, and even in the best regulated districts there has been, I think, more general drinking than under the permit system, and one result is established beyond contradiction, viz., that the half-breeds and Indians can get more liquor than under the old law. Under the permit system liquor was expensive and dealers were afraid to give to people they could not trust, and, consequently, the lower class of whites and half-breeds could very seldom get any. Now half-breeds with money can buy all they want, and as many of them are closely related to the Indians, and in some cases live with them, it is impossible, when liquor once gets into their possession, to prevent Indians camped with them from getting it also; again, it is impossible for any one not personally acquainted with them to tell, on sight, half-breeds from the better class of Indians, the latter, in many cases, dressing like whites, cutting their hair and speaking good English and

French. In some instances very little exertion is made to establish their identity, and undoubtedly Indians very often buy liquor as half-breeds. In some parts of the country, Battleford, Duck Lake, and Batoche in particular, the licences granted are out of all proportion to the inhabitants; in the former place with less than 400 male adults (outside of Indians), within a radius of fifty miles, there are two wholesale and two retail licences. As this district has during my term of office (seven years) never exported anything beyond a moderate quantity of fur and a few cattle, the exports of cattle being equalled in value by the imports of other stock, and generally does not grow enough grain and potatoes for its own use, importing also most of its flour, and as it has no mines or industries of any description, it is impossible to believe that these four licensed places can exist without impoverishing the district. To give you an idea of the consumption, I am credibly informed that between 1st June and 1st December, six car loads of liquor have gone into Battleford; in addition to this there can be little doubt that considerable amounts have gone in in smaller consignments not recognized as liquor. . . .

At Batoche and Duck Lake, with a joint population within fifteen miles of less than 400 male adults (outside of Indians) there are two wholesale and two retail licences; more than four-fifths of these residents are half-breeds and poor, cultivating from five to twenty acres of land, and owning generally about four horses and nine head of cattle each; the whole of the contents of each house being worth on an average less than $50. There is little or no outside travel at these places, and the question is how are these licensed houses supported? Some of these half-breeds have sold cattle at less than their value to obtain liquor with the proceeds, but not in sufficient quantities to support the trade; there is little or no money in either of the settlements, in fact in former years considerable relief has been required. Three of these licensees are half-breeds themselves and are also Indian traders, trading in the country north of the Saskatchewan, and outside the territory affected by the License Act. Under such circumstances it will be difficult, if they wish to trade liquor with Indians, to prevent it. So far, I do not think the Indians have got much liquor, as they have but little money or fur to trade, but one squaw has met her death near Duck Lake through liquor being supplied her, presumably for immoral considerations, as she was a loose character. . . .

While I have not the actual figures of liquor imported since 1st May, and under the permit system it was impossible to find out the actual quantity imported illegally, I have no hesitation in writing that the quantity of liquor used under the license system very greatly exceeds that under the permit system, and that while the heavy drinkers under the old system, except those who have taken the gold cure with advantage, still drink heavily, a considerable number of settlers who formerly seldom or never obtained liquor, are now using large quantities, and, as I stated before, half-breeds can get it whenever they have money, and consequently, in many cases, Indians, in spite of the closest watchfulness on our part.

Crime on the Prairies

Sessional Papers, Canada, 1891, no. 19, Appendix F: Annual Report of Superintendent S. B. Steele, Commanding Macleod District, North-West
Mounted Police, 1890.

To properly appreciate the orderly state of this district, it is necessary
to take into consideration all the influences that militate against a settled
state of order and which are to be found in their most developed state
in a western frontier town. The propinquity of the International boundary
and the sanctuary so long afforded by the North-West Territories (prior
to the new extradition treaty) to a large number of individuals to
whom residence on United States territory was fraught with more danger
than convenience, and whose immigration is by no means tended to raise
the moral tone of any district selected by them as a place of residence.
The neighbourhood of two large Indian Reserves, numbering altogether
over twenty-six hundred (2,600) Indians. The temptation to a certain class
to smuggle illicit whiskey of the worst description into the Territories.
The existence of a few individuals who for the sake of a dollar or two will
supply the Indians with all the intoxicants they desire, and a floating
population off the ranches, who frequently make up for their solitary life
on the ranges by making the most of every opportunity for conviviality
when they come to town. Yet in spite of these drawbacks, it is a notable
fact that no Eastern town of the same population can boast of a much more
orderly record and in no place in the Dominion are life and property more
respected. . . .

The crimes that are common in older and more settled countries are
happily rare or unheard of here: murder, robbery with violence or from
the person, arson, embezzlement, forgery, trespass, perjury, riot and rape,
and in their place we have to contend with cattle-killing, horse-stealing,
smuggling, breaches of the Indian Act and infringement of the liquor law
peculiar to a prohibition country.

Foreigners and Crime

Sessional Papers, Canada, 1893, no. 15: Annual Report of Superintendent R. B.
Deane, Commanding "K" Division, North-West Mounted Police, Lethbridge,
1892.

The Hungarian and Sclavish miners are quarrelsome people and do not
get on with each other at all well. They have a nasty habit of bringing
long-bladed knives into play, and one such offender would have been eligible
for the penitentiary had we been able to complete the evidence against
him. He was cleared by perjury on the part of his compatriots. It frequently
happens, in trying cases in which these people are concerned, that it is
necessary to have two interpreters, one to translate from Hungarian into
Sclavish, and the other from Sclavish into English, and when a witness
lays himself out to lie through two interpreters, of whose benevolent
neutrality he is assured, he has the game entirely in his own hands. Hun-

garians and Sclavs may be very good miners, but they are not altogether desirable citizens.   It is true they keep pretty much to themselves and wrangle principally with one another, but there have been one or two ugly knife wounds inflicted, invariably by a Hungarian upon a Sclav, for whom he seems to have a contemptuous dislike.   The Hungarians are said to have amongst themselves a secret society on the lines of the Italian Mafia, and that they dare not give evidence against one another.   In prohibition days they used to drink hop beer and become royally drunk on it in course of time; now they mix alcohol with their beer and can attain the desired result much sooner.

Rapid Growth of Population and Problems of Police

Sessional Papers, Canada, 1909, no. 28, Appendix C: Annual Report of Superintendent G. E. Sanders, North-West Mounted Police, Regina, November 1, 1908.

In my last report I referred to the difficulties of meeting the demands for police protection from all parts of my district; this difficulty still remains to an increased extent.   Comparing the number of constables to population with those employed by the older provinces, the question might naturally be asked why this should be the case, but a little consideration will show many causes.

The country is still young and its population has arrived quickly, it embraces many foreigners and is much scattered, large numbers of settlers and settlements are far away from railways and telegraphs.   To give adequate protection under these circumstances it is necessary to have men in every direction to deal with cases as they arise and to give that sense of security and safety which the isolated small settlements and lonely settler have a right to expect.   Along new lines of railway new towns spring up like mushrooms in the night, they have no organization and before their existence is barely known come demands for a constable backed up with stories of disorder caused by navvies and others connected with construction work. Several of these new towns have come into existence during the past year on the Grand Trunk Railway and I regret to say that, although you have instructed me to send men to Melville and other points as soon as possible, we have not at present been able to do so.   In the older provinces they grow gradually and spread gradually, the population is more condensed and municipal organizations exist, and people therefore protect themselves to a great extent.

Crime in the Cities

Report of the Commissioners Appointed to Enquire into the Prison and Reformatory System of Ontario, 1891 (Toronto, 1891), pp. 24-5.

From the copies of their annual reports furnished by the chiefs of police of the larger cities, we learn what number were arrested in each of those cities during the year 1889, and what offences they were charged with:—

HAMILTON.—The total number of arrests made and persons brought to trial during the year was 2,901. Of these 478 were brought to trial under warrant, 1,403 without warrant, and 1,020 by summons. . . .

Two hundred and ninety-five were charged with assault; 27 with aggravated assault; 20 with assault and robbery; 178 with disorderly conduct; 703 with drunkenness; 233 with drunkenness and disorderly conduct; 52 with fighting on the street; 4 with burglary; 26 with housebreaking and larceny, and 181 with vagrancy, etc.; other charges, 1,182. . . .

KINGSTON.—The total number of persons charged in the police-court was 552. Of these 379 were charged with drunkenness, 5 with disorderly conduct on the streets, 56 with larceny, 14 with other offences against property, 35 with vagrancy, and 63 with other offences. . . .

LONDON.—The total number charged with offences during the year was 1,640 males and 127 females—total, 1,767. . . .

Seventy-three were accused of common assault, 9 of assaulting and wounding, 101 of having been disorderly, and 1,045 of having been drunk. Of those accused of drunkenness, 516 were convicted and 529 were discharged. It is stated that the number arrested for drunkenness was 150 above the average of the five years, and the increase is attributed to the construction and opening of the C.P. Railroad. There was 1 case of arson, 1 of perjury, 1 of abduction, and 9 of assaulting and wounding. The other cases were of the usual character. 140 males and 43 females were charged with vagrancy.

The number of offences against property reported to the police was 123. In 89 cases the police made arrests. The number arrested was 107 males and 14 females. . . .

OTTAWA.—The total number arrested during the year was 1,032, of whom 136 were females. Three were arrested for murder, 1 for cutting and wounding, 64 for common assault, 8 for aggravated assault, 1 for shooting with intent, 1 for an attempt to commit suicide, 73 for breaches of the peace, 11 as insane, 1 for altering a note, 115 for larceny, 22 for other offences against property, 558 as drunk and disorderly, and 59 as vagrants. The other charges were of the usual character. . . .

TORONTO.—The police report for 1889 shows that the number of offenders apprehended or summoned by the city police for the year ending December 31st of that year, was 9,898 males and 1,689 females—total, 11,587. The drunk and disorderly numbered 4,570 men and 871 women; in all, 5,441. The number charged with larceny was 767 males and 111 females; in all 878. Those accused of burglary numbered 55; of housebreaking, 79; of highway robbery, 43; of fraud, 65; of forgery, 23; of trespass, 252; of other offences against property, 177; of common assaults, 650; of murder, 11; of manslaughter, 6; of other offences against the person, 153; of vagrancy, 333, of whom 125 were females; of breaches of by-laws and other offences, 2,621. . . .

Of the offenders, 527 males and 34 females—total, 561—were from 10 to 15 years of age, and 905 males and 115 females—total, 1,020—were from 15 to 20 years of age.

Growth and Character of Vagrancy

Report of the Commissioners Appointed to Enquire into the Prison and Reformatory System of Ontario, 1891 (Toronto, 1891), pp. 111-13.

To-day vagrancy is perhaps as great a nuisance in Ontario as in any state of the Union. Many of the lazy and worthless amongst our own people have adopted it as a profession. Under the system of assisted passages many have been brought to Canada from Europe who never intended to make a living by honest labour and a large number of inveterate vagrants still drift from the United States into this Province.

The number sentenced to confinement in the gaols of Ontario as vagrants during the year was 783 in 1869; 1,641 in 1875; 2,128 in 1876, and 3,888 in 1877. This was the largest number in any one year. For seven years after the number decreased. In 1878 it was 2,524; in 1879 it was 2,536; in 1880 it was 2,210; in 1881 it was 1,580; in 1882 it was 1,449; in 1883 it was 1,554. In the next year the number rose to 2,130; in 1885 it was 2,445; in 1886 it was 2,243; in 1887 it was 2,192; in 1888 it was 2,301, and in 1889 it was 2,164.

The number committed as vagrants in this Province in 1889 was 17.2 per cent. of all the prisoners committed. . . .

Toronto is the chief winter quarters of the army of tramps that infest this Province. During the summer they are scattered over the districts, not too remote from that city, in which experience has taught them that they can most easily make a living by doing small jobs, by begging or by pilfering; and as winter approaches they set out on their return, following almost invariably, the same tracks. Thus, while they swarm in some towns, they give little trouble in others. They visit Milton in large numbers, and as there is no lock-up, find their way to the gaol, where they obtain a night's shelter, room to sleep on the floor, and a meal or two. In some cases they are taken to the gaol by a constable, but in many cases they are themselves the bearers of the warrants for their own commitment which they procure from some accommodating justice of the peace or constable. They seldom remain in Milton more than one night, and they are "let go" in the morning as a matter of course.

Although the number of vagrants committed to the gaols is so large, that is by no means the whole number. Where there are police-stations and lock-ups, many receive a night's shelter of whom no account is made in the gaol returns. . . .

The evidence goes to show that these [tramps] may be classified as follows:

Those who are willing to work, who go from place to place honestly looking for work and who are unable to find steady employment.

Those who are willing to work and who do work occasionally, but who are dissolute or improvident, indulging in what they call sprees whenever they earn a few dollars, and finding themselves without money or resources of any kind at the beginning of winter.

The professional tramps who dislike and avoid work who roam over the country in summer, working only when they can not procure food by begging or stealing, and then doing only the lightest kind of work and as little of it as possible, and who flock to Toronto or other cities and towns in winter to take up their residence in the gaols or houses of industry, or to continue their habits of pilfering. In this class are to be found many who are drunkards and thieves, and who are capable of committing the most atrocious crimes.

Vagrancy in Toronto

Report of the Commissioners Appointed to Enquire into the Prison and Reformatory System of Ontario, 1891 (Toronto, 1891), Appendix, pp. 682-4: Evidence of the Rev. H. Baldwin, Rector of All Saints Church, One of the Representatives of the Trustees and Managers of the Toronto House of Industry.

It was on the subject of vagrancy generally that we came here to speak. I will be glad if you will allow me to give some statistics. I have come here and have asked certain members of the Board to come with me to-day, because I have found that in cities of the United States which have three times the population we have, there is only a tithe of the number of vagrants. It seems almost incredible that we had 1,481 tramps last winter in one institution in this city, and that some of these tramps actually stayed for nearly two hundred nights. Three hundred and fifty stayed for one night, three hundred for two nights, and one hundred and forty-seven for three nights, and so you go increasing until you come to get twenty and twenty-one staying one hundred and eight nights. I find also that we had last year one hundred and fifty who had been with us the year before, so that you have a regular army of these people. Now, our difficulty is just this; we are obliged to take them in every night, as we do not wish to have anybody in the city of Toronto begging for lodgings. . . . It seems a great pity that these people should be allowed to go in and dwell there and do nothing but cut a little wood, as we insist upon their doing, in the morning, as some return for the accommodation they have received. . . . We could not send them to the Toronto gaol, because that would simply be making criminals out of them, and if once we broke them into going there, these people would find the gaol ten times more comfortable than our quarters. . . .

A good many [of these tramps] are from the States, but there are also a good many from different parts of Canada, who flock to Toronto for their winter quarters. A great many are entered as having come from Hamilton. This might simply have been their last stopping place. A great number are strong able-bodied men who are quite capable of earning their living at occupations in any part of the country. . . .

These men are like bees, they go out through the country in the summer time and they are as great a curse to the Canadian farmer then as they are to us in the winter time. It is idleness they are looking for and not work. They pretend to be in search of work and when a farmer gives them anything to do they leave him in the lurch and go away at an awkward time. We have 100 people who come to us winter after winter, and then in the summer time go out and feed on the Canadian farmers.

Criminals from United States

Report of the Commissioners Appointed to Enquire into the Prison and Reformatory System of Ontario, 1891 (Toronto, 1891), Appendix, p. 503:   Evidence of J. C. Iler, Sheriff of Essex.

A great many in our county come from the other side; in fact, the majority of our criminals are from the other side. We are not responsible for that. I am glad to say that there is not one-tenth of the population of our gaol belongs to our own county. Of the prisoners there are fifty-eight from the United States—about one-third. They are professional crooks who make up the worst class of prisoners; burglars, robbers, and forgers. Not many of them are extradited.

Foreigners and Crime

Proceedings Eleventh Meeting of the Canadian Conference of Charities and Correction, Held in Guelph, Ontario, June 22nd-24th, 1910, pp. 35-6:   Paper Presented by Chief Constable Slemin, Brantford.

The great influx of foreigners into Canada materially affects social conditions. The foreigner, when he lands in this country, is in the same condition as an uneducated child. In order to educate them socially I adopted the system of visiting their homes, in company with our interpreter, and explaining the laws of Canada, at the same time confiscating revolvers, knives, etc., in their possession, and giving them to understand that as long as they obeyed our laws they would have the same protection as the Canadian, but in the event of their disobeying the law they would be dealt with accordingly. We assured them that we were their friends. Their condition in 1904 was very alarming owing to their ignorance of our customs, and the loose way in which their home life was looked on in their own lands. In 1907 we had 134 cases, mostly caused by liquor, one case, that of a new-comer, developing into manslaughter, but I am pleased to say this is the worst case up to the present time. In 1908 the number of cases was reduced to 124, mostly minor. In 1909 the population had increased to 2,229, and the cases before the court numbered 165, showing a reduced percentage. In 1904 we had 400 foreigners, and we had more trouble with them than we have with the present number. The trouble, I have found has been their fondness for liquor. Three drinking houses were broken up three years ago, and heavy fines imposed. Men keeping these places went back to legitimate pursuits, and through our efforts and constant visits their home and social life is becoming more naturalized every day, and to-day there is not a foreign home in Brantford in which liquor is sold. . . .

I think now the percentage of wrongdoers amongst foreigners compares favourably with other nationalities in Brantford.

Chinese Secret Societies and Crime

Sessional Papers, Canada, 1885, no. 54a: Report of Mr. Justice Gray, Member of the Royal Commission on Chinese Immigration.

There are grave objections to the Chinese as settlers or as residents in large numbers, which, apart from the question of competition with white labor, ought to be seriously considered.   Prominent among those objections is the undoubted existence among the Chinese of secret organizations, enabling them to act as compact bodies in any community where they may be, facilitating the evasion of local laws and the concealment of crime.   This constitutes a dangerous feature in the administration of justice where their personal interests are involved; our utter ignorance of their language and modes of thought placing the officers of justice in the power of interpreters, whose veracity is doubtful, and whose integrity there are no means of testing.   The power and extent of these secret organizations enable them to command a simultaneity of action throughout extended districts, and to inflict serious injury upon a community, while themselves not overtly violating any law so as to incur punishment. . . .

They are so entirely ignorant, so incapable of understanding our system of government that they are naturally suspicious, and resort to this mode of protecting themselves when it is not required.   Dangerous as is this element in their character, there is another which is worse, that is their disregard of truth where their feelings or passions are involved; and particularly in charges of a criminal nature, they care not what pain they inflict, or what they endure, so as their end be obtained. . . .

These two features of the Chinese character and habits are so objectionable that the utmost care is required to obviate the consequence.   No doubt, this want of truth renders unsatisfactory the administration of justice in all matters of a criminal nature affecting them, while the knowledge that such power of combination exists creates a sense of insecurity, particularly as to the permanency of engagements for domestic service or the privacy of the household.

The Chinese and Crime

Sessional Papers, Canada, 1885, no. 54a: Evidence of C. T. Bloomfield, Superintendent of City Police, Victoria, before the Royal Commission on Chinese Immigration.

Larceny is the principal crime amongst Chinese.   Next to larceny are assaults, cutting, wounding, and knocking on their heads, for the purpose of robbery, etc.   During the last eight years only one case had been brought to justice—Wong Foong—by evidence from themselves, and who got fifteen years, and is now in the New Westminster Penitentiary.

Crime in Vancouver

C. F. J. Galloway, *The Call of the West: Letters from British Columbia* (London, 1916), pp. 244-6.

In the residential sections the lighting is poor, an arc lamp generally being placed at each street intersection and the intervening distances of 150 to 200 yards being left in darkness. . . . It is usual when returning home late from theatres or dances to carry as little as possible on one in the way of loose cash or valuables, as "hold-ups" are not infrequent, more particularly for a short period each winter, when a number of "thugs" from across the line, having made Seattle too hot for them, come over and practise their calling in Vancouver. . . .

And it is not only at night that they practise; there are sometimes epidemics of purse-snatching in the West End; ladies are relieved of their vanity bags and purses in the middle of the afternoon in the most fashionable parts of the town! This generally, but not always, occurs during foggy weather. . . .

Sometimes the "thugs" go in for more daring exploits; street cars have been held up, one man wielding the revolver while another relieves the passengers of their valuables. On one occasion a restaurant in the heart of the city was the scene of a daring hold-up in the middle of the day. . . .

Banks have occasionally been robbed in a very bold manner . . . .

But I must not go on describing such things, or you will think that Vancouver is a dangerous place to live in. The possibility of being held up lends a certain spice of excitement to life, and makes one realize that one actually is in the wild and woolly West; but the real hold-up season is very short, the police soon get on their tracks, and the "thugs" are either caught or find it convenient to disappear back across the border.

Common Gaols in Ontario in 1890

Report of the Commissioners Appointed to Enquire into the Prison and Reformatory System of Ontario, 1891 (Toronto, 1891), pp. 121-2.

The common gaols of Ontario are in nearly every respect very unlike those which Howard described or those which Buxton visited. The appointment of the Board of Prison Inspectors in 1859 with large special powers led to great improvements in gaol structures. The work of improvement was continued actively after Confederation under the government of the Province until the gaols of Ontario, with scarcely an exception were so rebuilt or remodelled that the requirements of the Inspection Act were fully carried out. Now the gaols with very few exceptions are well built, well ventilated and well drained and the sunlight is admitted freely into corridor and cell. Unless when a gaol is abnormally crowded there is a cell for each prisoner and the yards in which the prisoners work or take air are sufficiently spacious. That which is the chief obstacle to the reformation of the gaol system of the United States does not exist in this Province. The municipalities construct the buildings, keep them in repair and provide for the maintenance and care of the prisoners, but the Government appoints the sheriffs and the sheriffs appoint the gaolers, subject to the approval of the government, and appoint the turnkeys.   The appointment of the gaoler is practically during good behaviour. Government inspectors are clothed with authority not only to determine how the prisoner shall be fed and treated and to recommend such changes and improvements in the buildings as they think desirable, but when necessary to compel the municipalities by process of law to give effect to their recommendations. Yet the moral evils of which the prison reformers of the United States complain, exist to a serious extent in some of the gaols of Ontario, in which prisoners of all ages and all degrees of guilt are allowed to mix together in the corridors and yards; in others classification is attempted, but is imperfect, and there is the same want of employment in all.   In very many of the gaols the only work the prisoners are required to do in addition to what may perhaps be called the housework, is the cutting, splitting and piling of the firewood used in the gaol, and the shovelling of snow from the walks and paths.

B. Juvenile Delinquency and Child Welfare Institutions

Effect of Bringing Children from Britain

(i)

Report of the Commissioners Appointed to Enquire into the Prison and Reformatory System of Ontario, 1891 (Toronto, 1891), p. 46.

Much evidence was taken as to the character and conduct of the boys and girls who, for some years, have been sent to this country from Great Britain.   The total number must be very large.   The official reports state that the number of those discharged from reformatories who emigrated from the year 1854 to 1888 inclusive, was 2,990 boys and 210 girls, and from Industrial schools from 1862 to 1889 inclusive, 1,432 boys and 324 girls. The reports do not state the number of these sent to Canada, but, no doubt, it was large.   Boards of Poor Law Guardians have sometimes sent out children from the work-houses.   Of these we cannot find any account.   The number sent out by benevolent associations is much larger than that sent by the British local authorities. . . . It may be very well for the boys who, coming here, obtain release from their former associations, and have better opportunities of earning a good living if they choose to be honest and industrious.   But it cannot be good for Canada to absorb such an element in such large quantities.   The importation of criminals half reformed, or reformed only in appearance, of imbeciles, paupers and persons of defective physique or tainted with hereditary disease, must necessarily increase the number of criminals and the volume of crime.   The evidence as to the girls who are sent to us by poor law boards and charitable organizations, was much less favourable than that received concerning the boys.

(ii)

Debates of the House of Commons, Canada, Session 1888, vol. II, p. 1168.

Mr. WILSON (Elgin) . . . I think the Government should seriously consider whether it would be in the best interest of the people of Canada to assist the majority of those children who are brought here. I have had frequent opportunities for a number of years of seeing and examining those who have been brought out by various institutions, and I have no hesitation in saying that they are not a desirable class out of whom to make citizens of this Dominion. I think the Minister stated that careful inspection was made to see that only proper children were brought out. I should like to know what arrangements are made for doing that. I do not know of any regulations of the department providing for any proper inspection of these children before they leave the old country. Many of these children are the offspring of a class of people whom we would not like to become citizens amongst us; many of them are diseased, and I think it should be seriously considered whether it would be wise to allow them to be scattered throughout the country, to mingle and associate with the children of our own people. I certainly think that the Government ought to decide either to exercise every diligence in the selection of these children or else not to render any further aid to that class.

Lack of Playground Facilities

Report of the Commissioners Appointed to Enquire into the Prison and Reformatory System of Ontario, 1891 (Toronto, 1891), Appendix, p. 251: Evidence of the Rev. Thos. Geoghegan, Rector of St. Matthew's Episcopal Church of Hamilton.

Some boys have no restraint at home. They are not restrained or punished probably for delinquencies in the public schools; they are on the street all the night. They have no place of recreation, and there are so many by-laws in the city that they can hardly play a game in the street without rendering themselves liable to be arrested. There are no playgrounds provided; they play cricket and base-ball on the market place; they break a window or a door and are taken in charge by the police, lodged in the police-station and get their first taste of the gaol, and thus do they begin their downward course. If another course had been pursued with these boys I do not think that one boy in ten who is a criminal now would have been a criminal. If they had proper home instruction, and if the Church had done its duty by them, and if the citizens had provided them with a place where they might have indulged in their boyish games. A boy is on the street playing base-ball and he has to steal his game; a policeman comes round and tries to run him down. This boy and some others run away and the next thing they do is perhaps to go into somebody's garden and steal fruit.

The Slum in Toronto

Proceedings Tenth Canadian Conference of Charities and Correction, Held at Toronto, October 19th-21st, 1909, pp. 10-12: Address by Miss Charity Cook.

I was asked to speak on the evils of overcrowding, how it affected the children.   I have the honour to represent the Toronto Mission Union, and we are right in the heart of things in Toronto.   We are told that we have no slum district in Toronto and know nothing about the tenement house; but we do know that there is a great deal of overcrowding, and the effect on the children is something that we will realize better later on.   I fear that Toronto is breeding a class of criminals that will keep it busy to take care of in the next few years, if nothing is done.   The effect on children as regards their health is very bad—our work is all among the poor. . . .

Children rooming with parents is a serious evil.   I could tell you of scores of cases where father, mother and children sleep in one room.   This is downright indifference, but more often it is because it is difficult for parents to realize that their children are grown up. . . .

The people who have the means and power to help don't believe it concerns them, though it does concern them.   The girls who are reared under these adverse circumstances too often go out to spread the contagion of evils.

In these homes there is a lack of proper sanitary conditions—one out-door closet for dozens of men, women and children.   It is simply disgraceful. Then looking out you can see the garbage piled up as high as the window. Nauseating odors and sights on every hand.   How can children grow up decently in homes like these!

. . . It is worse among the foreign element, for they are ignorant of our language and customs.   You can persuade the English-speaking people to improve their surroundings. . . .

Factory System and Child Labour

(i)

Sessional Papers, Canada, 1882, no. 42:   Report of the Commissioners Appointed to Enquire into the Working of Mills and Factories of the Dominion, and the Labor Employed therein.

The employment of children and young persons in mills and factories is extensive, and largely on the increase, the supply being unequal to the demand, particularly in some localities, which may partially explain why those of such tender years are engaged.   As to obtaining with accuracy the ages of the children employed, we found some difficulty, inasmuch as the employer has no record thereof, having no interest or obligation in so doing; consequently, in order to ascertain their ages, they were interrogated either by one of the Commissioners or some one in the factory.   We are sorry to report that in very many instances the children, having no education whatever, could not tell their ages; this applies more particularly to those from twelve years downwards—some being found as young as eight or nine years. . . . Occasionally, when we could gain the confidence of the very young children, we took the opportunity of ascertaining, as far as possible, why they were at work so young, with answers as follows:—"Having no father, had to help mother get a living."—"Would rather work than go to school." Some are there from the cupidity of their parents who have good positions as mechanics; others from the idle habits of the parents, who live on the earnings of the children, this being confirmed in one instance where three children were at work having a father as above described. Your Commissioners found this too often the case in cities and factory districts. It must be borne in mind that the children invariably work as many hours as adults, and if not compelled, are requested to work overtime when circumstances so demand, which has not been unusual of late in most lines of manufactures. The appearance and condition of the children in the after part of the day, such as may be witnessed in the months of July and August, was anything but inviting or desirable. They have to be at the mills or factories at 6.30 a.m., necessitating their being up at from 5.30 to 6 o'clock for their morning meal, some of them having to walk a distance of half a mile or more to their work. . . .

We find, in some trades where piece-work is done and where children are employed, that they are not engaged by the firm or managers of the shop or factory, but by the hands who take such piece-work to do, who arrange with the children as to the value of the labor, and who are solely interested in procuring the cheapest labor possible, irrespective of any other consideration as to the interests or condition of the labor employed. As to the attendance at school of children under fourteen years employed in the factories, there is no attempt to attend school at all, from the fact that the regulations under which they work would not allow it. We have observed with regret a serious lack of education in very many of the adult factory hands. In some parts of the country a large proportion are to be found who can neither read nor write.

(ii)

Report of the Royal Commission on the Relations of Labor and Capital (Ottawa, 1889): Second Report, p. 87.

To arrive at the greatest results for the smallest expenditure the mills and factories are filled with women and children, to the practical exclusion of adult males. The reason for this is obvious. Females and children may be counted upon to work for small wages, to submit to petty and exasperating exactions, and to work uncomplainingly for long hours. These are the inducements to employ this class of labor and why it is being utilized so largely. It would be wrong to blame any individual mill-owner or corporation for this state of affairs. It is entirely due to the system which all alike work by. So long as one employer is permitted to fill up his factory with this cheap labor, without any restrictions, the others are compelled to do likewise, or suffer the consequences of being undersold in the general market. There are, however, excrescences upon the system for which individuals are altogether responsible, and for which there ought to be some way of holding them to strict account.   One such presented itself in Montreal, where the conduct of a cigar manufacturer, in a large way of business, was under examination. . . . It is almost impossible to believe that such things should be done in the latter part of the nineteenth century, and yet it is very clearly proved that in this factory apprentices were imprisoned in a "black hole" for hours at a time. Occasionally the incarceration would stretch beyond the working hours, and a special visit would be made to the factory to release the poor little fellows. A special constable, who still wore his constable's badge, was employed to overawe and strike terror into the hearts of the juvenile offenders, and to carry out the punishment awarded by the proprietor and his foreman. Occasionally this Oriental despot would himself be the executioner of his own decrees, and did, upon one occasion, personally chastise, in a flagrantly indecent manner, a girl eighteen years of age. And for all this the law provides no remedy—nay, incredible as it may appear, law, in the person of the Recorder of Montreal, expressly authorized the punishment inflicted. This gentleman, on being examined, stated that he had authorized employers to chastise their operatives at their discretion, so long as no permanent injury was inflicted; and this evidence was given in the Year of Our Lord one thousand eight hundred and eighty-eight, much as it might be wished that it referred to some period of the dark ages, when servants had no rights which their masters were bound to respect.   The evidence describes a state of affairs which is simply astounding.   So vicious was it that a boy who was one of the witnesses before this Commission asked to be sent to the reformatory as a means of escape from the treatment he received.   The cigar manufacturer, when detailing his actions in the case of the young girl whom he so shamefully treated, seemed to think it a matter of very small consequence—a matter-of-fact, every-day occurrence, which it was not worth while making any ado about; and the Recorder was equally complacent when stating that he had empowered employers of labor to chastise their apprentices, because, in his opinion, it was "in accordance with common sense, which is the natural law, and conforms with positive Divine law and the civil law."   Comment on such evidence would be superfluous. But it may be said that if there is any civil law in existence which authorizes the infliction of corporal punishment, as stated by the Recorder, it ought at once to be repealed; for so long as it remains upon the Statute Book Canada has no right to class herself with the civilized nations of the earth.

Other cases of brute force resorted to by employers came before the Commission, but none of so flagrant a character.

Newsboys and Juvenile Delinquency

Report of the Commissioners Appointed to Enquire into the Prison and Reformatory System of Ontario, 1891 (Toronto, 1891), Appendix, pp. 723-8:   Evidence of J. J. Kelso, Toronto Humane Society.

I became interested in children through seeing them at the police court. One of the first things that caught my attention was the large number of boys of thirteen, fourteen or fifteen who were brought up for larceny, and in most cases convicted and sent to the Penetanguishene Reformatory. I found that most of these were newsboys. The profession of selling newspapers is in my opinion pernicious right through. There is no system of dealing with those engaged in it so as to bring out their moral nature. Those boys had reached an age when they were too large to sell papers. The general public buy papers from small boys in preference to large ones, and then again, as between boys and girls, the girls got the patronage, so that the profession of the larger boy was gone. These boys live like princes in their own way, and when they cannot sell papers they are driven to stealing to keep up their style of life. I have known dozens of cases where these boys made small boys break a window or unfasten doors, and would steal silk handkerchiefs and any fancy article that could be always disposed of. . . . I have studied this question in all its branches, and I have been watching these children closely for the past four years. There was no system of dealing with boys. Any one could leave his parents and go right into this business of selling papers. I drew up a law to license them and got it passed through the municipal council. . . .

The very first step taken was to prevent girls selling newspapers. I have frequently had evidence of how young girls who pursued this calling were ruined by designing persons. From the moment the law intending to keep them off the street was framed they disappeared. The boys would not go to the Newsboys' Home, which was specially provided for them, and there was no law to compel them to do so. There are nice clean beds there, with texts on the wall or over the bed, and appropriate mottoes. The boys are compelled to be clean, to have a bath. The average newsboy wants to go to the theatre and to entertainments of a not very desirable kind, and he would not submit to these regulations. These boys were scattered amongst the low dives. A gang went to a place called — — where, by paying five cents, they had the privilege of sleeping on the floor. They never took their clothes off from Saturday night till Monday morning. This man encouraged the boys to steal and to acts of rascality. They saw nothing there but evil, and were allowed facilities for indulging in all kinds of vice. This man's influence upon the boys was of the very worst character. He had a ready means of disposing of all the stolen articles. . . . The regulations regarding these boys are not in force to-day. The papers thought that it was going to hurt their business. . . . There is no training these boys to habits of industry. They will neglect their work, run away, and throw themselves out of a situation without the slightest regard of what is to become of them. My idea is that we ought to endeavor to do away with this system altogether, to stop entirely a large number of these boys from pursuing this occupation. I think that we ought to have stalls with old couples in charge of them for the vending of newspapers, just as they have in New York. . . .

There are at least two hundred of the boys licensed who have no responsible guardians or parents. In many cases the parents are drunkards and the boys drifted into this life as early as five or six years of age. I have known most heartrending instances of where children have been sent out to sell papers or beg, and the money has been taken away from them. . . .

Now, the fact is that here we establish schools for the respectable citizens' children, but no one is interested in these other children to see that they are educated. . . . It has been a source of great tribulation to me to see the way in which children are systematically manufactured into criminals. There is no other term can be applied to it. Take a child of seven or eight years of age and send it to gaol. By putting it there you break down the instinctive dread that every child has of prison. You habituate the child to this kind of thing. We have an Act passed for the protection and reformation of neglected children, but unfortunately the principle has not been carried out. . . . We have done nothing in the way of getting our own children on farms or in places where they may find comfortable homes either in this Province or in the Northwest, and yet we complain because other people are doing so. . . . There are a great many of these boys who live round these places, in the Model lodging house and cheap eating houses all over the city who might very well be drafted into the country. Then there are the boys about the theatre. I have seen a great deal about this, they go to the theatre and sit in the top place where they only pay 10c., and the class of plays they go to see is Irish comedy and Irish drama of the most sensational sort. That is the kind of play these boys go to see. There are large numbers—I am prepared to say that there are hundreds every night, between the ages of seven and fifteen, who go to witness the lowest kind of dramas. . . .

The Churches in Toronto don't do a solitary thing to save these boys. Another thing I would suggest is to try to have a play-ground for boys, a common play-ground. The play-grounds of the schools are all closed up the moment the schools are dispersed. Everybody knows that if a boy does not get a chance to develop himself physically, to work off his animal spirits, these spirits will find vent in some direction. There ought to be an entirely different system adopted to try to reclaim these boys who have fallen into crime. There is no society established for dealing with neglected children. We have an organization for taking hold of adult prisoners who get to gaol, but there is not a single effort made to prevent children from becoming criminals. . . . This system of ours has resulted in loss of property and danger to the community, and I declare most emphatically that we have got no system of looking after children to-day. Penetanguishene Reformatory was established at a time when this child question did not receive any consideration. I think it is a relic of a past age and is not adapted to the requirements of the world anywhere to-day.

Problem of Children in Rural Districts

Proceedings Fifth Canadian Conference of Charities and Correction, Hamilton, September 25th-27th, 1902, pp. 31-3: Address of the Rev. James Lediard, Owen Sound.

This Conference necessarily looks at these matters very largely from the standpoint of the city. We begin by thinking that rural districts have little

occasion for work of this kind.   As a matter of fact the protection of children
in rural districts is made a sort of secondary matter.   I want to speak this
morning on behalf of the rural districts in connection with this work among
children.   In the first place, rural children need protection.   During the
few years in which I have been engaged in this work, one of the things that
has astonished me is, that although I live in a busy town of 10,000, more
neglected children have been removed from the rural sections of the country
than from Owen Sound or the one or two other small towns or large villages.
I want to impress on you that there is a very large and important field of
work in the small communities.   Children in the rural districts are exposed
to precisely the same dangers as in the city.   The main line of difference
grows out of the fact, that the evil influences in the country are very largely
from the homes of the children rather than from the neighbors.   The three
things to which children are exposed in the country or city are, first neglect,
then cruelty, and the evil of vice and immoral surroundings. . . .

There is, as I have already intimated, a lack of protection in these rural
districts, because it is not supposed that these iniquities abound or exist at
all.   This lack of protection grows first of all out of the fact that the people
themselves and the authorities themselves being in the country do nothing
. . . .

My contention is the rural children can live in these conditions because
they are rural, because people are afraid of the law, of the lawyers, afraid of
publicity.

Juvenile Delinquency on the Prairies and Lack of Reformatory

Sessional Papers, Canada, 1909, no. 28, Appendix C: Annual Report of Superintendent G. E. Sanders, North-West Mounted Police, Regina, November 1,
1908.

Juvenile Offenders.—Although we show only four convictions under this
heading, the last year has seen a large number of these cases brought up by
the city police in Regina and Moosejaw.   The fact of there being no reformatory has been felt, and magistrates have had to content themselves in many
instances with giving admonition and allowing offenders to go free who
undoubtedly, for the public good and their own, should have been placed
in reformatories.   A few juvenile offenders, who were absolutely incorrigible,
have been sentenced to the penitentiary.   The erection of a reformatory for
the western provinces is urgently required.

Juvenile Reformatory Institutions in Ontario in 1890

*Report of the Commissioners Appointed to Enquire into the Prison and Reformatory
System of Ontario, 1891* (Toronto, 1891), pp. 87-103.

THE REFORMATORY FOR BOYS

A great mistake was made in the selection of the site of the Reformatory
for Boys at Penetanguishene.   When the Government found it necessary
to establish this reformatory they thought it would be economical to use

for the purpose a barracks which had been unoccupied since the war of 1812. This will not seem surprising when we remember that in those days the prevailing idea respecting reformatories was that they should be little else than prisons, in which juveniles, while receiving some education and industrial training, should be strictly confined, punishment being, at least, one of the chief objects of their incarceration. When the erection of the present massive structure was found necessary there seemed to be no reason for moving to another locality as the ideas as to what a reformatory school should be had undergone little change. The new structure was but a more commodious prison. The boys were every evening locked up in a triple tier of cells, with doors of iron bars and fastenings strong enough to hold the most desperate felons, and when allowed out during the day they were confined within a strong and very high close fence. And guards were set night and day to prevent escapes. . . .

The high fence and the rattle of the keeper's keys as he opens or closes the entrance gate still give the place much of the appearance of a prison on the exterior. Inside the fence things look much better. . . . Where those tiers of cells once stood they found a large, airy, well-lit dining room, admirably arranged, and a dormitory. . . .

The present state of the law is undoubtedly a great obstacle to the successful working of this reformatory. . . . Until full power to license deserving boys or place them out on probation be vested in a local authority the reformatory cannot do all the good it ought to do.

Ontario Industrial Refuge for Girls

This institution, which the commissioners visited and carefully inspected, appears to have thus far worked very satisfactorily. . . . A great obstacle to the success of the Refuge is that it is placed within the walls which also enclose the reformatory for women. The girls cannot be kept in ignorance of the character of the women whom they see several times every day from their playgrounds, and with whom several of the larger girls are brought in contact every day in the kitchen and elsewhere.

Ontario Industrial Schools

Industrial schools are regarded in Ontario as a part of its school system. The Act of 1884 (47 Vic. c, 46), provided that they may be established by "the public school board of trustees for any city or town, or the separate school trustees therein," or by any philanthropic society or societies incorporated under the Act respecting benevolent, provident and other societies, or any other Act in force in the Province, to whom any board of school trustees may "delegate the powers, rights and privileges conferred on such board" by the Act. . . .

By the provisions of this Act great progress has been made towards a thorough system of dealing with destitute and neglected children and those who have committed petty offences. The facilities afforded for placing all such children in the industrial schools are ample. The powers given to the boards or societies managing such schools, although not all that are necessary, are extensive.   They may make by-laws subject to the approval of the Lieutenant-Governor in Council and rules and regulations which when approved of by the Minister of Education have force of law.   They may place children out on licence or probation and recall them when such action seems necessary.   They may return children to their parents when they think proper or, the parents being dead, place them with other persons giving satisfactory security and in so doing discharge them from the custody of the board or society.   The Minister of Education may, by his own authority, order the discharge of any child at any time. . . .

The system created by this Act is, however, defective in some important respects.   It makes no provision for the reformation or preservation of children in their own homes as is done under the probation system of Massachusetts; no provision for placing in any other home, unless through the industrial school, the children of vicious parents or those who are destitute. . . .

The school at Mimico, still the only industrial school in the Province, is conveniently situated on a farm of 50 acres of good land a few miles from the city of Toronto and a short distance from a railway station. . . . The school was opened about three and a half years ago. . . . The school is conducted on the combined cottage and congregate plan.

Inadequacy of Machinery Dealing with Juveniles

Proceedings Tenth Canadian Conference of Charities and Correction, Held at Toronto, October 19th-21st, 1909, pp. 38-41: Statement of Mr. W. L. Scott, President of the Children's Aid Society of Ottawa.

Child-rescue work in Ontario, the betterment of the conditions of the neglected and dependent and delinquent children, is very largely in the hands of the Department of Neglected and Dependent Children and of the Children's Aid Societies, organized under its supervision and forming in fact branches or outposts of it. . . .

It must always be borne in mind that the children dealt with are of two classes, the neglected and dependent and the delinquent.   Not that this is a scientific division. . . . But the two classes must be treated as distinct, in this country at least, because the methods of dealing with them are necessarily somewhat different.   The status of neglected and dependent children is a matter within the exclusive jurisdiction of the Provincial Legislature, whereas a child who offends against the criminal law can be dealt with only under a Dominion Act.

For dealing with neglected and dependent children, the Children's Protection Act of Ontario provides an admirable system.   I do not know of its equal elsewhere.   Briefly put, it seeks to provide a good domestic home for every child whose home surroundings are not what they should be.   Every effort is made to improve the natural home, and where that proves impracticable, and only then, the children are removed under an order of the Court and placed in good foster-homes. . . .

And yet the work has not been half done. The Superintendent and the workers under him have been doing the very best possible under the circumstances. It is no fault of theirs; but it is true. . . .

The present Act does not make sufficient provision for the financial support of the work locally. Too much is left to voluntary effort and too great a tax is put on those who are willingly giving their time and effort and money in aid of the cause. When the Act was first adopted it was thought that the local societies would be generally endowed by wealthy persons in the several localities, and that this has not been so has been spoken of by Mr. Kelso as one of the disappointments of the work. It was also expected that the local municipalities would very largely take over the local support of the work. Experience has, however, proved that at least in the majority of cases the municipalities cannot be relied on to afford anything like adequate support. It is surely time for the Legislature to recognize that these are the conditions and that other means must be provided; for the present system places very serious limitations upon the work. In the first place, speaking broadly, the work is done only in those places where there happen to be persons willing to voluntarily undertake it. In most of these places, moreover, it is done in a desultory, haphazard manner and by no means thoroughly and systematically as it should be. In the large town of Pembroke, for instance, where there is a crying need for it, there is no society and nothing is being done. There is no society in any of the newer portions of Ontario, although there are plenty of neglected children there. In many towns and even cities where splendid work was once being done, societies no longer exist, or interest has largely subsided. The enthusiasts have moved away or lost interest. Really good and systematic work is being done only where a paid official is devoting all his time to it and in larger cities one paid official is not enough. . . .

Turning to the work with delinquents as such, we find our needs to be still greater. There is no use disguising the fact; we are at present far behind the age. We talk of our Juvenile Courts, but we have in fact no Juvenile Courts in the modern sense. We have separate sittings of our Criminal Courts for the trials of juvenile offenders, but these are not Juvenile Courts in the true sense. Probation, the essential element of the true Juvenile Court, is wanting. . . . Outside of the City of Ottawa the law does not provide for probation anywhere in Ontario. There is less excuse for this when it is remembered that the Juvenile Delinquents Act may be at once proclaimed in any place where facilities are provided for its proper enforcement. This Act has for some time been in force throughout the Province of Manitoba. It is before long to be put in force throughout the Province of Quebec. . . . In the City of Montreal probation has been in voluntary operation for two years. The Act is shortly to be put in force in Prince Edward Island, and probably in the three most Western Provinces also. . . . It is, therefore, time for Ontario to bestir herself.

C. Prostitution and Problems of Morality

Effect of Bringing out Children from Britain

Report of the Commissioners Appointed to Enquire into the Prison and Reformatory System of Ontario, 1891 (Toronto, 1891), Appendix, pp. 540-1: Evidence of W. T. T. Williams, Chief of Police, London.

Lots of girls who are prostitutes in this country are girls who have been brought from the old country.   They get out into the country, they become unmanageable at the schools, and the people who brought them out don't report them.   After a time they go into prostitution and drunken habits.   Old country girls of this class are more apt to get into the way of drinking than girls of the same class in this country.   I think very many of them go wrong through hereditary taint.   They are not strong enough to resist temptation.   They are physically weak.   I am not talking of children who come out with their parents.   I am talking of those brought up in the slums, and brought out for the purpose of being absorbed into the population here.   I would recommend prohibition altogether for them.   I would say, moreover, that besides being undesirable citizens in themselves, their presence has a bad effect upon others.   After they have been at work in the country they make for the cities, and sometimes they bring some country girls with them.   I have often known girls of the class I have described bring country girls into the city.   I can call to mind several cases; the police have found them here and have sent them home again. . . .

The careless way in which the sexes are allowed to mix together is productive of much harm.   When people come into the hospital I find that that is a cause of their going wrong.   There are lots of women who are picked up in the streets who come here for hospital purposes, and we have found that most of them, when they got into this way, had left farm houses.   A man and wife and family sleep down stairs in a house, and the hired man, perhaps, sleeps next to the girl and, of course, the temptation to immorality exists and no care is exercised in the way of protecting the girl.

Factory System and Morality

Report of the Royal Commission on the Relations of Labor and Capital (Ottawa, 1889): Second Report, p. 90.

Grave charges of immorality have from time to time been made against female operatives in the large mills and factories.   Whenever such charges have been made very serious apprehension has been felt by the public and careful enquiry has been made, in order to arrive at a correct conclusion upon this all-important subject.

In considering this matter it is necessary to look closely at the conditions of life in which—through no fault of their own—these young girls are placed. Stern necessity obliges them to earn a livelihood, and in pursuance of the avocation by which they earn their daily bread they are frequently compelled to toil for long, weary hours in close, ill-ventilated rooms.   In these rooms there is a general co-mingling of the sexes, which is partly necessitated by the nature of the work in which they are engaged, and which cannot be avoided so long as the division of the task between males and females remains as at present.   To this extent employers are not to blame, but when we find that in many cases the closet accommodation is lamentably insufficient, and that no attempt is made at the separation of these conveniences, grave censure is merited.   It has been sufficiently demonstrated that in some factories closets are used indiscriminately by the operatives of both sexes, and where the employer is thus careless of the moral feelings of his operatives it should be the duty of the State to interfere and see that the proprieties of life are strictly observed.   In further consideration of the cases of these girls it must be remembered that for a considerable period after commencing work in a mill or factory they are paid such small wages that it is almost impossible for them to live respectably and clothe themselves decently out of the amount.

Given these conditions, it is not a matter for surprise that one is occasionally driven in despair to a life of sin.   But it is monstrous to condemn a whole class because of an occasional sinner, as has been far too frequently done in this matter. . . .

The bare fact that a girl is willing to work hard during a long and tedious day for a very small allowance ought to be conclusive evidence that she is not inclined to a life of sin.

Immigration and Problems of Morality

Report of the Social Survey Commission of Toronto (Toronto, 1915), pp. 41-2.

The great tide of immigration that has of late years been flowing into this country has presented serious problems to our Canadian communities, especially the larger cities; and among these problems not the least is the complication of the social evil.

To begin with, it must be recognized that in some of the countries of Europe from which large numbers of immigrants are coming to us, the standards of sexual morality as well as the general standards of living, are not those of Canada.   And when these immigrants, speaking little or no English, are huddled together in crowded city quarters, in squalid surroundings, without wholesome recreation facilities, vicious conditions readily arise and are difficult to cope with. . . .

It is not alone the immigrant of foreign birth, however, whom this problem touches.   The facts show that in connection with young women immigrants from Great Britain there is a problem, for the protection of both the young women themselves and of the Canadian communities. . . . The fact remains a serious one that so large a proportion of this social wreckage should consist of young women who have recently come to this country from the motherland. . . .

Closely connected, probably, with the problem of immigration, is the fact, noted already, in another connection, that the commonest occupation of girls who go wrong is that of domestic service.

The Chinese

Sessional Papers, Canada, 1885, no. 54a: Report of Mr. Justice Gray, Member of the Royal Commission on Chinese Immigration.

With reference to Chinese prostitution the evidence shows that out of a total of 10,550 Chinese in the Province [of British Columbia] there are altogether only 154 Chinese women, of whom seventy are prostitutes, scattered throughout the Province entirely among their own countrymen, many as concubines, that relationship being among them deemed no offence, and no discredit.

It is doubtful whether a similar number of English or American people in a strange country would show any better record, though they might not use exactly the same terms.   In dealing with this question it is impossible to avoid plain language.

The evidence does not show reasonable ground for fearing in British Columbia, any contaminating influence from either one or the other of these vices, as coming from the Chinese.   It may safely be affirmed that the white associates (few as they are) of the low Chinese in these vices will be themselves found to come from the lowest and most degraded classes of the whites, persons so utterly dead to every feeling that becomes either a respectable man or a virtuous woman, that wherever they might be, in whatever city of the world, if it were possible to find any place lower than an opium den or a Chinese house of prostitution, it is there they would have to be sought.   It is a reflection upon the people of British Columbia to assume that as a people they could be led away by such degraded tastes.

In the police reports extending over five years from 1879, there are only two charges against the Chinese for prostitution, and none against any of the Chinese for the improper sale or use of opium, or for having misled, seduced, or enticed any white man, woman or child into their places of residence, or for having beguiled them in any way into their company for improper purposes, either of cohabitation or opium smoking.   It may here be observed that the police of the city of Victoria are a fine body of men, prompt in the discharge of their duties, vigilant as to offences against the laws, or infractions of the municipal regulations; and in no way tainted with love or affection for the Chinese.

In a country where whiskey drinking prevails to an unlimited extent, and where white and Indian prostitutes can be found and are known to exist in unknown numbers, it seems a contradiction to assume a dread of the white population becoming demoralized from the presence of seventy Chinese prostitutes, in a population of 10,550 Chinese people living in accordance with the customs of their country, and a practice of opium smoking among their own people, infinitesimally small, when compared with the practice of whiskey drinking among the whites.

Prostitution in Toronto

Report of the Social Survey Commission of Toronto (Toronto, 1915), pp. 9-17.

At the beginning of the investigation, it was a matter of surprise that the number of houses of ill-fame in the narrower sense appeared to be so small. It seemed incredible that the number definitely located (otherwise than by rumor) could represent the extent of commercialized vice in a city of this size. Further investigation, however, soon disclosed the explanation of this state of affairs. The bawdy house, as popularly understood, is only one of many methods adopted by this business, and by no means the most frequent or important one as far as Toronto is concerned. Moreover, these houses often do not conduct their business in a very open fashion. . . . In spite, however, of these precautions, it is comparatively easy to locate houses of ill-fame in considerable numbers, and scattered practically all over the City, though naturally they are more numerous in certain central districts, where there is a large floating population. . . .

That bawdy houses do not exist in greater numbers is explained by the existence of another class of houses, which may be described as houses of assignation. The house of this class usually keeps no prostitutes as inmates, but to it a number of prostitutes take the men whom they "pick up" on the streets or in other public places. The keeper of the house receives either a percentage of the prostitute's receipts, or a fixed fee for the use of the room for a short time. . . .

Besides those who are inmates of bawdy houses, or connected with houses of assignation, there is a very numerous class of individual prostitutes, who use their own rooms or apartments for immoral purposes. Sometimes this is done secretly, *i.e.*, without the landlady's knowledge or connivance. . . . In still other cases, the keepers of the house deliberately close their eyes to what goes on, but exact payment for their connivance in the form of higher room rents. It is only a step from this last-named practice to combining the business of keeping a rooming or apartment house with that of conducting a house of assignation, the legitimate business serving as a blind for the unlawful one.

When all these varieties of houses of ill-fame are included, the number, instead of being surprisingly small, is found to be extremely large. The Commission did not attempt a complete enumeration of them. . . . But from actual information in the possession of the Commission, it would appear that even the statements occasionally made about houses of ill-fame "existing by hundreds" in Toronto, while certainly grossly exaggerated if a house of ill-fame be understood in the usual sense, are not greatly exaggerated if the definition be extended, as it is in the statute, so as to include all houses or rooms which are used or resorted to for purposes of prostitution. . . .

The whole business of prostitution is attended by the practice of soliciting on the streets and in other public places. . . .

As to the prevalence of street soliciting, reports of a startling character were made by several investigators who were independently and on different occasions sent to investigate this matter. The Commission was not, however, content to base its conclusions as to this very important matter upon a few observations made under what might have chanced to be exceptional conditions. It accordingly had it kept under observation by a number of observers for a considerable period, with the result of proving conclusively that a number of the city streets are patrolled at practically all hours of the day and evening by many women and girls—often very young girls—plying their nefarious trade. . . .

It is not only the streets, however, that are frequented by prostitutes. They resort to certain hotels and restaurants, which become known as rendezvous. Four or five of the well-known hotels in the City are notorious in this regard. These are not of the lowest class of hotel—in fact, some of them are of distinctly high-class pretensions. . . . Some restaurants are used in a similar way, as rendezvous. Also the ostensible business of a restaurant or ice-cream parlor is sometimes used as a cloak for the traffic in vice. . . . Restaurants are in some cases not merely rendezvous for loose characters, but actually participate in their business. . . . Certain hotels rent their rooms in the daytime for immoral purposes. . . .

One of the very serious—if not from a social standpoint the most serious —of the many phases of the social evil in Toronto is the large number of what may perhaps be described as "occasional" prostitutes. By the "occasional" prostitute is meant a woman or girl who, while leading an immoral life, does not depend for her living wholly upon the proceeds of prostitution. . . . These "occasionals" are of many varieties. Some are married women who "sport" with or without their husband's knowledge or connivance; some are girls living at home, sometimes in quite respectable homes. Domestics, business or working women, chorus girls, are represented in this class. Their degrees of connection with the business are equally varied. . . .

As to the extent of this "occasional" prostitution, it is impossible to give definite statistics. The importance of the subject, however, was thought sufficient to warrant extended and careful enquiry and observation; and the conditions revealed were shocking. . . .

The conditions in Toronto are less favorable to the cadet than in some other places, and consequently this detestable specimen of humanity is less common here, but is not by any means unknown. An extension of the last-named phase of the cadet's business appears to exist in some of the foreign colonies in Toronto, in the form of what might almost be called a vice trust. A certain set of men, who by virtue of longer residence in this country plausibly represent themselves as "knowing the ropes" and possessing influence of various sorts, levy tribute upon prostitutes, keepers and cadets, partly by promise of aid in case of trouble, partly by threats of denunciation to the police, sometimes even by violence. In return for the tribute, they render, or pretend to render, service by influencing the police, by "fixing" the evidence in case of prosecution, etc. The existence and extent of this system are very difficult to verify, especially as its field of operation is among the non-English immigrants, but information concerning it has been received from several independent sources, closely in touch with conditions in those quarters of the city.

28

Closely connected with this local business, is that of transferring women from place to place to meet the demands of the traffic. . . .

A question to which the Commission has given earnest attention is that of the existence in Toronto of a "white slave traffic." . . . But while a considerable body of information has been accumulated as to the influences and causes by which girls are corrupted, and led to enter upon a life of professional vice, there has been no positive evidence secured of the existence in Toronto of a system of obtaining and retaining involuntary victims for the business of vice of such dimensions or character as to warrant the statement that a "white slave traffic" flourishes here. For such a statement implies not merely the occurrence of individual cases, but the existence of an organized system for keeping up the supply of prostitutes by such nefarious means. The mere fact that, so far as Toronto is concerned, the great majority of prostitutes are not inmates of resorts conducted by others, but are operating on their own account, is an indication that "white slave" methods are not a prime factor in the business here. There can be little doubt, however, that individual cases do occur. . . .

For a number of years, Toronto newspapers have been publishing advertisements of massage parlors. . . .

In all the massage parlors investigated, the operators were women, and, with one or two exceptions, the customers were men. In a few cases, the women professed to be trained nurses or beauty specialists and to carry on only legitimate massage, but, for the most part, the operators were wholly ignorant of scientific massage, and the prevalence of nefarious practices among the places advertising massage treatment was fully established.

Prostitution in the Small Town

Proceedings Eleventh Meeting of the Canadian Conference of Charities and Correction, Held in Guelph, Ontario, June 22nd-24th, 1910, p. 37: Paper Presented by Chief Constable Slemin, Brantford.

We have not a single known house of ill-fame in Brantford. All shady places are watched by the police and stamped out immediately. Anyone arriving in our city who is suspected of being a bad character is sent for by me, soundly advised, thus giving him or her an opportunity to do better, and leaving the impression that our city must be kept clean and free from immorality.

Prostitution in London, Ontario

The London Survey, Prepared under the Auspices of the Men's Federation of London, Oct.-Dec., 1913, p. 76.

Social vice exists in London in three forms—the house of prostitution, the house of assignation, and street soliciting.

The house of prostitution is conducted so as to avoid all suspicion. Usually it hides behind the "furnished rooms to let" sign. One of the most notorious of these places has two such signs in the windows. This is done more to throw off suspicion than to catch the unwary.   Everything is done to make the place look just like the neighbouring houses.   The front rooms are well lighted and the curtains never drawn.   The number of inmates vary. Usually not more than two or three women live in the house; although other women frequent it and are in constant telephone communication.

The houses of assignation are more widely scattered.   They are frequented by the women who solicit on the street.   Most of these women are intimate friends of the woman living in the house.

Street soliciting is more common than would be expected in a city the size of London.   Some of the hotel side rooms and the curtained rooms in certain restaurants are contributing factors.

Prostitution in Prairie Frontier Towns

Sessional Papers, Canada, 1891, no. 19, Appendix E: Annual Report of Superintendent R. B. Deane, Commanding "K" Division, North-West Mounted Police, Lethbridge, 1890.

Incorporation [of Lethbridge] will enable the town to provide for the "social evil," and it is to be hoped that the authorities will not allow themselves to be urged by fanatics into going too far.

As I say elsewhere, I have devoted a great deal of time and trouble to checking the prostitution of Indian women, but the evil cannot be abated altogether, the next best thing to abating it is to have it under control. . . .

The Indians have behaved very well on the whole in this District. . . .

Unless they have some work or means of livelihood we do not let them stay near town, although they know as well as we do that we have no right to interfere with them.

The principal trouble with them is in connection with their women. For instance, an Indian comes here with his family and says he has got work —probably just enough to swear by in connection with the slaughter house or something of the kind.   He then establishes his women kind in the river bottom and thither go all sorts and conditions of men, not unfrequently provided with whiskey which answers their purpose better than the cash value thereof.

Prostitution in the Lumbering Town

B. Pullen-Burry, *From Halifax to Vancouver* (Toronto, 1912), pp. 322-4.

Cranbrook [British Columbia] has a population of 3,500; out of this number 1,300 are employed in saw-mills in the district. . . . The town has an unenviable reputation.   Report says hundreds of undesirable women have made this centre their particular sphere of influence.   Formerly, it seems, they lived within the limits of the town municipality, but on the proposed erection of a Young Men's Christian Association building, they were instructed to quit, which they did, and created a colony of little houses the other side of the railway, but nearly opposite the new Y.M.C.A.!   As I was eating an unappetising meal, two remarkably well-dressed coloured women entered, and used the telephone a few feet from where I sat. The gist of their communication was as obvious as their profession. . . .

As I left this town early next morning, I observed from the train a number of small houses with lights in front of them of the colour of blood, and I thought of the perils the young of both sexes run in such places as these, where respectable housing for those who cannot pay hotel-rates is practically impossible to obtain.

Police Controls and Prostitution in Toronto

Report of the Commissioners Appointed to Enquire into the Prison and Reformatory System of Ontario, 1891 (Toronto, 1891), Appendix, pp. 101-4: Evidence of David Archibald, Staff-Inspector of Toronto Police Force.

The children of respectable, but poor parents, are sent out to sell newspapers; we prohibit girls from selling newspapers now, but they have gone out together in the past and they become contaminated by association with other boys and girls in various ways. Amongst the girls this contamination develops prostitution. I suppose that three-fourths of those girls developed into prostitutes. They were taken advantage of in the first place by disreputable people. That is the reason why such a strong effort was made to take the girls off the street altogether. . . .

[Importation of children from the old country] adds to the street walkers and prostitutes. A considerable proportion of the girls who fall into the hands of the police have been found in this line, but there have not been so many of the boys. The boys sent out under these auspices are principally sent to the country. If they are really bad boys they gravitate towards the city. . . .

My experience is that drunkenness is the result of prostitution more than prostitution is the result of drunkenness. My experience of this class is that those who are found in houses of ill-fame have been, as a rule, respectably reared, well educated, accomplished, perhaps, and that they never touched liquor until after their fall. . . .

As a rule they become demoralized, lose perhaps a fashionable position in life, and hide themselves and their shame from those with whom they had formerly been associated. They gradually become demoralized until at last they fall into drunkenness and the lowest form of street walking. . . .

When I was appointed to this special work six years ago, I made an official visit to the houses of ill-fame that then existed, accompanied by one or two other officers. I visited thirty-five known to be houses of ill-fame. I found on an average about four women in each house, and I found that two-thirds of this number were Americans. I took the name, age, nationality and length of time they were in this kind of life and I compiled a book containing the information. I gave them distinctly to understand that the law for the suppression of vice and houses of ill-fame was to be rigorously enforced in Toronto. . . . On my second visit I found that half the number had disappeared altogether. I was told by the officers on duty that they went in large numbers, with their trunks, to the station, and took tickets for the other side.   The law has been strictly enforced from that day to this, and the number of houses of ill-fame in Toronto has been reduced to a mini- mum, the number of women that are to be found in those houses is very few, and there is more trouble with the class of women who have become completely demoralized and have to be picked up as drunks and for soliciting on the streets. . . .

We find that there is not half the number arrested for prostitution that there was before.   Their houses have been broken up and soliciting is not carried on at all except in the worst parts of the city.   I don't think there are half as many now as there were in 1865, when the population was not more than a quarter of what it is now.   As a general thing citizens say that they find it a very rare thing to be solicited in the street by women.   In fact, unless you go to certain portions of St. John's ward, women will not solicit men on the streets at all, and a few years ago it was quite a common thing to be solicited in the most fashionable streets in the city. . . . The increased vigilance of the police, the increased number of policemen on duty, the increased facilities for dealing with prisoners, the patrol-wagon system have all contributed to diminish largely the number of this class of people on the streets of Toronto. . . .

I have been associated with the prison gate work commonly called the Haven, and also with the rescue branch of the Salvation Army, which is dealing especially with this class of females, and I have known some remark- able cases of reformation through both of these agencies.   Quite a consider- able number have been reformed. . . . I may say that in connection with the Salvation Army work, I have heard Commissioner Adams give statistics for three years showing that in dealing with this class, he had 80 per cent. of good results, and the work at the Haven has also been exceedingly good, as evidenced by the statement of the president of that association.

Immigration to the West and Growth of Immorality

Public Archives of Canada, S.P.G. in F.P., Canada, 1860-7; St. James, Assiniboia, July 13, 1860, the Rev. W. H. Taylor to Secretary, Society for the Propagation of the Gospel.

But I must not keep back the mention of that which is really a matter of regret, with an increase of useful settlers, we have also an increase of such as seek to get wealth by any means, especially by the sale of spiritous liquors.   There is an increase of those that drink them, and sad and sickening of late have been the consequences of an excessive indulgence in whiskey. We mourn, too, over a recklessness of temper in some of the young of both sexes—a disposition to spurn advice and counsel—to set at naught Minis- terial and parental authority, and to follow the bent of their own sinful or vicious inclination.   Perhaps there is an increase of crime, and as the Papers report the cases brought before the Court—it may go abroad that we are a most immoral and iniquitous set of people.   I have no doubt all the increase of immorality and disregard of human laws, may be traced to the influx from other lands—and the bad principles and practices they introduce and perpetuate. If all this with religion and the teaching and admonition of God's blessed word, what would the state of things be without it!

Gambling in Prairie Towns

Sessional Papers, Canada, 1891, no. 19, Appendix E: Annual Report of Superintendent R. B. Deane, Commanding "K" Division, North-West Mounted Police, Lethbridge, 1890.

Incorporation [of the town of Lethbridge] will enable one great nuisance to be suppressed here, viz.: gambling. Gambling is carried on openly and with impunity. The Dominion Statute does not apply now because Lethbridge is not a town, and the North-West Ordinance is *ultra vires*, on all of which points the professional gamblers are duly posted.

Saloons and Prohibition Law in Prairie Frontier

Sessional Papers, Canada, 1891, no. 19, Appendix C: Annual Report of Superintendent J. H. McIllree, Commanding "E" Division, North-West Mounted Police, Calgary, 1890.

The general state of prohibition in this district is as unsatisfactory as ever, both to the general public and to ourselves, who are supposed to enforce the provisions of the statute on the subject. Saloons are plentiful and the business of selling liquor is a profitable one, and instead of decreasing, the illicit traffic is increasing. Years ago this prohibitory law was a necessity, and fulfilled what it was expected to do, namely, rescued the native population from the state of degradation they were in, from being able to obtain unlimited supplies of alcohol in trade for robes. Since then the country has changed wonderfully. White people have swarmed into the country, and they expect to be allowed to judge for themselves by a majority of voices whether they shall have a prohibitory law or the contrary. In consequence, the present regulations are, I may say, universally unpopular. Every method is taken to evade the law, and men of responsible standing who would not think of breaking any other laws made for the government of the Territories, will go into the whiskey business without the slightest compunction, and no one appears to think any the worse of them for it. . . . It is no use to endeavor to convict a man for having liquor in his possession. If it is not an abnormally large quantity he can go and get all the permits he requires from friends to cover the liquor. The only chance for a conviction is when a straight case can be proved of selling intoxicants. . . . It is at any time extremely difficult to enforce the provisions of any law that has not the sympathy of the general public to uphold it, and this is the case in our endeavors to suppress the illicit liquor traffic. The mass of the people are against it, and there is no help to be got in that way. . . . We get abuse from the papers for not suppressing the evil, yet those who write the articles know perfectly well what we have to contend against. No large quantities of liquor have been seized during the past year. There are very large quantities of freight coming into Calgary in the course of a year, and it is an impossibility for one man on town duty to examine it thoroughly.

Opium Traffic in British Columbia

Sessional Papers, Canada, 1907-8, no. 36b: Report by W. L. Mackenzie King on the Need for the Suppression of the Opium Traffic in Canada.

In the coast cities of Vancouver, Victoria and New Westminster, there are at least seven factories carrying on an extensive business in opium manufacture. It is estimated that the annual gross receipts of these combined concerns amounted, for the year 1907, to between $600,000 and $650,000. The crude opium is imported from India in coconut shells, it is "manufactured" by a process of boiling into what is termed "powdered" opium and subsequently into opium "prepared for smoking." The returns show that large amounts of crude opium have been imported annually, and that the value of the crude opium imported in the nine months of the fiscal year 1906-7 was greater than the value of the amount imported in the twelve months of the preceding year; the figures for these periods being $262,818, and $261,943, respectively.

The factories are owned and the entire work of manufacture is carried on by Chinese, between 70 and 100 persons being employed. One or two of the factories have been in existence for over twenty years, but the majority have been recently established. It is asserted by the owners of these establishments that all the opium manufactured is consumed in Canada, by Chinese and white people, but there are strong reasons for believing that much of what is produced at the present time is smuggled into China and the coast cities of the United States. However, the amount consumed in Canada, if known, would probably appal the ordinary citizen who is inclined to believe that the habit is confined to the Chinese, and by them indulged in only to a limited extent.

The Chinese with whom I conversed on the subject, assured me that almost as much opium was sold to white people as to Chinese, and that the habit of opium smoking was making headway, not only among white men and boys, but also among women and girls. I saw evidences of the truth of these statements in my round of visits through some of the opium dens of Vancouver. . . .

I was told by one of the leading physicians of Vancouver that he has been shocked at the number of cases of women addicted to the habit which have come to his notice in the regular course of his practice during the past year. As for the Chinese, the casual visitor to their quarter of the city may see them in numbers at any hour of the night or day indulging in and under the influence of this drug.

What is hardly less surprising than the manufacture of opium is that its sale should be permitted, and this, in some districts without safeguards of any kind. It is true there is provincial legislation which to appearances should restrict the sale, but for some reason best known to the authorities, it seems to be openly ignored.

Saloon in the Urban Community

*The London Survey, Prepared under the Auspices of the Men's Federation of London,
Oct.-Dec., 1913, pp. 66-8.*

The liquor stores and the hotels except two on Dundas east, are all in a central area, bounded on the north by the Canadian Pacific Railway, on the south by the Grand Trunk Railway, on the east by Wellington street, and the west by Ridout street, a territory which is about a half-mile square. The centralization helps, together with an efficient police force, to make London an easier and a better policed city than many of similar population, as most of the drunkenness and disorder is within this small area.

While this centralizing of the bar-room is advantageous from the standpoint of patrol efficiency, it intensifies the social and moral problems of this district. Twenty-five out of the twenty-nine licensed places are bordering on or within an area half as large as the one mentioned above, namely, Talbot street on the west, Wellington on the east, Dundas and Carling on the north, and the Grand Trunk tracks on the south. Within this limited area are the homes of 1,500 people; or with the immediate adjacent territory, 3,137; of whom 102 are under 21 years of age. To counteract the demoralizing influence of the bars within this district, only two uplifting institutions are at work—the City Mission on Richmond street, and the Salvation Army on Clarence street. . . .

The first study pointed out some eight or ten hotels in which the evils and abuse of the business were most glaring. Repeated investigations of these during December and January have abundantly proved that at least six are worthy of the closest scrutiny on the part of the license commissioners. Especially is this true of the four so-called hotels on King street, between Richmond and Talbot, part of which is commonly known as "Whiskey Row"; the King Edward, the Queen's Park Hotel, and one or two others. . . .

"Whiskey Row" is notorious for its drunkenness, rivalling any district of any similar extent on "The Bowery"; and the side-rooms frequented by women too often are mere clearing houses for social vice.

3. CULTURAL ORGANIZATION AND EDUCATION

A. Ethnic Groups

Problem of Foreign Immigrant

*Report of the Standing Committee on Immigration, Canadian Conference of Charities
and Correction, September 23-25, 1917 (Ottawa, 1917).*

Canada's natural increase of population is only one-quarter of her incoming tide of colonists, 33 per cent. of those colonists do not speak our language, nor understand our institutions, and already in very many parts of the country we have large groups of foreign citizens, alien to our ideals. . . .

In a survey recently made by a member of the committee, of a typical rural community in Saskatchewan, the following nationalities were represented:—

Bukowinia	1,841
Galicia	562
Poland	187
Scandinavia	270
Iceland	28
Germany	19
Bohemia	8
Russia	5
Roumania	6
Jews	27
United States	56
Great Britain	163
Canada	124
Total	3,296

In an intensive survey that was made of one of the townships, 6 miles square, it was discovered that in a total school population of 102, there was not an English-speaking child of school age among them. . . .

Too often, however, our immigrants drift to the city, where we permit them to live amid housing and sanitary conditions which are a menace to themselves and to the health of all others living in the town in which they have settled. . . .

To educate our children thoroughly demands adequate school accommodation. It is notorious that in many of our larger cities our schools are scandalously overcrowded, but it is not so generally known that many of the schools in the rural districts of the West are similarly overcrowded. . . . It is desirable that there should be some Canadian influences operating in some of our more thickly settled foreign districts. We feel that it is a distinctly wise development in the Western Provinces that an Official Provincial Trustee should have been appointed. This officer now visits neglected districts; insists on schools being opened there; and sees that taxes are collected and the teacher paid. This has proved a wonderful success in the short period during which it has been operating.

It is impossible to dismiss the subject of schools without referring to the subject of adult education. . . . Your committee feels that it should draw attention to the many children and young people among our immigrants who have come to this country between the ages of 13 and 20. The members of this group are receiving little or no education, as no provision seems to have been made for their accommodation. As far as we could discover, no province has any definite policy regarding the education of the adult. The whole initiative is left to the local school boards, and what efforts are made are usually spasmodic and unintelligent. That some more energetic action should be taken is demonstrated from figures obtained in the survey already mentioned. The ten typical districts surveyed in the three Western Provinces report that of the 2,495 adults and children above school age investigated, 25 per cent. did not read or write at all, and 82 per cent. did not read or write English. . . .

One of the consequences of our neglect to introduce more adequate educational work among our adult immigrants is a frequent tendency to corruption in political affairs. . . . Instances could be quoted in which literally hundreds of immigrants who have been in this country less than three years have been given a vote through forgery and perjury. . . .

The Greek Catholic Church, the Greek Orthodox Church, and the Roman Catholic Church are all making some effort to help the foreign-speaking members of their respective communions, but compared with the need, this help is very ineffective. As these churches usually endeavour to teach their people by means of priests and others of the same nationality, the method does not bring the best and most prompt results in making them good citizens of Canada. The leadership is just as foreign to the institutions and traditions of this country as the people whom they are trying to lead. The Presbyterian, Methodist, Baptist, and to some extent the Anglican churches, have organized missions, but where their purpose is to transfer the allegiance of the immigrants from one denomination to another they are often looked upon with suspicion by the immigrant himself, which prevents their complete usefulness as Canadianizing agencies. The best work is undoubtedly being done by our Settlement and Church missions conducted on settlement lines. . . .

We should also like to consider in more detail, if space permitted, the work being done by the Y.M.C.A. and Y.W.C.A. Reading Camp Association, and some local churches, which are doing a great deal not only to educate the adult foreigner, but often furnish him with community leadership as well.

In conclusion, we feel we ought to mention the many national societies and clubs which the immigrants conduct for themselves. These range in ideals from those which exist merely to give their members a good time, up to those whose object is to instruct and enlighten the members of the race to which they belong. These are doing much better work in many cases than is generally known.

Chinese Immigrants

Sessional Papers, Canada, 1885, no. 54a: Return of D. W. Gordon, M.P. for Vancouver, Contractor and Builder, before the Royal Commission on Chinese Immigration.

So far as I have been able to gather from the most reliable Chinese and other available sources, the class of immigrants, or more properly speaking slaves or serfs, who are brought here from China, are gathered by the agents of the Chinese companies from amongst the criminal and poverty-stricken population of that overcrowded empire, largely from the seaports and rivers, where crime and poverty are the prevailing features. When they arrive here they follow any pursuit their owners can turn them to with advantage. The females, in ninety-nine cases out of a hundred, being prostitutes, are sold for that purpose to their countrymen on arrival.

Development of Race Prejudice against Chinese

Sessional Papers, Canada, 1885, no. 54a: Return of Sir Matthew Begbie, Chief Justice of British Columbia, before the Royal Commission on Chinese Immigration.

Those who stayed in Victoria and the lower country, chiefly engaged in domestic service, washing, etc.   These certainly supplied a want then felt; but I do not think they were ever much encouraged or welcomed, except that they found employment readily on terms satisfactory to themselves. The greater part took their picks and shovels to the gold mines.   I cannot say they were much wanted there; nor was their coming there, so far as I recollect, much welcomed or encouraged.   On the contrary, they were from the first thoroughly unpopular in the mines; the mining population being very Californian in its prejudices, its likings and dislikings.   Nor do I think that the feeling has much changed, although they now go quite freely to the Cariboo, and have for many years; also to the Cassiar.   They did not go to those districts at first, for obvious reasons; I think the police could scarcely have guaranteed them.

I do not think that the feeling of the whites against Chinamen has much changed; but I do not recollect anything that can be called "agitation" against them until Confederation.   The agitation is of the same description as that felt by the hand-loom weavers against the power-looms; by the flail-wielders against the threshing-machines in England fifty years ago; by the Solway fishermen against the stake-nets in the last century; by the lower orders in many parts of Europe against the Jews; and by the coal-miners in Pennsylvania against the machine-borers at the present day.

Chinese Recruited as Cheap Labour

Sessional Papers, Canada, 1885, no. 54a: Return of Samuel M. Robins, Superintendent of the Vancouver Coal Mining and Land Company, before the Royal Commission on Chinese Immigration.

When the Chinese first came to this Province they no doubt supplied a want then felt, and their coming was encouraged and welcomed, especially I may add by the Vancouver Coal Mining and Land Company (limited) which I represent; but the laboring population were always strongly averse to their introduction.   At the time of their coming here my company had been suffering from a strike of the white laborers, and we accepted the Chinese as a weapon with which to settle the dispute.   With a little more trouble we might, I think, have obtained Indians to answer our purposes equally well.

The encouragement given to the Chinese by employers of labor has not been withdrawn up to the present time, whilst the anti-Chinese feeling seems to have grown stronger every year.

Labour Opposition to Chinese Immigration

Sessional Papers, Canada, 1885, no. 54a: Statement of Knights of Labor L.A. No. 3,017, Nanaimo, B.C., Presented to the Royal Commission on Chinese Immigration.

Weighty though the above may be, we have other and higher reasons for desiring to exclude Chinese labor.   All history proves that a free, manly, intelligent, and contented laboring population, is the foundation and the source of the prosperity of any and every nation, and essential to the stability of free, popular institutions.   No nation has ever yet become or remained free and powerful, which degraded its labor or sought to deprive its workers of a just share in the produce of their toil.   Now, Chinese labor is confessedly of a low, degraded, and servile type, the inevitable result of whose employment in competition with free white labor is to lower and degrade the latter without any appreciable elevation of the former.   Their standard of living is reduced to the lowest possible point, and, being without family ties, or any of those institutions which are essential to the existence and progress of our civilization, they are enabled to not only live but to grow rich on wages far below the lowest minimum at which we can possibly exist.   They are thus fitted to become all too dangerous competitors in the labor market, while their docile servility, the natural outcome of centuries of grinding poverty and humble submission to a most oppressive system of government, renders them doubly dangerous as the willing tools whereby grasping and tyrannical employers grind down all labor to the lowest living point.

It is for this latter reason, chiefly, that we object to the Chinese, not altogether because they accept lower wages.   In many pursuits, in coal mining especially, Chinese labor is little, if any, cheaper than white labor: for while the individuals receive less the collective amount paid is little, if any, less than white labor would receive, while by the latter the work is almost invariably better and quicker done.   But white men demand the treatment of rational beings, while Chinese are contented to be treated like beasts of burden, consequently they are preferred by all who seek to tyrannize over their fellows, or who are resolved to keep together a great fortune, regardless of how their country prospers.

The Mennonites

Sessional Papers, Canada, 1891, no. 19, Appendix L: Report of Sergeant V. T. St. George, Reinland, Manitoba, to the Officer Commanding North-West Mounted Police, Regina, October 20, 1890.

On the whole, I may say that the Mennonites are in general prosperous and contented.   They certainly are a hard working and peaceful class of settlers.

Crime of any sort is almost unknown on the reserve.

They have a number of meeting houses and schools.   A regrettable feature about the latter is the fact that English is not taught, and the rising generation is growing up as ignorant of the language of the Dominion as those who came some eighteen years ago from Russia.

The elders of the communities exercise immense power, and their word is law, even in the most trivial matters.   For example: the members of one community are not allowed to paint their houses outside, and must wear one particular kind of heavy cloth cap in summer, and so on.

These elders are averse to any intellectual improvements or educational advance whatever among the Mennonites, and so long as they remain so these people will be what they are to-day—foreigners in language, customs and sentiments.

A few years ago an attempt was made by some of the more enlightened ones to introduce geographical maps into one of the village schools.   This led to a rupture in the community, and the result is, to-day two schools and two churches in the same village, the respective members of which often do not speak to each other, although in some cases they are brothers, or even father and son.

The Mormons

Sessional Papers, Canada, 1893, no. 15:   Annual Report of Superintendent S. B. Steele, Commanding Macleod District, North-West Mounted Police, 1892.

The opinion I have formed of the Mormon settlers is certainly favourable.   There is no doubt that they feel themselves on their probation and therefore are particular to make a good impression; I can, however, only judge them as I have seen them, and willingly give them credit for being enterprising, thrifty, industrious and most orderly.   They are self-contained and I believe their greatest wish is to be left alone.   The majority of them are ignorant, but probably not more so than a similar class the world over, and, as they have been recruited from many nationalities, I think that the Cardston colony of "Saints" are fair representatives of the labouring classes. They do not obtrude their opinions, are anxious to obey the laws and put themselves as far as possible in harmony with their surroundings.   Few communities that are not to a certain extent co-operative would have made so much progress in so short a time.   They are not rich, few of them having greater capital when they arrived in Canada than the settlers' effects and a few head of stock, yet without exception, all have gone ahead, and every year are diligently fencing and improving their lands and buildings according to their means.   All of this proves them to be good settlers as far as they have gone.

The Doukhobors

H. A. Kennedy, *New Canada and the New Canadians* (London, 1907), pp. 149-51.

About 30 miles along the [Battleford] trail we came upon a village of Dukhobors. . . .

The western settlers as a rule do not congregate in villages but live each on his own farm; and an ordinary western village, when it does come into existence, is a mere collection of separate units, no one house being built with any thought of general harmony. The Dukhobor ideal is communistic, and shows itself in the style and arrangement of the village as much as in the life of the inhabitants. . . .

These people are, as a rule, honest, inoffensive, and industrious. Most of them carry into practice their communistic ideal, with common ownership of the means of production, including work oxen and milch kine, and of the proceeds of their labour. Some, however, prefer to farm entirely on their own account, and are not excommunicated for their individualism. . . . The Dukhobors are strict vegetarians; or rather they are strict abstainers from anything killed, for in other respects their diet resembles that of their neighbours, including milk as well as tea and coffee and oatmeal and flour. A few of them speak good English. Large numbers of the men have worked on railway construction and have had other opportunities of learning the language of the country. Such instruction as the children get in the village seems to be entirely conveyed in Russian.

The Dukhobors are already losing most of their distinctive features, so far as dress is concerned.

B. Social Classes and Cultural Institutions

Social Classes in the Rural Frontier

Rural Survey, Turtle Mountain District, Manitoba, 1914, by Co-operating Organizations of the Presbyterian and Methodist Churches, pp. 24-5.

There is little class distinction to be found. Differences in the amount of property owned do not appear to have much influence in dividing the community into classes. Lines of cleavage, so far as they are drawn, are based upon ethical and religious standards rather than on ownership of property. The way a farmer voted in the Local Option campaign has more to do with group sympathy than the size of his farm. The dividing lines, as shown in the survey, are that one attends a church and the other does not, or that one takes part in questionable amusements and the other does not. This ethical and religious basis of rating friends in the country reflects very favorably upon our country population, and is in striking contrast to the money rating in most of our cities. This democratic spirit also extends to the hired help, who are treated on the basis of social equality.

The "Remittance Man" in the Rural Frontier

H. A. Kennedy, *New Canada and the New Canadians* (London, 1907), pp. 100-3.

There is only one class on the plains, and that is the working class. Here and there you meet a gentleman of leisure, but he is called a tramp.

Social distinctions as we know them in England and in the older cities of Canada have no existence on the plains. The farmer may have belonged to "the classes" and his man to "the masses," but they do the same work and eat at the same table. Or it may be the other way round, and the public school boy may find himself earning his experience and his wages from his father's ex-coachman.

Unhappily there are certain members of the English leisured class who find themselves in Canada without either the necessity or the inclination to work for their living. . . .

Many of these young Englishmen fail simply because they are not compelled to succeed. Born with the curse of money upon them, they know they can live whether they work or not, and the knowledge numbs their energy. . . . There are exceptions; but the average "remittance man," who knows that his allowance will come as surely as one month follows another, and expects that one of these days the capital producing this allowance will fall into his hands, is by universal testimony a failure.

Secret Orders in the Rural Community

Rural Survey, Swan River Valley, Manitoba, 1914, by Co-operating Organizations of the Methodist and Presbyterian Churches, pp. 25-6.

Among the secret lodges, the Orange and Foresters lodges are the most numerous, both having five lodges. A considerable number of farmers belong to both Orders. The Foresters is little more than an assurance association in most places. The Masons and Oddfellows have each a lodge in Swan River. There is only one purely rural secret society—the Royal Templars Lodge, at Pretoria. This lodge is at the centre of the social life of its community. . . .

The total membership of these thirteen lodges is 428, which represents about 25% of the adult male population. This relatively large proportion would seem to indicate that the secret orders would play a large part in the social life of the farmers. This is not true, however, for probably not one-half are farmers. The attendance of both village and country members, in relation to enrolment, is poor, being only 35%, and by far the larger proportion of these are from the villages. The lodges, even in their annual social functions, are very exclusive. They make no attempt to bring the community together. The aim of the lodge is to gather to itself a select group in the community. Among a dense population this has social value, but has little social value in the rural community. Those institutions that aim at reaching and helping all the people, such as the Grain Growers' Association, the Home Economics Society, the Boys' and Girls' Club, the School, and, above all, the Church, are the institutions that are destined to grow.

Reading Habits in Rural Districts

Rural Survey, Swan River Valley, Manitoba, 1914, by Co-operating Organizations of the Methodist and Presbyterian Churches, p. 23.

The following schedule shows the amount of and kind of reading matter coming into the farm homes:

Sixty-two per cent. of the farmers take some periodical. The Grain

Grower's Guide is by far the most popular. About 50% of the farmers interviewed subscribe for it. Almost all (96%) take some newspaper. The city papers have the largest circulation. There are more than four who subscribe for secular periodicals to one who subscribes for a religious periodical. Book-lovers are not very many. A few homes have well-selected libraries. It was a surprise to find the best English library in a Russian home. . . . The average purchase for those who buy books was seven per annum. This does not indicate necessarily the amount of reading, for there is much loaning of books. It is interesting to know that the people in the Bowsman district, where there is a good public library, buy more books than the districts without libraries.

Cultural Decadence in a Rural Sub-Marginal Area

Rural Survey, Turtle Mountain District, Manitoba, 1914, by Co-operating Organizations of the Presbyterian and Methodist Churches, pp. 31-2.

Without doubt the house-to-house investigation in the Marsden district shows one of the most backward rural communities in Canada. . . .

The people are more backward than their agriculture. . . . Eighty-five per cent. of the houses are of the poorer pioneer type. The average house has three low, small rooms for an average family of five persons. . . .

There is a rural school at the north-west corner of this district, where school has been held intermittently for the last five or six years. During this period it has never had a qualified teacher. The present teacher has been in this country less than a year, and as he had difficulty in getting work at his trade, which is that of a stationary engineer, he accepted a teaching position. While he is far from what might be desired in a teacher, by all reports he is much superior to the last one, who was in charge of the school for the previous three summers. . . . In looking over the enrolment of the thirteen pupils, more than half are over nine years of age and three are fourteen, and only one is above the first grade. Added to this there are half as many more children of school age in the district who have never been enrolled at all. Certainly racial degeneracy is partly responsible for this backwardness, but much of it is due to the fact that the children have never had a chance.

Forty-six per cent. of the families have, or once had, affiliation with some denomination. . . . Since there was no religious service being conducted, and as the only minister within reach was a Presbyterian student-missionary at Wassawa, it was arranged, after the survey had been made, to open a service in Marsden school.

Psychical Strain of Prairie Isolation

E. B. Mitchell, *In Western Canada before the War.* (London, 1915), pp. 148-51.

Farming was not, as a fact, generally popular, and many who had tried it spoke of it with a certain horror. People who came West deliberately intending to farm, some of them good hardy country-men, had given up their land or left it. Various causes were stated, besides the mere attractiveness of town life, principally the loneliness of the prairie and the impossibility of making farming pay. The loneliness of many parts is extreme. The farms are large, a quarter square mile at the least. In three districts I knew, blocks of empty "Company land" were constantly intervening, breaking up the settled country and harbouring gophers. These are lands granted tax-free to the Canadian Pacific Railway Company, as part of the bargain under which the line was built, and they have been held, for surrounding settlement to make them more valuable. The C.P.R. created Western Canada a generation ago, but now these empty lands are a perpetual irritant. Much of the rest of the land, for one reason or another, is not taken up, and in some districts much that is taken up is in the hands of foreigners. Roman Catholic settlers are influenced by their priests to settle together, but the true Anglo-Saxon of other communions shows his independence by wandering where he will. Thus an English-speaking family may be surrounded by Scandinavians or Galicians or Indian half-breeds, and there may be no neighbours at all, or no woman neighbours. I stayed with an Englishwoman on the borders of an Indian reserve in a most picturesque desolation, and I think she said the nearest Englishwoman was seven miles off; certainly the seven miles' trail by which we left their farm was bare of habitations. Far worse cases could be found; in this case there was a large family to keep things going. But I had an old-timer friend, a sort of mother to all her district, and at dishwashing time in the kitchen she told me stories of the prairie. It seemed as if her acquaintance might be divided into three sets—the "lovely" people, the "nice young fellows that don't know the first thing about farming," and the men and women who went mad. The prairie madness is perfectly recognized and very common still; the "bachelors" suffer most, and the women. For even if neighbours are not so impossibly far off, yet the homesteader has to work hard all day, and is in no great mood for exerting himself in the evening to walk to a neighbour's; if he is poor and has only oxen, their slowness is unendurable for a pleasure trip—they make about two miles an hour, and I was informed that a "converted man" had to sell his oxen, because it was impossible for an ox-driver not to curse. A woman alone in the house all day may find the silence deadly; in the wheat-farming stage there may not even be a beast about the place. Her husband may be tired at night, and unwilling to "hitch up" and drive her out "for a whimsy"; or the husband may be willing and sympathetic, but she may grow shy and diffident, and not care to make the effort to tidy herself up and go to see a neighbour—any neighbour, just to break the monotony. Then fancies come, and suspicions, and queer ways, and at last the young Mounted Policeman comes to the door, and carries her away to the terrible vast "Sanatorium" that hangs above the Saskatchewan. There is still that kind of loneliness on the prairie. Also, with the country only half filled up, no neighbourhood is populous. Twenty houses, perhaps, or thirty, within reach for social purposes, make a good neighbourhood. Not all can bear such lack of variety;

and cut-worms and your neighbours' ways lose their freshness at times as subjects of conversation.

Mixed farming is not so lonely or monotonous, because the pig falls mysteriously ill and has to be nursed, or a calf is born in a great frost, and has to be coaxed into life beside the kitchen stove, or a horse strays from the pasture over hill and dale, or the poultry get up a vast excitement because they see a white pigeon and think it is a new kind of hawk; but on the other hand the grind is worse.   Day in day out, in fair or foul weather, in health or sickness, the cows *must* be driven from pasture and milked, the team-horses watered and fed, the poultry fed and shut up, the eggs gathered.   No holiday or change is possible.   It is the singlehandedness of the average prairie farm and the distance from neighbours that makes it all so difficult.

Sharp Distinction between Town and Country

E. B. Mitchell, *In Western Canada before the War* (London, 1915), pp. 13-15.

Driving out to "the Lake" from town, one did not pass through seas of wheat.   This town (like others, I believe, in the West) is surrounded, not by smiling farms, but by a ring, four or five miles wide, of unbroken barren prairie.   Speculation has divided it into town lots, and sold it to distant investors; meanwhile it is useless.   Even beyond this belt, there was an enormous amount of uncultivated land, some owned by the great companies (C.P.R. and Hudson's Bay); while here and there lay ugly stretches of weeds, showing land that had been "broken" and allowed to fall out of cultivation again.   After the first five miles the rich smooth fields of the [immigration] posters really did at times appear—this part, one might be told, was taken up by farmers from Down East—and again other fields, with weeds rising above the wheat ears, or scantily covered and full of gopher-holes.   One saw little Noah's-ark lumber houses, or picturesque untidy hand-hewn log-huts.   But the motors buzzed past all the country doors to the Lake cottages, and country residents did not appear in the city parlours.   There was no conspicuous in-and-out class such as we have at home, with interests and friends and influence both in town and country: the vacant miles round the city might have been a cholera cordon or a Roman frontier wall for all the social intercourse that went on across it.

Observing these two sharply divided societies, the British mind is startled to discover that here business is socially at the top of the tree, and land-owning does not count at all.   Rough country clothes carry no suggestion of ducal circles.   The social convention is either that the country does not exist, or else that it is peopled by barbarians; and it is true that a homesteader who has driven twenty or forty miles in a heavy waggon over a hot dusty trail has a wildness in his look while he gets his groceries and enquires at the station for his machinery; in town he is not seen at his best.   I found, in fact, that thousands of miles of journeying might bring the travellers very little nearer Canadian rural life.

The Industrial Proletariat and Labour Organization

Report of the Royal Commission on the Relations of Labor and Capital in Canada
(Ottawa, 1889), pp. 111-13.

Among other matters brought out by this Commission is the interesting and important bearing on the labor question of the influence of workingmen's organizations. Nothing could be more striking than the contrast furnished between organized districts and others where as yet the principles of a trade organization are little known and still less acted upon. And if the progress that has been made towards uniting capital and labor in cities that are comparatively well represented in the ranks of labor bodies is to be taken as a criterion of the usefulness of such societies, we may well believe that they are destined to be a very important factor in the solution of the labor problem. And as the work of consolidating the ranks of labor makes progress, so will its influence extend and its usefulness become more apparent. . . .

That the wage question is the most prolific source of trouble there can be no doubt, and it is for the removing of this cause of friction in a friendly way that labor bodies have most strenuously persevered. The claim that workingmen do not receive full value for their labor, that they are too frequently unable to make ends meet, and that capital often takes advantage of their necessities to regulate the price of labor, appears to be well founded, when judged by the evidence given before the Commission. This state of affairs is, however, more apparent in the places that are not organized, and where wages are invariably lowered in the winter season. But in cities and towns where labor is organized, higher wages not only rule, but usually remain the same throughout the year. This is to be attributed to the fact that these societies claim an equal right with the employer in determining the amount to be paid for the labor given, the principle laid down being that the minimum rate shall be a living rate of wages for all. . . .

The principal objects of labor societies, until recently, were the protection of the worker in his wages and the prevention of undue competition among them by shortening the hours of labor. But these organizations have extended their field of usefulness, and their educational value cannot be overestimated. They have been very beneficial in promoting a spirit of self-control, in instilling a knowledge of parliamentary proceedings and in conducting meetings. A spirit of independence and self-reliance has grown with their progress, looking rather to their own efforts to accomplish their objects than appealing to the Government for assistance. Though much can be done by legislation, they themselves have, and can do, a great deal to better their condition by united action. In a mob men trample on each other, but in a disciplined army they brace one another up. So labor unions prevent disorder to trade. Nor should the character of those who compose these societies be overlooked. In nearly all of them, proficiency in their calling, as well as a good character, is made a condition of membership. . . .

To the persistent efforts of labor organizations may also be traced, very largely, the advanced state of public opinion in relation to the sanitary condition of factories, workshops, and dwellings of the working classes. It is now impossible in organized labor centres to neglect these matters. Employers find it difficult to carry on business where no attention is given to the health and comfort of their employees. In many places where these societies exist there is now an entire separation of the conveniences for the sexes, and care is taken that no corrupt influence shall gain any foothold where males and females are employed in the same building. The shortening of the hours of labor for women and children has for years been kept before the public by labor organizations, though as yet with indifferent success. Much progress has also been made in preventing the sending to this country, by interested people and charitable societies in other lands, an undesirable class of immigrants, and it is due to the reiterated persistency in protesting against this wrong, by organized labor, that the practice of sending the helpless and pauper classes to become burdens on our people and charities has been very much lessened and will, it is hoped, be prevented altogether.

Thus in many ways the influence of labor organizations has had a beneficial effect to those who have taken advantage of the opportunity they afford of discussing the whole labor problem in its economic, social and political aspects.

Some of the especial benefits are better wages, shorter hours of labor, better protection from accident, a more friendly relation to capital, prevention of child labor, higher education, a better knowledge of their trades through the discussion of their wants, voluntary and compulsory insurance, payment of sick and death benefits, and the extension of relief to the needy.

Social Isolation of Urban Business Groups

J. S. Woodsworth, *On the Waterfront* (Ottawa, n.d.), pp. 29-30.

In the background of the minds of the majority of the successful business men of Canada there is an old Eastern homestead. The successful business man may lunch at a high-class club or occupy a box at the theatre or spend his vacations in Europe, but as a boy he "did the chores," swam in the village millpond, cut his name in the desks of the little red school-house, and generally lived the all-round democratic life of a farmer's boy. . . .

In the nearer background of his consciousness is the life of the small town in which he experienced his early business struggles. Here he married and set up his first home. Here his children had measles and croup and he knew what it was to be on friendly terms with all sorts of neighbors. In his business, he called most of his employees by their first names and knew more or less of their personal affairs. There were few poor in the town, and they were generally shiftless or addicted to drink. If a man didn't make things go, it was more or less his own fault. Organized labor was unknown and Socialism was unheard of. A few constables represented the dignity of the Law and rounded up petty thieves and disorderly persons. The church stimulated men to overcome temptations to appetite, and to strive for a certain type of personal goodness.

Since our successful business man moved to the city and entered upon larger commercial and financial enterprises, the life has been very different.

The greatest change lies in his isolation from the common life about him. His offices in the fine new warehouses are open only to employees of the highest rank. He throws the responsibility for details upon managers and foremen. He studies the rise and fall of markets and analyses costs. Only privileged visitors get past the outer offices to trespass upon his time. At noon he lunches at an exclusive club with men of his own group and way of thinking. He drives or is driven in his own car, so that he does not even rub shoulders with the strap-hangers in the street cars. His home is in the best residential district, where building restrictions are rigidly enforced. After dinner with guests of his wife's "set" or "circle," he may accompany them to the theatre. On Sunday, he and his family occupy a pew in St. Mark's, where everything is in the best of taste. His isolation is complete, his class-consciousness assured.

C. Educational Institutions

School Attendance in Ontario

Proceedings Tenth Canadian Conference of Charities and Correction, Held at Toronto, October 19th-21st, 1909, p. 99.

Mr. J. J. Kelso:—Our school laws are designed to give every child born in the land an elementary education. The compulsory education law is supplementary legislation to compel the careless and indifferent to send their children to school and thus make sure this universal education. . . .

One difficulty in the past has been that many municipalities and township councils have neglected to appoint any truant officer, and at the present time it is safe to say there are at least 150 to 200 districts where the law is not put in force. Efforts have been made from time to time by the Education Department to have this important work more generally taken up, but there is always more or less indifference to contend with—the duties of truant officer have, in many instances, been added to the many other duties of the town constable and have not been taken seriously.

Failure on the part of parents to send children to school is often due to the poverty and wretchedness of the home life—lack of clothing and lack of good management in the direction of household affairs. Often there is the presence of drunkenness and vicious living, with children, under most baneful influences, rapidly acquiring an education of the wrong kind. . . .

The School in the Rural Frontier

Report of the Department of Education of the Province of Alberta, 1909, p. 46 Report of J. F. Boyce, B.A., Red Deer Inspectorate.

Taking the average rural school as a standard one is impressed with the fact that the standing of the pupils in the important branches of study is far from satisfactory. It must be said, however, that this backwardness is due to the conditions of pioneer life rather than to the failure of our system of education. No doubt there is room for improvement in the detail and the working out of our educational system and this will gradually evolve, but there is not much prospect of improving the work done in our rural schools until the conditions surrounding them become more favourable. Until the yearly school replaces the short term school, until qualified teachers take the place of "permits," until teachers remain longer than a few months in the same school, until the course of studies and the normal training of teachers are given a more practical turn, until the roads are improved and some plan of transportation of pupils becomes more or less general, until more money is forthcoming from taxation and until educationists and the citizens as a body give more energetic and zealous attention to the rural school, require more efficient work and insist upon better educational facilities for the country child, the outlook for the rural school is not bright. Increasing the usefulness of the country school by giving more continuity to the work and by rendering it more practical, more efficient and more vitalizing is the greatest problem in the educational world to-day.

Education among Foreign People in Western Canada

Report of the Department of Education of the Province of Alberta, 1909, pp. 60-1: Report of Robert Fletcher, Supervisor of Schools in Settlements of Foreigners.

An interesting feature of the work of the Alberta Government is the educating of the youth of foreign settlements, chiefly among the Ruthenians. A representative of the Department of Education devotes his whole time to this work. He organizes these settlements into school districts, acts as official trustee where needed, and in this capacity performs the duties of a board of trustees and its officers, and supervises the work of Ruthenian boards of trustees.

For a while at first very little progress was made. A number of meetings were called to get the people to organize into school districts and were well attended but they would express no opinion about schools or sign any papers. They misunderstood the aims of the department, and were averse to anything new. But as misapprehensions were cleared away and they began to realize the just and economical intentions of the department their opposition ceased and the work of organization spread rapidly. . . .

The greatest obstacle in the way of getting these schools in operation was the securing and establishing of qualified teachers. The Ruthenians, as was quite natural, desired teachers who could speak their own language but as none of these held qualifying certificates they were loath to engage the services of qualified teachers all of whom were English speaking. However, they reluctantly accepted a few and again misapprehensions began to vanish. . . .

In a few cases the board of trustees, being wrongly advised, held out against the acceptance of a qualified teacher until an official trustee was appointed by the department to administer the affairs of the district. After one term of such administration they became quite willing to conform with the requirements of the department and in two notable instances petitioned the Minister of Education to allow the official trustee to continue in office.

A growing interest in the education of their young is manifesting itself among the people. It is common for a parent to take his child to town to reckon up the price of a load of grain or a bill and his face brightens up if the youngster calculates correctly. The school term is lengthening. This year twelve districts, in which none but Ruthenians reside, have engaged teachers for the whole year, and as many more, that have a large percentage of foreign ratepayers, operate yearly schools.

Attendance and Standards in Schools among Foreigners

Annual Report of the Department of Education of the Province of Saskatchewan,
1914, pp. 92-3: Report of A. W. Keith, Rosthern Inspectorate.

Another matter which is constantly obtruding itself is the non-attendance of children of school age. This is especially noted in rural school districts. The worst offenders are found in the Galician settlements, where the children are kept at home to assist in the farm work and in the Mennonite villages in which a private "school"—so-called—is conducted by one of their own people. In these community schools, which are actively supported by a section of the Mennonite church, the German language only is used, and the chief text-book is the Bible, from which the children are taught reading, writing and geography. In this connection I have met parents who determinedly objected to their children attending the public school because in them they would learn the English language. In a third section the German Catholics have established parochial schools.

Arising out of these last two cases is the matter of the development of Canadian ideals and citizenship. Another phase arises in the Galician districts for in these the teachers in the public schools are usually young Ruthenians who have been granted Provisional certificates. After two years' experience I am not hopeful with regard to the success of this movement, *i.e.*, allowing unqualified teachers of the same nationality to take charge of these schools. The pupils undoubtedly acquire a smattering of knowledge, but their knowledge and use of the English language is extremely limited.

Non-Attendance in Rural Schools in the West

Annual Report of the Department of Education of the Province of Saskatchewan,
1911, p. 59: Report of A. J. McCulloch, Wadena Inspectorate.

The one great complaint with nearly all the teachers is the poor attendance of the pupils. School after school I found comparatively empty. Fifteen to twenty-five enrolled and from five to ten present. I drove eight miles to one school and found that the teacher had gone every morning for five mornings and not one child had come. He was a good teacher and the school was a splendid one, and there was a good stable in the grounds for horses, but the parents did not care whether the children came or not and so they didn't go. . . . People will keep their children from school for every conceivable reason but they have not the slightest compunction about making them work. Trustees will not fine their neighbours, and one cannot blame them when good neighbours and friends are few. The best attendance I found in the Ruthenian and Icelandic schools.

Immaturity and Transiency of School-teachers

E. B. Mitchell, *In Western Canada before the War* (London, 1915), pp. 68-73.

To return to the teacher, she is the belle of the prairie balls, the leading unmarried lady of her settlement. Often she plays her part in pretty comedies of courtship and disappears, as the Minister said, "into the sandy soil." Then her successor comes, as young and inexperienced as she was. Thus the average teaching may be bright and efficient and modern, but there can be no mature view of things or manly philosophy such as some of the old dominies of Scotland used to provide. There were dominies in Ontario too, I hear, not so long ago, and some of the men of to-day look back to the teaching of the village school as the inspiration of all their doings. Perhaps in one way the young school-mistress hastens the drift to the towns, though in another she undoubtedly adds attraction to country life. She is at an age when the gaieties of town almost necessarily seem the ideal, and young rustics are as quick as other children at catching an impression; there might be uses for some crusty old fellow to whom a great city should seem a mere scarlet Babylon and a sink for the offscourings of the earth. However, few men are found to offer for these posts, and the bachelor payers of school-rate are inclined to pass over those who do, and to wear the colours of the "school-marm," saying that, since they have no children to educate, in justice they ought to get *something* appreciable for their money.

But even outside of her classroom, the school-marm's life is not to be too rosily painted. I was in one district when a new teacher came, and the poor girl thought she would end by having to sleep upon the open prairie. There is no teacher's house. . . . This individual problem was solved; but one could see how very unpleasantly a teacher might be situated among foreigners with ways not too particular, or where few of the settlers were married. It is most difficult to get accurate information beforehand of anything on the prairie, except where the travelling clergy can help.

The prairie teacher is not troubled by too much inspection or interference from superior authorities who are very busy and very far away; and the local school-boards are usually glad to have got a teacher, and willing to leave everything to her; but if the local people should take a dislike to her, she will just have to go (I think a month is the notice required). . . .

Amidst much admiration for the Saskatchewan public schools, one doubt creeps in. Is the building perhaps over-emphasized in comparison with the teacher, who makes the school after all? For one thing, classes are too large, though probably not larger than the elementary schools at home.   Then everywhere there are these young teachers, mostly girls, while even head-masters are not far into the thirties.   Many men start life "teaching school," but turn off into law or business as offering greater attractions.   There is a difficulty coming if few men remain in the profession, and at the same time the higher posts are in practice closed to women, that is to the great majority of the teachers.   The women are discouraged from professional ambition, and the field for selection of headships is not wide enough.   The great schoolmasters who have influenced England so strongly have been selected members from a host of keen and able men devoting themselves for life to the profession of teaching; and it is possible that the comparative lack of such teachers may be the cause of a certain thinness of thought and absence of strong moving ideas sometimes to be noted in great new countries.   Canada has such a giant's task before her that she will need great ideas if ever a nation did.

Failure of School to Serve as Rural Cultural Centre

Report of the Department of Education of the Province of Alberta, 1914, pp. 87-8: Report of C. Sansom, B.A., Macleod Inspectorate.

The relationship of the rural school to the community is a matter of admitted importance in the development of a country.   In my inspectorate this relationship can scarcely be said to be of a kind likely to stimulate and foster the intellectual and cultural life of the community.   It is often asserted that the rural school should contribute to this end through its use as a centre where people may come together to take part in literary and debating socie-ties, concerts, etc., and to hear lectures on agriculture and other things. . . . In very few of these schools is work being taken beyond grade VIII, and our High Schools are receiving practically no recruits from this source.   Perhaps one reason for this may be found in the fact that as a rule the school does not create an educational atmosphere in the community.   Practically the only use made of most schools as "Social Centres" is for dancing purposes.   The theory of some educationalists is that if this use of the school is encouraged the social life of the community will be stimulated and the people thus brought together can be led to take a greater interest in educational affairs. But the weakness in the theory in this inspectorate is that the school activity ends in itself.   It is true, however, that this use of the school does tend to relieve the monotony and irksomenêss which many people, unfortunately, think necessary to attach to rural life.   An economic phase of the question is also disclosed in the fact that the admission fee to the dance constitutes the popular medium of contributing to any worthy cause, and large sums have been raised in this way for patriotic and benevolent purposes.   But that the educational and cultural influence of the custom is slight seems clear from the way the dance is usually conducted.

4. RELIGIOUS INSTITUTIONS

Religious Destitution in Isolated Prairie Communities

C. H. Johnstone, *Winter and Summer Excursions in Canada* (London, n.d., about 1892), p. 64.

I stayed with the Rogers [in Duck Lake] over Sunday. There was then no Episcopal church, nor as far as I know any place of worship within some miles; and as the inhabitants of Duck Lake have not yet become blue ribbonists, Sunday appeared to be passed in continuance of Saturday night revels, with the result that there were several broken heads and other catastrophes.

Religion in the Rural Frontier

Edward West, *Homesteading: Two Prairie Seasons* (London, 1918), pp. 195-6.

It would seem fitting to make some reference to what may be called the spiritual life of the prairie.

It may be frankly confessed at once that in the conventional sense, at any rate, this is at a low ebb. I am aware of the noble and self-denying labours of many men sent out under the auspices of the Archbishops' fund, . . . also of the zealous work of those who may be termed the apostles of the older Faith among the Indians and others, and also of the strong efforts put forth by various other denominations; but the fact remains that settlement has run as far ahead of the conventional work of the churches as it has of railroads. Besides this, the mere material pressure, the continual call for arduous and exacting labour in the subjugation of the new land, leaves little time for ordinary religious observances.

All this may not be without great good in the future, for there must be many faithful hearts who, through the dearth of time-honoured religious observances, may realize a deeper spiritual religion. This may bear noble fruit in time to come, especially if it helps those who experience it to see that the essence of Christianity does not consist so much in building beautiful churches and in paying good salaries to popular preachers as in doing justly and loving mercy; in fact, the opposite of that mere materialism which is so rampant.

It is only fair to add that among the settlers there is (apart from religious profession, and in spite of some littleness) very much of that spirit of mutual helpfulness and goodwill towards each other which is surely of the very alphabet of Christianity, and one longs that in this great new nation this spirit should permeate the Churches, and through them the State.

Church Attendance on Rural Prairies

E. B. Mitchell, *In Western Canada before the War* (London, 1915), p. 88.

Routine church-going almost disappears in the Western country, and a man may drive a very long way to find only five or six assembled. Here is a striking difference from older countrysides, the more remarkable because the cities are rather strict in their Sunday observance, stricter, I thought, on the whole, than either in England or modern Scotland. In some country stations a Church of England student would come one week, a Presbyterian the next, and a Methodist the third, and while certain people would attend only their own form of worship, others would share in all three. Kikuyu was at least sympathetically understood out there.

Church of England in Red River Colony

Public Archives of Canada, *S.P.G. in F.P., Canada, 1860-67:* Red River Settlement, November 10, 1865, Bishop of Rupert's Land to Secretary, Society for the Propagation of the Gospel.

The position of the church here is to my mind exceedingly unsatisfactory. As regards the great immediate object of the Ministry—the salvation of souls—I believe the efforts made here have been eminently blessed. There is much Spiritual profession and I trust Godly practice. The attendance at the churches considering the thin and widely-scattered people is satisfactory. The Number of Communicants is gratifying being far above any home experience—there is a very general maintenance of family Prayer— and no little individual Godliness. That is one side and a bright side. But there is for a Churchman another side gloomy enough. I fear there is hardly in any a hearty affection for the church that has been showering blessings on the land and there is no outward appearance of hearty entering into the privileges of our Form of Worship. The great body of the Protestant European Population come from Presbyterian Orkney and Sutherland in Scotland. Our Clergy when they came found the people writhing under a fancied wrong in not having been supplied with a Presbyterian Ministry. They come unwillingly to Church and our early Clergy tried to win their favour by engrafting the Presbyterian forms on our Liturgy. . . . Now happily we have the full order of the Church in our Services. But the Secession came. There are now 2 Presbyterian Ministers and by means of these and Elders scattered abroad they have services throughout our Parishes and they endeavour to take advantage of any weak place we may show. This adds seriously to our embarrassments. Now in looking back at the past I think (1) Too much concession has been made to Presbyterian prejudice and practice. (2) Too little prominence has been given to the distinctive principles and forms of our Church. (3) Too much has been done in laying hold of New Posts throughout the country and encouraging the formation of new settlements in this colony instead of concentrating our strength at the centre. But the grand and total error has been (4) Too little has been asked of the people so as to make the work their work. The Church here is to-day a foreign Church,—any gift by a Native to it is regarded as an obligation to the Clergyman and his Church. . . .

I promise to do all I can to bring out support from the people themselves, but I beg you to ask your Venerable Society to bear in mind:

1st. The peculiar position of this country. This poor isolated country with its scattered Indians—with its Colony 400 miles from any kind of market—is unlike any other. What a difficulty we shall have in getting any help out of our Vestries and Conferences. We have no gentlemen emigrants here—The only persons at all of the class of gentlemen by birth would belong to the Hudson's Bay Co.—But we have not above two or three in the settlement. . . .

2nd. The peculiar character and education of the people. They have never been yet taught to give—It has been felt that the people are rather inclined to another Communion. It has been with fear that anything almost has been done lest they should be driven elsewhere and the evils of schism already bad enough multiplied. . . .

Further the people here are mostly poor—those few that have some means have gained their property by hard industry and strong economy— These are not generally the class of persons that are most generous in giving —every little seems such a sacrifice—I fear a good many of the best off and most intelligent go to the Presbyterian services.

Denominational Rivalry in the Western Frontier

Public Archives of Canada, *S.P.G. in F.P.*, *Series D*, vol. 42: Edmonton, October 22, 1875, the Rev. Wm. Newton to the Bishop of Saskatchewan.

My present Sunday services are a Sunday School in the Mission House at 9 o'clock, Divine Service at 10, partly English and partly Cree. At 12 the horses are harnessed (sir) and I drive fast to "Fort Saskatchewan" where Colonel Jarvis and the Mounted Police Force are, I hold service as near 3 o'clock as I can manage it, the distance being about 20 miles. The Sunday evening is spent conversing with the men, reading with them, or doing anything which may arise to interest them in religious matters. So far as I can judge I am safe for a share of the people, and we have a foothold in the district. The Methodists are working fairly and unfairly to hold the supremacy their position has given them. Last Sunday Mr. McDougal I am told met the people coming to our service and drove them into his Chapel; but that sort of thing won't last—a Mr. Manning has settled at Edmonton in place of Mr. Warner who has been sent to Victoria. Mr. McDougal goes to Bow River. So with Mr. McDougal's son there are four Methodist Ministers in this district to one of our own Church, to say nothing of the Roman Catholics, who with the Methodists have been here for years. On arriving, I could not obtain a room at the Fort either for personal use or for permanent service, so the best and almost the only thing I could do was to take an unfinished house belonging to Mr. Hardisty and fix it up for Church and dwelling house.

Non-Enterprising Character of Church of England

Canadian Life as I Found It: Four Years' Homesteading in the North-West Terri- tories, by HOMESTEADER (London, 1908), p. 127.

We had our first Church of England service at the school-house last week, and a meeting afterwards to consider whether we should continue to have one. We decided to have a service every other Sunday, but we are only to have a layman to officiate. The Church of England is very slow in looking after its members; the Methodists and Presbyterians are much more active, and do not seem to mind what trouble they take.

Lack of Canadian Spirit in Anglican Church

E. B. Mitchell, *In Western Canada before the War* (London, 1915), pp. 83-7.

The Presbyterians struck me as much the most "Canadian" body, as distinguished from French-Canadian or Old Country; for, though many of the people come direct from Scotland, yet many of the people and most of the ministers seem to come from Eastern Canada. Presbyterianism seems to have a marked unity all over the Dominion, Western ministers having been educated down East and being personally acquainted with Church leaders in Montreal and Toronto. . . .

There is a direct Scottish influence on Canadian Presbyterianism, but it acts on the centres and through the centres. Scottish professors and preachers come to Halifax, Montreal, Toronto, Winnipeg, Vancouver, but there is no management of separate districts in the West by different branches of Presbyterianism in Scotland. Since the days of Dr. Robertson, the great superintendent of Western Missions, the Eastern Presbyterians have been awake to the Western opportunity, and have spared no effort to establish a strong hold, especially on the centres of population—the strategic points—in the West. The Presbyterian Church is most clearly one of the forces acting to bring scattered Canada together. . . .

In two ways at least the Presbyterian Church has definitely adapted itself to the special Western circumstances. The young student-evangelists in the scattered country districts need superintendence, and superintendents have been provided. A wind has blown from the prairie and has given back to Anglicans legislating Synods and strong lay representation, and to Presbyterians an office suggesting Prelacy. But an even more curious fact appears in connection with the Ruthenians. The Presbyterian Church has taken up the question of the Ruthenians, and is working for them at Vegreville, Alberta, and elsewhere; and it has been agreed that it is unnecessary to try to turn these Russians into Scotch-Canadian Presbyterians. The policy is rather to help them to keep up, as far as possible, their own religious ordinances. . . .

"The Church of England in Canada" makes no claim in its title to be a Canadian church, and in the West one cannot help seeing that in practice it is not Canadian but English. Had the Anglicans of the East no Dr. Robertson to rub in the fact that the New West was their own Canadian West, and church work there their work? I do not know the history, but apart from certain older men, chiefly missionaries among the Indians, the Canadian clergy of the Church of England in the West seem very few. I remember how surprised I was, a few days after arriving in M—, at a lunch following a deanery meeting, when the conversation ran persistently on Mr. Lloyd George and the Insurance Act, not a Canadian question! Listening and looking round I realized that almost all the men were English. The needs of English immigrants in the West have been met from England, with devotion and generosity, but with certain dubious accompaniments. It is not to be supposed that English authorities deliberately wish to maintain such a control as to prevent the growth of a genuine Canadian daughter of the English Church, but the present methods of helping do actually appear to tend that way; and the trouble is increased by the fact that there are two or three separate English connections, which tend not only to keep the West divided from the East, but to cut off one diocese from another on English ecclesiastical party lines. A diocese supported by the Society for the Propagation of the Gospel and a diocese supported by the Colonial and Continental Church Society have few dealings together, and the Archbishops' Fund Brotherhoods make a further complication. Instead of being encouraged to try to understand the Canadian mind, and to become Canadians, most of the young English volunteers in church work on the prairie are kept carefully within reach of the atmosphere of this or that English school of thought, and only the stronger minds can escape. Young Evangelicals are sent out West in batches—to an English Evangelical College, in the hands of an English society, with an English Principal; young High Churchmen are sent out in batches to a High Church Brotherhood redolent of Oxford. This is to change the sky, but not the mind; but the sky does tell in the end, in spite of all.

Weakness of Church of England in Western Canada

Bishop Ingham and C. L. Burrows, *Sketches in Western Canada* (London, 1913), pp. 122-31.

In regard to the present condition of the Church, then, we can see that she has great problems to solve and a hard, uphill road to pursue. She is completely out-distanced in numbers and wealth by the Romanists, Presbyterians, and Methodists, and in this country nothing succeeds like success. The very fact that the others are ahead to-day gives them a wonderful advantage, and assures them not only of holding their own members, but attracting many from the Church. The strong Church in town or village draws. . . .

The Church in Canada needs a real conversion, and if she does not seek for this, she will year by year drop back in comparison with the other bodies and yearly become of less force and power in moulding and building up a true Christian people. She needs at the present time a clergy caught up with the Pentecostal power that will lead them to go to work amongst the people with the sole desire of saving their souls—not carried away with some strange doctrine, or some idea that interests no one but themselves, but the plain Gospel, given by plain men in a way that plain people can readily understand. Elaborate music, early services (which household conditions here render difficult), strange vestments—and stranger doctrines—do not in the least interest people in this busy land. These things may be all very well for those wanting new sensations, but there are too many sensations of a practical nature in this country and the people are too desperately busy and earnest for them to care for, and least of all pay for, novelties in the Church.

The days of priestcraft and ecclesiasticism are long since over; they have, in fact, never arrived in this country. . . .

Above all, the future success of the Church depends on the individual clergy being strong men, and imbued with the power of the Spirit. . . .

It is only a waste of money to send out small second-rate men; they have no influence, and only cause the Church to lose in the esteem of the people.

Failure of Churches to Adjust to Changing Rural Population

Rural Survey, Turtle Mountain District, Manitoba, 1914, by Co-operating Organizations of the Presbyterian and Methodist Churches, pp. 53-8.

In Turtle Mountain District, as in many other parts of the prairie section of Manitoba, a large number of the old well-to-do settlers have removed to the towns and to British Columbia. . . .

Then with the increase in the size of the farms has come an increase in the number of hired help employed. Sixteen per cent. of the total population is represented in this class. In some communities the proportion is even higher. . . .

The removing of a large number of the old settlers has not meant a decrease in population. Rather there has been an actual increase of 12.1 per cent. in the rural sections and a net increase of 8 per cent. in both the towns and rural sections. The problem, therefore, is not that of rural depletion, but that of change in population. This change has increased materially both the burden and the opportunity of the Church.

The Church that spread over Manitoba was a splendid organization for pioneer society and the subsequent land farming period. Its individual emphasis gave color to its field organization and message. It rejoiced in and ministered largely to the man who joined field to field and who talked of his crops in terms of car-lots.

Naturally, when many wealthy farmers retired, and their farms fell into the hands of crop-payment buyers and tenants, both usually with little capital, the former almost invariably having great difficulty in meeting expenses, the minister and congregation became alarmed and too often overlooked the newcomer, who might have compensated largely for the loss of their wealthy predecessors. . . .

The Church is to-day apparently following the "lead" of the land farmers in joining circuit to circuit and mission field to mission field. The wisdom of this policy is doubtful. . . .

The Churches are becoming less intensive in their methods. They are often putting one man where they used to put two. . . .

Even in the face of a gain of 8 per cent. in population, the increase in church membership is only 2⅓ per cent.

Church membership is relatively smaller in the open country than in the towns and villages. . . . . One reason for this is not that the country people are less inclined to unite with the church, but that the ministers live in town and give more attention to town congregations. It is an inefficient distribution of religious leadership which places seventeen of the eighteen resident ministers in four towns and villages.

The Church that will meet the call of its ever-enlarging opportunity must needs minister to the whole community. The tenant and the hired help must have at least as large a place as the farm owner. . . . This is not the case at present. In Whitewater municipality 23 per cent. of the farmers are tenants, but only 13 per cent. of the church members are tenants; in Morton 26 per cent. of the farmers are tenants and only 13 per cent. of the church members are tenants; and in Winchester 33 per cent. of the farmers are tenants and only 17 per cent. of the church members are tenants.

Statistics are not available for an exhaustive study of hired help; it is true that a large proportion of hired help are church members. . . . Very few, however, have united with local churches or are actively engaged in church work.

Methodist Church in the Mining Frontier

James Woodsworth, *Thirty Years in the Canadian North-West* (Toronto, 1917), pp. 186-7.

The following is a quotation from my Quadrennial Report of 1898:

"The conditions of our work in British Columbia are different from those that generally obtain east of the mountains. The most marked progress has been made in what is known as 'The Upper Country,' covered by the Kamloops and Kootenay Districts. We have now a chain of missions across the mountains.

"The far-famed Kootenay country is undoubtedly rich in minerals. The boom stage has passed. Although the inevitable reaction has taken place, much that is real, solid, and promising remains. Such centres as Rossland and Nelson give promise of continued growth, while smaller towns, such as Trail, Kaslo, Sandon, and others, retain considerable vitality, and may yet grow to be centres of great importance. There is, however, much of the element of uncertainty in every mining country, which suggests the wisdom of practising the greatest caution in the multiplication of missions, the erection of expensive buildings, or otherwise committing the Church to an expenditure that may involve future embarrassment. At the same time economical considerations ought not to eclipse the obligation of the Church to preach and live the Gospel among the miners. Such is legitimate missionary ground. Without the presence of missionaries and churches life in the mining camps would be intolerable except to the very worst classes of society. No careful observer can visit such camps and make comparisons from time to time without being profoundly impressed with the wonderful results of the leavening power of divine truth. . . ."

Church of England in the Mining Frontier

L. Norman Tucker, *Western Canada* (Toronto, 1907), pp. 74-5.

The work in this diocese [Kootenay] is conditioned mainly by two things —the physical features and the chief industry of the country. The region is mountainous and mineral-bearing. In mining camps people necessarily live in close proximity to one another, and can readily combine to build their church and support their clergyman: all the more that their resources are easily available, being always in the form of monthly wages. Mountainous regions abound in valleys, lakes, and rivers, where travel is provided for by boat or by rail, which gives the communities easy access to one another. Compact communities, easily reached—these are the distinguishing features of the work in Kootenay, which explains the fact that, though one of the newest of our mission-fields, it is one of the most self-sufficing; out of eighteen clergy, no less than nine are entirely supported by their congregations.

The Churches and Foreign Groups in the Mining Frontier

The Acts and Proceedings of the Fortieth General Assembly of the Presbyterian Church in Canada (Toronto, 1914), p. 20: Report of District Superintendent, New Ontario.

Of the 418,000 newcomers into Canada last year, 140,000 could not speak the English language. . . .

That New Ontario is getting her share of non-English speaking may be seen from the mixed population of our mining and railroad towns. May we illustrate from Creighton Mine in the vicinity of Copper Cliff, and Hearst a railway town on the Grand Trunk Pacific, one hundred and thirty miles west of Cochrane. The figures are:

Creighton Mine		Hearst Mine	
Germans	20	Chinese	2
French	31	Syrians	6
Spaniards	35	Jews	9
Bulgarians	33	Germans	15
Polacks	168	French	28
Finns	209	Swedes	30
Italians	314	Bulgarians	44
English speaking	151	Spaniards	92
		Russians	115
Total	1,061	English speaking	51
		Total	392

When analysing these figures we must remember that the English speaking include men, women and children, Roman Catholic as well as Protestant, followers of the Stars and Stripes as well as lovers of the Union Jack. The inrush of these people by the hundred thousand constitutes one of the gravest problems in our national life. Freed from the restrictions of an arbitrary government, alienated from the tenets of their home church,

30

they are reading the rankest kind of literature, advocating the abolition of all authority in church and state, and everywhere preaching the doctrine of free love. The Finn is perhaps among the very best of those emigrants and yet I am informed that in Copper Cliff, Cobalt, and Porcupine there are between sixty-five and one hundred homes where the marriage tie has been disregarded. If the sanctity of the home is destroyed how shall the nation stand?

What are we doing to meet the situation? Wherever possible our regular missionaries are conducting English classes for the people in their localities and endeavouring at the same time to sow the seed of the higher life. In addition to our regular missionaries two special men were appointed, one to the Finns, the other to the Italians.

The Churches in the Rural Hinterland

Rural Survey, County of Huron, Ontario, 1914, by Co-operating Organizations of the Presbyterian and Methodist Churches, pp. 7-11.

In spite of all its wonderful natural resources the population [of Huron County] has decreased alarmingly since 1875. The total loss has been one out of every three persons (32 per cent.) and a loss in the country section of forty per cent. The town population has not increased since 1881. . . .

The effect on the country church is obvious. There is the disheartening influence of diminishing numbers, the continual loss of workers and of the young people of the church and the consequent loss of young families. . . .

In the diminished population the overlapping of different denominations is more painfully evident. . . . Regularly in the little village are found three, four, five or even more churches in the centre of a population sufficient to support one nicely. Several ministers often have to travel over the same ground among the same people. Divided into so many denominational groups, the work among young people in any one church is made difficult.

The Churches and Marginal Groups in the City

The London Survey, Prepared under the Auspices of the Men's Federation of London, Oct.-Dec., *1913,* pp. 45-7.

London is well supplied with churches and other organizations for carrying on religious work. In most cases each church is the centre of much and varied activity. . . .

The facts support the contention that church members who are vigorous in business are active and interested in the church, but that children of wealthy parents who may live without effort are not moral and spiritual forces. In almost every case the "big business" class, that is, wealthy members, were reported active in religious work; the largest proportion of inactive is among the "skilled" and "unskilled" labor classes. Of the whole membership 22 per cent., nearly one-quarter, are reported inactive. The proportion of male members is exactly one-third. . . .

Each church looks after its own poor. This means much over-lapping. . . .
Not one-half of the churches have discussions or make a study of social
and economic problems in any of their organizations. . . .

Only one church in London is carrying on organized mission or educational work among non-English-speaking citizens. This work was, by
convention, left to one denomination, the Baptist; but no definite work has
been done by them. . . .

In almost every church there is an organized effort to meet strangers at
the church door; but not one church reported an organized effort to find
strangers as they come to the city. The contrast between churches and
political workers in this respect is striking.

Church of England among Foreign Groups in the City

*First Annual Report of Church of England Mission to the Italians of Toronto and
Canada, 1899-1900.*

The Church of England Mission to the Italians has just closed the first
year of its organization and six months of its public work among the Italians
in Toronto for the salvation of men, women and children of that nationality,
and for the glory of our Divine Redeemer. . . .

During the winter months many among the poor have been supplied
with both food and fuel, many suffering from sickness have been relieved with
doctor and medicine, and a good deal of cast-off clothing has been distributed
among the destitute people with wisdom and care. The year has not been
without difficulties, and the faith has been tested, but prayers and labor have
overcome them.

The Sunday School has been well attended by boys and girls, and the
lessons were taught in the English language.

A free English-Italian night school has been conducted during the winter
with much success, and the boys were sorry to see it closed at present. An
English gentleman has faithfully and cheerfully engaged himself in this
work. . . .

The visitation at home has been constantly continued; and the Bible
and the Prayer Book can be found in many homes, where they never were
seen before.

Weakness of Church of England in the Urban Community

B. Pullen-Burry, *From Halifax to Vancouver* (Toronto, 1912), pp. 151-4.

The churches of Toronto are for the most part strikingly handsome
buildings, and in a stay of some weeks I found that if one wanted to hear
views expressed upon up-to-date subjects the Methodist and the Presbyterian churches were sure to provide you with something to digest at your
leisure. Nothing interested me more than a sermon preached in Broadway
Methodist Church upon the question of mixed marriages. . . .

In the Presbyterian churches I learnt something about Temperance . . . .

An Anglican Cathedral is in the course of building in the upper part of Toronto; lack of funds to complete it was much discussed by Bishop Sweeney of Toronto. At a dinner party at which I was present, his lordship alluded to the disinclination of the members of the Church of England to contribute to the building fund of the semi-completed cathedral, when the hostess declared they were all too fond of the world! Personally, I consider the apathy of many Anglicans arises from a weariness at the conservatism of our services. Why they should not be made as attractive as good music and fine oratory can make them, I fail to see. So long as we are treated to dull, if erudite, dissertations on Old Testament tribal data, so long will there be lack of interest in churches of unprogressive type.

The Churches and Labour

The Acts and Proceedings of the Fortieth General Assembly of the Presbyterian Church in Canada (Toronto, 1914), p. 44: Report of Presbyteries of High River, Macleod, and Kootenay.

The attitude of a large number of wage-earners and members of labour unions towards the church has not become more friendly. The influence spreading eastward and inward from the deplorable events of the prolonged labour disturbance on Vancouver Island, which brought representatives of labour into sharp conflict with government, has proved embittering and mischievous. The utterances of preachers and the deliverances of church courts, given forth with laudable intention of helping to heal the dreadful breach between the class interests involved, were belated, and sprang from imperfect knowledge of certain phases of the dispute. There was, however, a prevailing impression that the supineness of the church in face of an approach to anarchy was not creditable to our sense of social duty. . . . The vehemence and perseverance of the Socialistic attack on the church cannot be overlooked. It has to be studied and explained. It is closely related to the attitude of large sections of the people towards the church as an institution, and it affects any effort which the church may make in the direction of reaching numbers of people who are at present alienated from her. Our young missionaries are often much perplexed in endeavouring to meet the hostile criticism with which they are confronted; and even the most experienced men find it difficult to lead those who are subject to Socialistic influences into hearty alliance with the church.

The Churches and Problems of the Urban Community

The Acts and Proceedings of the Fortieth General Assembly of the Presbyterian Church in Canada (Toronto, 1914), pp. 316-17: Report of the Board of Social Service and Evangelism, 1913.

Our work in the congested down-town districts of cities for the past year has been along two lines.

(1) In co-operation with other bodies and departments of municipal life

seeking to right general conditions that are undesirable or hurtful, such as in housing, sanitation, temperance, suppression of vices, eliminating the unclean in commercialized amusement, promoting play-grounds, healthy recreation, an intelligent interest in good citizenship, etc., in which very much has been accomplished which it is impossible, in the space at our disposal, to give any intelligent report upon.

(2) In evangelical social settlements, evangelistic institutes, social service institutes, open-air preaching, etc., seeking to reclaim the wreckage of human life, and to improve the general character and conditions for the struggling masses, whether Canadians, Anglo-Saxons from the motherland, or other lands, or non-Anglo-Saxons.

The Churches and Growing Cities

The Acts and Proceedings of the Fortieth General Assembly of the Presbyterian Church in Canada (Toronto, 1914), pp. 389-90: Conclusions of the Joint Committee of the Methodist, Congregational and Presbyterian Churches.

The facts set forth in the above reports are evidence:

1. That church accommodation has fairly well kept pace with the growth of the English-speaking population in all our cities except Victoria and possibly Montreal.

2. That central and down-town churches are somewhat tardily adapting their equipment and the character of their work to the changed social conditions.

3. That while there is some tendency on the part of the working classes to let unions and trade associations take the place of church interests in their lives, and while there is a tendency on the part of many Old Country people to disregard church attendance on coming to Canada, the attitude of the people generally, including the working classes, continues friendly and responsive whenever the church goes to them with her ordinances in a practical, self-respecting, sympathetic manner.

4. That there is a growing tendency among the well-to-do classes and especially those who have become rich quickly to grow careless in their religious life and loose in their Sabbath observance, to attend one service on the Lord's Day or absent themselves altogether—a habit that has been greatly accentuated by the use of automobiles.

5. That throughout Canada the home mission propaganda of the various Protestant denominations has been adequate and effective so far as the English-speaking population is concerned. There may be scattered families in sparsely settled prairie districts uncared for, but no considerable community of English-speaking people is to be found anywhere in this Dominion without the Christian missionary, and the institutions of the Christian religion.

6. That the rural districts of the older provinces, where for some years past population has been stationary or declining, and the small towns of the western provinces are over-churched rather than under-churched. The immediate need is not more churches and more ministers, but fewer churches

and fewer ministers with larger congregations and more adequate financial support.

The reports tell of an over-churching in many villages and small towns, which, in view of the need elsewhere, is scandalous and criminal.

7. That the Protestant Churches have as yet scarcely touched the fringe of the non-English-speaking immigrants who have flocked in upon us during recent years and are becoming important factors in our national life. It is abundantly evident that the Protestant Churches have not yet seriously faced the problem of a large foreign population in our great cities and our western provinces. The incoming of well-nigh 100,000 annually from non-English-speaking countries is a fact the evangelical Churches of Canada must not ignore. The Lutheran and other Protestant Churches of northern Europe are not adequately meeting the need of our German and Scandinavian settlers, while the increasing multitudes from southern and eastern Europe, once they find themselves in the larger, freer life of this new land, do not readily submit to the authority of either the Greek or Roman Church, and are in danger of drifting away from the Christian Church altogether.

Religious Evangelism in the Urban Community

Clarence Mackinnon, *Reminiscences* (Toronto, 1938), pp. 173-4.

While I was in Winnipeg [1905-1909] the evangelistic type [of preaching] had passed its zenith. Other and aggressive interests began to crowd it out. The social problem, aggravated by trusts, combines, and a general tendency to disregard the rights of labour, was becoming more clamant. Had not the Church responsibilities for this age as well as for that which is to come? A study of the uncharted regions of the mind and its reflexes, complexes, brainstorms and what not, had created a new psychology. This in a highly diluted but quite novel form was bent on entering the Sunday School. Nevertheless the dominant note was evangelistic. After all, it came nearer to the heart of the Gospel. It held the comfort that human life in all its forms and conditions needed and it touched the emotions as well as the intellect and will. Skilfully organized simultaneous campaigns were instituted and large mass meetings encouraged. Dr. Wilbur Chapman conducted the one in the city—a man of earnestness, sincerity and prayer. Different centres were selected and the churches were packed. The results showed themselves in many changed lives. The excitement ebbed, of course, and a professor at Wesley College was heard to remark that if Dr. Chapman visited Winnipeg again there would hardly be a corporal's guard to meet him. He did come again, and on a wild, stormy night in mid-winter. His meeting was announced for Sunday evening after the regular service. It was held in the Walker Theatre, and there was not even standing-room left in the crowded aisles, hundreds being turned away. So much for the popular estimates of a revival.

I had another curious confirmation of this misguided judgement during a campaign we were holding in Minnedosa Presbytery. My special province was the little town of Hamiota. It was February, but every night the meetings were well attended. Some young bloods, unsympathetic to religious programmes, decided to give a popular entertainment in the town hall on one of the evenings. They were politely sorry to seem to interfere with our mission, but really a whole town could not be held up for a fortnight! So the concert was advertised; the day before the date of the performance, however, there was consternation among the organizers. Hardly a ticket had been sold. That, too, was an eye-opener. I took part in another revival as well at Moose Jaw which left very happy memories. Unquestionably the Church has become the poorer in spiritual intensity since it has abandoned the special meeting and the special appeal.

Salvation Army and Marginal Social Groups in the City

Canadian Advance (The Commissioner's Headquarters, Salvation Temple, Toronto, 1886), pp. 41-6.

We must be content with glancing very briefly at some of the more remarkable incidents that have made the history of the past year's work. The first incident that occurs to our mind was that wonderful gathering of saved drunkards in Toronto City in November, 1885. It was, perhaps, never till then that the Army had been recognized as the mighty instrument it really is for the reclaiming of inebriates. The testimonies that were then given as to the effects of Salvation and the reality of the power of the Grace of God not only to keep drunkards sober but to destroy the very appetite itself, awakened in a way perhaps never equalled, all thinking men as to the real cure for the nation's besetting sin. . . .

At this time, too, [May 24, 1886] there was a great inroad upon and awakening amongst the vicious and depraved of Toronto City. After the opening of the New Temple . . . it was a blessedly frequent sight to see bands of soldiers bringing drunkards and harlots into the barracks and getting them saved. Thank God this work continues, although much crippled for want of proper places to bring these reclaimed ones where they can have a fair chance to start for virtue and sobriety. . . .

Throughout the summer months very special effort was made to reach the masses of the city. A systematic work was carried on in the open-air; the Yorkville Corps visited each Sunday the crowds congregated in the Queen's Park, where they were listened to by thousands, and there is no doubt a work was done. Riverside soldiers, too, visited the public park in their district, and were greeted by orderly and respectful crowds who listened eagerly to the good news. The island, from time to time, was bombarded with "war cry" Brigades, and the Saviour of men was lifted in season and out of season with blessed results.

Work of Salvation Army in Canada

The Salvation Army Year Book for 1919 (London, 1920), pp. 54-5.

THE SALVATION ARMY was started in Canada in 1882, by a party of Officers sent from New York. Its history is a record of steady progress in Evangelistic and Social work throughout all the years since.

The administration of The Army's Work in the Dominion is divided into two distinct Territories—the East and the West. . . .

The League of Mercy has, since its inception here, spread to other countries. It is a carefully regularized work, in which women Officers and Soldiers visit and hold Meetings in hospitals, prisons, and other institutions.

Experience having demonstrated the value of the aid The Salvation Army can render in making effective the enlightened measures adopted by the Municipal and Provincial authorities for the reclamation of the "prisoners," our Officers are called upon to perform many and important duties in this connexion. They visit the various Prisons and Prison Institutions, and hold Meetings there, in some cases every week.

At Winnipeg one of our Officers has been appointed as a *woman police-constable*, while the Detention Home in connexion with the Juvenile Court has been placed under the care of The Army. There are between forty and fifty boys and girls in this Home, who are cared for and schooled, with a view to saving them from the life of crime into which many would otherwise inevitably drift. A court for dealing with offences by juveniles is held at the Institution twice weekly, and the Officer and his wife assist the judge in dealing with the cases that come before him. . . .

Other features of Canadian activity are the Immigration Lodges, and the system of people-distribution for which they stand; visitation of the workers in the *Lumber Camps;* the Industrial Stores, where salvage, made over into articles fit for service, is sold to poor persons at cheap rates; organization for winter relief, including the formation of Committees at Divisional centres which meet and discuss the needs and means to meet them, before the hard weather sets in; and special work among the large Scandinavian population.

In quite a number of towns Corps Officers serve in the capacity of local officials, such as police-court officers, and in one instance as chaplain to the fire brigade.

INDEX

DATE DUE
DATE DE RETOUR

LOWE-MARTIN No. 1137·